Visual Messages

Visual Messages

Integrating Imagery into Instruction

Second Edition

David M. Considine and Gail E. Haley

A Media Literacy Resource for Teachers

1999

TEACHER IDEAS PRESS
A Division of
Libraries Unlimited, Inc.
Englewood, Colorado

TEACHER IDEAS PRESS
A Division of
Libraries Unlimited, Inc.
P.O. Box 6633
Englewood, CO 80155-6633
1-800-237-6124
www.lu.com/tip

Library of Congress Cataloging-in-Publication Data

Considine, David M., 1950-
    Visual messages : integrating imagery into instruction / David M. Considine and Gail E. Haley. -- 2nd ed.
    xxiii, 371 p.   22x28 cm.
    "A media literacy resource for teachers."
    Includes bibliographical references and index.
    ISBN 1-56308-575-5 (softbound)
    1. Visual literacy--United States.   2. Mass media and children--United States.   3. Activity programs in education--United States.
I. Haley, Gail E.   II. Title.
LB1068.C66   1999
371.33'5--dc21   98-52727
                                                                              CIP

❖*Media literacy can play a positive role. These courses can help young people make sense of the many media messages that bombard them daily. This includes an awareness of how the media influences, shapes and defines their lives.*

—Richard Riley, U.S. Secretary of Education

In Memory of Don Considine
1923 – 1997

and for Michael Considine
Big brother, Friend,
Past President ATOM
(Australian Teachers of Media)

CONTENTS

PREFACE

"Reality has always been interpreted through the reports given by images, and philosophers since Plato have tried to loosen our dependence on images by invoking the standard of an image-free way of apprehending the real."

—Susan Sontag, *On Photography*

"Once, oh small children round my knee, there were no stories on Earth to hear. All the stories belonged to Nyame, the Sky God. He kept them in a golden box next to his royal stool." So begins the African folktale *A Story, A Story*. A trickster tale from a tribal culture, this Caldecott medal-winning children's book tells how Ananse, the Spider Man, uses his cunning to bring stories to the people of Earth. Today, we have seen a shift from a tribal culture to a technological society, but our stories remain locked in boxes called computers, television, and videotapes—created, owned, controlled, and distributed at the whim of technological titans with names like Eisner, Murdoch, and Gates. In the era of the oral tradition and tribal culture, stories were passed from one generation to the next, representing the collective wisdom of that culture through shared rituals, myths, archetypes, experiences, and values. Today, the purpose, form, origin, and influence of those stories have changed. George Gerbner, Dean Emeritus at the Annenberg School for Communication, explains this change very clearly. "These stories do not come from families, schools, churches, neighborhoods, and often not even from native countries. They come from a small group of distant conglomerates with something to sell" (Fox 1996, x11).

For Shirley Steinberg and Joe Kincheloe, the issue is nothing less than a struggle for the survival of childhood. In *Kinderculture*, they describe a crisis of childhood and "the corporate construction of childhood." Children, they suggest, are not only biological entities, but the cumulative product of the social and cultural forces operating upon them. What is needed, they suggest, in something tantamount to a call to arms, is "strategies of resistance" (1997, 5). Such concerns about media content and control need to be carefully counterbalanced by an understanding of our own role in the production-consumption cycle. While attention must rightly be focused on what the *media do to us*, it is just as essential that consideration be given to what *we do with the media*.

David Buckingham, one of the most respected voices in media education in the United Kingdom, challenges those who perceive children as passive pawns manipulated by media messages. "To all intents and purposes," he writes, "children appear to be regarded as not fully social—or indeed as pre-social beings" (1993, 11). The idea that children are the passive recipients of media messages has also been disputed by Australian researchers. A study of how elementary school age children responded to television depictions of kissing, swearing, and violence concluded that "primary school children were discriminating in their television viewing, made active choices about television programs and exercised self-censorship about things that concerned them" (Ramsay 1998, 14).

The limitations of the protectionist model within the United States were also recently addressed when the *Journal of Communication* devoted an entire issue to media literacy. Instead of restricting itself to reading the internal components of the page, screen, or frame, or attempting to protect students from manipulation by media messages, the authors argued that media literacy has to include "political education." The mass media "should be analyzed," they said, "as sets of institutions with particular social and economic structures that are neither inevitable or irreversible" (Lewis and Jhally 1998, 109-14).

Despite such misgivings, the protectionist approach to media literacy in the United States continues to gain momentum. In 1995, for example, The National Media Literacy Conference at North Carolina's Appalachian State University was billed as "an interdisciplinary approach to the impact of mass media on school, society, students, and citizens." By the time the conference convened in Colorado Springs in summer 1998, the agenda was considerably narrower, calling itself "a paradigm for public health." Personal behavior and public health policy are, of course, affected by media coverage, and these are legitimate areas of concern within the field of media literacy. The rich intellectual traditions of that field, however, with its roots in Australia and the United Kingdom, have a much broader agenda and methodology. For media literacy to fully flourish in the United States, those traditions must be recognized, respected, and then modified to local conditions and circumstances. That means identifying the widest possible constituency in order to energize and empower them. Although the prevention community has an important contribution to make, it is only part of the media literacy picture. Proponents of information literacy, digital literacy, and computer literacy, for example, are potential allies in responding to the communication revolution and the need for all of us to become better users and chosers of media and technology if our democracy is to survive.

Media literacy may well have a role to play helping at-risk students develop refusal skills and promoting resilience characteristics. It also has a major role to play in strengthening our understanding of citizenship and responsible participation in a democratic society. That means preparing today's students and tomorrow's citizens to understand the information forms of their culture, empowering them to selectively and effectively use those tools and technologies for their own purposes. It also means that while challenging media excesses, we need to guard assiduously against turning our students into cynics. Healthy skepticism and cynicism are two very different conditions.

Nonetheless, there is cause for cynicism. In an era dominated by media mergers and communication conglomerates, there is little doubt that story *selling* has become more important than story *telling*. In the name of profit, communication conglomerates are prepared to swamp our society in a rising tide of potentially toxic media messages, affecting not only our children and students, but their parents and teachers as well. While new media formats like the World Wide Web were initially hailed as a step forward and an information breakthrough, they have become, in some cases, tools for disinformation and mythinformation. Anyone with access to the technology can put any story into play.

The excessive and sensational press coverage given to the Lewinsky/Clinton White House sex scandal in 1998 was one example. Rather than applying journalistic tools of checking sources and verifying reports, much of the mainstream media picked up on the most lurid, unsubstantiated gossip from the web, repeating it, embellishing it, and validating it. The juggernaut of jaundiced journalism was in full swing. As *American Journalism Review* commented, "Standards were the first casualty. Innuendo quickly replaced hard facts . . . sparking a tidal wave of copycat journalism that pierced the heart of the big three—accuracy, fairness and balance" (Ricchiardi 1998, 31).

While presidential impropriety and an overzealous prosecutor may well have fed the story, declining journalistic standards and cutthroat competition from news media outlets exacerbated the tone, quality, and quantity of the coverage. Nothing succeeds like excess. Anyone who doubts this trend and the seeming inability of journalists to exercise restraint and responsibility within their own profession need look no farther than to the reporters themselves. Ann Compton, ABC's White House correspondent, has said that "fairness to the president, to all public figures, and even to private citizens is often ignored, especially under the pressure of deadlines and competition" (1998, 10). In the name of profit, anything goes.

As if to demonstrate the depths to which coverage had sunk in 1998, California viewers were able to watch a man commit suicide on a freeway, knowing that cameras were covering his final desperate act. One station actually interrupted children's programming to cover the incident. Nor are such episodes relegated to local stations or even to television. In summer 1998, CNN was forced to replace reporters and retract a story in which they had charged the U.S. government with using chemical weapons against deserters during the Vietnam War. At the same time, the *Cincinnati Enquirer* ran a front-page apology to Chiquita Brands International, admitting that part of the critical story it ran about the company was based on stolen voice-mail messages. The *New Republic* and the *Boston Globe* also were forced to admit that reporters Stephen Glass and Patricia Smith had fabricated stories and employed what *U.S. News and World Report* called "fictional techniques" (Leo 1998, 20).

When challenged about the content or influence of their products, programs, and reporting, the media moguls assert their First Amendment rights as an excuse to package, broadcast, and distribute their wares without the slightest consideration for the restraint and responsibility that should accompany those constitutional rights. "We're just giving the people what they want," becomes the clarion cry of the conglomerates. "If people didn't buy it, we wouldn't sell it," they claim, blaming their consumers. But consumers increasingly have fewer and fewer choices. While channels and outlets may proliferate, there is an increasingly narrower range of stories, storytellers, and story-sellers.

The 1998 American Booksellers Convention was abuzz with tales of flat and declining sales and the lawsuit independent bookstore owners brought against both Borders and Barnes and Noble, accusing the giant chains of antitrust violations. In another development that restricted access to information in the midst of the so-called information age, the Supreme Court damaged democratic discourse and limited access to alternative political points of view in a 1998 ruling that permitted television stations to prevent candidates from minor parties from taking part in televised political debates. The following week, Jane Seymour, star of the successful series, *Dr. Quinn, Medicine Woman*, lashed out at the cancellation of her show. The decision, she said, was not based on the merits or quality of the popular program, but on the calculations of the demographers and numbers crunchers at the network.

In a major development, the U.S. Justice Department also raised questions about the lack of consumer choices. Their concern was not with the television or publishing industry but with the brave new world of computer technology. In May 1998, they decided that one of today's storytellers and story-sellers had gone too far. They brought suit against Microsoft, claiming that it exerted undue pressure on the computer software market, limiting consumer choices and options. For his part, Microsoft owner Bill Gates proclaimed that his company represented innovation, equating innovation with both progress and America. Of course even a cursory glance at the 20th century provides any number of examples of innovations that have not always been regarded as steps forward. Nuclear weapons and nuclear power stations are a dual-edged sword, offering both promise and peril. The conception and birth of a sheep named Dolly as a result of cloning experiments is a more recent incident in which a so-called scientific and technological breakthrough was widely regarded as a moral and ethical abhorrence. And while Mr. Gates and his company may well be American, the influence of both is global, as evidenced by the fact that *www* stands for World Wide Web, not American web.

Although this book is intended for a North American audience, largely made up of readers in the United States who are concerned, naturally enough, with the role of media within our own domain, we need look no farther than our northern and southern neighbors to understand that our friends are concerned about the potential cultural contamination that exported American products and programs can create within their own countries. This was evident in summer 1998 when the United States was not invited to a 19-nation conference convened in Ottawa, Canada. The conference included Mexico, Britain, Brazil, and other American allies. The *New York Times* said that despite their differences, these countries shared "the fear that Hollywood and the rest of the American entertainment industry threatens their cultures" (DePalma 1998, B4).

TOOLS IN SCHOOLS

Beyond the world of entertainment and infotainment lies the classroom where teachers and students alike must come to terms with the new technologies. Unfortunately, such equipment frequently finds its way into our schools with more of an emphasis on acquisition than on application. Access to information so celebrated by cyberspace supporters cannot be automatically equated with success in understanding or evaluating the words and images at the disposal of web browsers. Many classroom teachers across the country have come to understand the perils as well as the promise of this new technology and the dreaded word, *accountability*, as their students have located nude photographs of Brad Pitt and offensive materials through searches for topics as innocuous as Amazon and rainbows. Furthermore, even when schools and universities are well equipped, they frequently fail to make the connection between teaching *with* the technologies and teaching *about* them. "There remains little recognition . . . that the means of information dissemination . . . might extend beyond print. The U.S. educational establishment refuses to recognize this fact, or is mystified as to how to retool and retrain in order to educate students and future citizens for the new realities of communication" (Kubey 1998, 61).

Foisted upon our classrooms and schools by a industry-hype and legislative mandates, the tools of the computer era have not yet lived up to the claims of their creators and purveyors. IBM may genuinely believe it offers "solutions for a small planet," but neither IBM, Apple, nor Microsoft have solved the problems of American education. Despite almost two decades of spending on computer-related equipment, the new technologies have not transformed the American classroom or the curriculum. A 1997 presidential report on technology in K-12 education identified success stories and pockets of progress but found no systemic shift in the day-to-day operation of the nation's schools. Despite all the promise and potential of the new technologies, the indisputable fact yet to be widely recognized is the simple idea that *tools don't change schools: teachers do.*

Yet, as the presidential report acknowledged, teachers are often left out of the process and forced to figure it out for themselves without adequate time, training, or administrative support. A consumer culture that celebrates the mystique of the machine fosters a mindset that makes it easy to ignore the nature and needs of the very people we expect to use these machines to bring about instructional innovation. In short, the technological tail continues to wave the educational dog. Colleges of education and universities, it is true, are experimenting with the new technologies and young teachers are being exposed to an increasingly wider range of tools and techniques. But institutional inertia continues to exert a strong force, limiting the power of technology to transform both schools and universities. A 1998 report from the Aspen Institute identified one such barrier as "the innate conservatism of academia," concluding that the Internet and distance learning "will complement rather than supplant on-campus traditional higher education" (Baer, 103).

Beyond the nation's colleges and schools, however, there is little doubt that communication technology is changing our nation and our world. Questions might well be raised about the nature of that change and who benefits from it. If our schools are yet to come to terms with the issues of whether the curriculum drives technology or technology drives the curriculum, there are equally crucial questions to be raised about the role of media and technology in a democracy. Any school system that meaningfully claims to prepare students for life as responsible citizens in a democratic society cannot afford to ignore the way that technology is shaping our view of ourselves and the world. Such an approach should be a balanced one, driven by neither the excesses of technophobes nor technophiles.

In what it described as the first national in-depth study of digital citizens, or *netizens*, *Wired* raised some crucial questions. Can these new technologies, they asked, build a new kind of politics, construct a more civil society and extend the evolution of freedom? The study categorized individuals as either superconnected, connected, semiconnected, or unconnected. It also dismissed several stereotypes about computer nerds and geeks. Connected individuals, they said, are more rather than less likely to read books. They are also more likely to be aware of important events and to vote. In an evaluation that bordered on hyperbole, the magazine announced that "far from being distracted by technology, Digital Citizens appear startlingly close to the Jeffersonian ideal—they are informed, outspoken, participatory, passionate about freedom, proud of their culture and committed to the free nation in which it has evolved" (Katz 1997, 72).

What Katz believes to be a free nation, however, is seen by many others as a media monopoly, restricting rather than expanding the choices citizens make whether choosing potato chips or presidents. Real freedom, they suggest, comes from critical education that "prepares students to be their own agents for social change, their own creators of democratic culture." The literacy implicit in such education is seen as a liberating experience that enables students to "separate themselves from manipulation" and "challenge their control by corporate culture" (Shor 1987, 48). While traditional literacy addressed the skills of reading, much of the new literacy education moves toward a form of resistance, as students and teachers alike are asked to question and challenge, even within the context of the printed page, "what that reading and writing does to them and their world" (Comber and O'Brien 1993, 2).

THE PURPOSE OF THIS BOOK:
Widening Our Understanding of Literacy

With the last decade of the 20th century just underway, Elliot Eisner argued in *Educational Leadership* that, "We think about literacy in the tightest most constipated terms" (1991, 10). For Eisner, what was needed was a broader, wider definition of literacy based upon the expanding and diverse communication forms of our culture, forms that are increasingly visual in nature. There is little doubt that our whole notion of literacy has historically been related to the major information forms of our culture, most notably, the printing press. As the *Journal of Curriculum Studies* has said, "Being literate has always referred to having mastery over the processes by which means of culturally significant information is encoded" (de Castell and Luke 1983, 173). Today, however, we live in an era that is no longer dominated by the primacy of print, even while our classrooms continue to privilege it. In the day-to-day world beyond our classrooms, most Americans get most of their information about themselves and their world from television, not textbooks—pictures, not print.

As such, we believe literacy must be expanded to include the ability to access, analyze, evaluate, and communicate information in all its forms. In a world dominated by the special effects mastery of computer-generated imagery, we can no longer afford to accept the illusion that seeing is believing, or what you see is what you get. Seeing is in reality a much more complicated process. Paul Martin Lester, for example, identifies six perspectives for analyzing images. These include personal, historical, technical, ethical, cultural, and critical readings or responses (1995, 123-24). Within the world of educational media, or instructional technology, Gavriel Salomon also argues that media are more complex than we initially admit. Media, he suggests, "are our cultural apparatus for selecting, gathering, storing, and conveying knowledge in representational forms" (1979, 3). Further, he argues, as an entity, media consists of "technology, contents, instructional situations, and symbol systems" (1). Successfully understanding and using media within an educational context, he believes, requires a holistic approach and a comprehensive examination of all its attributes.

Similarly, this book argues that the role of mass media, in what we shall call the curriculum of the living room, requires an equally rigorous examination. Throughout this book, we provide frameworks for critically analyzing news, advertising, film, and other media formats. We have successfully used these frameworks in seminars and workshops from Seattle to San Juan, including five years of programs for Wisconsin's Center for Excellence in Critical Thinking Skills, where media literacy has been prominently featured in staff development as part of its Facilitating the Future program. We have also heard from teachers throughout the United States who have successfully used these techniques in their own classrooms without the benefit of attending our workshops. These techniques provide a partial process for fostering the critical viewing, thinking, and listening skills necessary to understand the content, form, ownership, and organization of today's complex media messages. This book and the techniques it contains seek to empower students and citizens to be more autonomous decision makers. While that includes the idea that we become better users and chosers of media, it does not exclude the idea that one of our decisions is to disengage from the media, or to rely on less technology in our lives.

It is true that media literacy can be taught in traditional classrooms, using traditional methods, but it is our view that in subject matter and methodology, media literacy is both evolutionary and revolutionary. Though the term is likely to strike fear in the hearts of undergraduates, we believe that media literacy embraces a critical pedagogy. The view is evident in Wisconsin's critical thinking initiatives and pervades the Reich College of Education at Appalachian State University, which continues to pioneer media literacy education at the pre-service and in-service level.

New approaches to literacy and its impact on both students and their teachers were carefully described in *Reading Research Quarterly*. The new pedagogy, the authors wrote, "seeks to intensify student engagement [even though students may resist the intellectual work it entails] to increase student autonomy and authority [although it increases teachers' pedagogical responsibility to share power] and to invite co-construction of knowledge among all participants [which makes every day teaching terribly unpredictable]" (Roskos et al. 1998, 229).

In preparing this book, we continue to use the organizational format developed in the first edition. That is to say, we continue to organize the chapters around discrete media formats such as news, television, advertising, and motion pictures. We are, of course, cognizant of the fact that these different industries are frequently owned by the same companies and corporations and therefore share ideological and economic interests. We are also, of course, aware that in the United Kingdom, Canada, and Australia, media studies textbooks are likely to employ a format different from the one used here. In those countries, one is likely to encounter books that approach media studies from perspectives such as media languages, narratives, audiences, and representation. Each of these concepts can be found within each chapter of this book. However, it must be stated that beyond the United States, various school systems in numerous countries have had many years to evolve their own approaches to media education. In many cases, these classes are taught as separate courses with their own identity and intellectual traditions (cultural studies, women's studies) or housed within specific subject areas where their content has been approved and mandated by a ministry or department of education. Such conditions are, for the most part, not yet existent within the United States.

We continue to argue for an integrated and interdisciplinary approach to media literacy while acknowledging that some teachers may be able to offer discrete or separate courses (usually electives) in media studies or media literacy. Chapters 1 and 2 are intended to provide novice and advanced teachers alike with a broad overview of how media literacy has grown since this book was first published in 1992. This includes graphic representations of where it might most strongly be connected to the traditional curriculum, and how existing curriculum objectives in various subject areas are compatible with the goals of media literacy. In addition, these chapters also serve as the foundation for recognizing and explaining the key principles of media literacy. These principles share a common conceptual background with approaches used in Canada, the United Kingdom, and Australia.

WHO IS THIS BOOK FOR?

In preparing this book, we have had two broad audiences in mind. The first, as we have already suggested, is those teachers and library media specialists already in the classroom. The book can be used by teachers in elementary, middle, and high school. Activities and approaches throughout the book are consistently designated with *E, M,* and *H,* indicating to what age level we think they are most suited. As always, we encourage flexibility and experimentation in responding to these designations. With the same audience in mind, we have also geared the majority of this book to address traditional areas of the curriculum such as Art, English, Social Studies, History, Health, and Language Arts. The chapter on motion pictures, for example, is clearly divided into subject area headings. The television chapter, on the other hand, employs topics such as genres, stereotyping, political consequences, violence, sexuality, and substance abuse, which can easily be integrated into several components of the traditional curriculum.

The second audience for which the book is geared is pre-service teachers in colleges of education, along with their counterparts in departments of Library Science and Information Studies. The opening chapters of the book provide such readers with a firm foundation in the development of media literacy within the United States, anchoring these developments to support from various nationally respected institutions and individuals. The subsequent chapters are particularly useful at the pre-service level where students can be encouraged to integrate film, advertising, news, and television in assignments, papers, and portfolio projects developed for requirements in a variety of methods classes.

WHAT ARE THE OBJECTIVES OF THIS BOOK?

From the outset, it should be clear that we have an agenda. We are, and this book is, an unabashed advocate for media literacy within the American classroom and curriculum. We recognize that in this country we lag behind other countries who brought media literacy into the public schools long ago. While acknowledging their efforts and respecting their contributions, we have also brought something of our own interpretation to both teaching media literacy and implementing it. One such perspective is the strands that we describe as **PREPARATION, PROTECTION, and PLEASURE**. Again, it is contact with our readers and our workshop participants that has demonstrated to us that such concepts seem to resonate with you and to have value for you. In preparing this second edition of *Visual Messages*, we believe that our readers should be able to use this book to:

- define media literacy within the North American context;

- identify and explain basic principles of media literacy, including concepts such as media representations;

- acknowledge that media literacy includes awareness of how audiences use media, not just what media does to audiences;

- connect media literacy to key components of traditional and emerging curriculum;

- articulate a rationale for including media literacy in the curriculum;

- identify resources and support materials, including websites, books, journals, and videotapes;

- plan single lessons, units, or whole courses based on media literacy;

- integrate film, television, news, and advertising into courses; and

- use frameworks and strategies such as AIME (Amount of Invested Mental Energy) to help students become critical viewers and thinkers.

EVALUATING MEDIA LITERACY: The Early Evidence

In early 1998, *The English Journal* devoted an entire issue to media literacy. The first article in that issue was written by high school teacher Ellen Kreuger. Her article was aptly titled: "Media Literacy Does Work, Trust Me" (1998, 17). Anyone who has ever taught in the United States after having taught elsewhere is immediately struck by the obsession this country's educational establishment has with measurement and the constant demand that proof be provided. While espousing that children learn in different ways, too many educational administrators and state legislators are all too willing to require teachers to teach in one way and for their students to be tested in one way.

Asking if media literacy works requires an understanding of which types of media literacy we are talking about, in the same way that teaching reading skills needs to be assessed within the context of phonics, whole language, and other approaches. While these approaches may be perceived as divisions, it is more likely that they constitute healthy difference, dialogue, and debate about how best to teach a skill or set of skills. While reading teachers may disagree about how best to teach reading, they all agree that reading must be taught. Similarly, while media literacy advocates may disagree about which approach they should stress, they are united in the belief that media literacy has a legitimate role in the American curriculum.

Issues of educational accountability and economic feasibility are, of course, potential obstacles to media literacy's progress within the United States, but we must also realize that one of the greatest obstacles is not related to media literacy at all, but reflects the egocentric culture of the United States itself. It is a condition that the media play no small role in reinforcing by seldom validating or covering innovative practices outside the United States.

Beyond the field of education, distinguished futurist Alvin Toffler has acknowledged the damage this perception does to American management and business. Calling American managers ethnocentric and insular in an era of global economy, Toffler says that these managers, like Americans themselves, suffer "from the illusion that we have much to teach the world, but considerably less to learn" (1986, vii). His comments appear in the preface to Reinhard Mohn's *Success Through Partnership*. Although Mohn is hardly a household name in the United States, it is worth noting that he heads the Bertelsmann Group. Originally a small European publishing concern, it now ranks as one of the world's largest private media conglomerates, and it is increasingly expanding its operations within the United States.

With that in mind, any attempt to evaluate media literacy in the United States should at least begin with some curiosity about how it has succeeded in those countries that have already implemented it. In Australia, the Western Australia Ministry of Education has had no difficulty in developing evaluation mechanisms for media literacy courses. Among other outcomes, researchers have reported that girls perform better than boys and that students tend to score better at identifying key elements and components of programs and broadcasts, while not scoring as well in higher-order thinking that requires them to connect media content to broader cultural contexts (Quin and McMahon 1991). The British Film Institute has also developed authentic assessment instruments for media education courses in the United Kingdom, while in Canada, Chris Worsnop's (1996) methods are respected and widely used.

One of the most carefully scrutinized training programs within the United States has been the New Mexico Media Literacy Project based at Albuquerque Academy. The state Department of Education financed and mandated an independent evaluation. In part, the evaluators noted that the project was able to document "how their program either directly or indirectly positively impacts students through the efforts of . . . teachers, administrators and community members" (*NMedia Education Newsletter* 1996, 1).

The prestigious Aspen Institute has recognized the media literacy leadership role played by Appalachian State University's Reich College of Education. Throughout the 1990s, the college has formalized a core curriculum with media literacy first introduced to students in an interdisciplinary course: Literacy, Technology and Instruction. Since its inception, the faculty have conducted both formal and informal evaluations of the course. In addition to their journal commentaries and final evaluations, students routinely communicate through a listserv, which is open for observation by the dean, department chairs, and other faculty. Students have granted faculty permission to use their journals and listserv comments in academic writings. The first year found substantial evidence of student frustration and anxiety (frequently related to deadlines and workload), but subsequent semesters have revealed strong support for the course content, concepts, and competencies, whether designing web pages, critically analyzing news broadcasts, or developing their own motion picture study guides.

More formal research also tends to show promise for media literacy curricula within the public schools, including a role in health education. Initial efforts to teach critical viewing skills to third graders in an effort to deglamorize alcohol advertising have been shown to have both immediate and delayed effects and to increase children's understanding of persuasive intent (Austin and Johnson 1997). Another experimental and potentially promising program has been conducted by District Attorney Kevin Burke's office in Salem, Massachusetts. The audience for the program is juvenile offenders. The resulting product and process is a curriculum called *Flashpoint: Lifeskills Through the Lens of Media Literacy*. The program is particularly concerned with addressing violence, substance abuse, and racism in the adolescent community. Independent evaluators from Salem State College employed both qualitative and quantitative methods, which suggest the program may be deterring some of the participants. "It gave me time to think about the consequences," one student told evaluators. Results from the first year of the study were reported to the Annual Conference on Criminal Justice Research and Evaluation in Washington, DC, in summer 1998.

In short, in a relatively brief time, media literacy teachers, researchers, and students throughout the United States have begun the necessary process of documenting their methods and their outcomes. Portfolio assessment, learning styles research, site-based management, and concepts such as multiple intelligences offer them the opportunity to expand their base as school systems become more receptive to innovation. For that to happen, growth should be cautious, incremental, and based on a healthy blend of local autonomy and intellectual tradition. In particular, proponents of the protectionist and inoculation model should eschew any suggestion that media literacy is or might be a panacea for a plethora of social problems.

That being said, it should also be noted that the prevention community has a clear message for the media literacy movement, about how best to manage its growth. The most successful prevention programs, researchers have noted, are accomplished "when community leaders and opinion shapers have the opportunity to take ownership of the strategy and make it their own" (Hawkins, Arthur and Catalano 1995, 404).

Though our paths may differ, there is little doubt that we are fellow travelers on the road to media literacy. Three decades have now passed since Marshal McLuhan published *The Medium Is the Message*. In that landmark volume, he suggested that children of the television age were growing up absurd. Such children, he said, were educated in two worlds: the electronic world beyond the classroom and the chalk and talk, rear-view mirror, segmented, fragmented world of our schools. Neither environment, he charged, helped such children to grow up. With the millennium at hand, we can ill afford to enter a new century without preparing our students and citizens to confront, comprehend, and control the information technology that shapes the way they see themselves and their world. That is the task that now confronts media literacy proponents.

REFERENCES

Austin, Erica, and K. Johnson, (1997). "Effects of General and Alcohol Specific Media Literacy Training on Children's Decision-making About Alcohol." *Journal of Health Communication*, 2, 17-42.

Baer, Walter, (1998). Will the Internet Transform Higher Education? In *The Emerging Internet, Annual Review of the Institute for Information Studies*. Queenstown, MD: Aspen Institute.

Buckingham, David, (1993). *Children Talking Television: The Making of Television Literacy*. London: Falmer Press.

Comber, Barbara, and Jennifer O'Brien, (1993). Critical Literacy: Classroom Explorations. *Critical Pedagogy Networker*, 6:1 and 6:2, 1-10.

Compton, Ann, (1998). Rushing to Judgement. *Media Studies Journal*, 12:2, 10-13.

de Castell, Suzanne, and Allan Luke, (1983). Defining Literacy in North American Schools: Social and Historical Conditions and Consequences. *Journal of Curriculum Studies*, 15: 373-89.

DePalma, Anthony, (1998). 19 Nations See US as a Threat to Their Cultures. *New York Times*, July 1, B1, B4.

Eisner, Elliot, (1991). What Really Counts in Schools? *Educational Leadership*, 48:5, 10-11.

Fox, Roy, (1996). *Harvesting Minds: How TV Commercials Control Kids*. Westport, CT: Praeger.

Haley, Gail, (1971). *A Story, A Story*. New York: Atheneum.

Hawkins, David, Michael Arthur, and Richard Catalano, (1995). *Building a Safer Society: Strategic Approaches to Crime Prevention*. Chicago: University of Chicago Press.

Katz, Joe, (1997). The Digital Citizen. *Wired*, December, 68-82, 274-75.

Kreuger, Ellen, (1998). Media Literacy Does Work, Trust Me. *English Journal*, 87:1, 17-20.

Kubey, Robert, (1998). Obstacles to the Development of Media Education in the United States. *Journal of Communication*, Winter, 48:1, 58-69.

Leo, John, (1998). Nothing But the Truth? *U.S. News and World Report*, July 6, 20.

Lester, Paul Martin, (1995). *Visual Communication: Images with Messages*. Belmont, CA: Wadsworth.

Lewis, Justin, and Sut Jhally, (1998). The Struggle Over Media Literacy. *Journal of Communication*, Winter, 109-20.

Mohn, Reinhard, (1986). *Success Through Partnership: An Entrepreneurial Strategy*. New York: Doubleday.

Quin, Robyn, and Barrie McMahon, (1991). *Media Analysis Performance in Media in Western Australian Government Schools*. Perth: Western Australia Ministry of Education.

Ramsay, Gillian, (1998). Cool or Gross?: Australian Children's Attitudes to Violence, Kissing and Swearing on Television. *News on Children and Violence on the Screen*, 2:1, 14-15.

Ricchiardi, Sherry, (1998). Standards Are the First Casualty. *American Journalism Review*, March, 30-35.

Roskos, Kathleen, Victoria Risko, and Carol Vukelich, (1998). "Head, Heart and the Practice of Literacy Pedagogy." *Reading Research Quarterly*, 33:2, 228-39.

Salomon, Gavriel, (1979). *Interaction of Media, Cognition and Learning*. San Francisco: Jossey Bass.

NMedia Education Newsletter, (1996). State Department of Education Gives New Mexico Media Literacy Project the Highest Possible Evaluation, Winter 1 and 4.

Steinberg, Shirley, and Joe Kincheloe, (1997). *Kinderculture: The Corporate Construction of Childhood*. Boulder, CO: Westview Press.

Worsnop, Chris, (1996). *Assessing Media Work: Authentic Assessment in Media Education*. Mississauga, Ont.: Wright Communications.

ACKNOWLEDGMENTS

In writing the second edition of this book, we want to recognize the unique and invaluable contribution made to media literacy within the United States by our friends and colleagues in Canada's Association for Media Literacy. Their pioneering efforts throughout the 1980s and 1990s have served as a model, both inspirational and informational in nature. Of particular note are the leadership efforts of Barry Duncan and Father John Pungente, along with Neil Andersen and the evaluation efforts of Chris Worsnop. We also applaud The National Telemedia Council from Madison, Wisconsin, for its outstanding accomplishment in publishing *Telemedium: The Journal of Media Literacy*, which remains the pre-eminent voice of the movement within the United States.

On a more personal note, we thank Jeff Fletcher for photographic reproduction; Erin Simmons for computer-generated graphs and charts; Dave Bianculli for assistance with stills; and Bonnie Jung for her seemingly indefatigible good humor in preparing the manuscript despite changing jobs, homes, and marital status.

Finally, thanks must go to Charles Duke, Dean of the Reich College of Education, and Michael Jacobson, Chair of Curriculum and Instruction, at Appalachian State University in Boone, North Carolina, for having the vision and creativity to nurture media literacy within the college and to allow Gary, Jeff, Glenn, David, Kyle, Michael, Connie, Woody, and the rest of us to try the road less travelled.

Chapter 1

MEDIA LITERACY GAINS MOMENTUM
From Television to Telling Vision

When the first edition of this book was published in 1992, media literacy was little more than a dot on the horizon of American education. In isolated pockets of progress across the country, creative classroom teachers and some library media specialists labored to find resources and strategies that would enable them to help their students become "media literate." Today, media literacy is becoming increasingly mainstream. It has been endorsed by the Secretary of Education as well as the Secretary of Health and Human Services. Leaders of the movement have been invited to the White House. Media literacy has been the subject of conferences from Seattle to San Juan. It has also been addressed by the broadcast industry, including a 1996 PBS special, "Media Literacy: The New Basic?" and two reports on the "American Agenda" segment of ABC's *Evening News*.

In the United States in 1992, there was no widely accepted definition of media literacy, no clearly defined understanding of why students and citizens needed to be media literate, or where media literacy might be located within the American curriculum. But a consensus was beginning to form. Influential individuals and prestigious institutions were beginning to pay attention to the pioneering media literacy efforts of our nearby neighbors in Canada, where Ontario's Association for Media Literacy had made significant strides in locating media literacy within their own curriculum. The Canadians had been influenced in turn by scholars from the United Kingdom, most notably Len Masterman, Cary Bazalgette, John Fiske, and David Buckingham. These

academics had been instrumental in tracing the development of media education, as the British called it, locating it within a critical pedagogy that would be assimilated, modified, and incorporated within the emerging media literacy movement in the United States. Farther from home, the Canadians and Americans were well aware of the long-established roots of media education in Australia and the contribution made by ATOM (Australian Teachers of Media) through important publications like *Metro* and an outstanding series of motion picture study guides. For more than 20 years, Melbourne's La Trobe University had offered media education classes and degrees, preparing hundreds of classroom teachers. On the other side of the continent, Western Australia's Edith Cowan University also had an impressive track record and the Western Australian Department of Education was also a center for the research and publications of Robyn Quin and Barrie McMahon.

None of this, however, may have made much difference within the United States if the school reform/restructuring movements (Goals 2000, Site Based Management, Outcome Based Education, etc.) had not created an opportunity for institutional change and if traditional concerns about mass media influences had not been fueled and fanned by perceived media excesses that seemed to focus relentlessly on the sensational, the aberrant, the bizarre, and the violent, especially when it concerned sex, celebrity, money, or authority. These events included the Clarence Thomas/Anita Hill hearings, the trial of police officers charged in the videotaped beating of Rodney King, the assault on skater Nancy Kerrigan and frequently biased

❖**International concerns about the impact of media messages were evident in this headline from an Australian newspaper, warning of satellite technology bringing pornography into the nation's homes. Used with permission, the *Herald and Weekly Times*, Melbourne.**

coverage of her teammate Tonya Harding, the alternately tragic and humorous coverage of court cases including Lorena Bobbitt (charged with cutting off her husband's penis), Susan Smith (accused of drowning her own children), and the Menendez brothers (charged with murdering their own parents). The media feeding frenzy and the nation's seemingly insatiable appetite for such fare exceeded all previous coverage in the pursuit, arrest, and subsequent acquittal of

O. J. Simpson in what was perhaps the most sensational murder trial of the 20th century. Even the press seemed aware of their own excesses. CNN's *Media Circus* reported on the decline in journalistic standards and placed the blame on the profit motive. By 1996 there was growing evidence that the public was becoming increasingly concerned by media messages and their potential impact. A survey in *U.S. News and World Report* indicated that "two-thirds of the public

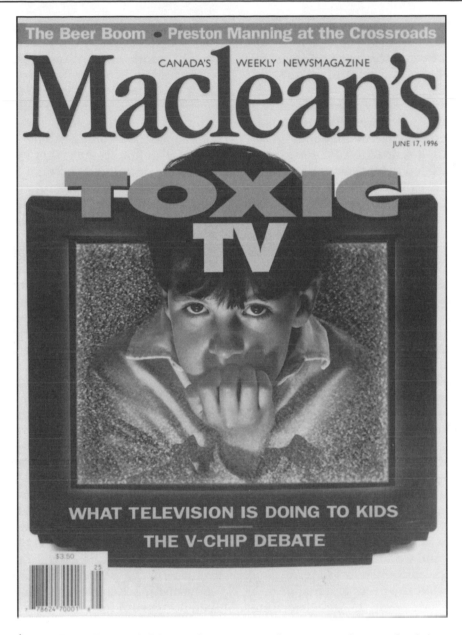

The Beer Boom • Preston Manning at the Crossroads

CANADA'S WEEKLY NEWSMAGAZINE

Maclean's

JUNE 17, 1996

TOXIC TV

WHAT TELEVISION IS DOING TO KIDS

THE V-CHIP DEBATE

$3.50

❖**Our Canadian neighbors also expressed concern about television content and V chip technology to control it. Used with permission of *Maclean's*, Toronto, ON, Canada.**

thinks TV shows have a negative impact on the country and huge majorities believe TV contributes to social problems like violence, divorce, teen pregnancy, and the decline of the family" (Impoco et al. 1996, 58).

Throughout the 1990s, television and the mass media were doing much more than simply entertaining or distracting a bored public. What they covered, what they ignored, and how they constructed their coverage affected not only average citizens in the privacy of their own homes, but also the political process and even the occupant of the White House. Through press pools and controlled coverage, George Bush rode an unprecedented tide of popularity as the commander in chief during the Persian Gulf War. Carefully selected images and commentary skillfully manipulated American public opinion in an extraordinary propaganda effort that rallied the country behind the cause and the commander. Only after the war would we begin to learn what we had not been told. In 1997, soldiers who served and who suffered from unexplained symptoms attributed to the war learned that documents related to the war and to chemical weapons were either missing or had been destroyed.

But there would be another casualty of the war. George Bush's interest and expertise had always been in foreign policy. When the economy took a nosedive, the president who had marshaled international forces for the defense of Kuwait seemed unable to recognize or respond to the growing financial worries of the American public. Smelling blood, the news media moved in for the kill. With the 1992 election just a year away, one network used Thanksgiving 1991 to suggest that the prospects of the turkey, traditionally donated to the White House, were positively rosy compared to the president's. Gloom and doom became the focus and forte of the nightly news. When the president went to a supermarket as a photo opportunity, the public saw a man so hopelessly out of touch that he was surprised by a cash register scanner. Glancing casually at his watch during a presidential debate in Richmond, Virginia, Bush signaled to the nation (at least in media spin) that he'd rather be somewhere else. His opponent that year was the largely unknown governor of a small southern state who had won the nomination of his party after his own war with the media. In one extraordinary season of politics, Bill Clinton was accused of pot-smoking, draft-dodging, and womanizing. In a startling press conference at the Waldorf Astoria, Gennifer Flowers told the press she had been in a long-term affair with the governor, and viewers heard a reporter ask if the governor had used a condom. This was to be a no-holds-barred campaign, not because the candidates wanted it that way, but because the rules of the game had changed and journalistic standards had declined. In media and politics, the press no longer distinguished between a candidate's private and public life. Image-makers, pollsters, spin-doctors . . . these forces now shaped the American political landscape. In February 1992, *U.S. News and World Report* commented, "America thinks it is a meritocracy, but in fact it has become a mediacracy. Mediacracy is not ruled by the media but by those who know how to manipulate symbols, information and the media" (Wolcott 1992, 6).

If our citizens and politicians were open to the distortion and distractions of the mass media, many of our impressionable teens and children were potential victims caught in a constant struggle between the visible and the vulnerable. In 1992 the Carnegie Council on Adolescent Development published *Fateful Choices*. The report opened with the announcement that by age 15 a quarter "of all young adolescents are engaged in behaviors that are harmful or dangerous to themselves or others" (21). They also pointed to the role the mass media played in "influencing attitudes and behavior of children and adolescents" (220). Of particular concern was the issue of media and violence. "The television and movie industries," the report said, "bear a heavy responsibility for making violence appear an acceptable, perhaps even normal way of life" (165). After describing problems associated with adolescent sexuality, substance abuse, violence, and other issues, *Fateful Choices* made it clear that if the media were part of the problem, media literacy was part of the solution. Despite the fact that teenagers find themselves "under a barrage of media messages delivered by television, radio, and pop music—usually in isolation from adults—schools have hardly begun to teach them how to view and listen critically." These abilities, they concluded, "ought to be a major component of life skills education" (53). At the same time, Theodore Sizer, one of the most influential voices in the school reform/restructuring movement, acknowledged the growing power and presence of television as a teacher and the need for schools to help students become better users and choosers of television. Calling television "the biggest school system, the principal shaper of culture . . . powerfully influencing the young on what it is to be American," he said, "what we need is to change the very nature of what it is to watch TV" (1992).

Similar concerns had already been voiced by Ernest Boyer, president of the Carnegie Foundation for the Advancement of Teaching. Tackling the whole issue of literacy head on, Boyer had written, "It is no longer enough to simply read and write. Students must also become literate in the understanding of visual messages as well. Our children must learn how to isolate a social cliché and distinguish facts from propaganda, analysis from banter, and important news from coverage" (1988, xxiv). The election of Clinton in 1992 further strengthened institutional support for the emerging media literacy movement. Speaking to a gathering of German and American educators at the University of Georgia in April 1994, then Assistant Secretary of Education Madeline Kunin told participants that our schools "have to teach critical viewing, listening, and thinking." What role, she asked, does the media play in our lives? Is the media a reflection of these times or does the media actually influence behavior? While Kunin acknowledged that the broadcast industry had to embrace more responsible production and programming, she also said teachers had a vital role to play. What we need, she said, "is to develop young people, young adults, who can themselves block out, analyze and evaluate media" (Considine 1995, 32). The following year, Richard Riley, secretary of education, signaled his support. Speaking at Julius West Middle School in Rockville, Maryland, Riley noted that young people spend four times as much time watching television as they do engaged in homework. Acknowledging that impressionable children and teens are bombarded by media messages every day, he said our students "need to stretch their minds and avoid being passive consumers. This is where media literacy can play a positive role. Media literacy courses can give young people the power to recognize the difference between entertainment, television that is just bad and the information they need to make good decisions." What they need, he concluded, is "a clear awareness of how the media influences, shapes and defines their lives" (12/13/95).

Rather than representing a top-down approach to media literacy, created within some centralized bureaucracy, the endorsements for media literacy from within the Department of Education and other branches of the administration were the result of the increasingly symbiotic relationship among educators, prestigious institutions, and of course, the growing public concern about the media. Lending considerable clout and coverage to the movement was Harvard University. In summer 1993 and again in 1994, Harvard's Graduate School of Education conducted media

education institutes that attracted teachers and administrators from across the nation. New York University's School of Education also offered Media Literacy and Education Institutes as part of its summer session. Part of the impetus for these programs was a 1992 gathering arranged by the influential Aspen Institute. The National Leadership Conference on Media Literacy called together prominent figures in the movement from both Canada and the United States. They included Barry Duncan from the Association for Media Literacy, Renee Hobbs from Harvard and Babson College, Marilie Rowe and David Considine from the National Telemedia Council, Kathleen Tyner from Strategies for Media Literacy, and Elizabeth Thoman from the Center for Media and Values. The gathering would serve to formalize the working definition of media literacy that has now become the established definition in the United States and Canada. While a term may vary here or there among various groups, it is now generally agreed that media literacy embraces the skills through which a person is able to *access, analyze, evaluate, and communicate* information in all its forms, including print and nonprint.

Exploring the components of both the German and Canadian approaches to media literacy, the think tank and its final published report also recognized emerging success stories in the United States. Particular attention was given to North Carolina's Appalachian State University. Described as "perhaps the most sustained institutional effort at preservice training within formal school" (Auferheide and Firestone 1993, 4), ASU's Reich College of Education was the only college of education in the country that required undergraduate teacher preparation in the key components of media literacy, including both analysis and production. While this was addressed in single courses such as Media and Learning, infusion was also evident in various offerings in several degrees and departments, including Library Science, Health Education, and Language, Reading and Exceptionalities. The success of the program, as the Aspen Institute commented, reflected some useful management strategies. These included connecting courses and competencies to existing and emerging state mandates, competencies, and guidelines. While documents from North Carolina's Department of Public Instruction (NCDPI) never used the term "media literacy," there was little doubt that what they did say was consistent and compatible with ASU's pioneering program and the media literacy movement as a whole. The Communication Skills curriculum, for example, included a Viewing Skills component. That document stated that "in a visually oriented world, the skills of viewing have assumed increasing importance. Visuals shape actions, promote thoughts, and occasionally warp meaning" (NCDPI 1992a). The Information Skills curriculum developed in 1992 made the connection even clearer. "The sheer mass of information and variety of media formats challenge every learner to filter, interpret, accept and/or discard information and media messages. The learner will identify and apply strategies to ACCESS, EVALUATE, USE and COMMUNICATE information for learning, decision making and problem-solving" (NCDPI 1992b). The state's superintendent of schools, Bob Etheridge, spelled out what the curriculum implied. "The influence of TV on our children has reached unprecedented levels; so it is important that we begin integrating media literacy into our critical skills curriculum" (1993).

North Carolina was not alone. Investigations of curriculum documents from dozens of states revealed that they contained language, goals, and objectives that were completely consistent with media literacy. Partial summaries of these documents were published in a series of articles, including a cover story on *School Library Journal* (Considine 1994), an extensive piece for *Educational Technology* (Considine 1995), and a management model included in an international perspective on media literacy (Considine 1997). English, Language Arts, and Social Studies documents consistently contained goals and objectives that addressed media influence and therefore the need for critical viewing and thinking skills. In Florida the Social Studies curriculum indicated that students should "recognize bias and stereotyping in the media" (1993). In Georgia they were expected to "evaluate the impact of mass media on public opinion" (1989b). New Jersey's English/Language Arts curriculum required students to "explore diverse print, nonprint

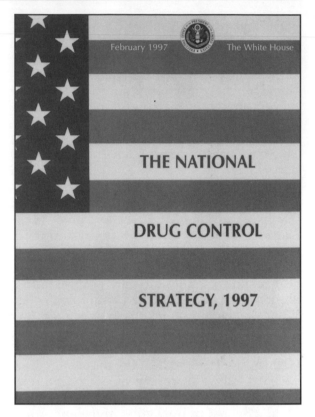

❖ **Since 1995 The Office of National Drug Control Policy has supported media literacy as part of the war on drugs. Used with permission of the Office of National Drug Control Policy, Washington, DC.**

and technological forms of communication and the means by which these influence people" (1991). In New Mexico students were expected to "recognize, analyze and respond to propaganda" (1993).

But it was the Health/Wellness curriculum that would become increasingly receptive to media literacy and its advocates. In Maryland the state documents said students should "analyze how the media influences sexual attitudes and behavior" (1993). In Georgia, advertising became a focus, with students required to "identify and analyze alcohol and cigarette advertisements" (1989a). In Virginia students were asked to "critique the way the media depict drug use" (1990). In April 1995 this approach was further validated by the Office of National Drug Control Policy (ONDCP). *The Executive Summary of The National Drug Control Strategy,* published by the White House, included media literacy initiatives as part of the war on drugs with the aim and intention of initiating programs that would "train young people to analyze media messages critically, whether commercial or entertainment, with the theme that one could and should think for oneself" (ONDCP 1995, 27). That summer, then drug czar Dr. Lee Brown convened a two-day meeting calling together leaders of the media literacy movement and the prevention community. Held at the White House, the event signaled that media literacy had at last come in from the cold. Articulating his department's perspective, Brown told participants, "Looking at the media as a risk factor in substance abuse makes sense. We need to know about the forces in our media culture as much as we know about the culture itself. We are committed to media education as part of our national drug strategy" (Considine and Rowe 1995). He would further add that he believed media literacy to be "a concept that will take hold in other federal agencies as well."

Brown was right. Health and Human Services secretary Donna Shalala would later distribute a publication to hundreds of thousands of students and schools throughout the country. In the introduction to *Substance Abuse Prevention Strategy: Media Literacy Skills*, Shalala said being literate in today's society "requires more than knowing how to read, write, or do arithmetic. Many of the media messages about tobacco, alcohol and other drugs entice youth with glamorous images. Teaching your students to be critical thinkers about media messages can help them . . . resist the temptation to become users" (1996, 2).

With federal support for media literacy growing and with so many states formulating curriculum documents that addressed media influences, Appalachian State University's College of Education convened the National Media Literacy Conference. Cosponsored by Wisconsin's National Telemedia Council, the event attracted participants from five nations and more than 30 states. It also attracted the attention of the ONDCP. Fred Garcia, the deputy director of Demand Reduction, and Alan Levitt from the same office provided both information and motivation. The success of the Boone, North Carolina, conference would serve as an impetus for subsequent national conferences, including

one in Los Angeles the following year and another in Colorado Springs in 1998.

But media literacy was not simply occurring from the top down. While important individuals and institutions were increasingly indicating support for the movement, it was also growing at the grassroots level. Father John Pungente from Canada's Jesuit Communication Project had studied media literacy success stories around the world, identifying key elements that had been necessary for success. At the top of his list was the involvement of teachers, with a sense of local autonomy and ownership in the process. Two examples of this kind of teacher involvement occurred in Billerica, Massachusetts, and Minnesota's Rocori School District. The Billerica initiative coincided with the introduction of the controversial program *Channel One*. *Channel One* provided a daily 12-minute Social Studies current affairs program and equipment to schools that subscribed to it. It also contained what critics called compulsory commercialization, with a captive audience of impressionable adolescents. If students and teachers were to benefit from the program, teachers would need support, time, and training to effectively use the materials. The Billerica School Committee recognized and supported the need for staff development. They developed training that would enable teachers to "gain new skills in analyzing, evaluating and producing messages in a variety of forms, using video, photography, graphics, texts, computers, radio and other forms" (Hobbs 1994, 17). Ultimately this would result in the nation's first master's degree in Media Literacy provided through the partnership of Fitchburg State College and the Merrimack Education Center.

Located in west-central Minnesota, the Rocori School District includes the towns of Cold Spring, Richmond, and Rockville. The District Values Statement articulated the desire to provide students with an excellent education and to produce students with high ethical and moral standards. But the community perceived barriers to achieving these goals, among them the breakdown of the family and the loss of values. Superintendent Tom Westerhaus and his teachers believed that the media were partially responsible for this, but also recognized that media literacy might provide a solution. So began the Minnesota Partnership for Media Literacy and Media Arts, designed to introduce media literacy and media arts education to teachers and students in the district's five schools. Teachers like Jennifer Meagher teamed with media artists like Laura Davis to develop skills in both analysis and production. "Their projects ranged from sequencing exercises using storyboards at the elementary level, to basic video production at the middle school and the development of a semester-long class at the high school" (Sorensen et al. 1994, 22). For many teachers, it was a stimulating and challenging experience that transformed the traditional teacher-centered classroom. Middle school English teacher Sue Tabaka-Kritzeck commented, "It was just as much a learning experience for me as it was for the students. I let them explore video for themselves rather than directing every aspect of their experience"

(22). Frequently and mistakenly perceived as the study of television, media literacy had instead begun to provide a telling vision and revision of American education. Armed with the right tools and techniques, a growing number of teachers were starting to realize that media literacy was more than just another subject. Effectively conceived and implemented, media literacy could transform a teacher from information dispenser to learning facilitator, from sage on the stage to guide on the side. The transmission model, with absolute knowledge passed from teacher to student, could be replaced with a transformational model in which learning was a collaborative effort between teacher and student. A poverty of pedagogy was slowly beginning to give way to the promise and potential of a new way of doing things, a way that could empower both teachers and students.

TOWARD A CRITICAL PEDAGOGY

In the wake of reports like *A Nation at Risk* (National Committee on Excellence in Education 1983), *A Nation Prepared* (Carnegie Forum on Education and the Economy 1986), *What Do Our 17 Year Olds Know?* (Ravitch and Finn 1987), and *Information Power* (AASL/AECT 1988), some of our schools have placed less emphasis on rote learning, memorization and drill, and practice, focusing instead on critical thinking skills and problem solving. Such skills are completely consistent with our definition of media literacy (the ability to access, analyze, evaluate, and communicate information). In fact, by definition it should not be possible to teach media literacy without at the same time teaching critical thinking skills, which in turn serves to engage rather than alienate students.

In *Control Theory in the Classroom* (1986), William Glasser sees a relationship between critical thinking and student involvement. There is, he says, "credence in the complaint of students that school is boring and I believe that the basis of this complaint is that they find it superficial. What makes knowledge both powerful and exciting is that, if it is knowledge, there is always a point of view" (72). By asking students to

examine media texts and explore their content, form, origin, ownership, ideology, and influence, media literacy implicitly fosters critical thinking skills. Barry Duncan from Canada's Association for Media Literacy has gone so far as to suggest that "for many young people media literacy discussions may be the only relevant critical thinking exchanges they receive in school" (1993, 278).

Clearly, in order for students to be engaged in critical thinking, their instructors must be engaged in reflective teaching. Here, too, the evolution of media literacy, or media education as it is best known in Australia and Europe, reveals a movement away from simple elements of aesthetics or comprehension. Too much of what was termed "analysis" or "discovery learning" was, critics have argued, predetermined, with students engaged in little more than a "sophisticated exercise in guessing what's in the teacher's mind" (Buckingham and Sefton-Green 1994, 130). Questions about ideology, power, social relations, and the way knowledge is constructed, carried, and conveyed by media representations necessitate a commitment to both critical thinking and a critical pedagogy. When a media literacy teacher asks, "How do media operate? In whose interests does the media operate? How is meaning created by the media?" higher-order thinking skills must be used. In the process the relationship between student and teacher is altered. Describing this evolution in media education in the United Kingdom, Len Masterman said, "It severely undermined the hierarchical role of the teacher as the accredited expert and purveyor of approved knowledge within the classroom. The teacher was no longer the arbiter of taste, but a partner or co-investigator in what was now a much more open-ended process" (1989, 13). Though some see this as radical, formulating a clash between static or absolute knowledge on the one hand and relativism on the other, the concept of knowledge as socially constructed is becoming increasingly mainstream. In 1997 *The Report to the President on the Use of Technology to Strengthen K–12 Education in the United States* made specific reference to reform efforts "on higher order thinking and problem-solving activities and on learning models based on the active construction by each student of his or her own knowledge and skills" (President's Committee, 87). The transformation of the teacher-centered classroom is the logical outcome of one of the key tenets of media literacy, which argues that audiences negotiate meaning, that rather than a single right answer, students may recognize and articulate a variety of perspectives on the same event or issue. In the process it is likely that they will come to realize that "how we experience our world is governed by assumptions of which we are not aware; it also becomes clear that any world view is but one of many" (Sarason 1983, 88). In fact, television technology has contributed to this liberation as "our children became consumers of possibilities . . . which stimulated the questioning-answering process we call curiosity" (93). There was, however, a problem. In the chapter "Schools as Uninteresting Places," Seymour Sarason observes that "the world of the school and the world of possibilities were in different experiential orbits" (95).

Media literacy represents an alignment of the curriculum of the classroom and the curriculum of the living room. While it is possible to teach about media in a traditional chalk-and-talk, teacher-centered classroom,

the principles of media literacy imply a methodology that changes both students and teachers. If audiences are actively engaged in constructing meaning rather than passively accepting it, the relationship among students, teachers, and the curriculum must inevitably change. As we have noted, Appalachian State University's Reich College of Education has been described as a national exemplar in undergraduate teacher training insofar as it addresses media literacy. While some of that success story can undoubtedly be attributed to the contribution, even charisma, of individual faculty, the college itself is receptive to a model that accommodates media literacy. The National Council for Accreditation of Teacher Education (NCATE) requires that all accredited colleges of education adopt a conceptual framework that provides the basis for their teacher education program. The framework at Appalachian provides an insight into the theoretical and philosophical context that accepts and nurtures media literacy. Initially developed by Gary Moorman and Bill Blanton, the model has been adopted by the college after a prolonged period that included debate, discourse, and dissent with members of the Core Curriculum Committee and the entire college. From the perspective of this model, the present generations use cultural content to solve problems and transform the culture for the next generation. "The role of the teacher in this process becomes one of organizing and guiding learners in activity leading to the acquisition and mastery of knowledge, skills, beliefs, values . . . cultural capital" (1997, 4–5). The model rejects behaviorist-reductionist models of the past because they have resulted in "a curriculum with little potential meaning and usefulness for students" (5). In its place, the college model argues that (1) knowledge is socially constructed, (2) a community of practice provides the context for learning, and (3) knowledge is a tool that guides teaching practice (7). The model considers "the importance of the teacher as co-active learner" and that the teacher "must have a meaningful professional relationship with pupils in order to recruit their assistance in planning and implementing instruction and co-constructing a democratic classroom" (11). Students are introduced to this model in one of their earliest core classes. This is further developed in Technology, Literacy and Teaching. The course examines the evolutionary nature of literacy, provides an introduction to media literacy, and offers hands-on experiences with a number of tools, including digital cameras and scanners. Student productions may include web site design, video production, and desktop publishing. The course also models Instructional Conversation as described by Claude Goldenberg. Shifting away from the traditional lecture or chalk-and-talk format, instructional conversation is a technique in which "the teacher manages to keep everyone engaged in a substantive and extended conversation weaving individual participants' comments into a larger tapestry meaning" (1992–93, 318). All students and faculty participate in a listserv, responding to readings, discussions, and screenings as they move toward establishing a community of practice capable of debating the issues that confront schools today. Though the course helps students explore contemporary issues and provides hands-on training, it is not a blanket endorsement of technology. Rather, the course proposes that through their readings and experiences, these young teachers will learn to "take an educational point of view regarding the computer" and other technologies so they can "raise not only questions of effectiveness, but also questions of values, alternatives and side-effects-ends as well as means" (Shelfer 1991, 82). The course, by nature, generates resistance, questioning, and discomfort. For some students lacking technical experience, the new tools seem very threatening. Still others find that religious values and teachings are challenged or threatened by multiculturalism and the growing presence of minorities in the classroom. For others, concepts of learning styles and multiple intelligences seem correct but unmanageable. They understand the implications for increased workload behind a philosophy that "everything can be taught in several ways." They also recognize Howard Gardner's truth that "so long as materials are taught and assessed in only one way, we will reach only a certain kind of child" (1997, 2). Exposing

these young pre-service teachers to a range of teaching tools and techniques opens their eyes, minds, and hearts to the need to teach and reach all students. By implication, it rejects the traditional chalk-and-talk, teacher-centered classroom where all students do the same thing the same way.

Recognizing the need for change, however, is not the same as knowing what change should take place or how to bring it about. Change is not a given. The culture and climate of schools as institutions frequently imprison teachers as well as students. Jonathan Kozol asks teachers, "How do we start to free ourselves from impotence and inertia" in order to "awaken students, to spark their curiosity and to open up their minds?" (1993, 3). Before teachers can permit students to speak out in the first person, to recognize their own role in constructing knowledge, Kozol believes teachers too must be liberated from a school system that "trains us not to speak in the first person" (10). While the teacher must always be a professional, practicing the art and craft of teaching, reaching students also requires a personal response. Kozol believes that teachers "need to be first persons in the eyes of children in the deeper sense of letting all our own complexities, our viewpoints, hesitations, dreams, and passions—and our vulnerable aspects, too—become apparent to the class" (12). It is a view endorsed by no less a figure than Jean Piaget, who clearly understood that stuffing facts into our children's heads was no substitute for touching their hearts and tapping their feelings. While the cognitive classroom conforms to the requirements of a system that stresses measurement and evaluation, Piaget realized that it addressed only part of the child. Our students, he said, are human beings "not partly cognitive and partly emotional, but in being and substance . . . both of these all of the time and indivisibly." Once we recognize this, he suggested, "effective teachers will see to it that emotion in some human interest form . . . does appear" (1970, 30). In both content and delivery, media literacy can facilitate this process by connecting kids to the curriculum.

STUDENT-CENTERED LEARNING: Putting the ME in MEdia and MEaning

In 1972 the Coleman Report, *Youth: Transition to Adulthood*, noted that schools deny students responsibility, as a result of which they become irresponsible. The following year, Cusick's study, *Inside High School*, said school "has systematically denied their involvement in basic educational processes and relegated them to the position of watchers, waiters, order-followers, and passive receptacles for the depositing of disconnected bits of information. They in turn have responded by paying only a minimal amount of forced attention" (1973, 222).

Three years later the New Secondary Education Task Force reported, "schooling of adolescents is often conducted in ways contradicting the nature and demands of human growth and development. Consequently, it loses power as a setting for learning" (Gibbons 1976, 49–50). Noting the impact of the media on adolescents, the task force said that schools "cannot ignore the hours adolescents spend dormant before television and other media. This time can be used by cultivating student involvement in action programs, by teaching students to relate actively to the media and by involving commercial television in the community's educational enterprise" (65).

By the late 1980s, the *Turning Points* report on the nation's middle schools concluded that adolescents are exposed to "massive impersonal schools" and "unconnected seemingly irrelevant curricula" (Carnegie Council 1989, 13). While instructional methodology clearly alienated many students, it was much more than a question of mere delivery. The very content of the curriculum lacked connectedness. Marieli Rowe, the executive director of the National Telemedia Council, put it succinctly when she said, "Task forces of two national commissions have looked at education in depth and with painstaking detail. What they have failed to consider is the child of the television age" (1985, 24). In the 1960s, Marshall McLuhan had said that children of the television era could not function within the confines of the traditional classroom. Two decades later *A Pedagogy for Liberation* (Shor and Freire 1987) continued to describe a mismatch between the world in which children live and the world in which they are schooled. Shor and Freire noted what they called "student resistance to the official curriculum." They also saw teachers and administrators refusing to change a curriculum that alienated students. Although school officials viewed student response as "mediocrity," the authors said it was actually "a performance strike" and that students "withdrew into passive noncompliance or offensive sabotage in response to disempowering education" (121–41). Elaborating on the gap between school and society, Shor and Freire said, "The world of American education, the school, is increasing the separation of the words we read and the world we live in . . . the world of reading is only the world of the schooling process, a closed world, cut off from the world we live where we have experiences but do not read about those experiences" (135).

Ray Browne has said, "We have been living in a democracy but educating towards an aristocracy of ideas and aesthetics" (1980, 12). The elitism evident in such schools drives many young people away. While educators typically refer to such students as dropouts, it might be more appropriate to call them "push-outs," repelled by and expelled from a system that ignores their very nature and needs as both people and pupils. In school systems where media literacy has been introduced, absenteeism has frequently declined while retention rates have increased. The reasons are quite simple. Media literacy by its very nature is a liberating experience that builds a bridge between the curriculum and young people. Its subject matter addresses the world of pop culture in which so many of our young people are steeped. But it is more than a matter of curriculum content. Key tenets of media literacy also result in classroom methods and practices that engage students and validate their own knowledge. Properly approached, it puts an end to what has been called "the Siberian syndrome" by which students are positioned as "exiles in the culture war of the classroom" (Shor 1996, 1). Canadian media literacy pioneer Barry Duncan has said, "Once teachers confront the popular culture of young people, they find media-generated issues are one of the best bridges to the world of their students" (1988). No longer the passive and disinterested consumers of school knowledge, students are now actively engaged in the exploration, discovery, and construction of their own knowledge. As such, media education "has the potential to challenge traditional notions of what counts as valid knowledge and culture" (Buckingham 1993, 285). But media literacy does more than change curriculum content. Teachers move away from the banking model in which they make deposits into their students' heads, instead becoming midwives delivering the ideas that are already there (Claxton 1990).

While it is possible for media literacy teachers to tackle their subject from a teacher-centered perspective, the ideas that audiences negotiate meaning and that knowledge is socially constructed should inevitably alter power relations within the classroom. Such classrooms are student centered, valuing participatory learning that is activist, affective, and democratic. David Buckingham describes such an approach by saying, "It implies a view of teaching and learning about the media as essentially dialectical and reflexive processes—as a constant movement back and forth between action and reflection—between practice and theory, between celebration and critical analysis and between language use and language study" (1993, 297). Ira Shor describes the liberation that results from a shift in classroom authority when teachers abandon the unilateral transfer of knowledge. "Empowered students," he says, "make meaning and act from reflection, instead of memorizing facts and values handed to them" (1992, 15). As might be expected, any change in power relations is bound to attract its critics. In a venomous essay called "Shakespeare Versus Spiderman," John Leo from *U.S. News and World Report* let loose on national standards for English language arts and the whole constructivist approach to education. He spoke derisively of "learning strategies," "gobbleygook education theory," and "multicultural claptrap." Describing the meltdown of traditional education, Leo attacked the idea that "meaning is not inherent in any text but is created in the mind of each child." The end result, he said, is that the teacher cannot teach. Instead, the teacher acts "as a marginal but friendly guide to critical thinking, which turns out not to mean the development of sharp and logical critical skills but the easy accumulation of divergent views on all matters. In effect learning becomes just another choice, a marketplace view of thought without thinkers" (1996, 61).

MEDIA ATTITUDES: *Advocates, Accomplices, and Adversaries*

Those who wish to promote media literacy within our schools should also take into account existing attitudes about mass media, educational media, and even library media specialists. Paul Saettler's *History of Instructional Technology* (1968) has some sobering lessons for anyone attempting to promote the use of media and technology within our schools. As early as 1923, researchers concluded that the infant audiovisual movement frequently placed too much emphasis on operator skills rather than helping teachers integrate the new tools into their own discipline. "The movement for visual education will progress in direct ratio to the number of teachers who are trained in the technique of visual instruction" (193). In the late 1980s, after more than a decade of spending on computer technologies and VCRs, *Educational Technology* said, "Very few universities currently prepare teachers to use instructional technology by modeling the use of technologies in classes . . . for most faculty in teacher education, technology is a bother, a mystery, a blur, a largely incomprehensible phenomenon" (Gooler 1989, 20). Sadly, the mistakes made with computers throughout the 1980s had little to do with the technology itself but mirrored the unsuccessful patterns of acquisition and application from the past. In 1969, *Audiovisual Communication Review* observed that "educational technology ends up doing little else but perpetuating the traditional system of education . . . despite their ability to revolutionize and upgrade the quality of education, they can by the same time mirror and prolong what is already going on in the school" (Hooper, 249). Almost three decades later, the presidential report on technology and education would note that while technology had transformed America's "offices, factories and retail establishments, its impact within our nation's classrooms has generally been quite modest" (President's Committee 1997, 11). Among other recommendations, the study called for "the use of new pedagogic methods focusing on the development of higher-order reasoning and problem solving skills" and a deeper understanding of "the ways in which technology should actually be used within an educational context" (7).

Of course, the use of media and technology cannot be isolated from the user and from the attitudes and perceptions that teachers, administrators, library media specialists, and parents have developed over a long period of time. Research suggests that these attitudes are crucial in determining the success or failure of technology in the teaching-learning process (Bellamy 1978; Pfister 1982; Smith and Ingersol 1984). Considine (1985) characterized these attitudes as media advocates, media accomplices, and media adversaries. The advocate is the teacher, administrator, or library media specialist who accepts as irrevocable the presence of an increasingly hi-tech culture and seeks ways to effectively incorporate the tools and techniques of this culture into the classroom. Media is viewed as a friend rather than a foe, as a means of complementing the instructional process rather than as a competitor. The accomplice is well-meaning but frequently misguided. While accomplices may incorporate media and technology into the classroom, it is often misused. It may be used as an electronic baby-sitter or a reward for students who have completed the real work. Accomplices seldom if ever preview videotapes or other media they use. Videotapes and other software are selected by what is termed the "have you got anything on? syndrome." This phenomenon occurs when a teacher arrives at the library media center and announces, "I'm doing marsupials today; have you got anything on it?" There are two real problems with such an approach. *Just because the program is about the topic, it does not mean that the program is suitable for the students or even the objectives.* The second problem is the direct result of failing to preview the program. Since the teacher has not seen it, students will not be provided with cueing and retrieval strategies. Feedback seldom follows a screening. As such, these teachers tend to perpetuate the passive and private pattern of viewing and consumption that too many students are already engaged in at home. Potentially they undermine the work of media and technology enthusiasts who must frequently account for ineffective or inappropriate use of media by their colleagues.

But the real barrier to media literacy is the media adversary. Saettler's *History of Instructional Technology* documents the presence of these hostile attitudes in the silent-film era of the 1920s. In the 1960s, Gans described the clash between school culture and media culture. "The school considers mass media fare uncultured, uncouth and because of its erotic and violent components, unwholesome. The mass media view school as dull, stodgy and unfashionable. Moreover the school preaches a culture of production and participation: the media one of consumption and spectatoring" (1967). Many beginning media literacy teachers have inadvertently activated these attitudes and found themselves accused of wasting valuable instructional time by watching television. Trying to explain to media adversaries that the process of watching is active rather than passive is a difficult task with this technological ostrich of the species, who possesses a Luddite-like resistance to media/technology, which is often perceived as an assault upon the primacy of print.

Nor are such views restricted to conservative teachers or even our schools. Media adversaries have no difficulty finding support in both the popular press and the academic press. *The Christian Science Monitor*, for example, has been critical of what it termed "edutainment," which it misguidedly believed to be incompatible with "that old fashioned learning process called reading" (1989, 12–13). In *Educational Leadership*, Harriet Shenkman invoked a military metaphor for the war with the media. The time has arrived, she said, "to marshal forces against the electronic demons that are having a damaging effect on the literacy of our students" (1985, 29). Never mind the fact that a substantial body of research suggests that when properly used, these same media can actually foster traditional literacy, including thinking, reading, and writing skills (Hortin and Teague 1984; McKim 1972; Sinatra 1986).

Research psychologist Kathy Pezdek has attempted to debunk some of the myths commonly associated with television and other media. Much of the opposition, she says, "comes from the aspect of human nature that causes all of us to split the world into halves—love and hate, safe and dangerous, good and evil" (1985, 41). In *The Closing of the American Mind*, Allan Bloom showed himself particularly hostile to popular music: "It ruins the imagination of young people and makes it very difficult for them to have a passionate relationship to the art and the thought that are the substance of liberal education" (1987, 79). Such elitist nonsense fosters conflict rather than cooperation between youth culture and school culture. This climate of hostility and confrontation does nothing to help young people understand mass media and its impact on their lives. Bloom claims MTV makes life "a nonstop commercially prepackaged masturbational fantasy" (1987, 75). Although he bemoans that situation and its impact on "the great tradition," he turns his back and closes his own mind to the idea of critical analysis of the media. Pop culture product is left to triumph over pedagogical process. This situation is part of a wider belief system that surrenders to the mystique of the machine and technology in our culture rather than recognizing that machines are created by humans and that what affects us are the decisions we make about the machines. Realizing that media representations may affect our opinions, attitudes, and behaviors implicitly involves realizing that we may not control our lives as much as we want to believe. Mark Crispin Miller suggests that many Americans do not recognize the media's impact on their lives: "Most Americans still perceive the media image as transparent, a sign that simply says what it means and means what it says. They therefore tend to dismiss any intensive explication as a case study of reading too much into it" (1988, 49).

Those who speak most loudly against the media invariably see only one side of the issue. In many cases such people seek to protect children from the media by banning or denying children access to certain forms of media rather than by teaching children critical thinking and viewing skills. Many of them, knowingly or otherwise, are also defending their own territory and traditions. These traditions and perceptions actually prevent them and their students from benefiting from these technologies and programs. Describing this situation, George Comstock said, "Educators have a tendency to be literary snobs, regretting the passing of an old order in which people really knew how to read and write. This attitude has prevented us from seeing the revolutionary promise of the electronic media that give new cognitive possibilities to disadvantaged groups" (1984, 46).

PARTNERS IN PROGRESS: KNOW-TV and Other Initiatives

As microcosms of society, schools are only as good as or as bad as the community they serve. The changing composition of the student population and the curriculum continues to place increased strains on school personnel and funding with the result that some programs are cut, others are watered down, teachers burn out, and students tune out. Rather than trying to go it alone, schools can begin to address some of their pressing problems through the process of partnership, forming coalitions of concern. Secretary of Education Richard Riley recognizes this need. "Schools cannot do it alone. But together we can improve American education—school by school and community by community." Arguing that "better education is everybody's business," Riley advocates building business and community partnerships for learning. Partners with the schools support education initiatives through funding, human and materials resources, and advocacy. One outstanding example of a partnership among business, the media industry, public schools, academia, and parents is the media literacy initiative developed by the Discovery Channel. It demonstrates what can be achieved when educators and the industry work with, rather than against, each other. KNOW-TV is a media literacy curriculum for analyzing non-fiction television developed by Dr. Renee Hobbs in collaboration with The Learning Channel and Time Warner Cable. It received the prestigious 1995 Golden Cable Ace Award for Public Service Programming. The program addresses "children's developmental needs and the process of designing speaking, listening, reading, and writing activities to help strengthen student analysis and communication skills" (Hobbs 1995, 7). It also provides a rationale and justification for including media literacy in the K-12 curriculum, by referring specifically to several components from North Carolina's state curriculum. But the program is only part of the process of promoting media literacy in the classroom and living room.

In 1996, Discovery Communications embarked on an ambitious series of media literacy workshops throughout the country. Coordinated by Anne Lamoureux, Discovery's executive director of Governmental Relations, the events have been held in Mississippi, Wyoming, Maryland, Tennessee, and elsewhere. Each event is carefully designed and developed around the concerns and issues addressed by the local community, frequently through their senator or congressional representative. Political support for the programs has come from both Democrats and Republicans, making media literacy a bipartisan issue. The influential politicians who have endorsed these programs include Billy Tauzin, chair of the House Telecommunications Committee, and U.S. Representative Jim McCrery, a member of the House Ways and Means Subcommittee. In Jackson, Tennessee, U.S. Representative John Tanner described the event as "one of the landmark days of our lives when it comes to educating our children" (9/15/97). No less enthusiastic was Connie Morello, who represents Maryland's eighth District. The former college English professor serves as chair of the Science Committee's Technology Subcommittee. Morello told a gathering of parents, administrators, teachers, and students that the media influences the way we see the world. Critical of the impact of negative advertising on the political process, she said media literacy was a necessary skill in the new information age. As a mother of nine and a grandmother of 15, Connie Morello believes in media literacy

and the work of Discovery Communications as they promote the KNOW-TV workshops. Others lending their support for the program by their active presence and participation have included Gerald Tirozzi, the assistant secretary for Elementary and Secondary Education, whose office oversees Title I; Goals 2000; and the Safe and Drug Free Schools Program. Hoover Alger, deputy director of the Office of National Drug Control Policy, has also taken part in KNOW-TV, further strengthening the bonds between media literacy advocates and the prevention community.

After a morning of introductions, lectures, and demonstrations, participants, including parents, teachers, principals, library media specialists, and even the occasional mayor or council member, are put to work as many of them begin, often for the first time, to think constructively and creatively about the media messages that surround them daily. It is a lively and frequently liberating experience. Assigned to different groups, they are asked to assume the characteristics and identity of different audiences or demographic blocks. Then they are given the task of creating a program about safe handling of food that will appeal to this market. Having spent years, even decades, as consumers of media messages, these parents and teachers suddenly become creators. The results are stimulating and informative. But that's just part of the program; when the teachers return to their classrooms, they are armed with readings, videotape resources, and most importantly, a new way of looking at the media, so in turn they can help children become better users and choosers of media messages. It is important to note that while experts and consultants conduct the program, ownership belongs to the participants. Dr. Hobbs tells them they are "encouraged to adopt, alter, modify, and adjust" the materials and methods presented in the program. Finally, the programs frequently include members of the local PTAs who have taken part in training provided as part of the "Taking Charge of Your TV" outreach. These sessions, which represent a partnership of the National PTA and the Cable Television Industry, have reached more than 100,000 parents. Parents like Sharon Weigh and Betsy Landers lend credence and support to these media literacy initiatives by demonstrating what they have learned and what they have done in their own families and living rooms. The message is clear: If we can do it, you can do it. Betsy Landers put it simply. After she took part in the media literacy training, she said she and her family had become more "intelligent and intentional viewers."

If KNOW-TV is the most ambitious media literacy road show, it is by no means alone, and it also limits its focus for the most part to non-fiction television. *Creating Critical Viewers*, on the other hand, is a concept developed by Dorothy and Jerome Singer under funding provided by the National Academy of Television Arts and Sciences (NATAS). This videotape and teachers' resource book explores health and safety issues, media stereotyping, commercials, news, and violence, among other subjects. The program intends to help students and teachers understand the conventions and formal features of television. Once again building a bridge between traditional literacy and media literacy, *Creating Critical Viewers* seeks to develop skills that "encompass the mechanics of writing—use of proper grammar, spelling, use of dictionaries, and of course, the ability to read with emphasis upon comprehension and interpretation" (Singer and Singer 1994). With regional conferences across the country, NATAS offers training and provides school visits by media professionals to talk about career choices in the media industry.

Undoubtedly the most comprehensive and potentially the most controversial coalition of concern is the Cultural Environment Movement (CEM). Created by legendary media educator Dr. George Gerbner, the organization convened its founding conference at Webster University in St. Louis in March 1996. Representing 150 independent organizations in every U.S. state and 63 countries on six continents, the organization seeks to promote freedom, fairness, responsibility, respect, diversity, and other values. It also believes that media creates an environment that frequently undermines such values. The founding convention created a Viewer's Declaration of Independence. Beginning with the familiar phrase, "We hold these truths to be self-evident," it went on to assert that "all children are endowed with the right to grow up in a cultural environment that fosters

responsibility, trust, and community, rather than force, fear and violence." Further, the declaration proclaimed independence from a media system that it said, "constrains life choices as much as the degradation of the physical environment limits life choices" (The People's Communication Charter 1996).

Though the document and convention delegates frequently employed the potentially alienating language of the left, which might lose support among more moderate parents and school administrators, the recommendations beneath the language were compatible with a responsible and comprehensive approach to the new information age. In fact, its vision of an informed, responsive, responsible, and active citizen monitoring both media content and ownership is a model for activism and advocacy in a democracy. The agenda for action published by the convention advocated media literacy programs supported by schools, churches, youth organizations, and the community. Further, it encouraged the support and election of school board members and candidates for office who supported media literacy endeavors of teachers and students. It also cast a critical eye on industry involvement, opposing "the use of media literacy as a public relations tool to rationalize the existing media system." As such, CEM might be seen to condemn the media literacy efforts promoted by Discovery Communications and NATAS, but it does not necessarily do so.

Among the diverse organizations and interests represented at the CEM convention, 15 working groups created recommendations for the governing body. Among these was a group that explored religion as a *cultural force* and media culture as *religion*. In an age of materialism and conspicuous consumption, religious people often wonder if it is still possible to raise a child to have spiritual values. Such a concern was evident in statements from this committee. In their recommendations to the board, they said it was time to "fight the media's reduction of our inner lives, our very selves to a totally material plane, and replace the notion that we exist mostly to consume, with the understanding that we are to serve, share, witness and celebrate." They also recommended that parishioners "practice media fasting to provide quiet periods for creative reflection on the human condition." Tellingly, they sought to support positive programming, to "avoid unwarranted and dispiriting criticism," and to "recognize the positive efforts of people of goodwill working within the media" (Working Committee 1997). Unfortunately, most of this modest language never found its way into the final report. A healthy, balanced view of the relationship between media and religion has, however, been developed at the University of Dayton. Led by Sister Fran Trampiets, the Institute for Pastoral Initiatives has introduced media education in the School of Education's Teacher Education Department, as well as the Faith and Values course in the Religious Studies Department. The Catholic Archdiocese of Cincinnati, in which the University of Dayton is located, has integrated media education into its programs and encourages the development of these skills in its teachers and pastoral leaders. At the national level, this has also been evident in the annual National Catholic Education Association conference, which draws 14,000 to 15,000 participants and regularly includes media literacy training. The Catholic commitment to media literacy operates on an international as well as a national level and has been endorsed by the Pope.

On World Communications Day 1994, Pope John Paul II articulated the need for parents to be critical viewers. He cautioned against parents who "surrender their role as the primary educators of their children," noting the "need for sound media education programs," and called upon parents to function as "discriminating television viewers" (Pope John Paul II 1994). In 1997, as a further sign of the growing cooperation between church groups, the National Council of Churches convened Media Awareness Year and hosted a national teleconference, Family, Media and Community Values. Ironically, while many church members express concern about media messages, they also understand that the ministry and "the word" can be spread through the same media and technology. While some may point the finger of blame at Hollywood and the media industry, as consumers and citizens, we must take a more proactive role in the way we choose and use media. Name-calling and the blame game, however entertaining, seldom create solutions for the problems we perceive, and frequently alienate those who would be our allies. The victim/villain model that presents the media as the bad guys and citizen/consumers as the good guys is far too simplistic. Rather than simply asking, "What does the media do to us?" it is now time to ask "What can we do with the media?"

REFERENCES

Adler, Mortimer, (1989). Our Students Must Learn to Think, Not Just to Take Tests (editorial). *Charlotte Observer*, September 23

American Association of School Librarians and Association for Educational Communication and Technology, (1988). *Information Power: Guidelines for School Library Media Programs*. Chicago: AASL and AECT.

Apple, Michael, (1979). *Ideology and Curriculum*. Boston: Routledge & Kegan Paul.

———, (1983). *Ideology and Practice in Schooling*. Philadelphia: Temple University Press.

———, (1986). *Teachers and Texts*. New York: Routledge & Kegan Paul.

Apple, Michael, and Linda Christian Smith, (1991). *The Politics of the Textbook*. New York: Routledge.

Auferheide, Patricia, and Charles Firestone, (1993). The National Leadership Conference on Media Literacy. Aspen Institute Communications and Society Program, Washington, DC.

Balli, Sandra et al., (1997). PreService Teachers' Field Experiences with Technology. *Educational Technology*, September-October, 40-46.

Bellamy, R. et al., (1978). Teacher Attitudes Toward Nonprint Media. Frankfort Kentucky State Department of Education. *ERIC Document #174*, 197.

Bloom, Allan, (1987). *The Closing of the American Mind*. New York: Simon and Schuster.

Boyer, Ernest L., (1988). Preface. In Edward Palmer, *Television and America's Children: A Crisis of Neglect*. New York: Oxford University Press.

Browne, Ray, (1980). Libraries at the Crossroads: A Perspective on Libraries and Culture. *Drexel Library Quarterly*, 16:3, 12-23.

Buckingham, David, (1993). *Children Talking Television: The Making of Television Literacy*. London: Falmer Press.

Buckingham, David, and Julian Sefton-Green, (1994). *Cultural Studies Goes to School: Reading and Teaching Popular Media*. London: Taylor & Francis.

Carnegie Council on Adolescent Development, (1989). *Turning Points: Preparing American Youth for the 21st Century*. New York: Carnegie Corporation.

———, (1992). *Fateful Choices: Healthy Youth for the 21st Century*. New York: Carnegie Corporation.

Carnegie Forum on Education and the Economy, (1986). *A Nation Prepared: Teachers for the 21st Century*. New York: Carnegie Corporation.

Chadwick, Clifton B., (1979). Why Educational Technology Is Failing and What Can Be Done to Create Success. *Educational Technology*, 19:1, 7-19.

Christian Science Monitor, (1989). Video Games Children Play. September 6, 12-13.

Claxton, Charles, (1990). Learning Styles: Minority Students and Effective Education. *Journal of Developmental Education*, 14:1, 6-8.

Coleman, James, (1972). *Youth: Transition to Adulthood*. Report of the Panel on Youth of the President's Science Advisory Committee. Chicago: University of Chicago Press.

Commonwealth of Virginia, Department of Education, (1989). Standards of Learning Objectives: Social Studies. Richmond, VA.

Commonwealth of Virginia, Department of Education, (1990). Standards of Learning Objectives: Health. Richmond, VA.

Comstock, George, (1984). Mind over Media. *Television and Children*, 7:3 and 4, 46-48.

Considine, David, (1985). Media Technology and Teaching: What's Wrong and Why? *School Library Media Quarterly*, Summer, 173-82.

———, (1990). Media Literacy: Can We Get There from Here? *Educational Technology*, December, 27-32.

———, (1994). The Media and the Message: How Librarians Can Bring Them into Focus. *School Library Journal*, January, 24-28.

———, (1995). Are We There Yet? An Update on the Media Literacy Movement. *Educational Technology*, July/August, 32-43.

———, (1997). Media Literacy: A Compelling Component of School Reform and Restructuring. In Robert Kubey (ed.), *Media Literacy in the Information Age*, New Brunswick, NJ: Transaction Publishers, 243-62.

Considine, David M., and Marilie Rowe, (1995). White House Convenes Media Literacy and Substance Abuse Forum. *Telemedium: The Journal of Media Literacy*, Fall, 41:2, 4-6.

Cultural Environment Movement, (1996). *Report from the Working Group on Religion and the Media*. St. Louis, March.

Cusick, Philip, (1973). *Inside High School*. New York: Holt.

Duncan, Barry, (1988). *Media Beat Education Forum*, Autumn.

———, (1989). Media Literacy at the Crossroads: Some Issues, Problems and Questions. *History and Social Science Teacher*, Summer, 205-9.

———, (1993). Media and Popular Culture in the Classroom: Perspectives on Media Pedagogy. Media Competency as a Challenge to School and Education. Compendium of a conference held by the Bertelsmann Foundation, Gutersloh, Germany.

Dwyer, Francis, (1978). *Strategies for Improving Visual Instruction*. University Park, PA: State College Learning Services.

Etheridge, Bob, (1993). News release from Citizens for Media Literacy. Asheville, NC, September.

Florida Department of Education, (1993). Social Studies Curriculum. Tallahassee, FL.

Gagne, R., (1980). Learnable Aspects of Problem Solving. *Educational Psychologist*, 15:2, 84-92.

Gans, Herbert J., (1967). The Mass Media as an Educational Institution. *TV Quarterly*, 16:20.

Gardner, Howard, (1997). An Interview with Howard Gardner. *Mindshift Connection*, April, 2.

Georgia Department of Education, (1989a). Quality Core Curriculum: Health and Safety. Atlanta, GA.

———, (1989b). Quality Core Curriculum: Social Studies. Atlanta, GA.

Gibbons, Maurice, (1976). *The New Secondary Education: A Phi Delta Kappa Task Force Report*. Bloomington, IN: Phi Delta Kappa.

Glasser, William, (1986). *Control Theory in the Classroom*. New York: Harper & Row.

Goldenberg, Claude, (1992-93). Promoting Comprehension Through Discussion. *The Reading Teacher*, 46:4, 316-26.

Gooler, D., (March 1989). Preparing Teachers to Use Technologies: Can Universities Meet the Challenge? *Educational Technology*, 18-21.

Grant, Carl, (1984). *Preparing for Reflective Teaching*. Boston: Allyn & Bacon.

Hobbs, Renee, (1994). The Billerica Initiative Brings Media Literacy to Middle School. *Community Media Review*, 17:1, 17, 19.

———, (1995). *KNOW-TV: Changing What, Why and How You Watch*. Bethesda, MD: The Learning Channel.

Hooper, Richard A., (1969). Diagnosis of Failure. *Audiovisual Communication Review*, 17:3, 245-64.

Hortin, J. A., and F. A. Teague, (1984). Use of Visualization in Problem Solving: A Comparison of American and African Students. *International Journal of Instructional Media*, 11, 135-40.

Impoco, Jim et al. (1996). TV's Frisky Family Values. *U.S. News and World Report,*. April 15, 58-82.

Kozol, Jonathan, (1993). *On Being a Teacher*. Oxford, UK: One World Publications.

Kunin, Madeline, (1994). Address, School Improvement Through Media Education Conference. Georgia Center for Continuing Education, Athens, April.

Leo, John, (1996). Shakespeare Versus Spiderman. *U.S. News and World Report*, April 1, 61.

Lortie, Dan, (1975). *Schoolteacher: A Sociological Study*. Chicago: University of Chicago Press.

Maryland State Department of Education, (1993). *Health Education: A Curricular Framework*. Baltimore, MD.

Masterman, Len, (1989). The Development of Media Education in Europe in the 1980s. *Metro*, No. 79, 13-17.

McKim, Robert H., (1972). *Experiences in Visual Thinking*. Monterey, CA: Brooks Cole Publishers.

McNeil, Linda, (1986). *Contradictions of Control*. Boston: Routledge and Kegan Paul.

Mecklenburger, James, (1990). Educational Technology Is Not Enough. *Phi Delta Kappan,* October, 105-8.

Merrow, John, (1995). *Promises, Promises*. Videotape. The Merrow Report, New York.

Miller, Mark Crispin, (1988). *Boxed In: The Culture of TV*. Evanston, IL: Northwestern University Press.

Moorman, Gary, and Bill Blanton, (1997). *Reich College of Education Conceptual Framework of Teacher Preparation*. Boone, NC: Appalachian State University.

Muffoletto, Robert, (1988). Reflective Teaching and Visual Literacy: Teacher Intervention and Programmed Instruction. *Journal of Visual Literacy*, 8:2, 53-66.

Naisbitt, John, (1982). *Megatrends*. New York: Warner Books.

National Committee on Excellence in Education, (1983). *A Nation at Risk: The Imperative for Educational Reform*. Washington, DC: U.S. National Commission on Excellence in Education.

New Jersey State Department of Education, (1991). Core Course Proficiencies: English/Language Arts, Division of General Academic Education. Trenton, NJ.

New Mexico Department of Education, (1993). English Language Arts Framework. Santa Fe, NM.

North Carolina Department of Public Instruction, (1992a). Communication Skills Curriculum. Raleigh NC.

———, (1992b). Standard Course of Study-Information Skills K-12. Raleigh, NC.

Office of National Drug Control Strategy, (1995). *National Drug Control Strategy: Executive Summary*. Executive Office of the President, Washington, DC.

Olympia School District, (1997). Communication Skills Curriculum. Olympia, WA.

The People's Communication Charter, (1996). *The Cultural Environment Monitor*, 1:1, 4

Perelman, L., (1988). Restructuring the System Is the Solution. *Phi Delta Kappan*, September, 20-24.

Pezdek, Kathy, (1985). Is Watching TV Passive, Addictive or Uncreative? Debunking Some Myths. *Television and Families*, 8:2, 41-46.

Pfister, Fred, (1982). Competencies Essential for School Media Specialists. *Journal of Education for Librarianship*, 23:37.

Piaget, Jean, (1970). *Science of Education and the Psychology of the Child*. New York: Orion Press.

Pope John Paul II, (1994). Television and the Family: Guidelines for Good Viewing. *Catholic Family Media Guide*, April-May, 20.

Popular Computing, (1983). Computers, the Next Crisis in Education, August, 83-84.

President's Committee of Advisors on Science and Technology, (1997). *Report to the President on the Use of Technology to Strengthen K-12 Education in the United States*. Washington, DC.

Ravitch, Diane, and Chester E. Finn, Jr., (1987). *What Do Our 17 Year Olds Know?* New York: Harper & Row.

Riley, Richard, (1995). Media Literacy for America's Young People. Speech at Julius West Middle School, Rockville, MD, December 13.

Rowe, Marieli, (1985). Educating Children in the Television Age. *Television and Families*, 8:2, 24-27.

Saettler, Paul, (1968). *A History of Instructional Technology*. New York: McGraw Hill.

Sarason, Seymour, (1983). *School in America: Scapegoat and Salvation*. New York: The Free Press.

———, (1996). *Revisiting the Culture of the School and the Problem of Change*. New York: Teacher College, Columbia University.

Schwebel, Milton, and Jane Ralph, (1973). *Piaget in the Classroom*. New York: Basic Books.

Shalala, Donna, (1996). *Substance Abuse Prevention Strategy: Media Literacy Skills*. U.S. Department of Health and Human Services, Washington, DC.

Sheffler, Israel, (1991). *In Praise of the Cognitive Emotions*. New York: Routledge.

Shenkman, Harriet, (1985). Reversing the Literacy Decline by Controlling the Electronic Demons. *Educational Leadership*, 42:5, 26-30.

Shor, Ira, (1992). *Empowering Education: Critical Teaching for Social Change*. Chicago: University of Chicago Press.

———, (1996). *When Students Have Power: Negotiating Authority in a Critical Pedagogy*. Chicago: University of Chicago Press.

Shor, Ira, and Paulo Freire, (1987). *A Pedagogy for Liberation*. South Hadley, MA: Bergin & Garvey Publishers.

Sinatra, Richard, (1986). *Visual Literacy: Connections to Reading, Thinking and Writing*. Springfield, IL: CC Thomas.

Singer, Dorothy, and Jerome Singer, (1994). *Creating Critical Viewers: A Partnership Between Schools and Television Professionals*. Denver: Pacific Mountain Network.

Sizer, Theodore, (1992). School Reform: What's Missing? *World Monitor*, November, 20-27.

Sleeter, Christine, and Carl Grant, (1991). Race, Class, Gender and Disability in Current Textbooks. In Michael Apple and Linda Christian-Smith (eds.), *The Politics of the Textbook*. New York: Routledge.

Smith, C. B., and G. M. Ingersoll, (1984). Audiovisual Materials in U.S. Schools: A National Survey on Availability and Use. *Educational Technology*, 24:9, 36-38.

Sorensen, Kristine et al., (1994). A Minnesota Partnership for Media Literacy and Media Arts. *Telemedium: The Journal of Media Literacy*. Fall, 21-22.

Sykes, Charles, (1996). *Dumbing Down Our Kids: Why American Children Feel Good About Themselves but Can't Read or Write or Add*. New York: St. Martin's.

Waggoner, Michael, (1984). The New Technologies Versus the Lecture Tradition in Higher Education: Is Change Possible? *Educational Technology*, 24:3, 7-12.

Washington Post, Weekly Edition, (1990). Waiting in the Wings: The Doofus Generation. July 9-15, 37.

Washington State Commission on Student Learning, (1997). Essential Academic Learning Requirements. *Technical Manual*. Olympia, WA.

Wolcott, John, (1992). Land of Hype and Glory: Spin Doctors on Parade. *U.S. News and World Report*, February 10, 6.

Woodward, A., and D. Elliott, (1990). Textbook Use and Teacher Professionalism. In D. Elliott and A. Woodward (eds.), *Textbooks and Schooling in the U.S.* 89th Yearbook, Part 1, of the National Society for the Study of Education. Chicago: NSSE.

Working Committee, (1997). Religion as a Cultural Force. Inaugural Conference of The Cultural Environment Movement, St. Louis, March 15-17.

Woronov, Terry, (1994). Six Myths and Five Promising Truths About the Uses of Educational Technology. *The Harvard Education Letter*, X:5, September-October, 1-3.

Chapter 2

MEDIA LITERACY
The Purposes, Principles, and
Curriculum Connections

Media literacy represents both a subject of study and a method of teaching. Both revolutionary and evolutionary in nature, it provides a philosophy and pedagogy for transforming traditional education while it affirms some of the most traditional goals and values of American education. Nowhere is this more evident than in the belief that schools should create productive workers and responsible citizens for a democratic society. Differences of opinion, however, may exist regarding the definition of responsible citizenship. Though some no doubt would view this as evidenced by law-abiding behavior, community involvement, obedience, and conformity, many media literacy advocates would have another vision. For these people, a responsible citizen would also be law abiding and involved with the community. But such a citizen would be more questioning. This citizen would practice healthy skepticism, constructive criticism, and, most importantly, be informed. In an era of spin-doctors, image-makers, pollsters, corporate mergers, and the special-effects mastery of computer technology, such skills are not only important, they go to the very heart and soul of responsible citizenship.

Spiral of Cynicism: The Press and the Public Good (Capella and Jamieson 1997) argues that this involves more than simply understanding issues or events. "Understanding the impact of social and political events requires understanding how the events are framed for the public in the stories the press tells" (229). If "our knowledge of leaders and institutions is a 'mediated'

one" (31), we need to ask "what effect if any does how candidates and public policy debates are covered, have on public cynicism about leaders and their performance?" From the perspective of the media literacy movement, this would involve an awareness of the process of both storytelling and story-selling. The content of the coverage could not be separated from the context of marketing or the culture of conflict evident in contemporary journalism. In *Seducing America: How Television Charms the Modern Voter* (1994), Roderick Hart asks if television enlarges or constricts political dialogue. Are we, he asks, "the captives of television . . . or its masters—complex negotiators of the meanings and interpretations it offers"? (9).

However one answers that question, Hart is clear in his belief that those who wish to further citizenship must take into account the way media, technology, and particularly television cover and control the political process. The media has changed both how politics is conducted and how it is comprehended. Television, he says, has altered the job description of civic leaders as well as "influencing who runs for office in the first place. Television suggests what legislation governors should endorse and how far their support should extend. Television helps form the attitudes that citizens take into the voting booth, as well as the criteria they use when exercising their franchise" (5).

In his 1995 State of the Union Address, President Clinton made specific reference to both citizenship and the potentially harmful impact the media can have on the democratic process. "More and more of our citizens," he said, "now get most of their information in very negative or aggressive ways that is hardly conducive to honest and open conversations." Nor did the president exempt politicians from the process. "For years, we've mostly treated citizens like they were consumers or spectators, sort of political couch potatoes who were supposed to watch the TV ads either promise them something for nothing or play off their fears and frustrations." Of course, as the 1996 campaign demonstrated, Clinton himself was quite capable of engaging in the very behavior he condemned. (See "The Clinton Campaigns" in Chapter 4.) Talking the talk without walking the walk breeds cynicism and alienation. If we wish to bridge this gap between rhetoric and reality, we must first recognize it. As citizens that means we must become increasingly vigilant in an age of visual and verbal volleyball where the camera not only can, but frequently does, lie.

❖**Many things to many people, media literacy involves a complex interaction between media messages, media formats, and media audiences. Properly understood, it has interdisciplinary applications and implications. Copyright © 1998 Gail E. Haley.**

PURPOSES OF MEDIA LITERACY

The Indian parable of the blind men touching the elephant has some relevance for those of us who work with media literacy. At the very least, it suggests that media literacy can be seen in different ways by different constituencies. It encourages us to recognize that one size does not fit all and cautions us against slavish replication of models, especially models from other cultures, that are not necessarily appropriate to the unique characteristics of American schools or society. This is not to reject those approaches, but rather to encourage exploration and modification of such models based upon local conditions. Within the prevention community, successful management strategies are ones that have empowered those at the local level.

Similarly, media literacy must be flexible enough to offer principles and guidelines without dismissing those programs that concentrate on one component or another, such as production over analysis, protection instead of preparation, television rather than computers. As prevention professionals have noted, the successful shift from innovation to implementation and integration is most likely to occur when "community leaders and opinion shapers have the opportunity to take ownership of the strategy and make it their own . . . and when diverse community members are involved in tailoring the intervention to their community" (Hawkins, Arthur, and Catalano 1995, 404).

Purpose 1: Preparation

For citizens to be informed and responsible, they need to be able to do more than merely access information. In a high-tech world with information saturation, students and citizens must learn to discern. They need the skills to critically analyze and evaluate information. In an age when most Americans get most of their information from television not textbooks, pictures not print, we need a wider and newer definition of literacy. Media literacy is that definition. Far from rejecting the world of print and our traditional notions of literacy, it builds on and strengthens those concepts. A student who uses the Internet to access information, for example, will employ new technologies to locate information but will still process print. As is the case with most web sites, however, the student will encounter images as well as text. Words and images will combine to create the message and its effect. Media literacy strengthens this student by providing communication skills for today and tomorrow. There is no difficulty finding these skills specifically addressed in various state curricula. In Oklahoma, for example, students access, organize, and use information with computers. Idaho expects students to communicate effectively in reading, speaking, writing, listening, and viewing.

As such, these students learn to participate in the process of democracy by accessing information that they are then capable of critically analyzing and evaluating. Further, they have the skills to verify and validate the information because they can access alternative points of view and perspectives from a range of sources. Today no single text, teacher, or website can be relied upon as the dominant source of information or authority on any given subject.

But media literacy is about more than accessing or analyzing information from other sources. Just as traditional literacy requires the ability to both read and write, comprehend and create, media literacy also has a production/communication component. At the most basic level, students would experience working with computers, developing skills with word processing as they engage in researching and writing term papers or in creative writing.

As we have already noted, computers consist of images as well as words. Students need to be taught graphic design skills so they can access, store, create, and display images, graphs, charts, maps, animation, clip-art, photographs, and other visual materials. Adobe Illustrator and Adobe Photoshop are two examples of software that provide this experience. Students can also work with video cameras, digital cameras, and other technologies as they develop new ways of both seeing and saying.

Students who have skills in these areas will not only do well in school, where they are likely to be both motivated and productive, they will also find themselves increasingly sought after by employers as they enter the workplace prepared with advanced techniques. This fact was recognized earlier in the decade when then secretary of labor Lyn Martin received the SCANS report (Secretary's Commission on Achieving Necessary Skills 1991). The document pinpointed the skills that the commission believed U.S. workers would need as they enter the 21st century. Among these are the ability to evaluate, process, and use information that closely approximates the informal definition of media literacy, and an awareness of how information technology affects society.

While media literacy can be taught without a production component, those who actively engage students in production suggest that theoretical concepts, aesthetics, camera angles, audience analysis, and other subject matter come to life and become more meaningful when students are given the opportunity to create. The result is that students are not only more connected to course content, but they are also becoming prepared for workplace skills, not the least of which is the ability to work cooperatively with others, one of the most consistent goals of any production process. "Preparation" also means preparation for responsible and informed involvement in a democracy, certainly relevant in all civics and social studies classes. In Oklahoma this is evident as students interpret and analyze political cartoons, while Georgia requires students to evaluate the impact of mass media on public opinion.

Purpose 2: Protection

In 1997, for the third year in a row, the Office of National Drug Control Policy included media literacy as part of its overall war against drugs. The document referred to "the pervasive power of the media, which collectively affects young people through words, actions, and narrative portrayal of specific activities" (41). Further, it argued, "Youngsters need the requisite skills to evaluate the messages they are receiving . . . Media literacy teaches critical thinking . . . This skill empowers individuals to modify their internal environment by affecting the way they see . . . and hear" (43). Nor is the ONDCP alone in its belief that media literacy can help students recognize, read, resist, and refuse potentially harmful media messages and the techniques that make them appealing. The Carnegie Council on Adolescent Development endorsed media literacy's role in the protection process in their report, *Great Transitions: Preparing Adolescents for a New Century* (1995). Taking note of media literacy initiatives in North Carolina and New Mexico schools, the Carnegie report said such efforts "deserve widespread consideration in schools and community organizations as an essential part of becoming a well-educated citizen" (118). The relationship between media literacy's agenda and the prevention community's agenda, including both substance abuse and violence, was explored in depth in an article in *Tele-medium: The Journal of Media Literacy*. "Sexuality, Substance Abuse and Violence: The Role for Media Literacy in the Prevention Process" not only addressed common concerns but also looked at various models (Information Deficit, Affective Education, Risk Reduction) and approaches to both prevention and media literacy, whether dealing with drugs, sexuality, or violence (Considine, David 1996). These concerns are clearly evident in *The National Health Education Standards* (1995). Media literacy was clearly seen as a viable strategy by a national task force seeking to address the problem of teen violence and school violence. *Safeguarding Our Youth: Violence Prevention for Our Nation's Schools* (1994) acknowledged the potentially harmful impact of media messages, but also recommended "that broad based media literacy education become a priority, implemented through an interagency, interdisciplinary approach" (93).

This interagency approach is alive and well in Washington State. The Teen Futures Media Network from the University of Washington's Early Childhood Teen Telecommunication Project was established in 1996. The primary goal of the network has been to support, foster, and make use of youth-driven media projects as a strategy for preventing teen pregnancy. Another of the network's goals has been to promote media literacy as a vehicle for addressing sexuality education issues. Working with the Department

❖**Whether using public service announcements or challenging media glorification of substance abuse, recognizing the impact of media messages and responding to them is now a valued part of the prevention process. Copyright © 1998 Gail E. Haley.**

of Health, the Office of the Superintendent of Public Instruction, and the Division of Alcohol and Substance Abuse, the network has presented conferences addressing media influences on areas such as suicide, violence, eating disorders, sexuality, and addiction.

Although the protection model is increasingly endorsed in the United States and increasingly evident in media literacy conferences with experts in public health and prevention programs working closely with media educators, it is not without its critics from abroad. David Buckingham points out that since research in the area has often been funded from the mental health budget, "the issue is primarily conceived in pathological terms" (1993, 11). Others suggest that however well meaning these attempts may be, they function from naive outdated communication models. Hypodermic theory or bullet theory tends to imply a passive audience being infected by media messages and images. The protection model they suggest sees itself as a means of immunizing vulnerable children and adolescents from toxic television and other infectious imagery.

Such concerns and complaints should not be ignored by those engaged in the protection process. Media literacy's credibility could be damaged if its advocates overzealously promoted it as a panacea for substance abuse, violence, or other social problems. Partnerships among media literacy organizations and Community Anti-Drug Coalitions, the Center for Substance Abuse Prevention, and the Center for Disease Control have already developed and are a necessary component of designing, implementing, and evaluating protection programs. While critics fear simplistic approaches, substance abuse is by nature a complex problem involving the substance itself, the host or individual engaged in the abuse, and the social, cultural, and psychological context in which consumption occurs. Cautious optimism might well be an appropriate description of the growing relationship between media literacy proponents and those who wish to provide children with protection from potentially harmful media messages. Fred Garcia, the deputy director of Demand Reduction, called media literacy "one more tool for the drug prevention community to put in

their tool box" (Osborn 1995, 7). Studies that used media literacy training to help elementary school-aged children reject alcohol messages suggest that it is a tool that promises success. After testing the program with third graders, researchers concluded that "these results provide support for the value of media literacy programs at the third grade level as a way to minimize the effects of alcohol advertising" on the development of alcohol expectancies and related behavior among children" (Austin and Johnson 1997). Once again, various state curriculum documents acknowledge the need for these methods. Kansas says that students should recognize advertising techniques that attempt to persuade them. In Virginia, students are expected to critique the way the media depict drug use, including advertisements for alcohol and tobacco.

The protection process is not restricted to chemical consumption or substance abuse. Many parents, teachers, citizens groups, and members of the clergy express concern about the values contained in today's media and seek to promote more positive values in impressionable children by protecting them from media values. Former vice president Dan Quayle was certainly in this category in May 1992 when he criticized *Murphy Brown*. "It doesn't help matters," he said, "when prime time TV has Murphy Brown—a character who supposedly epitomizes today's intelligent high paid, professional woman—mocking the importance of fathers by bearing a child alone and calling it just another lifestyle choice" (1992). In 1997 the Southern Baptist Convention condemned the Disney Corporation for lacking family values and called upon members to boycott the company and its programs, products, and theme parks. Later that year, when Disney-owned ABC premiered *Nothing Sacred*, the Catholic League collected more than 500,000 signatures objecting to the program's depiction of Catholicism and the priesthood.

Robert Bly has condemned television and its content as a toxic technology. Calling it "the thalidomide of the 90s," he said, "television provides a garbage dump of excessive sexual material inappropriate to the child's age, minute descriptions of brutalities, wars, and tortures all over the world;

an avalanche of specialized information that stuns the brain" (1996, 54). While such language certainly attracts attention, it's also highly possible that a blanket condemnation of the medium throws the baby out with the bathwater and does not predispose parents or teachers to seek examples of positive programs or constructive ways to help children view television and think about television. Though some think turning the set off serves as a form of protection, it will not, as Richard Riley suggests, give them "a clear awareness of how the media influences, shapes, and defines their lives" (1995). In trying to provide that awareness, teachers, particularly those working with teenagers, need to be very careful how they tackle the topic. For many teens, mass media is a source of pleasure. Attacking and condemning it is likely to render it forbidden fruit and hence more attractive in its appeal. Many teens are also likely to reject messages that seem more like preaching than teaching. Others quite simply deny that they may need or want protection. Helping them recognize and reject manipulative media messages, however, can be made enjoyable. *Adbusters* magazine, published in Canada is hugely popular with young people because it offers a forum and venue for deconstructing well-known ads, replacing them with satirical substitutes. By designing and creating their own counter-ads, young people fight fire with fire, turning the tools of the advertisers against them in a way that is both entertaining and educational.

While the process of protection is highly popular among parents' groups, media literacy advocates need to tread carefully in order to avoid exploiting fears and creating a climate in which it becomes impossible to develop the critical thinking and viewing skills that are at the heart of media literacy. Helping parents understand that they are both part of the problem and part of the solution is a delicate task that requires diplomacy. Properly managed, it results in a liberating experience as parents examine their own role in using and even abusing television and other media within their own homes. One outcome may be more selective and accompanied viewing, with parents and children watching together. Another may be more active detection and rejection of programs that contradict or undermine family values. Potentially even more liberating are the realizations that television, newspapers, magazines, and movies operate in a marketplace; that consumption feeds production; and that the creation of critical consumers may result in more constructive and positive programs and publications. The parent who contacts a network or publisher, who organizes a petition, or who constructively criticizes bad programs while praising and rewarding good ones not only provides protection for the child, but also prepares that child for responsible citizenship and responsible consumerism.

Purpose 3: Pleasure

The idea that the purpose of schools is to provide pleasure for students might strike some people as odd, silly, or inappropriate. However, the concept of pleasure, whether we call it appreciation or aesthetics, has always been in our schools, along with the loftier goals of creating responsible citizens and productive workers. Music, drama, and art classes have always fostered appreciation. Literature and English classes are not just for teaching students the basics of grammar; rather it is hoped that they will motivate students to read and to find personal enrichment and self-expression through art, literature, and the performing arts. If concepts related to preparation are addressed in Social Studies classes, and protection issues are subjects of Health Education, then clearly pleasure as an educational purpose can be integrated throughout the arts, including media arts. This concept is clearly recognized in West Virginia's English/Language Arts curriculum. Students are expected to view media for specific purposes, including pleasure, performance, communication, and information.

Such classifications are, of course, arbitrary and ignore the interdisciplinary nature of media literacy. They also ignore the interdisciplinary nature of art, as evident in the National Endowment for the Arts (NEA) publication *Eloquent Evidence: Arts at the Core of Learning* (1995a). Not content to banish the arts to the periphery of the curriculum to be tolerated as an elective, the report argued that the arts "can not only bring coherence to our fragmented academic world, but through the arts, students' performance in other academic disciplines can be enhanced as well" (1). Further, the report drew upon Howard Gardner's work with multiple intelligences to argue that the arts "can play a crucial role in improving students' ability to learn because they draw upon a range of intelligences and learning styles" (3).

Nor should the arts be limited to traditional concepts of fine and performing arts. The study of media was recommended by the NEA in its publication *Media Arts: Education Philosophy* (1991). Four years later saw its publication of *The Arts and Education: Partners in Achieving Our National Educational Goals* (1995b). Addressing the aims of the Goals 2000: Educate America Act, this report articulated a role for the arts. "Literacy," it said, "should be redefined to include media and symbol literacy. These are the languages of the arts, and they contribute heavily to the kinds of literacy required for all educated persons" (15).

As our information increasingly comes to us through a combination of sight and sound, training in the arts, including music, video, photography, and computer graphics, strengthens our ability to use these forms to both encode and decode information in a variety of forms. Further, as television's window on the world brings other countries and cultures into our living rooms, it offers the opportunity to reduce stereotyping, promote international understanding, and widen our appreciation of the arts, from the sandpaintings of Australia's indigenous people to the shadow puppetry of Bali.

In May 1997, participants in Seattle's Images of Youth: Teen Health and the Media Conference had an opportunity to listen to Raymond Soeung, Samantha Nop, and other teenagers from the Tacoma area describe the impact media production has had on their lives. For many of these young people, the STRIVE (Starting Teenage Responsibility in Video Environment) program not only provided a constructive outlet for after-school activities, but also literally saved them from the dangers of gangs, substance abuse, and other destructive behaviors. They learned video production, and some of the Asian-American teenagers drew upon the shadow-puppetry traditions of their native culture to tell their own stories. Many of them became so competent that they received more than $60,000 in contracts for video production. It is a real-life success story that demonstrates the interdisciplinary power and purposes of media literacy. By developing production skills, the students received job preparation and even earned money. But they also engaged in media production as an alternative to more negative behaviors, so their training not only prepared them but also protected them. Finally, their productions gave them an opportunity to succeed on their own terms, to tell their stories through their own words and images, to cooperate with their peers, to develop self-esteem, and yes, to experience the pleasure derived from all of that.

PRINCIPLES OF MEDIA LITERACY

Media literacy operates on a series of principles or concepts that are applied to studying key questions about the media. H. D. Lasswell (1948) provided a framework for understanding the content of media messages as well as the context in which they are both produced and consumed.

- **WHO?** he asked (Source, structure/organization/ownership of the media)
- **SAYS WHAT?** (Statement, content, values, ideology)
- **TO WHOM?** (Audiences)
- **IN WHAT WAY?** (Form, style, codes, conventions, technologies)
- **WITH WHAT EFFECT?** (Influence and consequences)
- **WHY?** (Purpose, profit, motivation)

Beyond this framework, media literacy functions on a series of principles that permit teachers and students to raise important questions about how the media operate and how different audiences interact with the media. Rather than existing in isolation from each other, these principles overlap. In Chapter 3, for example, Dan Rather attributes the rising "infotainment" values in network news to corporate takeovers and profit motives. In this way, content cannot be isolated from format, ownership, or economics.

Principle 1: Media Are Constructions

The old adage that "the camera never lies" is indicative of the way we have been conditioned to accept the representation of reality as reality itself. Take any glossy advertisement for a car from a magazine, show it to a group of students, and ask them what it is. Many of them will say, "It's a car." In fact, it is a representation or construction of a car. It looks like a car, but of course it is flat, two-dimensional, lighter than a car, smaller than a car, and cheaper than a car. If the point seems too obvious, it nonetheless begins to get us to distinguish between images, photographs, and pictures that depict people and places but are actually not those people or places. The image of the fashion model on the front of the magazine may look like her and be recognizable as her, but like most fashion images, it has been selected, altered, and enhanced. Likewise, the evening news presents accounts of real events, real people, and real issues. But the representations again have been selected, edited, designed, packaged, and presented. They may provide slices of life, glimpses at events on any given day, but they are not the events. They are reconstructions of those events seen from a particular point of view, juxtaposed against other stories, reduced in time, disrupted by commercials, and organized with an audience in mind.

Principle 2: Media Representations Construct Reality

This principle involves the realization that there is a relationship between the way the world is constructed by the media and the way we as media consumers perceive that world. If network news repeatedly features stories about violent crime or drug abuse, it is highly likely that the public will perceive these as major problems. In reality, neither violent crime nor drug use may be increasing. What may be increasing, instead, is news coverage of these issues since they frequently allow for conflict, graphic images, and the drama that makes news marketable. When we have no direct contact, no experience of, no im**media**te interaction with the people, place, or events depicted in media messages, these messages will **media**te our understanding and comprehension of the people, place, and events. Hence, if we have not visited Australia, we may perceive it as a combination of *Crocodile Dundee* meets the *Thornbirds*. Images of the bush, the outback, kangaroos, koalas, a land of wide-open spaces populated mostly by whites of European descent may fill our imaginations. In reality Australia is heavily urbanized, with most of the population clinging to the eastern coastal cities like Sydney and Melbourne. These cities have an enormous diversity of ethnic groups and nationalities, including a very strong and visible Asian presence. Similarly, if one was not alive during the Vietnam War, it is highly likely that media constructions of it (*Rambo*, *China Beach*, *Tour of Duty*, *Platoon*) have shaped our perception of the people, the place, and the issues of the conflict. Unless teachers help students deconstruct these representations, it is highly likely that left unchallenged and unquestioned, they will come to serve as reality rather than just a dramatic and commercial representation of it. Two brief moments in Spike Lee's *Malcolm X* demonstrate this point and are well worth using with senior students. Both take place in prison. In one scene, Malcolm is asked to consider how the dictionary defines the terms "black" and "white." Ultimately he realizes that the media (in this case a dictionary) reflects the values of the white male who created it. In another scene, he engages the prison chaplain in a discussion about the racial identity of Jesus and the apostles, asking why artists always depict Christ as white when there is evidence in the Bible that he had dark skin.

Principle 3: Media Constructions Have Commercial Purposes

While this concept seems obvious, it is not always evident to all our students, nor is it understood equally about all media. Though some understand immediately that movies are made to make money, others are likely to think that their primary purpose is to entertain. Advertisers routinely use celebrity endorsement to promote products, but not all students understand this. "Instead of seeing the athletes endorsing the products, many of the kids saw the products as endorsing the athletes" (Fox 1996, 2). In the case of news, some of our students think that the purpose of the news is primarily to inform. In reality, as part of a commercial network owned by a communication conglomerate, the news has to generate ratings and make money like any other program. Media messages must therefore be understood primarily as commodities created with the intention that they make money. Sometimes there may be a conflict of interest between this commercial imperative on the one hand and the secondary function on the other. This is quite typical in news, where entertaining the audience may be incompatible with informing the audience. If commercial values dominate the way the news is packaged and presented, news bureaus may give the people what they want, but not necessarily what they need. The glow and flow of television programs also mean that there is a carefully constructed sequence and strategy of programs, each meant to feed the other and either hold the audience or build it. Nielsen ratings measure how successful programs have been in attracting their audience. They are calculated on audience shares, with one ratings point equal to 980,000 homes.

In September 1997, *E.R.* hyped its premier season episode with the novelty attraction that it was going to air live. Clearly a marketing mechanism, the strategy succeeded, with the NBC show capturing a 28.5 rating. But that was only part of the process. The spillover effect was evident in the ratings records for the network's other Thursday night offerings. *Seinfeld*, which had always been popular, attracted its highest ever audience (33.9 million), and *E.R.*'s power accorded *Veronica's Closet* the biggest audience for a network premiere (35.1 million) since 1987. None of this was an accident. The decision to air the medical show live was based on marketing, as was the fact that the network chose to introduce its new series alongside the highly popular *E.R.*

Sales and marketing are also evident in newsmagazines. This is particularly apparent in looking at covers on magazines, since they will catch our eyes in a newsstand or while we are waiting in line at the supermarket checkout. The content of the cover as well as the graphic design and layout must get the attention of our eyes. Unseen is unsold. Sometimes these covers also raise ethical issues about profiting from pain. After the Oklahoma City bombing, some national magazines used an image of a fireman cradling a dead baby. Was this an invasion of privacy that derived income from the personal pain and tragedy of the child's family, or was it part of the public's right to know? Understanding the economic motives and the marketing strategies behind the mass media is a crucial component in helping our students become more thoughtful consumers.

Beyond the obvious fact that the aim of mass media is to make money, attention should also be focused on the issue of ownership of the means of production. In this sense, media content and the potential consequences of that content cannot be divorced from the domination of the industry by white middle-class males. Describing the effects of media messages about women on women, Susan Douglas says, "We feel ourselves to be both active agents and on-going victims of stories we never wrote and images we never drew" (1994, 294). Changing media representations of women, as Barbra Streisand, Goldie Hawn, Jessica Lange, Jodie Foster, and others have realized, means giving women ownership and autonomy in the process of creating, contributing to, and controlling those representations. The same, of course, is true for other minorities, including Hispanics and African Americans. Though media literacy frequently focuses on the content and form of media messages, older students need to consider the issue of ownership and what Ben Bagdikian calls the media monopoly (1990). In 1997, *Entertainment Weekly*'s list of the 100 most powerful people in the information/entertainment industry provided evidence of this importance. Of the top 10, only one person was either female or from a minority (Oprah Winfrey). While most Americans would be familiar with number 1, Steven Spielberg and number 6, George Lucas, how many of us would know Gerald Levin, Sumner Redstone, and other top 10 movers and shakers? If we don't know who

owns and controls the information received, we might well be able to enjoy it, but can we evaluate it or locate it in the commercial and corporate context from which it springs?

In the case of the motion picture industry, the question of control cannot be separated from the issue of creativity, especially when it comes to independent productions, including the early efforts of Stanley Kramer (*Inherit the Wind, Judgment at Nuremburg, Guess Who's Coming to Dinner?*) and contemporary independent successes, including *The Crying Game, The English Patient, Shine, Ulee's Gold*, and *Pulp Fiction*. As *Entertainment Weekly* suggested, it is simply impossible to consider the strikingly new voice and vision of independent films without acknowledging the crushing control and conservatism of corporate filmmaking. "Independent films are not only independent of big publicity departments to help sell the wares, but they're also free from the kind of audience testing, second-guessing and endemic messing around that so regularly makes big budget movies so safely boring" (Schwarzbaum 1997, 8-9). The commercial dictates of the entertainment industry frequently underestimate the audience, exerting a narrow and often formulaic influence on production patterns. In the process that means they frequently reject stories the industry believes lack audience appeal, especially representations of minorities. One example of this is evident in the rejections that greeted *Soul Food* producers. Despite the success of *Waiting to Exhale*, a story of middle-class, African-American women and their problems with men, several studios turned down *Soul Food*, which should have had similar audience appeal. Producer Robert Teitel said studio executives told him, "There's not enough killing, there's not enough action, no one will see it" (Ascher-Walsh 1997, 7).

Principle 4: Audiences Negotiate Meaning

This concept enables our students to recognize that they themselves are the targets of media messages and marketing. Demographics, psychographics, and other sophisticated tools and techniques are used by advertisers to identify and address different consumers. While we frequently talk about consumers as an audience, in reality there are many different audiences, and even within similar audience groups (teens, women, minorities) members of those groups process and perceive the same message in quite different ways. Two of the most controversial shows on television in recent years are *The Simpsons* and *The X-Files*. In 1997 they were both awarded prestigious Peabody Awards, much to the chagrin, no doubt, of their detractors, who perceive the programs from a very different perspective. Put simply, beauty is in the eyes and ears of the beholder, and we all bring our own personal filters to the media, accepting and rejecting messages and meaning based on a complex process that has been described as "situational mediators." These mediators include "the environmental conditions of exposure such as the presence of others while attending to the media, the presence of outside noise, and the division of attention between the media and some other task" (Stewart and Ward 1994, 343). These filters and distractions are very operative during television viewing when we frequently watch while engaged in some other activity. But negotiation also implies the emotional, psychological, intellectual, and physical environment. In the case of the latter, consider the difference between seeing a movie in the darkened environment of the theater with the image projected on a large screen and seeing the same movie on the smaller screen in the more familiar surroundings of our living room. Perhaps the most important concept derived from the idea that audiences negotiate meaning is that it rejects the idea of the audience as a passive pawn manipulated by the media. This principle enables us to recognize that audiences are "producers of meaning, not just consumers of media content. They decode or interpret media texts in ways that are related to their social and cultural circumstances" (Macbeth 1996, 8). Gender, race, education, age, and other factors all influence the way we construct meaning.

Principle 5: Each Medium Has Its Own Conventions and Forms

This principle draws attention to the discrete characteristics and attributes of each medium. While photography, motion pictures, and television share a common language (close-up, long shot, medium shot, point of view, etc.), only film and television also have the property of movement. This idea not only has significance for media literacy, but understanding it has major applications for the selection and use of educational media as well. Gavriel Salomon (1979) has addressed the symbol systems of media and indicated that these forms can be used to stimulate mental activity. For example, a split screen approximates the function of compare/contrast. The linear properties of traditional film and videotape are considerably different and more limited than interactive computer technologies that allow multiple points of entry and multiple approaches to similar tasks. Teachers who understand this will no longer pick a program simply by content or topic. Rather, they will take the form of the program into consideration, matching the characteristics and attributes of the medium with instructional objectives (cognitive, psychomotor, affective) and the nature and needs of the learner (visual, auditory, tactual-kinesthetic, etc.).

For the most part, however, media literacy draws attention to the form and style of film, television advertising, and other media. Simple examples are evident in Steven Spielberg's decision to shoot *Schindler's List* in black and white, not color. The black and white captured the look and feel of the documentary newsreel footage through which the world first learned of the Holocaust. *The Wizard of Oz* begins in black and white but then turns to color. Students invariably understand that this signifies the shift into the fantasy dreamworld beyond the Kansas farm. Even camera angles convey something of a character and circumstances just by the perspective or point of view they establish. The final scene of Richard Gere at the end of *Primal Fear* is an extremely high-angle shot that looks down on the lawyer. Arrogant and self-centered, he has spent most of the film absorbed with his own sense of self-importance. When he discovers he has been tricked by his client, the camera angle says it all, literally belittling him. Similarly, Frank Black is seen from the same perspective in the 1997 season opener of *Millennium*. In the episode in which Frank's family breaks up, Frank stares up at the heavens as we look down upon him dwarfed by the cosmos. "Is this the beginning of the journey or the end?" he asks. The use of a high angle typically renders a character weak, vulnerable, or threatened. Conversely, low-angle shots make us literally look up to characters. Their use typically empowers individuals who are shown this way. (See "Mise-en-Scene" and "The Four P's" in Chapter 6.)

There are also narrative conventions associated with various genres. In movies the gangster genre typically deals with the rise-and-fall format, tracing the climb to the top and the inevitable collapse of the gangster's empire. In the western, we are used to seeing the lone rider at the start and end of the film (*Shane*, *The Searchers*). Television crime shows also have their own codes. Despite the ensemble cast, we are now used to the emphasis on two cops as pals and partners (Hill and Rencko in *Hill Street Blues*, Bobby and Andy in *NYPD Blue*).

An awareness of the visual and narrative customs and conventions of the media enables our students to recognize, read, anticipate, appreciate, and even use these conventions themselves.

Principle 6: The Media Contain and Convey Values and Ideologies

Movies, television, and other media don't just tell stories, they also sell values, attitudes, and ideologies. The stories they tell, the plots they repeat, the dilemmas they construct, and the resolutions at which they arrive all represent a set of values. Whose story gets told and whose doesn't, whose perspective the story is told from—all these elements are at work, often invisibly, every time we turn on our television sets, rent a videotape, go to the movies, or even watch a commercial. Though viewers typically think they are relaxing, killing time, or being entertained, any exposure to media messages is also a learning experience. "The repetitive lessons we learn from television from infancy are likely to become the basis for a broader world view, making television a significant source of general values, ideologies, and perspectives as well as specific assumptions, beliefs, and images" (Gerbner et al. 1994, 30). One of the most consistent messages in commercials, for example, is the assumption that consumption is good. Underlying this assumption is the belief that our lives can be changed and made better by purchasing things. The populist movies of Frank Capra (*Mr. Smith Goes to Washington*, *It's a Wonderful Life*, *Meet John Doe*, *Mr. Deeds Goes to Town*) repeatedly valued the commonsense wisdom of the people (Jefferson Smith) versus the power elite. They frequently pitted small-town values, honesty, hard work, and optimism against the cynicism and corruption of the city. *Star Wars* rejects the technocratic coldness of the Empire in favor of the spiritual and individual goodness of the Force. Dorothy's journey to Oz ends with the lesson "There's no place like home." Fifties and sixties sitcoms often reinforced the patriarchy by suggesting that "*Father Knows Best*." After the establishment of the Motion Picture Production Code, gangster movies that had been criticized for glorifying the criminal now began to send the message that "crime doesn't pay." While audiences do not always get or accept these messages or ideologies, production patterns often reveal a consistent message, moral, or lesson beneath the plot and narrative chain of events. Teachers can use the above-mentioned examples to focus students on the message and meaning of the film or television program. While students usually respond to movies or television programs by describing what happened, this principle allows them to look beyond the narrative chain of events and to explore the manifest and latent message beneath the surface of a single production and the intertextual meaning evidenced in many movies or television series. Describing the ideology evident in Disney creations, *U.S. News and World Report* said, "Disney products consistently echo the same themes and values. The ideas that everything's going to be okay, that risks are required to make progress and that outsiders have a contribution to make run through virtually all the studio's films . . . they've set their stamp on our mainstream mythology" (Boroughs et al. 1995). One of the most obvious examples of intertextual reference and meaning occurs when a character is so successful in one television series that it spins off into a series of its own. Frasier Crane may well be known now as the host of a radio talk show in

Seattle, but television viewers first met him in a Boston bar called *Cheers*. *The Mary Tyler Moore* show featured such a strong ensemble cast that Lou Grant left the Minneapolis newsroom for a newspaper job in Los Angeles and Rhoda Morganstern also found a series built around her. More recently, Bob Newhart ended his highly successful *Newhart* series (1982-1990) with a dream sequence that explained that the Vermont Innkeeper had dreamed the entire show and was in reality still the mild-mannered psychiatrist who lived in Chicago and was married to Emily (*The Bob Newhart Show*, 1972-1978). In fall 1997, Newhart joined forces with Judd Hirsch, formerly of *Taxi*, in the new series *George and Leo*. One episode included guest appearances by a bevy of cast members from all three series, including most of Bob's therapy group, still in character from the original program, as well as Vermont's most famous brothers, Larry, Darryl, and Darryl.

Principle 7: Media Messages May Have Social Consequences

The final principle of media literacy shifts discussion from media content to social consequences, examining the potential impact and influences of these messages. This concept is explored in detail in the next section.

CONTENT AND CONSEQUENCES: From Image to Influence

Implicit in these broad principles of media literacy is the idea that media content has consequences. Two of the most consistent concerns that media literacy addresses are the way media create *representations* and the potential *influence* these media messages may have on different audiences. Historically, since the movie studies of the 1920s and 1930s, this audience has traditionally been impressionable children and teens. But the civil rights movement and the women's movement also focused attention on the impact of media messages on minorities, including women as well as various racial and ethnic groups. Though some public discussion still centers on the rather simplistic bullet theory, or one-way model of media influence in which passive audiences respond to incoming media messages, media literacy involves a more complex interaction among the media industry, media content,

media form and style, and various media audiences. Does the news media, for example, simply cover individuals and events, or does the construction of this coverage actually contribute to and influence events? Did television cameras merely record looting during the Los Angeles riots, or did coverage contribute to rioting and looting by showing locations where it was already happening? How might press coverage of issues like affirmative action and welfare mothers shape public perception and influence public policy? How might this coverage in turn be affected and shaped by assumptions the news media has about what interests the public? In the case of AIDS, since the media initially perceived this as a gay story and therefore outside of the mainstream, they minimized it. It represented "an excellent example of the power of the media to keep a sexually related topic off the agenda of both the public and policy makers" (Brown and Steele 1995, 15). The issue of representation and influence is integrated throughout this book in each section related to motion pictures, news, advertising, and television. However, it is worth taking some time now to explore these concepts in more detail.

For the most part, we are conditioned to looking at movies, television programs, and other media as though they are single, separate productions. In reality, while they may deal with different stories set in different times with different characters experiencing different dilemmas, they nonetheless represent a pattern of production that frequently emphasizes one group in our culture while minimizing others. Recognizing these production patterns is sometimes made easier by the bandwagon effect when a particular character or story type suddenly appears. In fall 1997, for example, shortly after *TV Guide* featured a cover story on television and religion, several new programs appeared on the schedule with church, priests, clergymen, and spiritual themes. These included *Nothing Sacred*, *Soul Man*, and *Teen Angel*. In the movies, John Travolta had already tested the religious waters, playing the angel in *Michael*. Using *TV Guide* or the television section of a newspaper, students can cut out programs and begin to classify by genre (story type), setting, occupation, and other categories as the initial stage in recognizing these patterns of production. Once they have started this process, they will be more receptive to seeing the continuity of characters, archetypes, stereotypes, and themes. For beneath what appears to be a group of different stories, these movies and television programs cumulatively construct an ideology and value system through the nature of the stories they both tell and sell. "Stories socialize us into roles of gender, age, class, vocation, and lifestyle, offering us models of conformity or targets for rebellion. Stories weave the seamless web of our cultural environment, cultivating most of what we think, what we do, and how we conduct our affairs" (Gerbner 1996, lx). In fact, the discussion of representation and influence is by no means restricted to electronic media. Jack Zipes is an expert on the meaning and influence of fairy tales. In *Don't Bet on the Prince*, he tells us that many

of the concerns about the influence of television and other media have traditionally been expressed about fairy tales. The struggle, he says, is between two different camps. "Away with smut and violence vs. let our children open their eyes to sex and resolve their Oedipal problems" (1986, 1). Just as media literacy explores representations of gender, class, race, religion, and other factors, fairy tales also empower and disempower members of these groups through the messages they carry and convey. "It is no longer possible to ignore the connection between the aesthetic components of the fairy tales, whether they be old or new, and their historical function within a socialization process, which forms tastes, mores, values, and habits" (Zipes 1986, 2).

Who creates, distributes, and profits from these stories is as central to the discussion as the nature of the representations themselves. A leftist perspective would regard this process of representation as one of "domination, resistance, subjugation, collusion . . . appropriation, interpretation, exclusion" (Bond and Gilliam 1994, 1). Through repetition and reinforcement, the mass media are actively engaged in the social construction of knowledge, which in turn "reflects the ways in which people are defined, apprehended, and acted upon by others and how those represented define themselves" (5). A more moderate view might avoid some of the potentially alienating language that implies the clear and deliberate maintenance of the status quo through the perpetuation and privileging of certain story types. A moderate view of representation might suggest that particular patterns of production, rather than being the conscious attempt to maintain the status quo, reflect a more complex process that involves audience research, the limited time in which to tell a story, social stereotypes, and so on. Nonetheless, the consistent and persistent message carried in these programs and productions, however well meaning, can also affect the way we think about ourselves and others. While Southern Baptists have objected to Disney's policy of allowing gay days at the theme parks, *Entertainment Weekly* raised a different set of concerns. "It's the thought that if you don't go along with the figurines and theme parks and the audio tapes and the CD-ROMS, that if you don't cave in to Mickey's cheery denatured omnipresence and just BUY ALL THE STUFF—then you must be un-American" (Burr 1997). What is needed, the author concluded, is not a boycott but perspective.

It is precisely that perspective that media literacy can provide by helping students recognize patterns of production and representation so they will begin to analyze and evaluate the media from a different point of view. No longer restricted to the narrative chain of events evident in the plot, or the form, style, and language through which the story is told, they are now capable of exploring the ideology present in the representation of different groups. Very rarely, the media actually help in this process by consciously disrupting typical patterns of representation. *Thelma and Louise* certainly generated controversy by creating a traditional buddy story about two women who had the male power symbols, including both the gun and the car. When Harry Belafonte comments that "white people are genetically inferior," in *White Man's Burden*, the shock comes from the fact that he articulates overtly the view of black people that literature and mass media conveyed in a more latent way for decades.

In Australia, where media literacy is an established part of the curriculum, the idea of media representation is connected to a study of Australian cultural identity not only in media education courses but also in Australian Studies. Using art, literature, and mass media, the Australian Studies course explores stereotyping and broad themes such as freedom and despair, refuge and menace, and the land and the people (Considine, Michael 1996). Australian identity is also explored through media representations in television commercials and movies such as *Gallipoli*, *Breaker Morant*, and *Crocodile Dundee* (Griffin 1994). Students are asked to explore their own identity in terms of national myths the media have both repeated and reinforced. The issue is not just academic. It focuses attention on where a nation has been, where it currently is, and where it is going. Exploring the myths of nationhood evident in media and literature, David Myers asks, "I wonder whether I am a typical Australian in my indecision about whether I should reach backwards nostalgically to anachronistic myths of the past or venture forward to the problems of the present and the future which sometimes seem frightening or repugnant" (1987, 1). He also makes a statement that has equal relevance in the United States today. "Now more than ever . . . in our multicultural society," he says, "we need an openness and an acceptance of many kinds of Australians" (1). Exactly the same can be said about Americans and their search for identity. In fact, just as American mass media has influenced the way Australians see the world, Australian directors and moviemakers now comment on the North American scene. Bruce Beresford, for example, has given international audiences the America of *Driving Miss Daisy* and the Canada of *Black Robe*. Peter Weir has depicted the Amish community in *Witness*. *Little Women* came to the screen under the direction of Gillian Armstrong. Following the success of *Muriel's Wedding*, P. J. Hogan explored matrimony American style in *My Best Friend's Wedding*. The work of Australian directors in the United States raises noncontroversial but nonetheless interesting questions about the ability of an outsider to tell the tale of another culture. It is but one issue in the complex and fascinating exploration of media representations. Teachers who wish to address the issue of media representations can use some of the following examples to introduce students to the concept, demonstrating the variety of groups depicted by the media as well as the potential influence these representations might have.

The Catholic Church

In 1997, ABC created a controversy by adding to its fall schedule a television program called *Nothing Sacred*. Depicting a priest in an unconventional and contemporary manner, the program alienated many Catholics, and more than 500,000 signatures protesting the show were sent to Michael Eisner, head of Disney, which owns ABC. Interestingly enough, the program actually acknowledged that Father Ray's view of the church alienated some of his parishioners. While the priest argues that "the church has got to change. We couldn't keep doing things the old way," not all of the congregation agree. Recently widowed and deep in grief, one parishioner refuses to allow the church to conduct the funeral service. He tells Father Ray that the new ways have ruined the church. "We had God then, Father. We knew that there was beauty and the wonder of the world . . . Father, there is no church anymore. It's all been downhill since you took Latin out of the mass." Perhaps the final word belongs to another priest, who tells Father Ray, "Bing Crosby's dead, so's Barry Fitzgerald. All we've got is you." Representations of religion, like those of any other group, need careful gathering of evidence and careful analysis of content before we can be sure how balanced or biased any representation may be.

Adolescents and Youth

One of the best ways to start getting students to think about media representations is to look at the teen screen, which is to say, the way movies, television, and other mass media depict teenagers themselves. In *Channel Surfing: Race, Talk and the Destruction of Today's Youth*, Henry Giroux describes the way the image and culture of youth are appropriated and exploited for pleasure. He also suggests that these images have an impact. "How American society feels about youth is partly determined by how they are represented and imagined in popular narratives" (1997, 2). Too often, he says, these images and narratives reject personal and social responsibility in favor of excessive hedonism. "A critically informed citizenry needs to raise questions regarding whose point of view is being legitimated by such representations" (30).

School and Teachers

Another representation to which young people can relate is the depiction of education as a process, school as a place, and teaching as a profession. *Stand and Deliver*, *Dangerous Minds*, *Mr. Holland's Opus*, and other contemporary movies provide an excellent opportunity for our students to compare and contrast their own experience of school with media representations of it. In what way are they similar? How are they different? But it's not just fictional representations in movies. The news media also cover school and education issues. How might this coverage affect public perception of the nation's schools and support for various bond issues? In 1996 and 1997 the mass media responded in an almost hysterical manner to the subject of ebonics, as a result of which they generated heat but very little light. George Kaplan regards this as typical coverage. The news networks, he said, "will head straight for the sensational, the pictorially vivid and the aberrant" (1990, 21). Beyond the depiction of teachers, students can also explore the concept of media representations by seeing which occupations (lawyers, police, judges, doctors) are frequently presented and which ones are typically absent.

Appalachia and the Mountains

Gone with the Wind, In the Heat of the Night, Evening Shade, Designing Women, Nell, The Coalminer's Daughter, and, of course, *Deliverance* are just some of the titles that come to mind when we begin to think about how movies, television, and other mass media have depicted the South in general and Appalachia in particular. It is frequently an alienating, frightening, and humorous world populated by coalminers and moonshiners. Unless we have actually visited these areas and had contact with the people, these media representations will shape our perception. In eastern Kentucky, Appalshop recognized the impact of these media representations and used media production as a way of addressing the problem they perceived. They developed a project whose aim was to "give access to the microphone and the camera to the people of the mountains who have been discussed and explained by outsiders so they can give their own account of their history and circumstances" (Gipe and Messner 1993, 130).

Media literacy may help students recognize these representations, detect distortions and stereotypes, and, as the Appalshop program demonstrated, use the production process as a means of giving personal voice and vision to those who have been the subject of stereotyping. How might this work, for example, in the Cajun culture or among various tribes of Native Americans?

Women

The Academy of Motion Picture Arts and Sciences designated 1994 as The Year of the Woman. The following year, the United Nations convened a world conference on women. How women are represented in the media cannot be separated from how women are treated in real life. One study of 167 movies released in 1995 showed just how narrow these media representations actually were. The report concluded that women were presented as "mothers and homemakers mostly; mostly women at a hearth, a stove, a crib, or a bedside," followed by students and prostitutes.

The article also connected these representations to the absence of powerful women in the film industry. Each year, *Premier* magazine releases a list of the 100 most powerful people in the industry. In 1995 there were only 11 women on the list and only one in the top 10. While more women were writing and directing pictures, they still accounted for only one out of every 10 films. For the most part, women also lacked the power to accept or reject which films were or were not made (Toppman 1995, F1).

Monkey See, Monkey Do?
The Issue of Influence

Discussions about media influence frequently imply a monkey see, monkey do mentality, as if the passive audience were somehow uniformly affected by the media to which they are exposed. In worst-case scenarios, we hear that a child burned down a house after watching Beavis and Butt Head play with matches, or that a teenager died after lying down on a highway, copying a scene from the movie *The Program*. While both events are tragic, it is also true that thousands, perhaps hundreds of thousands, of young people who saw the same TV program or movie did not act in the same way.

Nevertheless, a good deal of what passes as media literacy, particularly under the banner of the protection approach, continues to perceive the audience as "powerless victims of ideological manipulation" (Buckingham 1993, 243). Hence, Joe Camel makes kids smoke and Spuds McKenzie drives them to drink. Even if we are convinced that these advertisements do contribute to adolescent substance abuse (and there is evidence to support the claim), that belief in and of itself limits the power of the influence by suggesting that what is at work is not a monocausal media effect but rather the interaction or context of consumption, in this case the developmental stage of children and adolescents. It is also possible to suggest that the media audience actually influences program producers. "Receivers are not powerless . . . they wield influence within the institution . . . when they have been constituted as some effective audience such as an identifiable and desirable market segment" (Ettema and Whitney 1994, 11). Further, the perception of this audience, whether accurate or not, has some influence on the form and content of media productions. "Under certain circumstances, television writers and producers do hold information about their audiences 'in mind' when they work" (13). In this sense, we might suggest a symbiotic relationship between viewers and producers, arguing that the media both show and shape, reflect and reinforce, and mirror and make our society. We must also acknowledge that the discussion of how media influences the audience should focus on the fact that television and other media have not one but many different audiences, a point that becomes increasingly true as we move from broadcasting to the market segmentation evident in narrow casting.

It is not possible within the scope of this chapter, or even this book, to give an accurate and thorough accounting of the complex subject of media influence. That is a book in itself, perhaps best addressed in *Media Effects: Advances in Theory and Research* (Bryant and Zillmann 1994). It is necessary, however, to consider, at least briefly, some of what we know about the issue. Albert Bandura has suggested that in addition to the formal learning that takes place in the classroom, children also learn incidentally by observing their immediate environment in the process of social learning. Social learning theory indicates that this can include the process of both identification and imitation. In some cases, children may act like, talk like, and embrace the value system of their immediate role models, including their parents, their siblings, and other adults. Bandura also suggests that this observation can be extended to the media modeling represented in the process of viewing television. Extending this idea to social cognitive theory, he sees a two-way interaction between media and audiences. Describing the "bidirectionality" of the process, he comments

that "people are both producers and products of their environment" (1994, 61). Further, he suggests the influence is not sudden, but rather subtle, occurring over a period of time. George Gerbner has explored the extent to which viewing television influences and "cultivates" audience perceptions and behavior in areas such as race, gender, stereotyping, politics, religion, and other topics. Again, researchers dismiss the idea that this influence is a "one-way monolithic process" (Gerbner et al. 1994, 23). Television's influence is described as "subtle, complex, and intermingled with other influences. This perspective assumes an interaction between the medium and its publics" (23). Some theorists suggest the "drip model," with media influence taking place gradually over a prolonged period of time. Others describe heavy viewing as the "drench model." Priming theory argues that exposure to media messages primes the pump or activates existing attitudes and perceptions. "It essentially holds that when people witness, read, or hear of an event via the mass media, ideas having a similar meaning are activated in them . . . and that these thoughts in turn can activate other semantically related ideas and action-tendencies" (Jo and Berkowitz 1994, 45). In the case of media violence, for example, this might mean that "viewers will have hostile thoughts that will color their interpretation of other people . . . believe other forms of aggressive conduct are justified . . . or be aggressively inclined" (46). Uses and gratifications theory moves from a question of media content and influence to the active and selective process of how audiences use media. As such, the approach draws our attention to the fact that "there are selective patterns of exposure or preferential attitudinal dispositions toward certain kinds of media and vehicles within media that are not constant across all viewers" (Stewart and Ward 1994, 330). In the case of television, for example, research suggests that the consideration of what program to watch is secondary. The primary question is whether or not to turn the television on. Some of this research shifts the discussion away from the relationship between media content and cognition, and the acquisition of facts and ideas. In its place, it suggests that television and other mass media may be selected because of their ability to "maintain or change feeling states (moods) or excitatory states (arousal)" (335). The affective nature of media influence has been described as both the cost-benefit model (Atkin 1973) and the mood management theory (Zillmann 1988). In the case of the cost-benefit model, it is suggested that "media messages will be attended to when expected rewards exceed the expenditures and liabilities of exposure and will be avoided when liabilities are expected to predominate" (Hoffner and Haefner 1994, 194). Mood management theory argues along similar lines, stating that "viewers regulate their media exposure based on a tacit understanding of the emotional effects likely to be produced by various types of content" (195). The decision to watch or not watch the funeral service for Princess Diana is a contemporary example of a case in which the psychological and emotional state of the viewer would have been actively engaged not just while watching, but in the very decision to watch. Catharsis, empathy, grief, loss, curiosity, and closure are just some of the feelings that may have motivated different audiences around the world in their decision to tune in to that event.

What this body of research indicates is that the process by which media may influence audiences is complex. Those influences or consequences may be personal or public, cognitive or affective, immediate or delayed, psychological or even physiological. The following examples serve as a useful introduction to this topic and are reinforced throughout this book. They represent just a few ways in which the media may influence individuals as well as entire societies.

Types of Influence

- **Physical.** *The Journal of School Health* described a condition known as nintendinitis, or a pain in the right thumb developed as a result of playing video games excessively (Dorman 1997). Obesity has also been related to excessive television viewing (Dietz and Gortmaker 1985). This argument suggests that heavy viewers of television lack physical activity and tend to consume the high-sugar, high-fat foods advertised on television. As such, the influence is related not only to the content of the programs and commercials but also to the entire process of viewing.

- **Emotional.** Emotional arousal is a likely outcome of television viewing for both children and adults. TV news, for example, has been shown to exacerbate depression, but it is also argued that the news "helps depressives gain a sense of control over specific events" (Potts and Sanchez 1994, 79). Some children and adolescents have also been shown to experience "fright reactions," "enduring and intense emotional disturbances," and "severe and debilitating reactions" as a result of media exposure (Cantor 1996, 91). Horror movies and news stories such as on the Gulf War, the explosion of the *Challenger* space shuttle, and the Oklahoma City bombing are just some examples of media content that might create an emotional reaction.

- **Social.** The social and psychological influence of mass media messages can affect different audiences in different ways. In the case of messages about sexuality and adolescent audiences, for example, researchers have concluded that "adolescents who rely heavily on television for information about sexuality will have high standards of female beauty and will believe that premarital and extramarital intercourse with multiple partners is acceptable" (Brown et al. 1990, 62). Related to this are issues as complex as self-image, body image, eating disorders, and sexually transmitted diseases. Nor are teens the only group affected in this way. A study of men's magazines in *The Columbia Journalism Review* described "messages about social transformation . . . doing their part to re-shape masculinity." The interaction between the consumers and creators of *Esquire*, *GQ*, and other publications was also noted. "The culture works on the magazines as they work on it; today's more androgynous man has begun to see himself in the men's magazines" (Levine 1994, 31).

- **Environmental.** Mass media messages may influence the way we think about our environment and our willingness to address problems such as ozone depletion, recycling, and the greenhouse effect. Research has demonstrated that "specific media efforts can influence environmental knowledge (Shanahan et al. 1997, 306), though it has not yet been determined whether this knowledge translates into action and advocacy. It can also be argued that advertising, packaging, and the entire culture of conspicuous consumption are destructive to the environment. By contrast, billboards and public service announcements with Smokey the Bear alert the population to the problems of forest fires while a friendly owl urges us, "Give a hoot. Don't pollute!" As is so often the case, the media can be seen as both part of the problem and part of the solution.

- **Political.** The 1997 congressional hearings on campaign fundraising tactics focused attention on the need to raise huge amounts of money. While the news media gave extensive coverage to the story, for the most part they ignored the fact that the media, particularly the price of political advertising, are part of the very problem they are covering. Who runs for office and how they run are heavily influenced by traditional and emerging media formats, including the Internet. Techniques like negative advertising, widely used in contemporary campaigns, have contributed to low voter turnout and escalating cynicism. Their influence, it has been said, "convinces people that all politics is corrupt so there's no point in voting; since after all they are all as bad as each other" (Budiansky 1996, 30). But the political influence goes well beyond the candidates and includes the whole way we perceive a plethora of problems and issues. A 1997 study at Yale University explored the way *Time*, *Newsweek*, and *U.S. News and World Report* depicted the issue of poverty. Blacks were shown 62 percent of the time in stories dealing with this subject, despite the fact that only 29 percent of the U.S. population living below the poverty line are black. The consequence, the report suggested, was that "the pictures encourage stereotypes about race and fuel discontent among whites about the welfare system" (*U.S.A. Today* 1997). Describing the influence of the mass media on the political process, Doug Marlette has said that institutionalized religion has been replaced by "secular culture with encounter groups and talk shows replacing tent-style evangelism." In politics nineties style, appearance and theatricality are all that matters. President Clinton, he says, is "First Facilitator at our national panel discussion. First Therapist in our national encounter group session. Clinton's political genius was in recognizing that a talk show nation needed a host" (1993, 71).

SMOKE SCREENS: Cigarettes, Tobacco, and Principles of Media Literacy

"We must understand all elements which make up our customer, his wants and needs, translate these using product, pack imagery, advertising, into some specific brand direction that will inevitably meet those needs." (Vice President Research and Development, Imperial Tobacco Ltd. 1984)

Some 4.6 trillion cigarettes are smoked worldwide each year. In the United States, cigarette smoking is the single most preventable cause of death and disease. Yet for decades now, despite warnings from successive surgeons general and various health organizations, cigarette smoking has continued, aided and abetted by an advertising campaign that paints a portrait of consumption without consequences. Generations of adolescent males have succumbed to the myth of the Marlboro Man. Thousands of young women have accepted the message implicit in Virginia Slims and Misty's "Slim n' Sassy" slogan that smoking is an appropriate means of weight control.

Beneath the slick and glamorous world of cigarette advertising with its beautiful people and exciting locations, there exists an insidious propaganda machine. Using tactics that former Surgeon General Everett Koop characterized as both cynical and sleazy, the industry lawyers and public relations personnel dismissed medical and scientific evidence documenting the damage caused by its product, choosing instead to "discredit legitimate science as part of its overall effort to create doubt and controversy." Smokers and nonsmokers alike, Koop wrote, "should feel misled by the tobacco companies and their deceptive practices" (Koop 1996, xiv).

This situation might have continued unabated had it not been for the inside perspective suddenly made available to academics,

❖Used with permission of the *The Charlotte Observer*.

scientists, the press, the U.S. Congress, and the public in 1994. In May of that year, 4,000 pages of secret documents arrived at the office of Professor Stanton Glantz at the University of California, San Francisco. The internal documents came from the Brown and Williamson (B&W) Tobacco Corporation and its British parent, BAT Industries. They were the beginning of what would become an avalanche of previously secret documents made available under pressure from Congressional hearings, FDA investigations, and press scrutiny. Access to such data became even more readily available when the Liggett Group broke from the ranks of the other tobacco companies by making its own internal papers available.

These papers would become major evidence in the lawsuits brought by 40 states seeking to recover Medicaid costs associated with smoking-related illnesses. Liggett agreed to settle the actions, admitting that nicotine was addictive, that cigarettes are carcinogenic, and that the industry had marketed to minors. On June 20, 1997, these documents culminated in an historic accord. By terms of the settlement, tobacco companies agreed to pay $365 billion over 25 years, curtail advertising, and allow the FDA to control nicotine and additives in cigarettes.

Six months later, the proposal that required Congressional approval had still not been secured. The on-again, off-again nature of the landmark 1997 tobacco settlement underscored the financial, legal, and political complexity of trying to control the production and promotion of cigarettes. It involves extremely complicated issues that are relevant not only to cigarette advertising and marketing, but to the political power of tobacco lobbyists, the influence of special-interest groups, the freedom of the press, and, of course, the human suffering, illness, and death that result either from the direct consumption of tobacco products or the indirect, passive, or secondhand consumption of these products.

In a one-week period in 1998, four different developments highlighted the importance of the issue and dramatically demonstrated the fact that despite decades of concern, new evidence continued to emerge. In that period, Texas became the third state to accept a product liability settlement from the tobacco industry. The $14 billion price tag was the highest ever paid. At the same time, new evidence established a link between secondhand smoke and arterial damage. In addition, a biotech firm agreed to plead guilty to charges that it had conspired with a tobacco company to grow tobacco with double the amount of nicotine.

Finally, newly released documents stemming from a California action suggested that manufacturers had actively courted teen smokers, a statement the industry leaders had routinely denied. RJ Reynolds argued that the documents were taken out of context. The tactics, they said, were "unfair to the American people and serve only the agenda of some who seek to benefit from a broad misperception of how this company has conducted its business" (*U.S.A. Today* 1998). Former FDA head David Kessler called the revelations "the smoking gun," and Representative Henry Waxman raised the issue of charging tobacco executives with committing perjury in their earlier testimony before the U.S. Congress.

Behind all of the legal maneuvering and political posturing, the history of tobacco advertising clearly raises a number of issues

❖ In the 1996 presidential campaign the politics of puffing were evident as candidate Dole doubted the addictive nature of cigarettes. Used with permission of *Mother Jones* magazine, San Francisco.

that can serve as a case study in considering the principles of media literacy introduced earlier in this chapter. It offers an insight into how media influences young people and, just as importantly, provides evidence of successful and unsuccessful strategies when trying to combat these influences.

Principle 1: Media Are Constructions

Applied to cigarette advertising, this clearly refers not only to the creation and construction of advertisements in magazines and billboards, but to the wider, less recognized construction of marketing and delivery vehicles and venues whether sponsoring NASCAR events, tennis tournaments, or cultural programs. Associating the product with popular programs represents the construction in the public mind of an attitude that might be predisposed toward the company and its product. For the youth market, media construction includes T-shirts, play money, caps, and other merchandise actively displaying company logos. Our teens and children in effect become human billboards, espousing the cool image and attitude cultivated by characters in these ads.

It is important to understand that the media messages that supported the tobacco industry for decades were more than created or constructed. They were carefully researched, designed, and delivered to have the maximum impact. The advertising chapter of this book explains how clustering, psychographics, and other tools are used by

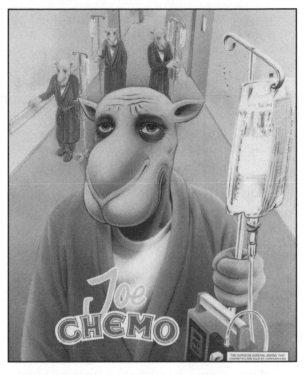

❖**Fighting fire with fire, Canada's Adbusters Media Foundation spoofs the controversial Camel commercial in a manner that is frequently appealing to adolescents. Used with permission of Adbusters, Media Foundation, Vancouver, BC, Canada.**

marketers. *The Cigarette Papers* (Glantz, et al. 1996) analyzes the B&W documents and provides an extremely thorough and revealing insight into how the tobacco industry went about constructing its message, including the consistent denial that tobacco contributed to cancer.

Principle 2: Media Representations Construct Reality

The old adage that what you see is what you get misses the point when it comes to most advertising that displays consumption without consequences. In fact, many impressionable teens don't get, that is to say, don't understand, what they see. For them, seeing is believing. What they see in the world advertising constructs for them are happy, socially popular people engaged in interesting activities, often in exciting locations like Joe's Place, a swinging night club where Camel's cartoon figure and his buddies hung out. Aspiring to the attitudes and lifestyle of

this invented media milieu, they buy into it through purchase and consumption of the product.

Of course, like all communication research, it is a little more complex and the flow of information is most assuredly not one way. If the tobacco companies appeal to young people, they do so because they have researched and exploited existing attitudes and anxieties adolescents already have. Talking to teens about what motivated them to smoke, *U.S. News and World Report* noted some interesting explanations. "For people who are insecure, it's something they have in common with other people." "A lot of people smoke to give the finger to the world." "I think there's some people who want to be bad but without being a criminal." "People don't stop because if they do, they're afraid they'll gain weight." Interestingly enough, they also can learn from experience. One sophomore commented, "I remember sitting there and thinking I was cool, I'm a rebel. Now I look back, and I was such a dork" (Roberts and Watson 1994, 38, 43).

In effect, the concept of reality is highly subjective. For many teens, there isn't one reality, rather there are realities. While they are cognizant of the facts about tobacco, their actions frequently reject these facts and this reality in favor of the more glamorous association and appeals the industry constructs for them. The Office on Smoking and Health at the Centers for Disease Control and Prevention puts it very aptly: "The Marlboro Man does whatever he wants to do. That appeals to the adolescent who's trying to break away from the rules."

It should also be noted that the tobacco industry has used more than advertising to construct reality. It has used intimidation, public relations, and litigation to silence critics. As we note in the advertising chapter of this book, the acceptance of tobacco advertisements in magazines implies that those magazines will not feature stories that are critical of the industry. Beyond this, the industry has also aggressively pursued its legal options when the news media, including *60 Minutes*, featured stories that were unfavorable to it.

Perhaps the most controversial example of this centered around a 1994 report called "Smoke Screen" on ABC's *Day One*. Researched by Walt Bogdanich, who had won a Pulitzer Prize as an investigative reporter for the *Wall Street Journal*, the story argued that the industry manipulated the nicotine content in cigarettes. When Philip Morris sued, ABC capitulated, paying millions of dollars in legal fees and offering an on-air apology. Philip Morris, for their part, blanketed the country with full-page newspaper ads proclaiming "Apology Accepted." One more critic had been silenced. Who knows how many other stories critical of the industry were never produced as a result of ABC's surrender? Once again the tobacco industry managed to create its own reality.

Principle 3: Media Constructions Have Commercial Purposes

It is obvious that the purpose of cigarette advertising is to make money. But this principle is considerably more complex than first meets the eye. Philip Morris's victory over ABC can best be explained in one word: money. Put more simply, ABC could not afford to run the risk of the case going before a jury that might not be sympathetic to it. The story had some holes in it, not the least being the fact that during the deposition stage, several sources indicated that their statements had been misconstrued or taken out of context. While ABC stood by and reiterated key elements of its report, flaws in the story severely undermined its credibility. It was the Achilles heel the industry needed for victory. Their legal action, filed in Richmond, sought $5 billion in compensatory damage and another $5 billion in punitive damages, despite the fact that Virginia law limited punitive damage to $350,000. The industry's ability to bully and bluff was strengthened by the fact that ABC was at that time in play with Disney about to take control. The prospect of a multibillion dollar settlement against new owners was less than attractive.

Analyzing the conflict, *Columbia Journalism Review* also noted another powerful weapon in the tobacco industry's arsenal. They threatened "to withdraw their $100 million Miller and Kraft advertising from the network" (Weinberg 1995, 37). The interrelatedness and symbiotic relationship between corporate America and the media industry was now at work. While cigarette advertising had been banned from television for decades, ABC and other networks routinely generated revenues by advertising products that were part of the giant holdings of the tobacco industry.

Once again, however, the profit motive meant more than simply competing and conflicting claims between the press and big tobacco. Even within the network itself, more than one agenda was at work. While truth and quality journalism were part of the motivation for covering the story in the first place, like all network programs, it was conceived in terms of its ability to generate interest, audience, ratings, and through ratings, advertising revenue. Hence it might be argued that the decision to cover the story in the first place was at least in part a financial one, and the decision to settle the case was also motivated by money.

For its part, the tobacco industry seeks to make money by promoting its product on the one hand and by aggressively protecting it on the other. In the mid-1990s, the size of this investment was staggering. Annual tobacco revenues were $48 billion. Some $339 million was spent each year on cigarette advertising. In 1996, 33 percent of total cigarette production in the United States was exported, resulting in a $5.3 billion trade surplus from tobacco. As *World Watch* put it, "Cancer sticks have become one of the country's most profitable exports" (McGinn 1997, 23).

But it has been the marketing of tobacco within America's own borders that has attracted the most controversy. Though the industry denied it for years, the 1990s brought increasing evidence that the tobacco industry viewed adolescents as a viable market. *U.S.A. Today* reported that RJ Reynolds's documents included the following observations: "To ensure increased and longer term growth for Camel filter, the brand must increase its share penetration among the 14- to 24-year-old age group." Further, the company's memos state "evidence is now available to indicate that the 14- the 18-year-old group is an increasing segment of the smoking population." The company documents indicate that they "must soon establish a successful new brand in this market if our position in the industry is to be maintained" (1998, 10a).

In the light of such strategy, it is easy to understand what forces led to the creation of Joe Camel. The success of the campaign became evident in the early 1990s when the *Journal of the American Medical Association* published a series of studies dealing with cigarette advertising. After the introduction of the cartoon figure, Camel income derived from sales to minors increased from $6 million to $476 million. Among adolescents, preference for Camel rose from 0.5 percent to 32 percent (Di Franza et al. 1991). Ninety-six percent of 6-year-olds recognized Mickey Mouse, only marginally more than the 91 percent who recognized Joe Camel. Recognition, many believed, was the first stage in the process of accepting the character and then the product he pushed. President Clinton believed that "the billions of dollars spent on advertising create a climate of friendly familiarity around tobacco and tobacco use" (*U.S.A. Today* 1997). The *JAMA* researchers were even more adamant. "Tobacco advertising," they wrote, "promotes and maintains nicotine addiction among children and adolescents" (Di Franza et al., 3152).

However, only part of the marketing strategy employed by the industry actually promoted the product. The rest of its effort was aimed at protecting it. In this process, they frequently found political protection. Having friends in high places must surely explain, at least in part, why George Bush and Ronald Reagan failed to endorse recommendations from Louis Sullivan, C. Everett Koop, Antonia Novella, and other health officials in their administrations. Beyond the federal level, the tobacco states certainly helped the companies defend their crop, even when it meant going against the party leader as was the case when North Carolina's Democratic Governor Jim Hunt disputed President Clinton's attempts to regulate the industry. Speaking at Elon College on August 22, 1996, Hunt said, "Tobacco farmers are not raising drugs . . . the cigarette company workers are not manufacturing drugs."

The 1996 presidential campaign provided further evidence of tobacco's political influence especially among southern Republicans. In fact, almost immediately after the Republicans took control of the Congress after the 1994 election, they terminated hearings into the tobacco industry and actively campaigned for the removal of FDA head David Kessler. Their standard bearer in the 1996 campaign was former Senate Majority Leader Bob Dole. During the campaign, Dole commented that he wasn't sure if tobacco was addictive, describing the scientific evidence as mixed. Turning his attention to

Ronald Reagan's Surgeon General, Dole suggested that Koop had been brainwashed, which prompted the response that Dole had either "exposed his abysmal lack of knowledge of nicotine addiction or his blind support of the tobacco industry" (5A). *Mother Jones* called Dole "Marlboro's Man," noting that "many of his political operatives and some of his largest contributors come from tobacco lobbies" (Kaplan, Sheila 1996, 32).

Dole was by no means alone in having industry support. In 1993, the year before they won control of the Congress, Republicans received $546,000 in soft donations. By 1995, the figure had increased to $2.4 million. Peter Jennings put the case to Dole himself in ABC's *Never Say Die,* a special investigation of the techniques that enabled the tobacco industry to turn adversity into opportunity for three decades. Jennings characterized the industry's contributions to the Republican party as a "seismic shift" from its previously bipartisan giving. He then asked Dole if the candidate felt comfortable with tobacco's support given the fact that it contributed so much to death and illness. Dole replied, "What they're doing is legal."

Among prominent Republicans accepting money from the tobacco industry was Senator Jesse Helms. According to *Common Cause,* Helms was given $77,000 while Dole's replacement as Senate Majority Leader, Mississippi's Trent Lott, received $54,000 (Kaplan, Sheila 1996). Two years later, as the mid-term elections got underway, the Republicans prepared to defend their control of Congress while the Democrats found themselves in financial trouble as a result of their legal bills from the fundraising scandals and the fact that many previous contributors had stopped giving. An editorial in *U.S.A. Today* worried that a "cash hungry Congress" would too readily accept the terms of the tobacco settlement, which would limit the industry's liability and shield it from punitive damages and class action suits. "In their eagerness to get their hands on the money," the paper said, Congress will be "more willing to settle for a bad deal" (1/16/98, 10a). As Jennings and ABC noted, "this is a very, very smart industry."

Principle 4: Audiences Negotiate Meaning

Those who wish to take on the tobacco industry have to learn to fight fire with fire. The sophisticated tools and techniques they use to attract young people to their product appeal to a complex mixture of social and psychological concerns. By contrast, the "just say no" message and method frequently fail to hit home. Those who wish to counter tobacco's pitch must understand as much about the culture in which consumption occurs as they do about the chemical itself. In other words, they must recognize the nature and needs of tobacco's youngest customers and develop countertactics that will meaningfully communicate with them. While this may seem obvious, the history of drug education efforts shows that it has not always been the case. A 1994 report from the Surgeon General, *Preventing Tobacco Use Among Young People,* makes this clear. Initially, prevention programs operated from the assumption "that these young people had a deficit of information" (216). What they needed, it was believed, was clear information about the harmful effects of tobacco consumption. Such programs believed that "improvements in knowledge levels of cognitive factors would thus lead directly to changes in behavior." Images and messages were employed that frequently aimed at inducing fear. Researchers concluded that the so-called "information deficit model" was not effective.

Nor was the affective model that followed any more successful. By the 1980s, researchers began to realize the complex context of consumption, including "sociodemographic, environmental, behavioral and personal variables" (217).

Just as media literacy moves from a simplistic discussion of media content, recognizing the social context in which meaning is constructed, prevention programs have also recognized the social and psychological elements at work when young people accept or reject pro-tobacco messages. Telling teens that tobacco is bad for them is no more likely to work than telling them that movies, television, or music are dangerous or unwholesome. Facts alone don't do the job any more than heavy-handed fear tactics. One of the reasons for the popularity of *Adbusters,* including its Joe Chemo campaign, is that it uses advertising tools and techniques satirizing the industry and its product. It should also be noted that while adults, teachers, and consultants have a contribution to make, the peer group is a very powerful player, often shaping decisions adolescents make about both tobacco and mass media. Actively involving the peer group in the prevention process through groups like SHOUT (Students Helping Others Understand Tobacco) has proved to be an effective strategy. So has the "Tar Wars" approach, which has student create their own posters and media messages to counter tobacco advertising.

Those who believe media literacy can somehow "protect" or immunize young people from harmful messages, including tobacco advertising, would do well to familiarize themselves with the history of prevention programs and the well-meaning but frequently misguided approaches that too often left the kids and their culture out of the process. If audiences negotiate meaning, we must focus on the context in which they construct meaning. The fact that millions of them choose not to smoke even though they are exposed to the same advertisements as their peers provides ample evidence that there are motivators beyond words, images, and slogans constructed by Madison Avenue and its clients in the tobacco industry.

Principle 5: Each Medium Has Its Own Conventions and Forms

In a western the audience expects the lone hero to ride in at the start and to ride off at the end. Television sitcoms are set in the home or office, feature a cast of characters in amusing situations, which we are cued to laugh at by canned laughter. Advertising, too, has its own codes and conventions. In television, this frequently includes the relatively rapid pace of cutting and, increasingly, using music and popular songs. Banned from television, the tobacco industry uses billboards, magazines, public places, even public transportation to carry its message.

During the 1980s, tobacco advertisement took on a new form, appearing in motion pictures in what became known as product placement. This included major hits appealing to young audiences such as James Bond's *License to Kill* as well as *Superman II.* Among the documents contained in *The Cigarette Papers,* there is a letter from Sylvester Stallone agreeing to use Brown and Williamson's tobacco products in his films for a fee of $500,000. Sporting events, stadiums, tournaments, and arenas have also routinely been a conventional form the tobacco industry has used to display its products. Cultural differences about this issue generated a controversy in Australia in 1997. The visiting Pakistani cricket team used cricket bats with the logo of their tobacco sponsor, Wills Kings, clearly visible not only to spectators in the stadium, but to the home viewing audience as well.

For the most part, however, discussion of tobacco advertising generally concentrates on messages in magazines and on billboards. These ads typically include an image of the packet but more importantly use people, place, and pitch to sell cigarettes. These elements are described in detail in the framework for analyzing advertising later in this book. These codes and conventions vary from brand to brand depending upon their target audience. Suffice to say that the models in the ads are frequently young and attractive and surprisingly healthy, given their choice to smoke. They appear to be socially popular or strong independent silent types like the Marlboro Man who reeks of the frontier ethos and rugged individualism. The locations are often exotic, idyllic, and escapist. What's wrong with this picture? Oddly enough, there's not a cancer ward, radiology room, doctor's office, or funeral home in any of them. Consumption without consequences!

Years ago, in simpler times, it was enough for a company to extol the virtues of its product: filter, flavor, fliptop box. In more competitive and creative times, there is less said about the product or its package and more emphasis on the values and attitudes associated with the product and those who use it. Recognizing and reading these subtle messages and the cultural codes they tap into is an essential part of any effort to combat the messages of advertising. In the case of young people, being cool and belonging is a driving force. Part of that comes from the social and biological changes they are experiencing with the onset of adolescence, but those feelings are amplified and exploited by the industry.

Principle 6: The Media Contain and Convey Values and Ideologies

A discussion of the values of tobacco advertising can take into account the values inherent in the ads themselves, as well as the values in the industry's public statements and private behavior. While Senator Dole described their behavior as legal, and the industry no doubt regards itself as primarily responsible to its shareholders, there is another view that raises serious moral and ethical issues. Critics of the industry are very clear on this point. In the case of B&W, for example, they have said that the company "has been well aware of the addictive nature of cigarettes." Despite this fact, "it chose to protect its business interests instead of the public health by consistently denying any such knowledge and by hiding adverse scientific information from the government and the public, using a wide assortment of scientific, legal and political techniques" (Glantz et al., 1996, 13).

Though the courts are now beginning to hold the industry accountable for some of this, for the most part, it is the industry that is being penalized, not the individuals who daily make the decisions by which the industry functions. Punishing these people as individuals, holding them personally accountable for the consequences of their decisions, may be overdue but is a long way off.

In the meantime, the message and values in their advertising cannot be missed. Newports is "alive with pleasure." More by both its name and pitch, it tells us to "Never settle for less." The Marlboro Man rivals the mystique of John Wayne. One of the most insidious messages at work in tobacco advertising is the strategy of "selling power to the powerless." In his testimony before the U.S. Congress, Dave Goerlitz, a veteran of 42 cigarette ads in the 1980s, made this point quite clear. "The other models and I were depicted as young and daring buddies and that's what young people relate to at 14" (Miller 1994, 22). Describing cigarettes' appeal to the young, *Extra* said it's not the smoke "but the smoker's toughness, his posture of defiance as he stands equipped to fight the world."

The combined statement of words and images, as we demonstrate in our framework for analyzing advertising, can best be understood by carefully considering factors such as posture, expression, gesture, and props. Joe Camel, for example, was frequently presented as "an entity of towering machismo by whatever big long tool or instruments he happens to be deftly wielding" (Miller 1994, 22). Mark Crispin Miller has very bluntly described this as the "big dick prosthesis." The Camel, he says, "is a mammal so redolent of fresh testosterone that he is himself a phallic symbol—his long thick snout and those two pendulous underglobes offer a vision of the male part so explicit that the term *symbol* might, in fact, be imprecise" (22). Whether we agree with this reading or not, there is little doubt that the values and attitudes conveyed in much cigarette advertising have a powerful impact on many impressionable young consumers. The consequences of that consumption, though invisible in the world of advertising, are all too real for those who get hooked.

Principle 7: Media Messages Have Social Consequences

According to *World Watch*, tobacco-induced illnesses will overtake infectious diseases as the world's greatest threat to human life within the next 25 years. For every 1,000 tons of tobacco produced, nearly 1,000 people will die from tobacco-related illnesses. Those illnesses include emphysema, cardiovascular complications, and various cancers, such as lung, mouth, larynx, pharynx, and esophageal. According to the Centers for Disease Control and Prevention, 16.6 million of today's young people will take up smoking and almost one-third of them can expect to die because of it. In Canada, a quarter million young people commence smoking each year, 85 percent of whom are 16 years of age. In the United States, 35 percent of student in grades 9 through 12 smoke, compared to just 25 percent of the total adult population. Studies indicated that those who start smoking at the age of 15 or earlier will lose eight years of their lives.

The consequences of the killer crop is, of course, not confined to North America. In fact, the U.S. companies banded together to create the United States Cigarette Export Association working under the free trade banner to break into Asian and Third World markets. In Japan, South Korea, and Taiwan, they were afforded greater promotional latitude than the domestic companies. In Taiwan, for example, there are no warning labels on the packets, and cigarettes can be advertised on television. In Malaysia, there is a ban on cigarette advertising, so the companies sponsor rock concerts with cigarette girls distributing their products. Cigarette imagery and advertising has shown up on kites, chewing gum packages, and children's school notebooks.

In 1990 the Senate Labor and Human Relations Committee held hearings on cigarette marketing in other countries. Senator Edward Kennedy commented: "Because of the aggressiveness of the tobacco industry, we are acquiring a different reputation in the Third World as exporters of disease and death." While some argue that tobacco was already popular in these countries, research suggests the American presence and promotion has exacerbated the situation. A 1996 study from the National Bureau of Economic Research concluded that the U.S. presence "encouraged heavier smoking in Asia" and that per capita cigarette consumption was "10 percent higher than it would have been under the previous closed-market system" (McGinn 1997, 23).

Beyond the issue of individual personal health, there are consequences that have national and international implication. These include economic consequences such as lost labor and productivity due to cigarette or tobacco-related illnesses. They also include constitutional consequences such as the delicate balance between rights offered under the First Amendment and responsibilities implicit with the planting, production, and promotion of a product that ultimately kills its consumers. Closely related to this is the relationship between the journalist profession and the tobacco industry. Magazines and newspapers that accept cigarette advertising are already compromised in their coverage of the industry. Any attempt to criticize or curtail the industry has frequently met, as we have seen, with litigation or inflammatory responses. One such full-page newspaper advertisement showed police arresting a driver in his car. The heading read, "Come Out Slowly With Your Cigarette Above Your Head." The accompanying text suggested that any attempt to prohibit tobacco would have "serious implications for America" and concluded that the advertisement was "brought to you in the interest of an informed debate." But the industry has seldom been interested in a debate, informed or otherwise. *Columbia Journalism Review* said their tactics in the ABC *Day One* lawsuit threatened the ability of reporters to get confidential information, since it challenged their ability to protect their sources. At stake is the delicate constitutional issue of the public's right to know versus the industry's right to privacy.

But there are more than legal consequences to consider. The production and promotion of tobacco continues to raise highly personal questions that go to the heart of our values as individuals and a nation. These include the moral and ethical corrosion of an industry and a nation that places personal profit and advantage over and above respect for human life. In fact, some people believe that one tool in the arsenal now combating the tobacco industry should be the weapon of divestment. When individuals, companies, and nations began to withdraw their financial support from South Africa as a means of opposing the policy of apartheid, the viability of the policy and the repressive government that enforced it was soon undermined.

Media literacy advocates believe that one outcome of media literacy will be the development of informed and responsible citizens and consumers. These citizens will be proactive not just reactive. They will recognize the interconnectedness of human ecology and assume responsibility not only for their own personal consumption but also for articulating and advocating policies that permit people to see how their lifestyle may impact on others. Such a day may seem utopian and far removed from reality, but 12-step programs and recovery groups know that success comes one day at a time. As the adage suggests, we are either part of the problem or part of the solution.

MEDIA LITERACY AND THE CURRICULUM CONNECTIONS: *Isolation or Integration?*

As we have already seen, the concept of media literacy has been embraced by prestigious institutions and individuals, including both the secretary of education and the secretary of health and human services. While this support is welcome, it does not in and of itself guarantee that media literacy will now easily find its way into either the existing or emerging curriculum. Any suggestion about bringing a new course or new content into our classrooms almost automatically sets off a battle over territory and the inevitable question, "If this is coming in, what are we going to get rid of to make room for it?" From the outset, media literacy proponents will need to give careful consideration to how they introduce the discussion to their colleagues, including whether it is best conceived as a competency or a course, and whether it is housed within one discipline or regarded as an interdisciplinary matter. In Ontario, media literacy initially began as part of high school English courses. In 1994, however, responding to the Provincial Language Standards from the Ministry of Education, the Association for Media Literacy (AML) articulated a wider role for the subject. "Media literacy," they said, "should not be considered as an add-on to the already crowded curriculum. A truly interdisciplinary activity, media literacy should be conceived as a means of facilitating the integration of critical thinking skills, aesthetics, the study of value messages, and study of the social and political implications of media texts. Media literacy should permeate many activities in geography and global education, science and language arts which will be conditioned by the mass media experiences young people bring to the classroom" (Duncan et al. 1994, 1; reprinted by permission). In their recommendations to the Royal Commission, AML argued that "media literacy should be introduced as a mandatory component in the primary and junior divisions," adding that "the intermediate level is far too late to begin education in this critical area" (12).

Exploring cross-curricular approaches, AML identified key areas where media literacy should be infused into education. These included critical thinking skills, interdisciplinary studies, citizenship, conflict resolution, information technology, mental health, environmental education, and creative expression. In the area of information technology, they also saw the need for teachers to make informed decisions about the presence and purpose of these tools in both school and society. "It is incumbent on educators to understand that the imminent arrival of the information highway is not just acquiring new hardware; rather, it is about understanding the social, psychological, political, and economic implications of this communications revolution" (15).

This comprehensive approach to media education has also been articulated in the United States. Wisconsin's Center for Excellence in Critical Thinking has integrated media literacy in its summer training sessions for several years. The state's CESA (Cooperative Educational Service Agencies) have been actively engaged with in-service media education for teachers, providing both training and the philosophical foundation. "Because of its tightly woven interdisciplinary nature, a comprehensive media education curriculum encompasses History, Mathematics, Language Arts, Critical Thinking, Technology, Philosophy, Logic, Citizenship, Classical Values, Social Studies, Political Science, Fine Arts, and other traditional pedagogical subjects. And it presents these themes in a way relevant to contemporary youth" (Downs and Knobloch 1992, 1).

One of the most recent and comprehensive state documents that clearly shows how media literacy is compatible with the traditional curriculum can be found in Washington State's Essential Academic Learning Requirements, published and approved in 1997. The Communication guidelines indicate that students will analyze mass communication, use a variety of media to illustrate and support ideas, identify messages in simple advertisements, and analyze and interpret the influence of media sources. History, Social Studies, and Civics guidelines state that students should investigate a topic using electronic technology and explain how cultural communication contributes to societal cohesion and/or division through television, books, and movies. Connections in the Arts curriculum include understanding different multimedia formats such as animation, photography, and video. As might be expected, the Health and Fitness curriculum also looks to media messages and their potential harmful consequences. Students are asked to apply skills to resist any harmful substance use and identify safe and unsafe messages, such as alcohol and tobacco advertising.

Modified at the local level by individual school districts, the state guidelines still serve to create media literacy-friendly curricula. In the Olympia school system, for example, local guidelines include statements that students identify and evaluate techniques used in mass media; use media and technology to browse, retrieve, and select information; and experiment with a variety of media to convey a message. In fall 1997, supported by the curriculum division and the technology division of the local administrative offices, teachers in the Olympia School District took part in their first media literacy training. The sessions were interdisciplinary in nature, emphasizing advertising, news, picture books, and state and local guidelines.

While the Washington example clearly makes a compelling case for a comprehensive approach to media education, it is possible that its very strength is also its weakness. Teaching media literacy within a single discipline such as Art, Social Studies, or Language Arts may provide administrative direction and support as well as academic rigor and consistency. Within the relatively small confines of one subject area, media literacy may be nurtured by a group of committed teachers. To be sure, this approach will also isolate the subject, focusing on its connections to just one discipline, but in some schools and some school systems this may be the best approach. It is better that media literacy be taught effectively and enthusiastically by a few teachers in a single subject area than that it be imposed on teachers and integrated throughout the curriculum if the support is not system-wide. In addition to housing media literacy within an existing discipline, it may also be possible to establish it as a separate discipline. As Len Masterman has indicated, this approach promises success when Media Studies is supported by a department "which has its own identity, its own funding, its own room and equipment, its own resources and library facilities, and an established status and permanent presence in the school" (1997, 48). Decisions about where media literacy belongs in the curriculum, who will be responsible for teaching it, and what level of administrative support is or isn't available must be taken into very careful consideration by each school. One size does not fit all, and what has worked in one system will not necessarily work in another. The organizational culture and climate of each school, the expertise and enthusiasm of the teachers, parental involvement, administrative support, and resources will all play a role in supporting or subverting media literacy as it finds its way into the classroom.

As Figures 2.1 (see page 52), 2.2 (see page 53), and 2.3 (see page 55) demonstrate, media literacy is compatible with numerous components of the U.S. curriculum. Teachers, library media specialists, and administrators can use these figures to identify and demonstrate these connections. But again, it must be emphasized that just because media literacy can be connected to the curriculum, it does not automatically follow that it will be. This requires a planning process that takes into account questions that are much more complex than the basic issue of whether or not media literacy should be taught. As *The Journal of Curriculum Studies* commented, "A literacy curriculum which is imposed, whether on individuals or entire cultures, cannot serve the same ends as one that is derived" (de Castell and Luke 1983, 174). For media literacy to take roots in the nation's

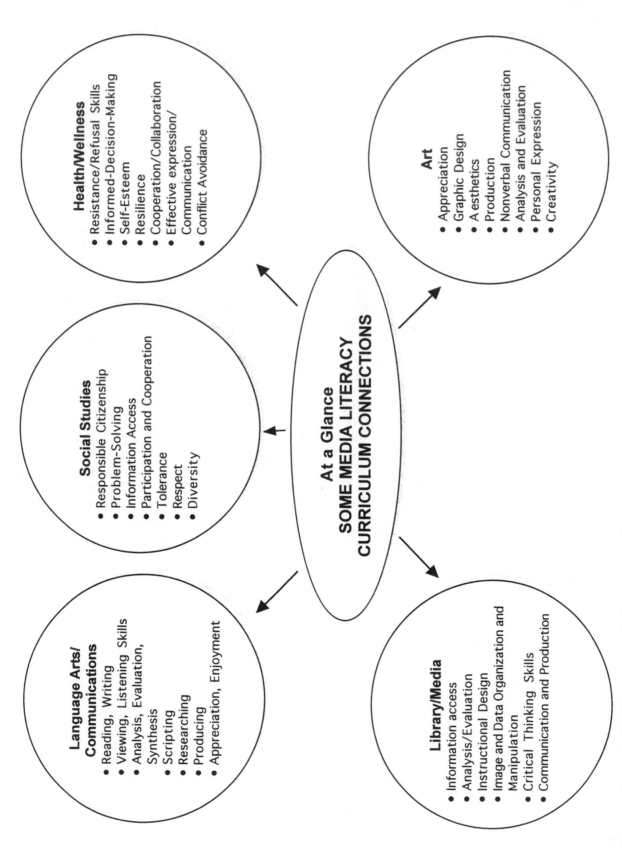

Fig. 2.1. Some media literacy curriculum connections.

English/Language Arts/ Communication	Social Studies/ Civics/History	Health/Fitness/Wellness	Art Education
Distinguish between fact and opinion, recognizing bias and stereotypes. [GA]	Recognizes bias and stereotyping in the media. [NJ]	Critiques the way the media depicts drug use in advertisements for alcohol and tobacco.[VA]	Understands different multimedia formats such as animation, photography and video. [WA]
Identifies the influence of mass media on individuals and society, becoming an informed receiver. [VA]	Analyzes mass media, interprets facts, distinguishes relationships ... cause and effect. [VA]	Identifies messages about safe and unsafe behaviors such as alcohol or tobacco advertising. [WA]	Identifies how camera shots, lighting, special effects and editing contribute to the design of videos. [GA]
Listens to and views media for a variety of purposes. [ND]	Evaluates perceptions, prejudices and stereotypes. [NJ]	Determines the validity of media marketing claims promoting fitness products. [TN]	Constructs meaning and or communicates ideas through the visual arts. [KY]
Makes Critical judgments as listener and viewer, providing constructive criticism. [IL]	Explains how cultural communication contributes to societal cohesion and/or division through television, books, and movies. [WA]	Analyzes how the media influences sexual attitudes and behavior. [MD]	Identifies processes and tools such as photography, computer art, and film used to create various types of visual art. [IL]
Explores diverse print, nonprint and technological forms of communication. [NJ]	Understands the impact of social institutions and media on individuals and groups. [MD]	Recognizes stereotypical roles advertisers use to influence adolescent consumers. [IL]	Employs technology and media to create art forms. [SC]
Identifies the accuracy, point of view and assumptions of media. [WA]	Interprets and analyzes political cartoons. [OK]	Identifies the effects of advertising on health product choices. [MI]	Identify uses of visual arts in popular media including television, film, and advertising. [OK]
Locates information by drawing upon media, technology and community. [KS]	Analyzes the interpretation of the same event from different news sources. [GA]	Recognizes and analyzes persuasion techniques in media advertisements. [ND]	Makes a video employing meaningful use of techniques and effects to create a special mood. [WI]

Fig. 2.2. Media literacy: some curriculum connections.

schools, it must begin at the grassroots level with the teachers. In his study of successful media education programs around the world, Father John Pungente has identified key variables that must be operative. Teacher autonomy and ownership is at the top of that list. Pungente also realizes that we must begin to build better bridges between the classroom, the living room, and the boardroom. "There must be," he says, "a collaboration between teachers, parents, researchers, and media professionals" (1993, 59). In the United States, as we have seen, there has been historical antagonism between schools and the mass media. If we are to go forward, there will need to be a new era of trust and mutual respect. We must put an end to the blame game and work together to improve both our schools and our society. The model for that partnership may already be evident in the KNOW-TV endeavors of Discovery Communications.

As teachers and parents, the challenge for us now is to find ways of working with the media in our own community, creating coalitions of concern that will help our children and ourselves become better users and choosers of media. The starting point in this process is to *recognize* the powerful and persuasive presence of media in the lives of our families and our children. Having recognized this presence, we must then begin to *respond* to these messages, helping our students resist and reject those that are inappropriate or that contradict our own values and teaching. How we go about this will differ from parent to parent and from one community to another. When we question, challenge, and reject these media messages, we enter the third stage of the process, which *rectifies* and *reconciles* the mixed messages our children might receive. Finally, we must also advocate quality programming and support it when we select a movie to attend, a videotape to rent, or a television program to view. When we do this, we recognize and *reward* quality programming, asserting our support as constructive media consumers in the realization that audiences can shape media messages. It is a powerfully liberating realization and a true exercise in responsible citizenship.

Library media specialists have customarily dealt with critical viewing and listening skills associated with traditional classroom media such as filmstrips and videotapes. Today they are likely to be responsible for helping students navigate the Internet to locate information, as well as evaluating and analyzing the authenticity and accuracy of the data, ideas, and opinions they find. These are some guidelines used by various states to describe skills that students need to master and that media specialists need to nurture.

- Develop the basic information-gathering, evaluation, analysis, and communication skills. (OR)

- Foster competence and stimulate interest in reading, viewing, and using information and ideas. (OR)

- Challenge every learner to filter, interpret, accept, and/or discard media messages. (NC)

- Recognize the power of media to influence. (NC)

- Identify and apply strategies to access, evaluate, use, and communicate information for learning, decision making, and problem solving. (NC)

- Recognize the selectivity of all media in news coverage. (MN)

- Draw conclusions about cause-and-effect relationships between the media's reports and the public's response. (MN)

- Recognize, interpret, and create visual images. (MN)

- Appreciate reading, viewing, and listening for enjoyment. (ND)

- Use technological tools to research, capture, and manipulate information.

- Exercise thinking skills to interpret relationships between events and media reporting of those events. (ND)

- Be a confident, responsible, and effective consumer and creator of information. (ND)

- Analyze and evaluate the effect of technology. (MI)

- Demonstrate critical viewing skills by selecting and analyzing media. (MI)

Fig. 2.3. Information skills, educational media and media literacy

REFERENCES

Ascher-Walsh, Rebecca, (1997). Recipe for Success. *Entertainment Weekly*, October 17, 6-7.

Atkin, C., (1973). Instrumental Utilities and Information Seeking. In P. Clarke (ed.), *New Models for Mass Communication Research* (2-5, 242). Beverly Hills, CA: Sage.

Austin, Erica Weintraub, and Kristine Kay Johnson, (1997). Effects of General and Alcohol-Specific Media Literacy Training on Children's Decision Making About Alcohol. *Journal of Health Communication*, Vol. 2, 17-42.

Bagdikian, Ben, (1990). *The Media Monopoly.* 3d. ed. Boston: Beacon Press.

Bandura, Albert, (1994). Social Cognitive Theory of Mass Communication. In Jennings Bryant and Dolf Zillmann (eds.), *Media Effects: Advances in Theory and Research* (61-90). Hillsdale, NJ: Lawrence Erlbaum.

Bly, Robert, (1996). Sibling Society: Adolescence from 15-35 and Beyond. *Utne Reader*, 75, June, 52-57.

Bond, George, and Angela Gilliam, (1994). *Social Construction of the Past: Representation as Power.* London: Routledge.

Boroughs, Don et al., (1995). Disney's All Smiles. *U.S. News and World Report*, August 14, 32-46.

Brown, Jane et al., (1990). Television and Adolescent Sexuality. *Journal of Adolescent Health Care*, 2:1, 62-70.

Brown, Jane, and Jeanne Steele, (1995). *Sex and the Mass Media.* Menlo Park, CA: Kaiser Foundation.

Bryant, Jennings, and Dolf Zillmann, (eds.) (1994). *Media Effects: Advances in Theory and Research.* Hillsdale, NJ: Lawrence Erlbaum.

Buckingham, David, (1993). *Children Talking Television: The Making of Television Literacy.* London: Falmer Press.

Budiansky, Stephen, (1996). Negative Advertising. *U.S. News and World Report*, February 19, 30-32.

Burr, Ty, (1997). The Kingdom Comes. *Entertainment Weekly*, May 16, 119.

Cantor, Joanne, (1996). Television and Children's Fears. In Tannis Macbeth (ed.), *Tuning in to Young Viewers: Social Science Perspectives on Television.* Thousand Oaks, CA: Sage.

Cappella, Joseph, and Kathleen Hall Jamieson, (1997). *Spiral of Cynicism: The Press and the Public Good.* New York: Oxford University Press.

Carnegie Council on Adolescent Development, (1995). *Great Transitions: Preparing Adolescents for a New Century.* New York: Carnegie Corporation.

Commonwealth of Virginia, Department of Education, (1990). Standards of Learning Objectives for Virginia Schools. Richmond, VA.

Considine, David, (1996). Sexuality, Substance Abuse and Violence: The Role for Media Literacy in the Prevention Process. *Telemedium: The Journal of Media Literacy*, 42:2, 3-9.

Considine, Michael, (1996). Using Aspects of Australian Land and Identity in Films for VCE and the SOS CFS. In *Practice No. 8.* Melbourne: Australian Studies Teachers Association.

de Castell, Suzanne, and Allan Luke, (1983). Defining Literacy in North American Schools: Social and Historical Conditions and Consequences. *Journal of Curriculum Studies*, 15, 373-89.

Di Franza, Joseph et al., (1991). RJR Nabisco's Cartoon Camel Promotes Cigarettes to Children. *Journal of American Medical Association*, December 11, 266:22, 3149-52.

Dietz, W. H., Jr., and S. Gortmaker, (1985). Television, Obesity and Eating Disorders. *Adolescent Medicine: State of the Arts Reviews*, 4, 543-49.

Dorman, Steve, (1997). Video and Computer Games: Effect on Children and Implications for Health Education. *Journal of School Health*, 67:4, 133-37.

Douglas, Susan, (1994). *Where the Girls Are: Growing Up Female with the Mass Media.* New York: Times Books.

Downs, Deidre, and Val Knobloch, (1992). *Comprehensive Media Education and Media Literacy—An Answer?* Cooperative Educational Service Agency, No. 10. LaCrosse, WI.

Duncan, Barry et al., (1994). AML Ensures That Media Literacy Is Represented in New Ministry Benchmark Standards Document. *Mediacy*, 16:21, 11-15.

Ettema, Jane, and D. Charles Whitney, (1994). *Audiencemaking: How the Media Create the Audience.* Thousand Oaks, CA: Sage.

Georgia Board of Education, Georgia Department of Education, (n.d.). Quality Core Curriculum. Atlanta, GA.

Gerbner, George, (1996). Preface. In Roy Fox, *Harvesting Minds: How TV Commercials Control Kids.* Westport, CT: Praeger.

Gerbner, George et al., (1994). Growing Up with Television: The Cultivation Perspective. In Jennings Bryant and Dolf Zillmann (eds.), *Media Effects: Advances in Theory and Research* (17-42). Hillsdale, NJ: Lawrence Erlbaum.

Gipe, Robert, and Ann Messner, (1993). Twixt the Holler and the Mall: Appalshop Films and the Politics of Image in an Eastern Kentucky Classroom. In Karl Heider (ed.), *Images of the South: Constructing Regional Culture of Film and Video.* Athens: University of Georgia Press.

Giroux, Henry, (1997). *Channel Surfing: Race, Talk and the Destruction of Today's Youth.* New York: St. Martin's.

Glantz, Stanton A. et al., (1996). *The Cigarette Papers.* Berkeley: University of California Press.

Griffin, Cheryl, (1994). Australian Cultural Identity in Australian Advertising. *Classroom Activities No. 1*, 1-9.

Hart, Roderick, (1994). *Seducing America: How Television Charms the Modern Voter.* New York: Oxford University Press.

Hawkins, David, Michael Arthur, and Richard Catalano, (1995). *Building a Safer Society: Approaches to Crime Prevention.* Chicago: University of Chicago Press.

Herman, Edward S., and Noam Chomsky, (1988). *Manufacturing Consent: The Political Economy of the Mass Media.* New York: Pantheon.

Hoffner, Cynthia, and Margaret Haefner, (1994). Children's News Interest During the Gulf War: The Role of Negative Affect. *Journal of Broadcasting and Electronic Media*, 38:2, 193-204.

Illinois State Board of Education, (1986). State Goals for Learning and Sample Learning Objectives. Springfield, IL: Department of School Improvement Services.

Jo, Eunkyung, and Leonard Berkowitz, (1994). A Priming Effect Analysis of Media Influences: An Update. In Jennings Bryant and Dolf Zillmann (eds.), *Media Effects: Advances in Theory and Research* (43-60). Hillsdale, NJ: Lawrence Erlbaum.

Joint Committee on National Health Standards, (1995). *National Health Education Standards: Achieving Health Literacy.* Washington, DC.

Kansas State Board of Education, (1994). Kansas Curricular Standards for Communication. Topeka, KS.

Kaplan, George, (1990). TV's Version of Education and What to Do About It. *Kappan Special Report*, January.

Kaplan, Sheila, (1996). Tobacco Dole. *Mother Jones*, May/June, 13-16, 32-34.

Keen, Judy, (1996). Dole Still Not Certain If Tobacco Is Addictive. *U.S.A. Today*, 13-16.

Koop, C. Everett, (1996). Foreword to *The Cigarette Papers.* Glantz, Stanton et al. Berkeley: University of California Press.

Lasswell, H. D., (1948). The Structure and Function of Communication in Society. In Lymon Bryson (ed.), *The Communication of Ideas.* New York: Harper & Brothers.

Levine, Judith, (1994). The Man in the Mirror: What *Esquire, GQ, Men's Journal* and *Details* Tell Us About the American Male. *Columbia Journalism Review*, March/April, 27-31.

MacBeth, Tannis, (1996). *Tuning in to Young Viewers: Social Science Perspectives on Television.* Thousand Oaks, CA: Sage.

Marlette, Doug, (1993). Never Trust a Weeping Man. *Esquire*, October, 70-77.

Maryland State Department of Education, (n.d.). A Maryland Curricular Framework. Baltimore: Maryland State Department of Education.

Masterman, Len, (1997). A Rationale for Media Education. In Robert Kubey (ed.), *Media Literacy in the Information Age: Current Perspectives* (15-68). New Brunswick, NJ: Transaction Publishers.

McGinn, Anne Platt, (1997). Cigarette Traffickers Go Global. *World Watch*, July/August, 18-27.

Michigan State Board of Education, (1992). Model Core Curriculum Outcomes and Position Statement on Core Curriculum. Lansing, MI.

Miller, Mark Crispin, (1994). Selling Power to the Powerless: How Cigarette Ads Target Youth. *Extra*, March/April, 22-23.

Minnesota Department of Education, (1994a). Model Learner Outcomes for Educational Media and Technology. St. Paul, MN.

———, (1994b). Minnesota Profile of Learning: High School Standards. St. Paul, MN.

———, (1994c). Proposed Graduation Rule. St. Paul, MN.

Myers, David, (1987). *Bleeding Battlers from Ironbark: Australian Myths in Fiction and Film 1890s-1980s.* Rockhampton, Queensland: Capricornia Institute.

National Endowment for the Arts, (1991). *Media Arts: Education Philosophy.* Washington, DC.

———, (1995a). *Eloquent Evidence: Arts at the Core of Learning.* Washington, DC.

———, (1995b). *The Arts and Education: Partners in Achieving Our National Educational Goals.* Washington, DC.

New Jersey State Department of Education, (1991). Core Course Proficiencies. Trenton, NJ: Division of General Academic Education.

North Carolina Department of Public Instruction, (1992). Standard Course of Study: Information Skills K-12. Raleigh, NC.

North Dakota Department of Public Instruction, (1993). North Dakota Curriculum Frameworks. Bismarck, ND.

Office of National Drug Control Policy, (1997). The National Drug Control Policy. The Executive Office of the President, Washington, DC.

Oregon Educational Media Association, (1993). Supplementing the Oregon Educational Act for the 21st Century Through School Library Media Programs. Beaverton, OR.

Osborn, Barbara Bliss, (1995). New Drug Busters: How Critical Viewing Skills Can Arm Kids Against Drugs. *Better Viewing*, September/October, 6-8.

Potts, Richard, and Dawn Sanchez, (1994). Television Viewing and Depression: No News Is Good News. *Journal of Broadcasting and Electronic Media*, 38:1, 79-90.

Pungente, John, (1993). The Second Spring: Media Education in Canada's Secondary Schools. *Canadian Journal of Educational Communication*, 22:1, 47-60.

Riley, Richard, (1995). Media Literacy for America's Young People. Speech at Julius West Middle School, Rockville, MD, December 13.

Roberts, Stephen, and Traci Watson, (1994). Teens on Tobacco. *U.S. News and World Report*, April 18, 38, 43.

Safeguarding Our Youth: Violence Prevention for Our Nation's Schools (1994). Report from the Department of Justice, Department of Education, Department of Health and Human Services, Department of Housing and Urban Development, Washington, DC.

Salomon, Gavriel, (1979). *The Interaction of Media, Cognition and Learning*. San Francisco: Jossey-Bass.

Schwarzbaum, Lisa, (1997). Independent's Day. *Entertainment Weekly*, November/December, 8-10.

Shanahan, James et al., (1997). Green or Brown? Television and the Cultivation of Environmental Concerns. *Journal of Broadcasting and Electronic Media*, 41:3, 305-23.

Stewart, David, and Scott Ward, (1994). Media Effects on Advertising. In Jennings Bryant and Dolf Zillmann (eds.), *Media Effects: Advances in Theory and Research*. Hillsdale, NJ: Lawrence Erlbaum.

Tennessee State Board of Education, (1994). Lifetime Wellness Curriculum Frameworks. Knoxville, TN.

Toppman, Lawrence, (1995). Mommies, Victims and Babes: On the Silver Screen Women Are Still the Second Sex. *Charlotte Observer*, October 29, F1, 6.

U.S. Department of Health and Human Services, (1994). Preventing Tobacco Use Among Young People: A Report of the Surgeon General. Washington, DC: Government Printing Office.

U.S.A. Today, (1997). January 31. (1997).

———, (1997). August 19, 3a.

U.S.A. Today, (1998). Kids Are Getting Lost in the Tobacco Deal Shuffle. January 16, 10a.

Weinberg, Steve, (1995). Smoking Guns: ABC, Philip Morris and the Infamous Apology. *Columbia Journalism Review*, November/December, 29-37.

West Virginia Department of Education, (1992). West Virginia Programs of Study: Instructional Goals and Objectives. Charleston, WV.

Wisconsin Department of Public Instruction, (1995). Art Education: A Guide to Curriculum Planning. Madison: Wisconsin Department of Public Instruction.

Zillmann, D., (1988). Mood Management: Using Entertainment to Full Advantage. In L. Donohew et al. (eds.), *Communication, Social Cognition and Affect* (147-71). Hillsdale, NJ: Lawrence Erlbaum.

Zipes, Jack, (1986). *Don't Bet on the Prince: Contemporary Feminist Fairy Tales in America and England*. New York: Methuen.

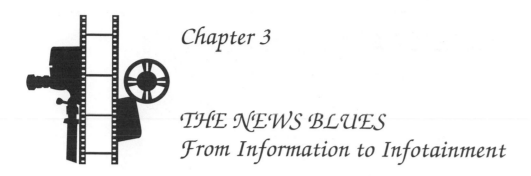

Chapter 3

THE NEWS BLUES
From Information to Infotainment

One of the most stated goals of American education has traditionally been the desire to create responsible citizens for a democratic society. Given the fact that most students and citizens now get most of their information about their own country and the wider world from television, not textbooks, it seems highly likely that these stories and pictures will shape their perception of themselves and the countries and cultures of the global economy. But how accurately does television function as a window on the world? What stories dominate local news coverage and national broadcasts? How representative are they of the way most of us lead our lives? Is journalism today, whether newspapers, talk radio, or television, really a reliable source of information to help citizens make informed decisions, or have we replaced information with infotainment? In summer 1996, *The Nation* made their opinion on the subject very clear. "No longer is it true that the medium is the message. More and more the media omit the message, suppress the message, homogenize the message, sensationalize the message or convert the message into entertainment, or worse infotainment" (1996, 3).

Interviewed later that year for the PBS broadcast "Media Literacy: The New Basic," former CBS anchor Walter Cronkite said he believed that we should be teaching skepticism. Cronkite, who had closed his nightly news broadcast with the declaration "And that's the way it is," has admitted that the closure was arrogant and implied an all-knowing authority that was inappropriate. Cronkite's successor, Dan Rather, also suggested in a 1997 appearance on *Larry King Live* that television news is often less than a credible source of reliable information. Discussing what he called "the volcanic era" of news, dominated by fierce competition, mergers, and corporate takeovers, Rather complained about "the continued fuzzing of the line between news and entertainment values." The ratings race means "fear runs rampant" in network news, he added, saying that even when a story is clearly tabloid, it finds a place in and on the news because of the fear that if they don't run it, somebody else will. In such an era, Rather said, "entertainment values overwhelm news values" (1997).

In February 1997, networks and newspapers alike found themselves caught in the struggle between conscience and commerce, professionalism and profit. As President Clinton prepared to deliver the first State of the Union Address of his second term, news arrived from Santa Monica that the jury in the O. J. Simpson civil trial had reached a verdict. The White House had already changed the date of the president's address to avoid a clash with the Miss USA Pageant. Now Press Secretary Mike McCurry spoke with the news media in an attempt to make sure that the ongoing Simpson saga did not take precedence over Clinton's address. Some networks used split screens to show the president speaking at the same time that Simpson's car was heading for the courthouse. Most canceled analysis of the speech, opting instead to go to California for the verdict and reaction. But the next day, when the verdict was no longer news, *U.S.A. Today* still pushed the president off the front page to run the headline "Jury: Simpson

❖**Used with permission of Fairness and Accuracy in
Reporting, Washington, DC.**

Liable" together with three color photographs. The president's extensive discussion of education was relegated to a less visible section. Rather than an isolated occurrence, this trend has been documented by The Center for Media and Public Affairs, which has shown that entertainment news and coverage of celebrities are more frequently provided by the news media than issues such as education and the environment.

The rationale for these decisions has been addressed by journalists themselves, including Cronkite and Rather, who have referred to the era of media mergers in which the once-sacrosanct news divisions were subsumed by the accounting mentality with the bottom line being profit. When new management canceled the CBS *Morning*

News, an angry Rather wrote to *The New York Times,* "The professionals at CBS News who are directly involved in news gathering, editing, broadcasting . . . refuse to allow any editorial decisions to be dictated by public opinion sampling. We base editorial decisions on journalistic experience and ethics, not on what polls and entertainment consultants say" (McCabe 1987, 290). Several years later, Rather found himself the symbolic subject for a report on the decline of quality news. Over several years, the article noted, he had been made "chattier, wrapped in sweaters . . . propped against desks, been forced to stroll through sets and wave pointers. He's been plunked down in front of globes that whirl, fade in and out. He has talked to faces on small screens that rise out of nowhere and to faces on large wall monitors" (Katz 1993, 13). All of these developments resulted from the very packaging and market research methods that Rather himself had attacked.

Hand in hand with the gimmicks, gadgetry, and marketing of news as infotainment is the increasingly combative, hostile, and polarizing coverage of jaundiced journalism. Perhaps nowhere has this been so blatantly and shamelessly stated than by *Newsweek*'s Eleanor Clift during an appearance on CNN's *Crossfire*. In today's journalism, she commented, "the natural instinct is to find the lie. The bias is, the name of the game is, to kill the king. You go after whoever is in power. That is the driving force of journalism; we're an adversarial body." If Clift speaks for her profession, and there is evidence that she does, the implications for our democracy cannot be ignored.

U.S. News and World Report has actually stated in an editorial that America has become "a mediacracy . . . ruled by those who know how to manipulate symbols, information and the media" (Walcott 1992, 6). In such an age, how might the ratings race, the drive for dramatic pictures,

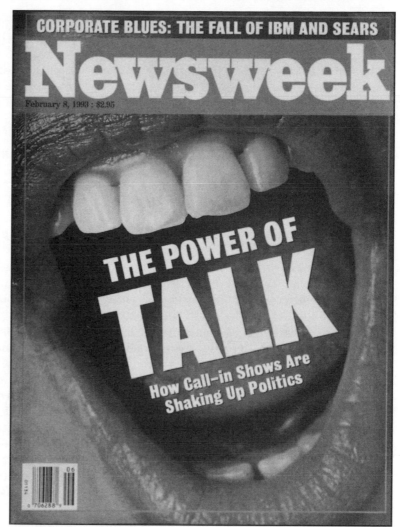

❖ **Power without pictures. Talk radio became a major political force throughout the 1990s, pushing a conservative agenda. But was this news or demagoguery that generated more heat than light? Copyright © 1993 Newsweek Inc. All rights reserved. Reprinted by permission.**

and the increasingly hostile and uncivil tone of news coverage affect the public's perception of their country and the world? Cynicism, fear, and withdrawal from the social and political process are three trends that have been observed. A 1995 article reported that "most people feel as though they have little to say about what government does," and an overwhelming majority of them "feel that the government is run by big selfish interests" (Grossman 1995, 13a). Two years later, on the eve of President Clinton's second inauguration, *U.S.A. Today* reported what it called a polling paradox that said much about the national mood. The report made it clear that news coverage is not only

capable of influencing the way we think about our world, but also the way we feel. In winter 1997, Clinton's approval rating stood at 62 percent, his highest score. While the public felt "personally better off," they were less optimistic about the state of the nation and the future of the country. Only in the depths of Watergate's constitutional crisis of 1974 had the public mood been so low, the report continued. But there was no constitutional crisis in 1997, the economy was moving steadily, and Wall Street continued to post record gains. Attempting to account for the bleak mood of the country, the report addressed "the mayhem index" of news coverage used by Rocky Mountain Media Watch.

Noting that "nearly half of local news stories are consumed by stories about crime, war and natural disaster," *U.S.A. Today* suggested a context in which the cumulative nature of negative news might shape public perception and discourage public participation. "Convinced that national problems never get better, Americans may be less likely to think it's worthwhile trying to solve them" (Page 1997, 21). It is in this context and against this backdrop that schools must rededicate themselves to the goal of nurturing responsible citizenship.

ACCESS ISN'T SUCCESS: *News, Citizenship, and Critical Thinking Skills*

The ability to access information should not be confused with success in comprehending or applying that information. As the so-called information age of the 1980s got under way, John Naisbitt warned in *Megatrends* that "we are drowning in information but starved for knowledge" (1982, 24). At the same time that CNN and other outlets were providing Americans with access to more news than ever before, Naisbitt feared that we lack the ability to comprehend or connect the story fragments. Neil Postman called this "a peek-a-boo world, where now this event, now that, pops into view for a moment then vanishes again" (1992, 70). In *Democracy Without Citizens: Media and the Decay of American Politics*, Robert Entman clearly addressed the consequences of such a state. "Despite any improvement in access to news, Americans do not know more about politics than they did 20 years ago. They vote less." While the news media has the power to make or break presidencies, Entman argued that they "cannot harness that power to serve democratic citizenship" (1989, 3).

Five years after the publication of *Megatrends*, Chester Finn, the assistant secretary of education, and Diane Ravitch published *What Do Our 17 Year Olds Know?*, a report of the first national assessment of history and literature. In the chapter "A Generation at Risk," the authors conclude that the younger generation "is ignorant of important things it should know" (1987, 201). Looking at the knowledge gap they discovered in these high school students, Ravitch and Finn asked, "Can they make sense of what they see and hear? Can they interpret the significance of the day's news?" (202). As we entered the last decade of the 20th century, evidence indicated that our students actually tune out the news and the world depicted in it. A report from the Times Mirror Center for the People and the Press suggested that what theoretically should have been the best educated generation in history had actually managed to grow up ignorant in an "information age." The study reported that only 24 percent of the under-35 population had read a newspaper the day before, compared to 67 percent 25 years earlier (Morin 1990, 35).

A 1993 Roper study commissioned by the American Jewish Committee concluded that "more than 1 in 5 people in the U.S. is open to the idea that the holocaust is a myth" (Stone, 1). Thirty-eight percent of adults and 53 percent of students didn't know what it referred to. A 1996 survey reported in the *Washington Post* described Americans as "tuned out, turned off and clueless." Conducted by the Kaiser Family Foundation and Harvard University, the study concluded that "the television news watchers were consistently less likely to know basic facts about politics, government or current affairs than those who depended mostly on newspapers . . . they see and hear the conflict but miss the content" (7). Further, the study noted that the TV viewers tended to see the world as a hostile and threatening place and that this perception shaped their view of foreign policy. Similarly, studies by Lewis (1992) and others indicate that the more television news viewers watch, the less they actually know about events such as the Gulf War and issues such as welfare and affirmative action. What they do tend to have is strong feelings about the world that television presents to them. It is a world where "emotion and imagery take precedence over reason," a world that "sets viewers adrift in a sea of images and an ocean of sensations." Such a world does not require "us to reason logically or to worry about the connection between evidence, premises and conclusions" (Dorman 1994, 35).

For some, no doubt, the simple solution to all of this might involve nothing more than turning off the television set. Journalist James Fallows understands the inclination. In *Breaking News: How the Media Undermine American Democracy*, he admits that the media have played a destructive role that "threatens the long term health of our political system" and "distorts the processes by which we choose our leaders and resolve our public problems" (1996, 6, 7). But he rejects the idea of tuning out or turning off. "Ignoring the news leaves people with no way to prepare for trends they don't happen to observe themselves, no sense of what is happening in other countries or even other parts of their own town, no tools with which to make decisions about public leaders or policies" (3). The remainder of this chapter attempts to raise issues related to the form, content, and ownership of the news and to provide teachers and students with tools and conceptual frameworks that will enable them to be more effective users and choosers of news media.

Special Note for Teachers

Walter Cronkite has suggested that we need to be teaching skepticism. In approaching news with young people, we need to be guarded about fostering distrust and cynicism. Define both cynicism and skepticism for your students. Make it clear that your aim is to foster independent critical thinking and that you want to encourage them to make up their own minds based on several sources of information. In studying news media with students, it is highly likely that you will encounter one or both of the following attitudes: "What's it got to do with me anyway?" and "I can't do anything about it anyway." Your first challenge is to connect the subject of news stories to the real world in which students live, making it meaningful and relevant for them. The second challenge is to empower them and provide them with the belief that their feelings and actions can change both situations and coverage. Aware, informed citizens participate in the community and society and make a difference through their involvement. Informed and aware consumers monitor the media, accepting and rejecting coverage according to their own criteria. These consumers can also shape media coverage by their letters to the editor, calls to the networks, and other means to both challenge and reward coverage.

GETTING STARTED: The Nature of News

What is news? There is no better way to begin a study of the news media than to ask this question. The question leads to a series of other questions:

1. Is news new?

2. To whom is it news?

3. Who determines what is newsworthy?

4. Is it *all* the news?

For students, particularly those in middle school and high school, these questions are crucial if they are to begin to understand the communication process and the way the media operate as gatekeepers, filtering information before passing it on to society or closing the door on it.

News Formats

- Newspapers
- Newsmagazines
- Radio
- Television
- Internet

What News We Use

Two surveys in 1996 suggested differences and declines in the way the U.S. public uses various news sources.

- 59 percent of people indicate most of their news comes from television.

- 23 percent indicate that their main source of news is newspapers.

- Network news is regularly viewed in 26 percent of homes, a decline from 41 percent 15 years earlier.

- 18- to 29-year-olds also appear to be tuning networks out. Viewership dropped from 36 percent to 22 percent between 1995 and 1996.

- Radio is also reported to be a regular source of news by 61 percent of women and 71 percent of men.

- Newsmagazines are used by 45 percent of women and 51 percent of men.
  (Sources: *Time*, 10/21/96; *U.S.A. Today*, 8/26/96)

NEWSPAPERS

(ELEM/MID) — Have students bring in an example of each one of these types of newspapers: national, morning, evening, weekly, local, tabloid, and special interest. Divide the class into groups and have each group study a different type of paper. Compare and contrast the papers for:

- Size (number of pages and size of pages)
- Color/black and white
- Cost
- Front page (content—stories' covers, types of headlines, etc.)
- Back page (whole paper or of sections)
- Editorials
- Features
- Cartoons/comic strips
- Photographs (size, content)
- Advertising
- Classifieds
- Circulation
- Sports

In what way do the differences in these elements suggest something about the community and consumer group for whom each paper is intended?

Have students research life in their own community based on the elements they find in their local newspaper. Remember that they are looking at all of the newspaper, not just the stories. What, for example, do they learn about their community from display advertising and help-wanted ads and other classifieds?

Have students examine the Sunday edition of one of the larger newspapers in the state. In what way is it different from the regular weekday edition? Why is it different? Make a display board that compares the Sunday edition to the daily paper.

Obviously the Sunday paper will be larger and will cost more, but why is it larger? Is there more news every weekend? If that's the case, why is there actually less television news coverage in a weekend? These questions provide a useful framework for considering how the definition of news changes on a weekend and how the consumer influences news.

The fact that many Americans do not work on Sunday means we have more time to read. Because we have more time to read, the newspaper creates a bigger edition, which includes not only weekend sports but also features designed for different members of the family.

Content and Discontent

Michael Gartner, the former head of NBC News, has noted that there is a mismatch between what the news media tell us about and what we want to know about. Drawing from a study by Pew Research Center for the People and the Press, he notes that the content of news typically addresses subjects few of us are interested in. For example:

- 16 percent of us closely follow politicians and politics.

- 9 percent are interested in culture and the arts.

- 13 percent are interested in famous people and celebrities.

- 14 percent follow consumer news.

- 15 percent express a preference for entertainment news.

(Source: U.S.A. Today, 6/4/96)

Gartner concludes that the press does not adequately cover our main interests, which are local news, crime news, and health news. Should the press give the public what it wants? What is the difference between what the public wants to know and what it needs to know?

Use these figures above and have the class analyze a newspaper by seeing how much space is given to each category. Compare and contrast a midweek edition with a weekend edition.

Viewpoint and Opinion

Many people usually assume that because it is news, it is real and therefore true. They also assume that the story consists of a series of facts that are reported neutrally for viewers' consideration. Often, however, stories are presented in such a way that viewers are actually led to draw a particular conclusion. We are being encouraged to adopt the perspective and point of view of the writer, reporter, or anchor rather than to draw our own conclusions.

Have students read editorials on several key issues to try to develop a sense of the views and values of the newspaper editor. Are these views and values reinforced throughout other sections of the paper written by other journalists?

See whether the newspaper regularly features two opposing points of view on important issues. Such columns usually appear on the editorial page. In *U.S.A. Today* this section is called "Face Off."

Cut out a series of photographs from newspaper articles and give them to students. Make sure to keep a record of the article, the accompanying photographs, and whether it was a positive or a negative story.

Have the students look at the photos and indicate what they think the story was about and whether they think the person pictured was presented positively or negatively in the story. Then ask them to explain how they reached their answer. Facial expression and body language can be read and interpreted as clues in this process. Props can also play a part. For example, was there a gun in the picture, or perhaps a police car or a sheriff's badge? What about the camera angle? Is it objective, or does it impose a point of view and perspective? Does it, for example, tilt down or up at the subject?

How often are the pictures truly neutral, needing words to establish a context, and how often do they speak for themselves? Is the role of the photograph to decorate or elaborate? Does it contain and convey meaning independently of the story?

(ELEM/MID) — Give students a list of stories and ask them to decide where they would place the stories in a newspaper and to explain their choices. Possible stories might include:

- Death of a senator
- Plane crash
- Coalminers' strike in England
- United States loses America's Cup
- Coup in overseas nation
- President visits flag factory
- Former president has surgery
- Stock market closes down
- Baseball star arrested in drug raid
- Storm damages wheat crop
- Animals saved from forest fire

- AIDS cure found

Now give students a series of stories and pictures that you have cut out of several newspapers. Make sure you have removed any evidence of what pages the stories came from, but keep a record of the pages for yourself. Have the students arrange the stories in the order they think they would have appeared in the paper, and compare the students' arrangement to the actual positions you have recorded. Students must be able to explain their decisions. Do students make the same decisions as editors and publishers?

Writing Headlines

(ELEM/MID) — Journalists typically use catchy headlines to grab our attention. These headlines often involve literary devices such as metaphor, simile, or alliteration. A newspaper report of an unstable vehicle in the solar car race across Australia read "Sun Setting on US Car." When a student's automobile engine design won a scholarship, the story was headed "Engine Design Drives Student to Success." During the Iraqi invasion of Kuwait in 1990, one headline declared Saddam Hussein the "Bully of Baghdad." Later headlines read "Butcher of Baghdad."

In 1997, when scientists in Scotland cloned a sheep and named her Dolly, the American headline read, "Hello Dolly!" *Time* billed the same story as "Clone on the Range." Referring to the old song title, another source called the story "There Will Never Be Another Ewe." When Queen Elizabeth knighted Paul McCartney, several press reports used Beatles song titles as their lead-in, including "Let It Be" and, of course, "It's Been a Hard Day's Knight."

The McPapering of the United States

(MID/HIGH) — In *Unreliable Sources* (1990), Martin Lee and Norman Solomon write, "Stuffed with celebrity gossip and other bite-sized light items, the innards of many newspapers largely resemble fluffy bonbons" (14). *U.S.A. Today*, which started in 1982, is often cited as an example of this type of newspaper. How much news do these papers contain? In what way have they influenced the form, content, look, and coverage of other newspapers? Are these papers more useful or less useful than television as a source of news?

NEWSMAGAZINES

(MID/HIGH) — Give students a selection of newsmagazines such as *Time*, *Newsweek*, and *U.S. News and World Report*. Have the students analyze the form and content of the magazines, including the following criteria:

- Size of pages
- Number of pages
- Price
- Type of advertising

Using issues of the three magazines from the same week, have students compare and contrast:

- Cover story

- Editorial

- International stories

- National stories

- Coverage of business

- Coverage of education

- Coverage of sports

- Coverage of entertainment

Which magazines do students believe provide a better and more informative view of the week, and why?

Based on the type of advertisements appearing in each magazine, ask the students to develop a profile of the primary readers of each magazine. Would the readers, for example, be more likely to be male or female, working class or middle class, college-educated or with no college education? These questions help students understand the concept of targeting audiences. In looking at the advertisements, they are actually looking at the audience. How do the products, pictures, and form of persuasion reflect the audience for the newsmagazine?

Time Out: Pictorial Prejudice and Newsmagazine Covers

In June 1993, *Time* magazine admitted that their "Incredible Shrinking President" cover story (June 7) had generated an enormous amount of negative mail, including one letter from a Republican who said the only thing shrinking was *Time*'s reputation as a credible news source. Exactly one year later, the magazine would once again come under fire, this time for its "enhancement" of its cover image of O. J. Simpson. The photo illustration that *Time* used was based upon the photograph of Simpson released by the Los Angeles Police Department. *Newsweek* ran the photo as is. *Time* altered it, darkening the skin, blurring the image, and creating a heavier beard. The National Association for the Advancement of Colored People (NAACP) complained that the photo "plays into the stereotype of the African-American male as dangerous and violence prone." Dorothy Gilliam, head of the National Association of Black Journalists, said, "It does make him look more sinister, more macabre" (Hoverston and Kanamine 1994, 1d).

The covers of newsmagazines are clearly designed and intended to capture our attention and promote sales. But is successful marketing strategy compatible with objective and responsible journalism? In many cases, special effects, amusing captions, and other devices that grab our attention also telegraph the magazine's perspective and influence us, whether we read the article or not. Shoppers standing in a checkout lane at

a supermarket, and commuters browsing through a magazine stand at an airport or train station, are likely to see these covers with their pictorial prejudice. Sometimes an image is so powerful that there may be an ethical question about running it. After the Oklahoma bombing, several news outlets ran a story featuring the photograph of a dead baby in the arms of a rescue worker. The photo was taken by an amateur, and it went on to win the Pulitzer Prize. It was also very private and painful for the family of the dead infant. Ask students to discuss the use of this image, including the family's right to privacy, the public's right to know, and the commercial benefits of running the picture. Other examples of this issue include images of the family and victims of TWA Flight 800 and of the child beauty pageant winner who was murdered in Boulder, Colorado.

(MID/HIGH) — Use the following examples of covers from *Time* to help students understand the design decisions that are involved in creating a magazine cover. Then have them find recent issues of major newsmagazines that reflect some of these design decisions.

January 19, 1993. Fighting Back. The story deals with spousal abuse. The decision has been made to use a black and white photograph of the woman whose story is featured. This lends authenticity and a documentary quality to the story. A box with a small image is integrated into this cover. The person in this picture is shown in much smaller proportions than the woman. Why? What impact does this have?

March 15, 1993. In the name of God. This is an excellent cover to work with. It features David Koresh of the Waco compound and Sheik Abdel-Rahman, whose followers were blamed for the bombing of the World Trade Center in New York. The page is split into three parts, with an image of each man at the left and right, while the title of the cover story runs down the middle between them. Both portraits, however, have been elongated, distorted, and presented out of proportion. Why? What impact might this have? How fair or accurate are these images? Were these prejudicial pictures taken before or after juries had investigated the cases to which the stories allude?

May 10, 1993. Ascent of a Woman. This cover deals with the increasing power of Hillary Clinton and gets its bounce by referring to Al Pacino's Oscar Award-winning film. Facial expression is interesting also.

May 17, 1993. Anguish over Bosnia. This is a very useful cover to work with in terms of color and positioning/placement. The story raises the possibility that Bosnia is Clinton's Vietnam. The president is in the foreground of the frame, positioned on the left of the page, depicted in color and in profile (quite different from most images of him). He looks from left to right as though facing the future. In the background, shown in black and white, we see LBJ. His expression and body language pick up on the cover's caption.

May 31, 1993. Dr. Death. Despite the grim title, this story about Jack Kevorkian shows a smiling and seemingly relaxed individual whose appearance belies all "Grim Reaper" associations.

February 21, 1994. The Star Crossed Olympics. This is another very strong cover that has some things in common with the Clinton/LBJ cover already mentioned. Nancy Kerrigan dominates the cover. She is skating. Her facial expression, posture, and body language are all positive. She wears white. In the shadowy background, imperceptible from some angles, is the face of Tonya Harding. The use of positioning for the two skaters, combined with the light and darkness, serves as a fairly clear commentary on the two women. Was this picture presented before or after Tonya Harding's plea bargain? How fair or unfair is this image? See also the use of background/foreground positioning as well as soft and sharp focus in the Bush/Quayle cover (8/29/88).

April 4, 1994. Deep Water. This was a controversial cover that the *New York Times* called "another doctored grimly monochromatic *Time* magazine cover, misleadingly cropped, 5 month old photo of a seemingly doomed president" (Rich 1994, 13a). The whole design of the picture weighs very heavily on a conclusion of guilty, at which the magazine seems to have already arrived without benefit of judicial process. The cover alludes to Whitewater and how the "president's men" attempted to cover up the investigation. The most obvious and striking thing about the cover is that it is black and white. Clearly the magazine had no shortage of color photographs to work with. Hence, the decision to use black and white said something about the subject. The cultural expression "It's right there in black and white" makes it clear that truth and black and white are associated. Therefore, by using this style, the magazine attempts to reinforce the veracity of its story. This is further strengthened when we take into account the documentary style and the cultural assumptions we also have about the validity of these forms. *Time*'s historical account of D-Day (5/28/84), for example, went black and white, as did *Newsweek*'s cover for a week in the life of President Clinton (7/12/93). The body language of the president on this April 4 cover is clearly negative. Does he seem worried? concerned? thoughtful? We are meant to think he is worrying about Whitewater, but we have no idea when this picture was taken or what he and George Stephanopolous (in background) were thinking about. The language is also loaded, characterized as "deep" and, more importantly, with a reference to the "president's men," an allusion to Nixon and Watergate.

Narrowing of News

(MID/HIGH) — Several times in recent years, all three major newsmagazines have featured the same cover story. When a major event like the Oklahoma bombing galvanizes the attention of the nation, it is likely that all news outlets will concentrate on the same story. But frequently this happens without a major incident. As such it represents the narrowing of news, which in turn limits our access to other stories. Some examples of this narrowing of news can be found on the following covers. On February 12, 1996, all three major magazines (*Time, Newsweek, U.S. News and World Report*) featured a cover on Magic Johnson coming out of retirement. On April 8, 1996, all three featured an image of Jesus Christ and two used the same heading, "In Search of Jesus." The following week, all three had an image of Theodore Kaczynski, the alleged Unabomber. Have students anticipate which story will be featured on the magazines. Compare and contrast the stories the magazines select. Develop a criterion for assessing the national significance and impact of the stories they cover.

(EL/MID/HIGH) — Body language has been referred to on several of the covers that have been analyzed. In June 1995, Scott O'Grady, an American flier, was rescued after being shot down in Bosnia. Newsmagazines selected strikingly different images of the pilot to showcase their stories, as a result of which their covers, while similar in content, were so different in form that they conveyed distinct meanings. *Newsweek*'s heading was "The Right Stuff" and they showed a jubilant and elated soldier. On the other hand, *Time*'s theme was "A Pilot's Story" and they showed a grim-faced close-up of O'Grady.

❖ The *New York Times* was critical of this misleading, prejudicial picture. Copyright © 1994 *Time* magazine, April 4, 1994. All rights reserved. Used with permission.

Minorities Matter: Stereotyping, Distortion, and Ethnocentricity

(MID/HIGH) — Obviously the news in a newspaper or news broadcast is not all the news that happened in the world on a given day, or even all the news that happened in the immediate environment of the viewer/reader. Rather, it is the news the publishers and editors think will be of interest to their readers. Whether this news has utility and can actually be applied to current issues, concerns, or problems facing these consumers is another matter. By the very nature of both selecting and rejecting types of stories, the news becomes ethnocentric. Rather than dealing with all countries and all cultures equally, it presents stories that are perceived to be of interest to people sharing a common background and value system. Although this makes good marketing sense, it might also limit the scope of the news, and in the process, by ignoring certain news stories, it may prevent consumer citizens from more fully understanding minority elements in their own country as well as international issues and perspectives. This has been particularly controversial in terms of issues related to race. Ishmael Reed charges that local TV news "polarizes whites and blacks by racializing issues such as welfare, affirmative action, and crime" (1993, 22). In *The American Journalism Review*, Reed has argued that the images television selects distort the reality of these issues. Only 39 percent of welfare recipients are black and 85 percent of drug users are white, says Reed, but "when reporting about such issues, local television news will air tapes of blacks." Students can be divided into groups and assigned various news stories such as crime, welfare, and drugs and asked to monitor the types of images used in both television and newspapers. It is interesting at this point to take note of a research study related to viewer perceptions of television news along with their suggestions about improving the quality of coverage. Among the suggested improvements were fuller presentation of minorities, less stereo-typical presentation of minorities, and more minority reporters and anchors (Lind 1995).

Other groups have also complained about distorted reporting and representation. An article in the *San Jose Mercury News* asserted that "TV Coverage Cheapens Arab Lives" and provided examples of words and pictures that distorted Iraqi and Arab life (Husseini 1991). A 1989 article in *TV Guide* asked, "Is TV News Guilty of Japan Bashing?" The article reported studies that found "stereotypes everywhere. Japan as a closed society, at once hostile and indifferent; the clannish-driven Japanese; the anthill lifestyle" (Diamond and O'Neill 1989, 25). Given Japan's economic power in the world and the significance of the trade relationship with the United States, it is important that Americans have much more than a simplistic and stereotypical image of the people and culture.

From a Distance

Ironically, as America's ties to other nations continue to grow and our standard of living depends upon developing markets in the Pacific Rim and Third World, news coverage of these countries has actually declined. Despite the presence of CNN's *World View*, coverage of foreign and international news has decreased since the 1970s. In 1971, 10 percent of editorial space in the nation's 10 leading newspapers was dedicated to foreign news. By 1986 the figure had dropped to 2.6 percent. Writing in the *Humanist* in 1990, Dan Rather said this trend had occurred at "the very time it has become indisputably clear that America's future depends upon having a better understanding of that great big world beyond our shores" (1990, 6). Sometimes what we don't know about other people and places can actually hurt them. Examining the relationship between Africa and the American press, *Extra* suggested that by failing to cover the famine in Ethiopia, Sudan, and Somalia in 1990, the media made the situation worse. Though the United Nations and the U.S. Agency for International Development had warned that the situation was becoming alarming and had requested international help, the story fell on deaf ears. "The blame for inadequate coverage," said the report, "does not lie primarily with the few reporters covering Africa for the US, but with editors, publishers and news directors who make Africa their lowest priority" (Hunter and Askin 1991, 10). In the case of television news, although we frequently see stories about Japan, Mexico, China, Bosnia, and Russia, they are often filtered through a U.S. prism; as a result, we are encouraged to look at other countries and cultures only from our own perspective. Americans are typically surprised and shocked when they see themselves through other eyes. Though this can be painful, it is a necessary process of maturation and one that the news media often preempt. Most Americans, for example, were never exposed to confrontational photographs or footage of President Bush's trip to Australia. In Sydney one newspaper occupied almost the entire front page with the headline, "Bush Fury." The story addressed the anger Australian farmers felt about unfair U.S. trade policies. When Bush spoke at the World Congress Center in Melbourne, police and demonstrators clashed violently in what one officer described as "the most ferocious demonstration" he had seen in 18 years on the force. The front page of the *Jakarta Post* ran a photograph of the riot and the heading, "Violent Clashes as Bush Ends Australian Visit" (1/4/92, 1).

By Mike Smith, Las Vegas Sun, for USA TODAY

❖ Used with permission of Mike Smith, *Las Vegas Sun*, 1996.

Though the subject matter should clearly have been of concern to Americans, the event was largely ignored by the U.S. media. Several years later, during the Olympic Games in Atlanta, an Australian newspaper had occasion to comment on the inward-looking nature of U.S. coverage. The reporter complained about the cultural bias evident in the way the American media covered the event. Not only were athletes from other countries marginalized, but in the case of Ireland's swimming sensation, Michelle Smith, they were also practically criminalized. When a world event dedicated to international harmony is reduced to a self-centered celebration of one country, everyone suffers from it. "Sadly," wrote the *Herald-Sun*, "it seems that those who call the shots in the U.S. media work on the principle that if the Yanks aren't doing it, it isn't happening" (Sheahan 1996, 92).

Later that year, both *The Guardian* in England and *The Age* in Australia featured a piece by British playwright Harold Pinter that launched what could only be described as a scathing attack on the United States. Ostensibly a piece about American foreign policy and the failure of the United States to recognize the overwhelming international

opposition to its policy on Cuba and its support for the Helms-Burton Bill, the article also took aim at American politicians, the American public, and the news media. "Brutal, indifferent, scornful, ruthless . . . biased, arrogant, and ignorant" are just some of the terms Pinter used to describe American society. "The US has educated itself to be in love with itself. Language is employed to keep thought at bay." Successive presidents, aided and abetted by the media, claimed Pinter, have kept truth and reality from the American public while creating a society of haves and have-nots. The haves are cushioned by comforting language and the constant mantra "the American people." "The cushion may be suffocating your intelligence but you don't know that. Nobody tells you. It is probably more than a newspaper or a TV channel's life is worth to do so" (Pinter 1996, A11). While Pinter's tone may be excessive, he has a point, particularly when discussing the window on the world that television supplies for some and denies for others. While British and Australian viewers, for example, can routinely tune in to CNN and broadcasts of various networks' news programs from the United States, American viewers must rely almost entirely on American visions and voices to present the rest of the world to them.

Not only does the American media serve to silence difference and dissent among our allies, but too often it polarizes our own people, pitting one group against another. Discussing this trend, journalist Susan Estrich accused the media of "turning every issue into a yes/no proposition, as articulated by two people representing the furthest extremes and pushing the most emotional buttons." While some may see the process as ideological, Estrich believes it is financial, driven by ratings and sales. "They do it because it is the easiest way to produce hot television, hot radio, hot talk." While such coverage may generate heat, it seldom sheds light and forgets the most basic fact that on most issues, there is always a middle ground (1995, 13a).

But the media does much more than polarize; it also manages to both marginalize and minimize, rendering some sectors of society invisible, insignificant, and powerless. *Selu: Seeking the Corn-Mother's Wisdom* explores Cherokee culture, including values such as respect, cooperation, and balance. It also addresses the impact the news media have had on the way the public perceives Native Americans. "Somewhere down the line our information system is breaking down. How can the press be the watchdog of the people, if we are blind in one eye . . . Who focuses the good eye of the press? Who decides which issue is worthy of attention?" (Awiakta 1993, 58)

(ELEM/MID/HIGH) — Introduce students to the following terms and have them locate examples. Students should work in pairs and develop a criterion for these definitions. Newspaper stories are easier to work with than the images, words, and speed of television coverage.

- **Polarize** (present opposite extremes with no middle ground)

- **Marginalize/Minimize** (give little or no coverage to events, issues, or groups)

- **Trivialize** (employ a light, mocking, or amusing tone that discounts or disrespects an event, issue, or point of view)

Whose Window, Whose World?: Content Analysis of News Coverage

Create a chart as a way for students to monitor the frequency with which the media represent various groups in our society. Students can also begin to classify stories as + (positive), – (negative), or N (neutral) in terms of how these various groups are represented. By using one symbol for each story they log, they can begin to develop both a quantitative and a qualitative table.

(ELEM/MID/HIGH) — People with Disabilities

The passage of the Americans With Disabilities Act in July 1991 brought the issue to the attention of the American public. But FAIR (Fairness and Accuracy in Reporting) noted the distorted way in which the press responded to both the issue and individuals with disabilities. "For the press, disabled people are either tragic, hopeless cases constantly bemoaning their fate, or incredibly brave, courageous, and inspiring. For this reason people with disabilities are almost invariably described as 'overcoming' their disability, or 'afflicted by' or 'suffering from' it" (Johnson 1991, 15). Assign students to explore the way the media represent the issue of disability and those who have disabilities. Are the claims made by FAIR still valid criticisms? Refer to Chapter 6 and the depiction of disabilities in movies.

(MID/HIGH) — Contemporary court cases, including the Simpson murder case and the police beating of Rodney King, have both exposed and exacerbated race relations in this country. Former president Jimmy Carter has clearly addressed the role the news media can and should play in such matters. Television and radio, he has said, "can play a long-term role in defusing and moderating ethnic tensions." Further, they can "help reduce conflict from occurring by identifying tensions and needs. But this requires media organizations to recruit and advance members of minorities whose insights can expand the outlook of the entire organization" (1994, vi).

- Assign students the task of analyzing coverage of major court cases in which race is a factor. Look for issues of balance and bias. Identify the race of each of the journalists.

- Monitor local and national news broadcasts for minority representa-

tion in terms of the anchors and reporters.

- Invite a minority (black, Hispanic, Asian) journalist to speak to your class and encourage minorities in your class to enter the profession.

- Contact your nearest university with a journalism department and collect data on the racial composition of students majoring in journalism. Apply the same concept to other minorities such as women.

Wrong About the Religious Right

(MID/HIGH) — Though people frequently assert that the media are biased, traditionally regarded as meaning "liberal," bias can sometimes result from ignorance rather than opposition. A 1995 report indicated that among the leading members of the country's so-called media elite, 80 percent said they rarely attended religious meetings and 50 percent claimed no religious affiliation. This is in contrast to the public at large among whom 40 percent say they regularly attend church and 90 percent express some religious affiliation (Mattingly 1995, 5). With little or no connection to religious communities, how can journalists accurately report about such congregations? Evidence of this problem appeared when a *Washington Post* reporter described evangelical Christians as "poor, uneducated and easy to command" (5). In fact, a survey conducted for the *Post* and published under the

heading "Wrong About Religious Right" showed much greater diversity in the group. Based on a Virginia sample, the poll indicated that those who called themselves evangelicals, or born-again, included 39 percent Democrats and 41 percent Republicans. Half of them characterized their politics as moderate, as distinct from the right-wing claims constantly used to describe them (Morin 1993, 37). Students can monitor the way religion and religious issues are presented by the news media. They can also check with both local and network news and see if a reporter is actually assigned to cover religion in the way that some journalists specialize in medical, science, business, or education news. What credentials do religion reporters have? What credentials should they have? Refer to Chapter 6 for the depiction of the church and clergy in movies.

Crime Time: If It Bleeds, It Leads

(MID/HIGH) — A 1997 national survey indicated that 61 percent of the country believed the United States was losing the war against crime. This perception came at the same time as the discovery that crime statistics in New York had declined 50 percent in four years, and reductions had also been reported in other areas of the country (*U.S.A. Today*, 21). The reason for the gap between reality and perception is summed

up in a statement from FAIR: "There is no more violent crime today than there was 20 years ago. What there is more of, much more of, is crime coverage and the coverage has taken on a shrill tabloid tone" (Jackson and Naurekas 1994, 10). Media coverage of the so-called drug wars of the 1980s also affected public perception of the seriousness of the problem. Monitoring press coverage and public perception of the drug issue, Richard

Morin found a correlation between the frequency of the coverage and how seriously the public rated the problem. In January 1989, 19 percent of those surveyed said it was the number-one problem facing the country. By August it had increased to 44 percent, and by October it was 53 percent. While the public seemed convinced of the growing menace, "this was largely the result of the media's sudden interest in the subject, rather than an increase in the prevalence or use of illicit narcotics" (Morin 1994, 27). As was the case with the crime story, statistics contradicted news coverage. Reliable research, said Morin, indicated "that drug use during this period was, if anything, flat, or perhaps even going down slightly—anything but up" (27).

Excessive press coverage of crime is evident not only in tabloid coverage of the trial of public figures such as O. J. Simpson, but also in the personal and private family tragedies involved in the Menendez brothers' murder trial, the killing of JonBenet Ramsey, the murder trial of Susan Smith, and countless others. Personal tragedies become a sideshow carnival attraction for a seemingly insatiable public. In the meantime, broadcasting is reduced to narrowcasting, with fewer options available to those not interested in these subjects and most of the mainstream media following each other story by story. On August 2, 1993, for example, three of the main newsmagazines in the country all featured stories about crime and violence. *Newsweek* led with "Teen Violence: Wild in the Streets." *Time* opted for "Big Shots: An Inside Look at the Deadly Love Affair Between American Kids and Their Guns." *U.S. News and World Report* gave us "Super Cops: Can They Solve America's Crime Problem?"

The Institute on News and Social Problems believes "the media is the principal source of the public's information about crime" (Gilliam and Lyengar 1995, 2). They also suggest a relationship between public perceptions and both the form and content of crime coverage. News coverage, they suggest, "links the issues of race and crime" and heightens the public's fear of crime, "increasing their enthusiasm for get-tough solutions" and providing "an incentive for self-serving politicians to gain political advantage from" (4). Describing what he calls "the mean-world syndrome," George Gerbner et al. (1994) has demonstrated that heavy viewers of television news are more likely to believe their world is a dangerous and threatening place. The consequence of this television content is that viewers believe the world that television constructs for them rather than the reality about it. They are more likely to support tougher prison sentences, support the death penalty, and be aggressive in foreign policy. Yet their stands on all of these issues have been shaped not by reality but by marketing decisions made by news executives who have discovered that coverage of crime, and violent crime in particular, is good for ratings and sales. But what price do we pay for that decision?

- Compare the quality and quantity of crime coverage in local, state, and national newspapers.

- Use FBI, Justice Department, and other statistics to compare national trends to media coverage. Which provide the most accurate picture?

- It has been suggested that crime coverage is linked to race. Examine the way the press presents minorities when dealing with crime.

- Local news in California has been accused of "providing a distorted picture of youth and youth violence" (Dorfman and Woodruf 1995, 4). Examine the representation of young people and crime.

- Contact your local news sources to discuss their coverage of crime.

- Analyze news stories of crime to see how much attention is given to both causes and solutions.

❖ Used with permission of Fairness and Accuracy in Reporting, Washington, DC.

Welfare Mothers and Battered Women

News coverage of crimes against women often plays down the seriousness of the crime and frequently blames the victim, particularly in cases of rape and sexual harassment. When Paula Jones first complained about sexual harassment from then governor Bill Clinton, an editorial in *U.S. News and World Report* dismissed her claims. "It does not pass the smell test," they noted, adding that "the smell intensifies with the information about attempts to profit from the alleged incident" (Zuckerman 1994, 82). In January 1997, as an appeals aspect of the case made its way to the Supreme Court, *Newsweek* featured the woman on its cover. Throughout the period of soul-searching, much of the press engaged in a form of media mea culpa, admitting that they had dismissed the seriousness of her charges because of stereotypes and prejudices related to trailer trash and big hair.

In the case of battered women, FAIR has also documented news bias. In some cases the press downplays or minimizes the frequency of such attacks and in other cases minimizes the seriousness of the assaults. They "describe violence in ways that mirror the batterer's own rationalizations" and "often use language which is euphemistic, gender-neutral and evades the issue of blame" (Devitt and Downey 1991, 10). While the media seem preoccupied with the question, "Why didn't you leave?" victims of abuse frequently ask, "Why do you want to hurt me?" The growth of date rape on college campuses and evidence of sexual harassment in our armed services cannot be isolated from the content in which attitudes and behaviors develop. While the news media frequently headline sexual scandals in Congress and the military, evidence suggests that their overall record of covering the topic is less than balanced.

Stereotypes of single mothers living off welfare have also been part of traditional media coverage, and once again they have provided only part of the picture and little context. Seeking to correct the image, Richard Morin has pointed out that there are actually more white single mothers than there are black, and that the biggest growth is in the suburbs and rural areas, not the inner city that is typically presented. Interestingly enough, he has also shown that the number of single mothers in the United States is actually lower than in Sweden, France, Denmark, and the United Kingdom (1995, 34). What the press has tended to concentrate on when addressing this topic has been shame, promiscuity, and "the pathology of out of wedlock births" (Flanders and Jackson 1995, 13). In the process of presenting the issue this way, the media have repeated and reinforced, but not challenged, a series of stereotypes and myths about women and welfare. These include the belief that poor women have more children because of financial incentives, that the public is fed up spending money on the poor, and that $5 trillion spent on welfare since the 1960s hasn't worked. FAIR has examined and dismissed these and other media mythconceptions (Flanders and Jackson 1995).

(MID/HIGH) —

- The death of Nicole Simpson focused media coverage on battered women. Whether that coverage remains vigilant, balanced, and thorough after the case has yet to be seen. Monitor press coverage of violence against women. Analyze the tone and content of the stories. Compare and contrast coverage when presented by a female and a male reporter. Conduct surveys in your school or community to detect gender differences in attitudes about this issue.

- Encourage groups in the school, including the newspaper producers, counselors, and others, to provide a forum on the issue.

Just Another Pretty Face?

Sometimes the way female journalists are treated reflects the deep-seated bias of a male-dominated industry and society. One female sports reporter was subjected to insult and abuse by players and management for the New England Patriots, resulting in a heavy fine for the club. In January 1991, *TV Guide* ran a cover story with a picture of Jane Pauley. The heading asked, "Is She Tough Enough to Make It in Prime Time?" The cover recalled the August 1989 cover of *Time*, which featured Diane Sawyer and the heading "Is She Worth It?" Both women's credentials were implicitly challenged by even asking the questions. When Peter Jennings, Tom Brokaw, or Dan Rather get a raise, one seldom finds cover stories questioning their value or contribution.

Ina Bertrand (1994) says that the way the news media represent and present women confirms "their own lack of self-esteem" and encourages them "to assume that it is white men and their concerns that are really important" (47). Female anchors and reporters are presented for the viewing pleasure of men. "What they look like is more important than what they say" (48). On the other hand, men are positioned as authority figures and, as a result, "what he says is more important than what he looks like."

In U.S. society, women constitute approximately 50 percent of the workforce, 45 percent of the labor force, and 50 percent of newspaper readership. Does the press provide an objective reflection of women in society? A 1989 study concluded:

- Female journalists contribute only 27 percent of front-page bylines.

- Only 24 percent of front-page photographs featured females.

- The average percentage of references to women on the front page is only 11 percent (Bridge 1989, 11-13).

- A 1995 study reported a decline in stories covered by and about females (Reynolds 1995, 13a).

Figures released in 1997 showed a decline in the presence of women and minorities in the evening news broadcast by the networks. Stories presented by women fell from 21 percent to 16 percent. Stories presented by Hispanic, Asian, or black correspondents slipped from 12 percent to 9 percent. The composition of newsrooms at the local level showed slight improvement. Women made up 36 percent of editorial staff. Minorities represented 11 percent of newspaper staff, and 40 percent of newsroom employees were women (*U.S.A. Today*, 2/21/97, 11a).

(MID/HIGH) — Break students into groups and assign each group one copy of various large city and national newspapers. The students should select an area of interest, such as bylines, photographs, or story content, and tabulate the proportion of each that is contributed by men or deals exclusively or largely with men. This concept can also be applied to analyzing television news.

Identify a series of issues of particular concern to females. The so-called "soccer moms" of the 1996 election were interested in health care and education. Other concerns for women are child care, contraception, and abortion. What are other issues for women? Are these issues well represented in the news media? Are they typically represented by women or men? Are their issues for which the gender of a reporter would enhance or hinder his or her ability to accurately and fairly cover the story?

(MID/HIGH) — Invite a woman journalist to your class to discuss journalism as a career and coverage of women's issues.

Women in News

(MID/HIGH) — The presence of women in the news industry has enormous implications for our society. As a growing industry, news offers career opportunities for young women. Communication research suggests that the female perspective is often lacking in an industry largely owned by men and in which men make most of the decisions. The question of women and the news involves a discussion of both visibility and viability. The absence of women from the news is often explained in terms of their low profile in national politics and in the policy-making process. "Women's absence from the public sphere as well as their lack of status as authority figures or experts gives the news media a ready-made justification for women's absence from news programs" (Rakow and Kranich 1991, 13). This is essentially a chicken-and-egg argument that claims women are not covered because they are not powerful enough. Obviously, it could conversely be argued that women's viability as authority figures is minimized by the amount of coverage they receive. But the question of coverage must address quality as well as quantity and explore how women are covered. When Pat Schroeder chose not to run for the presidency in 1988, the media made much of her tearful announcement. Her femininity was covered by men as if it were a political handicap and liability. It might equally have been argued that a nurturing, emotionally honest candidate could have been refreshing. So often women are seen through male eyes and perspectives. One report suggests that when women do appear on the news, they do so as examples of uninformed public opinion, consumers, housewives, spouses to the men in the news, or as victims of crime, political decisions, or disasters. "Thus not only do they speak less frequently, but they tend to speak as passive reactors and witnesses to public events, rather than as participants in those events" (Holland 1987, 139). Students can test their findings as they monitor and analyze news broadcasts. For most of them, the issue of how women are represented in the news media will be something they have never considered.

How aware are students of women in the news industry? Is the most famous female journalist they can name Lois Lane or Murphy Brown? Although women appear to be well represented in television news, visibility does not necessarily indicate power. A 1990 report in the *New York Times* suggested that an increasing number of female anchors were becoming "evening stars," particularly in newsmagazines. But journalist Linda Ellerbee told the newspaper that the trend was not necessarily a positive one. "They put the star before the show. All they really want people to watch is the person . . . this trend does no good for women and it doesn't matter if the show's good or not. It's all based on the person. Then if the show fails, the woman gets blamed" (Carter 1990, H-27).

Ellerbee's comments seemed particularly apt several years later, when CBS decided to team Connie Chung with Dan Rather as co-anchors of the evening news. When the network slipped from second to third place in the ratings, it was Chung who was blamed and replaced, while Rather stayed on.

TELEVISION NEWS

(ELEM/MID/HIGH) — When we talk about "television news" we are referring to news on television, and most of the time we think about network evening news. Actually the term *television news* refers to many different types of programs broadcast at many different times. Give students copies of *TV Guide* or the television listings in daily newspapers and have them compile a list of all programs that would be classified as news oriented. These programs should include:

- Morning news programs from networks, such as *Good Morning America*

- Evening news programs from networks

- Late-night network news programs, such as *Nightline*

- Lunchtime news programs

- Weekly news programs/news-magazines, such as *Hard Copy, 20/20,* and *60 Minutes*

- Weeknight news forums and discussions

- Local news, A.M. and P.M.

(ELEM/MID) — Have students conduct a survey of their parents, relatives, and other adults to find out which news programs the adults regularly watch and why. Compile the results and display a chart showing the news-viewing preferences in your area. Compare your results to Nielsen ratings for these programs. (Ratings appear regularly in *U.S.A. Today*.)

(ELEM/MID/HIGH) — Break the students into groups and assign each group the task of viewing and analyzing one of the types of programs listed above. Things to look for include:

- Broadcast time

- Length of broadcast

- Number of presenters, such as anchors, reporters, sports, film reviewers, meteorologists, etc.

- Gender balance of presenters

- Types of stories covered, such as international, national, regional, state, local

- Format, such as interviews in the studio, on-location footage, anchors' and other reporters' commentaries, etc.

Local News

Writing in *American Journalism Review,* Howard Rosenberg said that local newscasts present their on-air personalities "not only as a family unto themselves, warm, cuddly, and complementary, but also as the community's extended family" (1993, 19). One consequence, he noted, has been that "the message of news has inevitably shrunk to a tiny gray blimp against their blinding gloss." Studies in *The Journal of Broadcasting and Electronic Media* tend to substantiate the claim, suggesting that sensational stories about crime and conflict have increased "at the expense of information related to local government, politics and public policy" (Slattery and Hakanen 1994, 214).

Initially, the idea of local news was that, in contrast to national network news, which addressed the big picture, it would focus on the immediate concerns of the local community. As such, broadcasters were to further the democratic process by increasing community awareness and understanding of local issues. Deregulation throughout the 1980s, however, along with technologies that provided access to stories outside the community, resulted in a dramatic change in the content of local news. With profit maximization as the guiding principle, newscasters found themselves "forced to program for the broadest possible audience at the lowest possible cost. Stories that provoke an emotional response, such as human interest stories, are favored over those that enhance an understanding of current events, but have not historically drawn large audiences" (Slattery et al. 1996, 405).

(ELEM/MID/HIGH) —

- Study local on-air news teams in terms of Rosenberg's description of the friendly family. Who are the members of the team? (News, sports, weather?) How do they interact with each other? Is there banter among them about their weekends, local events, or community happenings? How would you characterize the mood they establish?

- Marjorie Williams (1990) uses several terms to describe local news personalities and content. One term is "salt and pepper anchor team." This is a reference to the black and white composition of the anchor team that is likely to be evident in an area with a large minority population. Introduce students to the concept and the marketing idea behind it.

Another term that Williams uses is "landscaping of news . . . with peaks and valleys." This refers to the emotional ebb and flow of the program content. Students can monitor the mood of the stories to see if this peaks-and-valleys pattern can be tracked. One thing usually avoided is a very serious story coming immediately before or after a very lighthearted story; some transition is preferred. Sometimes the break for commercials can be used as the buffer/transition between moods.

- Survey adults in the local community to see what types of stories they prefer to see on local news and what their favorite news outlet is.

- Compare and contrast the types of stories covered in a single week on local television news to those featured in local newspapers. What are the differences? What factors might explain the differences?

- Link Slattery's research findings with concepts of responsible citizenship and with the media literacy principle that all media constructions serve commercial purposes.

Science and Medical News

(ELEM/MID/HIGH) — Most networks have correspondents who specialize in particular areas. Viewers are familiar with the ones who cover the White House, the Supreme Court, or the Pentagon. In the background, however, are correspondents who specialize in scientific or medical news. Despite the enormous impact of medicine and science on our lives, these stories are seldom covered in depth, and they are nowhere near as numerous as stories about politics or the economy. Because scientific research is comparatively slow and a medical laboratory is not visually exciting to most people, these stories tend to rate low in the priorities of network executives who make decisions about what to show on a visual medium. Yet the impact of the new invisibility of these stories could be quite significant. The United States lacks scientists and engineers. Our schools do not turn out enough students skilled in science and math. Many students are not motivated to enter these areas. How

does the public perception of science shape our society, and how do the media contribute to this perception? How is medical news constructed? Most news originates in publications such as *The New England Journal of Medicine* and *The Journal of the American Medical Association (JAMA)*. They provide copies to science reporters on Tuesdays, embargoed for release on Thursdays. In essence the journals control what the press has access to and when. One result of this is episodic reporting. The journals try to limit journalistic speculation and exaggeration. The editor of *JAMA* has said, "There's a tendency on the part of some journalists to be cheerleaders, to hype advances that might not be as big as they seem" (Kurtz 1991, 38).

Break the class into groups, with each group responsible for monitoring TV news coverage of medicine and science. If there are seven students per group, each student could watch the news just one evening per week. Over a month, a fairly good analysis should be possible. Students could document the stories by covering elements such as:

- Topic of story

- Position of story in news (first, last, etc.)

- Running time of story

- Anchor's lead-in

- Reporters' comments

- Visuals

- Positive or negative depiction of science or medicine

The *Wall Street Journal* and *Forbes* dominate economic and business reporting. The medical world also has major sources. What is *The New England Journal of Medicine*, and why is it so consistently cited in medical news? What other medical or scientific sources are consistently cited?

Gloom and Doom: No News Is Good News

Thirty years ago on their album *Sergeant Peppers Lonely Hearts Club Band*, the Beatles sang, "I read the news today, oh boy." Today, more than ever, there is reason indeed to exclaim "Oh boy!" *U.S.A. Today* has said, "The morning paper hits the doorsteps sex saturated. The nightly news is chockablock with explicit language, lust, and perversion" (Edmonds 1993, 9a). *Newsweek* commented that "the dread t-word—tabloidism—is increasingly seeping into the respectable networks, but it is gussied up and disguised with slick packaging and the imprimatur of Diane Sawyers, Barbara Walters or Tom Brokaw" (Reibstein 1994, 62). Beyond the networks, research also indicates that local television news has become increasingly negative (Stone and Gruisin 1984; Whetmore 1987; Zillmann et al. 1994). Harry Schwartz, a member of the editorial board of the *New York Times*, said, "Newspapers and TV are peddling political pornography and the nation suffers. . . . The media claim to be performing a public service, but everyone knows their motives are mercenary. Scandals sell newspapers and build television audiences" (1994, 8a).

Schwartz's comments came in the wake of a series of hostile exchanges between the press and public figures, including Bobby Ray Inman's withdrawal of his nomination for secretary of defense following criticism of him by William Safire. When White House attorney Vince Foster killed himself in 1993, his suicide note included a bitter statement regarding the news media. "Here ruining people is considered sport." The view was shared by *Newsweek*'s Jonathan Alter, who described the transformation taking place in journalism as "sharper writing . . . shouting on television and a general coarsening of public dialogue" (1993, 33). Anyone who witnessed the hostile exchange between Dan Rather and then vice president George Bush during a live interview in the 1988 presidential campaign certainly understands the concept of journalism as combat. Some even believe that what *Time* referred to as the "ambush" was set up by one side to boost ratings and by the other side to dispel the image of Bush as a wimp. Four year later, during another campaign, the media engaged in a feeding frenzy, albeit a lighthearted one, castigating Vice President Quayle for suggesting that TV character Murphy Brown contributed to the decline of family values. Minnesota governor Arne Carlson has made it clear that he thinks press coverage has hurt and misrepresented his state. Speaking at an event in 1996, he was sharply critical of the news media in the Twin Cities, charging that their "thirst for profits" drive them toward a negative and sensational view of life. Far from limiting himself to the content of news reports, Carlson actually argued that this content had consequences. The press, he said, was "guilty of spreading cynicism about politicians, corporations, and other institutions." This steady diet of negative news contributed to an unrealistic and unrepresentative depiction of life in Minnesota (Berg 1996, 16a). *U.S. News and World Report* also sees consequences from the relentlessly negative coverage. "It is a process that has bred a double cynicism, one about the media and the other about the integrity of public figures. The scandalizing may attract the people as viewers and readers, but it alienates them as citizens" (Zuckerman 1996, 64).

Zuckerman is correct. While the public may object to negative news, there is also plenty of evidence that they are attracted to it. As David Broder wrote, "People curse the messenger even as they hungrily consume the message" (1987, 12). When the O. J. Simpson story broke in summer 1994, *Time*'s sales increased 50 percent, and during major days covering the Simpson case, circulation for *U.S.A. Today* rose by 100,000. Public interest, registered in sales and ratings, makes the case for the press—that they are only giving the public what they want. While there is some truth to the argument, there are also clear differences evident when we analyze the audience for the Simpson case. Approximately a quarter of the public watched the case and followed it regularly. The audience was female by a ratio of 2 to 1. It included twice as many nonwhites as whites, and five times as many people earning less than $20,000 a year as those making over $50,000. Twenty-eight percent of the regular viewers did not have a high school diploma. Only 8 percent of the regular viewers were college graduates (Kurtz 1995c, 36).

The Simpson case contained key elements of tabloid news: sex, violence, racism, and a celebrity. While such stories might be expected on newsmagazines such as *Hard Copy* or *20/20*, the amount of time dedicated to the story during network news took time away from issues that may have been less interesting but ultimately more important for the day-to-day lives of average citizens. It should also be noted that in the excessive coverage given to the case, there were also notable exceptions. *60 Minutes*, for example, never dealt with the story.

The Simpson case also revealed the desperate ratings race and the drive to scoop the competition regardless of the validity of the story. Judge Lance Ito complained about what he classified as "incorrect," "prejudicial," and "irresponsible" reporting. In a statement from the bench, he said, "I am so saturated by the irresponsible behavior of the media that I am beyond being outraged, I'm almost numb to it at this point." Ito's complaints were triggered by false news reports that Marcia Clarke, the prosecutor in the case, had been at Simpson's house, and that police were looking for a bloody ski mask. When challenged from the bench, the press, such as station KNBC, were extremely qualified in admitting any errors or wrongdoing. Even when the press admits to lapses of judgment, it fairly quickly returns to the same modus operandi. "Like a guilty alcoholic the morning after a binge, the media are now engaging in the identical ritual of self-flagellation. . . . If the press really took any of these bouts of soul searching seriously, surely it wouldn't indulge in the same behavior over and over again" (Rich 1994, 13a).

Balanced reporting has increasingly given way to hostile, combative "gotcha journalism." It is a process that seemingly exempts no one so long as ratings and sales benefit. Reportedly upset because he was served a cold breakfast on the press plane, Brit Hume challenged Bill Clinton in his early days in office. Accusing him of a certain "zigzag quality in his decision-making process," Hume provoked the following reply from the president: "I have long since given up the thought that I could disabuse some of you of turning any substantive decision into anything but political process" (Thompson 1993, 11a). Nor has the First Lady been free from this form of jaundiced journalism. Perhaps the most infamous example of this took place when Connie Chung interviewed the 68-year-old mother of House Speaker Newt Gingrich. Chung prodded the woman into revealing how her son felt about Hillary. "Why don't you just whisper it to me, just between you and me?" When the woman confided that her son thought Mrs. Clinton was "a bitch," Chung had her sound bite. Despite the fact that she clearly implied the statement was in confidence and off the record, the network not only ran the comment, but actually used it as a tease to promote the show. Anything for ratings! "And we wonder why they hate us," wrote Joe Urschel in *U.S.A. Today* (1995).

Why We Hate the Media

Dan Rather, Walter Cronkite, Bill Moyers, and other media insiders have all recognized and lamented problems with the press. James Fallows, who has written for *Atlantic Monthly* and the *Washington Post*, has described what he calls "an astonishing gulf between the way journalists—especially the most prominent ones—think and the way the public does" (1996, 45). In the case of press coverage of President Clinton, for example, he traces the issues that most concern the public, as evidenced by the questions they raise in town-hall-type forums with the president. In contrast to these issues and topics, the press aggressively and disdainfully pursues its own agenda. While the public reacted positively to Clinton's marathon 1995 State of the Union Address, the press dismissed it. Although some Democrats might suspect a bias against Clinton, in reality, says Fallows, "it reflects instead the instincts, pressure and incentives of the modern news business" (51).

The emphasis on business, the bottom line, and profit seems to emerge as a consistent theme in trying to understand what has gone wrong with the news media. In 1994, CNN produced an hour-long special called "The Media Circus," which examined tabloidism. The program looked at the way rumor, gossip, and sensationalism, formerly the province of *A Current Affair*, *Inside Edition*, *The National Enquirer*, and others, had entered into respectable mainstream newspapers and network broadcasts. Ken Auletta from *The New Yorker* said that journalism had become "just another carnival barker trying to get more people into a smaller tent." In the new news era, the function of a journalist was no longer limited to informing the public about significant issues of the day. The dominant drive, the program suggested, was to serve the economic interests of the company by building the largest audience possible. Ironically, while sensational stories frequently result in increased circulation and ratings, there is a price to pay in terms of respect and credibility.

In April 1995, for example, the American Society of Magazine Editors hosted a forum called "Why Everyone Hates the Media." Opening the first session, Henry Muller, editorial director for *Time*, used recent polling to prove just how poorly the public perceived the press. According to a Harris poll, only 15 percent of the public expressed a great deal of confidence in the press, down from the post-Watergate high of 30 percent. Asked whether the press helped or hurt the nation solve problems that confronted it, 71 percent believed the media got in the way of problem solving. In terms of trust and reliability, the public rated journalists 13th out of 26 professional groups, behind pharmacists and ahead of the senators and congresspeople on whom they frequently reported. Mike Wallace, Bill Moyers, David Gergen, Mandy Grunwald, and other panelists appearing in the forum all agreed that cynicism and sarcasm were rampant in the news media. Gergen, who had served in the Nixon administration, noted that cynicism and hostility were very high during the Watergate and Vietnam era. What he found odd about the current situation was the fact that cynicism "is so much more pervasive at a time when there's less to be cynical about." *60 Minutes* correspondent Mike Wallace said he himself had been a victim of this type of coverage. Describing press portraits of Newt Gingrich as "an attack dog," "smart but dirty," and a "precocious buffoon," Wallace said he was startled to find the Speaker intelligent, thought-provoking, and engaging. The press, he said, often carries "a cynical baggage that blinds us to what is actually taking place in front of us."

In addition to cynicism, Mandy Grunwald described a tone of sarcasm and a drive to celebrity. Glib, speculative, hard-hitting reporting full of sound bites has become the order of the day. Journalists are rewarded for nailing a public figure (rightly or wrongly) by appearances on the weekend talk shows that are so valued among the East Coast press. Programs like *Crossfire*, *The Capital Gang*, and *Washington Week in Review* have turned many journalists into household names with celebrity status and the high incomes that go with it, not only for their on-camera appearances but on the lucrative lecture circuit as well. In 1996, for example, Sam Donaldson's and Ted Koppel's salaries were reportedly $2 million.

William Safire and Cokie Roberts were both able to command some $20,000 per speech. Addressing this issue in the *Washington Post*, Howard Kurtz said, "The essence of journalism, even for the fiercest opinion mongers is supposed to be professional detachment. The public has a right to expect that those who pontificate for a living are not in financial cahoots with the industries and lobbies they analyze on air" (1996, 9). But it goes beyond the issue of potential conflict of interest. The era of journalists as talking heads has resulted in a contradiction. "The way to become most successful as a journalist was to give up most of what was involved in being a reporter" (Fallows 1996, 53).

Who's to Blame? Or, He Who Pays the Piper . . .

It seems that both the public and the press agree that something has changed in the way journalists conduct themselves. Understanding what that change is and knowing why it has taken place are two related pieces of the same puzzle. Recognizing the forces and factors that shape the news is an important part of any attempt to become media literate, since it moves the discussion from a rather simple but important analysis of content to an examination of the social, cultural, economic, and political context in which news is both produced and consumed. Though the majority of this book addresses the subject of the message the media sends, serious attention should also be given to the nature of the messenger itself. Though the American public could no doubt name Peter Jennings, Dan Rather, and the other national anchors who present the news, it is highly unlikely that they are aware of what Ben Bagdikian called "the private ministry of information and culture" involved in both the telling and selling of news. In *The Media Monopoly*, Bagdikian argues that awareness of the powers behind the media is central to responsible citizenship in a democratic society. "Instead of control by governments, public opinion is increasingly controlled by a small number of corporations . . . it is time for Americans to examine the institutions from which they receive their daily picture of the world" (1990, xx111). By the middle of the same decade, media ownership continued to be concentrated in fewer and fewer hands. Addressing the result, *The Nation* said the nightly national news had been "Disneyised, Murdochized, Oprahized, and Hard Copyized" (Miller 1996, 3). Describing the ownership of CNN, NBC, ABC, and CBS, the paper continued, "Two of these four corporations are defense contractors (both involved in nuclear production) while the other two are mammoth manufacturers of fun 'n' games. Thus we are the subject of *a national entertainment state* in which the news comes to us directly from the two most powerful industries in the United States" (9). How likely is it, Miller asked, that news bureaus owned by the defense and nuclear industries would seriously investigate the practices and policies of these industries? What conflict of interest is presented in the way news addresses foreign policy and military involvement when the parent companies have connections to both?

Accompanying the special issue was an extensive diagram that detailed the ownership and holdings of these news organizations. NBC Network News was part of the General Electric group. Holdings here included GE Lighting; GE Transportation Systems; GE Power Generation, including nuclear reactors; and GE Aircraft Engines, in addition to numerous television, radio, and cable operations. CBS News was part of the Westinghouse group. This includes Westinghouse Remediation Services and GESCO, which is responsible for the operation of four nuclear facilities, including Savannah River, which had been the subject of earlier critical media coverage. Other holdings include various banking, insurance, and communication organizations. ABC Network News is part of the Disney empire. That includes more than 400 Disney stores, Hyperion books, numerous newspapers, magazines, record companies, and sports teams, including their California Angels and the Mighty Ducks. Ted Turner's CNN includes MGM and RKO, the Atlanta

Braves and Hawks, all under the umbrella ownership of Time Warner, including HBO, Cinemax, and Warner Brothers, and magazines such as *Time, Fortune, People, Life,* and *Sports Illustrated,* among other interests. In this complex conglomerate of communication industries, it is easy to see why news bureaus have been swallowed up by the profit motive and entertainment values that Dan Rather described to Larry King.

If new ownership and corporate values have played a role in transforming news, so, too, have the tools and toys of a high-tech age. Though we frequently think of technologies as neutral tools, technology has played a major role in shaping the form and content of today's news. The advent of electronic news-gathering technology in the 1970s served to decentralize national news and expand local coverage. Satellite technology further eroded national ownership and control of the pictures that drive television news. While one result was clearly improved local news with access to a wider pool of stories, there were other less favorable outcomes. "Get it fast" and "get it first" became more important values in news production than the traditional admonition to "get it right." Eye Witness News, Live at 5, and other marketing mechanisms became indicative of the "we're on top of everything syndrome in which the message becomes the technology" (Rosenberg 1993, 19). With local stations now having access to their own powerful pictures and with competition from CNN and newsmagazines like *Hard Copy,* the network news divisions found themselves under increasing pressure to grab viewer attention, even if it meant dumbing down the news. Window dressing and slick packaging with a high-tech theme found their way into both local and network news. CBS's set for the 1996 presidential election was one such example. The cyberset was meant to display state-of-the-art technology, which of course meant accurate, fast, and reliable. Instead viewers saw an obviously uncomfortable Dan Rather surrounded by gimmicky gadgetry that had more style than substance. At one point the anchor commented that it was easier in the old days when all they had to work with was a string and two tin cans.

The new technology also put to rest once and for all the old adage that "the camera never lies." ABC's Cokie Roberts found herself in the middle of one controversy created by technology. After the 1994 State of the Union Address, viewers saw the reporter standing on what appeared to be the lawn of the Capitol. In fact, Roberts was in the studio and computer imaging had been used to create the illusion that she was at the Capitol. Organizations charged with reporting the truth found themselves faced with a credibility crisis when they used the new technology to deceive. In a warning to consumers, the *Washington Post* wrote, "The latest technology makes deceptions much easier and faster and much harder—if not impossible—to detect" (Sawyer 1994, 24). What resulted was an overzealous preference for pictures, secret surveillance, hidden camera techniques, and sting operations that would further challenge the credibility of the news media. In the age of newsmagazines, a new style and method took over. These broadcasts presented "morality tales of black hats and white hats, with the reporters as avenging US marshals. Instead of a six gun, his or her weapons are a hidden camera and a hand-held mike thrust at a reluctant witness before they slam the car doors. It's gottcha journalism" (Zoglin 1993, 51).

(MID/HIGH) —
The previous section raised numerous issues and provided several specific examples that can be used to help students understand the changing nature of news. Introduce them to key terms:

- **Gotcha journalism.** Style of reporting that pits journalist against subject and specializes in getting or catching the subject making a mistake.

- **Feeding frenzy.** Basically a pack attack with a "kick 'em when they're down" mentality. Frequently results in overkill and overcoverage. Snowballing story.

- Discuss the ethics of Connie Chung's "just between you and me" incident.

- Explain the concept of conflict of interest with reference to (1) journalists making speeches for organizations they cover and (2) ownership of news organizations by groups with military and industrial holdings.

- Discuss the ways in which economics and new technology has affected news.

Food Lyin'? ABC Versus the Supermarket

In December 1996, a jury awarded Food Lion $5.5 million in punitive damages in an action brought against ABC's *Prime Time Live*. The grocery store chain was the subject of a 1992 undercover report that was particularly critical of food-handling procedures. Hidden cameras provided viewers with an opportunity to see and hear Food Lion employees altering the "sell-by" date on various fresh food items and mixing out-of-date and potentially harmful meat with fresh meat. The day after the program aired, Food Lion stock dropped 15 percent. Food Lion, who later obtained all 40 hours of footage, argued that the content of the program was taken out of context and was unrepresentative of policies and procedures in their stores.

In one of those peculiar moments that television is capable of creating, *Prime Time* took the opportunity in February 1997 to present its case to the public. That program explored the history of investigative journalism and the ethics of hidden camera techniques. The public, it has been said, has an insatiable hunger for this "kind of documentation that looks good on screen. Palatial homes, incriminating memos, revealing audiotape—these have always been the truffles of the producers of the hunt. But secretly recorded video, where the viewers see the action with their own eyes, may be the tastiest delicacy of all" (Baker 1993, 26). While ABC allowed Sam Donaldson and Diane Sawyer to describe and justify the techniques used in this and other stories, they also included a statement from Chris Ahearn, Food Lion's spokeswoman, and a fascinating interview between Diane Sawyer and the jury that had convicted ABC.

From the outset, ABC indicated that they intended to appeal the case. From their perspective, they argued, "we like to think we've effected some real change." At the time the original story ran, *Columbia Journalism Review* saw both sides of the issue. While concluding that "the show did its job, successfully illustrating part of a problem," it also raised ethical issues. "When," they asked, "does investigative journalism become spying and is spying always wrong?" (Baker 1993, 28)

Following the verdict and during the 1997 broadcast, ABC repeatedly stressed that the verdict and the ruling did not challenge the truth of their initial report. Instead, the case centered on the techniques they had used to get the story. In particular, they were found guilty of fraud and trespassing, having falsified and lied about the credentials and previous work experience of ABC's employees who infiltrated Food Lion stores. Every juror appearing on the February program said they thought hidden cameras were necessary under some circumstances, and five of them indicated that the Food Lion story warranted the use of hidden cameras. While the final award the jury recommended was for $5.5 million, they stated that their recommendations had ranged from zero to $1 billion.

(ELEM/MID/HIGH) —

- Explain the concept of hidden cameras and investigative/undercover reporting.

- Discuss privacy versus the public's right to know.

- Under what circumstances do students think it is acceptable to deceive by using these techniques?

- If your students were the jury in the ABC-Food Lion case, how would they rule?

Where There's Smoke There's . . . ?
NBC Versus General Motors

If ABC's coverage of the supermarket was controversial, NBC's coverage of GM trucks was nothing short of inflammatory. The story was featured on the program *Dateline* and the subject was an allegedly unsafe GM pickup truck that was supposedly prone to burst into flames upon collision. The subject matter of the story was interesting in itself for the simple reason that GM was an NBC client, which is to say they advertised with the network.

The story producers crossed the line between covering a story and creating the story. According to the *Washington Post*, the fuel tank did not rupture during the initial test. "The collision produced some dramatic footage—gasoline spraying from the tank's filler neck and igniting—but the fire lasted 15 seconds, went out by itself, and caused no major damage to the truck" (Weiser 1993, 6). Although the network had several means of verifying and checking a story for both accuracy and legality, they failed in this case even when one of those objecting to the shape the story was taking was their own reporter, Michelle Gillen.

The commercial culture of the new newsroom has created an era in which "the quest for hot visuals can overwhelm ethical concerns and shatter credibility," according to *American Journalism Review* (Zuraik and Stoehr 1993, 27). Unhappy with the visuals they had, the producers of the story "improperly enhanced the shown crash story by using igniters to ensure a videogenic burst of flame." The reason for the decision was a simple matter of the marketing ethos that dominates so much of today's news. "The producers decided they needed a climactic moment to jolt the audience" (Diamond 1993, 18).

In addition to contributing to the fire, the program used techniques of more down-market newsmagazines like *A Current Affair* and *Hardcopy* to add to the dramatic look and feel of the story. This included a POV (point of view) positioning of the camera inside the truck, so the moment of impact was perceived by the viewer from the perspective of the driver. The controversy created by the story led to an on-air apology by the network and the replacement of Michael Gartner as head of NBC News. Even then, the network still continued to manipulate its use of images. Sometime later in a story related to Idaho's Clearwater National Forest, they showed images of dead fish, even though the footage came from a completely different site.

❖ Used with permission of Wayne Stayskal, *Tampa Tribune.*

Industry Guidelines: What's Your Opinion?

(MID/HIGH) — The Society of Professional Journalists has a set of guidelines that address the issue of hidden cameras and media representation. Study some of these with your students and use the criteria to evaluate the Food Lion, GM, and other stories. In general, the guidelines suggest that hidden cameras and other forms of misrepresentation are appropriate under the following conditions:

- When the subject is of vital public interest and covering it may prevent harm to others

- When other alternatives for covering the story have been exhausted

- When the journalists covering the story are prepared to disclose/discuss the deception

- When individuals covering the story and the news institution involved make a commitment to excellence through a commitment of adequate time and funding

- When the damage prevented by revealing the story outweighs damage resulting from the story

- When the story was constructed as a result of meaningful collaboration, discussion, and decision making

(Source: Russ W. Baker, *Columbia Journalism Review*, August 1993)

Photo Opportunities: A Picture Is Worth a Thousand Words

(MID/HIGH) — Former Reagan advisor Michael Deaver was superbly adept at getting the president's picture in the most positive perspective. Interviewed on the PBS broadcast "Illusions of News," Deaver described the way in which he and other White House aides skillfully selected symbolic backdrops and other settings to complement the story they wanted to both tell and sell. But putting a positive spin on the story by effective photo opportunities was only part of the picture. Deaver freely admitted that the images often contradicted more unpleasant and unpopular aspects of administration policy. In an extraordinarily candid moment, he said the audience wouldn't remember what the reporter said. A reporter could actually appear on camera criticizing a policy or position, but the public would be distracted by the engaging and appealing image the White House presented. In the battle between the eye and the ear, Deaver said, the eye wins all the time. Further support for this belief is evident in Sam Donaldson's *Hold On, Mr. President*. The reporter said that he and his colleagues were frequently criticized during the Reagan years for not being tough enough on the president. From Donaldson's perspective, the press did their job and told the public. The problem was that the public wasn't listening. What

emerged during the Reagan administration was a relationship between the president and the press, best expressed by Deputy Press Secretary Larry Speakes: "You don't tell us how to stage the news and we won't tell you how to cover it" (Donaldson 1987, 123).

The preference for pictures that now pervades the news media is not restricted to the Oval Office, nor to controversial coverage of Food Lion and the GM pickup truck. Looking for compelling footage for a story on underage drinking, one crew actually supplied the subjects of their story with drink. On another occasion, *U.S.A. Today* suspended a reporter who staged a front-page photo of weapon-toting gang members. The young men were actually sent home to get their guns for the picture. ABC News showed what appeared to be actual footage of a diplomat supposedly handing over secrets. Only later were viewers told that the picture was staged with an actor. Some argue that television is a visual medium that by necessity requires pictures. "Television is so focused on pictures and so limited by time that in the normal run of reporting, it cannot provide the context that gives meaning and perspective. On the contrary, distortion is inevitable" (Zuckerman 1994c, 64). Dan

Rather has taken a similar position. "Television," he says, "has difficulty with depth. We have troubles with stories of complexity. I'm not sure that we're all that good at covering the issues" (Weisman 1984, 4). Such a view seems predicated on the nature of television as a technology, as if the lights and wires that make up its glow and flow were somehow incapable of broadcasting words, talking heads, or thoughtful prolonged discussion.

These limits, of course, are not inherent in the technology itself nor in its mode of transmission, but are rather the result of the deliberate marketing and production decisions producers make about what stories to tell and how to tell them. While it is true that television is a visual medium, this does not explain or justify the sound bites, fragmented stories, or the growing tendency to run with questionable images. It also ignores the consequences of an information society that privileges pictures over print and the spoken word.

John Leo at *U.S. News and World Report* worries about this "marriage of fact and fiction, news and entertainment." Such a trend, he argues, replaces logic with emotion, substituting the very concept of truth with "image-based truths." Leo also very bluntly addresses the people behind the pictures and this philosophy of news making. "The business is now in the hands of a new generation whose members don't think of themselves as reporters or producers, but as filmmakers with little interest in words and heavy interest in dramatic effect" (Leo 1993, 24).

If the Food Lion and GM stories raise serious questions about the way we perceive events in our own country, the role of image-based stories on the international front is equally disturbing. A study of 661 television news stories about Central America concluded, "One ends up knowing almost as little about Central America, and why the United States is involved there, as one knew before" (Weisman 1984, 4). Similar complaints were made about coverage of the Iranian hostage crisis in 1979-1980. Despite such questions and concerns, foreign policy seems to be increasingly entangled with public perceptions and the role television pictures play in shaping those perceptions.

Perhaps nowhere was this more evident than in Madeline Albright's declaration on CNN that "television has become the 16th member of the Security Council." Then U.S. ambassador to the United Nations and now the first woman secretary of state, Albright was discussing America's intervention in Somalia in the early 1990s. From the outset, dispatching American troops was in part driven by television images of starving women and children with big eyes and bloated bellies. While the viewing audience may have had a very limited understanding of where Somalia was or what events precipitated the crisis, such matters were cognitive concerns. Television pictures shape our perceptions on an affective level. As such, they frequently leave us susceptible to the most compelling, painful, and dramatic image, no matter how representative of the larger story it may be.

From the moment troops landed in what was supposed to be a stealth operation, the cameras went along. It was, in fact, the first-ever, live, televised amphibious landing. The pursuit of pictures also posed a risk for our troops. The Pentagon complained about the bright lights of the television cameras and their ability to temporarily blind marines and helicopter pilots. If images had evoked U.S. pity and compassion going into Somalia, pictures also enraged politicians and citizens alike who demanded the withdrawal of our troops. In October 1993 the viewing public saw images of dead U.S. soldiers being dragged through the streets of Mogadishu. They also saw the bruised and beaten face of captured Chief Warrant Officer Michael Durant, and asked, as did the *U.S. News* cover, "What Went Wrong?" Pictures alone could not provide the answer. In an editorial called "The Blind Eye of Television," Mortimer Zuckerman wondered about the impact of television on national policy and public perception. Had we now entered an era, he mused, when foreign policy and the involvement of American troops would be affected whenever "guilt-inducing TV images move the American audience beyond tolerance to action. What if duty is suddenly made unpopular by TV images of body bags coming home? Where does it all end when it begins with the astigmatic lens of a television camera?" (1993a, 84). Two years later with another group of American troops entrenched in Bosnia, foreign policy by CNN seemed to many observers to remain the order of the day. While the real wars were always fought with bullets and tanks, the *Washington Post* said, "the war for public opinion is waged through faxes, newspaper articles, and, above all, television images" (Dobbs 1995, 25). Nowhere was the triumph of the image and the control of information more obvious than during the 1991 Persian Gulf War.

The Persian Gulf War and the News Media

The context in which the Persian Gulf War was both covered and, some would say, created was best summed up by a television reporter's description of the first day of the war: "It looked like *Top Gun*, and it sounded like half time at the Superbowl." Both the sporting reference and the entertainment allusion were typical of a conflict that was consistently portrayed to the American public as a matter of good guys, bad guys, winners, losers, shoot 'em ups, and the painless precision of a video game. While the war is now a faded memory to many of our students, those whose parents were involved with the conflict are still likely to relate to the events that affected them personally. Any attempt to discuss whether the war was right or wrong might well create conflict for these families. It might however be possible to discuss whether or not the war was necessary. With Saddam Hussein still in power and the emotional events of the war behind most of us, enough distance has now been created for teachers to explore the war and the way the media covered the event and the relationship between this event and public perception. Rather than simply dealing with an event from several years ago, this topic provides a forum for the wider exploration of the role the media could or should play during a war.

Those who question the entertainment/sporting metaphor used to describe the war have no shortage of primary and secondary materials from which to draw for documentation. "The Gulf War was packaged as an aesthetic spectacle. The prowar constituency rooted for the US team as if it were a sports event and from the beginning there was a close relation between war and football" (Kellner 1992, 257). Former Reagan aide Michael Deaver described the war as "a combination of Lawrence of Arabia and Star Wars" (Schiller 1992, 23). The best sources for an in-depth exploration of the media's role in covering the war include *The Triumph of the Image: The Media's War in the Persian Gulf, A Global Perspective* (Mowlana et al. 1992), Douglas Kellner's *The Persian Gulf TV War* (1992), and a very informative short videotape, *Lines in the Sand*. Even an apolitical mainstream magazine like *TV Guide* raised questions about war coverage. Columnist Jeff Greenfield expressed concern about "the most significant, most troublesome aspect of television's first real-time war—the uneasy blend of instant, immediate, around the world, round the clock access to information that is inherently incomplete, fragmentary or downright wrong" (1991, 5). Three years later, describing similar coverage of events in Bosnia, *U.S. News and World Report* recognized part of the legacy of Gulf War coverage: "Foreign affairs is especially vulnerable to compression and emotionalism . . . the pictures we don't have may be as critical as the ones we do have" (Zuckerman 1994c, 64).

There is certainly some reason to believe that during the war itself, the American public either perceived or received only part of the picture. A study by the University of Massachusetts Center for Studies in Communication concluded that "the news media have failed quite dramatically in their role as information providers. Despite months of coverage, most people do not know basic facts about the political situation in the Middle East" (Jhally et al. 1991). The study suggested that support for the war was "built upon a body of knowledge that was incorrect or incomplete" and that "the more people know the less likely they are to support the war." From the outset, the public failed to perceive the complex history of events leading up to the ground war. Most Americans first learned about the danger of the situation on July 21, 1990, when Iraq moved 30,000 troops and tanks to their border with Kuwait. Irritation between the two nations had been brewing for some time since Kuwait had begun to sell oil at below the agreed-upon OPEC figure, which in turn created financial losses for Iraq. But the seemingly local issue had deeper roots.

Throughout the war between Iran and Iraq, the United States had supported and armed Iraq, hoping to curtail the spread of Islamic fundamentalism in the area, which had culminated in the 1979 Iranian hostage crisis and seizure of the American embassy. Thus, for a period of several years, American policy had contributed to an arms buildup by the very country they were about to go to war against. For its part, Iraq believed that its war against Iran had been an Arab effort to control Iranian Islamic fundamentalism. Hence, it viewed Kuwait's oil policies as less than an act of gratitude.

Even so, events in the gulf may not have escalated had it not been for signals some believe the U.S. government sent to Hussein. On July 25, 1990, the U.S. ambassador to Iraq, April Glaspie, met with Saddam Hussein. At that point, she told him her government had "no opinion" on the border dispute between the two countries. The impression was furthered in Washington during a July 31 speech by John Kelly, assistant secretary of state for Middle Eastern Affairs. Kelly stated that the United States had no formal commitment to the defense of Kuwait. Douglas Kellner suggests that both events raise the question as to whether the United States "purposely led Iraq to believe there was no major U.S. objection to invading Kuwait" (1992, 13). Further, Kellner contends, the Bush administration "set the stage of the Gulf War by failing to warn Iraq of the consequences of invading Kuwait and then by quickly sending troops to Saudi Arabia while undercutting diplomatic efforts to resolve the crisis" (17).

If the U.S. administration manipulated events for their own ends, the mass media went along for the ride. "In retrospect and on balance, the remarkable control of American consciousness, during and after the war, must be regarded as a single achievement of mind management" (Schiller 1992, 22). How and why the media cooperated with the government in shaping public perceptions of the war and events leading up to it are perhaps best understood by the term "manufacturing consent" (Herman and Chomsky 1988). Edward Herman and Noam Chomsky have written that the mass media "serve as a system for communicating messages and symbols to the general populace" (1988, 1). In the case of the news media, although they "serve the ends of a dominant elite," this is often difficult to see because they "periodically attack and expose corporate and governmental malfeasance" (1). Although the news media may be critical of the establishment, they are part of it, deriving income and profits from it. The Persian Gulf War was a crisis that promised profit or prestige through special bulletins, 24-hour coverage, and information saturation. For Ted Turner's Cable News Network (CNN), it provided a spectacular international showcase. CNN, said *The Nation*, "represents a new dimension of an emerging global culture that is already heavily Americanized" (Rosen 1991, 622-25). Whereas politicians and average citizens were impressed by CNN's coverage, *The Nation* cautioned against the impact of "dramatic visuals deployed for their oomph value rather than their importance in any exploratory scheme" (623). Such coverage, the magazine suggested, would promote international competition in which news coverage on the global level could be reduced to the triumph of the image over the issue. As a result, "political deeds that lack a visual dimension may tend to escape world notice because they bore the image hungry producers" (623). In attempting to reflect on coverage of the war, it is therefore necessary to consider the form as well as the content of the stories.

As a backdrop to these elements, one must raise the crucial question of ownership, or what we have called the origin of media messages. Understanding the ownership and origin of the news provides some context for understanding why particular stories are ignored and others are stressed and the forces and factors affecting the coverage. *Manufacturing Consent* addresses what it calls "news filters" that shape coverage (Herman and Chomsky 1988). These filters include:

- *Size and ownership:* As part of the corporate United States, the mass media, including the news media, have ties to big business. That relationship must affect how stories are selected. What, for example, are some likely effects of the fact that General Electric owned ABC?

- *Advertising:* It keeps programming on the air. At the most basic level, however, it could be argued that he who pays the piper calls the tune. How would the profit motive and the needs of the consumer culture influence coverage?

- *Reliance on government perspectives:* Unnamed sources and official government representatives feed news bureaus' points of view, values, and policies that are often uncritically reported as fact. When coverage is censored and controlled, as it was in Grenada or the Persian Gulf, reporting is invariably slanted.

- *Flak:* This simply refers to an institutionalized form of discrediting alternative perspectives. Spiro Agnew served as a hit man who constantly condemned media coverage. President Reagan criticized the media's role in affecting public opinion. By using flak, government officials can create a climate that induces a more positive form of coverage. The result, of course, is to stifle alternative points of view. What range of perspectives was provided about the Persian Gulf War?

These filters affected the coverage of the war in the Persian Gulf and continue to affect the way news is presented on a daily basis. At times the bias is evident, but often it is much more subtle. Throughout the war and the events leading up to it, President Bush continually referred to a "new world order." According to one source, he used the phrase 42 times in public statements. It was a vague, undefined reference that the media seldom questioned, despite Bush's earlier vagaries, evident in phrases such as "a thousand points of light." By not challenging the expression, the news media followed the administration line and allowed the president to project himself as an international visionary. By July 1991, *U.S. News and World Report* said, "The president has almost entirely dropped the words ["new world order"] from his lexicon, indicating another turn in US foreign policy" (21). The news media did more than simply report the war. They presented it from a particular perspective that contributed to the climate of acceptance. In covering the war with such intensity, they also distracted the public from pressing domestic problems. On April 7, 1991, Peter Jennings on *ABC Nightly News* almost acknowledged this when he asked, "Remember the way it was before the war?" As war euphoria and postwar parades gave way to domestic concerns, the public began to focus on pocketbook issues and the growing recession. While George Bush had skillfully led the nation and its media to see the crisis in the gulf from his perspective, gloom-and-doom coverage of the economic downturn would question his leadership and undermine his bid for a second term.

Censorship, Capitulation, and Pentagon Propaganda

On one level, despite all their power, the news media essentially found themselves caught between a rock and a hard place in which they would be damned if they did and damned if they didn't. Keenly aware of the way media coverage of the Vietnam War had fed and fueled the antiwar movement, the Pentagon had no intention of allowing negative media coverage to shape foreign policy. Before the press could cover them, they had every intention of first controlling the press. If the press wanted to cover events in the gulf, they would cover them the way the Pentagon wanted. Using the basic weapons of propaganda (keep it simple and keep repeating it), the military had for some time now perfected the way the media covered military events. The Center for Defense Information has documented this in the program "The Language of War."

In Grenada, for example, the Pentagon did not refer to an invasion; rather, they called it "a pre-dawn vertical insertion." Equally, by the time the buildup in the gulf took place several years later, terms like "Desert Storm" and "Desert Shield" were employed to project the expedition in a positive light for the U.S. public.

Reporting pools were established so that journalists on the ground in the gulf could only get access to places and personnel that the military approved. Access was limited to about 90 journalists in 11 approved pools, all guided by military press officers and reporting back to the larger press corps of more than 500. The military restricted access to Saudi telephone lines, banned cellular phones, and attempted to control all television images and other pictures. Reporters could not forward their material until it had been approved, which is to say, until it had been subjected to inspection and censorship by the military. CBS News President Eric Ober understood the implications quite clearly. Writing in the *Wall Street Journal*, he said, "Will we really find out what is happening in the desert? I have to conclude that the answer is no" (Kellner 1992, 81). But the press went along with the restrictions because it was the only way they could cover the story and because those who didn't, like Chris Hedges from the *New York Times*, had their credentials lifted. The results were quite apparent: "Instead of the media recording and analyzing every step, the American public and the world was allowed to see only a limited and antiseptic war" (Young 1993, 9). Since the war seemed to be clean and for the most part without casualties or even consequences, public support for it increased.

While the public's growing enthusiasm for the war was partly the result of government orchestration of coverage, it resulted as well from the media's role as war booster and, amazingly enough, from Saudi selling of the war through an American public relations firm. One of the most bizarre episodes of the war is generally referred to as "the baby incubator story." In testimony before the House Human Rights Caucus, a tearful teenage girl described stories of Iraqi soldiers removing babies from incubators and killing them. Both the president and vice president picked up on the story and repeated it. In the vote authorizing the war, several senators referred to it as an example of Iraqi atrocities. As it subsequently turned out, the teenager was the daughter of Kuwait's ambassador to the United States. She had been coached for her appearance by the public relations firm of Hill and Knowlton. The president of that agency was Craig Fuller, who had previously been Bush's chief of staff. The agency's account on behalf of Kuwait was said to be in excess of $11 million. In the period after the war, *60 Minutes*, *20/20*, the *New York Times*, and other reports verified these claims, but the story had already been successfully told and sold to the American public and the world.

If the media can be excused for falling prey to a well-orchestrated public relations campaign, they cannot so readily be excused for their errors in judgment. *Unreliable Sources: A Guide to Detecting Bias in News Media* (Lee and Solomon 1990) addresses the way the language the media employs can influence public perception. The authors describe what they call "a lexicon of buzzwords and catchphrases that range from the vaguely factual to the questionable to the ridiculous" (11). Rather than being neutral, these words and phrases that we hear over and over again "shape our language and guide our thoughts" (10). Reports that originated in the United States were not subjected to the censorship and control experienced by those coming directly from the gulf, so the government cannot be blamed when looking at the loaded language the press used to demonize Hussein or to marginalize the antiwar movement in this country. Clearly the government controlled our understanding of the war by using terms like "collateral damage" as a euphemism for civilian casualties. But the media passed such phrases on aiding and abetting the propaganda process by employing inflammatory terms like "the butcher of Baghdad" to describe Hussein. In the process, by demonizing one man, they personalized the war into a struggle between Bush in the white hat and Saddam in the black hat, in such a way that the American public never had to understand the impact of the war on the women and children of Iraq.

But the media went beyond simplifying the conflict. They "engaged in a frenzy of jingoism" (Young 1993, 9) while downplaying alternative solutions to the conflict. In the period leading up to the war, rallies of more than 100,000 demonstrators gathered in cities like Washington and San Francisco to express opposition to war. The events were covered by the press, but once the conflict got under way, such opposition tended to be silenced or minimized. One study from Fairness and Accuracy in Reporting (FAIR) found that "of 878 on-air sources, only one was a representative of a national peace organization—Bill Monning of Physicians Against Nuclear War. By contrast, seven players from the Super Bowl were brought on to comment on the war" (Naurekas 1991, 5). Despite the fact that opposition to the war came from mainstream groups like the National Council of Bishops and the National Council of Churches, media constructions and representations of the antiwar group tended to concentrate on its members as "unshaven counter cultural and violent" (Kellner 1992, 253). The consequences of such coverage and construction are clear. "Relying as network TV did on random protesters to present a movement's view is to deny that movement its most articulate and knowledgeable spokespeople" (Naurekas 1991, 5). Hence, the telling and selling of the war was anything but neutral. Within the context of media literacy, coverage of the Gulf War represents an outstanding study. Principles of media literacy discussed at the beginning of this book include the idea that media are constructions, that these constructions shape reality, and that they have commercial purposes. Involving key components of communication theory, the concepts suggest that media messages have their greatest impact when audiences have no direct experience of the people, places, or events depicted and no other source of information. Douglas Kellner described just these conditions. Most Americans, he suggested, had little awareness or understanding of the complexities of Middle Eastern politics. As a result, "Their pictures of the events in the Gulf were a product of the Bush administration's discourse and media frames through which the crisis was constructed . . . the mainstream media fostered the military solution through its framing

of the images" (1992, 56). In the final analysis, the war in the gulf took the media to that ethical crossroads where information meets entertainment. Much of what we were told about the war subsequently proved to be untrue. We were, for example, repeatedly told about smart bombs hitting their targets with great precision. After the war the military indicated that some 70 percent of the bombs missed their targets. But the preference for pictures that now controlled our newsrooms would accept whatever images and ideology the government would feed it, and we had no choice but to go along, not so much as citizens but as members of the international viewing audience. The problem, however, came with the price of admission. For even though "it might have been great theater and great television, it was not great journalism" (Young 1993, 9).

Questioning the government or challenging the accepted version of events is seldom a popular course upon which to embark, especially if you work within the essentially conservative confines of our classrooms. As we have cautioned earlier, such questioning by its very nature may backfire, resulting in rampant cynicism rather than the healthy skepticism we seek to nurture. Some people will argue that the very act of challenging or questioning our military and our government is unpatriotic and un-American. We believe this questioning and constructive criticism are at the heart of informed responsible citizenship. There is little doubt that we did not have the information or access to all the facts during the Persian Gulf War. Many no doubt would argue that this is the necessary trade-off in a time of war, and that censorship and control of information are the price we pay for national security. But there are other prices and other consequences too, once we surrender our right to know. More than six years after the end of the war, those who served their nation are still trying to find out the truth about the illnesses from which many of them suffer, the truth about what they were or were not exposed to during their time in the gulf. The same government that asked them to answer the cause is now causing them to question it as it changes and modifies its own story, moving from denial to limited acknowledgment, as more and more pieces of the story come to light. It is ironic that much of the new information about what really happened in the gulf comes to us today through the very media agencies that failed to shed more light on the war itself.

(MID/HIGH) —
Coverage of the Gulf War raises substantive questions that go to the heart of the U.S. constitution, our understanding of democracy, and the entire concept of responsible citizenship.

- Press pools and euphemisms raise Orwellian specters of Newspeak and totalitarian truths. Explain the terms to students and link them to *1984*.

- Discuss the First Amendment with your students.

- Assign a debate in which one side argues that freedom of speech and the public's right to know are the most important principle, while the other side argues for censorship

and control of the press in the interests of national security.

- Explore the concept of "national security." Is a nation secure if it does not have free access to information or if its citizens can't distinguish between fact and propaganda?

- Earlier in this chapter we discussed terms like "marginalize," "minimize," and "polarize." There is much evidence that Hussein and Iraq were "demonized" by the U.S. media. Explain this term and use your school and public libraries to find examples of this in magazine covers from late 1990 to early 1991.

- Douglas Kellner says the "mainstream media were cheerleaders and boosters for the Bush administration and Pentagon policy" (1992, 1). Explain the concept of "booster" and have students find other examples in contemporary press coverage.

POLITICS, THE PRESIDENCY, AND THE PRESS

"The great leader image," writes Joshua Meyrowitz, "depends on mystification and careful management of public impressions." While many Americans today may long for the old-style political leadership, "electronic media of communication are making it impossible to find one. There is no lack of potential leaders but rather an overabundance of information about them" (1985, 270). The up-and-down, roller-coaster Clinton White House of the first administration cannot be explained simply by referring to an inexperienced young president who had to grow into the job. Nor is it possible to deny that Clinton and his team made mistakes during the first few months in office. But the mistakes were frequently magnified and blown out of proportion by a press obsessed with the negative and the game of "gottcha journalism" played at the presidential level and at public expense. On February 1, 1993, for example, with Clinton in office less than 30 days, *Time's* cover proclaimed "Clinton's First Blunder." Zoe Baird had been nominated for the position of attorney general, the first woman to receive this nomination. When

it was disclosed that she had hired an undocumented nanny and not paid the woman's Social Security or worker's compensation taxes, there was public outrage fueled by the increasingly powerful forum of talk radio. Clinton, who had campaigned on a platform of ethical conduct, fairness, and a philosophy of "people first," found his feet well and truly held to the flames, as his predecessor, George Bush, had been pilloried by the press and the public alike when he had reneged on his famous utterance "Read my lips, no new taxes." *Time's* cover was hardly the exception to the rule. The same month, *U.S. News and World Report* said, "The president has emerged as the champion backpedaler, blown off course by any breath of hot air" (Zuckerman 1993b, 70). The *Washington Post* said, "No politician is more masterful at the one-on-one encounter with the average citizen in the flesh or on the tube . . . but Clinton has yet to show that he can become a master at the business of governing as well as talk-meistering" (Rowen 1993, 5).

While presidents have never been immune from the criticism of the press, those who have occupied the Oval Office during the period that Dan Rather calls "the volcanic news era" have been subjected to a rigorous and potentially destructive scrutiny. Alarmed by media coverage of Bill Clinton's first few months in office, David Gergen noted that five of the past six presidents had been driven from the White House "in defeat or despair." "We are," he added, "making politics a spectator sport. When our hero first arrives we stand and cheer. But when we see he has feet of clay, and they all do, it's 'Throw the Bum Out.' No democracy can succeed as an entertainment" (1993, 92).

In *The Making of the President, 1960*, Pulitzer Prize-winner Theodore White wondered whether "the hallowed doctrine of freedom of the press can be responsibly applied to the modern reality of American broadcasting" (1961, 280). Two decades later, in *America in Search of Itself*, he concluded that "American politics and television are now so completely locked together that it is impossible to tell the story of the one without the other" (1982, 165). Seeing a relatively unknown governor from a small southern state elevated almost overnight to the presidency, White said, "There could have been no Carter presidency without television" (195). Television, with its national audience, delivered Jimmy Carter to the American people, turning him into a household name more quickly than any mass mailings, townhall meetings, or whistle-stop tours could have done. In the post-Watergate era, Carter was perceived as an honest, down-to-earth man and a Washington outsider. The very strengths that helped get Carter elected soon became weaknesses once he assumed office. The outsider now seemed like an amateur. When Americans were taken hostage in Iran and the news media dwelled on the president's inability to free them, Carter seemed weak and ineffectual. The damage was done.

In 1992 another relatively unknown southern governor made his bid for the Oval Office. Once again, television would be instrumental in bringing the candidate to the attention of the American public. In the process, it presented him, warts and all. During the painful primaries, Bill Clinton staggered from one scandalous revelation or accusation to another until it seemed inevitable that his campaign would collapse under the cumulative weight. Accused of womanizing, draft dodging, and pot-smoking, Clinton and his war-room warriors confronted the charges, including an extraordinary interview with the candidate and his wife on *60 Minutes* on the post-Super Bowl show. By the time the election rolled around, Clinton and his team had immunized him against further assault. No matter how hard George Bush and the Republicans tried to tell the public that Clinton had fatal character flaws, the public had their own priorities. Four years later, another Republican candidate warned the country about Clinton's character. Independent Ross Perot predicted the administration was so scandal-ridden that Clinton's re-election would result in a Watergate-style constitutional crisis. It wasn't that the public didn't hear or care. Exit polls in 1996 clearly indicated that the public did not trust the president and did not believe he was honest. For more than four years now, the news media had raised serious questions about William Jefferson Clinton. Perhaps the media had overplayed their hand and turned the public off. Perhaps the American public had begun to distinguish between a candidate's personal life and his public record. In 1996, voters seemed ambivalent. While they believed the media spent too much time covering the personal side of politics, they also believed overwhelmingly that coverage of the Dick Morris scandal was appropriate (Woodhull et al. 1996).

Is This Any Way to Choose a Leader?

The last three presidential elections and the way the media have covered and contributed to them might well raise the question "Is This Any Way to Choose a Leader?" Such a question was raised in the 1992 campaign when *U.S. News and World Report* asked, "Why does the world's greatest democracy conduct a national election as if it were a barroom brawl?" (Zuckerman 1992, 76). While much can be said about the quality of media coverage, something should also be said about the quantity of coverage. In the 1968 primary season, the average time a candidate appeared on network news was 42 seconds. By 1996 it had shrunk to 7.2 seconds (Cronkite 1996). The 1996 campaign was the least covered presidential campaign in recent memory. Press coverage between January and July of that year was down 43 percent from the 1992 campaign and 51 percent from the 1988 election (Tyndall 1996). About 12 minutes of network news during the period was about politics, which was about 50 percent less than during the 1992 election (*U.S. News and World Report* 11/18/96). If the press wasn't paying attention, there was evidence that the public, too, was tuned out. The viewing audience for the Republican convention was down 25 percent from 1992. When Jack Kemp delivered his acceptance speech, NBC aired a re-run of *Seinfeld*. When former president Gerald Ford made his speech, the networks ignored it. "Don't blame the networks for the bleak political coverage," said Andrew Tyndall, "blame the parties" (5). Both the Republican and Democratic conventions lacked spontaneity and tension. Tightly scripted and controlled, they were intended to shut out any sign of dissension or disunity in the ranks and to project an image of each party united behind its leader. The riots of the 1968 Chicago convention, the communication chaos that marred McGovern's nomination in 1972, and the acrimony and alienating language of the 1992 Republican convention in Houston were all banished. So, too, was the essence of American politics: debate, discussion, disagreement, and discourse. Elizabeth Dole wowed delegates with her Oprahesque speech as she wandered through the audience. The Democrats went for emotional symbols and appeals. Reagan Press Secretary Jim Brady and actor Christopher Reeves, each with profound disabilities, spoke on behalf of society's victims. One critic described it as "an airless pageant full of bogus emotionalism that was thematically akin to some overwrought Victorian melodrama in which tragic maiming and dying young are the dramatic centerpieces" (Baker 1997, 2). Both parties attempted to portray themselves as the party that put families first. In 1992 the Republicans had raised the issue of family values. In her 1996 convention address, Hillary Rodham Clinton said it was more than a matter of family values; it was a matter of valuing families. *U.S.A. Today* complained, "It sounds like a campaign for patriarch-in-chief not president . . . every candidate wants

Anthony Lewis vs. Charles Peters: Should losers pay?
Brooks Jackson slays the PACs
Just Say Nonsense: Nancy Reagan's drug programs don't work
The not very reassuring past of Ira Magaziner

The Washington Monthly
May 1993/$3.50

Rock and Rule

Think MTV's videos are rotting your kids' brains? Check out its political coverage.

By Christopher Georges

❖In 1992 candidate Clinton skillfully exploited the youth vote through MTV appearances. One result was a record turnout by youthful voters, but was their decision an informed one? Reprinted with permission from *The Washington Monthly*. Copyright by The Washington Monthly Company, 1611 Connecticut Avenue, NW, Washington, DC 20009.

to play the helpful next-door neighbor of so many old TV series" and "each party implies the other is somehow to blame for everything that undermines family stability" (1996b, 14a).

Did party orchestration of the 1996 campaign and media coverage of it hurt or help as the public attempted to understand the issues and make a decision? Forty percent of the public said that coverage "does not help them decide how to vote. That's two out of five people who say they need better coverage to help them carry out their most important duty as a citizen in a democratic society" (Media Studies Center 1996b, 2). In 1988, advertising played a major role in how the public perceived the candidates and the issues. By 1992, candidate Clinton used talk shows and the youth-oriented MTV to get his message across. Twelve percent of MTV's substantial 18- to 29-year-old viewing audience said that

MTV coverage had influenced their vote (Georges 1993). While talk shows and MTV could energize the electorate and get out the vote, there were serious questions as to whether such media coverage provided voters with the type of information they needed to make an informed vote. "Despite voters' proclaimed desire to base their votes on the issues rather than on the more trivial information about the candidates, most people knew very little about the former and a great deal about the latter" (Lewis and Morgan, 1992). Surveys found that 86 percent knew the Bushes had a dog called Millie and that Dan Quayle had criticized *Murphy Brown*. By contrast, when it came to issues, only one-third knew that Clinton supported the death penalty and cuts in capital gains taxes. According to FAIR, only 13 percent of coverage of the 1992 election dealt with an exploration of policy and issues.

What voters want to know, what they need to know, what coverage they access, and how this affects their vote, including their decision whether or not to vote, are central to the discussion of media and democracy. In the 1996 campaign, "voters rated debates—where candidates talk with little interference from journalists—as the single most important source of information that helps them learn about a campaign" (Woodhull et al. 1996, 2). They also expressed disdain for commentary, analysis, endless chit-chat, and too much emphasis on a candidate's personal life. Walter Cronkite and others have advocated free time provided by the networks to the candidate. In 1996, this was used to a limited degree, most typically as part of the network news. For Cronkite, this was not enough. Cronkite believes these pieces need to run during prime time when there is greater likelihood of reaching the disengaged. The networks, for their part, were reluctant to give up the lucrative revenue that comes from prime-time programming. Sixty-seven percent of the public believe that providing free access for the candidates would be helpful. The press themselves seemed sure that the candidates had avoided real issues. Among topics that needed addressing and that were missing in action were urban unemployment, the disappearing welfare net, and potential problems in North Korea. Writing for

the *New York Times* shortly after the election, Tom Brokaw complained about the campaign's failure to seriously address "truly vexing issues such as race relations, education, out-of-wedlock births, and the growing income gap between the top and bottom." Ominously, he added, "If we don't begin to address these underlying anxieties seriously, they will erupt in ways we cannot begin to control" (Baker 1997, 6). If the press blamed the candidates for not addressing the issues, the public had a different reaction. In a remarkable commentary, voters blamed neither the candidates, nor the parties, nor the media for their lack of knowledge. Seventy-eight percent said voters are to blame if they do not have enough information to make a choice (Woodhull et al. 1996, 2).

But accessing information is only part of the process. The quality, accuracy, and reliability of the information are central to the democratic process. In part, the nature of the information is dictated by the political parties themselves, and in part it is dominated by the self-serving interests of the media. During a 1997 press conference, 15 out of 17 questions President Clinton was asked dealt with the subject of campaign finance. For months, questions and allegations abounded regarding foreign money and illegal fund-raising as part of the 1996 presidential campaign. Ironically, the very media that seemed obsessed with asking where the money came from gave very little attention to the media's role in driving campaign expenses. Huge media markets like New York, California, Texas, and Florida require enormous amounts of money to purchase advertising time. During the 1996 election, the 75 biggest media markets in the country received $400 million from political ads, an increase from the $300 million spent in 1992. Arizona's Senator John McCain wants to free politicians from the need to raise money for these ads, arguing that free airtime would solve the problem. His efforts are opposed by The National Association of Broadcasters. If all candidates, not just major party candidates, were provided with free access to the airwaves, several major benefits could occur. Candidates would be able to devote more time to discussing the issues and less time on the road raising money. If all candidates, not just major party candidates, had equal access there would be more room for minority points of view. Candidates would be less likely to be in debt to lobbies, PACs, and special-interest groups. Advertising, frequently despised by the electorate and hardly a reliable source of political information, could be replaced by forums, discussions, and debates in which candidates took real questions from real people, outlined their policies, and avoided campaigning by sound bites and photo opportunities.

One of the basic principles of media literacy tells us that audiences negotiate their own meaning, making up their own minds, not simply in terms of media content but within the context of their viewing/listening experience and their own personal, emotional, social, and psychological nature and needs. When we look at how men and women receive and perceive news, there are some clear gender differences. Women are less likely than men to regularly tune in to Sunday morning talk shows like *Meet the Press*, as well as *CNN Headline News*, CSpan, and radio news. On the other hand, they are more likely than men to access newsmagazines like *20/20* and morning news broadcasts. Given the role of the so-called soccer moms in the 1996 campaign,

reaching female voters will be of increasing importance to both parties. This market research also raises serious questions about how men and women see the role of government and the political process as a whole. If women favored Clinton overwhelmingly in the 1996 election, as gender gap statistics suggest, it was angry white southern males who turned against him and his party in the Republican landslide of the 1994 campaign. In many cases, these voters had their own medium of choice: talk radio. "Political talk radio appeals to a powerful elite white male audience" with three times as many listeners likely to be Republican as Democrat (Media Studies Center 1996a). If talk radio provides some listeners with information, it is also full of opinion rather than facts. In an extensive analysis of Rush Limbaugh's broadcast, FAIR documented numerous untruths and characterized much of the commentary as an assortment of "sloppiness, ignorance and fabrication" (Eaglemen et al. 1994, 11). In many cases, talk radio has been filled with anger, accusations, denials, and outrageous remarks. One commentator told a caller he wished he could get him up against a wall and shoot him, and also expressed the hope that President Clinton was HIV-positive.

Restoring the Bond and the Digital Democracy

Harvard University's Center on the Press, Politics and Public Policy has analyzed media coverage of the presidential process, identifying key problems and making a series of recommendations to restore the bond by connecting campaign coverage to the voters. Among the problems the report documented were the following:

- There is too much distance between voters' concerns and press coverage.

- There is too much coverage of the horse race (who's ahead) and strategy rather than issues.

- There is too much theater coverage— the candidate as performer rather than validity of policies and platform.

To a large degree, the Harvard report argues that television has been responsible for a good deal of this type of coverage, and that the failure to vote is in turn based upon perceptions about how politics is conducted. In particular, the study says, "the modern technology of television has shaped a new political reality that is defined more by images than facts and more by emotions than rational deliberation" (1991, 41). Further, "the production demands of television which places a premium on symbolic visual elements and powerful emotional moments have come to dictate the daily activities of presidential candidates and drive out the extended explanation of important issues" (10-11). Improving the nature of campaign coverage will depend upon the media having a plan, sticking to the plan, and not getting caught up in the fray in which they themselves become victims.

In 1988, when the press tried to expose the claims of both parties and the manufactured news they disseminated, it was them who the public attacked. "The voters, readers, viewers felt they saw a rude elite group with its own agenda tearing down the candidate in a gladiator show" (127). The Harvard study said that improved reporting would come from greater balance, greater research, more emphasis on outsider perspectives, greater relevance to the voters and less emphasis on images and photo opportunities. Such a strategy, they suggested, would elevate the level of political discourse and encourage citizens to participate in the democratic process.

Historically, such participation has always been lauded and encouraged in this country. Yet responsible citizenship surely implies more than merely the act of voting. Surely a responsible voter is also an informed and aware citizen who has made a judgment after careful consideration. Given the data we have seen from several recent elections and surveys, there is substantial evidence to suggest that many of those who vote do not understand the issues of the campaign or even the day-to-day workings of their own government. While MTV and other groups routinely promote participation through Rock the Vote and other campaigns, the 1996 election found a solitary voice speaking against the act of voting. "Uninformed voters going to the polls are even more dangerous than apathetic nonvoters staying home. Those who can't be bothered to educate themselves jeopardize democracy with their ignorance. All of us would be better off if the ill-informed stayed home on election day" (Chavez 1996, 14a).

Staying home on election day may be the course of action many Americans take in our high-tech future. In fact, election day may be every day in the coming digital democracy, or what *Time* described as the "cyberdemocracy." As more and more computers and interactive technologies enter our homes and workplaces, polling stations and long lines may become a thing of the past. Representative democracy itself might be challenged by a series of electronically conducted national plebiscites as every issue is put to the people and instantly voted on. While such an era remains the stuff of science fiction, the tools and technologies that could create it are already in place and at work. Today, various lobbies and special-interest groups for particular causes are able to energize their constituencies and affect congressional votes through the skillful combination of websites, mailing lists, E-mail, radio, and television broadcasts. It is a courageous politician indeed who can remain impervious to an onslaught of faxes, mail, and telegrams from his or her own district, no matter how clearly orchestrated or unrepresentative it may be. Although the traditional response to this form of participation by citizens has acknowledged grassroots and populist movements, the technologies they use, and that in turn use them, are not of the people or by the people. Such technologies can very easily represent the emergence of an electronic elite as the gap between the information-rich and the information-poor widens. While such technology may give citizens greater access to their representatives, they could just as easily swamp our senators and congresspeople in a tidal wave of attitudes and opinions that strangles rather than facilitates government. Such a view was held by Robert Wright, who argued that the problem in American politics today is not that Washington is out of tune with the public, but "too plugged in" (1995, 15). "When town halls become call-in shows, deliberation loses and slogans become laws" (16). In such circumstances, while the technology may give citizens instant access to their candidates and representatives, they frequently use it without the time for quiet reflection and contemplation needed to resolve an issue. Said Wright, "Protest has gone from the street to the fax, further hamstringing the capital's lawmakers" (19).

(MID/HIGH) —

- Monitor media coverage of a local, a state, and a national election to see how much attention is devoted to issues and how much to the personality or personal life of the candidates.

- Discuss the purpose of national political conventions and how they have changed in a television age.

- Do the networks have a professional responsibility to show an entire convention, even if it's scripted and the audience is small? Discuss.

- Debate who is to blame if (1) people don't vote and (2) voters don't understand the issues.

- Discuss the idea that ignorant people shouldn't vote.

- Using the media data related to gender differences, have students survey people in their communities to see where they get most of their political information. Then compare and contrast these sources of information.

- In 1991, Harvard University identified several major problems in the way the press covers national elections. Use these to monitor coverage in the next national election.

- Study a source like MTV to see what issues seem to be of importance to young people. Do your students agree with these concerns? If not, contact MTV and express your own questions and concerns.

- Explain the idea of digital or cyber-democracy to your students. Ask them to discuss potential benefits and detriments of the new technologies.

- Monitor the cost of an election in your own state or during a presidential election.

- Debate the advantages and disadvantages of providing candidates with free television time.

- Contact national and state candidates and ask them to address the media's role in the increasing cost of campaigns.

Covering Clinton

Bill Clinton's relationship with the press has been both controversial and contradictory. Toward the end of the 1996 presidential election, Bob Dole accused the media of keeping Clinton in office. "We're not going to let the media steal this election. The country belongs to the people, not the *New York Times*," he told an audience at Southern Methodist University in Dallas. In Pensacola, Florida, Dole said that editorial decisions had been made to ignore and play down scandals and problems within the administration. "We know the liberal media is not going to report all things. They want him re-elected. They like it the way it is." Both the *New York Times* and the *Washington Post* ran excerpts from Dole's speeches including his criticism of the press. Dismissing the criticism, Frank Rich pointed out that the same press that exposed Watergate and the Pentagon papers had taken on this administration. The *LA Times* had broken the Whitewater story, and the *Washington Post* had been highly critical of the failure of the Democratic National Committee to fully disclose their finances. He also referred to the conservative media holdings of Rupert Murdoch and the anti-Clinton focus of Reverend Sun Myung Moon's *Washington Times*. In the 1996 campaign, more newspapers throughout the country endorsed Republican Bob Dole than they did Bill Clinton, and many who did endorse Clinton, like the *New York Times*, did so with reservations and without enthusiasm.

Since he appeared on the national political scene in 1991, Bill Clinton has engendered both love and loathing in the news media, whose treatment of him has been condemned as both fawning and hostile. With the 1992 election season barely under way, Clinton had become the favorite of the press corps. Young, good-looking, charismatic, a bright Rhodes scholar with a good organization and good policies, he was favored by the press over others like Jerry Brown and Paul Tsongas, whom they dismissed as unelectable. The support for Clinton was evident in Sidney Blumenthal's writing for *The New Republic* and Joe Klein's influential cover story in *New York*. Tom Rosenstiel called it "the invisible anointment of Clinton in the media" (1994, 53). Klein would later anonymously pen a

❖ **Used with permission of Wayne Stayskal, *Tampa Tribune*.**

less than flattering portrait of a Clinton-esque character in the best-seller *Primary Colors*. The publication and its circumstances would raise questions about the ethics and neutrality of the press. But as campaigning for the New Hampshire primary got under way, Clinton and the press corps were comfortable with each other. Within a few short weeks, a member of the Democratic National Committee would say, "Clinton's biggest problem now is that 90 percent of the press corps think he is a liar" (Rosenstiel 1994, 80).

If the press had changed their opinion of Clinton, it said as much about their character as it did his. Before he announced his candidacy for the presidency, Clinton, his wife Hillary, and their advisors had been aware that the question of alleged womanizing might come up. They also had an answer. "What you need to know about Hillary and me is that we've been together nearly 20 years. It has not been perfect or free from problems, but we're committed to our marriage and its obligations to our child and to each other. We love each other very much" (Germond and Witcover 1993, 170). Under normal circumstances and the normal rules

of play, that should have been enough. But this was journalism 1990s style. The rules had changed. No topic was taboo, no question too outrageous. In the 1988 campaign, Paul Taylor of the *Washington Post* asked Democrat Gary Hart if he had committed adultery. In 1992, during a press conference at the Waldorf Astoria, a hitherto unknown woman named Gennifer Flowers was asked if Governor Clinton had used a condom.

When the *Miami Herald* tracked Gary Hart (following a challenge issued by the senator himself), a journalistic tradition was broken. In the past, journalists had made a clear distinction between the private life of a politician and his or her public duties. Nowhere was this more evident than in the Kennedy administration. If the private habits and passions of a politician did not interfere with his ability to conduct the business for which he had been elected, the press tended to ignore it. It was equally established within the media that rumors, gossip, and unsubstantiated charges or accusations would not be covered. In January 1992, as Clinton and his Democratic rivals campaigned through New Hampshire's snow, a tabloid called *The Star* ran a story claiming that then governor Clinton had been involved in a long-term affair with a woman called Gennifer Flowers. The story had actually run earlier in London's *Daily Mail*, but had been ignored by the American press. *The Star* ran further stories revealing the existence of a number of tape-recorded phone conversations between Flowers and a man it alleged was Clinton. Slowly, inevitably, the story began to be repeated by other media outlets. By repeating it, they validated it. "It was a textbook illustration of how the media worked. This faint buzz of coverage gave the allegations of infidelity enough weight that reporters saw them as a potential political liability for Clinton even though they had no substantiation" (Rosenstiel 1994, 59). During a televised debate among the Democratic candidates, Cokie Roberts further escalated coverage of the story. Addressing Clinton, she asked him to respond to fears held by members of his own party that "allegations of womanizing" would bring him down. The fear, she said, was that "the Republicans will find somebody and that she will come forward late, and that you would lose the all important democratic woman's vote" (Germond and Witcover 1993, 175). When Ted Koppel and *Nightline* picked up the story, the Clinton team sent Mandy Grunwald to assail the host on his own broadcast. Accusing him of sleazy journalism, Grunwald said, "You're setting the agenda and you're letting *The Star* set it for you" (182). Four years later, on the night Clinton accepted the renomination of his party for his second term, the sleaze factor, as NBC called it, once again emerged. This time a prostitute came forward to reveal her relationship with Dick Morris, a longtime Clinton friend and the architect of his 1996 recovery.

Between the Gennifer Flowers story and his election in November 1992, Bill Clinton dodged more than his share of bullets, including controversial questions about draft dodging, pot-smoking, and mysterious trips to the Soviet Union. There is little doubt that Clinton's character, equivocation, endless efforts to empathize, and need to please and be liked have created much of the unflattering press attention that he has attracted. Without exonerating him from his own role and responsibility in this process,

it is also necessary to attempt to explain the coverage by recognizing the changing character of the American news media. Throughout this chapter, we have explored the preference for pictures and drama that now drives much that passes for journalism in this country. Like Dan Rather, Walter Cronkite, and others, we have connected this ethos to the changing ownership of broadcasting. While Clinton's conduct and character explain some of the negative coverage he has received, changes in our communication conglomerates explain it too. In *Strange Bedfellows: How Television and the Presidential Candidates Changed American Politics in 1992*, Tom Rosenstiel says that the emergence of CNN and local access to pictures meant that "the networks lost their oligopoly over news and their ability to set journalistic standards" (1994, 63). Clinton himself has acknowledged the shifting power of the media. "You know why I can stiff you on press conferences?" he asked a group of reporters. "Because Larry King liberated me by giving me to the American people directly" (Phillips 1993, 10a).

Clinton's suspicion of the media was more than justified. NBC's White House correspondent, Andrea Mitchell, admitted, "There's a gotcha mentality to a lot of what we do. Reporters coming in to this administration felt they had blown it with Ronald Reagan and George Bush, that they had let them get away with murder, and they were going to be tougher on this new guy" (Kurtz 1994, 10). Todd Gitlin said, "The stampede to condemn Clinton as a failure when he had been in office less than two weeks was breathtaking." Were these journalists, he wondered, the same ones who only recently had described the Clinton campaign as "unprecedented in its brilliance" (1993, 36)? *Esquire* described the new president and his relationship with the press as "the new media ice age, the most distant president since Nixon." Bill Clinton, they said, "will touch, hug and listen patiently as some stranger in McDonald's spills out his life story . . . is eager to charm anyone in the world except the correspondents who now cover him" (Shapiro 1993, 66). Even the book industry benefited from Clinton baiting and bashing. Less than 16 months into his administration, the president found himself the subject of Bob Woodward's *Agenda*. The reporter who had helped bring down Richard Nixon now seemed to have another president in his sights. Lesser presses and authors continued to turn out less than flattering accounts of the administration. Clinton was analyzed as the adult child of an alcoholic and his administration was characterized as the dysfunctional presidency. Reviewing one such effort and the national appetite for such fare, the *Washington Post* accused the author of "spewing venom in over 800 pages of gibberish without even penning a memorable line; shamelessly dissecting the Clintons' private lives like voyeuristic buzzards swooping down to eat and regurgitate previously discredited tabloid stories" (Brinkley 1995, 35).

A comparative analysis of networks news coverage of the first few months of the Bush and Clinton administrations reveals the new negativity. Sixty-two percent of the coverage of Bush had been positive, compared to 42 percent positive coverage of Clinton. The study conducted by The Center for Media and Public Affairs reported wide differences among the three major networks. While coverage at CBS ran at a very balanced 40 percent for both Bush and Clinton, coverage at the other networks revealed greater differences. Sixty-seven percent of NBC's coverage of Bush had been positive, compared to 46 percent for Clinton. At ABC, Bush's coverage was 86 percent positive, compared to just 38 percent for Clinton (Phillips 1993, 10a). A simple explanation for this is that Bush made fewer mistakes in his first few months in office or, conversely, that Clinton screwed up more frequently. Given the fact that Bush was a Washington insider who had been vice president for eight years, this seems like a reasonable claim. Once again, however, the context of the new news media cannot be ignored. Todd Gitlin has described what he calls "the manic depressive melodrama of new beginnings." He also blamed much of Clinton's negative coverage on "the cynical editors who write the headlines and decide which stories go on the front page and the equally cynical producers who arrange the sequence of the evening news" (1993, 36). Perhaps Perry White got

it right. In a 1990s episode of *Lois and Clark* he told Jimmy Olson, "This is a newspaper, it's either catastrophe or atrophy."

The so-called Republican revolution of 1994 was widely interpreted as an anti-Clinton vote. In fact the majority of Americans of voting age stayed home. The revolution that put the Republicans in the majority was a revolution executed by a minority of the U.S. public. If Newt Gingrich's ascendancy was based on disappointment or dismay about the first two years of Clinton's term, both the president and the press were responsible for the outcome. The manic-depressive reporting Todd Gitlin describes does not end with the publication or broadcast of a story, but is fed into the wider society. Here it shapes public perceptions, which, in turn, show up in polling, which then loops back into both political policies and more press coverage. In the wake of the Republican takeover of the Congress, Bill Clinton's role and future seemed grim. In one speech, he was actually forced to articulate his belief that he was still relevant, still a player, and still the president. Perhaps Newt Gingrich and the Republican majority now gave the press new targets. Perhaps, as many charge, Clinton skillfully maneuvered to the middle with a me-too strategy that blunted many potential attacks. Whatever the reason, Clinton easily won re-election in 1996. He did so in the midst of widespread criticism and concern from the press and continued doubts from the public. The press, for their part, remained ambivalent. Though many respected and admired his skills as a candidate and a performer, they were less sure about his presidency. Perhaps that ambivalence shows up in the numbers analyzed from national network news. Throughout the 1996 campaign, 50 percent of the stories about Clinton were positive in tone. In different circumstances, with a weaker economy and a stronger opponent, those numbers may have made Clinton vulnerable. In 1996, however, Clinton was safe. Only 33 percent of network news stories about his opponent, Bob Dole, were positive (*U.S. News and World Report*, 1996).

(MID/HIGH) —

- A president is usually accorded a so-called honeymoon period by the press. During the first few months in office, heavy criticism is muted. Clinton was not given this period. Discuss the concept with students, including its relative advantages and disadvantages.

- Have students locate newsmagazines like *Time* and *Newsweek* for the period January-May 1993. Analyze coverage of Clinton for bias and balance.

- Examine similar news sources for coverage of Newt Gingrich and the Republican Congress for the first four or five months of 1995.

- Watch a presidential news conference with students. Point out key reporters like Helen Thomas. Listen carefully for tone and emotion in both the questions and the answers. Compare the entire conference to the diluted and summarized version given in newspapers and network news.

Fig. 3.1. A Framework for Analyzing Broadcast News (TRANSPARENCY MASTER)

- STORY

- SEQUENCE

- SCOPE

- STRUCTURE

- STYLE

- SLANT

- SPONSOR

Elements of the Framework for
Critically Viewing Broadcast News

This framework has been used with teachers and students from elementary school through college. While it is by no means the only way of deconstructing news, it does represent a format that seems user-friendly and that can be used at different age levels with varying degrees of sophistication. The transparency master (Fig. 3.1) can be used to introduce students to each element. Or the transparency master can be duplicated and students can take notes in the space provided under each heading.

(ELEM/MID/HIGH) —

Story. The start of the analysis is quite simply a log or record of what stories were contained in the broadcast. Since this is a linear process, the log should represent the order in which the stories were presented. Typically, students start the study of news by suggesting that the news contains the most important stories on any given day. Several stories on any given night, however, may be either unfolding events, not specifically related to the day of the broadcast, or investigative reports about issues designated as significant, but again not restricted to any single day. If we start with the concept of a story, this is also an opportunity to introduce the concept of the anchor as storyteller.

Sequence. Sequence is related to the story log since it indicates in what order the stories were presented. Ask students what the sequence indicates and most of them will tell you that it shows how important the story is. This provides the teacher with an opportunity to ask, "Important to whom?" Sometimes students will say, "Important to the viewer or reader," and sometimes students will say, "Important to the editor or producer." The discussion provides an opportunity to explore the concept of priorities and ranking. It is also the time when we can start to examine the relationship between what the public *wants* to know and what it *needs* to know. This opens up the whole area of accessing information, responsible citizenship, and the marketing of news. The expression "If it bleeds, it leads" has frequently been used to describe priorities at work in local news. If that philosophy is still true, the sequencing of news should verify the fact.

The selection, omission, and sequencing of stories can be used to develop critical thinking skills. On Earth Day 1990, for example, would the lead story be Earth Day or the release of a hostage from the Middle East? How many people would be directly affected or influenced by Earth Day? How many people would be directly affected or influenced by the release of Robert Polhill? Which story was most likely to produce the best pictures, the greatest conflict, and the highest emotional response? Although Earth Day had ecological significance to the world, the Polhill release was more dramatic, and that story was elevated to the lead that evening. Posing questions such as these is the real purpose of the exercise. Students are not meant to simply record what was presented and how it was presented, but also to analyze the decisions behind those presentations. For a more in-depth study, the television logs can be compared to newspapers from the same day or the next morning. For example:

1. May 1990: ABC opened with the deaths of puppeteer Jim Henson and Sammy Davis, Jr. These stories ran ahead of both a confrontation between President Bush and the Congress and a visit to Moscow by the secretary of state, Jim Baker. CBS opened with Dan Rather in Moscow.

2. June 1990: ABC led with the opening of an international AIDS conference in San Francisco. Peter Jennings reported from that city. CBS opened with Nelson Mandela's visit to New York City, and the AIDS conference was not among their top three stories.

3. Summer 1991: ABC began its top story by declaring, "Alarm bells are ringing" in northern Iraq. They chronicled a threat to the

Kurds. CBS did not cover the story at all.

Scope. Like the first two elements, scope is still essentially a logging exercise that does not require higher-order thinking skills. Scope measures the time or space devoted to a story. In theory, the more time devoted to a story, the more important it is. Students can clock the running time for each segment. If they were working with newspapers, they could do this by measuring column inches. Scope and sequence are clearly related, but it must be pointed out that the longest stories are not always at the start of the broadcast (the lead), nor are the shortest stories always at the end. National network news typically includes thematic segments such as "American Agenda" (ABC) and "Eye on America" (CBS) that occur 15-20 minutes into the broadcast but take up a good deal of time. Hence, while they rank low in sequence, they are high in scope.

Structure. By this point, the framework is being used for analysis and evaluation. Students will need to see segments of the news several times in order to effectively analyze this aspect of the broadcast. The concept of structure involves all the different decisions that have been made in putting any story together. Typically, for example, a story commences with a head-and-shoulder shot of the anchor. The anchor typically has a news graphic or news box behind his or her head with a visual indicating what the story is about. An outline of the map of California with flames in it would, for instance, indicate fires out west. A cross made out of television sets was a graphic one network used when covering the televangelist scandals of the 1980s. What happens after the anchor has introduced the story? Do we go live to the scene, where a reporter brings us up to date on events? Does the reporter have a conversation with the on-air anchor? Do we have footage of the actual events, such as picketing airline pilots, collisions on icy interstates, the president a making speech, etc.? Do other people get to comment? Who are they? Experts, well-known talking heads, man-in-the-street interviews, comments by the person or persons who are the subject of the story? Is all of the video that is shown current, or is some file (dated) footage used? How is the story handed back to the anchor, and does the anchor bring closure or simply move on to the next story?

Analysis of story structure also allows students the opportunity to see if the story remains on track or turns into something else. By listening critically to the anchor and reporter, students can usually begin to spot the segue. One extraordinary example of this happened in a CBS story about a fire at Windsor Castle. Initially the story provided a series of neutral facts about where the fire started, when it started, what financial damage had been done, the contents of the building, and so on. Then, quite abruptly, reporter Martha Teichner announced that the fire was "a timely metaphor for the crises that have engulfed the British royal family lately." What followed was a blatant piece of tabloidism completely irrelevant to the fire. The network discussed the future of the monarchy, the unhappiness of the queen, and the failed marriages of several of her children, turning a once credible news report and a factual story into the stuff of soap operas. NBC, in a rather self-serving piece of reporting, also started with one story and spun off into something else. When a distraught father shot his children and then turned the gun upon himself, the network featured the story as its second piece for the night. Fairly quickly, however, it degenerated into some soul searching about the role of journalists who find themselves caught up in events. The transition may have been excusable if NBC had simply stuck to events of the day and the reporter who was contacted by the man. Unfortunately, they used the opportunity to pull out dramatic file footage, sure to keep the audience in their seats as we got to relive such events as the New York Trade Center bombing and the Waco siege. With a stretch of the imagination, one could say the network was just putting the events of the day in context. Unfortunately, it was *their* context and *their* concerns. The story quickly stopped being about the Tampa tragedy that they announced, and too soon became a story about the news media itself.

Style. Style and structure are related. The best way to begin to approach the concept of style is to isolate the beginning of the news, asking students to concentrate on the types of things they typically see and hear as a network news broadcast commences. Students normally make a reference to music. Ask them to describe the type of music, the mood, and the feeling it creates. If they are not sure, ask them if it is quiet, classical, soft, or soothing. Students normally know that this is not the way news begins, and this prompt fairly quickly results in comments about loud, dramatic music. It is worth the time to introduce them to the music used by ABC, CNN, NBC, and CBS at this point. Now ask students what they see when a broadcast begins. Some time ago it was typical for a broadcast to begin with a voice-over announcing the network and introducing the anchor, who would be seated at a desk with the network logo in the background. Now it is much more common to find entertainment production values at work. The broadcast often begins with a hook or, if you will, scenes from tonight's episode designed to keep us tuned in. Typically that means stories about crisis and conflict are likely to open the news. The themes of the stories therefore blend with the dramatic style of the music. When the anchor does appear, it is typically within the context of the studio set. This set is shown not because it has to be, but because showing it confers power on the anchor and the network. It is a set full of monitors, computers, telephones, and people moving back and forth in the important business of keeping us informed. The psychology of the set tells us to trust and believe these people at mission control who are on top of it all. This idea of the working newsroom was developed at ABC in the late 1970s when Frank Reynolds was anchor.

The concept of set decoration goes well beyond where the anchor is positioned. Merely placing a reporter against a specific symbolic backdrop also conveys status and authority. "Everytime they do a standup on the White House lawn, the subliminal message is that they are privy to everything that goes on inside" (Shapiro 1993, 66). Look for the Supreme Court, the Pentagon, and other backgrounds that convey power on the reporter. Also look for the decor when professional groups like doctors or attorneys are interviewed. A row of bookshelves, a busy hospital corridor—these and other sets serve to add dramatic context to the story. Camera angles are also part of the message. High-angle (tilt-down) shots frequently suggest a sense of vulnerability or weakness. A CBS piece on the danger of contracting AIDS from dentists used this shot, looking down on the patient in the chair as the dentist probed her mouth. Low-angle (tilt-up) shots tend to convey power and authority. These are seldom selected accidentally. Explore these concepts further in Chapter 6 and then have students locate the shots in news broadcasts and explain the relationship between the style of the story and its content.

Style can also include the language used to describe events. Literary techniques like alliteration are particularly easy to spot. They grab the attention of the ear in the same way that the set and cutting hold the attention of the eye. An NBC broadcast opened with a shooting in Florida that they called "Tampa Tragedy," and problems with radon in schools, which they billed as "Radon Risk." Not only were the words used by the anchor, but they were actually printed on the screen as titles for the lead stories. When a major hurricane hit the East Coast, Dan Rather opened the news with these three words: "Huge Hurricane Hugo." When a British businessman caused a banking collapse in Singapore and escaped to Germany, Rather announced his capture this way: "Finally Fingered in Frankfurt." A report from Los Angeles after a major earthquake described it as "a city divided by color and culture and cash." Flooding along the Mississippi River in Iowa was presented as the "Defense of Des Moines." Any number of problems in Russia have been built up under the title "Crisis at the Kremlin." Alliteration can also be detected on radio news. A riot in Indonesia was reported as "a mostly Muslim mob." Use these phrases to introduce students to the concept so that they can recognize when it is being used and why. Sometimes language is used as a play on words, typically for lighthearted reports. In a CBS report on a growing controversy about fox hunting, Dan Rather began, "Should fox hunting be hounded out of existence? The fur is flying."

Slant. This section addresses the issue of balance or bias in news reporting. It is typically one of the most difficult areas to work with because people perceive stories, including their bias, in different ways based on their own beliefs and attitudes about the topic, person, or events covered. A criterion therefore needs to be established as well as a rating scale as a shorthand code for classifying each story. In this case, students can designate stories they analyze as P+ (positive), N- (negative), or B- (balanced). The rating can be applied to both words and images used during a broadcast. Throughout this chapter, terms such as "marginalized," "polarize," "minimize," and "demonize" have been used and explained to indicate various biases in the way stories are constructed by the news media. The concept of marginalizing and minimizing is fairly easy to explain to students, and they seldom have trouble detecting it. If a teacher asks them to analyze coverage of an issue to see if (1) both sides were covered, (2) both sides were given equal time, and (3) both sides were presented objectively, most students are capable of identifying imbalance in reporting. Research indicates that coverage of the Persian Gulf War typically privileged pro-war forces, giving them time and space to express their views while giving little time or space to opponents of the war. In the coverage of social issues, *USA Radio Network News* frequently stresses one side by allowing its point of view to be heard, but not others. When Congress re-introduced legislation to ban partial-birth abortion in March 1997, the radio network allowed Republicans Dick Armey and Illinois representative Hyde to speak, but did not present anyone opposed to the measure. Similarly, when Patricia Ireland, president of the National Organization of Women (NOW), spoke at a midwestern campus, the coverage was again skewed. Students opposed to NOW's support of abortion were allowed to condemn NOW and the university for endorsing the "abortion holocaust." No representatives from the university or NOW were heard from. When the Hemlock Society promoted a bill in Illinois related to doctor-assisted suicides, the radio broadcast provided a forum for Lutherans for Life, but the listening audience did not hear from sponsors of the bill. Since *USA Radio Network News* is frequently heard on Christian radio stations, its coverage of social issues tends to reflect the philosophy and therefore bias of its target audience. It should not, however, be mistaken for balanced and objective reporting that

equally and fairly presents both sides of an issue.

"Loaded language" or "weighted words" is another term that can be used to help students recognize bias in the way a story is expressed. If a report opens with the phrase "an already rattled White House" or "dire doings in Washington," an entire mood and context have been created before the viewer even attempts to process the story. The reaction has, in fact, been prepackaged by the opening tone and phrasing. There is a big difference between using the phrase "abortion rights advocates" and the phrase, "the abortion industry." Likewise, consider the negativity of "anti-abortion advocates" compared to the positive image of "pro-life supporters." The term "Desert Shield" used during the lead-up to the Gulf War was not a neutral term but one clearly intended to convey athe sense of protection. As such, the use of this language justified the action. Describing the "semantic swamp" in the affirmative action controversy, columnist Barbara Reynolds believed that the language used actually shaped public perception. "If the press and politicians would stop using the explosive and disingenuous words, preferences, and reverse discrimination, the angst over affirmative action would be diffused" (1995a, 134a).

At times, loaded language can seem rather harmless, especially when the anchor seems to be relating to a widely held concern or celebrating a popular event along with the audience. During a broadcast of the program *48 Hours*, Dan Rather told viewers in the path of Hurricane Hugo, "We care about you. We're thinking about you." One can understand the sentiments and even applaud the anchor's empathy, but once this pattern of speaking for the audience—speaking on behalf of the audience—begins, it is very difficult for news to remain neutral.

When the space shuttle program got back into space after the long delay caused by the explosion of the *Challenger*, many news broadcasts seemed to abandon objectivity and functioned instead as national cheerleaders, in the process actually serving to create the mood and response they were at the same time reporting. Some journalists tend to identify themselves and their reports with the nation, personifying the country, as a result of which they speak for the country and establish themselves as the arbiters of national opinion. ABC's "American Agenda" nightly news segment often provides excellent coverage of important social issues, but the packaging should really read "ABC's Agenda." ABC and the United States are not synonymous. In April 1990, when U.S. hostages were released, Peter Jennings opened the news by saying, "Good evening. There's nothing Americans would like more than to see it [release of hostages] become a trend."

Whether an anchor correctly or incorrectly gauges the national mood is not the point. The issue is whether network news should seek to speak for the nation. When the stock market fell dramatically in the late 1980s, the news media presented the story with a sense of gloom and doom that may have actually made people more pessimistic than the event merited. By early 1991, media coverage of the recession and the Persian Gulf crisis was being blamed for an increase in reported cases of anxiety and depression.

One of the most obvious and outspoken examples of bias in a news broadcast occurred in 1988. During a live interview with then vice president Bush, Dan Rather said, "Mr. Vice President, you've made us hypocrites in the face of the world. How could you sign on to such a policy?" The public reaction was interesting. Fifty-one percent thought the anchor had been rude, but 59 percent thought he was correct in challenging Bush on his role in the Iran Contra controversy. Asked whom they trusted to tell the truth more, Rather or Bush, 49 percent opted for the anchor and 22 percent for the future president of the United States (Stengel 1988, 19). It's not just the words an anchor or reporter uses in a commentary or question; sometimes the tone and visual cues and clues can clearly signal his or her own opinion. Michael Gartner, former head of NBC News, has said, "A raised eye-brow, an ad-lib to the anchor, a question in a shouting or threatening tone of voice, all can add a perception of unfairness."

Even sporting events, like the Olympics or the Super Bowl, can be the occasion for boosterism and bias, especially in local news. When the Yankees won the World Series in 1996, the *New York Times* took exception with the comments of reporters and anchors at WNYW-TV. "The station has shamed itself," said the *Times*, adding that "Penny Crone's gushing and burbling flew in the face of any pretensions to the practice of journalism, often an alien concept in local news" (Sandomir 1996, c4).

Sponsor. Like most programming, broadcast news is intent on selling as well as telling. Students intuitively understand the concept of targeting an audience. If you ask them what programs would feature advertisements for cereal, toys, and action figures, they will reply cartoons. If you ask them what programs would feature ads for trucks, beer, and insurance, they will typically refer to sports shows. Obviously advertisers sponsor shows that reach the audience they want to buy their products. But most marketing involves more than the simple matter of providing information about a product. While part of any purchase is a rational decision, another part of it is psychological and motivational. If news, as we note throughout this chapter, concentrates on gloom and doom, crisis and conflict, a threatening world with events frequently out of control, what state of mind are viewers likely to be in? To what sales techniques and pitches might they respond? How Do You Spell Relief? While advertisements in network news include items such as tiles, contact lenses, automobiles, and other relatively innocuous products, the psychology and consistent message under the majority of advertisements play on security, fear, and pain by promising some form of cure, relief, or escape. News broadcasts are heavily sponsored by insurance companies; headache relief remedies; sleeping aids; indigestion and heartburn products; various pills, rubs, ointments, and medicines to ease pain, not to mention laxatives and hemorrhoidal suppositories. Those not busy tranquilizing themselves in search of some chemical cure for the woes of the world can escape by means of an ocean voyage on a Carnival Cruise or Royal Caribbean. Over and over, the message and words beneath the ads create a cumulative picture of a fearful, insecure, threatening world and the promised safety and security of the sponsor's product. The scene: a dark city street at night. The character: a lone white woman. The dilemma: Her car battery is dead because she, incompetent that she is, forgot to turn her lights off. Vulnerable and alone on our menacing city streets, she finds relief and safety through a Diehard battery.

An NBC news broadcast from March 1993 opened with three quick overviews of stories featured that night. The top story dealt with the family fight between Woody Allen and Mia Farrow, including allegations of child abuse. The second story addressed the risk to the nation's schoolchildren from radon in building materials. The third major report came from Tampa where a distraught father had killed himself and his children. The first block of ads after news segments clearly based on a theme of risk and uncertainty in our living rooms and classrooms played off that message. Dupont promised "better things for better living." In this case, they had a product that protected the lives of the nation's police officers. Grainy video images and real police testified about being shot in the line of duty. The punchline: "Being a police officer is always going to be dangerous, but it doesn't have to be fatal." A momentary respite from the gloom and doom of the ads and the news seemed to be offered in a snowy landscape with a rather cute squirrel. Quickly, however, dramatic menacing music told us that things are not safe in our garden. Weeds and other unwanted, unseen nasties lurk beneath the surface. Lucky for us that Ortho has a product with which we can kill. Their consistent message is, "We help you from the ground up, showing you the way. It's our nature to help." Even a seemingly harmless toothpaste commercial for Arm and Hammer tartar control repeatedly stresses the promise of "control," which is the very thing we need in the insecure world the news brings to our living rooms. The promise of relief we find in the advertisements during the news sometimes pervades the report itself as the all-knowing anchor promises to help us. Discussing the risk of getting AIDS from our dentists, Dan Rather said, "We'll tell you what you can do to protect yourself."

A CBS broadcast from November 1996 reveals a pattern of perilous stories interspersed with commercials that offer safety, sanctuary, and relief. Top stories that night dealt with another institution that was unsafe, in this case the military, where charges of sexual harassment continued to grow. Oddly enough, this was the top story on Veterans Day. Our corporations were also out of control. Texaco executives were accused of racist policies and remarks. Our hospitals were becoming less than hospitable, and women were being sent home too soon after having mastectomies. Among other stories that night: major problems from wintry weather in the Midwest, a menacing sex offender in Florida, unsafe minivans, and starving refugees in Africa. Commercials included Imodium AD, Alka Seltzer, Ensure, ExLax, GasX, Sustacal, Fibercon, and Robitussin. While all the products offer relief from the problems that plague our bodies and our world, they also connect very directly to the aging population who watches the evening news. In fact, the very week of this broadcast, CBS featured a week-long series on the highs and lows of "Facing Fifty."

Remind students that by looking at the people in the advertisements, as well as the products, they can begin to construct a portrait of who is watching the news and who it is aimed at. Ken Auletta, author of 3 Blind Mice, spotted the trend in the early 1990s. "The slow death dance of network news is reflected in the ads interspersed throughout the nightly newscast. All those Maalox and denture commercials reveal a painful truth; network news has become the preserve of old people" (1991, 6).

REFERENCES

Alter, Jonathan, (1993). Journalism as a Blood Sport. *Newsweek*, August 23, 33.

Atkin, C., (1973). Instrumental Utilities and Information Seeking. In P. Clarke (ed.), *New Models for Mass Communication Research* (205-42). Beverly Hills: Sage.

Auletta, Ken, (1991). Look What They've Done to the News. *TV Guide*, November 9, 4-7.

Awiakta, Marilou, (1993). *Selu: Seeking the Corn Mother's Wisdom*. Golden CO: Fulcrum.

Bagdikian, Ben, (1983). *The Information Machine*. New York: Harper & Row.

———, (1990). *The Media Monopoly*. Boston: Beacon Press.

Baker, Ross, (1997). Frustrated Journalists in a Quiescent Campaign. *Media Studies Journal*, 2:1, 1-8.

Baker, Russ, (1993). Truth, Lies and Videotape. *Columbia Journalism Review*, August, 25-28.

Barber, Ben, (1994). Wolves Gather as Clinton Licks His Wounds. *The Sunday Age*, August 14, 12.

Barone Center on Press, Politics and Public Policy, (1991). Restoring the Bond: Connecting Campaign Coverage to Voters. A Report of the Campaign Lessons for 92 Project. Cambridge, MA: Harvard University.

Benedict, Helen, (1992). *Virgin or Vamp: How the Press Covers Sex Crimes*. New York: Oxford University Press.

Berg, Steve, (1996). Carlson Cites Media for Feeding Public Cynicism. *Star Tribune*, May 19, 16a.

Bertand, Ina, (1994). Women in the News. *Metro Magazine*, No. 98, Winter, 47-50.

Bridge, Junior, (1989). No News Is Women's News. *Media and Values*, Winter, 11-13.

Brinkley, Douglas, (1995). *Washington Post*, weekly edition, June 5-12, 05.

Broder, David, (1987). *Behind the Front Page: A Candid Look at How News Is Made*. New York: Simon & Schuster.

Carter, Bill, (1990). Women Anchors Are on the Rise as Evening Stars. *New York Times*, August 12, H-27.

Carter, Jimmy, (1994). Foreword. In *Television, Radio News and Minorities*, ed. Donald Browne and Charles Firestone. Queenstown, MD: The Aspen Institute.

Center on the Press and Public Policy, (1991). *Restoring the Bond: Connecting Campaign Coverage to Voters' Concerns*. Cambridge: Harvard University Press.

Chavez, Linda, (1996). The Clueless Voter Ought to Stay Home. *U.S.A. Today*, October 30, 14a.

Cole, Williams, (1995). Readers for Sale: What Newspapers Tell Advertisers About Their Audiences. *Extra*, May-June, 6-7.

Considine, David M., (1993). Media Literacy and the Political Process. *Telemedium: The Journal of Media Literacy*. 1st/2nd Quarter, 9-12.

———, (1994). A Cure for the Bad News Blues: Critical Thinking Skills in an Age of Infotainment. *Telemedium: The Journal of Media Literacy*, 40:2, 7-11.

Cronkite, Walter, (1996). Why Free TV Airtime Is Good Politics. *U.S.A. Today*, May 7, 11a.

David, William, and Jung Sook Lee, (1993). Television News Technology: Do More Sources Mean Less Diversity? *Journal of Broadcasting and Electronic Media*, 37:4, 453-64.

Devitt, Tiffany, and Jennifer Downey, (1991). Battered Women Taking a Beating from the Media. *Extra*, May-June, 10-11.

De Witt, Phillip Elmer, (1995). Porn on the Internet. *Time*, June 3, 38-42, 190.

Diamond, Edwin, (1993). Auto Destruct. *New York*. March 15, 18.

Diamond, Edwin, and Katryna O'Neill, (1989). Is TV News Guilty of Japan Bashing? *TV Guide*, May 20, 24-27.

Dobbs, Michael, (1995). Foreign Policy by CNN. *Washington Post*, weekly edition, July 31-August 6, 24.

Donahue, Deidere, (1994). The 4 L's for Selling Magazines. *U.S.A. Today*, January 10, 1d.

Donaldson, Sam, (1987). *Hold On, Mr. President*. New York: Random House.

Dorfman, Lori, and Katie Woodruf, (1995). Local TV News, Violence and Youth: Who Speaks? *Media Matters: The Institute on News and Social Problems*. Waltham, MA: Brandeis University.

Dorman, William, (1994). Mass Media and Logic: An Oxymoron. *Educational Vision*, 2:2, 35.

Eaglemen, Jonathan et al., (1994). The Way Things Aren't: Rush Limbaugh Debates Reality. *Extra*, July-August, 10-15.

Edmonds, Patricia, (1993). Real Sex: News Is Making Life a Little Sleazier. *U.S.A. Today*, November 18, 9a.

Edmonds, Patricia, and Richard Benedetto, (1994). Angry White Men. *U.S.A. Today*, November 11-13, 2a.

Entman, Robert, (1989). *Democracy Without Citizens: Media and the Decay of American Politics*. New York: Oxford University Press.

Estrich, Susan, (1994). Fear Sells and We're to Blame. *U.S.A. Today*, October 19, 13a.

Estrich, Susan, (1995). Hey There's a Middle Ground Too. *U.S.A. Today*, October 19, 3a.

Fallows, James, (1996). *Breaking the News: How the Media Undermine American Democracy.* New York: Pantheon.

Flanders, Laura, and Janine Jackson, (1995). Public Enemy No. 1: Media Welfare Debate Is War on Poor Women. *Extra*, May-June, 13-16.

Franklin, Gilliam, and Shanto Iyengar, (1995). Violence and Race in Television News Coverage of Crime: Does It Matter? *Media Matters: The Institute on News and Social Problems.* Waltham, MA: Brandeis University.

Gartner, Michael, (1994). Dump On Air TV News Reporters. *U.S.A. Today*, February 10, 11a.

———, (1995). Ignore ABC Apology: Cigarette Makers Kill. *U.S.A. Today*, August 29, 13a.

———, (1996). Boring Media Fails to Cover Real Interests. *U.S.A. Today*, June 4, 14a.

Georges, Christopher, (1993). Mock the Vote. *Washington Monthly*, May, 31.

Gerbner, George et al., (1994). Growing Up with Television: The Cultivation Perspective (17-42). In Jennings, Bryant and Dolf Zillmann (eds.), *Media Effects: Advances in Theory and Research.* Hillsdale, NJ: Lawrence Erlbaum.

Gergen, David, (1993). Give Clinton a Chance. *U.S. News and World Report*, May 10, 92.

Germond, Jack, and Jules Witcover, (1993). *Mad as Hell: Revolt at the Ballot Box 1992.* New York: Time Warner.

Gitlin, Todd, (1993). Whiplash. *American Journalism Review.* April, 35-36.

Gleick, Elizabeth, (1996). Read All About It. *Time*, October 21, 66-69.

Grossman, Lawrence, (1995). Beware the Electronic Republic. *U.S.A. Today*, August 29, 13a.

Hanson, Christopher, (1994). The Triumph of the Fuzz and Wuzz. *Columbia Journalism Review*, December.

Herman, Edward, and Noam Chomsky, (1988). *Manufacturing Consent: The Political Economy of the Mass Media.* New York: Pantheon.

Hoffner, Margaret, and Margaret Haefner, (1994). Children's News Interest During the Gulf War: The Role of Negative Affect. *Journal of Broadcasting and Electronic Media*, 38:2, 193-204.

Holland, P., (1987). When a Woman Reads the News. In H. Baehr and A. Dyer (eds.), *Boxed In: Women and Television*, 133-50. New York: Pandora.

Hoverston, Paul, and Linda Kanamine, (1994). Time Criticized over OJ Cover. *U.S.A. Today*, June 22, 1d.

Hunter, Jane, and Steve Askin, (1991). Hunger in Africa: A Story Untold Until Too Late. *Extra* 4:5, 8-10.

Husseini, Osama, (1991). TV Coverage Cheapens Arab Lives. *San Jose Mercury News*, February 27.

Jackson, Janine, and Jim Naurekas, (1994). Crime Contradictions. *Extra*, June, 10-13.

Jamieson, Kathleen, (1992). *Dirty Politics: Deception, Distraction and Democracy.* New York: Oxford University Press.

Jhally, Sut, Justin Lewis, and Michael Morgon, (1991). *The Gulf War: A Study of the Media, Public Opinion and Public Knowledge.* Summary Report by the Center for Studies in Communication, University of Massachusetts, February.

Johnson, Mary, (1991). Media Miss the Disabled Rights Issue: Courageous Cripples Instead of Access Activists. *Extra*, 4:4, 15.

Johnson, Peter, (1993). Local News Directors Clear the Air About TV Violence. *U.S.A. Today*, October 6, 3d.

Katz, Jon, (1993). Dan Rather in Defeat: A Symbol of Our Times. *Sunday Oregonian*, October 3, 13.

Kellner, Douglas, (1992). *The Persian Gulf TV War.* Boulder, CO: Westview Press.

Kinh, Anthony, (1997). Running Scared. *Atlantic Monthly*, January, 41-44, 61.

Klein, Joe, (1996). *Primary Colors.* New York: Warner Books.

Kurtz, Howard, (1990). A Note to Fellow Newsies: How About Some Self-Restraint. *Washington Post*, weekly edition, May 28-June 3.

———, (1991). Calling the Shots on Health News. *Washington Post*, weekly edition, July 1-7, 38.

———, (1994). Rolling with the Punches. *Washington Post*, weekly edition, January 24-30, 10.

———, (1995a). There's Anger in the Air. *Washington Post*, weekly edition, October 31-November 6, 8-10.

———, (1995b). Inside the Media Spin Machine. *Washington Post*, weekly edition, August 21-27, 6.

———, (1995c). Putting the Squeeze on the News Media. *Washington Post*, weekly edition, April 10-16, 36.

———, (1996). Money Talkers. *Washington Post*, weekly edition, February 12-18, 6-9.

Larry King Live, (1997). CNN, January 13.

Lee, Martin A., and Norman Solomon, (1990). *Unreliable Sources: A Guide to Detecting Bias in News Media.* Secaucus, NJ: Carol Publisher.

Leo, John, (1992). All the News That Fit to Script. *U.S. News and World Report*, May 4, 26.

———, (1993). Spicing Up the Ho-Hum Truth. *U.S. News and World Report*, March 8, 24.

Levine, Daniel, (1993). The Truth About TV News. November, 87-91.

Lewis, Justin, (1992). What Do We Learn from the News? *Extra*, September, 16-17.

Lewis, Justin, and Michael Morgan, (1992). Issues, Images, and Impact: A FAIR Survey of Voters' Knowledge. *Extra*, December 7-11.

Lind, Rebecca Ann, (1995). How Can TV News Be Improved? Viewer Perceptions of Quality and Responsibility. *Journal of Broadcasting and Electronic Media*, 39:3, 360-75.

Lines in the Sand: A Video Essay, (1992). Syracuse, NY: Griffin-Wirth Associates.

Mattingly, Terry, (1995). Religion in the News. *Media Ministry*, Winter, 4-5.

Mauro, Tony, (1995). Prosecutors Ran from the Evidence. *U.S.A. Today*, October 4, 1a.

McCabe, Peter, (1987). *Bad News at Blackrock: The Sell-Out of CBS News*. New York: Arbor House.

Media Studies Center, (1996a). *The Media and Campaign 96 Briefing, No. 2*.

———, (1996b). *The Media and Campaign 96 Briefing, No. 3*.

Meyrowitz, Joshua, (1985). *No Sense of Place: The Impact of Electronic Media on Social Behavior*. New York: Oxford University Press.

Miller, Mark Crispin, (1996). Free the Media. *The Nation*, June 3, 9-12.

Morin, Richard, (1990). Waiting in the Wings: The Doofus Generation. *Washington Post*, weekly edition, July 9-15, 37.

———, (1993). Wrong About the Religious Right. *Washington Post*, weekly edition, January 24-30, 37.

———, (1994). They Only Know What They Don't Like. *Washington Post*, weekly edition, February 5-11, 6-8.

———, (1995). The Face of the Single Mother. *Washington Post*, weekly edition, May 1-7, 34.

Mowlana, Hamid et al. (eds.), *Triumph of the Image: The Media's War in the Persian Gulf—A Global Perspective*. Boulder, CO: Westview Press.

Naisbitt, John, (1982). *Megatrends*. New York: Warner Books.

Naurekas, Jim, (1991). Gulf War Coverage: The Worst Censorship Was at Home. *Extra*, 4:3, 3-10.

———, (1992). Unfair to Bush, Unfair to Clinton? Campaign Coverage Was Unfair to Voters. *Extra*, December, 5-7.

Ornstein, Norman, (1995). So What's Wrong with a Self-Critical President? *U.S.A. Today*, November 8, 15a.

Phillips, Kevin, (1996). Debates Build Up. *U.S.A. Today*, October 3, 13a.

Phillips, Leslie, (1993). Presidents and Media Stay at Arms Length. *U.S.A. Today*, April 26, 4a.

Pinter, Harold, (1996). Brutal, Ruthless and in Love with Itself. *The Age*, December 31, A11.

Postman, Neil, (1992). *Technopoly: The Surrender of Culture to Technology*. New York: Vintage Books.

Potts, Richard, and Dawn Sanchez, (1994). Television Viewing and Depression: No News Is Good News. *Journal of Broadcasting and Electronic Media*, 38:1, 79-90.

Puette, William, (1992). *Jaundiced Eyes: How the Media View Organized Labor*. Ithaca, NY: Cornell University Press.

Rakow, Lana, and Kimberlie Kranich, (1991). Women as Sign in Television News. *Journal of Communication*, 41:1, 8-23.

Rather, Dan, (1990). Journalism and the Public Trust. *Humanist*, 50:6, 5-7, 42.

Rather, Dan, with Mickey Herskowitz, (1977). *The Camera Never Blinks: Adventures of a TV Journalist*. New York: William Morrow.

Ravitch, Diane, and Chester E. Finn, Jr., (1987). *What Do Our 17 Year Olds Know?* New York: Harper & Row.

Reed, Ishmael, (1993). *American Journalism Review*, September, 22.

Rehm, Diane, (1994). Can We Talk About Talk Radio? *Washington Post*, weekly edition, September 19-25, 23.

Reibstein, Larry, (1994). The Battle of the TV News Magazine Shows. *Newsweek*, April 11, 61-65.

Reynolds, Barbara, (1995a). Affirmative Action Sinking in Semantic Swamp. *U.S.A. Today*, June 23, 13a.

———, (1995b). Connie Chung's Biggest Problem Is She's Not a He. *U.S.A. Today*, June 2, 13a.

Rich, Frank, (1994). Another Media Morning After. *New York Times*, June 30, 13a.

———, (1996). It's the Media Stupid. *New York Times*, October 30, 21a.

Rodriguez, Richard, (1994). Is it Really Because OJ Simpson Is Black? *U.S. News and World Report*, July 4, 7.

Rosen, Jan, (1991). The Whole World Is Watching CNN. *Nation*, May 13, 622, 625.

Rosenberg, Howard, (1993). Bad News. *American Journalism Review*, September, 18-19.

Rosenstiel, Tom, (1994). *Strange Bedfellows: How Television and the Presidential Candidates Changed American Politics in 1992*. New York: Hyperion.

Roush, Matt, (1991). *U.S.A. Today*, January 17, 1d.

Rowen, Hobart, (1993). Clinton, Master of the Direct Sell. *Washington Post*, weekly edition, February 22-28, 5.

Sabato, Larry, (1991). *Feeding Frenzy: How Attack Journalism Has Transformed American Politics*. New York: Free Press.

Saffire, William, (1993). A Virgin No More. *New York Times*, March 25, 15a.

Sandomir, Richard, (1996). *New York Times*, October 28, 4c.

Sawyer, Kathy, (1994). Down to a Photo Refinish. *Washington Post*, weekly edition, February 28-March 6, 38.

Schement, Jorge Reina, and Charles Firestone, (1995). *Toward an Information Bill of Rights and Responsibilities*. Washington, DC: Aspen Institute.

Schiller, Herbert, (1992). Manipulating Hearts and Minds. In Mowlana et al. (eds.), *Triumph of the Image: The Media's War in the Persian Gulf—A Global Perspective*. Boulder, CO: Westview Press.

Schwartz, Harry, (1994). Media Abuse Their Power. *U.S.A. Today*, January 20, 8a.

Seelye, Katharine, (1996). Dole Imploring Voters to Rise Up Against the Press. *New York Times*, October 25, 1a.

Shales, M., (1992). Television's Beachhead in Somalia. *Washington Post*, December 9, 1c.

Shapiro, Walter, (1993). No, Mr. President, I'm Britt, He's Wolf. *Esquire*, July, 66-67.

Sheahan, Mike, (1996). If It Ain't American, It Ain't Happening. *Herald Sun*, July 31, 92.

Sherill, Robert, (1993). Murdock: "Man for the 80s." *The Nation*, May 10, 613, 642-44.

Slattery, Karen, and Ernest Hakanen, (1994). Sensationalism Versus Public Affairs Content of Local TV News: Pennsylvania Revisited. *Journal of Broadcasting and Electronic Media*, 38:2, 205-16.

Slattery, Karen et al., (1996). The Expression of Localism: Local TV News Coverage in the New Video Marketplace. *Journal of Broadcasting and Electronic Media*, 40:3, 403-13.

Starobin, Paul, (1995). A Generation of Vipers. *Columbia Journalism Review*, March-April, 26.

Stengel, Richard et al., (1988). Bushwhacked. *Time*, February 8, 16-20.

Stepp, Carl Sessions, (1993). How to Save American Newspapers. *American Journalism Review*, April, 18-24.

Stone, G. C., and E. Gruisin, (1984). Network TV as the Bad News Bearer. *Journalism Quarterly*, 61, 517-23.

Thompson, Bill, (1993). The President Shoots Back. *Charlotte Observer*, June 17, 11a.

Time, (1996). Cover on Clinton's next cabinet before election. October 21.

Tyndall, Andrew, (1996). Why Network TV Campaign Coverage Is Down in 96. Media Studies Center: *The Media and Campaign 96, Briefing No. 3.*

Ungar, Sanford, (1994). Sensationalizing the Sensational. *U.S.A. Today*, October 25, 13a.

Urschel, Joe, (1995). Chun-Gingrich: and We Wonder Why They Hate Us. *U.S.A. Today*, January 6, 11a.

U.S.A. Today. April 20, 1993.

———, (1996). Credibility Nose Dives When Rumors Replace Facts. March 7, 12a.

———, (1996). August 26, 1a.

———, (1996). August 29, 14a.

———, (1997). January 17, 21.

———, (1997). February 21, 11a.

U.S. News and World Report, (1991). N.t., July, 21.

———, (1996). Did the Media Tilt Towards Clinton? November 18, 32.

Walcott, John, (1992). Land of Hype and Glory: Spin Doctors on Parade. *U.S. News and World Report*, February 10, 6.

Walsh, Kenneth, (1993). The Unmaking of Foreign Policy. *U.S. News and World Report*, October 18, 30.

Weiser, Benjamin, (1993). TV's Credibility Crunch. *Washington Post*, weekly edition, March 8-14, 6-8.

Weisman, John, (1984). Why TV Is Missing the Picture in Central America. *TV Guide*, September 15, 2-7.

Whetmore, E. J., (1987). *Mediamerica: Form, Content and Consequence of Mass Communications*. (3rd ed.) Belmont, CA: Wadsworth.

White, Theodore, (1961). *The Making of the President 1960*. London: Jonathan Cape.

———, (1982). *America in Search of Itself: The Making of the President 1956-80*. New York: Harper & Row.

Williams, Marjorie, (1990). Behind the Screens. *Washington Post Magazine*, May 13, 15-19, 34-41.

Woodhull, Nancy et al., (1996). Voters to Media-Deliver the News Live and Unencumbered. Media Studies Center: *The Media and Campaign 95, Briefing No. 4.*

Wright, Robert, (1995). Hyper Democracy. *Time*, January 23, 15.

Zillmann, Dolf, and Jennings Bryant, (1985). Affect, Mood and Emotion as Determinants of Selective Exposure. In Zillmann and Bryant (eds.), *Selective Exposure to Communication* (157-90). Hillsdale, NJ: Lawrence Erlbaum.

Zillmann, Dolf et al., (1994). Effects of Upbeat Stories in Broadcast News. *Journal of Broadcasting and Electronic Media*, 38:1, 65-78.

Zoglin, Richard, (1993). The Magazining of TV News. *Time*, July 12, 50-51.

———, (1996a). The Last TV Show. *Time*, August 26, 22.

———, (1996b). The News War. *Time*, October 21, 58-64.

Zuckerman, Mortimer, (1992). The Politics of Trivial Pursuit. *U.S. News and World Report*, February 24, 76.

———, (1993a). The Blind Eye of Television. *U.S. News and World Report*, January 18, 84.

———, (1993b). Clinton's Shaky Start. *U.S. News and World Report*, February 22, 70.

———, (1994a). It Does Not Pass the Smell Test. *U.S. News and World Report*, May 23, 82.

———, (1994b). *U.S. News and World Report*, July 12, 64.

———, (1994c). Limits of the TV Lens. *U.S. News and World Report*, July 25, 64.

Zuraik, David, and Christina Stoehr, (1993). Money Changes Everything. *American Journalism Review*, April 27-30.

Chapter 4

BROUGHT TO YOU BUY
America, Advertising, and the
Culture of Conspicuous Consumption

OVERVIEW

Starting in 1995 and for three successive years, President Clinton used the State of the Union Address to urge the tobacco industry to employ restraint in their marketing methods and in particular to refrain from the practice of using advertising and other techniques to promote cigarettes to children and teenagers. The president had every reason to be concerned. Those who doubt the ability of mass media to influence children and teens need only look at the case of Old Joe the Camel. After the cartoon camel figure was introduced, Camel income from sales to minors rose from $6 million to $476 million and adolescents' preference for the brand increased from 0.5 percent to 32 percent (Di Franza et al. 1991). The advertising blitz with funny money, T-shirts, and other paraphernalia featuring the cartoon logo provided the double whammy of all successful advertising: information and *motivation*. For an increasing number of America's young people, Joe Camel was *cool*, and they wanted to be like Joe. "There is no doubt," said Clinton, "that the billions of dollars spent on tobacco advertising creates a climate of friendly familiarity around tobacco and tobacco use" (1/31/97).

While millions of Americans supported the president's efforts to regulate the industry and make it more responsible, the attack on tobacco advertising has, for the most part, been an isolated one that has left other harmful products like alcohol virtually unchallenged.

❖**Reprinted from July 1, 1996, issue of**
***Business Week* by special permission.**
© 1996 by McGraw-Hill Companies.

From the perspective of some people, it is not only the products themselves that are harmful but the entire process and place of advertising in American society. Comparing advertising to a vampire and a virus, Leslie Savan argues that advertising "infects just about every organ of society" (1994, 1). In *The Sponsored Life* she describes a society in

119

which "commercial culture sells our own experiences back to us . . . reconstituted inside us, mixing the most intimate processes of individual thought with commercial values, rhythms and expectations," with the result that citizens are replaced by consumers "slowly recreated in the ad's image" (3). The Consumers Union believes that the continuous barrage of advertising assailing us has an impact on both young people and the environment they live in. It "encourages continuous consumption and acquisition at the expense of reasoned decision-making, thrift and environmental sensitivity. At a time when kids need to learn how to consume thoughtfully, numerous promotional messages are teaching the opposite" (1990, 5). This voice is echoed in *PTA Today*, the publication of the nation's parent-teacher organizations. "It is vital," they wrote, "that we help our children understand how to distinguish between **wants** and **need** and to be able to put them in a balanced perspective" (Rosenberg 1994, 5).

Ironically, while some look to the curriculum and classroom to help young people develop such skills, our schools themselves are increasingly becoming the site for advertising and commercial campaigns. In 1997, *U.S.A Today* reported that an increasing number of the nation's school systems, faced with declining tax dollars, had turned to selling advertising space in their schools. The Seattle system anticipated that they could create $1 million a year from such revenue. The idea was pioneered in Colorado Springs, Colorado, in 1993, and although the income has been less than they expected, they have still generated $226,000 from advertising in their system. Vending machines in schools have always been a form of promotion, but an increasing number of school buses, classrooms, and hallways now feature promotional materials for a variety of companies reaching out to the lucrative $100 billion market that teenagers alone represent.

While revenues gained from such advertising may help some schools provide better facilities and equipment, it is highly unlikely that those schools will foster an educational environment that asks students to critically distance themselves from the commercial culture that engulfs them. Comedian Dana Carvey quickly discovered the meaning of the adage "Don't bite the hand that feeds you" when he made fun of his

sponsor, Pepsi Taco Bell, only to discover soon after that he no longer had a show. Of greater significance is the ability of advertisers to silence and limit any unfavorable coverage of their methods, product, or industry. In the case of cigarette advertising in women's magazines, "editors confide that by accepting advertising, a magazine has entered into an implicit agreement not to criticize the product" (Whelan 1995, 13a). Publications are more likely to risk the health of their readers than their own fiscal health. This is not only true in broad-based entertainment magazines, but also in the mainstream press. FAIR (Fairness and Accuracy in Reporting) has documented soft coverage of the tobacco industry in publications like *Forbes* (Naurekas 1994). Any attempt to help students understand the content and form of television and other mass media without also exploring advertising ignores the context in which such messages are created and consumed. Estimates suggest that newspapers receive 75 percent of their revenues from advertisements, while mainstream magazines get about 50 percent and broadcasters almost 100 percent (Dines and Humez 1995). Those who bring us the program and publications also bring us the products. As one might expect, there is a clear relationship between the selling and the telling. In the case of television, "networks avoid that which will offend or dissatisfy advertisers. An advertiser's preferred program is one that allows full use of the products being advertised. The program should be a complimentary context for the ad" (Butsch 1995, 407).

While much attention in recent years has focused on the promotion of potentially harmful products like alcohol and tobacco, educators are increasingly addressing the attitudes and values behind the products. For some, it is the entire ethos and ideology of consumption that is problematic. David Korten (1995) describes the vicious cycle of alienation and spiritual emptiness associated with advertising. Marketing techniques continually suggest a problem/solution, desire/gratification process in which our personal void and emptiness can be solved by spending and consuming. Our personalities and our private selves are equated with products. In the words of Aurora Oldsmobile, "Is what you drive a reflection of who you are?" Believing that we can make our lives better by consuming, we seek to fill our emptiness or lack by purchasing a product. The purchase in turn requires that we spend more time making money in order to pay for the object of desire, which further alienates us from connection with our inner or authentic selves. For religious educators, a constant question and concern is how we raise children to have spiritual values in an era of rampant materialism. In the secular world of big bucks where he who dies with the most toys wins, "salevation" has become an acceptable substitute for salvation.

Wally Bowen at Citizens for Media Literacy believes that the message to consumers has even more subtle consequences. "An advertiser-driven popular culture emphasizes stories of individual conflict and gratification, and rarely tells the stories of citizens joining together to challenge the status quo" (1995, 7). Nor does Bowen believe the problem ends at America's borders. The global economy and the mass marketing of American products and values contribute to "the disappearance of authentic local cultures in a rising tide of

❖Advertising's impact on the spirit and presentation of the Olympic games in Atlanta in 1996 and the winter games in Nogano, Japan, in 1998 drew criticism. Used with permission of Grant E. Wilmoth.

global McCultures" (1). Mass media resistance to messages that question consumption is evident in the fact that American television networks and stations have routinely refused to run advertisements from groups promoting International Buy Nothing Day.

The expression "brought to you by" is more than a glib acknowledgment of the sponsor of a particular program or event. Increasingly, it describes American society and culture, as anyone who witnessed the commercial overkill of the Olympic Games in Atlanta can verify. Media literacy advocates are also quick to point out that any attempt to understand journalism, film, television, the Internet, or other media outlets requires a dedicated commitment to the principle that all media are commercial constructions. Scottish media educator Eddie Dick emphasized this fact to participants at the New Literacy conference in Canada in 1990. He asserted that advertising is central to the study of media, adding that the movement toward media education tends to be indicative of the health and open-mindedness of an education system as a whole.

Those who seriously wish to understand America, and to help others understand it, must sometime in their course of study explore the relationship between the nation and its advertisements. Writing in *The Image Makers: Power and Persuasion on Madison Avenue*, William Meyers says, "Ad Alleys wizards have firmly established themselves as *both the creators and controllers of our consumer culture* . . . they are virtually able to dictate the food we eat, the soda or beer we drink, the cigarettes we smoke, the cars we drive, even the Presidents we elect" (1984, 3-4). From the political perspective alone, any attempt to understand the controversy and scandal of foreign contributions in the 1996 presidential campaign must ultimately address the cost of campaigning, including political advertising budgets in key states like California and Florida. If the health of the nation is threatened by the commercial culture's stranglehold on the political process, the health of our children, adolescents, and minorities is also compromised. Naomi Wolf believes that images of women in advertising and mainstream media "flatten the feminine into beauty without intelligence or intelligence without beauty," noting that "women are allowed a body or a mind but not both" (1991, 59). Prisoners of perception, she says, will escape from this bondage not through lobbyists and placards, but by learning to see things differently. The Office of National Drug Control Policy also saw a relationship between liberty and literacy, endorsing media literacy in 1995 because "one can and should think for oneself" (27).

Helping students recognize, read, and reject manipulative messages in advertising is a vital and strategic way of fostering critical thinking skills, resulting in more responsible citizens and consumers, whether selecting a car or electing a president. While teenagers are frequently in denial, often rejecting the possibility that advertising might influence them, the evidence suggests otherwise. Research in this area indicates that "adolescents may have difficulty separating puffery from substantiated ad claims" and that "they appear to accept advertisers' claims as relevant criteria for their own and other's decisions" (Linn et al. 1984, 383). Adolescents also frequently derive pleasure from advertisements, and teachers need to be careful to avoid any heavy-handed approach that tells students advertising is bad. While adults often complain about commercials, there is evidence that here, too, we like them more than we are willing to admit. A 1996 study reported in *Advertising Age* said that about 57 percent of us think commercials are as enjoyable and entertaining as the shows, and 58 percent of us say the ads are helpful in keeping us informed.

Of course, just because we enjoy the advertisements is no reason to believe that we should accept the veracity of the claims they make or purchase the product they promote. In fact, techniques that entertain us while distracting us from logical consideration of the product or pitch may be the most valuable tools of persuasion. The ability to analyze and evaluate advertising, while clearly necessary, has become increasingly difficult because of both the growing number of these advertisements and the changing nature of commercials. A *Business Week* cover story called "The New Hucksterism" said, "In the postmodern advertising, sales pitches once clearly labeled have now been woven subtly into the culture, redefining what an ad is and where it takes place" (Kuntz 1996, 76). One case in point was Elizabeth Taylor's appearance on *The Nanny* and *High Society*. The story lines of these television programs advanced both a celebrity and her products. The cast of *Friends* appeared in character as part of a promotion for Diet Coke. Product placement, evident in movies, has also found its way to television. Helen Hunt reaches for a package clearly recognizable as Tums. Characters in *NYPD Blues* prefer Snapple. Kitchen Aid products and appliances are given prominence during episodes of *Cybill*. While these examples may seem harmless, they are all ways of manipulating objects and products into our consciousness without our knowledge. In the process, they avoid the distancing and tuning-out that many of us engage in when the commercials run. Just as significantly, by placing the objects in the homes and workplaces of characters with whom we are familiar, they create a form of celebrity endorsement that we do not consciously recognize or read as a sales pitch.

The Center for Media Education has also raised concerns about camouflaged commercials children and teens are likely to encounter on various websites. On-line microtargeting by companies like Frito-Lay and Nabisco often merge entertainment and commercial content and style, with the result that younger users may not know when they are being sold something. Lines or publications from companies like *Colors from Benetton* and *Guess Journal* are another innovative way of keeping a company name, image, and product in front of young consumers without the traditional appearance of an advertisement. One of the latest trends in the selling and promotion of products is what might be termed "virtual advertising." This form of electronic billboard not only operates in the United States, but is now marketed globally where areas of stadiums, sport sites, and arenas are sold to various markets, and ads targeted to those markets are programmed into that screen space. Once again, while we may tune in to watch a competition or event, we will be constantly reminded, consciously or otherwise, that this program has been brought to us buy.

Some Starting Statistics

Various estimates suggest that an average American is exposed to some 16,000 ads daily. In one form or another, these ads assail us from billboards, buses, park benches, public toilets, television, radio, newspapers, and magazines. More recently, this has included the Internet and audio advertising, to which we are subjected while waiting for our phone calls to go through. In a supermarket, we are surrounded by advertising in the form of packages. By the middle 1990s, 30,000 different packages could be found in supermarkets, an increase from 17,500 just a decade earlier. Networks ran 6,000 commercials a week, a 50 percent increase from 1983 (Kuntz 1996). The Olympic Games contributed to a record year for Madison Avenue in 1996. Advertising spending jumped more than 11 percent to $66.7 billion. Among the biggest spenders were Intel and Compaq computers, both spending in excess of $60 million. GM, an Olympic sponsor, spent the most of any company, forking out more than $1.7 billion for advertising. The beer industry spent $0.72 billion, while the tobacco industry budgeted $0.49 billion to promote its products (Wells 1997). On-line and website spending increased from $55 million in 1995 to $301 million the following year, of which $241 million was for promotional websites. The television advertisements also tout the websites. In one ad for laundry detergent, a young father explains that no one is ever really prepared for parenthood. His new chores include doing the laundry. Lucky for this young dad, he found the Tide website, which helps him understand what to do about chocolate pudding and other stains.

Curriculum Connections and Concerns

Drug Education. The drug problem in this country emerged in part out of a consumer culture that pushes and promises quick fixes and instant solutions. The consumer culture is a chemical culture that sells highs and lows from caffeine to sleeping pills. Trying to address the problem of illegal drug use necessitates consideration of the socially sanctioned drugs, including those that we generally regard as harmless. Attention should be given to how advertising promotes socially sanctioned drugs and our perception of them, as well as to the role PSAs (Public Service Announcements) can play in combating the drug problem. When Excedrin runs a campaign that says, "Life Got Tougher, So We Got Stronger," what message is being presented? Doesn't the statement, along with the accompanying image of a stressed-out woman, suggest that a chemical cure rather than a lifestyle change is an adequate response? Do messages like this perpetuate a reliance upon pharmaceuticals rather than asking us to take an inventory of our lifestyle and the way it contributes to our stress?

Alcohol Awareness. In 1989, Surgeon General C. Everett Koop called for a ban on alcohol advertising and was particularly critical of its impact on impressionable adolescents. Groups such as Mothers Against Drunk Driving (M.A.D.D.), Students Against Drunk Driving (S.A.D.D.), and Stop Marketing Alcohol on Radio and Television (S.M.A.R.T.) have all expressed concern about the social sanction afforded alcohol consumption in media and advertising that associates drinking with social success, athletic prowess, sex appeal, and good times. But in 1990, William Bennett said that he had been appointed drug czar, not health czar. Bennett argued he needed to focus on illegal hard drugs and that, although alcohol was a problem, it would only confuse and cloud the issue.

The Clinton administration waged a vigorous campaign against the tobacco industry's marketing techniques while leaving the brewing industry largely unchallenged. If Old Joe the Camel targeted children, similar claims could have been made about Spuds McKenzie or the Budweiser frogs. Why has alcohol advertising been less subject to challenge when a good case could be made that drunk driving, date rape, and other behaviors involving alcohol are just as dangerous if not more so than those associated with tobacco consumption?

Tobacco. In April 1997, a judge in North Carolina attracted national attention by ruling that tobacco was a drug and that as such, it could be regulated by the Food and Drug Administration (FDA). While the judge said the FDA had no power to regulate the advertising methods and techniques of the tobacco industry, his decision to classify tobacco as a drug was a blow to an already beleaguered industry. For President Clinton and former FDA head David Kessler, this had been a long, hard-fought battle. Previous Republican administrations had made similar recommendations that were rejected by Presidents Bush and Reagan. In 1990, then secretary of health Louis Sullivan had been particularly vocal in his criticism of cigarette advertising, drawing special attention to strategies used to target young women and blacks. While most discussion of cigarette advertising invariably shows up in health education courses, some consideration should also be given to the political process and lobbying that has protected the tobacco industry for years. This includes the role of the southern states in national politics and the ties of the tobacco industry to the Republican Party. Finally, tobacco could and should also be considered from a global perspective. Fighting tobacco's impact on American children while ignoring the damage it does to the people of the Third World ignores the ethical and moral considerations implicit in profiting from the export of a killer crop.

Sex Education. Attempting to address complex issues such as teen pregnancy, sexually transmitted diseases, and AIDS without considering the impact of advertising and the media in these areas ignores the entire cultural context in which sexual attitudes and behaviors are created. The Kaiser Foundation has concluded that "the media do play an important part in shaping American s' sexual beliefs, attitudes, and behaviors" (Brown and Steele 1995). As such, they are capable of challenging, contradicting, and subverting the curriculum of the classroom. Whether a school program stresses abstinence or safe sex, it will be a more effective program if it takes into account the sexual messages advertising sends to young people, providing them with the resistance/refusal skills necessary to avoid being manipulated by these messages.

Health Care. Beyond the world of tobacco, alcohol, and illegal drugs, the nation's health is strongly linked to marketing products and perceptions. This includes our physical fitness and appearance, as well as our self-esteem and self-image. Advertising has an impact on what we eat. It sells fast foods and a fast lifestyle. But do we really know what we eat and can we make informed decisions? On July 15, 1991, the cover story of *Time* was "Misleading Labels! Why Americans Don't Know What They're Eating." Advertising promotes diets and weight-loss programs for the overweight and creates an image of the ideal body for both men and women. The pursuit of "the look" keeps the consumer culture running, through the marketing of everything from cosmetics to exercise equipment. Bulimia, anorexia, and other eating disorders need to be considered at least in part against this background. For athletes, the competitive edge can be chemically induced, resulting in drug scandals that taint runners such as Ben Johnson or steroid abuse by football players such as Lyle Alzado. The greatest drug of all, and perhaps the most addictive, is the illusion of the quick fix promised by so much of the media.

Ecology, the Environment, and Pollution. Our lifestyles contribute to the problems of pollution and environmental damage. The products we use and the materials they are packaged in are often harmful and destructive. Twenty percent of the world's population in the industrialized G7 nations consume 70 percent of the world's resources, create two-thirds of the greenhouse gases, and release some 80 percent of CFCs and 65 percent of the sulphur and nitrogen gases. Legislation can change business and industry, but education is more likely to change human behavior. That means first recognizing our own role and responsibility in the ecosystem, acknowledging that if we are not part of the solution, we must be part of the problem. Consumer awareness has an important role to play in this process. The case of dolphin-safe tuna is an important one that shows how public perception and opinion can change industry behaviors. Green consumerism is a movement that has had success in changing production and marketing methods through education. Many environmental advocates believe that marketing methods must be changed if the environment is to be safe. "For American society to become ecologically sustainable, the narcissistic wounding of the public by the advertising industry will have to stop" (Kanner and Gomes 1995, 25).

The Political Process. U.S. schools traditionally assert that one of their functions is to prepare responsible citizens for their role in a democratic society. Given that the political process is now completely infused with advertising, marketing, image consultants, and polling, it is not possible for us to prepare students for an active role in this process without also helping them to become both critical viewers and critical thinkers.

Defining Advertising

(ELEM/MID/HIGH) — The best way to start a class that addresses advertising is quite probably to see what the class already knows or thinks it knows about advertising. Ask your students to develop a definition of advertising. Compare it to a dictionary definition. The American Marketing Association defines advertising as "any paid form of nonpersonal presentation and promotion of ideas, goods, or services by an identified sponsor" (Mandell 1984, 3). Jib Fowles picks up on this idea suggesting that "advertising refers to paid-for-messages that attempt to transfer symbols onto commodities to increase the likelihood that the commodities will be found appealing and be purchased" (1996, 3). For Stuart Ewen, advertising is "a process of creating commodity images for people to emulate and believe in" (1988, 91). These last two definitions suggest that while the purchaser thinks he or she is buying a product, in reality that product and its packaging symbolically represent a lifestyle, ideology, and value system that the consumer, consciously or otherwise, relates to.

Older students can explore these concepts while younger students can begin to distinguish between key terms in Mandell's definition, such as ideas, goods, and services. The Yellow Pages can be a very useful tool here, especially when students begin to think about advertising for services. Mandell also makes reference to "an identified sponsor." While consumers typically know what product or service is being advertised, we do not always know who is bringing us the ad. In the case of the milk mustache ads, we recognize the product, and in many cases the celebrity promoting the product, but how many consumers could correctly indicate that these ads are presented by the National Fluid Milk Processor Promotion Board?

Types of Advertising

(ELEM/MID/HIGH) — We have already learned that advertising promotes ideas, products, and services. These commercials are produced in many forms. Have the class develop a list of the various forms of advertising. The list should include:

- Print: Magazines and newspapers, including display and classified advertising.

- Radio: Commercial radio exists because of the presence of advertising.

- Billboards: Includes giant highway billboards as well as advertising on buses and other public transportation.

- Television advertising: This should include emerging forms of commercials, such as those that are now often in videos we rent or buy. The videos *Rain Man* and *Top Gun* both begin with this type of advertising.

- Product placement in movies and television: The deliberate visual and sometimes verbal reference to products during programs and movies. The manufacturers have paid to have their products seen in such situations. (See *Mr. Destiny*.)

Advantages and Disadvantages of Advertising

(MID/HIGH) — In a statement that would surprise some and alarm many, Joseph Turow has said that the advertising industry "exceeds the church and the school in its ability to promote images about our place in society—where we belong, why and how we should act towards others" (1997, 2). Further, he suggests that advertising talk and techniques have "been driving a profound sense of division in American society" (2). Is this what we think? Is this what our students think? Is it possible that advertising could be doing much more than providing products to people who want them?

Once our students have arrived at a definition of advertising, break them into groups so they can brainstorm the potential positive and negative effects of advertising. Older students might actually tackle this topic in the form of a debate. The following list touches on some of the topics that might be examined during this discussion.

Advantages

- Provides information about goods and services available
- Pays operating costs for television, newspapers, and magazines
- Employs thousands of people
- Reduces cost of goods by competition
- Improves the standard of living by supplying goods and materials
- Keeps the economy active

Disadvantages

- Trivializes the political process
- Promotes unhealthy products
- Encourages materialism
- Manipulates consumers
- Ruins the environment

TARGETING AND OTHER TOOLS AND TECHNIQUES OF THE TRADE

(MID/HIGH) — The next several pages explain various tools and techniques advertisers use in researching and preparing a campaign. Teachers can use this information to introduce students to appropriate marketing methods. The section also raises issues about the ethics of some forms of advertising and the possible consequences of these advertisements. Teachers can locate a selection of print and/or television ads to demonstrate these issues or assign students the task of locating ads of their own.

Distinguishing between two different media approaches and philosophies, Joseph Turow says, "Society-making media have acted out concerns and connections that people ought to share in a larger national community" while "segment-making media are those that encourage small slices of society to talk to themselves" (1997, 3). So long as both groups operated in balance, society, he suggests, was reasonably well served. Unfortunately, this balance is no longer operative. "The fundamental changes taking place in the television industry have been leading national advertisers, along with their ad agencies and media firms, in unprecedented attempts to search out and exploit differences between consumers" (4). Driving this, he says, is the shift from mass marketing to targeting, "which involves the intentional pursuit of specific segments of society" (4). Pick up a copy of any major marketing magazine (*Adweek, Advertising Age*) and you're likely to see the strategy at work along with all the tools of the trade arrayed to attract advertisers to particular programs and outlets.

Fox network promotes itself with an image of a flying stork carrying a television set. "We deliver almost as many kids as he does" the copy reads. Going on, the network declares, "We're good at hitting below the belt." NBC marketing announces that it's "The best way to find teens and tweens since the invention of the mall." Competitive Media Reporting warns its clients: "Technology is on the move. Don't get left at the dock. We can put strategic information in your hands in minutes—manipulated and organized in the way you want it. Our new digital encoding techniques track your commercials with near perfect accuracy." The *Chicago Sun Times* markets itself very skillfully in order to attract advertisers. In the county that counts, they say, "our bite is bigger." Using a graphic of a pie, the advertisement in *Advertising Age* (July 19, 1994, 39) plays on a series of references to food, appetite, and hunger. Their paper "delivers the biggest piece of Cook County . . . it not only carves out all of Chicago, but also the key affluent suburbs with a full 70 percent of metro area residents and over $440 billion in annual retail sales."

Generation X. One of the more recent examples of targeting by marketing differentiation is the so-called Generation X phenomenon. Karen Ritchie of McCann Erikson is generally credited with recognizing or creating this target group during a 1992 speech that proclaimed that there was life beyond baby boomers. What she identified was a segment of the population born between 1961 and 1981, 80 million strong, single, frequently still living at home, and with spending power of $150 billion. So came Generation X, the Twenty Somethings, or the Baby Busters, as they have variously been described. While it is relatively easy to analyze the number of individuals born during this period, their level of education, and their income, the attitudes frequently ascribed to the whole group are a generalization at best and a stereotype at worst. Alienated from mainstream culture, they have been described as overeducated, underemployed, and paradoxically "constituted by a group that deny its existence" (Hicks 1996, 74). Karen Ritchie, author of *Marketing to Generation X*, says they have a sense that "no one will look out for you so you have to look out for yourself" (1995, 5b). They learned not to believe what they saw on TV, and they have a penchant for the offbeat and obscure. They are, suggests Carolyn Hicks, "the archetypical post modern generation born and raised in a whirlwind of images with referents, at home in a world where everything is a commodity and simulations are more real than reality" (1996, 76). Reaching this group has often required extreme approaches and unconventional styles. Levi's Dockers enlisted *Spin Magazine* to promote block parties in major cities to sell their new line of Authentics khakis. The pants, they announced, were khakis with "a blue jean soul." Nike created an elaborate four-fold gate in unconventional type, on unconventional stock, that boldly asked, "Who the Hell Does Nike Think They Are?" It was followed inside by "Who the hell do you think you are?" Reebok introduced a silver-painted lesbian mountain biker. Mountain Dew enlisted Andre Agassi in a bungee-jumping piece, and Taco Bell followed the extreme marketing methods with a cliffhanging drama in which the hero is saved by the sheer strength of the company's cheese.

Psychographics and VALs (Values, Attitudes, and Lifestyles)

Most of us have a basic knowledge of demographics, or the science of statistics as applied to the composition of the human population. For marketers, demographics provide some useful information about the size of particular markets. This essentially means that advertisers have some sense of the number of potential customers or purchasers. When this is applied to television, networks guarantee advertisers a specific price per 1,000 viewers (CPM) in any designated demographic group. In 1997, for example, the cost of a 30-second spot targeted to 18- to 34-year-olds was $23.54 (per 1,000 viewers). On the other hand, viewers over 35 could be purchased for $9.57 (Vinzant 1997, 21).

Psychographics moves beyond raw numbers and broad categories based upon age or income. This process provides insights into the nature and needs of consumers, establishing elaborate psychological profiles for segments of the population. These profiles enable segmentation and fragmentation of the market so ads can be targeted more specifically to each broad consumer group. This means that the techniques used in the ads are specifically targeted at each group and run in magazines or during programs that would appeal to the group. Developed by the Stanford Research Institute, psychographics divides the nation into a series of VALs (Values, Attitudes, and Lifestyle) profiles. These include Belongers, Emulators, Societally Conscious Achievers, and other categories. Belongers are described as "the typical traditionalist, the cautious and conforming conservative. The lifeblood of the Belonger's world is a strong sense of community consciousness. Change is his arch enemy (Meyers 1984, 19). Constituting about 20 percent of the population, they are experimental and "will try anything" innovative so long as it fits in with their lifestyle. One way to begin spotting the psychology in the sales is to look at the way similar products are marketed with profoundly different moods or appeals. In the case of insurance, for example, there is a vast difference between the blunt, down-to-earth assurance provided by Prudential—"The Rock"—and the humorous comfort of an old friend offered by Met Life's use of Snoopy. While the clients being targeted will both purchase the same product, a very different psychological mind-set is being appealed to.

Clustering and PRIZM
(Potential Rating Index by Zip Markets)

Clustering is a process of computer-generated market research that arranges the country's 250,000 neighborhoods into 40-48 varying lifestyles. Developed by Jonathan Robbin and his Claritas Corporation, it took the country's postal zip codes and developed a marketing philosophy that essentially argued, "where you live determines how you live" (Weiss 1989, xvi). "Within each cluster of neighborhoods," it is argued, "inhabitants tend to lead similar lives, drive the same kind of cars to the same kind of jobs, discuss similar interests at similar social events" (2). The neighborhoods were assigned a quality rating, or ZQ, which expressed the value of life in that neighborhood, at least in terms of advertisers, on a scale from 1 to 40. The classifications included "Pools and Patios," "Furs and Station Wagons," "Back Country Folks," "Norma Rae Villes," "Blue Blood Estates," "Coalburg and Corntown," "Heartland America," "Young Influentials," and "Shotguns and Pickups." Such classifications, while broad and frequently offensively stereotypical, nonetheless provide a sociological and scientific strategy and "framework for making sense of our pluralistic society and finding our way around it" (3). Michael Weiss, author of *The Clustering of America*, says the technique can be used to "predict the lifestyle of residents with startling accuracy—from the brands of bread likely to be found in the pantry to the political bent of magazines on the coffee table" (40).

MARKETING RESEARCH

Any purchasing decision is based upon a combination of factors. Some of these are logical and rational, such as cost, quality, and relative usefulness of the product. We tend to be aware of these elements when making purchasing decisions. Part of the decision, however, depends upon less obvious factors such as the motivations and associations already discussed in this chapter. Advertisers have a clear picture of their audience. *Mirabella* magazine, for example, knows that 96 percent of its readers are women; 51 percent are married, and 49 percent are widowed. The median age is 41.4 and the median household income is $68,800. Eighty-three percent of the readers are college-educated and 69 percent own their own home. In addition to these demographics and psychological factors, advertisers are interested in the physiology of perception, particularly areas related to how the eye sees, what attracts its attention, and what factors influence recall and recognition. All of this information helps them determine how to package and display products. The technological approaches they use include:

1. Eye scanner: This machine reads eye movement and helps advertisers understand where the eye looks on a page or a TV screen so they can design advertisements to match this.

2. T-Scope: This machine measures recall, including objects and brand names. Ads are tested to make sure that they draw attention to the product and that the audience can recall the product or the brand, rather than only some person, phrase, or image in the ad.

3. Analog machine: Television commercials are tested by the analog machine. This is a form of joystick measurement device. People watch commercials and indicate a score for them, ranging from very dull to very good. The results are tallied by a computer and serve as an indication of the potential success of the commercial.

Hence, by measuring consumers and their reactions, marketers are more likely to develop techniques that get us to respond positively. It must be stressed that many of these techniques influence us without our knowledge. Several examples from real life demonstrate this. When Betty Crocker put a spoon on the packet, sales increased. Packaging changes for Scotch transparent tape, K Mart film, and Bubble Yum bubble gum also resulted in increased sales. People perceived that the products were somehow better, even though only the packaging had changed.

HIDDEN PERSUADERS AND SUBLIMINAL SEDUCTION

The foregoing discussion of VALs and market research indicates that advertisers know more about us than we know about them. They know what makes us tick, and because of that they are able to bombard us with messages that influence us without our knowledge. Sometimes what advertisers say to us is very direct, and the meaning of a commercial is obvious. An ad may tell us, "Use this product and you will appear to be wealthy and sophisticated." Or "Drink this and you will be young, athletic, and socially attractive." Other times, however, the meaning of a commercial is much more subtle, with the message embedded in the image or the text. These advertisements often appeal to us on the subconscious or unconscious level and induce responses of which we are not aware. Sometimes this occurs through the use of symbolism and other times through various subliminal images and messages embedded in the ad in such a way that we are not consciously aware of being exposed to them. The very concept of subliminal advertising is disturbing to many individuals. It is not uncommon to find students and adults who flatly deny even the possibility of such a technique. The reasons behind such denial are crucial. One has to do with the fact that recognizing the existence of subliminal advertising implies that we can be manipulated and, at the same time, that we are powerless against the media. Given our basic human need for security and self-direction, the concept of subliminal advertising can be quite threatening. Another reason the subject evokes such hostility and denial has to do with the fact that these hidden messages are often sexually oriented. Bryan Wilson Key articulates some of the problems associated with this topic in his book *Subliminal Seduction.* "Any investigation of the techniques of subconscious communication involves first an investigation into one's own fantasy systems, self-images, illusions, personal vanities, and secret motives. This is an investigation that might make even the toughest of us extremely uncomfortable" (1972, 1-2).

In *The Clam Plate Orgy and Other Subliminal Techniques for Manipulating Your Behavior* (1980), Key documents the widespread academic, political, and industrial opposition and denial he encountered in trying to raise consciousness about this process. Interestingly enough, *The Hidden Persuaders,* written by Vance Packard in 1957, addressed many of these concerns without provoking such opposition. One of Packard's chapters is called "The Psycho-Seduction of Children," and the opening of the book clearly recognizes the hidden forces at work in the marketplace. "This book is an attempt to explore a strange and rather exotic new area of American life. It is about the large scale efforts being made, often with impressive success, to channel our unthinking habits, our purchasing decisions, and our thought processes" (1957, 1).

Teachers who wish to introduce students to subliminal advertising must recognize some of these problems. In addition, most students go through a stage of reading too much into advertisements. This overenthusiasm needs to be tempered. It is, however, significantly better that they recognize the existence of subliminal advertising than it is for them to turn a blind eye to it. In subliminal advertising, more than in any other area, we need to acknowledge that, as consumers, not only is what we see not what we get, but also we do not "get" (understand) what we see. By the early 1990s, advertisers were beginning to spoof the idea of subliminal messages. Absolut vodka created an ad that read "Absolut Subliminal" and had a message in ice cubes. Seagram's gin created a print ad that asked, "Can You Find the Hidden Pleasure?" *Sports Illustrated* (7/15/91) featured a similar ad that urged readers to "Find the Hidden Refreshments" by connecting the dots in the glass. A more serious essay in *U.S. News and World Report* asserted that Newport's "Alive with Pleasure" cigarette campaign has "a strong undercurrent of sexual hostility, usually directed at women" (1991, 18). Tobacco and alcohol companies, the article said, "seem to resort to subliminal themes most frequently. Despite the industry's attempt to dismiss the whole idea of subliminal techniques by lampooning it, the reality is that advertising often works covertly, by playing on social symbols and cultural codes that we are not fully aware of."

Teachers wishing to pursue this topic with students should consult the books cited in the "References" section of this chapter. They have excellent visual examples of symbolism and subliminal techniques. Some examples of subliminal advertising are listed below.

1. Gilbey's gin, *Time*, July 5, 1971. This famous advertisement has been widely analyzed for its subliminal techniques. Among these, perhaps the best known and most discernible is the spelling of *sex* by placing one letter in each of the three ice cubes in the glass shown in the ad. Key's (1972) work also talks about the subliminal imagery of drowning faces in liquor ads. These images supposedly appeal to the death wish of alcoholics.

2. Benetton clothing. This more recent print advertisement is likely to appear in magazines such as *Rolling Stone* and *Premier*. The ad draws upon biblical symbolism by invoking the story of Adam and Eve. In it, a teenage male and female are depicted from the waist up. The male wears blue jeans but no shirt. The female wears an open jean jacket with nothing on underneath, and the top button of her jeans is undone. She is offering the boy an apple. A snake is wrapped around her neck, and its head, with the mouth open, hovers over her breast. Nothing is said at all about Benetton or their products. The entire ad operates upon a mythical and symbolic level.

3. Edge shaving cream featured a startling ad for a brief time in *Rolling Stone* magazine. The slogan of the ad is "Not Your Ordinary Shave." The top half of the page is dominated by a man's face covered with shaving cream. His eyes are closed, and he has a pleasurable smile on his face. In the bottom right of the frame, a hand holds a can of shaving cream. To the left is an image of a surfer with a mountain sunset behind him, and to the surfer's left is the image of a woman's face partly obscured in shaving cream and surf. The real activity, however, is in the man's face. Although the ad was eventually airbrushed and toned down, initially it featured quite discernible sexual images. What appeared to be mountains was actually a naked woman on her back with her knees raised. The shaving cream on the man's upper lip contained several pictures of naked women and at least one penis. Perhaps this is what the ad meant when it said, "You get everything you might expect in a clean close shave and something you didn't."

"Baad Sells": Information, Motivation, and Feelings

As a recent cover story in *Forbes* noted, "Baad Sells." While the story alludes to a basic marketing method used to push products, it must be noted from the outset that it is often very difficult for young people to distinguish between the product they purchase and the attitude, lifestyle, and value system that promote the product and vice versa. Herein lies the failure of the cognitive classroom and curriculum to address the substance-abuse problems associated with the consumption of tobacco, alcohol, and other harmful materials. The child sitting in such a classroom can dutifully record, repeat, and explain all the negative facts and dangerous consequences involved in the use and abuse of these products. The same child can score very well on a test regarding these dangers and then go home to indulge in the use of the products. The problem in the cognitive classroom and with the information deficit model is that it assumed that once kids knew something, it would change their behavior. In reality their behavior is not based on what they *know* about products, but rather on how they *feel* about them. Hence, if cigarettes make them feel cool, or proclaim their independence and individuality, they are likely to incorporate them into their behavior. One very obvious example of a television ad that celebrates attitude and lifestyle at the same time that it sells its product was created for Apple computers in 1997. Shot in black and white and consisting of a series of images of famous people, including Einstein, John Lennon, and Muhammad Ali, the voice-over promotes individualism. "Here's to the crazy ones . . . the rebels . . . the misfits." The punchline said simply, "Think Different."

Any attempt to understand how advertising works must go well beyond the products and information that advertising provides the consumer, addressing the real punch, which lies in the motivation provided by the ads. In *Advertising and Popular Culture*, Jib Fowles describes these two aspects at work within the industry as "an unresolved conflict between research information and creative execution" (1996, 79). In seeking to reach the consumer, he says, the advertising agency and its client must recognize two components: "One is the area of the mind governing the individual as a social creature, and the other is the area of the mind housing basic instincts, impulses, drives, and needs" (93). Almost nothing in the strategy involves the quiet, thoughtful, rational articulation of a series of facts designed to persuade the consumer to use the product. "Increasing numbers of commercials provide the viewer with an entertainment experience rather than information about tangible product attributes" (Hitchon and Thorson 1995, 376). If viewers vote with loyalty or channel changing, they clearly endorse this approach. "The least zapped commercials on TV are the fast paced lavishly produced soft drink spots that lean heavily on entertainment and little on product attributes" (Kuntz 1996, 78). What works then—and the research is clear on this—is a series of skillfully edited images, with an appropriate soundtrack that will first get the viewer to pay attention and then get the viewer to respond. This effective avenue has proved to be an important strategy. Researchers have concluded that "emotional messages were significantly better remembered than non emotional messages" (Hitchon and Thorson, 386). It is important to recognize that adults as well as children are targeted by this process. Our feelings and emotions are frequently exploited, often in thoroughly enjoyable ways, by products we tend to regard as acceptable. In the case of Hallmark greeting cards, one company spot is a combination Currier and Ives meets the Waltons. Set on Christmas Eve somewhere in the snowy landscape of middle America, it presents a portrait of an extended family and a young boy awaiting the return of his older brother. By the time the two boys sing "Oh Holy Night," there is not a dry eye in the house. Dupont co-opted Beethoven's "Ode to Joy," a piece normally associated with religion, for their own commercial purposes, using it against a montage of Alaskan wildlife. Both of these television commercials are enjoyable and entertaining. They are also emotionally moving and therefore potentially harmful because they make us feel. Only the most hardened cynic can resist the skillful combination of image and music presented in these commercials. If these techniques can be used to sell us relatively harmless products like greeting cards, the same devices can be used to promote products that are much more problematic. A powerful advertisement for Apache helicopters, for example, employs images reminiscent of Batman and the hymn "Amazing Grace" to sweep its target audience up in the emotion of the moment. In *Selling Weapons*, a program from America's Defense Monitor, critics complain that techniques such as these enable munitions manufacturers to bypass logical questions such as what the weapon will do, why it is needed, and of course, what the money could be spent on if it didn't go for weapons. If it feels good, buy it!

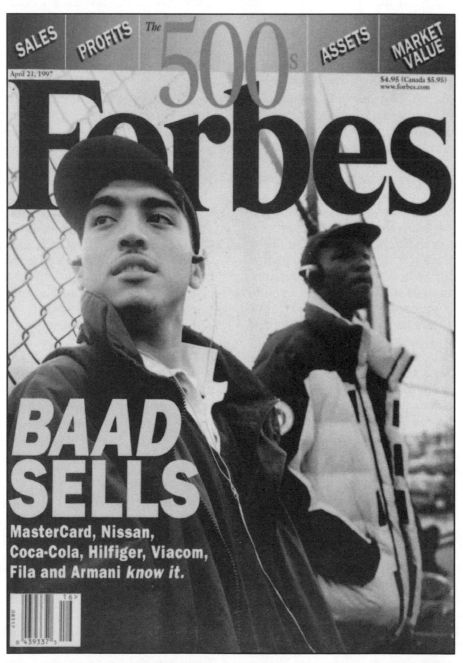

❖**Reprinted by permission of FORBES Magazine © Forbes Inc., 1997. Photography by Danny Clinch.**

The Ideology of Indulgence:
Live with Abandon

"How can I fill the void of emptiness?" the ad for Boston Market asks. The answer, for anyone conversant with the world of advertising in the late 1990s, is to consume conspicuously. But it will take more than fast food to fill our void. Only through the relentless pursuit of the look and the label can we establish our identity and proclaim it to the world. Niche marketing or lifestyle advertising assures us that we are what we consume. One of the most consistent messages pervading advertising today, irrespective of whether the product is a car, a cologne, or a hamburger, is the theme of individuality, indulgence, and a complete absence of self-restraint. Parents, teachers, counselors, and those concerned with providing young people with a focus, a framework, and a future that involves working hard and delayed gratification, should look beneath the surface of seemingly harmless products and examine the philosophy being espoused. Burger King says, "Whatever lights your fire," "Express yourself," and boldly proclaims its philosophy, which seems to be "Give the people what they want." AT&T promises that "it's all within your reach." Calvin Klein tells us to "Just Be." Of course, we are all better at being with CK on our backsides, chests, and elsewhere. Allegra, an anti-allergy product, advises us to "Live with Abandon." But abandonment comes with an attitude and consequences. Mary Pipher, a therapist and the author of *Reviving Ophelia*, believes that mass marketing to children turns their dreams into shopping lists. Moreover, these kids don't just purchase products, they buy into the attitude the products represent. Increasingly, she reports, teachers across the country tell her that children are "less polite, less able to approach another child in a friendly manner, more likely to use the 'F' word, say something sexual, or interrupt when others are talking" (Donahue 1996, 2). While parental influence and home life obviously play a major role in the way children behave, there's little doubt that Madison Avenue, in the name of profit, markets and models some questionable values and behaviors. Urban black culture, initially ignored by marketers, has now become fashionable. *Forbes* put it this way: "Main Street meets Mean Street. The badass attitude that springs from the pavement cracks sells everywhere these days" (Levine 1997, 142). More cynically, they said, "Corporate America's inner city lust is really about . . . a black market with $325 billion in spending power that cares intensely about brand names and the pipe dreams they inspire" (144). But if young people find Tommy Hilfiger and Fila inspiring, others are less impressed. Writing in *U.S. News and World Report*, John Leo complained about these messages and advertisers who are "focusing more and more on the emerging market of people who do only what they want to do; that is people who yearn to be free of all restraint, expectations and responsibilities" (1995, 31). Citing Nike's "Just Do It" and Burger King's "Sometimes You Gotta Break the Rules" as examples, he describes the growth of a hedonistic, self-centered society that represents the rise of individual indulgence and the decline of core values. In a strongly worded attack on the industry's techniques and consequences, Leo said: "By pushing self-obsession, narcissism and contempt for all the rules, they strike at the sense of connectedness that any society needs to cohere and to care about its common problems. It's time to call the corporations and ad agencies on this. They are busy financing our social meltdown" (31).

THE NEED TO READ ADVERTISEMENTS:
A Critical Framework

(ELEM/MID/HIGH) — This is a crucial component of the chapter that can be used in great depth with middle and high school students and with less detail with elementary school students. Using the transparency master (Fig. 4.1), teachers can introduce students to each component of the framework and either provide their own examples of these techniques or assign students the task of finding ads that demonstrate the concepts.

In their hit song "The Grand Illusion," Styx provided a message suitable for any introductory class on advertising. "Don't be fooled by the radio, the TV, or the magazines. They'll sell you photographs of how your life should be, but they're just someone else's fantasy." Helping young people recognize and read the communication tools and propaganda techniques employed in advertising can provide them with the skills to resist potentially harmful messages. It can also deepen their understanding and awareness of commercial communication so they can more fully appreciate and value these methods when they are used in constructive ways. At the outset, while young people are typically interested in advertising, they tend to resist or deny any assertion that they themselves are manipulated by ads. Many of them also tend to believe that what you see is what you get. In reality, as media educators know, there's more to it than meets the eye.

Beginning to teach young people to think critically about the form, content, and consequences of advertising is a process of distance learning that asks them to step back from the commercial culture that surrounds them and look at it from a different perspective. The problem, of course, is that advertisements are omnipresent. "They are woven so tightly into everyday life that to hold them at an objective distance and to comprehend them is not easy. The scrutineer is lulled into complacency by their familiar surfaces" (Fowles 1996, 20). It is also apparent that when properly presented, critical viewing skills curriculum initiatives can "have far reaching results" proving that previously held "beliefs are not immutable to change" (Austin and Johnson 1997). Interestingly enough, it has also been shown that the use of saturation advertising, that is, using fire to fight fire, can be effective in combating and changing attitudes. In the case of cigarettes, for example, anti-tobacco advertising "was accompanied by significant normative changes over one year" and "more negative attitudes towards drugs" (Hawkins, Catalano and Miller 1992). While advertising may therefore be seen as a problem by many people in our society, it can also be part of the solution. For that to happen, we need a more critical understanding of how it works.

Fig. 4.1. A Critical Framework for Understanding Advertising (TRANSPARENCY MASTER)

- PRODUCT   - PLACEMENT

- PACKAGE   - PURCHASER

- PITCH/PERSUASION

Elements in Understanding Advertising

Product. Most children, especially younger ones, will start with the perception that advertising is used to promote things in packages they can find on shelves. Given the way they themselves are targeted by advertisers, it is likely that any initial list of products advertised generated by students will include toys, soda, and fast food. One way to expand this list is to ask them to think about what type of products are advertised during particular programs such as football and basketball broadcasts. By now your list should start to include cars, trucks, insurance, and, of course, beer. Using Mandell's definition of advertising, we also note that ideas and services are promoted. If students struggle with this, give them copies of pages from a Yellow Pages directory so they can identify services that are advertised. Older students can discuss effective and ineffective PSAs such as "This Is Your Brain. This Is Your Brain on Drugs." In election years, they can also explore political advertising and monitor and watch features in national and state newspapers. There are also plenty of opportunities for them to explore public relations and the way major corporations try to present themselves to the public through PR campaigns. Examples of these slogans are Dupont's (Better Things for Better Living), Dow's (Lets You Do Good Things), and GE's (We Bring Good Things to Life).

Package. Understanding that the package is part of the promotion is essential to any understanding of how advertising works. As we have already seen, techniques such as the eye scanner and Tscope (used to measure recall of images) are important in shaping an ad. They also provide input and guidance that determines the shape, size, and color of the package in which the product comes. Some of the principles involved are technical considerations related to visibility and graphic design. Restaurants, hotels, and many businesses, especially those on busy roads and highways, frequently use combinations of yellow, black, and orange on their signs and billboards so they can be read from a distance by drivers in moving vehicles. Foreground and background in such signs and in smaller packages must have high contrast for readability. But beyond the science of optics,

there is also the psychology in sales and packaging. Men tend to be attracted to images that are hard ("Like a Rock"?), while women prefer softer images. Cool and hot colors must be clearly distinguished and applied to appropriate products. Red, for example, would not be appropriate in the promotion or packaging of a sun-care product. Cereal packets are almost uniformly common in their size, shape, and appearance. Perfumes, colognes, and antiperspirants, on the other hand, vary quite a lot though they are frequently sensuous and often phallic. Once a particular marketing trend has proven to be successful, many manufacturers of the same product will follow the pattern. The success of the longneck beer bottle is one example. CDs initially came in a long narrow package, with the disc at the bottom of the rectangular-shaped packaging. This has been phased out at considerable savings to the manufacturer, not to mention the environment.

Pitch/Persuasion. Most of the time advertising tends to be consumer-centered rather than product-centered. In other words, advertising increasingly tells us less factual information about the actual product, concentrating instead on packaging attitudes and values that appeal to the consumer and are associated with the product and its possession and/or consumption. Jib Fowles distinguishes between commodity advertising when the promotion connects directly to the commodity and its properties, and compound advertising when, in addition to the product or commodity, we are also given characteristics and connections that are external to the product but that become associated with it. Typically this involves some form of symbolism. It was not an accident that Energizer chose a rabbit for its successful battery campaign. "The symbolizing rabbit has always dwelled in the thicket of intertextual references . . . a powerful and ready made symbol for potency, renewal, endurance" (Fowles 1996, 4). In the case of cigarettes, Marlboro, initially targeted at women, failed, only to re-invent itself through the Marlboro Man. Frederick Jackson Turner's frontier thesis, with its emphasis on rugged individualism, is inherent in the American character and psyche that Marlboro tapped into. The cowboy motif and masculinity also became part of a pitch for Chevy Malibu that asserted, "this is not a country for wimps."

An extremely simple way to help students distinguish between commodity and compound advertising is to give them a series of magazine advertisements to work with. Whether dealing with cigarettes, alcohol, clothes, or most other products, much of the text and a good deal of the image will be about something other than the product. Frequently the product and the package are small, while the people and the place are emphasized. An ad for Capri cigarettes shows a woman in an exotic and elegant setting, dressed in a sumptuous gown. The text tells us that she's going to Capri and is going to stay there. While it is clearly a reference to changing brands, very little in the picture or print contributes to providing factual information about the product. Even when a product is visually emphasized, dominating a page, it is typically surrounded by other detail that contributes heavily to the message and the meaning. The bottle in a Passport Scotch ad dominates the frame, but the meaning is carried and conveyed by the props, which include silver coasters, crystal glasses, a castle, a passport, a park bench, two people, and a series of crests and insignias on the label of the bottle. The presence of people within the frame and sometimes out of the frame is crucial to setting the social milieu in which consumption occurs, which is one reason why attempts to regulate cigarette advertising in the United States and other countries have included removing people from the commercials. Cigarette, alcohol, and even fast food advertising tends to show us healthy, energetic, popular individuals consuming these products. In reality, of course, consumption of these products can frequently have very different consequences, including both unhealthy and unsociable results. Examination of still and moving advertising can help students recognize the various pitches and persuasions the advertising industry uses to promote their products. The following list includes some of the approaches most commonly used.

1. *Humor.* This is used very successfully for a wide variety of products and will frequently show up as a favorite type of ad when talking to students about what appeals to them. Joe Isuzu and the Energizer Rabbit are two examples. Pepsi's ad featuring bears dancing in the main street of a U.S. town is another popular campaign. Recently, there has been a tendency to include what might be termed "bathroom humor" in this approach. A squadron of birds flies in formation to soil a car while the background soundtrack plays "Danger Zone." Grey Poupon employs sounds of flatulence promoting their squeeze bottle in the "Pardon my Poupon" spot. Infiniti attempts to laugh at death by creating a television ad set during a funeral. A grieving widow cries as her husband is lowered into the grave. The humor comes from the fact that he's buried sitting up in his car. It's not the spouse she has lost that she cries about, it is the car she is really going to miss!

2. *Everybody's Doing It.* Ironically, as Leslie Savan notes, advertising involved in the process of shepherding masses is riddled by a basic paradox, which "is to say 'Join Us and Become Unique' " (1994). The sales pitch essentially uses peer pressure and the need to belong as a method of promoting the product. It often tends to focus on belonging to the "in crowd." Dr. Pepper got good mileage out of a campaign that asked, "Wouldn't You Like to Be a Pepper, Too?" Oddly enough, the consumer here was completely associated with the product, ultimately becoming one of Pepper's people.

3. *Fear and Insecurities.* Slice-of-death commercials that draw on fears and insecurities are often grainy and shot with a hand-held camera to create an unsteady cinema verité look. People in the ads appear threatened and uncomfortable. They are often sitting in boardrooms talking about the failure of a computer or

telephone system and the competition they face. AT&T and Macintosh have created good examples of this technique. Unfortunately, it is a method that is too often used to sell technology. As such, it is highly manipulative, selling by intimidation and often preventing consumers, including teachers and educators, from asking real questions about the technology. An IBM print ad shows a worried executive. The text asks if a 14-year-old sociopath will bring the company to its knees. The pitch is for a security system that hackers can't penetrate. The method, however, is potentially quite disturbing. A television ad for technology depicts a young girl (Anna Pacquin) in a snowy roadside scene beside an abandoned outdated car. She is lost, alone, and stranded in the wilderness, and the camera moves in on her face as she speaks these words: "On the information superhighway, there are no hitchhikers. There are no speed limits. There are no rest stops. There are no troopers. But there will be a passing lane; a passing lane." On the screen, the words "Network MCI" appear. Otherwise we are told absolutely nothing about the product or service. We are clearly, nonetheless, meant to believe that without that service, we will be in a technological wilderness. Home security systems also frequently market themselves through fear, anxiety, and insecurity, as does The Club, a product used to prevent automobile theft. Even Listerine now presents itself in an ad shot partly in black and white as protection from that mouth menace, gingivitis. Financial fear and insecurity are the subtext of an advertisement for Charles Schwab, which contains the line "Maybe somebody made some money. It wasn't me."

4. *Celebrity Endorsement.* The testimonial approach, represented by the use of famous people, is easily recognized and particularly influential with children and teens who frequently equate liking a person with a good product. Of course, just because a celebrity promotes a product does not mean that either that person or the product are necessarily what they purport to be. When the real-life persona of the celebrity clashes with the image of the product and the company that creates it, the celebrity is typically dropped. Michael Jackson and O. J. Simpson, who have made millions from product endorsements, now make very little because of problems in their private and public lives. In the 1990s, lipsticks have been created using the names of celebrities Madonna, Rosie, Anjelica, and Whoopi. One of the most enduring promoters for a product has been Bill Cosby's association with Jello. With the company since 1974, the entertainer and his image have contributed to the success story, which brings in $775 million a year and has the product in three out of four American homes. Another area where celebrity endorsement is evident is sports. Golf sensation Tiger Woods is doing extremely well from this connection. Interestingly enough, not all sporting success results in endorsements and sponsorships. Asian Americans like tennis star Michael Chang and skater Kristi Yamaguchi, while attracting some interest, have not attracted the advertising dollars of other sports heroes. The Olympic Games are now routinely scrutinized in terms of which athlete will end up on the Wheaties box. After the games in Atlanta, the honor was shared by Kerri Strug, Michael Johnson, and Dan O'Brien. Even politicians have

gotten into the act. Following his loss in the 1996 presidential election, Bob Dole debuted in a credit card spot during the 1997 Super Bowl. The line he uttered: "I just can't seem to win." In the campaign itself, both President Clinton and Senator Dole showed up in print ads with milky mustaches.

5. *Sex Appeal.* Like it or not, sex sells, and advertisers have long recognized and exploited the fact to sell everything from cars to toothpaste and underwear. Burger King even used the song "You Sexy Thing" to promote their chicken sandwich. Given concern about teen pregnancy, AIDS, and other STDs (sexually transmitted diseases), advertisers should exercise restraint and responsibility in using sexual situations and scenarios to promote products that would appeal to young people. Calvin Klein has pushed the boundaries of good taste and exploitation to such an extent that his images and methods have been accused of being kiddie porn, and he has been the target of criminal investigations. A lot of the time, however, sex appeal in advertising is less blatant, based less on the display of nude or semi-nude bodies. Frequently, innuendo is used in the text to imply a sexual situation. In England, a bed manufacturer claimed their product would be pleasing "everytime you make it." The language of sex and sport has often intersected in the United States, with manufacturers talking about sexual success in terms of "scoring" and various degrees of success described as "getting to first base" and so on. It is hardly surprising, then, to find this ambiguous copy in an ad for Jockey briefs: A handsome male model, wearing only the manufacturer's product, looks out at the viewer with a self-satisfied smile. The text reads: "Hot streak. Made the point. Played it right. Couldn't miss. I was in that zone. When things are right. Things are right." Health and sexuality are often combined in a sales pitch. Soloflex promoted their fitness equipment with an image of a taut male torso and the slogan "a hard man is good to find." Today, some shampoo manufacturers suggest by the oohs and aahs emitting from the shower stall that their product is not only organic but quite simply orgasmic. Though women have traditionally been positioned as sex objects for the gaze of men, there have been times when the male has been positioned this way or even sexually deflated. Hyundai featured an ad that equated a man with a car. Women in the spot reflected on how a man's choice of automobile said something about him. The dialogue included phrases such as "Wonder what he's got under the hood" and "He must be overcompensating for a shortcoming." This gender-bending message was not appreciated by some males. John Leo complained that "the traditional phallic symbols of the ad business—pool cues, hoses, cameras, and so forth are mostly held by women," and he added, "We don't need sexual sniper fire from the ad industry" (1993, 25).

6. *Exotic Places.* These ads tend to blend fact and fantasy to sell a "lifestyles of the rich and famous" escape. Carnival Cruises is a simple example of such escapism.

7. *Something for Nothing.* These include standard "buy one, get one free" claims as well as all sorts of premiums and give-aways. Competitions and the chance to win something are also part of this technique. In summer 1990, Coca Cola's "magic" cans promised money and prizes.

8. *Plain Folks.* Essentially, these ads operate on a populist, no-frills approach and tend to present average-looking people to convince us of the honesty and authenticity of the product. Ads for Bartles and Jaymes wine coolers, with their laid-back style, demonstrate this technique quite well. So, too, does a recent McDonald's ad in which a teenage boy explains to his date that he has simple tastes. This leads into the "food, folks, and fun" McDonald's slogan.

9. *Happy Families.* These often tend to use a slice-of-life approach, creating vignettes of family life to sell a product. This might include parents seeing a teenage daughter off on her first date or an older brother taking his sister out for hamburgers.

10. *Value and Reliability.* These ads stress logic over associations, pitching both the quality of the goods and their reasonable prices.

11. *Science and Statistics.* These are usually recognized through claims such as "9 out of 10 dentists surveyed" or "recommended by more people." Students need to be introduced to the ways in which such statistics and claims can be misleading. Scientific persuasion tends to include phrases such as "new and improved" or "secret ingredients" or images and phrases that promote a technological and scientific mystique that preempts critical evaluations of the claims or the product.

12. *Health and Nature.* These ads either state or imply that a product contributes to your health and well-being. Claims such as "all natural" or "no preservatives added" are typical. So, too, are suggestions that use of the product will somehow improve your performance. One example is the beer slogan "Bring Out Your Best." Sometimes the claims that a product is natural are quite the opposite. Just For Men hair color, for example, promises "the look of your *natural* color in just 5 minutes." Of course, gray is the natural color being disguised.

13. *Negative and Comparison.* Other appeals tend to include "tastes good," "good for you," and the promise of status or a successful career. Negative or comparison ads have dealt with everything from political mudslinging to selling cars. They are interesting because they actually name the competition. One hamburger chain featured a clown in the background, obviously to invoke the image of McDonald's in an ad suggesting that some hamburger places packaged food in funny boxes and charged prices that were less than funny. A recent television ad for Volkswagen compared the car favorably to both Volvo and the Honda Accord. Imodium A-D disparagingly referred to its competition as "the pink stuff." A radio spot for Ovaltine specifically names the competitor, Quick, when the female character announces, "I'm not a kid anymore." Her point, quite simply, is that she has outgrown the competition and needs a more adult but equally chocolatey drink.

Placement. As we have seen, techniques such as clustering, demographics, and psychographics are employed as part of the science, psychology, and sociology of advertising. They are used not simply to design a good package or develop a great pitch, but to make sure that the message is placed in a position where the potential consumer will see it. Students intuitively understand this. Ask them what type of show will feature ads for cereals, toys, fast food, and action figures, and they will pinpoint Saturday morning cartoons. Ask them what programs will feature ads for douches and feminine hygiene products, and they will tell you soaps. Reverse the process and tell them they are creating ads for trucks, beer, and insurance.

Their task is to determine where they will place those spots to reach their target audience. If they conceptualize advertising as an arrow, they can have a great bow and a great arrow, but until they learn to aim, they will not hit their target. How do advertisers position and place their commercials in order to maximize the penetration of this message?

Purchaser. Closely related to the concept of placement is the purchaser targeted by the ad and the way it has been positioned. *Essence*, *Ebony*, and *Jet* magazines are clearly not intended for the majority of the reading public. The stories they contain and the ads in them address the African-American community and certain economic and gender segments of that community. *Young Modern* and *Seventeen* are obviously for a very different group of consumers. While this seems obvious, many students would look at advertisements in these magazines only in terms of the products they promote. By applying the purchaser component of this critical framework for analyzing advertising, we can get them to see that looking at the product actually helps them see the people at whom the product is aimed. Frequently this can be achieved by simply looking at the people in the ads. How old are they? What type of clothes do they wear? What do they drive? What is the setting or location in which we find them? What does any of this tell us about their income, social circumstances, or occupation? This technique can be used with still advertisements in magazines as well as with television commercials. Remember, in the case of TV commercials, the reflection of the people in the ads is likely to serve as a fairly good signal of the type of people sponsors think are watching the program.

Decoding Advertising Images: Visual Literacy Techniques

(ELEM/MID/HIGH) — Much of the previous discussion, which provides a critical framework for analyzing advertising relies upon the words used in commercials and what is actually said in these ads. But a lot of what goes on in commercials happens visually. Nonverbal communication constitutes a good deal of the communication at work in commercials. The techniques and visual vocabulary employed in advertising have their origins in art and photography. These techniques are quite evident in children's picture books (Considine, Haley, and Lacy 1994). Teachers in elementary school can compare and contrast the presence of posture, position, point of view, and other elements in both picture books and advertising. These techniques are described in detail in Chapter 6.

Decoding advertisements with these techniques moves through a series of stages:

1. *Image:* The initially constructed picture.

2. *Identification:* The simple process of recognizing the various objects used in constructing the composition, such as two people, a bottle of wine, a sports car, and a highway. This process is restricted to recognizing the internal elements of the frame.

3. *Interpretation:* In this process, we move from isolating the individual elements and their literal meanings to a consideration of their cumulative statement and cultural context. This includes the symbolic, metaphorical, and mythical meanings of any ad. In this step we move from recognizing to reading and comprehending. It includes reading the relationships among figures and objects in the frame as well as reading their external, social, and cultural references.

4. *Influence:* Our ability to recognize and read the process by which advertisements and other visuals are constructed potentially empowers us. It helps to demystify the media and reveal the ideological messages embedded in advertisements. It helps us recognize the concealed and cumulative nature of these messages and their potential social impact. Finally, we have

the opportunity to use such visual techniques in our own creations and communications.

Several visual devices can be isolated that enable us to analyze the composition and content of visual messages in still or moving form. A basic beginning might be called the "four P" approach.

1. *Posture:* Gestures, facial expressions, and posture often convey a lot about moods, feelings, and attitudes. Students can be taught to "read" this body language and act out their own moods through posture.

2. *Point of view:* Generally established by the placement of the camera. Tilt-ups make the subject strong, forceful, sometimes threatening, and very often masculine. Tilt-downs render the subject weak, vulnerable, sometimes frightened, and more often than not, feminine.

3. *Position:* The location of an object or person in the frame often contributes to the meaning. A person at the head of a staircase, for example, is usually in a stronger position than one at the foot of a staircase. A bottle on a table is one thing, but a bottle placed in a man's crotch, as it is in a Salem cigarette ad, says something else altogether.

4. *Prop:* When the physical object has a symbolic or metaphysical meaning. This can be something as simple as color symbolism or as loaded as sexual symbolism invoked by images of the biblical apple and snake. (For more information, see the "Mise-en-Scene" section in Chapter 6.)

Sample Decoding

(MID/HIGH) — An example of this process of decoding can be seen in a print ad for Passport scotch. The key slogan of the ad is "Because You Enjoy Going First Class." This could actually be covered or cut out of the ad, and students would still be able to read the visuals to see how status and sophistication are used to promote the product. At the identification stage, students would analyze the elements of the picture. These consist of a bottle of scotch, glasses, serving trays, a passport, and a building in the background. Having the students interpret the elements develops their analytical skills and their critical thinking, as a result of which they decode the meaning behind the ad. The bottle dominates the frame. However, the label on the bottle is deliberately designed to reiterate the message. It consists of a series of shields and insignias that suggest nobility or royalty. The glasses are expensive crystal, and they sit on silver coasters. The building in the background suggests a European castle or estate. Every element in the frame, therefore, contributes to the elite message. Using this example with students, ask them to develop a profile of the consumer this ad targets and the type of magazine in which it might appear.

So far, we have looked at the broad stages involved in reading advertisements. But what exactly are we reading? Applying the four P's to the broad elements of advertising helps us to translate both static (print) and dynamic (television) advertisements. These elements are:

- *Graphics.* The graphics consist of picture and print or text. Attention is focused on the design and composition of the frame. This might include the number of words, the size of the print, the position of the print, the shape of the package, the color of the object or text, and the sharpness or softness of the focus. Graphic design includes shapes of objects and their position or place within the composition. When dealing with words, consideration should be given not just to what is said or stated, but also to how it is said (tone, mood, etc.) and who says it. In the case of television ads, for example, one study of 1,000 commercials using voice-over found that 86 percent of the voices were male. What does this suggest about the structure of the advertising industry, the targeted consumers, and social relations as a whole?

- *People.* What sort of people appear in the ad? What age are they? Are age groups evenly represented in advertisements, or do they tend to represent segments of society? What gender is most evident in ads, and how is that sex depicted? This element can be used to analyze the content of ads for their social implications, such as racial composition and the visibility or invisibility of various body types. Increasingly we find evidence in both print and television advertising of positive representations of the physically impaired. Target, K Mart, and other stores depict these

groups who have previously been invisible. Can students find any examples of this? This method allows students to consider the ways in which advertisements construct representations of society. How truly representative are they? One study indicated that women were seven times more likely to appear in personal hygiene ads than men. Other studies found that 79 percent of ads using women were for kitchen or bathroom products, that 56 percent of women were depicted as housewives, that women were shown in 18 occupations whereas men were shown in 43 occupations, and that men tended to be depicted in business settings or outdoors. Have students try to confirm or refute these findings by their own analysis of magazine or television advertising. A simple chart could be used to facilitate this study.

Picture This: Social Relationships in Advertising

(MID/HIGH) — So far, we have addressed the depiction of people in advertisements in quantitative terms. But what is the quality or nature of the human relationships represented in ads? How do the posture, body language, position, and point of view used in ads convey meaning about social relationships? T. Millum (1975) provides an interesting system for categorizing the social relationships depicted in magazine advertising.

1. Reciprocal relationships, in which each person is the focus of the other's attention.

2. Divergent relationships, in which each person is directed to something different.

3. Object relationships, in which the people focus on the same object.

4. Semi-reciprocal relationships, in which one person focuses on the other, who focuses on something else.

Describe these broad categories to students and have them find examples of magazine advertisements for each group.

GET THEM WHILE THEY ARE YOUNG: Advertising, Children, and Youth

The August 1982 cover of *Advertising Age* features an article on the youth market, extolling the advantages of "getting them while they are young." Similar sentiments are expressed in a 1987 issue of *American Demographics*. "Don't be put off by the

strange language, the purple hair and the one dangling earring," says the author. "In a few years, today's teenagers could be wearing three piece suits, working for an investment bank, or managing a supermarket. Make friends with teenagers now and you may have customers for life" (Guber 1987, 42). Using information drawn from Teenage Research Unlimited, a research group, the article pointed to the conservative nature of teens, indicating that boys in particular equate success with money and money with happiness. Two-thirds of teenagers reported getting a lot of information about new products from television. The report also noted the emphasis on macho and muscles in males and a general adolescent concern with speed, including the food they eat and their forms of entertainment. The peer group exerts enormous pressure on teens, and being accepted by the crowd is important to them. For advertisers, the peer group offers a powerful ally.

Boys in particular tend to be more influenced by peer group attitudes when making purchasing decisions. Twelve- to 19-year-old females, on the other hand, are more likely to think about price and parental advice. Whether male or female, the advertising industry has these young people firmly in their sights, and they have a formula for reaching them. According to Paul Kurmit (1992), a specialist in juvenile marketing, the basic rules of pitching television commercials to kids are quite simple. The rules of the game include:

1. Talk the talk.

2. Put it to music.

3. Move it along at a swift pace.

4. Don't preach.

5. Make it fun.

6. Pictures sell, including those that seem to have nothing to do with the product.

Adolescents are particularly susceptible to marketing strategies because of their developmental stage and their need for security. Although their clothing and appearance sometimes suggest rebellion, it tends to be a rebellion more about image or appearance than about ideas, and within the confines of their cliques, individuality and deviance are not rewarded. At the very period that teens are in the process, consciously or otherwise, of defining who they are and what they want, advertisers can subvert the search for self through the marketing of prepackaged identities. This process often implies to adolescents that unless they look a particular way or can afford to wear particular labels and clothes, they are not as good as those who can. Although this may not be the intent of advertisers, a very real distinction must be made between intent and impact. Willingly or not, advertisers might be suggesting to children and teens that they live in a culture in which images and appearances are more important than ideas and substance. Is it possible that we are creating a consumer culture that increasingly believes we really can judge books by their covers?

The youth market is extremely lucrative, and there is great competition among advertisers to attract young buyers. The purchasing power of teens is substantial. In 1989 they spent $71 billion. Females spent an average of $55 a week, and males spent $48 per week. Breaking the figures down further reveals the relative affluence of the young consumer. Twelve- to 15-year-olds spent $35 per week, compared to $53 per week for 16- to 17-year-olds and $78 per week for 18- to 19-year-olds. The child market is also extremely lucrative. In 1990, *American Demographics* reported that the number of 4- to 12-year-old children in the United States stood at 33 million and was growing. In 1989 these children represented $9 billion in sales, an 83 percent increase from 1984.

These children spend $2 billion a year on candy, soft drinks, frozen desserts, and snacks. They spend $1.9 billion on toys, games, and crafts. They spend $700 million a year on clothing, and over $600 million on movies, live entertainment, and spectator sports.

Given the enormous profits the child and youth markets represent, it is no wonder that advertisers target them. Given this targeting and the purchasers' relative inexperience, it is time schools began to help these young consumers make intelligent and informed decisions. Teachers working with very young children might find *The Berenstain Bears Get the Gimmies* (Berenstain and Berenstain 1988) a simple way to start talking to children about selling.

Purchasing Profile: What I Buy: The When, Where, and Why

(ELEM/MID) — It is important to realize that a lot of the marketing aimed at young people comes in such pleasant and entertaining forms that neither the children nor their parents would necessarily include it in a list of advertising that targets kids. The link between movie merchandise and fast food outlets is one of the most insidious examples of this. Because of long-term contracts between the studios and the fast food franchises, this process is not likely to go away soon. The result is that parents taking their family out for pizza, hamburgers, or Mexican food are likely to find themselves assailed by children wanting and expecting a collection of cups, glasses, puppets, and, of course, various figures. In recent years, this marketing has found Pocahontas and the cast at Burger King, Casper at Pizza Hut, Power Rangers at McDonalds, Congo watches at Taco Bell, and the 1997 Star Wars trilogy at all the outlets under the Pepsico banner (Kentucky Fried Chicken, Pizza Hut, Taco Bell). At the very least it increases the cost of a family meal. It also obviously means that exposure to movies reinforces the food outlets and vice versa in a cycle that is increasingly difficult to break. A purchasing profile is a useful way of helping young people begin to keep a log of their spending decisions so they become more conscious of not only what they buy but also when, where, and why.

Modify this profile format to meet your own requirements and the nature of the students with whom you are working. Typical items on the list might be shoes, clothes, records (tapes, CDs), fast food, cigarettes, and, of course, entertainment expenses such as movies. In the fast food category, the students should specify not only hamburgers, pizza, etc., but also the chain they patronized and their reasons for doing so. Those reasons could include everything from convenient location to price, flavor, give-aways, etc.

Slime Time: Pitching to Kids

John Lyons refers to television advertisements aimed at children as "slime time," suggesting that "this is the closest advertising ever comes to brainwashing" (1987, 291). Lyons is particularly critical of the violence and mayhem in Saturday morning cartoons and the products associated with them. The result of this viewing, he says, "if not brain washing, is brain damaging." Peggy Charren, from Action for Children's Television, shares this opinion, calling such advertising "unique brainwashing." In Quebec, television advertising aimed at children is banned. In this country, however, our youngest citizens are seen as future consumers who are certainly capable of influencing the purchasing decisions made by their parents. As we become more aware of the impact of media in our society, targeting children is likely to become increasingly controversial. In July 1991 the American Academy of Pediatrics, for example, called for an end to low-nutrition, high-sugar product advertisements aimed at children.

Concern about television advertising and child consumers hinges on four factors:

1. The developmental level of the child, which renders him or her particularly vulnerable to the claims of commercials.

2. The content, form, and style of the commercials themselves, which often make products appear more dynamic, exciting, or larger than they actually are.

3. The relationship between the program and the products, particularly in the case of animated series with a complete toy line based on them or that have actually developed out of a toy line, resulting in the charge that these are not really programs but thinly disguised 30-minute commercials.

4. The views and values implicit in both the programs and the products, especially when they represent violence and sexism.

No doubt exists that revenues and rewards can be reaped from advertising to children. The toy market alone generates some $12 billion a year. The success stories include hot new items such as Nintendo as well as old standbys such as Barbie. The Barbie Doll line, including all the accessories, was grossing in excess of $325 million annually during the 1980s, and Barbie's accessories included a designer wardrobe by fashion giant Oscar de la Renta. Another success story was Teddy Ruxpin, an example of animated plush manufacturing, which grossed $100 million in its first year. Although Barbie and Teddy Ruxpin have both been criticized for their social implications, the real criticism has been leveled at the more visible and violent products of the toy industry. Mattel's *Masters of the Universe* program and products grossed some $1 billion in 1985, including a line of bedroom slippers for toddlers featuring the skull head of Skeletor. The war toy industry, well fueled by *Rambo* and other movies, grossed $1.3 billion by midyear in 1980 alone, causing alarm among groups and individuals who believed that such playthings afforded social sanction to the use of violence to solve problems. By Christmas 1990, with the deadline for the Iraqi withdrawal from Kuwait in the Persian Gulf approaching, the toy industry had hit the market with several games and products based on the conflict.

Of course, the concept of licensed merchandise based on cartoon, television, or movie characters is not new. Disney had great success with Mickey Mouse before the advent of television and, in the 1950s, generated a national craze with Davy Crockett merchandising. The new wave of merchandising really began with the phenomenal success of *Star Wars* in 1977. Today, thanks to corporate mergers and highly sophisticated marketing strategies, children and their parents are confronted by products pushed through films, television, and magazines. This strategy creates a toy line rather than a single product and relies upon multiple purchases within the same product category by the same child. Hence, Barbie needs Ken and a dream house, and He-Man requires Skeletor. Action figures are a staple element of this marketing strategy, and Star Wars, Batman, Beetlejuice, and other toy lines come with their own unique carrying cases. In recent years, the movies *Dick Tracy*, *Total Recall*, *Back to the Future*, and *Days of Thunder* have all been turned into video games, yet another extension of media mergers and new marketing methods. Although there is not space to address the phenomenon in this book, both teachers and parents need to think about how children are socialized by these toys. If our society is violent, is it possible that the origins of that violence lie in our sanction of explicitly aggressive action figures? If young women avoid careers in math and science or become obsessed with their appearance, are they merely responding to the cosmetic culture foisted upon them in childhood?

(ELEM/MID/HIGH) — Have students develop a list of Saturday morning or after-school programs aimed specifically at children. Develop a list of the products advertised on these programs. Which ads do the students find appealing and why?

(ELEM/MID/HIGH) — Develop a list of animated series with their own line of toys. These will probably include *Voltron*, *Transformers*, *He-Man*, *She Ra*, *Princess of Power*, *Go Bots*, and *G.I. Joe*.

Ask the students which of these programs they watch or have watched. Ask them if they have bought any toys based on these programs. Have them bring some of the toys to class and discuss whether they were satisfied or dissatisfied with the purchase.

This unit, when tackled with teenagers, provides an interesting opportunity for students to look back on themselves as children or to comment on the differences between themselves and younger or older brothers and sisters. It also can be used for an eye-opening sociological study of the differences between toys aimed at males and those aimed at females.

Food for Thought: Advertising, Nutrition, and Dieting

(ELEM/MID) — The saying "You are what you eat" is a useful starting point when trying to help children and adolescents understand the relationships among their bodies, their self-image, the food they eat, and the packaging and promotion of that food. An outstanding ABC special, "Diet of Danger," looked at U.S. nutrition and the medical impact of our food choices. Among other things, the program noted:

1. By the time students are 18, they have seen 20,000 food commercials, 80 percent of which advertise food that is low in nutrition.

2. Seventy-eight percent of children influence the purchasing decisions of their parents.

3. Cereal advertisers spent $654 million in one year.

4. Fast food advertisers spent $1 billion in one year.

5. Gum and candy advertisers spent $405 million in one year.

6. Soft drink advertisers spent $389 million in one year.

These figures represent spending in the late 1980s. By the time of the Olympic Games in Atlanta in 1996, advertising expenditures had continued to expand. That year alone, the soft drink industry invested $0.67 billion in advertising. Coke spent $305 million, a 57 percent increase from the previous year. The fast food industry spent $2.95 billion to promote their products with McDonald's paying out $599 million. The Olympics provided a perfect forum for many of these producers and in the case of McDonald's, paid off, with one of their ads (Boy/track star) being judged "uplifting, inspirational" and the most popular ad of the Games. Of course, not all commercials can be described as either uplifting or inspirational.

These advertisements represent a powerful and attractive inducement to consume. The people in these advertisements are young, fit, and healthy, despite their apparently poor eating habits. Consumption is shown without consequences. Any attempts to alter patterns of consumption are challenged by the food industry. In 1991, "yielding to pressure from the meat and dairy industries, the Agriculture Department . . . abandoned its plans to turn the symbol of good nutrition from the 'four wheel' showing 'The Basic Food Groups' to an 'Eating Right' pyramid that sought to de-emphasize meat and dairy products in a healthful diet" (Sugarman and Gladwell 1991, 39). Nutritionists seek to provide us with one set of information while advertising consistently erodes this advice. How can we address this contradiction in the classroom? A simple starting point might be to go over the basic food groups with the class and discuss the concept of nutrition. Having established a list of the foods that are beneficial, it might then be useful to see what food is advertised most frequently on television. You might want to develop a chart listing products such as fish, beef, poultry, dairy, eggs, fruit, vegetables, and grains.

How frequently is each group advertised? Which elements of a particular group are stressed? For example, is milk advertised more than eggs or cheese? How often are these foods advertised as products of fast food chains? For example, is meat most frequently advertised in hamburgers? How are the products promoted? This can include the models used (age, race, socioeconomic situation) as well as the persuasive techniques, such as "all natural," "it's good for you," "new and improved," "happy families," etc. (Each of these techniques is treated earlier in this chapter.)

(ELEM/MID) — Have students concentrate entirely on the selling of fast foods. What types of fast foods are advertised on television: pizza, hamburgers, seafood, fried chicken, tacos, and others?

(ELEM/MID) — Divide the class into groups. Each group should study the promotion and packaging of one of the fast foods listed. The assignment should include completing a chart.

❖**Researchers identified marketing techniques, advertising, and packaging as contributing factors in what *Time* once called "the girth of a nation" as America grew heavier and heavier. Reprinted with permission of *American Demographics*, Ithaca, NY.**

Make sure students are familiar with the various persuasion techniques as they work on this assignment. Older students can conduct sophisticated analyses of each ad. The younger students, however, are quite capable of understanding how stuffed toys, character merchandise, and food specials offered for a short time are used to attract customers.

(ELEM/MID) — Conduct a class poll to see what the favorite fast food is. You might want to conduct this as an election, with one candidate speaking for each group. See if students prefer one particular chain to the others and find out why. Is it the food, the prices, the location, the give-aways, the advertising? Which of these factors seems most influential in shaping the class's preference?

(ELEM/MID) — Develop a class survey of families and food. Each student should be given a sheet and asked to list the members of their family and each person's favorite food when they eat out. The survey could include the number of times they eat fast food each week, the type of food they eat, and their reasons for selecting that food. This process not only develops a profile of the eating behavior of families in your community, but it also provides insights into the lifestyles of the parents. For example, it can provide information about how busy mothers and fathers are during the day, how much time they have for lunch, the type of area in which they work, and so on. Potentially, this can open up an entire exploration of the relationship between the food we eat and the lifestyles we live. Questions about drive-in windows or food "to go" can further develop this process. Ultimately, you can develop a picture of not just what people eat, but also why they eat it.

WHAT'S IN THIS, ANYWAY? *The Need to Read*

Most students are aware that cigarettes contain warning labels, but do they know that some of the food in their kitchen cabinets also contains warnings? Sweet 'n' Low, for example, contains saccharin and carries a warning that use of the product may be hazardous to humans. Equal, on the other hand, can also be used to sweeten coffee and drinks but contains no saccharin, no sodium, and no warning. After the Food and Drug Administration (FDA) allowed advertisers to promote their products by making health claims, consumers were bombarded by statements about the benefits of all types of food. Many of these claims were misleading because they did not provide consumers with the full picture. Campbell's, for example, said its soup was high in fiber and stressed those benefits. The same soup, however, was also high in fat and sodium, which promote heart disease. Land-O-Lakes stressed the vitamin A in its butter and its benefits for the skin. But the product was also high in less beneficial cholesterol. Crisco advertised that its oil had no cholesterol, but it was high in saturated fats, which can clog arteries. Pepperidge Farm said its pound cake was cholesterol-free, but it was also high in fat. Lean Cuisine's Chicken Cacciatore was low in calories but high in sodium. The half-truths contained in this type of advertising generated complaints from the American Medical Association, the American Heart Association, and the American Cancer Society. These complaints prompted David Kessler, head of the FDA, to introduce new guidelines for labels, packaging, and advertising. In spring 1991, the FDA made Citrus Hill remove their orange juice from store shelves and told them they violated regulations by calling processed juice "fresh." The problems implicit in this type of marketing necessitate that we help students become critical thinkers and consumers by reading labels, asking questions, and watching advertising carefully.

(ELEM/MID/HIGH) — A simple way of examining labels is to have each student bring one packet of food to class. In class, students should examine the box, bottle, or packet to see how it is made to look attractive. Wesson oil, for example, comes in a tall, clean, clear bottle with a bright label. The label stresses, in large letters, the fact that the oil is "100% all natural" and "Light and Natural." Many products today claim to be natural, but we seldom even ask what that means anymore. If it is processed, can it be natural? Wesson's label says it has no additives, no cholesterol, and no salt. It also says it "tastes light." Does that mean that it is actually light or that it just tastes as if it were? The expression "salt free" does not mean the same thing as "sodium free." The term "sugar" can actually mean any number of ingredients, including glucose, dextrose, lactose, and fructose. Direct your students' attention to the small print about the contents of their packages. This is an excellent way for health, science, and biology teachers to help students understand such concepts as calories, U.S. Recommended Daily Allowance, body fat, etc. Most packages also contain the address of the company. If your students have concerns or questions about the way a product is packaged or promoted, have them write to the company. Given the obscure phrasing on so much labeling, a simple request might include putting information on packets that the average citizen could understand. Minority students might request labeling in Spanish or other languages. Students might also write to the FDA to ask for the existing guidelines concerning advertising and food and health claims. This process not only encourages students to be thoughtful consumers but also promotes responsible participation in a democracy. This exercise develops critical thinking skills that are badly needed in this area. George Bush's secretary of health, Louis Sullivan, said, for example, that to understand today's labels consumers must be "linguists, scientists, and mind readers."

DANGEROU.S. DIETS: If Looks Could Kill

In 1990 the American Dietetic Association reported that Americans' diets reflected a desire for quick fixes for bad habits. Although Americans were taking more vitamins, using more olive oil, and eating more oat bran, for example, only 8 percent reported eating more vegetables and only 6 percent said they were consuming more fruit. In the same year, congressional hearings were held regarding the largely unregulated weight-loss industry. Representative Don Wyden called the industry and its claims "a scam on the American public." Skillful advertisements used celebrities such as Tommy Lasorda and Susan St. James to promote the benefits of various weight-loss programs. The congressional hearings, however, provided evidence of the potential danger of some programs, including heart attack, brain damage, and gall bladder injury. Despite the high visibility of the diet and fitness industry, a 1991 report from the Centers for Disease Control suggested, "Americans are just as likely to be overweight today as they were in the 1960s." Twenty-four percent of men and 27 percent of women are significantly overweight. Obesity was also more prevalent among the poor and minorities. The study suggested "little progress . . . in educating people about good nutrition and weight loss" (Booth 1991, 37). Spas, aerobics, jogging, Jazzercise, light beer, and Lean Cuisine have had little or no impact on "the national prevalence of fat."

By the middle of the decade in a cover story called "Girth of a Nation," *Time* reported that 58 million Americans weigh more than their ideal body weight. Twenty-one percent of teenagers are in this category. Eighty percent of women and 25 percent of men are on a diet at any given time. Fifty percent of nine-year-old girls have dieted.

Unfortunately, there is growing evidence that while we are unhappy with the way we look, we seem unable to do much about changing it. In 1972, 23 percent of women reported dissatisfaction with their body. By the mid-1990s the figure had doubled. Seeing ourselves clearly, putting our body image and physical appearance in perspective, is increasingly difficult given the way we are bombarded with advertising's idealized body images. In the real world, the average height and weight of American women is 5-foot-4 and 142 pounds. In the glamorous world of modeling and advertising, it is 5-foot-9 and 110 pounds. A 1996 cover story in *People* magazine discussed the impact of these media images on our self-esteem. "Many Americans are feeling worse and worse about the workaday bodies they actually inhabit. The people being hurt most are the ones who are most vulnerable: adolescents" (Schneider et al. 1996, 66). The following year, *Psychology Today* reinforced these findings as they reported the results of their national body image survey. "For the past three decades," they noted, "women and increasingly men have been preoccupied with how they look. But the intense scrutiny hasn't necessarily helped us see ourselves more clearly" (Garner 1997, 32).

Of all the victims of dangerous dieting, those suffering from serious eating disorders are the most vulnerable both psychologically and physically. According to the American Anorexia and Bulimia Association, 150,000 women die of these maladies each year. Those suffering from bulimia exhibit symptoms such as repeated episodes of purging and bingeing; feeling out of control during bingeing episodes; purging through excessive dieting, vomiting, use of laxatives or diuretics; and an obsession about their

❖ **"PEOPLE" Weekly is a registered trade-mark of Time Inc. Used with permission.**

weight and shape. While family conditions and interpersonal relationships are part of the background of the illness, the self-loathing and self-destructive behavior implicit in the disorder cannot be isolated from their cultural context, including media messages and images that establish unrealistic and idealized body images in our society. Naomi Wolf, author of *The Beauty Myth*, says, "We deserve the choice to do whatever we want with our faces and bodies without being punished by an ideology that is using attitudes, economic pressure, and even legal judgments regarding women's appearances to undermine us" (1991, 1).

(MID/HIGH) — This exercise is particularly interesting with adolescents and adults. Give each student a blank index card. They are not to write their names on it. What they have to do is write an answer to the following question: "If you could change your appearance, who would you most like to look like and why?" Collect the cards. Read through them and place the names on the board. Did anyone say they were happy the way they were? If not, you have just established that as a culture, we are generally

dissatisfied with the way we look. The real task, however, is to think about why. Typically, most of the names you have in front of you will come from the worlds of film, music, modeling, or television. If you have sports figures, stress that these people actually look this way. The media figures, on the other hand, not only use makeup, but they also have body doubles or stand-ins.

(MID/HIGH) — Collect a series of magazines and have students look for examples of products related to weight loss and dieting. These might include pills, liquid diets, and clinics. Have them study the ads to see what type of people the ads are aimed at, how much weight they claim can be lost (extreme, average, etc.), the persuasive techniques they use (before-and-after photographs, social inferiority, etc.), and the type of magazine in which the advertisement appeared. Be sure to note that statistics suggest that 75 to 90 percent of people who lose weight gain it back. Perhaps the most visible example of this is in the case of talk-show host Oprah Winfrey. She lost 67 pounds on a highly-publicized liquid diet, but also gained a lot of it back. The public and the press's fascination with dieting was evident in the tabloids' treatment of Elizabeth Taylor and *Designing Women*'s Delta Burke. Why is the media so concerned with overweight women, whereas it ignores men such as William Conrad, Raymond Burr, and John Goodman? Is this a double standard, or does it address the role of women as sex objects in a media industry that is controlled by men and caters to male fantasies? This question can be tackled by older students in a content analysis of images of obesity in the media.

(HIGH) — Doctors are reporting an increase in the number of teens seeking plastic surgery because they are unhappy with their looks. Discuss this trend with your students. What do they think of it?

(MID/HIGH) — Collect examples of magazine ads that realistically reflect the diversity of body types. Compare them to ads that promote an idealized body type. When the magazines are aimed at adolescent females, encourage students to write to the publishers praising balanced images and criticizing idealized images.

SEX ROLE STEREOTYPES AND ADVERTISING

Naomi Wolf's suggestion that images of women also contain, carry, and convey an ideology seems to be substantiated by research. *Psychological Reports* explored advertising representations of endomorph, mesomorph, and ectomorph body types. They concluded that personality characteristics and attributes were clearly assigned by body type, with mesomorph presented favorably and endomorph appearing unfavorably (Spillman and Everington 1989). Hence, it might be argued that media representations of female body types stereotype lifestyles by associating personal as well as social success and happiness with physical characteristics. But Wolf sees even more danger and damage in the narrowly prescribed roles that advertising and other media provide for women. The emphasis upon images of glamor and beauty, she says, "is not that they exist but that they proliferate at the expense of most other images and stories of female heroines" (1991, 2). In the process of selling, the argument goes, these advertisers, along with the newspapers, magazines, and television programs they sponsor, also engage in a relentless and restrictive process of telling women who they are and how to behave. At the same time, of course, they also define the way men see females. "The beauty myth tells a story. The quality called beauty objectively and universally exists. Women must want it and men must want to possess women who embody it" (12). For Wolf, the content of these messages cannot be separated from those who own and create the messages; "it's all about men's institutions and institutional power" (12).

A simple example of a seemingly harmless commercial that clearly addresses both power and powerlessness can be seen in a television spot for car batteries. A woman is seen alone on a city street at night. She is therefore already positioned in a vulnerable and threatening environment. Her car will not start. She is trapped in the mean streets. More to the point, she confesses that she forgot to turn off her car lights. Now she is not only vulnerable but careless as well. The solution, of course, is a battery with a longer life. The fact that the battery is presented in overtly male language—"Die Hard"—further emphasizes the insecurity of women and the strength and safety of men.

Of course men are not always represented as competent or in charge. In the mid-1980s, television advertising began to feature a series of images of men in unusual circumstances. In each case the men appeared to be losers, jerks, wimps, or hapless individuals, particularly—and here is the key point—compared to the women in the ads. In one spot for Kellogg's Bran Flakes, a husband and wife play doubles tennis. His main contribution is to return the ball when it bounces off his head. Midas, Draino, Nutri-Grain, and Rice Chex ads all featured men who acted more like children in need of guidance and discipline. During the 1990s, men's bodies have become increasingly objectified. A commercial for Diet Coke featured a group of women watching from an office window as a construction worker in the street took off his shirt and drank a soda. Discussing the trend in the *New York Times*, Jean Kilbourne argued that the advertisers were still extraordinarily guilty of a double standard in the images and words they used. Referring to an ad for a styling product, she said the copy included the following words: "Make the most of what you've got, even though your breasts may be too big, too saggy, too pert, too flat, too full, too far apart." The outrageousness of such a message, she suggests, is best understood if we reverse gender representations and address men the same way. Now the copy reads, "Your penis may be too small, too droopy, too lopsided . . . two inches" (1994, F13). It is difficult to imagine any mainstream magazine carrying such a message to men, but Kilbourne and others argue that women are continually addressed in such demeaning ways. In the process, rather than furthering our understanding of ourselves and others, advertising inhibits and impedes our personal and social growth. "What makes us men and women?" asks Katherine Dodds. "Those trapped in the gaze," she says, "have no way of knowing. They mirror back and forth reflections of each other's loss and longing. Advertising doesn't just create images, it constructs differences between men and women" (1996, 37).

These differences are apparent in a report from the United Nations Commission on the Status of Women. Among the findings, the study concluded that

- Women tend to lack intellectual independence and defer to males.

- Women use and need products to attract the attention of men.

- Women tend to be obsessive about cleanliness.

- Women are shown in a narrower range of roles than men.

- Commercials in children's programs depict more men and boys than women and girls. (Fox 1996, 14)

By looking at a body of other studies, it is evident that these messages pervade programming at all age levels. A study of gender stereotyping in MTV commercials found that they empower men and seldom use women as voice-over authorities. The products advertised also had clear gender delineations. While products aimed at males tended to be entertainment based, "the product type most often oriented to females was personal products—products with the primary purpose of improving or enhancing the physical attractiveness of the buyer" (Signorielli et al. 1994, 99). The target audience for these messages was 12- to 34-year-olds. MTV was in 6 out of 10 households, and 25 percent of its audience were 12- to 17-year-olds. In fact, this group represented the largest adolescent audience for any television program. How might these narrow and restrictive gender roles affect and influence an audience experiencing puberty and actively seeking sex role information? The researchers concluded that although the feel and style of MTV were nontraditional, its gender depictions were heavily stereotypical. As such, they concluded, commercials on MTV "preserve and perpetuate stereotypes about women" and "adolescents receive warped views of the roles and responsibilities of women in society" (100).

If the age of the audience should be considered when discussing the impact of advertising, it is equally as important to consider the age of the models or characters in the commercials. Again, the data available tend to suggest that advertising constructs a very narrow perspective that constricts the way we see ourselves and others. Seventy percent of women in ads are between 18 and 34 years of age (Busby and Leichty 1993). Beyond the pages, screens, and scenarios that Madison Avenue constructs for us, real people in the advertising industry fall victim to the stereotypical visions they themselves have helped construct. In 1997 a jury found one agency guilty of age discrimination against an employee. Far from being an isolated occurrence, the event prompted *U.S.A Today* to observe, "Age bias cases gush from fountain of youth culture." On Madison Avenue, they said, "one thing is clear, the man or woman in the gray flannel suit must not have hair to match" (Wells 1997, B1). Youthful imagery and cutting-edge technology are perceived as incompatible with an aging, albeit mature and experienced workforce. Nor is age the only impediment to success in the world of advertising. As one might expect, an industry so narrow in its representation of women might also have problems with women workers. Jerry Della Faminia, a well-known authority inside advertising, puts it bluntly: "The industry is about as backward in its treatment of smart women as any industry there is" (Wells 1995, B1). The number of women in the advertising agency business has grown more than 40 percent in the last decade. Many of them are enormously successful and in responsible positions. Abby Kohnstamm, for example, is IBM's vice president for corporate marketing and responsible for a worldwide advertising budget of $500-700 million. Despite the presence and performance of women like her, females in advertising frequently still find themselves filtered through frames that are less than flattering. When *U.S.A. Today*'s business section reported on women in the industry in 1995, they presented them as "the divas of Madison Avenue." Webster defines "diva" as a prima donna. Beyond the world of opera, the term comes with its own baggage, most of which is negative.

(ELEM/MID) — Ask students to find out who makes the purchases in their families. This can be broken down into individual family members, as well as individual goods, such as food, gasoline, furniture, clothes, etc. Try to find out why the dominant buyer in the family has that job. Is it because one parent works and the other does not? Is it a question of preference? Is it a matter of tradition?

(MID/HIGH) — Select a series of magazines and have students look for the ways that men and women are depicted. They can create columns and divide the ads into traditional and nontraditional roles. Typical traditional roles would include:

Men	Women
sportsman	housewife
father	mother
businessman	sex object/
authority figure	femme fatale

Typically, ads assign males an aura of competence and control, either physically or financially. Are there ads in which the woman appears to be assertive and involved in decision making? What sorts of things do the women make decisions about? Are there ads in which men appear to be in a nurturing or supportive parental role?

(MID/HIGH) — Use the same exercise for television advertisements. It might be useful to keep a list of what programs the ads are featured in. Is there such a thing, for example, as women's programs? How are women depicted in the ads during these programs? How does this relate to the way women are actually depicted in the program? One useful example might be *Dr. Quinn, Medicine Woman*. How does the representation of women in ads during women's programs compare to the way women are depicted in ads for a different audience?

(MID/HIGH) — Select television programs that would appeal to an adolescent female audience, for example, *Party of Five*. Explore the types of products advertised and the representation of females in these commercials.

(HIGH) — Assign an essay or a debate based on Katherine Dodds's assertion that "advertising doesn't just create images, it constructs differences between men and women."

Back-Handed Compliments

(MID/HIGH) — Sometimes advertisers assert or advocate one thing but contradict themselves in the process. Virginia Slims, for example, developed the slogan "You've Come a Long Way, Baby" for its cigarettes. On the one hand, the ad seemed to congratulate women on the strides they had made, but on the other hand, the use of the word "baby" infantilizes women and diminishes their prestige and power. The ad also stresses an idealized body image. Show students one of these ads and ask them to find the back-handed compliment. Can they identify other examples?

Pieces-Parts

(MID/HIGH) — Advertisements for lingerie, perfume, lipstick, stockings, shoes, and a range of other products are consistently presented by showing only parts of the female body. The process robs the woman of her identity and reduces her to a collection of prime parts displayed in a meat market. Can students find examples of the male body treated in this manner? Using magazine advertising, have students find examples of this technique, for both sexes if possible.

There are likely to be significantly more examples of body-part female models. Discuss with the class the social and cultural factors that lead to this different depiction of the sexes. How does it show up, for example, in movies, television, and art? The entire concept of nudity also might be addressed here. Why are there so many female nudes in the world of art and so few male nudes? How does this tie in to the gender of the artists, cultural convention, and patronage of the arts in a patriarchal society?

Body Billboards

It is not uncommon to find women's bodies used as billboards adorned with slogans, logos, and graffiti. Tanqueray sells alcohol by displaying a beautiful woman in a bikini with the words "Imported Tanqueray Special Dry" on her torso. Budweiser turns three women into a giant label for their product. Have students find other examples of body billboards. Are men ever depicted this way?

Androgynous Advertising: Gender Blenders

(MID/HIGH) — The pop world has created images of androgyny in the various persona assumed by David Bowie and in performers such as Boy George, Michael Jackson, Mick Jagger, Sinead O'Connor, and kd lang. Each of these performers emerged at a time when the sexual revolution of the 1960s and the women's movement of the 1970s and 1980s were redefining traditional gender notions. As pop icons they influenced fashion, style, and appearance. Today, advertising shows signs of sexual ambiguity and uncertainty. This is most evident in magazine advertising, where it is often difficult to tell whether the models are male or female.

Show examples of such androgyny to students, or have them find their own examples. What products are advertised this way? In what magazines do the ads appear? At what type of consumer are they aimed? Do your students find the ads interesting, attractive, offensive, etc.?

Women in Advertising: Female Executives

(MID/HIGH) — Have students research the advertising industry to see how many women hold executive positions in advertising agencies or run their own agencies. Have the students track down some of the products the women promote and the way they promote them. Is there any evidence that ads produced by women are less stereotypical than those produced by men?

Validating Violence

Jackson Katz comments that "one need not look very closely to see how pervasive is the cultural imagery linking various masculinities to the potential for violence" (1995, 134). While most discussions about media violence concentrate on the graphic excesses of cable television, networks, and of course, movies, advertising also frequently uses words and images that stress aggression, power, and the downside of weakness and vulnerability. Among the most obvious and worst examples are ones in which men seem to dominate women. "Blame It on Taboo" depicts borderline rape as the nude male model seduces the female artist. Beer and alcohol products with slogans like "the silver bullet," and names like Powermaster and Colt 45 cannot be disassociated from the aggressiveness often manifested by male drinkers who have consumed too much.

But such messages are overt and relatively obvious. Identifying words and images in advertising that play off action, combat, military metaphors, and sporting symbolism offers us an entire array of products that are promoted by stressing strength. These include everything from Trojan condoms to Dell computers and the Chicago Mercantile Exchange. In addition, as noted earlier in the chapter, posture often conveys its own messages. Images of men and, increasingly, boys are frequently cold, insular, and sullen. Arms are folded, eyes are hidden behind dark glasses, while the pose and posture portray men who are hard, erect, in control. In contrast, women are often shown with very vulnerable body language, their arms, legs, and mouths open, the camera or point of view looking down on them. The cumulative messages in these advertisements construct a lesson in what it is to be male and what it is to be female.

(MID/HIGH) — Using a variety of magazines (some aimed at men, some at women, and some at both), collect a series of ads that use aggressive images or words to promote their products. What type of products, if any, are typically sold this way? Locate ads in which women appear to be physically threatened or victimized. Are these images in magazines aimed at men or women? If students find such messages offensive, encourage them to write to the publisher to complain about them. In the process you might also encourage them to praise the publisher for ads they think are gender fair and nonviolent.

CONDOMNATION: Selling Safe Sex and Abstinence

According to the Guttmacher Institute, advertising contraception is likely to lower the rate of teen pregnancy. Certainly teens receive plenty of messages about sex from the mass media. Magazines targeting teens frequently contain stories about human sexuality. Advertisements in these magazines, as noted earlier, have traditionally used sex appeal and suggestiveness as a major pitch and persuasion. "Paradoxically," as researchers have observed, "many of the same advertisers who have exerted pressure to keep responsible sex information out of the media, often use sexual appeals to promote their products" (Brown and Steele 1995, 14). Sexual messages in magazine advertisements have increased both quantitatively and qualitatively. There are more sexual messages per issue, and the messages are more overt and explicit (Soley and Kurzbard 1986). While teens have no trouble locating messages that contain sexual themes, they do not so readily obtain or locate clear and responsible sexual information. This includes information that would help sexually active adolescents engage in safe sexual behavior, and also messages that would encourage and support teens who choose to remain sexually abstinent. Too much of the message the mass media sends young people tells them that "everybody's doing it." In fact, sexual activity among teens is declining. A 1997 government report indicated that 50 percent of girls ages 15 to 19 had had sex at least once, a 5 percent decline since 1990. The figure for males also showed a 5 percent decline from 60 percent in 1988 to 55 percent. Responding to the report, Secretary of Health and Human Services Donna Shalala said we need to continue to "change the cultural messages that have been accepted too long" about teenage sex (*New York Times* 1997).

As an increasing number of school systems throughout the country endorsed a curriculum promoting sexual abstinence in the 1990s, many began to realize that teens receive mixed messages about sexuality. While church, school, and family may promote one message, the mass media in general, and advertising in particular, frequently tell another story. Recognizing and reconciling these messages must play an integral role in such curriculum initiatives if they are to succeed. It is equally necessary that young people who are sexually active are not denied information that will protect them. Nowhere has the American media been more hypocritical regarding sexuality than in the stance they adopted as AIDS spread during the 1980s.

In the mid-1980s, as the severity of the AIDS crisis really became known, government and health officials around the world turned to advertising to alert the public to the need for sexual safety and responsibility. At times the ads were highly successful. Perhaps the best example were Scandinavian ads that used humor to get the message across. Sometimes scare tactics were used. One Australian ad featured a figure of Death bowling and knocking down pins that were people. A highly controversial Australian poster depicted two young men kissing and the words "When you say yes . . . say yes to safe sex." In England some of the ads were so obscure that people mistook them for gardening commercials.

In the United States, the real controversy has centered on getting condom advertisements on television. The American College of Obstetricians and Gynecologists had to delete references to the word "contraception" in an ad they submitted. NBC helped them re-create the ad in a blander format, saying that they did not want "to put off people who were concerned about a pitch for contraception." The advertising campaign for Lifestyle condoms also ran into objections, and all three networks blocked it. An ABC vice president said the ad was "contrary to our policy of accepting products which related to controversial issues." The condom ads were rejected because they dealt with birth control, which the networks regard as a moral and religious issue. The ads did begin to appear on about 30 of 1,200 local television stations, usually late at night.

When congressional hearings were held on the issue, Representative Henry Waxman of the Health and Environment Subcommittee accused the networks of hypocrisy, saying they would not depict sexual responsibility, but they regularly depicted scenes of sexual titillation and seduction. Surgeon General Koop testified at the hearings, saying advertising was a necessary weapon in the fight against AIDS. Koop said television advertising was particularly necessary because high-risk groups such as blacks and Hispanics relied heavily on television as a source of information. The Fox Network responded in November 1991 that they would run condom commercials after Magic Johnson, the professional basketball player, announced he was HIV-positive. CBS and NBC said they would review their opposition to such commercials.

(MID/HIGH) — The controversy over condom commercials could be explored in sex education classes, as well as in English and Social Studies classes. The essence of the dispute hinges on the public's right to receive information during a health crisis and the right of the networks to determine what they do or do not broadcast. Today, groups such as Musicians for Life advertise condoms on MTV. Where else do our young people get their information about AIDS prevention? Isn't it ironic that potentially harmful products such as alcohol and tobacco can be advertised, but potentially life-saving products such as condoms are restricted? What does this say about our culture's contradictory messages about sex?

Teachers should be able to connect this issue to basic principles of media literacy. How, for example, can we connect reluctance to run condom commercials with the idea that (1) media are commercial constructions, (2) media messages represent values and ideology, and (3) media messages have social consequences? If the media are as liberal as we so often hear, why wouldn't they run these ads?

ALCOHOL ADVERTISING: *Through a Glass Darkly*

For a number of years now, various groups including S.A.D.D. (Students Against Drunk Driving), M.A.D.D. (Mothers Against Drunk Driving), and SMART (Stop Marketing Alcohol on Radio and Television) have campaigned against alcohol advertising, particularly marketing methods that are likely to attract children and teenagers. Support for these initiatives has come from high offices. C. Everett Koop, Ronald Reagan's surgeon general, objected to targeting techniques that equated the consumption of alcohol with social, sporting, and sexual success. This view was also shared by Antonia Novello, George Bush's surgeon general. In the second Clinton administration, General Barry McCaffrey, head of the Office of National Drug Control Policy, described alcohol as America's number one drug problem.

Yet, despite this statement, the Clinton administration was much more aggressive in the war it waged against the tobacco industry than in efforts it made to curb underage drinking. Unlike tobacco advertising, which was first linked to the consumption of cigarettes in the mid-1960s and finally banned from television in the 1970s, alcohol advertising continues to be afforded social sanction on the nation's television screens, during sporting events, on billboards, on radio, and in magazines. In December 1996, faced with a 28 percent decline in sales, the Distilled Spirits Council made the decision to ignore its self-imposed ban on liquor advertising on television, as a result of which American children, teens, and adults found themselves exposed to an entirely new form of alcohol advertising.

❖Photograph by Jeff Fletcher, Appalachian State University, NC. Used with permission.

Anyone who believes teenage drinking is just a case of boys being boys, a rite of passage, or letting off a little steam needs to take a long sobering look at the statistics and stories behind the consumption. The Department of Health and Human Services has estimated that there are 15-18 million alcoholics in this country, compared to 3 million cocaine or crack addicts. In 1997, drug czar Barry McCaffrey told an audience at American University that 47 percent of us have a loved one, family member, or employee who is engaged in addictive behavior. Hands down, he said, the number one drug in this country is alcohol, with 10 percent of those who use this "mildly addictive substance" becoming addicted to it.

In 1987 the Centers for Disease Control estimated that there were some 105,000 alcohol-related deaths in the United States that year. In 1989 nearly 2 million Americans were arrested for drunk driving. Estimates suggest that each year, drunk driving results in 23,000 road deaths, 1 million personal injuries, and $5 billion in property damage. Approximately 46 percent of homicides have been shown to be alcohol related. Fetal alcohol syndrome damages the fetus in the womb and promotes mental retardation. Possible results of fetal alcohol syndrome include escalated medical costs, increasing strain on schools to provide special education, undermined future productivity of impaired infants, and new burdens for taxpayers. A 1991 survey by the Department of Health and Human Services reported that 8 million junior and senior high school students are weekly drinkers, and some 454,000 are binge drinkers, consuming 15 or more drinks each week. Despite the fact that all states prohibit sales of alcohol to anyone under the age of 21, the survey estimated that 6.9 million teenagers have no problem obtaining alcohol. The report said the brewing industry had confused and compounded the problem with fruit-flavored wine coolers packaged as fruit drinks. At the same time, the Bush administration had proposed cutting the budget for the National Institute on Alcohol Abuse and Alcoholism (Iskoff 1991, 37).

A 1993 report found that 12 million college students consume in excess of 430 million gallons of alcohol a year, and 40 percent of them report binge drinking. U.S. Secretary of Education Richard Riley said, "We cannot pretend that binge drinking is just an isolated event" (Wellborn 1993). The year before and again in 1996, *U.S.A Today*'s national survey of U.S. high school students found that the students themselves rate alcohol and apathy as the major problems they confronted. Behind the statistics of alcohol consumption, one finds a staggering array of statistics addressing the consequences of that consumption. Researchers have concluded that heavy use of alcohol (and other drugs) "appears to increase risk for both commission and victimization of homicide and other acts of violence as well as predatory crimes" (Catalano, Hawkins, and Arthur 1995, 352). The report, *Youth and Alcohol: Dangerous and Deadly Consequences*, outlined some of the overlapping attitudes and behaviors related to the abuse of alcohol.

- 34 percent of drivers aged 18-20 in fatal automobile accidents had been drinking.

- 18 percent of drivers aged 15-17 in fatal automobile accidents had been drinking.

- 31 percent of youth involved in the commission of crime had alcohol in their systems.

- 18 percent of high school females and 39 percent of males agreed that it was "acceptable for a boy to force sex if the girl is drunk or stoned."

- Alcohol is the strongest predictor of rape among college-age women.

- Alcohol consumption is a major predictor of at-risk sexual behavior (Kusserow 1992).

Consumption of alcohol, the study reported, "frequently leads to crime, sexual misconduct, personal injuries, higher school drop-out rates, and other consequences that hamper the ability of adolescents and children to stay healthy, to stay in school, and to take charge of their futures" (2).

These studies make clear the consequences that can result from alcohol abuse. Researchers have also focused on the context in which consumption occurs, particularly as it relates to the nature and needs of the user/abuser. "Most adolescents who consistently use alcohol and other drugs, lack social and peer resistance skills and have less than optimal bonds with their families, schools, and communities. They often want desperately to belong, even to the extent of doing things that go against their better judgment" (OSAP 1991a, 53). It is precisely this sense of alienation, this need for approval, that alcohol advertising addresses. In a variety of ways, the words, music, and images of the brewing industry tell young people that "using alcohol is normative; using it to make relationships and life easier is appropriate; connecting alcohol to intimacy and sex is de rigueur. Alcohol solidifies men's resolve about finding sexual partners. . . . People drink and have sex, or drink and do exciting things that break a variety of rules . . . without poverty, incarceration and death" (Keeling 1994, 245). Too often teenagers and their parents suffer from mythconceptions about alcohol. Researchers, for example, dismiss the view widely held among parents that "behaviors such as AOD (Alcohol and Other Drugs) use are simply signs of adolescents' normal need to rebel against parents, teachers, and other authorities" (OSAP 1991, 15). Adolescents, for their part, often believe they can sober up by drinking coffee or getting some fresh air. Aiding and abetting the misinformation is the world of Madison Avenue. The Center for Substance Abuse Prevention believes that "the glamorization of alcohol and mixed messages about its use have a very real effect on our community. Advertising," they argue, "is a very powerful educational tool in America." "Too often," they state, "a teenager's only information about alcohol comes from advertising and his or her peers. Neither is a very reliable source" (CSAP 1995, 21).

As a final comment it should be noted, particularly by those teachers not routinely involved in substance abuse education, that there is a body of evidence indicating that the subject of teen drinking needs to be introduced well before the onset of adolescence. Researchers have concluded that "pure liking of alcohol commercials was a strong predictor of behavior" (Austin and Nache-Ferguson 1995, 17) related to the consumption of alcohol. They have also concluded that advertising is frequently more effective in reaching young people than are parents, teachers, and other adults. "Young children may be gaining their knowledge about alcohol more quickly from commercials which are intended to teach viewers the benefits of drinking particular brands than from real life sources who would be more likely to provide more balanced information" (15). The expectations and perceptions that young people have about alcohol seem to be shaped at the time they are in the third, fourth, or fifth grade. Children and their parents need to be aware of this so both the classroom and the living room provide an environment that counters the claims made by alcohol advertising.

(ELEM/MID/HIGH) — Earlier in this chapter we provided a list of persuasion techniques and visual elements (props, posture, point of view, position) that advertisers use to promote their messages. Introduce these concepts to students and apply them to alcohol advertising in magazines when students complete the following preliminary questions:

- What type of alcohol is promoted in the ad(s) (beer, wine, spirit, liqueurs)?
- What age group and gender are depicted in each ad?
- What is the setting or location for each ad?
- What activities are the models engaged in?
- Why were these people and this place chosen for the ad?
- How do body language and facial expression contribute to the message?
- What socioeconomic group is the ad depicting or targeting?
- What doesn't the ad tell you about consumption of alcohol?

See if students can determine what type of magazine would feature individual ads. Remember, it is important that they understand the concept of targeting so they learn to distinguish between the message and the consumers of different magazines like *GQ*, *Esquire*, *Cosmopolitan*, *Glamour*, *Essence*, etc. Just as magazines target different audiences, so do the manufacturers of alcohol. In general, Michelob can be said to be for a younger, more middle-class market than is the blue-collar, working-class image of Budweiser. This, of course, is not to say that taste and price are irrelevant, or that some middle-class people drink Bud while some working-class people drink Michelob.

Personal Inventory

(ELEM/MID/HIGH) — Many schools now routinely ban the wearing of T-shirts and other clothing that promotes alcohol and tobacco. Develop a profile survey that enables students to inventory their own wardrobe to see what alcohol-related clothing or merchandising they or other family members may have. If your school is actively involved in alcohol awareness in your community, this may be a starting stage for helping parents recognize and realize how many pro-alcohol messages the home environment may provide. Moving from awareness to activism and advocacy, your school could promote an event in which alcohol-related merchandise is collected and burned at your school. Such a high-profile event promoted through community newspapers and media can widen awareness of alcohol-related problems. Tragedies like the drunk-driving death of students can also become catalysts for this form of personal inventory and activism.

Battling Billboards and Counter-Advertising

(MID/HIGH) — Another way of addressing the impact of alcohol advertising in your community is to monitor the number of alcohol advertisements children see on billboards and other displays in their community. Sometimes the local government and council are not aware of the number of these signs or their proximity to schools and other areas frequented by children. In Seattle, students actively campaigned against the presence of a Marlboro advertisement in the Kingdome; as a result, it was removed. In this sense, children not only learn about the presence and power of advertising, they also learn a basic lesson in democracy through grassroots organization and activism. In addition to monitoring and challenging the presence of billboards in their community, students can develop counter-advertising strategies, seeking the support of local businesses that might promote, sponsor, or display such messages. These messages can be displayed in your school and heavily promoted during events such as prom night. On a more advanced level, this concept can also be used in video production with students creating their own counter-advertising commercials. In Washington State, health educators work with several examples of this type of commercial. One features two teenagers on prom night all dressed up and ready to have their official photograph taken to preserve the happy moment. Drinking, however, ruins it. In an alternate gender fair effort, one commercial shows the female slumping drunkenly to the floor while the embarrassed boyfriend complains that his night is ruined, and in the other the boy is the intoxicated party. A clever and more sophisticated production shows two young men heading off to the beach well loaded with their supply of beer. They uncap each bottle with the wild anticipation of all the promised rewards they have seen in real alcohol advertising. But no cheerleaders arrive, no Scandinavian bikini babes materialize, and no instant party commences. In the end they conclude "This sucks!" The punch line on the screen: "Alcohol. It's Not as Cool as They Say."

Warning Labels

(ELEM/MID/HIGH) — In the late 1980s, federal law required warning messages on beer and other alcohol. The label specifically warns pregnant women that drinking alcohol can create birth defects. It also says consumption of alcohol impairs an individual's ability to drive a car or operate machinery. Discuss these warnings with students. Were they aware of them? Examine a can of beer. Is the warning clear and visible, or is it overwhelmed by the label and logo?

Sample Slogans and Pitches from Print Ads

(MID/HIGH) — The previous analysis of alcohol advertisements in magazines focuses on the visual components. In addition to the power of the picture, some attention should be given to the pitch made in print: the slogan or phrase used to sum up the statement. The following list reflects some approaches. You might want to have a group of students concentrate on slogans used to market alcohol and have another group try to develop a slogan or pitch targeting a specific market. Are there potentially misleading or negative consequences from the slogans? For example, does the claim that a beer has more flavor and is less filling suggest that consumers can actually drink more? Why is it less filling? If it has fewer calories, does it also have lower alcohol content?

1. "America's Pop Hero" (used by Miller Lite). Picture shows close-up of can in hand, thumb opening pull-top, and foam exploding. Clearly targets a young audience and would appear in something like *Rolling Stone* magazine.

2. "Seduce a Slice" (used by Seagrams Extra Dry Gin). Close-up of glass with slice of lemon. Clearly uses sex to sell. Placement of print

on label might even be scanned rapidly and read as "sextra dry."

3. "Party Right with Bud Lite" (used by Budweiser). Features Spuds McKenzie, a dog, as party animal with a guitar around his neck. Although some might claim it supports cautious drinking, its overall appeal to the college crowd evokes the film *Animal House*.

4. "He'll Be up Here with Us Someday" (used by Johnny Walker). This interesting line is uttered by Teddy Roosevelt to Abraham Lincoln in a depiction of the faces on Mt. Rushmore. Clearly the ad stresses success and political power, with alcohol somehow being part of that road to success.

5. "Johnny B Very Good Indeed" (used by Christian Brothers brandy). A clever association with rock legend Chuck Berry. Not only does he have the same initials as the company (C. B.), but the ad also invokes one of Berry's hit songs ("Johnny B. Goode") to promote the product. Highly likely to appear in *Rolling Stone*.

ALCOHOL ADVERTISING ON TELEVISION

Magazine and billboard advertisements for alcohol are restricted to a single frame or picture. On television, these ads come to life. The director is able to create a mini-movie with a scenario, sequence, characters, setting, and even a score. These elements immediately give the advertisement power that is lacking in a magazine. They have the ability to get not only the attention of our eyes but also that of our ears through the use of music, voice, and sound effects. These ads can be lavish, million-dollar productions set on an estate with a large cast, an enormous banquet, and an aria from a famous opera. Or they might be less opulent but nonetheless effective, pitching light beer to armchair quarterbacks by evoking images of male bonding and buddies.

(MID/HIGH) — Have students analyze a variety of alcohol ads on television using the following guidelines.

- What type of alcohol is advertised (beer, wine, spirits, liqueur)?

- What age group, sex, and race are depicted in the ad?

- What is the setting or location of the ad?

- What socioeconomic groups are the people in the ad from? What factors What socioeconomic groups are the people in the ad from? What factors in the ad lead to this conclusion (clothes, cars, language)?

- What activities are the characters in the ad engaged in?

- How do body language and facial expressions create the mood established in the scene?

- How does the use of music contribute to the atmosphere created by the ad?

- Using the list of persuasive techniques provided earlier in this chapter, identify the various associations and persuasive techniques employed in the ad.

- How realistic or true to life is the scene presented in the ad?

- What program is sponsored by the ad? What relationship is there among the product, the program, the persuasion or pitch employed, and the people likely to be viewing this program? For example, beer is more likely to be advertised during football games. What types of programs feature ads for wine?

(MID/HIGH) — Use a storyboard sheet provided earlier to have students sketch the visual structure of an ad. Then have them use a separate sheet to develop a storyboard for their own television ad. Give them the choice of making an ad to market to a specific group or of making an ad pointing out the dangers of alcohol abuse, the need for a designated driver, or responsible drinking behavior.

If you have the facilities, you might be able to produce a public service announce-ment (PSA), or you might try resource sharing with your local community-access television station to produce a PSA. Broadcasting provides the basis for a classroom discussion on advertising's purpose. The quote can also be applied to techniques used in marketing alcohol.

TARGETING MINORITIES

Some of the country's leading manufacturers of wine use elaborate advertisements showing sophisticated middle-class people enjoying their drinks and conversation at lavish dinner parties or intimate gatherings. There is, however, a darker side to these glamorous images. That side is not depicted in magazine or television advertising, but it is quite clearly targeted. The target group is winos, and the product is any number of inexpensive and potentially harmful cheap wines. In San Francisco, opposition to this form of marketing led to withdrawal of the products from particular areas of the city. In a free-enterprise economy, there is no doubt that companies have the legal right to market their product. What, however, are the ethical implications of companies creating a product that is the drug of choice for people already in need of help? This became a highly controversial issue in 1991 when the G. Heileman Brewing Company tried to introduce a malt liquor called Powermaster. The company was accused of targeting minority groups with their campaign. They were challenged by groups such as the Coalition Against Billboard Advertising of Alcohol and Tobacco and the National Association of African-Americans for Positive Imagery. These groups had successfully prevented RJ Reynolds from targeting tobacco ads at minorities in 1990. Statistics indicate that alcohol contributes to 60,000 deaths in minority communities, and 90 percent of billboards are also located in minority communities. In a stinging editorial in *U.S.A Today*, the surgeon general attacked advertising "campaigns that are designed to keep our minorities enslaved by taking away their good health, freedom and dignity" (Novello 1991). She dismissed the industry's charges that free speech was being censored, saying there is a difference between political expression and commercial expression. In a call to arms against advertisers, she urged Americans to "get informed, to get involved and to get in charge. Tell the purveyors of alcohol and their hired-gun persuaders that we have had enough disease, disability and death. Tell them that we simply will not tolerate marketing that distorts and deceives." Within days of the column, the Bureau of Alcohol, Tobacco and Firearms withdrew permission for the company to use the name "Powermaster" because it violated laws against marketing alcohol by "kick." The company later withdrew the product.

THE SPORTING LIFE

The National Coalition to Prevent Impaired Driving is opposed to the use of beer company logos in sporting events. In 1990 they focused attention on the race-car industry and alcohol images at the track, on the cars, and on the clothes the drivers wear. The group believes that the association between drinking and fast driving sends a potentially harmful message. Miller, Anheuser-Busch, and Coors spend some $50 million on promoting their products at racetracks. The president of the Beer Institute defends the practice, arguing that race-car drivers do not drink while they drive. He also says the opponents tend to suggest that race-car fans cannot think for themselves. The advertising industry, of course, is well aware that many people have not been taught to think about advertising or the choices they make as consumers.

(MID/HIGH) — Divide the class into groups and have each group cover a different sport such as football, baseball, soccer, ice hockey, tennis, and golf. Each group must find examples of advertising links between their sport and alcohol. They can use both magazine and television advertising and should look for elements such as:

- Endorsements by sporting figures

- Advertising alcohol during sporting events

- Billboard or similar structural advertising at stadiums, arenas, etc.

Collect a series of sport/fitness-related magazines, such as *Sports Illustrated* and *Men's Health*, and monitor the magazines for the presence of alcohol-related advertising. Help students see the contradiction between the content of the magazine and these types of ads. Use this contradiction to inform parents about the mixed messages young people receive about alcohol and a healthy lifestyle. Encourage parents and students to engage in a letter-writing campaign asking the publishers not to accept alcohol advertisements.

Product Placement

(ELEM/MID/HIGH) — In *Terms of Endearment* (1983), Shirley MacLaine visits a restaurant with Jack Nicholson. Rather than simply ordering a drink, she specifies the brand, asking for Wild Turkey bourbon. Although most movie-goers do not remember this moment, they were all being pitched to buy a product in the middle of a movie, which is not supposed to have advertisements. This process is known as product placement. Advertisers actually pay film companies to have their products referred to or shown. Have students develop a list of movies they have seen in which characters not only consume alcohol, but also the brand name is shown or referred to. Remember this can happen in what appears to be a casual setting, including a street scene, a store scene, or in a kitchen, bar, or dining room. Teachers wishing to introduce students to this concept will find the movie *Mr. Destiny* to be a good example of this technique since it includes overt references to cereal, coffee, and beer in its early scenes. *Fargo* also contains specific reference to a fast food outlet and a major hotel chain. *Caution:* Before showing the film, check your school district's policy on films.

MARKETING AND MINORITIES: *Demographics Is Destiny*

Thomas Burrell is head of the largest black-owned advertising agency in the world. While promoting products, he also consciously constructs positive images of African Americans, especially intact families with fathers present. The images are intended to counter and challenge "stereotypes of Blacks like the lazy ni—er [sic], the welfare mother, the irresponsible father, the ghetto drug dealer, or the violent, unemployed youth" (Cassidy and Katula 1995, 94). Whatever the product or pitch, there is little doubt that advertising reflects the society it serves. In the process, it also helps to perpetuate the views and values of that society by repeating, and therefore reinforcing, stereotypes. In their book *Gender, Race and Class in Media,* Gail Dines and Jean Humez state that "eliminating racism in advertising imagery is not just a matter of changing the numbers of course, but also of reexamining and changing the codes and conventions of representation" (1995, 72).

Irrespective of the product or pitch, advertising reflects the dominant society it serves. By selectively selling that segment of the society images of itself, it also filters out, ignores, and marginalizes other elements of the population. In the process it helps to preserve, repeat, and perpetuate majority views and values by reinforcing stereotypes of minorities outside the dominant culture. The "Frito Bandito" is one classic example of an offensive image used to sell to white America. Aunt Jemima is another. Paul Newman is not Mexican, but Bandito Salsa depicts him with a drooping moustache in another ethnic stereotype. No one is suggesting that these images are deliberately racist, stereotypical, or offensive. Nonetheless, whatever the intent, the impact remains the same both on the group represented and on the way the majority culture perceives members of that group.

The changing composition of the American public, including the rapid growth of the minority population, is already altering these advertising images, both in mainstream publications and in magazines targeting minorities. In 1997 the black population was about 33 million, and expected to reach 40 million by 2010. The Asian-American population of 10 million was expected to reach 15 million by the same time. The most rapidly growing segment of the population, however, was Latinos. Consisting of 29 million in 1997, it was expected to grow to 41 million by 2010, thus becoming the majority minority population in the United States. Frequently ignored in the past by mainstream media, these groups are now being actively courted. In addition to traditional publications like *Ebony, Essence,* and *Black Enterprise,* new publications include *Black Child, Inside Asian America, Latino, Hispanic,* and *Vietnow.*

(MID/HIGH) — Collect a series of magazines aimed at white readers and another series aimed at minority readers. Have students compare and contrast images of minorities in both. They can be charted both quantitatively and qualitatively, looking for positive versus negative images, variety of settings, lifestyles, and occupations depicted, etc.

Once the issue of racial representation has been explored, return to some of the key concepts of this chapter and explore the types of products and pitches used in minority publications. In what ways are they similar to and different from methods and approaches used in white publications?

Pictures of Pluralism: TV Advertising and Minority Children

Ellen Seitter says, "When television commercials are set in the home, in the domestic sphere, we can predict with certainty that only white children will be shown." Further, she suggests that "children of color are orphaned on television commercials, excluded from the loving grasp of parents, restricted to token membership in a peer group, relegated to the status of neighborhood kids" (1995, 101). The presence of parents or grandparents, she suggests, automatically segregates children by race. Domestic scenes, including kitchen table, living room, front porch—all of these areas are zones where "whites are pictured alone." The childhood world constructed by advertising confers favor upon whites and blondes. While children of color can be shown interacting and playing with white children, typically they are "shown as passive observers of their white playmates" (100). Looking at commercials on Saturday morning cartoons, Seitter further documents ways in which minority representation is minimized. Whites outnumber minorities, the minority children seldom have lines, and they are consistently shown in the least dynamic section of the screen.

(MID/HIGH) — Using both magazine and television advertising, have students monitor the portrayal of minority children to support or refute Seitter's claims. A more advanced approach could involve examining these images in programs aimed at minority audiences.

National Stereotypes

(ELEM/MID/HIGH) — A Wendy's commercial made fun of the lack of choices available to citizens in the Soviet Union. A Kentucky Fried Chicken ad featured an image of a wise old Chinese man and a group of children calculating on an abacus. An ad for Kaopectate featured a Mexican family promoting an anti-diarrhea formula. Several contemporary ads featured unflattering images of the Japanese. Several contemporary commercials have used images of Italian nuns, Buddhist monks, and other denominations to promote products. Find examples of ads that draw on stereotypes of national characteristics and discuss these ads with students. Discuss the problems associated with stereotyping and the promotion of images of national groups.

THE GRAYING OF AMERICA

The number of Americans who are 65 or older is increasing and will continue to increase for many years as baby boomers move beyond middle age. Just as the youth market dominated the 1960s when baby boomers were in their teens, the gray market will exert a dominant influence throughout the 1990s and into the 21st century. Ask students to identify products and services that are likely to increase as a result of this development.

(MID/HIGH) — Magazine and television advertising is not only beginning to market products for senior citizens, but also increasingly featuring older people in ads. McDonald's created an ad called "New Kid." Shot in sepia tones, it featured an elderly man going off to his first day on the job at McDonald's, where he impresses the younger workers. "Don't know how they got along without me," he tells his wife at the end of the day. Geritol-Extend uses the slogan "50's Nifty" to promote its product, adding, "because you're as young as you feel." Have students look for examples of ads aimed at consumers who are 50 or older. Network news is a good example. What type of products are advertised, what pitches do they use, and what magazines or TV programs have the commercials?

(MID/HIGH) — Look at a program such as *Golden Girls* that is clearly aimed at an older audience. What types of products are advertised during this program? How do they differ from commercials aired during *Friends* or similar programs targeted to a younger audience?

(ELEM/MID) — Have students interview their grandparents to get their opinions of advertising. Some students might want to shop with their grandparents to compare what their grandparents buy with what their immediate family buys. Are there goods and services their grandparents need that they find difficult to locate?

THE GAY MARKET

(MID/HIGH) — Homophobia in both school and society is frequently fueled by intolerance based on ignorance. Homophobic attitudes at school can create a hostile learning environment that makes it difficult, if not impossible, for gay and lesbian students to pursue their studies. In part the homophobia is based on negative media stereotypes. With the growing visibility of the gay population, some segments of the advertising world are actively courting these consumers. Estimates suggest that Miami, San Francisco, and New York receive about $17 billion a year from expenditures related to gay travel and tourism. Advertisements promoting such travel and locations are likely to be found in gay publications such as *Out* and *The Advocate*. Network television, however, while gradually accepting gay characters (*Ellen*, *Spin City*), remains unwilling to run ads for a gay audience. In 1997, ABC, for example, turned down a spot for a lesbian cruise planned to run during the coming-out episode of *Ellen*.

One automobile manufacturer has discovered that lesbians are four times more likely to own a Subaru than the rest of the population. In a magazine ad targeted at the group, the spread showed two women, a car, and the text "It Loves Camping, Dogs and Long Term Commitment. Too Bad It's Only a Car." The music industry, through both its performers and album covers, has used androgynous images and messages since the

1960s. It is not surprising, therefore, to find gay images appearing in music stores. Teledec's *Sensual Classics Two* depicted two men embracing.

Sex education and health classes that discuss gay lifestyles can use images like these and others located in gay publications to examine all of gay life, not just the question of sexual preference. By concentrating on ways in which gay people are similar to heterosexuals, this approach can break down stereotypes frequently repeated in the mass media.

Principles of media literacy can also be explored, especially those that relate to media messages as commercial constructions, the values and ideology of media messages, and the social consequences of media messages.

THE PACKAGED PRESIDENT: Advertising and the Political Process

During the 1984 presidential campaign, a member of the Reagan team told a television commentator, "It's the images we care about most, the balloons, the flags, the symbols." By the time of the 1990 election, pollsters reported widespread voter apathy and low turnout. Many people, they said, were turned off by the process. Although voters became increasingly disenchanted with the political process, they also had dramatic, even historic choices to make. In 1989, Virginia elected Douglas Wilder as the state's first black governor, and a black was elected mayor of New York City. The following year, North Carolina Democrats selected Harvey Gantt, a black, to challenge conservative senator Jesse Helms. Women were becoming increasingly visible, both at the voting booth and as candidates, highlighted by the campaigns of Ann Richards and Diane Feinstein for the governor's office in the key states of Texas and California. Controversial issues, including abortion and flag burning, also provided the opportunity for voter involvement. Yet, despite strong personalities and sharply different policies, there is substantial evidence that the U.S. political process itself fails to attract the interest or active involvement of millions of citizens who stay home on election day. To begin to understand the reasons behind this apathy, we have to take a new look at how the business of politics is

conducted in this country. Presidential historian Theodore White has noted, "American politics and television are now so completely locked together that it is impossible to tell the story of one without the other" (1982, 165). White describes the U.S. electorate as a vast television audience divided into major television markets known as ADIs (Areas of Dominant Influence). These markets provide national hubs for the focus and flow of images and information about the candidates. At the center of this process we find advertising, which provides the bread and butter for network television and now dominates U.S. politics. Kathleen Jamieson says:

> *Political advertising is now the major means by which candidates for the presidency communicate their messages to voters. As a conduit of this advertising, television attracts more candidate dollars and more audience attention than radio or print. Unsurprisingly, the spot ad is the most used and the most viewed (1984, 446).*

In 1992 and again in 1996, Bill Clinton successfully told and sold his message to the American public. His victory in both cases is made all the more significant because of his

❖**Photograph by Jeff Fletcher, Appalachian State University, NC. Used with permission.**

come-from-behind strategy. In 1994, for example, the Republican revolution had seized control of both the Senate and the House of Representatives, leaving many observers convinced that Clinton's days were numbered. The message that he himself crafted, including his political advertising, was part of his formula for victory. So, too, were the markets he chose to address. This is true of both the states where he bought heavy amounts of television time and his middle-class message of values and optimism, frequently couched in deceptively negative ways. Alex Castellanos, who worked for Bob Dole in the 1996 campaign, complained, "We've counted 44,000 Clinton ads run against us and 97.5 percent are negative" (Thomas et al. 1997, viii). In his foreword to *Back from the Dead: How Clinton Survived the Republican Revolution*, Joe Klein discusses the power of advertising. "It may be all you need to know about the presidential campaign of 1996," he concludes (vii).

Like Theodore White and Kathleen Jamieson, Klein believes the mass media plays a pivotal role in the U.S. political process. Since the first televised presidential debates were held in 1960, television, advertising, and today the Internet have offered voters greater access to the candidates and their messages. Whether this access is substantial or merely an illusion dominated by style and the politics of personality needs to be considered carefully. Recent elections, including the 1994 mid-term election that brought the so-called Republican revolution to Congress, have been characterized by low voter turnout. What is the relationship between the voters' disinterest and the way in which they receive their political information, not only during an election but throughout the year? Both the news media and the world of political advertising have a role and a responsibility in the way voters perceive politics as a process and the presidency and Congress as institutions.

But what is it about the nature of the process that turns these viewers/voters off? Two potential responses are worth exploring. One suggests that political ads are dishonest or deceptive and that viewers are inherently suspicious of them. George Bush, for example, campaigned in 1988 by saying, "Read my lips. No new taxes." Although Bush was elected, polls suggested that many Americans did not believe he would keep the promise. More generically, political ads tend to promise and promote slogans, clichés, slick solutions, and quick cures to problems such as the national deficit that do not go away and are even ignored after elections are over. The result is cynicism and a widespread suspicion that what you see is not what you get, or that it really doesn't matter for whom you vote anyway. A second concern expressed by viewers/voters centers on the nature of the ads themselves, specifically the tendency toward "negative" advertising. At its simplest level, the negative ad concentrates on attacking an opponent rather than extolling the abilities and policies of the candidate. In the worst scenarios, the election degenerates into name-calling, smears, and mudslinging. In the 1989 gubernatorial contest in New Jersey, both Democratic and Republican candidates used images of Pinocchio to accuse each other of lying. The vicious 1990 Texas gubernatorial primary was also waged with negative ads.

When candidates do not attack each other, their campaigns and strategies are often based on creating fear and polarization, distracting voters from the exploration of real issues, and avoiding solving key problems through devices such as wrapping themselves in the flag. The flag-burning issue was widely criticized in the national press as a cynical and manipulative exercise exploited for partisan purposes. The use of fear to intimidate voters is not new. The Lyndon Johnson campaign of 1964 gave birth to the negative commercial with the notorious "daisy" spot. The ad showed a young girl picking petals from a daisy, while an ominous voice counted down from 10 to 1, culminating in an atomic explosion. The Republican candidate, Barry Goldwater,

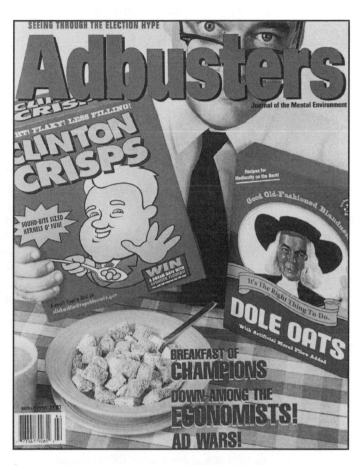

❖ **Candidates packaged and presented like any other product promise the triumph of image over issue, style over substance, and undermine our whole notion of a democracy. Used with permission of Adbusters, Media Foundation, Vancouver, BC, Canada, 1996.**

was thereby associated with the atomic apocalypse and lost in landslide proportions. In 1988 Republican Party candidate George Bush used the Willie Horton spot and images of black inmates and a revolving prison door to play on voters' fear of crime. By 1990 the issue was being tapped in Florida and Texas with death penalty ads that one newspaper called electric chair one-upmanship.

In addition to overt advertising, consideration must be given to the ways that staged news, photo opportunities, and media events increasingly allow politicians, particularly incumbents, to receive favorable coverage. In this chapter, the concept of product placement has been discussed as it applies to cigarette and alcohol advertising.

It is now necessary for us to consider this concept in terms of how it is used in the political process. In the Reagan White House, Michael Deaver was extremely effective in making sure that the president appeared frequently on national television and in the most favorable light. Central to this was the framing of presidential appearances against symbolic backdrops such as the flag and the Statue of Liberty. The composition of the picture was deliberately constructed to eliminate from the frame any sense of opposition or discord. During coverage of the 1984 presidential campaign, for example, television cameras were consistently placed where they could not show hecklers or demonstrators. The networks, eager for good footage, were unknowingly co-opted into consistently presenting orchestrated images of the president, thus compromising their neutrality and objectivity. At the time, reporters such as Lesley Stahl believed that strong, critical commentary would get through to viewers. Later, as reported in both Martin Schram's *The Great American Video Game* (1987) and the outstanding PBS series *The Public Mind,* Stahl realized she was wrong. In the television age, a picture is worth a thousand words, and with the White House controlling the pictures, the reporters' words were overwhelmed. Richard Cohen, senior political producer at CBS, came to realize that Reagan's right-hand man was really an executive producer of network news. "He suckered us," Cohen admitted.

This is the backdrop against which the U.S. political process and advertising's role in it must be considered. As the last decade of the 20th century began, discontent with the process was evident in voter apathy and in media scrutiny promoted by watchdog groups intent on finding a better way. The *Long Beach Press and Telegram* had created a hotline in 1984 for readers to report on unfair or untrue campaign tactics. By 1990 the *New York Times*, the *Washington Post*, the *Philadelphia Inquirer*, and Cable News Network, among other groups, had established a critical approach to campaign tactics. The Center for National Independence in Politics focused on negative, issueless campaigns, and the same theme became the focus for forums at the Annenberg School of Communication and the Harvard Kennedy School. PBS announced plans to provide airtime to candidates in 1992 as an antidote to commercials that avoided issues, stifled debate, and marred campaigns. In politics the national debate has clearly begun to address the very process itself. It is important in teaching about the political process in this country that educators focus not only on the structure of the legislature but also on the very process by which those legislators are elected. In looking at presidential campaigns, attention should be given not only to who ran and won, but also to how the campaign was conducted and the role of television, advertising, and the media in the process. New technologies now promise the cassette candidate in VHS or Beta, direct-mailed to a letter box near you. This trend, perhaps more than any other development, fuses the content and competencies of the traditional curriculum, with the emerging curriculum, and provides an opportunity for developing both critical thinking skills and critical viewing skills. By studying campaigns from the past, we can trace the growth of advertising in the political process and help students recognize various tactics and strategies used in packaging the president and all our politicians.

Any school system or individual teacher who genuinely wants to promote responsible citizenship for a democratic society cannot afford to ignore the relationship between advertising and the American political process.

THE CAMPAIGN TRAILS: Teacher's Overview of Selected Case Studies

1960: Kennedy Versus Nixon

Historian Theodore White won the Pulitzer Prize for his book *The Making of the President 1960* (1961). Interestingly enough, the book's index makes no mention of media or advertising. The term "television," however, is used and is central to any understanding of the election and the result.

Between 1950 and 1960, the number of television sets in U.S. homes had grown from 4 million to nearly 40 million, or 88 percent of the population. The presidential debates were the first televised debates in history and immediately gave the underdog, John Kennedy, national visibility.

On paper and in print, Richard Nixon, a two-term vice president in a popular Republican administration (that of Dwight Eisenhower) had more experience, was better known, and was favored to win. Kennedy had several negatives with which to contend. He was Catholic and no Catholic had ever been elected president. He would have been the youngest president ever elected, and this reinforced the claim that he was inexperienced. Finally, he came from East Coast money and privilege, which contrasted sharply with Nixon's middle-class background.

The impact of the televised debates has been well documented. Research suggests that those who heard the debates on radio thought Nixon won, whereas those who saw the debates on television believed Kennedy won. Looking at the debates today, it is easy to see why Kennedy's ratings went up rapidly. Despite his youth and his relative inexperience, he appeared calm, cool, and controlled, whereas Nixon, recently released from the hospital after an illness, looked awkward, tense, uncomfortable, and sweaty. Addressing the style of the debates, White suggests that Nixon used television less effectively than Kennedy. "Nixon was addressing himself to Kennedy, but Kennedy addressed himself to the audience that was the nation. . . . It was the sight of the two men side by side that carried the punch" (1961, 287-88). White also acknowledges the powerful role television had begun to play in the U.S. political process and the emergence of being "telegenic" as a criterion for high office.

Kennedy campaigned under a simple slogan: "Kennedy: Leadership for the 60s." It was a progressive, forward-focused theme that addressed a nation entering a new decade and facing the space age. By implication, it suggested that Nixon was yesterday's man. His tired television image reinforced that. The Republican slogan, "Nixon-Lodge: They Understand What Peace Means," promised security and strong leadership and implied that Kennedy's inexperience in foreign affairs was dangerous. Yet, in a country buoyed by the Baby Boom, Kennedy's attractive wife and his father image were in keeping with the times and promised a new look after the aging image of Dwight and Mamie Eisenhower.

The popular vote was very close and not decided until well into the early hours of the following morning. In terms of electoral votes, Kennedy won 303 to 219. In terms of the popular vote, however, Nixon missed becoming president in 1960 by just 112,000 votes. Kennedy received 49.7 percent of the popular vote over Nixon's 49.5 percent. Looking at Nixon's campaign, White says it had neither philosophy nor structure, offering no whole picture either of the man or of the future he represented. Kennedy's people promised optimism, epitomized in their use of the song "High Hopes," which was frequently associated with the campaign.

1964: Johnson Versus Goldwater

Taking place so soon after the assassination of Kennedy, the 1964 election gave voters the chance to both commemorate and consolidate. The country needed security and was in no mood for a change. A vote for Lyndon Johnson represented a continuation of the Kennedy program. That choice was made easier when the Republicans selected conservative Barry Goldwater as their standard-bearer. Goldwater's off-the-cuff remarks and strong statements alarmed many people and set him up as a prime target for negative advertising. His statement that "extremism in the defense of liberty is no vice" continued to feed the critics.

Johnson liked the commercials for Avis and Volkswagen that had been created by the Doyle, Dane, Bernbach firm, and they were given charge of getting the unelected president elected. The campaign's advertising is most notable for two spots. The "daisy spot" developed by Tony Schwartz was an exercise in fear. The picture showed a small girl playing with the petals on a daisy. At the end the picture changed to a nuclear explosion. Behind the images, Johnson's voice said, "These are the stakes—to make a world in which all of God's children can live, or to go into the dark. We must either love each other, or we must die." The other spot used Goldwater's words against him and showed a saw slicing off the eastern seaboard and the region floating away from the rest of the country. When the nation needed calming, the images of holocaust and fragmentation frightened the electorate and doomed the Goldwater campaign.

Goldwater's campaign slogan was "In your heart you know he's right." Many responded with the saying, "In your guts you know he's nuts." Relying on scare tactics, Democrats used the slogan "The stakes are too high for you to stay at home." Goldwater carried only six states—his home state of Arizona, as well as Louisiana, Mississippi, Georgia, Alabama, and South Carolina. In the electoral college, Johnson piled up 486 votes to 52. The Democrats got 61 percent of the popular vote and the Republicans, 38 percent.

During the campaign, Johnson had said he would not send American boys to Vietnam. It was a pledge he would not keep, and that decision would stop him from seeking office again.

1968: Nixon Versus Humphrey

By 1968, advertising and the political process had become increasingly fused. The rebirth of Nixon and the role of advertising in that process were documented in *The Selling of the President 1968*. Among other things, Nixon's creative people were told, "Voters are basically lazy, basically uninterested in making an effort to find out what we're talking about" (McGinnis 1970, 36).

Nixon had lost to Kennedy in 1960 and was subsequently defeated in the California governor's race. He had turned bitterly on the media, saying they would not have him to kick around anymore. He was widely referred to as "Tricky Dick," and yet, here he was running again for the highest office in the land. He had been unable to sell himself successfully in the past. If he was to get his message across this time, something would have to change. In *The Selling of the President 1968*, Joe McGinnis reported the thinking of Nixon's people as they pondered this: "The response is to the image not the man. . . . It's not what's there that counts, it's what's projected . . . it's not what he projects but rather what the viewer receives. It's not the man we have to change, but rather the received impression" (1970, 38). This account by McGinnis has been challenged by Jamieson. But however accurate or inaccurate the report, there is no doubt that the 1968 campaign saw a growth of the use of both advertising and television. The campaign was also the first presidential campaign in which Roger Ailes, an advertising and media specialist, played a major role. Ailes was in charge of Nixon's television appearance. He would also be a major player in the media campaigns of Reagan (1980, 1984) and Bush (1988). But in 1968, Nixon was his client and his problem. Ailes said, "Let's face it. A lot of people think Nixon's dull. Think he's a bore, a pain in the ass. They look at him as the kind of kid who always carried a bookbag. . . . That's why these shows are important. To make them forget all that" (103).

If Nixon's image was a problem, the Democrats were in worse shape. Johnson had deepened the country's involvement in Vietnam, "the living room war." The draft had sharply divided the country. On the domestic front, Johnson's vision of the Great Society and the War on Poverty had taken second place to the Vietnam War. Riots in Watts, a Los Angeles suburb, in 1965 escalated racial unrest, which exploded again in major rioting in April 1968 following the assassination of Martin Luther King, Jr. Facing humiliation at the polls and challenges from within his own party, Johnson announced in March that he would not seek reelection. The Tet offensive that January and Walter Cronkite's critical broadcast about Vietnam further eroded public confidence in Johnson and the Democrats. Attention shifted to Robert Kennedy's bid for the White House. When he was assassinated in June 1968, the country seemed to be plunging deeper into chaos and violence. By the time the Democratic convention assembled in Chicago, the national theater of the absurd played out nightly on the nation's television screens.

Overzealous police attacked, clubbed, and gased demonstrators in the Chicago streets. Tear gas found its way into the convention and the hotels. Dan Rather was roughed up on the air by Democratic Party workers. Hubert Humphrey's nomination for the presidency was marred by the images that flooded into America's living rooms while demonstrators in the streets chanted, "The whole world's watching." There was little doubt that the country was in turmoil and that Richard Nixon offered some promise of unity. The key issues of the campaign were Vietnam and crime and lawlessness. Nixon's theme was simple: "This Time Vote Like Your Whole World Depended on It." The Democratic slogan was "Humphrey: There Is No Alternative."

Advertising and the media played a major role in the campaign. Nixon outspent the Democrats two to one on television. He also outspent them four to one on radio and two to one in print. The television spots were strong, bold, and controversial. Nixon's words hammered with these themes on television:

We see Americans dying on distant battlefields abroad. We see Americans hating each other; fighting each other; killing each other at home. We see cities enveloped in smoke and flame. We hear sirens in the night. As we see and hear these things, millions of Americans cry out in anguish. Did we come all this way for this?

Against the background music of "Hot Time in the Old Town Tonight," viewers saw Republican ads with montages skillfully juxtaposing the Democratic convention and candidate with images of rioting, violence, and the Vietnam War. A shot of Vietnam carnage followed by the smiling face of Humphrey led to protests by the Democratic National Committee. Despite Nixon's media blitz, his numbers in the polls remained constant between May and November, staying at around 42 percent.

The Democratic campaign is probably best remembered for two spots, both created by Tony Schwartz and both centering, interestingly enough, on Nixon's choice of Spiro Agnew as running mate. Given Agnew's future fate and the role he took on, attacking the media as "nabobs of negativism," the Schwartz strategy was interesting. One spot called "Heartbeat" asked voters to consider whether they wanted Agnew to be that close to the presidency. The other, generally referred to as "Laughtrack," showed Agnew's face as raucous laughter grew louder, only to terminate with the voice-over "This would be funny if it weren't so serious." The strategy of attacking a popular candidate through his choice of running mate would again be used in 1976 to question Gerald Ford's choice of Robert Dole, and in 1988 in attacks on Dan Quayle as George Bush's running mate.

Despite an early wide lead, Nixon saw his advantage dwindle. Many believe a media overkill by the Republicans energized sluggish Democrats into voting. President

Johnson announced a bombing halt late in the campaign that further helped Humphrey's standing. On November 2, both the Harris and Gallup Polls gave Nixon a slim 42 to 40 percent lead. Considering his financial advantages and the Democratic disarray, Nixon had come close to blowing a commanding and irreversible lead. In the final outcome, Nixon received 31,770,123 votes (43.40 percent) and Humphrey got 31,270,333 votes (42.72 percent). In electoral votes, Nixon received 302, Humphrey 191, and George Wallace 45. The Wallace campaign had succeeded in carrying Arkansas, Louisiana, Mississippi, Alabama, and Georgia.

1976: Ford Versus Carter

The most important point about the 1976 campaign is that the winner, Jimmy Carter, began with 3 percent recognition in the polls and ran against the power of the incumbency. It has often been said in parliamentary democracies that oppositions do not win elections; rather, governments lose them. The Republican administration of 1976 was tainted. Gerald Ford was the unelected president who had taken office when Nixon resigned. At the time he addressed himself to what he called "the long national nightmare." Ford thought it was over. In pardoning Nixon, however, he angered many and reminded others of a time they would rather forget.

Nineteen seventy-six was also the nation's bicentennial. Americans wanted to believe in their system. They wanted their faith, hope, and optimism renewed. The Oscar for best picture that year would go to *Rocky*. Although its cinematic merit may be questionable, its values were in keeping with the time. The cinematic fantasy that reenergized the American dream was the story of an outsider, an underdog who triumphed. It is an important social barometer to read when viewing Jimmy Carter's emergence from obscurity to become president of the United States.

But good timing and the national mood alone would not have gotten Carter elected. First and foremost, he needed visibility, and television offered it. Writing in *America in Search of Itself*, Theodore White noted, "There could have been no Carter presidency without television" (1982, 195). In 1976 the television set made Jimmy Carter a household name and gave him what he needed. But four years later, it would also destroy him.

Jamieson (1984) describes 1976 as "a watershed year in campaign advertising." The campaigns stressed personal appeals and person-in-the-street testimony. Using the polling strategies of Patrick Caddell and the media skills of Gerald Rafshoon, Carter was able to develop spots and strategies that contrasted his pluses with Ford's negatives. He campaigned as an outsider, against Washington corruption. He invoked images of small-town, rural, populist sentiment against the cynicism and greed of the city and the corporations. The Carter campaign had the flavor of Frank Capra's *Mr. Smith Goes to Washington*. But if Carter was country and a peanut farmer, he was neither redneck, cracker, nor hayseed. He was a born-again Baptist, a theme that was to emerge more strongly as the New Right grew in the 1980s. He was educated. He had been in the armed services, and he had been governor of Georgia. If southern stereotypes were still present in the media (*Deliverance* [1972] and *Macon County Line* [1974]), Carter's candidacy addressed the New South and assuaged northern fears.

In the 1976 campaign, federal financing laws awarded the candidates $21.8 million each. Both Ford and Carter spent more than 50 percent on paid media, including 30- and 60-second spots. Ford's spots often asserted, "He's making us proud again." Unfortunately the slogan invoked a time voters did not want to remember. In addition, many Americans got their impression of the president from television, and the cameras were not kind to Ford. He was shown falling down airplane steps, hitting spectators when he played golf, and as the butt of jokes in comedian Chevy Chase's parodies on *Saturday Night Live*.

He also had to face a challenge from within his own party in the person of Ronald Reagan. It was a bruising, damaging process that Ford narrowly won, racking up 992 delegates to Reagan's 886. The power of the incumbency redistributed uncommitted delegates in Ford's favor, but nonetheless he remained damaged goods.

Carter's ads addressed the broad themes of his campaign. His slogan was simple: "Leadership for a Change." The man from Plains, Georgia, delivered "plain folks" ads. They talked of "a president who is not isolated from our people but who feels your pain and shares your dreams and takes his strength and wisdom and courage from you." So Carter wore his heart on his sleeve. He told *Playboy* magazine he had lusted in his heart. He assured the nation, "I'll never lie to you." He delivered a major speech from the porch of Franklin Roosevelt's home in Warm Springs, Georgia, symbolically fusing the New South with the New Deal and the popularity of the Roosevelt legacy. But the campaign was not all positive. Ads questioned Ford's choice of Dole as a running mate, and polls showed that the choice did influence some voters. Carter was also able to forcefully articulate the failures of the Ford administration in television spots:

> *We have been a nation adrift too long. We have been without leadership too long. We have had divided deadlocked government for too long. We have been governed by veto too long. We have suffered enough at the hands of a tired, worn-out administration without new ideas, without youth or vitality, without vision and without the confidence of the American people.*

When the votes had been cast and counted, Carter had 297 electoral votes to Ford's 241. The South had fallen in line solidly behind Carter, disrupting a major voting block that had gone for Republicans Nixon and Goldwater. With the exception of Texas, the West went solidly Republican, and Texas, of course, could well be counted as part of Johnson's and Kennedy's southern strategy.

1980: Carter Versus Reagan

Theodore White notes television's role in making the Carter presidency; he also sees its role in Carter's destruction. "He who comes to power by television must be prepared to be destroyed by television . . . though he [Carter] might control camera attention, he could not control events" (1982, 195).

Jimmy Carter's presidency was in trouble well before 1979, when Iranian radicals seized the U.S. embassy in Tehran and took U.S. citizens hostage. For a moment, it even seemed as though the crisis might help the embattled president by unifying the nation behind him in his attempts to free the prisoners. Certainly Carter needed a distraction. The country was beset with an 18 percent interest rate and 18 percent inflation. The national mood was sour, variously described as a malaise, and Carter himself, in a televised address to the nation, described a "crisis in confidence." Compounding the problem, the Soviets had invaded Afghanistan. Carter boycotted the 1980 Olympic Games and imposed a grain embargo in retaliation. Meanwhile, just as Ford had had to battle Reagan before facing Carter, Carter now found himself fighting off a challenge inside his own party in the person of Edward Kennedy.

But the real attrition in the Carter campaign came from the nightly news as it covered the hostage crisis. Night after night for more than 300 nights, national attention was focused on U.S. impotence. "Day 222 of the hostage crisis," Frank Reynolds would intone as he anchored *ABC Nightly News*. Day after day, week after week, little changed but the number of days. It was April 25, 1980, when the last real chance of the Carter administration died on the desert floor in Iran. The president was forced to go on television and admit that the rescue mission had failed; the technology had malfunctioned, and the most powerful nation in the world could do little to free its own people from foreign captors. Still stinging from the loss of the Vietnam War, many Americans, raised on John Wayne movies, questioned what on earth had gone wrong with the country's leadership. When Carter's secretary of state, Cyrus Vance, resigned in protest of the attempted rescue mission, the administration's credibility was further eroded.

Against this background, Ronald Reagan appeared. For Reagan, his time had come. There would be challengers such as George Bush, who called Reagan's financial views "voodoo economics," but Reagan was an old war-horse with a strong, well-financed organization. In addition, Carter and the times had handed him the issue on which to run. Whereas Carter seemed weak, Reagan had always seemed strong. Carter's inexperience was balanced against Reagan's record as governor of the major state of California.

Reagan had been an actor and president of the Screen Actors Guild. He knew how to work a crowd and how to face a camera. His presidency consistently used television to bypass Congress and appeal directly to the American people. Like Roosevelt's use of radio and his famous "fireside chats," Reagan entered U.S. living rooms and invoked elements of U.S. mythology. "Win one for the Gipper," recalled the legendary Notre Dame football player, and this became a standard tool in Reagan's repertoire. When he debated Carter during the 1980 campaign, he was able to brush the incumbent aside and score points with one-liners such as "There you go again." Reagan

looked and sounded secure and in charge throughout the campaign. Although the Democrats tried to depict Reagan as an extremist with a dangerous foreign policy, the electorate was more concerned about inflation, interest rates, and the declining prestige of the United States. The widespread public perception was that Carter was incompetent. Although many Americans liked Jimmy Carter as a person, they did not want him to be president. Late in the campaign, when his attacks on Reagan became more strident, many people even began disliking Carter the man, and the Democrats' own polls began to record the dive. Carter and Mondale won only their home states of Georgia and Minnesota, plus West Virginia. In electoral votes, the Reagan-Bush ticket won 489 votes to 49.

One footnote in the 1980 campaign should acknowledge the role the media played in first launching and then destroying the Kennedy challenge to Carter. Media polls, pundits, predictions, and projections created the climate for Kennedy to challenge Carter. But once Kennedy announced his candidacy, the same media that had seemed to favor him turned against him. Kennedy's campaign was not helped when he could not explain to Roger Mudd why he wanted to be president. In media circles the interview became known as the "Muddslide." Finally, it must be noted that only 53.9 percent of Americans voted in the 1980 election.

1984: Reagan Versus Mondale

In many ways the record Reagan landslide in 1984 merely reaffirmed the judgment the electorate had made in 1980. Walter Mondale had been Carter's liberal vice president, and he was perceived as being a rehash of old views that the "Reagan revolution" and the New Right had wiped out.

In looking back at the 1984 campaign, three points need mentioning. The campaign was historic because Mondale selected a woman, Geraldine Ferraro, for his running mate, which was a major breakthrough. Second was the way the media looked for conflict and competition to make even the primary process seem interesting. Mondale's election was a foregone conclusion in

the primaries, and that would not generate ratings or newspaper sales. The media were attracted to Gary Hart, and the sudden surge in Hart's campaign can be traced in large degree to this. Hart's debate with Mondale gave the former vice president his best line for the campaign when he asked, "Where's the beef?" thus invoking a hamburger slogan to undermine Hart's credibility. Third, the morning after the election defeat, in a televised speech, Mondale acknowledged that television had not warmed to him and he had not warmed to television. He lamented the growing tendency for the U.S. political process to be controlled by sound bites, photo opportunities, and "hooks." The next election, in 1988, would be described as the most negative in presidential history. At the end of the 1984 campaign, the Democrats won only Minnesota and the District of Colum- bia, accumulating 13 electoral votes to 525. Mondale-Ferraro got 40 percent of the popular vote, compared to 58 percent for Reagan-Bush.

THE CLINTON CAMPAIGNS: Bush and Beyond

The last two presidential campaigns of the 20th century are notable for the fact that the winner, William Jefferson Clinton, not only joined Woodrow Wilson and Franklin Roosevelt as the only Democratic presidents re-elected in this century, but that he won in both 1992 and 1996 despite the fact that he had been written off. In 1992, as one of the numerous Democratic candidates in the primary field, Clinton was initially perceived as the leader among an uninspiring group. He was, however, up against George Bush, the popular sitting Republican president who had led the United States and much of the world in the Gulf War, an event many believed had restored the nation's willpower, resolve, and self-image that had been battered in the post-Vietnam War years. Clinton's chances were further diminished when in rapid succession he was accused of womanizing, draft dodging, and pot-smoking. The womanizing charge had destroyed the candidacy of Gary Hart in the 1988 campaign. A bitter Hart had retreated to Colorado where he proceeded to attack the media for covering the story of his personal life. Clinton, however, together with his wife Hillary, used the media to defuse the story. Appearing on *60 Minutes* immediately after the Superbowl, the political couple presented themselves to the nation for inspection and confession. The courage, honesty, and commitment that seemed evident during the interview went a long way in convincing voters that this was a private and personal matter that would not impinge upon Clinton's ability to govern.

To a very real degree, though carrying more baggage from his past than most presidential candidates, Clinton also benefited from the mood of the country. The 1988 campaign had been widely regarded as one of the dirtiest and most negative presidential elections in recent memory. The public had expressed their displeasure with negative campaigning, even though, ironically, the growing body of evidence suggested it was a powerful and effective tool. The recession that gripped America throughout 1991 and 1992 also had voters concentrating on personal issues that would have a direct impact on their income, pocketbooks, and ability to make ends meet. In such a climate, they seemed willing to ignore matters of morality, the personal foibles of a candidate, and the character question that the Republicans misunderstood and misused to their regret in both 1992 and 1996.

However, 1988 was a different matter. Ronald Reagan, the Great Communicator, ended his eight-year presidency and handed the reins over to George Bush, his heir apparent. But Bush, even after eight years as vice president, was still an unknown to much of the American public. Many believed he was a wimp. To win the White House, Bush would need to dispel that perception, increasing his own positives while, at the same time, driving up the negatives for his Democratic challenger, Massachusetts governor Michael Dukakis. Though it is now often forgotten, Dukakis led Bush by high double digits following the Democratic convention. How that advantage collapsed has more than a little to do with political advertising, much of which was negative in nature.

Dirty Politics: Deception, Distraction and Democracy is without doubt the best account of the impact of political advertising. Kathleen Hall Jamieson writes, "William Horton and Michael Dukakis are now twinned in our memory" (1992, 16). For those who do not remember, William Horton was not a candidate in 1992. He would, however, greatly affect the fortunes of the Democratic nominee. Horton was a black criminal who had been furloughed, during which time he once again engaged in violent crimes. The Bush campaign did not create the so-called Willie Horton spot that informed viewers and voters of this story. It was, however, created on their behalf by pro-Bush forces intent on softening up the governor's lead. The Bush campaign added to the power of the ad by picking up on the subject and style. Their theme of a prison turnstile with violent criminals being released on weekend passes resonated with fearful white voters, and the destruction of Dukakis was under way. In the process, truth got lost. In fact, Jamieson suggests that the fragments of facts, images, and implied truths contained in ads are constructed and comprehended in a very creative way by voters. "Like pack rats, voters gather bits and pieces of political information and store them in a single place. Lost in the storage is a clear recall of where this or that fact came from. Information contained from news mixes with that from ads for example" (17). It gets "fuzzed up," she observes, "because it all comes into the home through the same little piece of glass" (23). One fact very "fuzzed up" in the Willie Horton issue was the record of Dukakis and his Republican predecessor, who had actually introduced the practice of furloughing prisoners. Despite the fact that both a Democratic and a Republican governor used the practice with statistically similar results, Dukakis was singled out in the public mind as being soft on crime. The governor exacerbated the situation during one of the presidential debates, expressing almost no emotion when asked how he would feel about the death penalty if his wife, Kitty, were raped and murdered. In the public mind, Dukakis quickly deteriorated in credibility. Not only was he soft on crime, but he was also portrayed as soft on defense. When his handlers tried to create a photo opportunity, placing the governor in a tank, he appeared awkward, uncomfortable, and terribly out of place. The perception was so compelling that the image initially designed as a pro-Dukakis piece was actually co-opted by the Republican campaign and used in the commercials they ran against him.

To be sure, 1988 was not all negative. Taking his cue from Reagan's ebullient 1984 "Morning in America" spots, Bush employed flags, children, music, and low angles to make himself appear compelling, presidential, and personable. Just four years later, Americans would indicate they found him distant, detached, and unable to understand the impact of the recession on their lives. If the tank spot diminished the credibility of Michael Dukakis, George Bush also discovered the way a picture could be worth a thousand words. Trying to convey the impression of a down-to-earth, in-touch president, Bush's strategists went for the common man strategy. The concept backfired when they took the president to a supermarket where, in front of millions of U.S. viewers, the chief executive expressed his astonishment about the wonders of an automated check-out line. As Dukakis stumbled during the debates, Bush, too, sent all the wrong signals. Struggling with a question from a black woman during the Richmond encounter, he admitted what many Americans already believed when he told her, "I don't get it." When he glanced at his watch, something debaters routinely need to do, the perception in living rooms across the United States, and in post-debate network spins, was that the president had somewhere else he would rather be. For Bush, time was running out in more ways than one. Too much of his campaign "was tied to events of the past in a country and at a time when voters were hurting economically and fed up with harping on personal questions about the candidates" (Germond and Witcover 1993, 434).

The arrogance of presidential power also isolated Bush. Throughout the campaign, no matter how many polls his own people showed him, George Herbert Walker Bush simply found it difficult to believe that voters might reject him for a gadfly like independent Ross Perot or Bill Clinton, whose character, he was sure, disqualified him from serious consideration. Bush had come from behind to beat Dukakis, and Clinton had more than enough negatives to be exploited for a similar victory. In the end, Bush believed, while the American public may have concerns about the economy, even his handling of it, they would re-elect him commander in chief, rejecting what he described as the failed governor of a small southern state. All he had to do, he believed, was keep hammering away at the character question. Bush saw the election as a choice between the security of his service and integrity on the one hand, and the inexperience and insecurity represented by Clinton, on the other hand. When his spots hammered away at Clinton's character flaws, they not only told viewers something about the younger governor, they also spoke volumes about their president. "The spots were missing the point. The voters were looking for evidence that the president had a plan for dealing with the economic situation, and there was no such evidence in the commercials. On the contrary, they reinforced the suspicion that Bush was playing the old fashioned negative politics" (Germond and Witcover 1993, 449). The American public, for its part, was not in the mood for a repeat of the Willie Horton campaign. This fact was made abundantly clear to Bush and his challengers during a town hall-style presidential debate. In front of millions of viewers, Bush was forced to abandon the negative strategy when the studio audience made it clear that they wanted the candidates to explore issues and avoid personal attacks.

In such a context the Clinton campaign excelled. The themes of "Change" and "People First" resonated with an electorate that had begun to believe 12 years of Republican leadership was enough. The youthful image of the Clinton/Gore families with their children was in sharp contrast to Bush, his silver-haired wife, and Millie the dog. The Democratic convention in New York defied all expectations of in-fighting and division, becoming instead a love fest to the theme of Fleetwood Mac's "Don't Stop Thinking About Tomorrow." So powerful was the picture of unity presented to the nation that Ross Perot announced his withdrawal from the race. The Clinton/Gore buses barnstormed across the nation's heartland in a populist gesture that drew huge crowds. Back home in the Little Rock War Room, a new generation of political operatives were about to unseat a president, using a new type of campaign, captured on film in the Oscar-nominated documentary *The War Room*. James Carville, Dee Dee Myers, Mary Grunwald, and George Stephanopoulos were the principal players. Aided by an influential group of FOBs (Friends of Bill), they developed a rapid response team that monitored Republican attacks and had effective responses on air within a quick turnaround period. They took their energetic young candidate to MTV, Arsenio, and other youth media markets Bush eschewed as being unpresidential. They skillfully exploited the Kennedy connection the press were quick to seize upon, using an image of a

16-year-old Bill Clinton meeting JFK. The mythic nature of the campaign and the sense of destiny seemed evident in a cover story one national magazine ran, which represented Al Gore and Bill Clinton as Huckleberry Finn and Tom Sawyer. But the dynamic duo were very much 1990s guys, as evidenced by their marketing strategy. Ignoring the major national media markets, the Clinton/Gore strategy targeted the battleground states. Grunwald declared, "We wanted to define Clinton in the battleground states before they defined us" (Germond and Witcover 1993, 436). It was a strategy they would employ brilliantly four years later in the same battleground states to preempt the campaign of Bob Dole. In 1992 they used polling figures to risk their lead in major states, pulling advertising or running no advertising in several big states while pouring money into closer races where airtime cost less. It was one more ingredient in a successful formula that from the very beginning had been nothing if not daring.

The week before the election, a CNN/U.S.A Today poll showed a virtual dead heat with Clinton clinging to a one-point lead over Bush. It was to prove a major polling aberration. When election day rolled around, 55 percent of eligible voters turned out to cast their votes. Clinton took 370 electoral college votes, while Bush garnered 168 and Perot none. Clinton won 43 percent of the vote compared to 38 percent for Bush, and an impressive 19 percent for the independent candidate. Throughout the campaign, Bush had eschewed MTV and the talk show format in which Clinton revelled. The decision was costly. Among young voters in the 18- to 24-year-old group, Clinton carried 46 percent of the vote compared to Bush's 33 percent. Clinton had used television skillfully throughout the campaign to project the image of himself he wanted the public to see. Among the first interviews he granted after winning, he bestowed his favor on MTV and *TV Guide*. Talking to *TV Guide* shortly after the election, he provided a telling insight into his campaign and the distinction he drew between print journalists and television. "Anyone who lets himself be interpreted to the American people through these intermediaries [journalists] alone is nuts. Arsenio and MTV give me a chance to communicate directly with young voters who might or might not watch news shows or read newspapers" (Olson and Ross 1992, 15).

The winning ways of 1992 would once again prove their strength as candidates lined up for the 1996 election, which would choose the final American president for the 20th century. The 21st Century Express carried Bill Clinton into Chicago and the Democratic convention, where music from 1968 told delegates it's "Only the Beginning." The train ride was a whistle-stop tour of middle America, rolling out of Virginia and across the heartland for several days of photo opportunities. At every stop, Clinton hammered away at the contrast between Bob Dole's nostalgic vision of a country whose better days were behind it and his own belief that the glory days were ahead, if only Americans would help him "build a bridge to the 21st century." He avoided press conferences and hard questions from journalists, relying instead on images and advertising to carry his message to the people.

In a highly unusual development, "Clinton was intensely involved in the ads. He not only approved them but he also helped to write them and knew their timing and audience" (Thomas et al. 1997, 39). Losing Congress to the Republicans had hurt him. He had bounced back from that earlier loss, and he was determined to survive the defeat of 1994. Advertising would play a key role in his political fortunes. So, too, would Newt Gingrich, architect of the Republican revolution who overplayed his hand, notching up record negatives with the electorate. Throughout fall 1995, using stealth methods, Clinton's team began to run a series of ads, largely undetected by the national media in the key battleground states. They had defined themselves in 1992 before George Bush could move in for the kill. Now they intended to define Bob Dole by linking him to the unpopular Gingrich. For months these markets were saturated with messages that told voters Dole and Gingrich were one and the same. Stylistically, Clinton was shown in color from flattering and well-lit angles. His opponents appeared in grainy black and white, often depicted with menacing posture and body language. But it was not all black and white. In fact, Clinton's ads were often negative without seeming so.

They "weren't traditional chain saw massacre negatives. They sandwiched a negative message between positive images" (viii), said Joe Klein, who described some of the spots as masterpieces of the Empathic Negative genre. The message was simple. Only the president could protect them from these extremists. When Gingrich orchestrated the shutdown of the government at the end of 1995, Clinton was able to present himself as someone who stood up for seniors and would not allow cuts in Social Security and Medicaid. In 1996, improving on his victory four years earlier, Clinton would carry the senior-heavy Republican states of Florida and Arizona.

Clinton also positioned himself clearly in the middle. A series of "neuro polls" had told him that his typical voter was "a single woman, a watcher of MTV and Oprah. She was often afraid at night and admitted to being an overeater. Clinton did well with feeling, intuitive types" (Thomas et al. 1997, 16). But he was losing the family vote of the thinking, judging type of voter. Gun control, school uniforms, attacks on tobacco advertising, criticism of cop-killer bullets—these were some of the issues Clinton would co-opt to seize middle America from the Republican Party. The ads immediately began to produce results well before Bob Dole ever emerged victorious from his primary battle with Pat Buchanan and Steve Forbes. In August 1995, Clinton's numbers had stood in the mid-40s. By December they were in the mid-50s. He cemented that with a strong State of the Union Address at the start of the new year.

But it was more than just cynical opportunism. Clinton had grown on the job. He had faced down both Congress and the American public on foreign policy issues, including his unpopular positions on Haiti and Bosnia. Leading the nation in mourning after the Oklahoma City bombing, he assumed presidential stature as he did when greeted by thousands of well-wishers on a visit to Ireland. His opponent had stature as Senate majority leader, but was hopelessly mismatched against the younger, more energetic Clinton. *Newsweek* reporters who covered the election commented that Bob Dole "ran one of the most hapless campaigns in modern political history" and was "so ill-suited to the role of presidential candidate that it seems a wonder anyone let him try" (Thomas et al. 1997, 4). It is indicative of the weakness of the Dole campaign that it received its highest burst of energy when his wife, Libby, addressed the San Diego convention and when he announced that the popular Jack Kemp would be his running mate. When Vice President Gore scored a clear victory over Kemp in the televised debates, that brief surge also faded. In fact, the Clinton/Gore team decisively won all the debates, a feat not even Ronald Reagan equaled.

After shocking losses in the early primaries, Dole fired part of his team. Throughout the campaign, he frequently ignored the advice and directions of his managers. He fell off a stage in California. He rambled in several speeches. He set off a controversy by suggesting that tobacco was not addictive. On occasion he forgot what city he was in, such as the time he stood in Los Angeles and made reference to the Brooklyn Dodgers. Clinton, too, faced controversy. His friend and consultant, Dick Morris, was discovered to be involved with a Washington hooker whom he allowed to listen in on presidential phone calls. Dole and the press raised serious financial and ethical questions about illegal contributions to the Democratic campaign. But the economy was good, and the voters were now used to the sleaze factor. They had heard it all before. On election day, it was not a question of who would win but rather a matter of by how much they would win. The lack of suspense drove the numbers down. Ten million fewer people voted in 1996 than had turned out in 1992. Clinton received 49 percent of the vote, while Dole got 41 percent and Perot just 8 percent. The president carried 379 votes in the electoral college compared to Dole's 159. Clinton and Dole each received 44 percent of the male vote. The president, however, exposed the gender gap, claiming 54 percent of the female vote, compared to 38 percent for his challenger. He also got 83 percent of the black vote, while Dole got just 12 percent. First-time voters went for the president 54 percent to 34 percent. Seniors also rewarded the president, casting 50 percent of their votes for him compared to 43 percent for Senator Dole. Victories in California, New York, and Florida put large numbers in Clinton's column. His decisive early ad campaign in the battleground states of the industrial East and Midwest locked up Ohio, Illinois, Michigan, Missouri, Wisconsin, and Pennsylvania, making it mathematically impossible for Dole to break through.

It should also be noted that while voters gave Clinton a decisive victory, they returned a Republican Congress, apparently accepting the message Gingrich turned to late in the campaign when he asked voters not to give the president a blank check. In May of the following year, six months after the election, the president's popularity, buoyed by a robust economy, continued to grow. His approval ratings moved above 60 percent, his highest level of support recorded. But the dichotomy between his public performance and his private life that characterized much of his administration continued to be evident. At the same time he visited Europe to promote a new NATO, newspapers back home headlined two strikingly different stories. Consumer confidence had reached a 28-year high. Not since the late 1960s had the country felt so upbeat about the economy. Low unemployment, low inflation, and record highs on Wall Street fed the optimism. The same week, the Supreme Court unanimously ruled that the president could not postpone the sexual harassment case that Paula Jones had brought against him. The accusations were not new to the American people. They had heard about womanizing when Clinton first ran in 1992. Then, and again in 1996, they seemed to ignore such matters, concentrating instead on the state of the economy and the leadership Clinton provided. For some the vote for Clinton in 1992 and 1996 represents evidence of the moral decline of the nation. For others it signifies a process of maturation in which the electorate made a clear distinction between a candidate's private life and his public duty. Whatever our perspective, there is little doubt, as Theodore White noted, that those who come to power through the media can also be destroyed by the media. Such is the nature of the American political process. In January 1998, it was the Internet, the newest technology, that first broke the Lewinsky/Clinton sex scandal. The networks and newspapers soon followed. Special prosecutor Ken Starr was not far behind. Before long, the whole world was watching.

ACTIVITIES

This brief history of campaign advertising and the media's role in the political process provides a background to the study of current elections. It helps students conceptualize the election process in a fundamentally different way. Rather than simply knowing who ran and who won, students now have an opportunity to realize the increasing roles that advertising, television, and technology play in U.S. politics. They can study the personalities, the policies, and the process. Until voters become aware of the ways the process influences the outcome, including the very decision as to who will run in the first place, elections in this country are likely to continue to be more image than issue and more style than substance, governed by impulse and emotion rather than by logic and rational decision making. The authors cited in this chapter do not believe that the complex domestic and global issues of today or of the 21st century can best be addressed by such a political process.

(HIGH) — Discuss the political process in your school. What offices can students run for and vote for? What is the level of student interest or apathy in these elections? What qualities does a typical candidate have? Are the looks of the candidates important? Do candidates actually campaign, make speeches, and use publicity?

Study a recent political television advertisement. You might actually show the class an ad from a current campaign, or you may have access to ads from older campaigns. Remember, even if you can't get an actual ad, several slogans and ads are quoted in this chapter.

If you are working with a videotape of an ad, show it to the class without the sound. Have them concentrate on the images, including both the content and the form. What type of camera angles are used? Look at the posture, facial expression, and body language of the candidate. How do these affect our impressions of the politician? Does the spot use montage and rapid editing to juxtapose the candidate with themes and issues with which he or she wants to be associated? Are there any strong graphics, props, or backdrops such as stars and stripes, the U.S. flag, or the Statue of Liberty? Do we see images of a multiracial society and the young as well as the old? At what target audience do students think the ad is aimed?

When they have developed strong responses to these questions, show them the ad with the sound. How does the sound contribute to the message? Direct their attention to music, words, sound effects, and the tone of the narrator's voice. Could the soundtrack be successfully used as a radio spot? That is, can it stand independently from the images?

Locate a negative or adversarial commercial. Introduce students to the concept by describing the "daisy" spot and several other negative ads referred to in this chapter. Have them analyze the new commercial to determine what makes it negative. Issues that should be discussed include the difference between truth and fairness and the relationship among distortion, deception, and dishonesty. For example, the 1988 Bush campaign hit Michael Dukakis for not cleaning up Boston Harbor, but the ad did not tell us what role the federal government played (or didn't play) in funding the cleanup. In another example, the controversial Willie Horton spot painted Dukakis as soft on crime but ignored the fact that when Ronald Reagan was governor of California, he also had a furlough policy and that, in fact, Dukakis merely followed a common practice. Neither of the ads lied—they simply did not provide all the information. It should be noted that for all that is written about them, negative ads are not always successful. Despite Roger Ailes's successful campaigns for Nixon and Bush, his 1989 candidates for mayor of New York City and for governor of New Jersey both lost.

Break your class into groups, each representing an advertising agency. Each group has to come up with the best strategy, slogan, radio spot, TV spot, and print ad for the 2000 or 2004 presidential election. Have them conceptualize the work in terms of personality; policy, slogan, and themes; and process. They should attempt to use the turn of the century to sell their candidate. What type of candidate do they believe will be successful at this time? How will the changing composition of the U.S. population shape the choice of candidates and issues? Will new technologies allow new forms of advertising?

Will they run a positive or negative campaign? Look over some of the slogans from past campaigns that were not successful, such as Ford's "He's Making Us Proud Again." What are the potential pros and cons of using a slogan such as "The Dream Team"? It sounds good and it's catchy, but do people want to believe in the dream? Doesn't it leave the campaign wide open to negative attacks suggesting the candidate and the party are asleep or are even creating a nightmare? As students develop their own spots, have them use the storyboard format from this chapter.

If you have the facilities, the class could actually record a radio spot or television spot. Footage from old campaigns could be cut and re-edited with new voice-over to re-market a candidate.

Have the class debate the advantages and disadvantages of political advertising. Use the following lists as idea generators. They can actually have the debate, or you might want them to develop a paper on this topic.

Advantages

- Encourage voters to vote
- Bring the issues directly to the people
- Are cost-effective in that TV ads reach more people for a lower price than do direct mail and newspapers
- Don't change voters' minds but simply confirm their existing beliefs and attitudes (see the previous section on Nixon's 1968 campaign)
- Are quick and simple

Disadvantages

- Create apathy and alienation
- Substitute images for issues
- Make campaigns so expensive that only the rich can run
- Make campaigns so expensive that political action committees (PACs) and special-interest groups influence the candidate
- Rely on emotion, not logic
- Manipulate a visually illiterate electorate
- Require candidates to be "telegenic" or attractive, thus disadvantaging average-looking candidates who are otherwise well qualified. Could Lincoln or Franklin Roosevelt be elected in a TV age?
- Rely increasingly on negative techniques

MISCELLANEOU.S. STRATEGIES AND ACTIVITIES

Most of the instructional activities suggested in this chapter have been arranged around themes. The following activities represent single-concept lessons that can be used without a thematic approach.

And the Winner Is . . .
Glad Advertising and "Badvertising"

(ELEM/MID) — The advertising industry presents many awards for outstanding commercials, including awards for television commercials and print and billboard ads. The CLIO awards recognize high achievement in advertising. Other awards, such as the Baddies and the Trumpet, are given for ads that were not well received by the industry. Have students discuss their favorite and least favorite ads. Develop critical criteria for voting for and evaluating ads. Conduct a class poll for best and worst ads. Have students create their own award certificates for best and worst ads. Send the winning and losing certificates to the relevant companies, along with a letter from the class saying what they liked and disliked about each ad.

Clean Dreams

(ELEM/MID/HIGH) — An enormous number of ads that appear on U.S. television emphasize the need for cleanliness. Have students develop a list of the products that are advertised by emphasizing cleanliness. What type of people appear in these ads? What are the rewards of cleanliness? Younger students will be likely to concentrate on household cleaners. Older students, however, might discuss how the "clean dreams" approach is applied to people as well as to sinks and dishes. Teeth must be whiter than white, armpits must be heavily deodorized, and any number of feminine hygiene products marketed as "natural" actually disguise a woman's natural odor.

Green Consumerism

(ELEM/MID/HIGH) — In recent years, consumer activism has led to protests against commercials and companies and has often resulted in organized efforts to boycott products. This movement suggests that consumers are beginning to think more critically about marketing and its impact. One example has been the emergence of "green" consumerism. Exxon found itself in trouble with the way the public perceived the company following the *Valdez* Alaska oil spill of 1989. Various tuna distributors have been attacked because traditional methods of catching tuna resulted in killing or hurting dolphins. By 1990 the tuna industry had begun to produce ads addressing these concerns. McDonald's was criticized for the use of polystyrene food containers, and Coca-Cola was criticized for its ties to South Africa and that country's policy of apartheid. AT&T was criticized for contributions to Planned Parenthood.

Sometimes putting pressure on a company has no impact on sales or productivity. Companies are merely forced to address a public relations problem. Nonetheless, critical consumers tend to be active citizens exercising the rights afforded them in a democratic society. Until we begin to see a relationship among the products we purchase, the way they are packaged and promoted, and the way we dispose of them, we cannot hope to solve national and international problems such as pollution, acid rain, and the greenhouse effect. Teachers might want to talk to students about their own behavior and the choices they make as consumers. What do they do with their soft drink cans? Do they buy fast food in polystyrene packages? What is the impact on the environment? To which companies can they write about packaging and the ecological consequences? Can they set up recycling at home, at school, or in their neighborhood?

Teachers should also help students question the claims made by advertisers and manufacturers that their products are environmentally safe. Are the claims true or just another sales pitch?

Advertising and the Telephone Directory

(ELEM/MID) — The phone directory offers a cheap, readily available source of advertising for classroom use. Using it in the classroom not only helps students understand advertising but it also provides them with practical, day-to-day skills necessary to live in this culture. For students from different cultures, understanding the icons and information in a phone book can serve as useful survival skills.

Depending on the age level with which you are working, you can introduce students to the organization and alphabetical format of the directory. What logos, images, and icons are used to represent different businesses, industries, and professions? Photocopy some of the various corporate logos. Cut the name of the companies out of the ads and see which ones students can identify. The front of the directory also uses logos and icons for emergency numbers. Familiarize the students with the images that represent services such as doctors, firefighters, ambulances, and police.

Looking at Logos

(ELEM/MID) — Many major companies and corporations are instantly identified by the images or logos they use. Shell Oil, McDonald's, Paramount Pictures, and Arm & Hammer detergent are all examples of high name recognition. Cut logos from various ads, packets, or boxes. Make sure there are no names on the ads, and see which images the students recognize. You might create a mismatch game, giving labels the wrong names and asking the students to reclassify them. Have students design and draw logos for various companies and products you make up, such as Sunshine cereal, Bluewave detergent, Knight car polish, and Crown carpeting. In each case, ask the students to explain why they chose the logo they did. You can reverse this exercise by having each student show his or her logo to the class and asking the class to correctly identify the concept of the logo.

Selling Seasons

(ELEM) — Most elementary school teachers develop materials, activities, and displays to observe Thanksgiving, Halloween, Valentine's Day, and other holidays, celebrations, and special days. Almost all holidays and observances, including Presidents Day, Memorial Day, and Labor Day, are used by retailers and advertisers for special sales. Older students might explore how commercialization affects the true spirit of these holidays. Younger children can collect and study advertisements from local and state newspapers to see how the holiday is linked to selling. Have the students make a list or a display board of the keywords and pictures advertisers use to promote their products. At Christmas, for example, we commonly see images of Santa Claus and reindeer. At other times of the year, we see images of Abraham Lincoln and George Washington, witches, the U.S. flag, and so on. For Memorial Day 1990, McDonald's promoted a red, white, and blue special for those who had served their country, and the special included free apple pie.

"Shelf-Help"

(MID) — In 1990 a study by the Center for Science in the Public Interest reported that the organization and display of products on supermarket shelves was designed to attract the attention of children. The report concentrated on sugar-heavy breakfast cereals. It indicated that brands such as Fruit Loops and Cocoa Puffs tended to be placed on shelves at children's eye level. More nutritious brands such as Total and All Bran were placed on the higher shelves. Is this a manipulation of shoppers, or is it simply an effective sales technique? Have students study the organization of cereal on shelves in their own supermarkets to see if this pattern is repeated. A more advanced study could include observations and interviews to determine what cereals people buy, why people buy them, how children influence the choice of cereal, and the sugar content of cereals. Finally, the exercise can be extended to introduce students to the ways that display influences purchases. How, for example, are weekly specials highlighted in local supermarkets? What is impulse buying, and why are candy, magazines, and cigarettes so consistently arranged near the cash registers in supermarkets?

TEACH YOUR CHILDREN WELL

The world of children's advertising offers unique opportunities to help young consumers become critical viewers and thinkers. Here are some simple suggestions to help you get started.

Food for Thought

(ELEM/MID) — Select breakfast cereals such as Barbie or Batman. Take some packets to school and ask children why these cereals have these characters on the boxes. Present price information about these cereals as compared to more traditional cereals. Try a taste test to see if the children can distinguish between character cereals and more traditional brands.

"Some Assembly Required"; "Batteries Not Included"; "These Parts Sold Separately"

(ELEM/MID) — Discuss the above phrases with students to see if the children know what they mean. Study toy packages and magazine or television toy ads to see if they contain such phrases, and see how much the phrases are emphasized or minimized. Consider the size of the print, the location of the print, the speed or volume with which the phrase is said, and so on.

Special Effects and Visual Techniques

(ELEM/MID) — Think about the ways toy ads are presented on television. Are there a lot of sound effects or special effects such as explosions? Does the toy seem to move by itself? Is it shot from an angle that makes it appear larger than it actually is? Is the toy shown being used by several children all having a very good time? Does the commercial feature a song, jingle, or music that creates a mood? If so, what is the mood?

Color Counts

(ELEM/MID/HIGH) — Have students conduct a series of surveys to explore the role of color in advertising and packaging. You might want to divide the class into groups to study different aspects of this subject. Students could examine products found at home, dividing them into different categories such as food, cleaning supplies, drinks, etc. They should note what the most commonly used colors are, for what products these colors are used, and if there seems to be any difference in the colors used for products aimed at men versus women. The same assignment could be given to students during a field trip to a supermarket or a hardware store, or they might be assigned the task for homework. On the field trip, students could be assigned to specific aisles and products. Students could also be asked to determine the dominant colors used in billboards and various signs for hotels, restaurants, fast-food outlets, and businesses in their own community. Finally, students could cut advertisements from magazines and arrange a display by colors.

(ELEM/MID/HIGH) — Watch a series of television ads with the color turned off. After watching the commercials in black and white, discuss the colors that should be used in each ad and the reasons for the choices.

Strike a Pose

(ELEM/MID/HIGH) — This is a simple exercise from which young children, teens, and adults can benefit. The purpose is to promote awareness of body language and the ways that advertisers structure social and human tableaus that express gender attitudes and relationships. Collect a series of magazine ads aimed at both men and women. Look for striking differences in facial expression, gesture, stance, and posture. These will not be hard to find. The male look tends to be closed, stern, sullen, hands on hips, arms folded. The female look tends to be open, provocative: arms, legs, and mouth open, the body often reclining. Break the class into groups of two or three. Give each group a picture and have them mimic the postures in the picture. Then have them change gender roles, so the boys strike the pose of the females and the girls strike the pose of the males. A variation on this is to keep the pictures with you at the front of the room and call upon individual students to come forward and mimic the pose in one of the pictures. The rest of the class has to guess whether the pose belongs to a male or a female.

What's in a Name?

(MID/HIGH) — The choice of a name for a product often involves as much decision making as naming a child. The name must be memorable, simple, and communicate something about the individual nature of the product. Sanitary napkins, for example, promise women they will not be restricted by the problems associated with menstruation, so the names chosen include such words as "Freedom," "Stayfree," and "Security." The dirt associated with dishes is handled by selecting names that invoke freshness and cleanliness, such as "Dawn," "Sunlight," "Cascade," and "Ivory." Shampoo promises a better appearance and greater social acceptability, so it is marketed as "Finesse," "Style," and "Agree." Select a series of products and have the class develop a list of all the different names used to sell those products. Discuss the reason each name was selected. Divide the class into small groups and assign each one a specific type of product. The group must come up with a name for the product and justify their choice. Finally, older students might discuss what happens when human values and emotions such as love, joy, passion, and liberty are turned into promotional vehicles and brand names. Does this process trivialize these values and feelings?

Songs That Sell

(ELEM/MID/HIGH) — A major marketing device to draw our attention to products is the use of a song or jingle. The first jingle used for marketing was developed in 1923 for the Happiness Candy Company. Today, an enormous number of songs are used to promote a wide range of products. One of the most successful campaigns to use this technique was the California Raisins spot that featured "I Heard It Through the Grapevine." Many of today's ads feature yesterday's songs, particularly those from the 1960s and 1970s. But why? One reason is that some of these songs are old and are often relatively cheap to use. A more significant reason, however, is that the songs are instantly recognized by a generation that now has major spending power; they are, in fact, the songs with which this generation grew up. The widespread use of pop music has included some of the following:

"Like a Rock," Chevy Trucks

"Natural Woman," Clairol

Theme from *A Man and a Woman*, Chevy Ventura

"The Look of Love," Snackwells

"Morning Train," Burger King

"Can't Explain," Taurus

In the mid-1990s, television viewers included large numbers of baby boomers and the music of the 1960s was used to motivate them. Buick Le Sabre opted for "Stand by Me." Eggo Waffles used "Little Surfer." Pepto Bismol used "Mama Said There'd Be Days Like This." Nissan, with animation reminiscent of that in *Toy Story*, went back to the days of the British invasion and "You Really Got Me," by the Kinks. Burger King drew its musical material from the 1970s and 1980s, including "Urgent." One of the most successful advertising campaigns to use rock music was created for GM Chevy trucks. The spot relied on just three words from a Bob Seeger song, but the pitch was so powerful that the truck is now firmly identified in the public mind with the expression "Like a Rock." Beyond the mainstream of rock and pop, fringe music, including rap, has also been used as part of advertising.

In 1990, rap music found its way into advertising. Rapper Young M.C. did a pitch for Pepsi, Miller Lite beer used Run D.M.C., McDonald's "Fries Surprise" campaign used rap music, and Jovan perfume sponsored a "Write Your Own" rap tune contest. Compile a list of songs used to promote products. Mismatch the list and have students match the correct product to its song. Have students make their own list of all the pop songs and jingles they know that are used to promote products. Have the students select a song with which they are familiar and write new lyrics to make their own jingle. Give students a current list of Top 40 songs. Look at the titles. Discuss which songs might be used to promote particular types of products. Select "oldies" that could be turned into product pitches. For example, Roy Orbison's "Only the Lonely" might become an Oscar Mayer theme, sung as "Only Bologna."

ADS AS HISTORICAL ARTIFACTS

The American Advertising Museum in Portland, Oregon, has an outstanding collection of print and television advertising in addition to an extensive display of packaging and premiums. The museum is currently developing plans to expand, including the prospect of arranging traveling exhibits. The existence of the museum serves to demonstrate and document the social and historical significance of advertising. History and social studies teachers who recognize the relevance of advertising to the curriculum can draw upon magazines and newspapers from the 20th century and teach students how to uncover the past by analyzing the advertisements. A recent example demonstrates just how clearly advertising is tied into political and economic developments. When the Berlin Wall fell in 1989, several leading U.S. companies were quick to send production crews to Berlin in time to have ads running on U.S. television before the Christmas shopping rush. During the Vietnam War, Kodak created a spot featuring a soldier returning home to his family and fiancée. By fusing images of the Grain Belt, middle America, farmland, soldier, and the lyrics of "The Green, Green Grass of Home," the commercial created an indelible record of the national mood at a particular moment in time. In *Advertising the American Dream*, Roland Marchand addresses the historical evidence that advertising affords us. "Once we have placed the advertisements in the same category as many traditional historical documents, it may be possible to argue that ads actually surpass most other recorded communications as a basis for plausible inference about popular attitudes and values" (1985, xix). Marchand believes ads reveal social values, the state of technology, fashions, styles, and insights into the economy.

Most communities today have one or more flea markets or antique and collectible fairs. Often, these travel to various malls once or twice a year. It is quite common for dealers to have dated copies of *Life*, *Look*, *Saturday Evening Post*, and other magazines rich in advertising. University and public libraries can also be good sources for such magazines. In addition, your students may have parents or grandparents who collected some of the magazines, and you might be able to draw on them. Country craft and collectible stores are now also quite common, and they often feature antique advertising for wall display. These can be particularly good examples of racial stereotyping in advertising. Finally, old tins, boxes, cans, and packets also provide good historical materials, and if the originals are not available, many of them are now sold as reproductions.

(ELEM/MID/HIGH) — Before starting the study of a historical period with stu-

dents, provide them with magazines, newspapers, or other advertising from the time. Their assignment is to find out about the period by looking at the pictures. If you like, you can divide the class into groups and have each group make a class presentation on one of the following topics:

- Fashion and clothes (men, women, children)

- Food (prices, packaging)

- Appliances and furnishings

- Recreation and leisure (movies, sports, theater, etc.)

- Transportation and communication (cars, trains, planes, telephones, etc.)

- Occupations (shown in display ads, positions vacant in classifieds, wages)

- Family life (size of family, number of children, type of home)

- Views and values (how were social ideals reflected?)

(HIGH) — Older students might extend this process by investigating whether these materials provide an accurate or representative picture of that period and society. Might they not reflect the middle-class society of the advertisers or magazine subscribers, but ignore other levels of society? Might they not reflect social aspirations and fantasy, rather than social reality? These questions are crucial to the consideration of popular culture as historical evidence, and exploring these issues promotes critical thinking skills, which have applications in all areas of the curriculum.

REFERENCES

Advertising Age (1994). How Teens Shop. July 18, 3.

Atkin, C. K., (1990). The Effects of Televised Alcohol Messages on Teenage Drinking Patterns. *Journal of Adolescent Health Care*, 11:1024.

Atkin, C. et al., (1984). Teenage Drinking: Does Advertising Make a Difference? *Journal of Communication*, 34:2, 157-67.

Atlat, James, (1984). Beyond Demographics: How Madison Avenue Knows Who You Are and What You Want. *Atlantic Monthly*, October.

Austin, Erica Weintraub, and Heidi Kay Meli, (1994). Effects of Interpretation of Televised Alcohol Portrayals on Children's Alcohol Beliefs. *Journal of Broadcasting and Electronic Media*, Fall, 417-35.

Austin, Erica Weintraub, and Beth Nache-Ferguson, (1995). Sources and Influences of Young School Age Children's General and Brand Specific Knowledge About Alcohol. *Health Communications*, 7:1, 1-20.

Austin, Erica Weintraub, and Kristine Kay Johnson, (1997). Effects of General and Alcohol-Specific Media Literacy Training on Children's Decision Making About Alcohol. *Journal of Health Communication*, Vol. 2, 17-42.

Berenstain, Stan, and Jan Berenstain, (1988). *The Berenstain Bears Get the Gimmies*. New York: Random House.

Booth, William, (1991). Quit Nagging and Pass the Cookies. *Washington Post*, weekly edition, July 22-28, 37.

Bowen, Wally, (1995). Ads, Ads Everywhere: Are There Any Limits? *New Citizen* 2:2, 1, 7.

Brown, Jane, and Kim Walsh Childers, (1994). Effects of Media on Personal and Public Health. In Jennings Bryant and Dolf Zillmann (eds.), *Media Effects: Advances in Theory and Research*. Hillsdale, NJ: Lawrence Erlbaum.

Brown, Jane, and S. Newcomer, (1991). Television Viewing and Adolescents Sexual Behavior. *Journal of Homosexuality*, 21:1 and 2, 77-91.

Brown, Jane, and Jeanne Steele, (1995). Sex and the Mass Media. Kaiser Foundation, Menlo Park, CA.

Busby, L., and G. Leichty, (1993). Feminism and Advertising in Traditional and Nontraditional Women's Magazines 1950s-1980s. *Journalism Quarterly*, 70:2, 247-64.

Butsch, Richard, (1995). Ralph, Fred, Archie and Homer: Why Television Keeps Recreating the White Male Working Class Buffoon. In Gail Dines and Jean Humez (eds.), *Gender, Race and Class in Media*, 403-12. Thousand Oaks, CA: Sage.

Cassidy, Marsha, and Richard Katula, (1995). The Black Experience in Advertising: An Interview with Thomas Burrell. In Gail Dines and Jean Humez (eds.), *Gender, Race and Class in Media*. Thousand Oaks, CA: Sage.

Center for Substance Abuse Prevention, (1995). *The Challenge of Participatory Research: Preventing Alcohol Related Problems in Ethnic Communities*. Washington, DC: U.S. Department of Health and Human Services.

Christiansen, B., and M. Goldman, (1983). Alcohol Related Expectancies vs. Demographic Background Variables in the Prediction of Adolescent Drinking. *Journal of Consulting and Clinical Psychology*, 51, 249-57.

Chuck, Ross, (1996). Blacks Drawn to Indy TV. *Advertising Age*, 3/4, 8.

Considine, David M., Gail Haley, and Lyn Lacy, (1994). *Imagine That: Developing Critical Viewing and Thinking Through Children's Literature*. Englewood, CO: Libraries Unlimited.

Consumers Union Education Services, (1990). *Selling America's Kids: Commercial Pressures on Kids of the 90s*.

DeVaney, Ann, (1994). *Watching Channel One: The Convergence of Students, Technology and Private Business*. Albany: State University of New York.

Di Franza, Joseph, et al., (1991). RJR Nabisco's Cartoon Camel Promotes Camel Cigarettes to Children. *Journal of the American Medical Association*, 266:22, 3149-54.

Dines, Gail, and Jean Humez, (eds.), (1995). *Gender, Race and Class in Media*. Thousand Oaks, CA: Sage.

Dodds, Katherine, (1996). Interventions in the Belly of the Beast. *Adbusters*, Spring, 35-37.

Donahue, Deidre, (1996). No Nonsense Therapist Takes Society to Task. *U.S.A. Today*, April 9, D1-2.

Ettema, Jame, and D. Charles Whitney, (1994). *Audiencemaking: How the Media Create the Audience*. Thousand Oaks, CA: Sage.

Ettenberg, Elliot, (1985). Psychographics: The Art of Finding Out Who. *Sales and Marketing Management in Canada*, August 16.

Ewen, Stuart, (1988). *All Consuming Images: The Politics of Style in Contemporary Culture*. New York: Basic Books.

Fowles, Jib, (1996). *Advertising and Popular Culture*. Thousand Oaks, CA: Sage.

Fox, Roy, (1996). *Harvesting Minds: How TV Commercials Control Kids*. Westport, CT: Praeger.

Garfield, Bob, (1994). Rating Corporate Slogans. *Advertising Age*. July 18, 3.

Garner, David, (1997). The 1997 Body Image Survey Results. *Psychology Today*. February, 30-34.

Germond, Jack, and Jules Witcover, (1993). *Mad as Hell: Revolt at the Ballot Box 1992*. New York: Time Warner.

Guber, Selina, (1987). The Teenage Mind. *American Demographics*, 9:8, 42-44.

Hawkins, David, Michael Arthur, and Richard Catalano, (1995). *Building a Safer Society: Strategic Approaches to Crime Prevention*. Chicago: University of Chicago Press.

Hawkins, J. David, Richard Catalano, and Janet Miller, (1992). Risk and Protective Factors for Alcohol and Other Drug Problems in Adolescence and Early Adulthood: Implications for Substance Abuse Prevention. *Pychological Bulletin*, 112:1, 64-105.

Hicks, Carolyn, (1996). The Only Things That Aren't Fake Are You, Me and Sprite: Ironies and Realities in Generation X Advertising. *Metro Magazine*, No. 106, 71-82.

Hitchon, Jacqueline, and Esther Thorson, (1995). Effects of Emotion and Product Involvement on the Experience of Repeated Commercial Viewing. *Journal of Broadcasting and Electronic Media*, 39:3, 376-89.

Ingrassia, Michelle, (1995). Calvin's World. *Newsweek*, September 11, 60-65.

Iskoff, Michael, (1991). Just Say Alcohol. *Washington Post,* weekly edition, June 17-23, 37.

Jamieson, Kathleen, (1984). *Packaging the Presidency: A History and Criticism of Presidential Campaign Advertising*. New York: Oxford University Press.

———, (1992). *Dirty Politics: Deception, Distraction and Democracy*. New York: Oxford University Press.

Jernigan, David, and Patricia Wright, (1995). *Making News: Changing Policy Case Studies of Media Advocacy on Alcohol and Tobacco Issues*. University Research Corporation, The Marin Institute for the Prevention of Alcohol and Other Drug Problems.

Kaid, Lynda Lee, (1996). Presidential Ads as Nightly News: A Content Analysis of 1988 and 1992 Televised Adwatches. *Journal of Broadcasting and Electronic Media*, 40:3.

Kanner, Allen, and Mary Gomes, (1995). All Consuming Self. *Adbusters*, Summer, 21-25.

Katz, Jackson, (1995). Advertising and the Construction of Violent White Masculinity. In Gail Dines and Jean Humez (eds.), *Gender, Race and Class in Media*. Thousand Oaks, CA: Sage.

Keeling, Richard, (1994). Changing the Context: The Power in Prevention Alcohol Awareness, Caring and Community. *College Health* 42. May, 243-47.

Key, Bryan Wilson, (1972). *Subliminal Seduction*. New York: Signet Books.

———, (1980). *The Clam Plate Orgy and Other Subliminal Techniques for Manipulating Your Behavior*. New York: Signet Books.

Kilbourne, Jean, (1994). Gender Bender Ads: Same Old Sexism. *New York Times,* May 15, F13.

Kleusch, Mary, (1992). *A Guide to Curriculum Planning in Alcohol and Other Drug Abuse Programs*. Madison: Wisconsin Department of Public Instruction.

Korten, David, (1995). *When Corporations Rule the World*. West Hartford, CT: Kumarian Press.

Kuntz, Mary, (1996). The New Hucksterism. *Businessweek*, July 1, 76-84.

Kurmit, Paul, (1992). Ten Tips from the Top Agency. *Advertising Age*, February 10, 36.

Kusserow, Richard, (1992). *Youth and Alcohol: Dangerous and Deadly Consequences*. Washington, DC: Office of the Inspector General, Department of Health and Human Services.

Lasn, Kalle, (1995). Our Consumptive Way of Life Is Poisoning the Air and Water. *Adbusters*, Winter, 3:3, 25-28.

Leo, John, (1993). Madison Avenue's Gender Wars. *U.S. News and World Report*, October 25, 25.

———, (1995). Decadence the Corporate Way. *U.S. News and World Report*, September 4, 31.

Levine, Joshua, (1997). Badass Sells. *Forbes*, April 21, 142-48.

Linn, Marcia et al., (1984). Adolescent Reasoning About Advertising: Relevance About Product Claims. *Journal of Early Adolescence*, 4:4, 371-85.

Lowry, D. T., and A. Shindler, (1993). Prime Time TV Portrayals of Safe Sex and AIDS. *Journalism Quarterly*, 70:3, 628-37.

Lyons, John, (1987). *Guts: Advertising from the Inside Out*. New York: American Management Association.

Mandell, Maurice, (1984). *Advertising*. Englewood Cliffs, NJ: Prentice-Hall.

Marchand, Roland, (1985). *Advertising the American Dream*. Berkeley and Los Angeles: University of California Press.

McGinnis, Joe, (1970). *The Selling of the President 1968*. London: Andre Deutsch.

Meyers, William, (1984). *The Image Makers: Power and Persuasion on Madison Avenue*. New York. Times Books.

Millum, T., (1975). *Images of Women: Advertising in Women's Magazines*. London: Chatto and Windos.

Molnar, Alex, (1994). 10 Questions to Ask About Advertising, Marketing Programs and Curriculum Materials in Your Schools. *PTA Today*, May/June, 8-9.

Montgomery, Kathryn, (1991). Alcohol and Television: And Now for Some Mixed Messages. *Media and Values*. Spring-Summer, 55-56.

Naurekas, Jim, (1994). Smoke Screens: When Journalists Boost the Tobacco Industry, Follow the Money. *Extra,* September-October, 18-19.

New York Times, (1997). Sexual Activity Among US Youths Is Declining, Report Shows. May 2, A15.

Novello, Antonia, (1991). Liquor Industry Must Stop Targeting Minorities with Alcohol Ads. *U.S.A. Today*, July 1.

Office for Substance Abuse Prevention, (1991a). *Turning Awareness into Action: What Your Community Can Do About Drug Use in America*. Washington, DC: U.S. Department of Health and Human Services.

Office for Substance Abuse Prevention, (1991b). *Preventing Adolescent Drug Use: From Theory to Practice*. Prevention Monograph No. 8. Washington, DC: U.S. Department of Health and Human Services.

Office of National Drug Control Policy, (1995). *National Drug Control Strategy: Executive Summary*. ONDCP, White House, Washington, DC.

Olson, Barry, and Peter Ross, (1992). Clinton on TV. *TV Guide*, November 21, 15.

Osborn, Barbara Bliss, (1995). The New Drug Busters: How Critical Viewing Skills Can Arm Kids in the War Against Drugs. *Better Viewing*, September/October, 6-8.

Packard, Vance, (1957). *The Hidden Persuaders*. New York: Pocket Books.

Pener, Degen, (1996). Extreme Advertising. *Entertainment Weekly*, Summer, 67.

Petersen, Corlice, (1995). Kids Exploited as Sex Objects. *U.S.A. Today*, October 2, 13a.

Riche, N., and Martha Farnsworth, (1989). Psychographics for the 90s—The News VALS Psychographic System Could Be a Boon for the Market. *American Demographics*, July 1989, 25.

Ritchie, Karen, (1995). X Marks Moving Target for Marketers. *U.S.A. Today*, May 17, 5B.

Rosenberg, Ellen, (1994). From Barney to Supernintendo: What to Do When Your Child Wants It All. *PTA Today*, May-June, 5.

Savan, Leslie, (1994). *The Sponsored Life: Ads, TV and American Culture*. Philadelphia: Temple University Press.

Schneider, Karen et al., (1996). Too Fat, Too Thin: How Media Images of Celebrities Teach Kids to Hate Their Bodies. *People*, June 3, 64-74.

Schram, Martin, (1987). *The Great American Video Game: Presidential Politics in the Television Age*. New York: William Morrow.

Seitter, Ellen, (1995). "Different Children, Different Dreams: Racial Representation in Advertising." In Gail Dines and Jean Humez (eds.), *Gender, Race and Class in Media*. Thousand Oaks, CA: Sage.

Shorris, Earl, (1994). *A Nation of Salesmen: The Tyranny of the Market and the Subversion of Culture*. New York: Norton.

Signorielli, Nancy et al., (1994). Gender Stereotypes in MTV Commercials: The Beat Goes On. *Journal of Broadcasting and Electronic Media*, 38:1, 91-101.

Soley, L., and G. Kurzbard, (1986). Sex in Advertising: A Comparison of 1964 and 1984. *Journal of Advertising*, 13:3, 46-55.

Spethmann, Betsy, (1990). Marketing to Kids. *Advertising Age*, February 10.

Spillman, Diana, and Caroline Everington, (1989). Somatypes Revisited: Have the Media Changed Our Perception of the Female Body Image? *Psychological Reports*, 64, 887-90.

Sugarman, Carole, and Malcolm Gladwell, (1991). Once Again the Foxes Set Policy in the Henhouse. *Washington Post*, weekly edition, May 6-12, 39.

Thomas, Evan et al., (1997). *Back from the Dead: How Clinton Survived the Republican Revolution*. New York: Atlantic Monthly Press.

Tinkham, Spencer, and Ruth Ann Weaver-Lariscy, (1993). A Diagnostic Approach to Assessing the Impact of Negative Political Television Commercials. *Journal of Broadcasting and Electronic Media*, 37:4, 377-400.

Turow, Joseph, (1997). *Breaking Up America: Advertisers and the New Media World*. Chicago: University of Chicago Press.

U.S. Department of Education and Health and Human Services, (1995). *Health for Success. National School Health Education Standards: Achieving Health Literacy*. Washington, DC.

U.S. News and World Report, (1991). N.t., n.d., 18.

U.S.A. Today, (1991). N.t., September.

Vinzant, Carol, (1997). Discounting the Elderly: Why TV Slights Its Most Faithful Viewers. *Extra*, 10:2, 21-22.

Weiss, Michael, (1989). *The Clustering of America*. New York: Tilden Press.

Wellborn, Kellie, (1993). *The Appalachian*. October 21-24, 1.

Wells, Melanie, (1995). Divas of Madison Avenue: Women Are Moving Up on Madison Ave. *U.S.A. Today*, June 12, B1-3.

———, (1997). Age Bias Cases Gush from Fountain of Youth Culture. *U.S.A. Today*, March 18, B1.

Whelan, Elizabeth, (1995). Tobacco Rules in Too Many Women's Magazines. *U.S.A. Today*, November 14, 13A.

White, Theodore, (1961). *The Making of the President 1960*. London: Jonathan Cape.

———, (1982). *America in Search of Itself: The Making of the President 1956-80*. New York: Harper & Row.

Wolf, Naomi, (1991). *The Beauty Myth: How Images of Beauty Are Used Against Women*. New York: Anchor Doubleday.

Wright, Patricia, (1995). *Organizing for Change: Confronting Alcohol, Tobacco and Other Drug Issues at the Grassroots Level*. U.S. Office of Personnel Management for the Center for Substance Abuse Prevention, Washington, DC.

Chapter 5

FROM LIVING ROOM TO CLASSROOM
Taking Television Seriously

This instrument can teach, it can illuminate; yes and it can even inspire. But it can do so only to the extent that humans are determined to use it to those ends. Otherwise it is merely wires and lights in a box.—Edward R. Murrow

Someone once suggested that television is called a medium because it's rare when it's well done. The joke is symptomatic of a media mind-set that has historically undermined the willingness and ability of teachers and parents alike, whether in the classroom or the living room, to address television's ability to teach. To a very real degree, it might now be argued that ignoring television in the education process not only ignores the nature and needs of children weaned in this electronic environment, but also ignores the nature of America as a nation. President Clinton, the first viewer and the first president raised in the television era, has acknowledged television's role in his personal life and in the life of the nation. "Television has been an integral part of my life, and I've always believed that it has enormous influence upon our culture. And also reflects our culture. It's a reflection of what's happening in America and where we're going" (Murphy and Redicliffe 1996, 46). It is hardly surprising, then, that Clinton has focused much attention on the impact of media messages on impressionable children and teens, whether addressing cigarette advertising or violence on television.

Nor is the president alone in his belief that television exerts an important influence upon the nation, including the way we see ourselves and the way others see us. In *U.S. News and World Report* it was observed that "TV has become the closest and most constant companion for American children. It has become the nation's Mom and Pop, storyteller, babysitter, preacher, and teacher" (Zuckerman 1993, 64). For many Americans, television is simply indispensable. A 1996 *TV Guide* survey found that 52 percent of Americans said they would not give up television viewing forever for any amount of money.

It is ironic that a technology that occupies such a powerful and pervasive presence in our homes is so consistently ignored in our classrooms and curricula. Television has now been present in the nation's schools for almost half a century. The VCR revolution of the 1980s increased the promise and potential of television technology. Yet, despite the presence of the equipment and the promise of the technology, there is almost no sign that the content and form of television are ever integrated in any systematic way into the curriculum. Television and its related technologies tend to be used for delivery systems for presenting the traditional curriculum in a marginally new way, in the same way that motion pictures replaced radio in the classroom and videotape signaled the demise of filmstrips. The nation's schools may teach *with television* or *through television*, but with the exception of isolated pockets of progress, they do not teach *about television*. Any school system that claims to be child-centered surrenders all credibility if it chooses to ignore the fact that these children have seen 5,000 hours of TV before they ever arrive at school for their formal

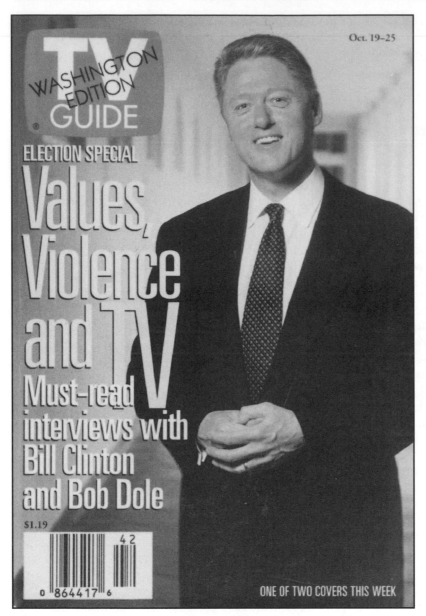

❖**Reprinted with permission from News America Publications, Inc., publisher of *TV Guide* magazine, copyright, October 19-25, 1996, News America Publications, Inc.**

the best" (Leifer 1974, 221). Further, viewing television promotes children's recognition of letters and numbers, encourages language acquisition, and potentially undermines their ability and willingness to learn in the static, sterile chalk-and-talk environment that still characterizes too many of our classrooms. Sadly, researchers have argued this point for more than 20 years with minimal impact on teachers, and, just as importantly, on those professors and academics charged with the responsibility of preparing teachers to reach today's children. For the most part, colleges of education continue to celebrate the primacy of print, exhibiting all the characteristics of institutions of inertia. Conclusions from two decades ago continue to ring true today:

> *Not enough time is spent in our schools helping students to cope with the symbology of visual media; few relationships between television viewing at home and teaching in the school have been established. The resultant "cultural gap" leads to minunderstandings between students and teachers as well as re duced learning (Barton and Miller 1977, 229).*

education. The window on the world that television provides for these young people aids their cognitive development, shaping their perceptions of people and places beyond the security of their own homes and immediate families. According to the *Harvard Educational Review*, "It socializes children into a fictitious social system, where criminals are always caught . . . minorities and elderly are rarely seen and problems are solved in an hour and usually worked out for

In many ways, television is its own worst enemy, not so much because of the questionable and often controversial content, but because of its inescapable omnipresence. It's a case of not being able to see the technological forest for the technological trees. David Bianculli, author of *Taking Television Seriously: Teleliteracy*, makes such a point. "The common and easy thing to do," he says, "is to dismiss TV entirely and attack it for its obvious excesses and weaknesses. Because of the pervasiveness and familiarity, it is either taken for granted or targeted for abuse." Those who dismiss the medium as inferior, illiterate pop culture, he argues, "haven't checked out the scenery in quite a while" (1992, 4-5). Bianculli also recognizes the gulf these attitudes create between students and those who must both teach and reach them. "The students of today already take television quite seriously . . . the teachers have only to catch up and, given the chance, the children shall lead them" (6, 287). While it is perfectly plausible that children can teach teachers about television, Bianculli seems to assume that taking television seriously somehow confers understanding and comprehension of the medium upon its young viewers. Exposure to television may well acquaint children and teens with plotlines, genre conventions, even editing and camera techniques, but for the most part, deeper understanding of the content and impact of television will require the presence of an intermediary, whether a parent or a teacher. To assume this role, adults need to be more attuned to the pleasure that they themselves derive from television, to look and listen for the very best the medium has to offer. Incongruous as it may seem, the very best of this visual medium often has its roots in very good writing. The pilot episode of Emmy Award-winner *The Wonder Years* closed with the voice-over narration of Kevin Arnold as he looked back upon the turbulence and pain of coming of age in the 1960s. It is a speech these authors have seen bring tears to the eyes of grown men and women in our media literacy workshops. As the episode ends, Kevin searches a private place in the woods to find his childhood sweetheart, Winnie Cooper. Winnie has just been told that her brother Brian died in Vietnam. Kevin struggles with feelings of love, death, and desire. He comforts the girl, offering her his jacket, and they share their first kiss. The camera draws back and Percy Sledge sings "When a Man Loves a Woman," as we hear the voice of the adult Kevin looking back on his childhood:

> *I think about the events of that day, again and again. Whenever some blowhard starts talking about the anonymity of the suburbs or the mindlessness of the TV generation, because we know that inside each one of those identical boxes with its Dodge parked out front, and its white bread on the table and its TV set glowing blue in the falling dusk, there were people with stories. There were families bound together in the pain and the struggle of love. There were moments that made us cry with laughter and there were moments like that one of sorrow and wonder. (Wonder Years pilot episode, aired 1/31/88).*

Of course not all television writing is this tender, not all episodes this exemplary, but it is not difficult to find quality programming. Teachers who do nothing more than browse *TV Guide, Entertainment Weekly*, or the regular reviews in *U.S.A. Today* will be alerted to quality programs and to episodes and characters that might resonate with their students and connect with the curriculum. Our failure to identify such programs robs us of effective teaching tools, denies students a deeper appreciation of television, and results in a blanket condemnation of the industry, which is demeaning to many of the men and women who write, create, and produce television, because they believe it can be an uplifting human experience that both entertains and educates.

❖Whether in the living room or the classroom, parents or teachers who view with children become instructional intermediaries who can put the messages in context for impressionable young viewers. In short, it's not just what they watch, but how they watch and who they watch with. Copyright © 1998 Gail E. Haley.

PAGE Versus SCREEN and Other PROS and CONS

Douglas Rushkoff writes, "To appreciate the media as a facilitator rather than hypnotizer, we must learn to decode the information coming into our homes" (1994, 6). It is equally true that we must learn to recognize and respond to the arguments that have marginalized and undermined the serious study of television in the classroom. Among the more pervasive negative beliefs about television established in both academic research and the public imagination, we find some of the following:

- Television causes and/or contributes to violence in society.

- Television, whether in advertising or programs, uses sex to sell.

- Television promotes a culture of conspicuous consumption that ignores the spiritual side of human nature in favor of materialism.

- Television is cheap, vulgar, and anti-intellectual.

- Television disrupts family life and communication.

- Television impedes literacy and discourages reading.

- Viewing television promotes passive acceptance of its message.

After 50 years of scrutiny, it is not difficult to find research that points the finger of blame for many social ills clearly in the direction of television. A good deal of the research, however, suggests that it is not the content of television alone that contributes to any effects, but rather the social and psychological context in which viewing occurs. In the case of violence, for example, researchers have noted that "viewing violence leads to aggression and aggressive tendencies lead to viewing television" (Huston et al. 1992, 56). The chicken-and-egg nature of the argument demands that we look at the cycle in which these media messages are not only produced but also consumed. Equally, when we address aspects of physical health such as obesity, it is difficult once again to establish which comes first. While studies have reported that "the prevalence for obesity increased by 2 percent for each additional hour of television viewed" (Dietz and Gortmaker 1985), the question once again goes beyond television content and demands consideration of the viewing context, which, in this case, could include the sedentary lifestyles of the couch-potato culture.

Other opponents of television have much broader concerns about its impact. Writing in *Esquire*, Bill McKibben, author of *The Age of Missing Information*, suggested that what television really does is to promote a narcissistic culture. "Self obsession is what comes through the TV set—the ceaseless preoccupation with keeping us from becoming bored for even an instant. Reminding us at every break that our immediate satisfaction is the purpose of a consumer culture" (1993, 67). Neil Postman is even more damning in his criticism. For Postman, television not only indulges our self-obsession, but it does so in such a way that it infantilizes the entire culture. Despite the fact that we are a nation of chronological grown-ups, says Postman, television undermines maturity and authority. "It is biased towards the behavior of the child-adult. TV promotes as desirable many of the attitudes we associate with childishness: an obsessive need for immediate gratification, a lack of concern for consequences, an almost promiscuous preoccupation with consumption" (1981, 24).

But far and away the greatest educational concern raised about television's impact on children has been the belief that it promotes passivity and discourages reading. Even a sacred cow like *Sesame Street* is not safe from the critics. Jane Healy, author of *Endangered Minds: Why Our Children Don't Think*, has focused her attack on this beloved children's program. Describing it as a "peripatetic carnival," she argues that "the habits of the mind necessary to be a good reader are exactly what *Sesame Street* does not teach: language, active reflection,

persistence and internal control" (1990, 220). Further, she concludes, "I am convinced it is not merely a coincidence that our faith in it [*Sesame Street*] has coincided with a major decline in reading and learning skills" (221). Among 10 reasons she gives for why the program is bad for reading skills, a major concern is that it establishes false expectations about how print on a page behaves. "Words in books do not jump about, transform before one's eyes or call attention to themselves" (226). Confronted with this disappointing reality, many children, she says, simply turn off "when informed that they must bend their brains around the hard job of attacking the words, rather than having a barrage of letters, words and pictures attacking them" (226). Pity the poor parent or pedagogue apprised of Healy's perspective. If *Sesame Street* is so damaging, everything else must be horrendous, ergo turn off the television.

Of course, depriving the child of television also deprives the child of a window on the world, albeit a distorted window. The child without television is denied a perspective beyond the immediacy of the family, neighborhood, state, and nation. The child who lives in a house without television is deprived of the social cement that binds the nation and provides a common meeting point and experience for children and adults alike who may not share a common religion, language, or economic background, but who still gather in front of the same glowing box. The child, teenager, or adult deprived of television not only misses the information that can foster cognitive development, but is also denied the emotional highs and lows that resonate across the nation when we come together in a shared experience of an event. Such an event happened when children and adults across the country watched in dismay and disbelief as the space shuttle *Challenger* exploded. The nation grieved and mourned together through the presence of the roving eye of television as we learned about the Oklahoma City bombing and witnessed the memorial service. On a more uplifting note, a teenage gymnast named Kerri Strug showed she had the right stuff at the Olympic Games in Atlanta. In a remarkable display of courage, she battled the pain of damaged ankle ligaments to perform one final vault that gave the U.S. team the first-ever gold medal for women's gymnastics. It was an inspiring sight, an affirmation of human determination, that television provided not only to viewers in this country but around the world. When the television lens focuses beyond our shores, it is equally capable of compelling our attention, whether showing us the collapse of the Berlin Wall, a lone demonstrator standing in front of a tank in Tiananmen Square, or the atrocity and human misery that civil war or famine can create.

But it is not just news or sporting events that offer the opportunity to educate and inspire. At its very best, television can teach, motivate, and move. *All in the Family* provided such a lesson when Edith was raped. In an episode called "My Name Is Alex," *Family Ties* chartered new territory for a sit-com as teenager Alex Keaton painfully explored the death of his friend, the meaning of life, and his own faith in God. Similarly, *Sesame Street* used the real-life death of storekeeper Mr. Hopper to introduce Big Bird and, by implication, the young audience to an awareness of dying. Sherwin Nuland, author of *How We Die*, has studied the way television depicts death. Among exemplary episodes, he singled out *NYPD Blue* for its story line that dealt with the death of Andy Sipowicz Jr. Referring to a "depth of empathy and even wisdom displayed by the entire superb cast," he adds that the program sets a remarkable standard for dealing with the complexity of death. Addressing loss, anger, grief, and healing, he says, "The writing in this episode is suffused with the sorrow of ordinary people—the sorrow of all of us. The direction is meticulous, there is not a false emotion or superfluous action" (1996, 69).

So once again, as we learned with *The Wonder Years*, exemplary television programming often means exemplary writing. It's not just the words the characters speak, but the very same codes, conventions, and elements that constitute a good novel. Good television and good film, like good literature, tells us something about the human condition through the common elements of plot, conflict, resolution, characters, setting, protagonist, and antagonist. None of this, of course, is to suggest that television and books are the same. *Reading Television* makes some clear distinctions between the two. While the written work "promotes consistency, narrative development from cause to effect . . . clarity and a single tone of voice . . . television is ephemeral, episodic, specific, concrete, and dramatic in mode" (Fiske and Hartley 1978, 15). These differences, however, should not constitute divides. Being pro-television does not mean being anti-book any more than being pro-book necessitates hostility toward television. The TV production of *Gulliver's Travels* no doubt introduced millions of children and their parents to the Lilliputian world of Swift's novel, which they would otherwise never have encountered. Similarly, 1997's screening of *The Odyssey* no doubt introduced many viewers to the idea that Homer was someone other than the head of the Simpsons' household. Rather than setting the page against the screen, it is much more constructive and beneficial to see the way television and books can complement each other. Children's author Mem Fox operates from such a perspective. "Television and books," she says, "have one thing in common. It's what the child gets out of them that matters. Reading is not inherently good. Television is not inherently bad" (1993, 103). Further, she suggests, "The child who loves books will gain enormously from watching television—much of the unknown world will be revealed, giving the child valuable insight and information to assist later in understanding more demanding literature" (101). Finally, for those who remain concerned that reading requires more concentration and effort than viewing, there is a growing body of evidence that challenges the notion that children watch television passively, or that they derive little from it. In the case of children's programs, for example, viewing has been shown to "be positively related to young children's vocabulary, letter and number skills as well as their later school achievement" (Macbeth 1996, 199). In addition, researchers continue to challenge the idea that children are not intellectually engaged by television. "Children are often cognitively active when watching television . . . they attend when the content is comprehensible and interesting" (Huston and Wright 1996, 38). Well beyond the question of program content, the whole social and psychological context in which viewing takes place continues to demand further study. This fact cannot be overemphasized, whether addressing the role of the parent in the living room or the teacher in the classroom. There is now considerable evidence indicating that what we get from the television-viewing experience is related to the expectations we have of it. If teachers and parents fail to challenge children and teens as they encounter the medium, it is likely they will process it on a shallow and superficial level. While much needs to be said about offensive or inappropriate programming, one of the greatest barriers to television's success as a teaching tool is the attitudes that we as a society have about television. "One reason that viewers do not concentrate much mental effort on television is a widespread belief that television is easy. When you watch television, you expect it to demand little so you do not invest much effort in understanding it. That attitude is especially pervasive in the United States" (Huston et al. 1992, 93). Changing television's role in our schools and homes requires that we first change the way we ourselves think about the medium.

10 WAYS TO THINK ABOUT TV

1. *Agent of Socialization.* Television has long been regarded as a window on the world that socializes young viewers into the views and values of the dominant culture. In a multicultural society it is crucial that media models provide fair, accurate, and reporsentative images of all groups in the culture. How television depicts gender roles, occupations, religious groups, races, nationalities, the elderly, the impaired, and the disadvantaged, among other groups, can in large part determine society's response to these groups. When such depictions are accurate and informative, teachers can use them to help students understand society. If the representations are biased, unrepresentative, or distorted, teachers need to put them in context and teach students to critically evaluate the images and locate alternative sources of information.

2. *Source of News and Information.* Television has replaced the newspaper as the main source of information in our culture. That information comes in many forms, including news programs, newsmagazines, current affairs broadcasts, news specials, talk shows, and the widely condemned "trash" or "tabloid" TV. News specials, documentaries, and other information-oriented broadcasts now frequently make transcripts and videotape copies available, providing schools with a potentially invaluable resource. Although the evening news may cover the same stories as a newspaper or magazine, television's form and style invariably shape the way viewers receive and perceive the story. Teachers can help students understand the roles played by print, picture, visual, and verbal presentations of a story. Reading and analyzing news are covered in Chapter 3 of this book.

3. *Merchandising Mechanism.* Commercial television exists because of commercials. Programs are presented to provide advertisers with the opportunity to address a vast audience. Various technological and programming developments have led to the creation of shop-at-home services, which are potentially beneficial to shut-ins but may also represent another step toward the cabled cocoon as more and more of us withdraw from society into the safety of our high-tech homes. Those who do venture forth are increasingly likely to find video vendors on elevators, escalators, store shelves, and even supermarket

shopping carts. Whether these new marketing mechanisms will actually benefit shoppers or induce consumer confusion and media manipulation depends upon how prepared we are to understand these increasingly sophisticated media marketing techniques.

4. *Political Process and Propaganda*. Television technology has increasingly become an agent for patriotic propaganda and televised terrorism. The concept is hardly new. Demonstrators during the 1968 Chicago Democratic convention chanted, "The whole world's watching" and used pictures of police brutality to make their point. Many observers believe the United States lost the Vietnam War because it was the first "video," or "living room," war, and people were convinced by pictures that undermined official government statements. When the United States invaded Grenada, the military controlled media coverage of the operation. Throughout the 1980s, various governments, including those of Israel and South Africa, attempted to control the way television covered events in those countries. The massacre of civilians in Tiananmen Square in 1989 and the resulting worldwide condemnation of China again emphasized the power of the picture in the political process. The collapse of Eastern Europe's Soviet bloc can in many ways be attributed to the power of the picture as portable video cameras, VCRs, and various new technologies provided alternative media messages to those of the traditional, state-controlled media. The impact of television technology on foreign affairs and international politics was the subject of a 1989 *Nightline* broadcast called "Revolution in a Box." During the 1990 Gulf crisis, Iraq's Saddam Hussein used television as a tool of terrorism, broadcasting pictures of the women and children he was holding hostage in an attempt to influence public opinion. Beyond the international scene, television also remains an integral part of the democratic process. It allows the nation to watch congressional deliberations and special hearings, provides access at the local level for diverse individuals and groups to express their own ideas, broadcasts town and school board meetings, and generally makes the process of government more visible to the electorate. The high cost of television and the expectations we have of the medium also make it a potentially harmful agent of the political process. Although it can promote democracy by exploring issues and giving free expression to candidates and individuals, it can also stifle debate, replace issues with images, and substitute slick slogans and advertising strategies for serious discussion and examination. It should also be noted that while this process is most evident during presidential elections, it also affects local races, impacting the way propositions are presented to voters on a range of issues. During the 1997 off-year election, for example, Oregon voters struggled with the issue of repealing the nation's only Right to Die law, passed in 1994. While thoughtful debate and careful deliberation were needed, as usual the complexity of the issue was reduced to television ads between dueling doctors. Next door, in Washington, the National Rifle Association heavily funded the "Vote No" advertising, opposing Initiative 676, which would require that all guns have security locks and that some million handgun owners be licensed.

5. *Teaching and Training*. The video revolution has brought major growth in the home education market and in the application of

video in teaching and training in all areas of society. Airline emergency procedures have become much more meaningful now that video is frequently used to demonstrate procedures, replacing the previous instructions from flight attendants that lacked clear visuals. Cybervision represents a new approach to training for a range of sports including tennis, golf, and skiing. Ski schools now frequently use video to help clients ascertain their own skiing ability, and video provides instant feedback for sporting enthusiasts in areas as diverse as white-water rafting, golf, and skiing. For the less active, self-help and do-it-yourself videos now address everything from potty training to plumbing. Although these applications of television technology are potentially beneficial, consumers have almost no criteria by which to effectively evaluate such products before purchase.

6. *Educational Video.* The home market is being inundated with instructional programs and so, too, is the classroom. Cable and satellite technologies have brought the growth of educational instructional programming, including the Arts and Entertainment Network, the Learning Channel, and the Discovery Channel. Some of these ventures, such as Whittle Communications' "Channel One" newscast, have been controversial, resulting in litigation between educators who want to use the broadcasts and educational administrators who oppose it. In many such cases, the real issue has less to do with the programs themselves than it does with the media mind-sets we bring to them. The VCR is a deceptive technology. It entered the home market in the 1980s more rapidly than television did in the 1950s. The potential danger of our familiarity with the technology is that we mistake consumer convenience for instructional effectiveness. Teachers and media specialists need to be particularly wary of companies who transfer former filmstrips and slide/tape programs to video format. Although this strategy makes sense for the producers, it is potentially harmful in the classroom. Filmstrips and slide programs are designed for larger screen projection than is possible when they are reduced to video format. Filmstrips and slide programs usually produce single, still, clear pictures, which are particularly useful for objectives involving visual recognition, recall, and discrimination. These factors may all be impeded when these programs are transferred to video in the name of convenience.

7. *Surveillance, Security, and Law Enforcement.* Television technology is increasingly being used for security and surveillance purposes, from eye-in-the-sky spy satellites to video cameras mounted in banks, businesses, and homes. Recent applications of the technology have included new forms of evidence resulting in lower legal costs and less congested court calendars. This has been particularly effective in the case of drunk-driving arrests that were videotaped by cameras mounted in the front of police vehicles. Applying television technology in this manner has obvious administrative and managerial benefits, but continued use of these techniques must be weighed carefully to protect individual privacy. The issues raised are ethical and Orwellian, and as a culture we need to understand the implications of a society in which surveillance is no longer questioned. Although video can be used by security forces as an agent of control, it can also be turned against those forces. In March

1991 the nation witnessed Los Angeles police officers beating a man who offered no resistance. That incident, captured on videotape by an amateur, provided irrefutable evidence of the event. The spread of citizen surveillance was featured in the July 22, 1991, cover story of *Newsweek*, which announced the arrival of "video vigilantes."

8. *Televangelism.* The growth of television technology has brought religion and church services into the homes of thousands of Americans. For the infirm, shut-ins, and other groups who cannot get about easily, these broadcasts provide a potentially important service. But as with so much of television technology, the benefits must be considered against the potential damage. The televangelist scandals of the 1980s revealed financial corruption and fraud, often at the expense of thousands of Americans who had given generously even when they could not afford it. But the problems ran deeper than that and revealed the danger of using sophisticated technology to address and manipulate an audience that is vulnerable because it is visually illiterate. Sophisticated mailing-list techniques and a fusion of computer and television technology enabled religious broadcasters to target potential converts and contributors. Despite the doctrine of separation of church and state in this country, some of these broadcasters defined social and political agendas, registered new voters, and attempted to influence political platforms at the state and national levels. The recruiting and persuasion were often done through propaganda that played on the fears and uncertainties of the television congregation. Televangelism, perhaps more than any other development, provides evidence that any movement toward media literacy and critical viewing skills should address the adult population as well as the young people in our schools.

9. *Family Member, Friend, and Companion.* For many Americans television is and has been for some time, like a member of their family. It provides a constant background presence in our homes and is often highly visible in our living rooms, kitchens, and bedrooms. Television programming often influences decisions about where we eat, when we eat, and even what we eat. Meal times are often planned around the evening's programs, and the microwave, like TV dinners of the 1950s, provides instant feeding for the fast-food, instant gratification culture that television has nurtured. Studies suggest that television has contributed to a decline in family communication, and Neil Postman (1985) argues that it has eliminated serious discourse in our culture. Advances in technology have made television omnipresent in our society, such that it has become almost a constant companion. It is now so portable that it can go with us wherever we are. Campers in a pristine national park or forest can watch television, staying in touch with the very culture from which they are seeking a vacation. Spectators at a baseball or football stadium often have their eyes glued to their portable televisions, as though actually attending the event somehow is no longer real enough. There is little doubt that developments in telecommunications will continue to increase the role of video in our lives. For example, we may soon be able to see the person to whom we are talking when we make a phone call. Whether these developments make our culture more human and our communication more personal and meaningful will depend less on the technology than on the way we use it.

10. *Vintage Video.* Television has experienced both a "golden age" and a "vast wasteland." Recent years have seen evidence of broadcast television in transition, with strange but innovative programming such as *Twin Peaks, Dream On, Cop Rock,* and *Ally McBeal* responding to the challenges of cable and the VCR. Those not satisfied with current broadcast fare have the opportunity to return to the past by buying or renting the increasing number of vintage television programs now available on videotape. These include episodes of *Gunsmoke, Bonanza, The Outer Limits, The Twilight Zone, Star Trek, The Honeymooners, I Love Lucy,* and *The Beverly Hillbillies.* These programs serve as historical evidence of the culture that both created and consumed them. Properly used, they can be effective teaching tools to show the state of technology in the 1950s and 1960s, as well as examples of fashion, furniture, consumer appliances, and prices, and to provide extraordinary insight into the views, values, and attitudes of the characters and culture. *Nick At Night* and *TV Land* also continue to broadcast classic television, including *The Patty Duke Show, I Dream of Jeannie, Bewitched,* and contemporary classics like *The Wonder Years.*

WHO WATCHES WHAT? Age, Race, Class, Gender, and Other Viewing Variables

America's fascination with television is well documented. Our children spend more time watching television than they do attending school, and the only thing we spend more time doing than watching television is sleeping. In 1983, Maurine Doerken, in *Classroom Combat: Teaching and Television,* observed that 9- to 12-year-olds attended school for 980 hours per year, compared to 1,230 hours spent watching television. By the time they graduate from high school, it is likely that most students will have had 11,000 hours in the classroom and 22,000 hours in front of the television. A 1988 longitudinal study conducted by the Department of Education found that eighth graders spent 21.2 hours per week watching television, compared to 5.5 hours per week spent on homework. At the same time, the average family was reported to watch television for 7.2 hours per day. By the early 1990s, statistics indicated that 60 percent of households with television also had cable. Remote control was present in 87 percent of households and 65 percent had VCRs (Xiaoming 1994). By the middle of the decade, the networks were losing some of their attraction. In the 1995-1996 season, evening viewership dropped from 65 to 61 percent, the lowest level ever recorded. The Internet and video games were draining some viewers, but many were looking to other options on cable or VCR. Despite the decline, for the most part, in one form or another, Americans still spent their evenings watching a screen.

Yet, despite all of this viewing, it must be noted that we do not all view the same things, and, equally as important, we do not all view in the same way. Sex, race, class, gender, and other factors all influence what, when, and how we watch. A 1990 report in *American Demographics* indicated that educational attainment was related to television viewing, with high school dropouts watching 20 hours of television a week compared to college graduates who watched less than 12 hours per week. Research from the 1990s documented increased time spent viewing by "socially disadvantaged groups (black people, the poorly educated and with low occupation prestige)" (353). Those with less than high school educations were watching 5.5 percent more television than in earlier decades. Parental viewing habits in such households clearly affect the viewing behaviors of their children. Children who are the heaviest viewers tend to come from families where parents have little education or have low occupational status (Huston and Wright 1996).

David Buckingham made a meticulous and major scholarly contribution to our understanding of how children process and perceive television, including differences among them. His in-depth interviews with British children provide fascinating insights into uses and gratifications children derive from the medium. As expected, he found differences between middle-class and working-class children. However, he also found very interesting differences along gender lines. It is, he noted, "the girls who engaged in the most complex debates about modality or character, for example, or whose judgments were generally the most fluent and elaborate" (1993, 267). Equally, when Buckingham focused their attention on video games, the girls once again seemed more insightful. "The boys like all the fast games," one female student offered, " 'cause they don't have to use their brains, it's something they can do without thinking about it" (Buckingham and Sefton-Green 1994, 25).

While boys enamored of video games would no doubt defend themselves, arguing that such games require dexterity and hand-eye coordination, gender differences are also apparent in the way adults interact with television. Researchers have indicated that males prefer "viewing attentively, in silence, without interruption, in order not to miss anything." Further, they seem puzzled and perplexed by the viewing behavior of their wives and daughters. "For the women, viewing is fundamentally a social activity, involving ongoing conversation and usually the performance of at least one other domestic task" (Dines and Humez 1995, 364).

If gender accounts for both what we watch and how we watch, age and race also need to be taken into account. Elderly viewers are heavy viewers. In fact, this age group watches more television than any other segment of the population. Other than the fact that most of them are retired and have time to watch, television serves other functions. It is a means of "involvement, companionship, filling time, structuring time" (Huston et al. 1992, 14). Researchers have described television viewing for this age group as "a parasocial activity that allows isolated older persons to maintain the illusion of living in a populated world" (David and Kubey 1982, 202).

Black viewers tend to have more favorable attitudes to television than whites, and they tend to rely more on television for news and information. This group is "apt to perceive programs as reflecting reality; and they often use television to learn social codes of conduct" (Huston et al. 1992, 16). Differences between white and black viewers are evident in examining preferences during the 1996 season. For white viewers, the top 10 shows were:

1. *E.R.*
2. *Seinfeld*
3. *Friends*
4. *Caroline in the City*
5. *Single Guy*
6. *Home Improvement*
7. Monday night football
8. *Coach*
9. *NYPD Blue*
10. *60 Minutes*

The top 10 favorite shows of black viewers were:

1. *New York Undercover*
2. *Living Single*
3. *The Crew*
4. *In the House*
5. *Fresh Prince of Bel-Air*
6. *Martin*
7. *Family Matters*
8. *Martin* (Sunday nights)
9. Monday night football
10. *The Preston Episodes*

The only common meeting point for both groups was football (*Time* June 3, 1996, 68).

Beyond the issue of race, regional differences also have an impact on what, when, and how audiences watch. Southerners love to watch shows that are set in the South, whether urban or rural, and they are fond of series that feature black characters. *In the Heat of the Night* attracts 40 percent more viewers than the national figures, while *Matlock*, set in Atlanta, and *Evening Shade*, set in the Ozarks, also increase the national audience. The South watches 26 percent more soap operas than other regions of the country and 13 percent more college sports. If the South knows what it likes, it also knows what it dislikes. New York humor, evident in programs like *Seinfeld*, is not as popular south of the Mason Dixon line. While it was on the air, the NBC hit, though still popular, dropped 22 percent from national ratings, and *Home Improvement* showed a 35 percent decline from national numbers.

Children ages 6 to 17 also clearly have their own preferences for programs. According to *TV Guide* and Nielsen ratings, the top 10 programs for this age group during the 1995-1996 year were:

1. *Boy Meets World*

2. *Family Matters*

3. *The Simpsons*

4. *Muppets Tonight*

5. *Lois and Clark, The New Adventures of Superman*

6. *In the House*

7. *Friends*

8. *Fresh Prince of Bel-Air*

9. *Boston Common*

10. *The Single Guy*

Young people also have their own perspective on television and its impact on their life and society in general. A nation-wide study of children ages 10 to 16, conducted by Children Now, reported that:

- 82 percent think TV shows should help them distinguish right from wrong.

- 77 percent say there is too much sex before marriage on TV.

- 62 percent say these images influence kids to have sex too early.

- 69 percent say TV kids don't face the same problems that they do.

- 66 percent of them live in households with three or more TV sets.

- 54 percent have television in their own rooms.

- 55 percent watch alone or with peers, not family.

(Connect 1995)

Like all surveys, the data in these reports need to be scrutinized. Lumping 10-year-olds together with 16-year-olds is problematic in terms of their level of sophistication in interpreting the question. Equally, Nielsen surveys that lump the entire developmental years 6 to 17 in one category do little to help us distinguish between the taste of children and that of adolescents, which parents and teachers certainly know are very different. In fact, the entire basis of the Nielsen surveys has been challenged by the industry. In April 1997, *Entertainment Weekly* reported that disputes centered upon the accuracy and reliability of the so-called Nielsen households. About 5,000 homes are used as the basis of the Nielsen ratings. Among the areas of dispute, it has been claimed that selection of the households underrepresents single-person homes by 15 percent, low-income households by 26 percent, and overrepresents households with college graduates by some 31 percent. Given that a single rating point can represent $150 million per year in revenue, the stakes are not small. Since these figures also provide patterns and profiles of potential viewers, and therefore consumers, they are likely to influence advertisers, which in turn influences the types of programs that are either accepted or rejected.

A Student Television Viewing Survey

(ELEM/MID/HIGH) — A "Student Television Viewing Survey" handout is a useful and simple data-gathering tool that can be used with individual students, single classes, or entire school populations to ascertain how much time students spend watching television and what they watch. Until we have the answer to these questions, we are ignorant about the role television plays in students' lives, and we are unable to tap into their existing viewing patterns to enable them to process their viewing more effectively. Once we are aware of what our students routinely watch, we can attempt to develop instructional tie-ins.

The survey also allows us to understand viewing conditions because students record whether they view the program alone or in the company of family and friends. This information can be useful in trying to develop parental support and involve parents in the concept of critical viewing at home. By modifying the survey, teachers can also attempt to find out why children watch TV. For example, do they watch for escape, entertainment, information, relaxation, or company? The survey can be taken home and kept as a journal that records viewing behavior for a week, or teachers may prefer to hand out *TV Guide* and newspaper listings of television programs so the assignment can be completed in class.

This simple instrument can be kept as part of student records. It may provide some correlation for teachers when they compare high and low academic achievers with high and low viewing profiles. It can also be a useful pre-program instrument for teachers wishing to influence both what students watch and how much they watch. A second survey completed after a critical viewing skills or media literacy unit might show, for example, some changes in these areas.

TV or Not TV

(ELEM/MID/HIGH) — TV is often blamed for the following:

- Making students passive
- Promoting violence
- Concentrating on the negative
- Stressing materialism
- Making children hyperactive
- Discouraging reading
- Reducing concentration span
- Promoting stereotypes

Ask students to develop a list of all the positive and negative things they can think of about television. Have older students consider whether these things are actually caused by television or by the way people use television. High school students could research the topic and then debate it.

Turn Off TV Week

(ELEM/MID/HIGH) — For the past several years now, one week each April has been designated as "national turn off television week." While turning off the television does not help us become critical viewers or thinkers of television content, it does provide the opportunity for us to reflect on the presence of television in our lives, the habits we have developed relating to it, and alternative ways to use this time. The student television survey mentioned earlier in this chapter might serve as a springboard for this event, whether conducted in a single class, or planned and coordinated as a school-wide activity. Students who participate in the event can develop journals and reports related to the way turning off the television for a week affected them and their families.

IT'S NOT WHAT THEY WATCH, IT'S HOW THEY WATCH

There is no doubt that some television programs are beneficial and educationally effective. Everyone acknowledges the role the Public Broadcasting Service (PBS) and the Children's Television Workshop play in this work. Prime-time programming and other special broadcasts on network television can also be powerful instructional tools. ABC's "The Day After" was a controversial made-for-television movie that widened community discussion of nuclear power and provided teachers with materials and techniques to explore the controversy. In 1990, ABC's "Earth Day Special" brought together an all-star cast and used humor to seriously explore ecological and environmental issues. Television history was made that same year when the three networks all broadcast the same program at the same time. "Cartoon All-Stars to the Rescue" was a 30-minute anti-drug animated special featuring leading cartoon characters such as the Teenage Mutant Ninja Turtles, Alf, Kermit, Garfield, the Smurfs, Bugs Bunny, and the Chipmunks. Supported by U.S. First Family, the program was broadcast over 1,000 stations in Canada, the United States, and Mexico, reaching some 20 million children and an estimated two-thirds of the under-12 population. Animation and education also joined forces in fall 1990 when Turner Broadcasting introduced *Captain Planet and the Planeteers*, an environmentally based cartoon series. Each episode concluded with a message telling viewers how they can help the environment. Putting its money where its mouth is, Turner Broadcasting contributed 10 percent of all royalties to environmental causes. In a different vein, both *The Wonder Years* and *Doogie Howser, M.D.*, featured classroom sequences with characters speaking in French and the use of English subtitles.

Each of these programs represents a positive example of television's role as a teacher. Although we need to recognize this contribution, we must be wary of simply relying on television producers to make good programs. This response renders teachers and students little more than passive consumers dependent on the networks for educational materials. It also deprives teachers of the strategies necessary to transform all television viewing into a learning experience. As such, it deflects our attention from two key general research findings:

1. As learning facilitators, teachers can have a major impact on what children watch and how they watch.

2. How children watch, including their expectations, attitudes, and attention, affects the way they process television. This includes their ability to recognize, recall, and comprehend information (Salomon and Leigh 1984).

To build on the implications of these findings, we must break away from traditional mind-sets. We must let go of the idea that for children to learn from television the program must be good. That perception is product- rather than process-oriented. By developing effective cueing and retrieval strategies, teachers can turn almost any broadcast into a learning experience. The dominant media mind-set to be challenged is that television is somehow in conflict or competition with the classroom. This perception promotes an adversarial relationship between teachers and television, which clearly limits cooperation.

The following list provides some positive suggestions regarding the potential of television.

1. "The classroom and TV should not be in competition with each other" (Ernest Boyer, former U.S. commissioner of education, in Palmer 1988, xxiii).

2. "Rather than abolish television, we should find ways of harnessing its tremendous power in the direction of more effective education for children" (Singer, Singer, and Zuckerman 1981, 16).

3. "For many preschoolers TV may represent the only learning curriculum they have, and we must be sensitive to its vast potential for influencing their future behavior

through observation and imitation" (Doerken 1983, 22).

4. "It [television] can be a powerful educational force in children's lives if we carefully select appropriate programs and make sure that children make an effort to reflect on what they watch" (Kelley 1983, ix).

TEACHERS TAKE "AIME" AT THE FRAME

If a positive outlook is a successful beginning to using television as a teaching tool, a postive strategy supported by research is even more successful. Research clearly suggests that teachers can change the level of learning from television viewing by changing children's perceptions and attitudes regarding the viewing experience. This is a potentially revolutionary approach to teaching with television for many teachers because it shifts the emphasis and onus from the program producers and the program content to instructional strategies and the nature and needs of young learners.

Writing in *Television, Sex Roles and Children*, Kevin Durkin acknowledged the vital role played by the viewer in any learning experience: "As much depends upon what the child brings to TV viewing as upon what it extracts" (1985, 3). Research suggests that what the child brings to television is directly related to what he or she processes from it. Gavriel Salomon, Tamar Leigh, and other researchers have introduced the AIME (Amount of Invested Mental Energy) model. Essentially the theory suggests that most television viewing engages only part of the attention and participation of the audience, resulting in cognitive economy or shallow processing. To a large degree this half-hearted approach "strongly depends on their preconcepts rather than on any necessary limitations imposed by the medium" (Salomon and Leigh 1984, 122). The implications for teachers are clear: Change the way children think about television and you change the way they process television. At its most basic level, this means that teachers who provide children with cueing and retrieval strategies before any screening will potentially change what and how much a child retrieves from any screening. To do this, preview the program, make sure children expect to learn from the viewing experience, then provide them with key scenes, ideas, or content you want them to pay attention to and remember. At a more sophisticated level, the theory implies that such viewing behavior and attitudes can be integrated into the child's total viewing experience, changing the way the student perceives and processes all visual media both in the classroom and the living room.

Thoughtful Viewing

(ELEM/MID/HIGH) — These starting exercises can be used at all levels. Select a 5- to 10-minute clip from any television program, including classic programs that are now available on video. Carefully preview the program, taking notes on what happens, the order in which it happens, camera angles, special effects, interesting vocabulary, and so on. Select several of these areas that seem appropriate for your students and then show the clip. You may decide to show the clip without any preparation (cueing and retrieval) to see how students respond to a before-and-after approach. By finding a second clip of similar length and style, you could then see how cueing and retrieval influence students' processing. If you have time, or if you can work with other teachers, you might actually set up a control group experiment. You could, for example, divide the class in half, showing each group the same clip but providing one group with pre-screening guidelines and the other with none. The benefits of this approach are that the feedback is fairly quick and the input or material shown is exactly the same, which restricts processing differences caused by program differences and not by instructional strategies.

The various elements you might ask students to recall or comprehend will vary with the age group, but the following areas should provide some guidelines.

- *Sequencing:* Have students develop a list of the sequential order of events.

- *Characters:* Have students develop a list of the names of the characters in the clip.

- *Clues and cues:* Can the students find visual and verbal cues that tell them where or when the story is set? This can be something as basic as a calendar in the set; a reference to a day, month, or year; fashions; furnishings; automobiles; or weather.

- *Comprehension:* If the clip involves a character making a particular decision or choice, ask the students to explain the motivation, causes, or consequences of the action.

- *Visual style:* See if the students can remember specific techniques, camera angles, and special effects. Can they remember what techniques were used at specific moments in the clip, and can they suggest why these devices were used?

- *Verbal recall:* Give students several key phrases from the clip and see if they can correctly identify the character who said the lines. If the program used words or phrases that might not be familiar to your students', see if they remember such words and understand what they mean.

Short exercises like this promote visual discrimination and processing, encourage students to become more critical listeners and viewers, increase their concentration spans, and change their expectations and appreciation of television as a recreational and informational tool.

TELEVISION, READING, AND LITERACY

One of the most frequent charges levelled at television is that it distracts children from print and discourages reading. In *The Plug-In Drug*, Marie Winn describes "the incontrovertible fact that children's viewing experiences influence their reading in critical ways, affecting how much they read, what they read, how they feel about reading, and, since writing skills are closely related to reading experiences, what they write and how well they write" (1977, 65). Yet, there is growing evidence that when properly used, television can foster language acquisition, general knowledge, and extend the viewer's vocabulary, and actually promote interest in reading. In *What Do Our 17 Year Olds Know?* Diane Ravitch and Chester Finn reported that minority students were likely to gain in these areas from television viewing (1987, 151). In *Television and America's Children*, Edward Palmer argued that "television is not the antithesis of reading; on the contrary, used well it can encourage and instill a life-long love of literature" (1988, 87).

It is not difficult to find examples of television promoting reading. Project Literacy U.S. (PLUS) Public Service Announcements feature young stars such as Neil Patrick Harris (*Doogie Howser, M.D.*) and Fred Savage (*The Wonder Years*) espousing the joys and benefits of reading. Programs such as "The Reading Rainbow" draw attention to books and stories and promote interest in reading among young viewers. Many students probably received their first exposure to Shakespeare when they saw *Moonlighting*'s startling "Atomic Shakespeare" episode, which was based on *The Taming of the Shrew*. Often, reading and writing are addressed as themes in prime-time programs that provide good models for school-age viewers. When Fonzie (*Happy Days*) took out a library card in one episode, there was a reported 500 percent increase in applications for library cards, testifying to the enormous impact television can have on the attitudes and behavior of young viewers. More recent programs have integrated the issues of literacy and reading and writing into their plots. *Head of the*

Class based an episode on a black basketball star who was illiterate. Caught between the conflicting pressures of athletics and academics, the young man finally faced his problem and stayed on at school to learn to read. *Roseanne* featured an episode in which Darlene found success and self-esteem in writing a poem. An episode of *Brewster Place* entitled "The Poet" recognized the poetry of Margaret Walker and Langston Hughes. The story centered on Lewis Cross, a young black boy whose father died in the Vietnam War. Writing became a cathartic creative process that allowed the boy to express the feelings he had for the father he lost.

How can classroom teachers use television and video to foster literacy? The first step is recognizing that children process different media in different ways, even when the narrative and content remain the same.

Child Development reported studies with the well-known children's books *A Story, A Story* and *Strega Nona* that indicated that "memory and comprehension were generally better for television than text" (Pezdek, Lehrer, and Simon 1984, 2080). Video versions of stories, therefore, are a powerful instructional ally for strengthening children's ability to both recall and comprehend aspects of a story. Research by W. Collins et al. (1978) shows dramatic improvement in the ability of students in late elementary school years to comprehend narratives presented in movies, television, and other audiovisual formats. Appropriate instructional strategies can help children "read" such programs; the result is "continuous efforts during viewing to select, order and make inferences about the narratives" (390). Remember, the emphasis is not on what they watch, but how.

Stories and the Screen

(ELEM/MID) — Marie Winn wrote that reading is "a two way process" but "television is a one way street; the viewers cannot create television images" (1977, 64). However, video technology is now available that enables students to become directors. Have the class act out a scene from one of their favorite stories and videotape it. Or, have students write their own stories and videotape the one they like best. You might show students what a script looks like and have them use this writing format. If you want to keep it simple, have the students write stories that can be told visually without words or by using bold printed titles to explain the action.

(HIGH) — Students in Boston studied George Orwell's *1984* and made their own video Newspeak broadcasts, fusing traditional literature with the new visual literacy. In North Carolina, a teacher assigned her class the task of writing a current version of the *Canterbury Tales* with modern-day pilgrims snowed in at an airport. Students came in costume and acted out the roles. The video camera often acts as an incentive, encouraging students to participate and "star" in their own interpretation of literary episodes.

Recreational viewing of television outside the classroom can also be used to develop reading skills. In their article "Using Television to Teach Specific Reading Skills," Anne Adams and Cathy Harrison said, "If we develop activities that stress the printed words on the TV screen, not only do we gain by having the student complete a specific assignment, but it will also cause the student to notice and perhaps read more of the words on TV" (1975, 48).

Television as Text

(ELEM) — Using television clips from commercials, news broadcasts, or educational programs, develop recognition and reading activities related to any of the following areas:

- Consonant cluster recognition
- Letter sizes
- Dictionary definitions
- Meaning of phrases
- Alliteration

- Maps, charts, and graphics

Having previewed the program, develop worksheets telling students that they will hear or see particular words and graphic devices. The class can work on all the exercises, or you can divide students into groups that each focus on different elements of word and phrase usage in the broadcast. Exercises such as these may encourage more active processing of print and graphic information during recreational viewing at home.

TELEVISION GENRES

Students who have already been exposed to literary genres and the typical elements, codes, and conventions of folktales and fairy tales can also apply these concepts to the elements of various television story types. This analytical approach fosters their understanding of differences and similarities between print and nonprint media.

Defining Genre

(ELEM/MID/HIGH) — Introduce students to a simple definition of genre as a type of story. Drawing from literature, you can give them examples such as folktales, fairy tales, science fiction, and fantasy. Chapter 6 refers to movie genres like westerns, war/combat films, and horror movies. Now have the class come up with classifications for television genres. This can be done as a class discussion or, you might distribute copies of *TV Guide* or the television section of a newspaper, asking students to identify and label programs by genre. Key genres they might be expected to label would include:

- Cop/Crime (*Law and Order, Homicide, NYPD Blue, Murder One, Nash Bridges*)
- Science Fiction/Fantasy (*The X Files, Millennium, Sliders, Profilers, Alien Nation, Forever Knight, Hercules, Xena Warrior Princess, Roar*)
- Medical Dramas (*E.R., Chicago Hope*)
- Sitcoms/Domestic Comedies (*Fresh Prince of Bel-Air, Home Improvement, Frasier, Seinfeld, Roseanne*)

Other possible formats that conform to the narrative conventions of genre would include soap operas, which are very popular with some young audiences. While we typically expect to find soaps running during the day, students might want to compare and contrast these traditional soaps with prime-time fare such as *Party of Five* and *Friends*. In what way are they similar and in what way are they different from each other? Beyond narrative structure, television has also invented its own types of program such as the talk show. In recent years these programs have been widely criticized for their controversial, sensational, and often tasteless subject matter. Some people argue that Jenny Jones, Sally Jessie Raphael, and others have created a cult celebration of the bizarre, the aberrant, and the dysfunctional. Jane Shattuc offers another view. In her book *The Talking Cure: TV Talk Shows and Women*, she argues that these programs represented "a participatory form of TV devoted to the public debate of everyday issues by women" (1997, 1). As such, she says, "they empowered an alienated class of women to speak" (198). High school students will be familiar with some of this type of programming. Where do they stand on the issue? Are these shows really liberating or just another example of trash and tabloid television? What differences, if any, exist in the attitudes expressed by your male and female students?

(HIGH) —

Shattuc refers to "the Oprahfication of America." How influential can one talk show host be? Who are the most popular hosts among your students? What reasons do they give for liking these individuals? When Oprah recommends a book, national sales for that title normally soar. Use this concept to move from a discussion of genre to media literacy principles that deal with the effects of media. How else might talk shows influence us?

E.R. and medical shows like *Chicago Hope* also provide composite portraits of life and death in big-city hospitals. How accurate are these representations? *The New England Journal of Medicine* reported that the programs provided a false impression of cardiopulmonary resuscitation rates. On both of these popular programs, some 65 percent of patients were revived, and 76 percent survived long enough to leave the hospital. In real life, complications and disabilities are much more likely, with just 2 to 30 percent of patients surviving (Levy 1996, D1). Why is the success rate so much higher in these dramas than in real life? Dines and Humez suggest that reliance upon familiar formulas is necessary to attract television audiences, arguing that "it is vital to place any genre analysis in the context of the political economy of television" (1995, 396). What role might economics, audiences, and marketing play in the outcome of these stories? How might these stories shape our perceptions of doctors as individuals and hospitals as institutions?

The question of television influence has also extended to other genres. In the case of *The X-Files*, which has attracted a cult following, that influence has spread overseas. In 1997 the national president of the Lutheran Church in Australia accused the program of contributing to community fears and restlessness. "With its 'trust no one message,' " the program was charged with "preying upon distrust, suspicion and uncertainty in the community" (Peggler 1997, A5). When the fifth season of the *X Files* opened in November 1997, *U.S.A. Today* featured the story on the front page, not in their entertainment section. They also commented that the show cashed in on anti-government sentiment, tapping Americans' distrust of institutions. In the process, of course, *The X Files* might reinforce and magnify, not just reflect, these attitudes. Once again, profit and patterns of production are evident when one genre produces a major hit. *The X Files'* success encouraged similar programs, including *Millenium, The Pretender, Profiler,* and *Sleepwalkers.* Ask students to discuss the popularity of these types of programs, including their formats, themes, and potential influence. In what way might the end of the century be shaping public interest in these types of programs as well as in movies like *Contact* and *Independence Day*?

CRITICAL VIEWING AND THINKING SKILLS

A growing body of research suggests that if we teach children to become critical viewers, we do more than give them the ability to analyze the construction of isolated images; we also give them the ability to think critically about the composition of the picture, enhancing their ability to read words and worlds. Although many continue to regard television viewing as a passive process, others see the potential of the video age to develop new literacies while reinforcing traditional literacy. A 1990 issue of *The Harvard Education Letter*, for example, reported, "The video screen is helping children develop a new kind of literacy—visual literacy that they will need to thrive in a technological world . . . in television or film, the viewer must mentally integrate diverse camera shots of a scene to construct an image of the whole" (Greenfield 1990, 1).

Although television can be used to develop reading skills and promote traditional literacy, it is essential that educators also recognize that television is a unique medium and that to understand it fully, we must be conversant with its codes, conventions, and characteristics. That means acknowledging the power of the picture and accepting the fact that seeing is not believing. Jack Solomon said, "Television images lull us into thinking that they are real, that they aren't iconic signs at all but realities. Since we see them, we trust them, often failing to realize that, like all signs, they have been constructed with a certain interest behind them" (1988, 144). Deconstructing these media representations requires relinquishing the powerful and pervasive notion in our culture that seeing is believing, that what you see is what you get. The real issue, however, is whether we "get" (understand) what we see. The process of reading television addresses some of the following elements.

1. *Interpreting the internal content of the program:* Essentially this involves a narrative analysis or the ability to recall and recognize what happened and why, with reference to genre codes and conventions.

2. *Interpreting the internal construction of the frame:* This process focuses attention on media form and style. It includes the overall design and look of the picture and involves such things as camera angle and the various shots used.

3. *Recognizing the external forces and factors shaping the program:* This industrial/sociological approach looks at issues such as media ownership and control in an attempt to understand how these factors shape programming. A simple example would address the relationship between media ownership and the depiction of women and minorities in the media. Can a patriarchal white industry depict women and minorities fairly?

4. *Comparing and contrasting media representations with reality:* This might include comparing television's depiction of the Vietnam War (*Tour of Duty, China Beach*) with documentaries or histories of the war. It might also include studying incidents of violence on television compared to national crime statistics or examining the depiction of groups, races, religions, and nationalities to detect stereotyping and bias.

5. *Recognizing and responding to the potential impact of television form and content:* This focuses attention on appropriate responses and viewing behavior, including writing to producers and sponsors, as well as using television more selectively.

Learning to Look: A Visual Vocabulary

(ELEM/MID) — Mind-sets about the primacy of print have traditionally impeded the contribution visuals can make to the reading process. In reality our students need skills in interpreting both words and images. In the case of young children, an imbalance in one area results in problems in the other. *The Reading Teacher* has commented, "When the capacity for interpreting imagery is weak, comprehension is at best superficial" (Goldstone 1989, 594). *Words About Pictures: The Narrative Arts of Children's Picture Books* sees a two-way traffic between reading words and images. "Reading a picture for narrative meaning is a matter of applying our understanding of words. We are engaged in an act of turning visual information into verbal" (Nodelman 1988, 211). While some still believe that the classroom must stress print, *School Library Journal*, a bastion of books and a staunch defender of literacy, has also acknowledged the power of the picture and the need to help young people process the ideas embedded within them: "The skills and abilities needed to decode and interpret visual images are probably as demanding as those required for print" (Vandergrift and Hannigan 1993, 20). Learning the language of television enables students not only to spot the shot but also to understand why a director used that point of view and composed the frame in that manner. The following components, along with the discussion of film style and mise-en-scene in Chapter 6, should help students recognize and read visual language, whether in film, television, advertising, picture books, or other formats.

Introduce students to the following definitions of camera movements and shots. Then watch a brief clip from anything on television and have them find examples of each technique. Increase the level of sophistication by asking them to explain why the director chose that shot. Ask them to develop a one- to two-page script indicating what shots they would use. If you have access to a video camera, demonstrate each shot to the students or break them into groups and have each group record an example of one specific shot.

- *Wide shot:* Entire subject and surroundings are shown. Often referred to as establishing shot, giving information about setting and location.

- *Medium shot:* Traditionally focuses on one or two people or objects in frame. Usually head, shoulders, and half-torso shot. Often used during conversation.

- *Close-up shot:* This is used for details. Often an important prop such as a gun, a phone, or a letter is shown this way to draw viewers' attention to its strategic importance to the plot. When people are shown in close-up, it is usually done to highlight facial expression and reactions.

- *Extreme close-up shot:* Dramatic effect, often a tight shot of an eye, a screaming mouth, or a trembling hand.

- *Point-of-view:* The camera is used to develop the perspective from which we, as viewers, see. Usually the camera is objective, which means we see as an outsider looking on or in. Occasionally, the camera is subjective, assuming the position of a character. An entire episode of *M*A*S*H* was shot this way. The point-of-view technique also includes low-angle (tilt-up) and high-angle (tilt-down) camera work, each of which conveys a particular meaning.

Although television uses many of the same shots as motion pictures, it is important to recognize how the different screen format affects the composition and impact. Epics such as *Lawrence of Arabia*, *Dr. Zhivago*, and *Reds*, all made for the big screen, suffer in the claustrophobic confines of television. Marketing strategies now mean that many movies are shot with cable or VCR in mind, as a result of which more close-ups are used than in classic Hollywood cinema. Other directors feel so strongly about the difference between film and television that they insist video versions of their movies be released in letter-box format—the format of the film is in the same proportion as it appeared on the movie screen; this may leave a black border around the projected image on the television screen.

(ELEM) — Show children a clip from a movie such as *Star Wars*, *Platoon*, *Lawrence of Arabia*, or *Dr. Zhivago*, and ask them whether it would look better at the movies and why. Ask students if they can think of a movie they saw in a theater that lost something on television and what the difference was. *Caution:* Before showing the film, check your school district's policy on films.

Why Bother with Critical Viewing Skills?

For many educators, the concept of interpreting and reading television is a foreign or flimsy one banished to the periphery of learning and accorded, at most, the status of an educational elective. Like many of our perceptions of the media, this one stems from social attitudes about television and the scant attention given television and media during teacher education.

In one study documented in *The Journal of Communication*, a critical viewing curriculum was developed for children in the third, fourth, and fifth grades. These children were selected because they are traditionally heavy viewers and because "their stage of mental development makes them potentially more vulnerable than children of other ages to TV's influence" (Rapaczynski, Singer, and Singer 1982, 46). Areas of particular vulnerability included the ability to distinguish reality from fantasy, confusion concerning moral judgments, and literal understanding of language. The critical viewing skills curriculum addressed these concerns as well as teaching children to recognize the purpose and power of television in areas such as advertising, stereotyping, and aggression. The study reported that students and teachers were both enthusiastic. The children "enjoyed using their newly acquired knowledge for the class and home activities," and teachers believed the lessons "not only helped to reinforce concepts related to TV, but also promoted language arts skills" (54).

The development of effective critical viewing skills can also contribute to critical thinking skills, which go beyond the ability to simply remember and understand visual information. Raphael Schneller reported a field experiment with ninth graders and concluded, "Our research has shown that it is indeed possible to change youth's credence attitudes towards mass media generally and specifically towards TV" (1982, 104). Kathy Krendl and Bruce Watkins supported these findings, concluding that "the perceptual set with which the messages are received and interpreted affect how it is processed" (1983, 211). Thus, with appropriate strategies, children can be taught to question the form and content of television. As always, teachers should focus on the context in which children view, including their attitudes and expectations.

Problem Solving from Prime Time

(ELEM/MID) — Most stories, including those on television, focus on a character or group of characters confronted with a dilemma to resolve. Particularly in crime programs, which are so prevalent on television, the solution to the problem is physical or violent rather than intellectual or rational. These programs, therefore, are potential models of problem solving in society. By directing children's attention to such programs, we can help them develop critical thinking skills for conceptualizing problems and a repertoire of appropriate responses and solutions. When our students are being pressured by peers to engage in potentially risky behavior, rehearsing responses and discussing the circumstances of television characters can become part of the overall approach to the development of resistance/refusal skills. When the behavior is less problematic, students can still empathize with characters they relate to in programs such as *Home Improvement*, *7th Heaven*, *Party of Five*, *2nd Noah*, and others.

Select a program that features a dilemma and a resolution. Ask students to identify the following elements of the program: conflict, causes, course of action, and consequences. Select a second program. Allow the conflict and the causes to emerge. Stop the program before the course of action and consequences have developed. Break the class down into groups and have them discuss the course of action they would take and the projected consequence. This can be used to support values education projects with strategies such as STAR (Stop, Think, Act, Review). These approaches help children think about their own behavior, placing introspection before impulse.

In the article "Problem-Solving in TV Shows Popular with Children," typical plot problems or conflicts are divided into five key areas:

1. Physical

2. Property

3. Authority

4. Self-esteem

5. Sentimental romantic (Dominick, Richman, and Wurtzel 1979).

Ask students to think about the main problems or conflicts in their own lives. Have them create a list of these items. Introduce them to the five categories identified in television programs popular with the young. Which problems that your students listed show up in television? Which problems show up in television that don't show up in your class survey? Teachers may wish to develop an anonymous survey for students to encourage them to be more honest. A student facing a physical problem with a bully, for example, will probably not want to admit that in class. The discussion of a similar event found in television may, however, help both the victim and the bully think about their behavior.

Show students an episode from a program or assign them a program to view at home. Ask them to identify conflict, causes, course of action, and consequences, and to analyze the presence of particular conflict types in the program.

Encourage parents to watch such programs with their children and discuss the causes and resolutions of conflicts. This is particularly useful when the characters are children or teens or when they are role models for young viewers.

IF LOOKS COULD KILL: Television and Stereotyping

In 1995, *U.S.A. Today* reported that 8 out of 10 students believe their peers are racially prejudiced (August 17, D1). The following year, in an editorial discussing allegations of racism in corporate American boardrooms at Texaco and sexual harassment charges in the military, the same paper wondered if this nation would ever grow comfortable in its modern skin, commenting that "a lot of us still don't seem to get it, still don't seem to grasp the value of respect and diversity" (November 8, 1996, 14a). While demographics continue to demonstrate diversity in our society, too often the media stress difference and deviance from the norm, potentially dividing the nation into the majority culture and "others." While the mass media normally does not create or invent social stereotypes, repeating them does play a role in reinforcing public perceptions about ethnic groups, religions, members of particular occupations, and entire countries and cultures. Television news, as noted earlier, is quite capable of marginalizing and polarizing, pitting one group against another. But mainstream television, including sitcoms, dramas, and soap operas, can also present people in narrow and negative ways.

The nagging wife, the dumb blond, the jock, the nerd, the threatening black, the miserly Jew, the butch lesbian, the alcoholic Irishman, and the effeminate gay—these are just some of the stereotypes present in our society and employed for dramatic or comedic convenience in our entertainment media. These characters model attitudes and behavior. As such, they are potentially powerful influences because (1) they enter our homes where they are afforded social sanction; (2) formula and format result in repetition, which is a key ingredient for the acceptance of media messages; (3) viewing these programs frequently occurs without parental supervision and without the intervention of an adult intermediary to help young audiences recognize and reject these stereotypes; and (4) there is a prevalent social belief that TV is just entertainment and we should not take these messages seriously.

The principles of media literacy, however, remind us that media representations affect reality, creating personal, social, economic, and political consequences. In *Channeling Children*, Betty Miles wrote, "Beyond its particular plot, the program tells the child something about the way the world is:

whether it is that men kill each other and women cook, or that women spend their husband's money on ludicrous hats, or that some women and men live happy single lives" (1975, 3). More important, young viewers tend to form a bond with the media models they select. Timothy Meyer said, "Favorite characters are seen as behaving quite consistently with the child's description of his own behavior, his own judgments of what is right or appropriate, and his perceptions of a friend's behavior" (1973, 3).

Two decades after the publication of *Channeling Children*, researchers are still able to document both the content and potential consequences of television stereotyping. Writing in *Gender, Race and Class in Media*, Janet Rhodes commented, "Instead of using its potential to reverse ridicule and misinformation [television] has perpetuated the worst stereotypes of Blacks found in American popular culture" (1995, 424). Though many expected cable to bring diversity and difference to programming formats, evidence suggests that mainstream stereotypes persist beyond the networks. Looking at representations of race, gender, and age in cable programs, researchers concluded, "There has been relatively little movement toward more accurate proportional representation of historically underrepresented demographic groups" (Kubey et al. 1995, 459). Beyond the controversial and contentious issue of racial representation, research also suggests narrow classification by class or socioeconomic status. Describing the blue-collar males evident in *The Simpsons* (Homer), *All in the Family* (Archie), *The Flintstones* (Fred), *The Honeymooners* (Ralph), and others, Richard Butsch concludes: "The working class is not only underrepresented; the few men who are portrayed are buffoons. They are dumb, immature, irresponsible or lacking in common sense. . . . He is typically well-intentioned, even lovable, but no one to respect or emulate" (1995, 404).

Why do these images matter? Why should teachers help students develop the critical thinking and viewing skills necessary to reject these cumulative portraits of entire segments of our society? Understanding this issue shifts the discussion from media content to social consequences.

According to the American Psychological Association, media stereotypes have the potential to influence the "self perceptions and aspirations" of the groups depicted, as well as inter-group attitudes (Huston et al. 1992, 7). The portraits that television constructs constitute a form of visual validation or nullification. They render some groups important and powerful, and others invisible or negative. As recently as 1996, one report concluded that "regardless of the type of programming . . . the window on the world is European, American, middle class and male" (Graves 1996, 77). Hence television not only recognizes particular segments of society, but in so doing, it confers respect upon them. Conversely, while it recognizes other groups, they are consistently demeaned and diminished by negative and narrow representations. Hispanic actor Marco Sanchez has experienced this restrictive view of his own people. "I can't tell you how frustrating it was to go on auditions and know I'd be considered for one of four roles: the drug dealer, the gang member, the lover, or the streetwise youth with a heart of gold" (Gabe 1993, D1). Non-recognition of groups, or negative stereotypes of groups, can potentially have two major outcomes: (1) the creation or maintenance of negative inner-group attitudes (i.e., prejudice and racism); and (2) negative effects on the self-esteem of members of the minority groups (Huston et al. 1992, 25). Teachers, administrators, counselors, and parents need to work very hard to create a school and classroom environment that reflects tolerance and acceptance, values diversity, and fosters positive self-esteem among all students. When our children feel bad about themselves, their academic performance is likely to suffer. If classrooms, bathrooms, and hallways become environments in which those who are different are allowed to become isolated and alienated, our schools have failed in their job of providing equal educational opportunity. While television is clearly not responsible for all social hatred and prejudice, it can become part of the picture in helping students respect and value themselves and others. Young women trapped in dangerous diets in a desperate attempt to achieve the look of media supermodels can certainly be helped if teachers challenge these stereotypical body images.

Tormented teenagers coming to terms with their own sexuality can also be hurt or helped by the messages television and other media send them and their peers. While it is possible to find gay characters on television (*Will and Grace, Ellen, Spin City, Veronica's Closet*), it is extremely difficult for adolescents to find images of people their own age, struggling with their own emerging sexual identity. With rare exceptions like Ricki (*My So Called Life*), this group is largely invisible. Is it any wonder that suicide seems an option for gay and lesbian teens who find little support at home, at school, or in the media?

Defining Stereotypes

(ELEM/MID/HIGH) — Introduce students to a definition of "stereotypes." Elaborate on the definition by suggesting that the media use this mechanism for dramatic purposes knowing that audiences will recognize the characters immediately, which leaves more time for the development of the plot and action. Although the media usually do not create stereotypes, they repeat them and, therefore, reinforce them. By articulating stereotypes, television and other media affirm such attitudes in our culture. This can prevent us from thinking critically and fairly about issues and individuals because we become distracted by labels and clichés. George Bush used this technique successfully against Michael Dukakis in the 1988 campaign. The stereotype constantly invoked was "liberal," and Dukakis was placed on the defensive battling "the L word" and the charge that he was "a card-carrying member of the American Civil Liberties Union." This latter charge, of course, invoked images of a card-carrying Communist. The presence of stereotyping on television must, therefore, be placed in the broader context of stereotypes in this culture and the way they impede the ability of our students to understand the country they live in. If the media distorts, stereotypes, or misrepresents the elderly, the impaired, the disabled, or any other group in society, it is difficult for students to understand and value these individuals.

Elements of Stereotyping

(ELEM/MID) — Introduce students to elements of stereotyping such as physical characteristics, manner of speech, beliefs, attitudes, and clothing. Provide them with a simple example such as nerds, yuppies, bikers, or jocks. Have them describe the elements of the stereotype using some of the headings developed. See if they can think of an example from television of such a stereotype. The ABC series *Coach* offers several variations on the jock stereotype. The program clearly acknowledges that not all jocks behave in one way and even explores the interaction between the jock stereotype and the feminist stereotype.

Examples of Stereotyping

(ELEM/MID) — Have the students develop a list of groups, individuals, or institutions that might be stereotyped in the media. Broad headings could include racial stereotypes, national stereotypes, gender stereotypes, religious stereotypes, regional stereotypes, occupational stereotypes, generational stereotypes, and disabled/differently abled stereotypes. Have students break these broad headings into more specific questions. For example:

- *Racial stereotypes:* How are blacks, Hispanics, Native Americans, and Asians depicted on television? Name programs in which they appear.

- *Regional stereotypes:* How is the U.S. South depicted in television programs? In what ways are Southerners represented differently from those of other regions? Develop a list of programs set in the South.

- *Religious stereotypes:* Does television show a variety of religious affiliations? How are various religions represented? Do we see characters observing holy days and partaking in rituals, or are we simply told what their religion is? How is the relationship between faith and science expressed in life-and-death dramas such as *E.R.* and *Chicago Hope*? When we see family life in sitcoms such as *Roseanne, Home Improvement, Fresh Prince of Bel-Air*, etc., is the family's religion rendered invisible, or do we see them actively express their religious convictions? *Touched by an Angel, Soul Man*, and *7th Heaven* provide very good examples of programs in which religion and faith play a dominant role. How typical are these shows? When creative programs try to break from shallow stereotypes and display the complexity of characters or issues, they often run the risk of being attacked and misunderstood. One case in point was ABC's controversial series *Nothing Sacred*. The program centered on Father Ray Rayneaux, a contemporary, compassionate, and questioning young priest. It should also be noted that the series drew on the work and experiences of a Jesuit priest. Despite this fact, it was challenged by The Catholic League and more than 500,000 signatures were sent to ABC's parent company, Disney, complaining about the representation of the priest, the priesthood, and Catholicism. Beyond the complaints, the show's detractors also encouraged corporations including Sears, K Mart, and Chrysler Plymouth not to sponsor the series. Television reviewers, on the other hand, found the representations and writing to be relevant and balanced. *U.S.A. Today*'s Matt Roush called it "that rarest of TV dramas, with the courage of conviction, able to express compassion with passion while wrestling with all manner of red flag issues: abortion, homosexuality, drugs, liberalism, and not least, faith" (September 18, 1997, 3d). The "Faith and Values" page of the Minneapolis *Star Tribune* called the boycott of the show misguided, saying that no entertainment series in memory had treated religion more thoughtfully. The program, it said, "is about real human beings applying their beliefs to real problems and living with the consequences." It also noted that, unlike *Touched by an Angel* and similar popular series, *Nothing Sacred* provided no miracles and no pat solutions. "For a show this well-written and well-intentioned to be smothered when there's so much irredeemable trash on TV, now that would truly be a sin" (Holston October 18, 1997, B9). Teachers can use controversial programs like *Nothing Sacred* as case histories to understand the relationship between media representations and the commercial context and constraints that support or subvert innovation and complexity.

Content Analysis and Stereotyping

(ELEM/MID/HIGH) — Content analysis is a relatively complex process that can be modified and used at all levels of schools to help students monitor the media, recognize distortion, and identify stereotypical representations. It involves observing, coding, recording, and analyzing television data; when properly developed, it fosters media literacy, critical thinking, and statistical analysis. At its most basic level, content analysis can work quantitatively to determine such things as the number of Hispanic, Catholic, or adolescent characters on television. By dividing students into groups, with each group looking at a single program, a reasonably accurate count of such elements can be made. For more involved studies, these figures could be tabulated against national statistics based on the census and other sources. A more involved form of content analysis and one more suitable for middle and high school students involves quantitative and qualitative analysis. Rather than simply describing the number of particular characters represented on television, this focuses attention on how they are represented.

❖Slammed by conservative Catholics as an assault on the church, ABC's controversial *Nothing Sacred* explored new territory and won critical praise but poor ratings. The creation and the destruction of the program says much about television as an industry and provides a media literacy case study of the importance of both representations and ratings. Used with permission of ABC Television Network. Photography by Bob D'Amico. © 1997 Bob D'Amico/ABC, Inc.

THE WORLD OF WORK ON TELEVISION

If television serves as a window on the world for young children, providing them with pictures and perceptions of how their society functions, one primary presentation in almost all television fare is the world of work. What occupations and professions are most frequently depicted? What occupations and professions are ignored or underrepresented? What forces and factors influence how the working world is represented? How accurately does television depict the actual work involved in any job or profession? How do these images influence children's concept of work, and how, if at all, do they shape children's career choices? Gerbner's research on television found significant misrepresentation of the workplace. He noted the depiction of 12 doctors, 30 police, 7 lawyers, and 3 judges per week, but only 1 scientist or engineer (1981).

Gerbner's conclusions were reinforced in the 1990s by Lichter et al., who described an imbalance in television's representation of the workplace. "The world of prime time television has always been weighted towards the upper middle class. Doctors, lawyers, and other professionals, not to mention business executives, are much more populous on television than in real life" (1994, 186). For the most part, women on television have traditionally occupied "low status white collar jobs" (189). Researchers have also begun to ponder the potential consequences of the way television represents work. This has been particularly specific in the case of both doctors and attorneys. Television's portrayal of the legal profession, it has been argued, "influences the public's perception of attorneys" (Pfau et al. 1995, 442). Researchers also suggested the possibility that "prime time network television depictions may contribute to an erosion of public trust in physicians" (455).

(ELEM) — Ask students to develop a list of all the occupations or jobs they know of. Have them write a brief description of what they think the job entails. Discuss how accurate their impressions are and where they got their impressions. Many children will describe the jobs their parents have. Because most children do not actually observe their parents working, their impressions will be based on what they have heard and how they have interpreted it.

Next, have the students develop a list of the professions and jobs they most frequently see on television, or ask them to name their favorite programs and the work the characters do in these programs. Using only television programs, have the students describe the type of work the characters do, what it involves, how long it takes, how much money they make, the work environment, and so on. Discuss how accurately television represents this work. Invite a real-life doctor, lawyer, nurse, etc., to talk to your students and discuss the work they do compared with how television represents it.

(MID) — Have the class develop a list of the jobs most commonly depicted on television. Issue the students current copies of *TV Guide* or the television section of daily newspapers and have them compile a list of programs that feature the jobs they have identified as well as programs depicting jobs they did not identify. When the lists are complete, have the class discuss some of the jobs that are seldom or never seen on television. Is Gerbner's finding that engineers and scientists are seldom seen still true? Does television depict dentists, architects, mechanics, or carpenters? If these professions and occupations are invisible on television, have the class discuss why they think this happens. Does it, for example, mean that being an architect or a dentist is boring or unimportant?

Break the students into groups and have each one study how a different job is represented on television. Students should watch relevant programs and describe the work environment, the various tasks involved in the job, the attitudes and morale of the workers, the level of income, and how accurate they think the depiction is. In addition, they could research that job in the real world by visiting workplaces, talking to people who hold such jobs, writing to professional associations, and finding out what it takes to enter that job or profession. Have each group report their findings to the class.

CASE STUDY ACTIVITIES

The Legal Profession

(ELEM/MID/HIGH) — One of the most frequently depicted professions on television is the legal profession (*Ally McBeal, Homicide, The Practice, Picket Fences*). Potentially, children can learn about a range of jobs in law, including judge, prosecutor, public defendant, paralegal, and attorney. How many of your students are familiar with these terms, and what do they think each type of work involves? What types of crimes do they think most commonly come before the courts, and how accurately does this reflect national crime statistics or the statistics in their own town or county? Can legal issues addressed in television programs be used to facilitate students' awareness of controversial and constitutional issues? These questions can provide a focus for studying the accuracy of the image of the legal profession and the impact that image has on the way young people perceive the law. In a March 1990 article, *TV Guide* interviewed attorneys and asked them to discuss television's depiction of the legal profession. Their comments are worth sharing with students. Jerry Spence, who successfully prosecuted Kerr-McGee in the *Karen Silkwood* case and successfully defended Imelda Marcos, was critical of one aspect of *L.A. Law*: "Most of their lawyers are young and competent. Well, in law, you can't be both! To be a good trial lawyer takes years and years, maybe twenty of ugly hard work before you're competent to stand for an hour before a jury" (*TV Guide*, 1990, 8). Alan Dershowitz, a professor of law at Harvard University, asked why 90 percent of the lawyers spent 90 percent of their time representing 1 percent of the population. "The show's cases rarely deal with the issues of social significance like whether there is a right to beg on the subways, or cases involving the homeless. If you can't resolve a case in twelve minutes, they don't do it" (5). Other complaints about *L.A. Law* suggested that "it creates a terrible impression for young lawyers. It suggests that if you go to work for a large firm like that, you'll get fun work" (5).

In exploring television images of attorneys, teachers should also direct students' attention to the distribution of power in legal firms. How many female partners are there, for example, in *L.A. Law*'s McKenzie, Brackman, Chaney, Kuzak, and Becker firm? Are the female attorneys shown as being equally competent as their male counterparts? Do they receive as many major cases and the same financial bonuses as the men? If they are not treated equally, does this reflect the bias of the program producers or is it a reflection of the real world? *L.A. Law* has been such a successful program that some law professors credit it with increased enrollments. Mike Kelly, dean of the law school at the University of Maryland, teaches an ethics course in which he uses clips from the program. Bill Simon of Stanford University Law School told *U.S.A. Today*, "Lawyers are influenced by the show and held to the high standards of *L.A. Law* because it is so plausible" (May 9, 1991b, 10A). If television's depiction of occupations can influence adults, what impact would these images have on more impressionable children and adolescents?

Teachers on Television

One profession that students should be very familiar with is teaching. School has consistently found its way to television either for comedic purposes (*Our Miss Brooks, Welcome Back Kotter, Head of the Class, Davis Rules*) or for drama (*Mr. Novak, Room 222, The White Shadow*). The consistent presence of school on the screen offers the potential for these media representations to shape the public's perception of teaching as a profession, schools as institutions, and of course, the students who attend these schools. As such, they might well affect the public's response when school boards and districts appeal to the voters for support on various bond issues. The representation of teachers also has the potential to affect the self-esteem of members of the profession and the way young people think about teaching as they formulate their career plans. Ken Reeves, Charlie Moore, Peter Dixon, Gabe Kotter—these are just some of the names of television teachers that spring to mind. Interestingly enough, they all worked with high school students. Television, and for that matter the movies, seldom sees any interest in setting a story in an elementary school. Kids and conflict work much better when the student population can be angry, articulate, and adolescent. But what about the teachers who worked with these kids? How did they come off? "Teachers tend to be shown as calm, caring, morally concerned individuals who are first and foremost interested in their students' well being. They are warm and benevolent in their personal lives and dedicated professionals in the context of their work" (Lichter et al. 1994, 253). A study by Judine Mayerle and David Rarick analyzed images of school on television over a 40-year period. They concluded that the images were restricted and stereotyped but were becoming more realistic. Comparing television teaching to the real world, they wrote, "The television world of education is dominated by male teachers and administrators and as such, has a much lower proportion of students than in the real world" (45). During the 40-year period, 20.8 percent of all lead or supporting characters were administrators, 36.8 percent were teachers, 37.5 percent were students, and 4.9 percent were other staff such as counselors and coaches. Educational census data from fall 1985 show that only 1.4 percent of participants in U.S. education at all levels were professional or administrative staff, 5.2 percent were teachers, and 93.4 percent were students.

From a statistical basis, it is therefore apparent that television does not accurately reflect the world of teaching. Have students discuss typical teaching tasks, events, and incidents depicted on television compared to their own experiences of school. In what way are television teachers different from typical teachers (dress, personality, attitudes, teaching styles)? Is there a stereotype of school administrators or principals? If so, what is it (bumbling fool, stern disciplinarian) and how does it relate to the real world?

Although the images of teachers and teaching can be inaccurate, several television programs have tried to create positive images and dismiss negative stereotypes. Jack Neuman, creator of *Mr. Novak*, worked closely with teachers and principals in developing his stories. "The school teachers that I talked to were suspicious, if not downright hostile. I couldn't blame them. Motion pictures and television have treated education as a farce comedy too many times. I said I was going to make a high school teacher the most popular hero ever seen on film."

Head of the Class is a more recent attempt to provide positive images of teaching and students. Charlie Moore's instructional strategies often represent a multimedia approach to teaching that his students find highly challenging. In one episode, his materials included the movie *Medium Cool*, Bob Dylan's *Bringing It All Back Home* album, and books by Eldridge Cleaver and Martin Luther King, Jr. When interviewed for this book, Michael Elias, one of the show's producers, talked about the way the program was conceptualized. Aware of traditional approaches such as *Welcome Back, Kotter* that stressed laughter over learning, the producers tried to depict an amusing but serious view of teaching and learning.

> *We wanted to do a show about bright students and they're . . . let me see . . . they're bright but somehow insulated students who are long on study and short of life experience. Then into their lives comes a sort of freer spirit; a teacher, a substitute teacher. He's a guy who has sort of done a lot and been around; a guy who wants them, urges them to look at the world a little differently, loosen up, not be quite as dogmatic in their studies and the way they look at the world.*

Although Charlie Moore does represent a positive image of teaching, the character is stereotypical to the extent that he is the hero-teacher, the loner who succeeds by being a nonteacher, by breaking the rules. As such, he deals with the principal as a buffoon (Dr. Samuels), and we seldom see other teachers or any real peer reinforcement. Responding to these suggestions, Elias accepted the stereotyping charges and said, "You've got to stay funny to stay on," thereby acknowledging the commercial and industrial constraints that control television images. Despite this, *Head of the Class* has consistently promoted a positive image of teaching and learning, including the programs it did from Moscow, which were produced in part to combat stereotyping in the miniseries *Amerika*.

General Hospitals: The World of Doctors and Nurses

Two very popular medical programs throughout the mid-1990s have been *E.R.* and *Chicago Hope*. Both feature big-city hospitals and explore the economics and politics of hospitals as institutions. Both also feature ensemble casts full of professional skill as doctors and nurses, but subject, too, to human weaknesses. Dr. Peter Benton on *E.R.* is brusque and frequently cold and aloof. Skillful as a surgeon, he lacks people skills and a bedside manner. Equally troubling is *Chicago Hope*'s Kate Austin. Brilliant and driven, she is forced almost every episode to try to balance her role as a surgeon, a would-be administrator, and a mother. When the pressures get too great, she breaks a court order and flees to New Zealand with her daughter. While the doctors on these programs are dramatically engaging, they seem to have more than their share of failures and inadequacies. They drink too much, are addicted to gambling, leave instruments inside patients after surgery, treat sex casually, falsify research, and obsess over their material possessions. This seems to be a marked departure from the world of *Marcus Welby*, *Dr. Kildare*, *Ben Casey*, and other television doctors from the past. "Doctors have always been prime time's consummate good guys, who dispense healing and wisdom in equal measure" (Lichter et al. 1994, 243). In the 1970s, television presented "supersuccessful doctors who could cure both somatic and social ills . . . they were saints not only in their personal lives but also in their miraculous success rates" (245-46). Today's doctors are less successful both personally and professionally. Why television now shows the complexity of the medical profession may have much to do with the complex ethical, legal, and moral issues facing scientists, doctors, and the public. *Picket Fences* frequently takes controversial social issues such as the right to die, cloning, and fetal tissue transfer, allowing its doctors, judges, attorneys, and private citizens to debate the issues.

Students can monitor medical programs such as *LA Doctors* to study representations of doctors as individuals, medicine as a profession, and hospitals as institutions. These depictions can be related to contemporary issues related to health care reform and the aging American population. In fall 1998, for example, *LA Doctors* tackled the controversial issue of medical use of marijuana. They can also explore gender politics, especially in terms of the way male doctors interact with female nurses, and the way female doctors are treated by their male colleagues.

A WINDOW ON WOMEN: Television's Representation of Females

George Gerbner has suggested that disproportionate representation on television can contribute to "acceptance of minority status as natural, inevitable, right, or even deserved" (1981, 4). Researchers have also documented a relationship between television viewing and sex role socialization of both males and females. Girls who watch the most television have "the most negative attitudes toward their gender" (Huston et al. 1992, 29). Heavy television viewing by both boys and girls has also been shown as a predictor "of a later tendency to endorse traditional sex role divisions of labor with respect to household chores" (30). Television is clearly capable of modeling independent and assertive female characters (*Roseanne, Murder She Wrote, Murphy Brown, Maude, Designing Women*). In 1995, *TV Guide* announced "the invasion of the prime time boss ladies." "All of a sudden," they noted, "strong female characters in power suits are invading the male bastions of prime time. They are district attorneys, detectives, advertising executives, and star fleet commanders. Never before have so many women been placed in positions of power" (Murphy 1995, 12). Yet, despite the visibility of Jill Brock (*Picket Fences*) and Maggie, the bush pilot (*Northern Exposure*), longitudinal studies tend to suggest that such characters are more the exception than the rule. The authors of *Prime Time: How TV Portrays American Culture* provide both a quantitative and a qualitative analysis of women in television since the 1950s. Among other things, they note that since 1955, men have constituted 72 percent of all television characters and 85 percent of all characters with a college education. Summarizing the depiction of female television characters, they conclude, "They are less likely to be mature adults, are less well educated, and hold lower-status jobs. Their activities tend to represent the private realm of home, personal relations and sexuality, while men represent the public realm of work and social relations" (Lichter et al. 1994, 120). Further, the authors seek to explain the conditions and assumptions that affect such representations. "Television's view of women is influenced partly by what its creators think the audience wants, partly by what they think it needs, and partly by the stereotypes and assumptions they inadvertently project into their creations" (147).

Since media literacy is concerned not just with media content but also with the possible consequences of the representations and context in which they are both created and consumed, knowing who writes and creates these programs is as important as knowing who watches them. The television industry is still largely a patriarchal institution. Among the highest-rated sitcoms (*Seinfeld, Home Improvement, Single Guy, Coach, Frasier, Murphy Brown, Grace Under Fire, Ellen,* and *Roseanne*), the overwhelming majority have males as head writers or producers. One exception is *Ellen,* for which Eileen Heisler and DeAnne Heline served as executive producers and head writers. It is also worthwhile to explore similarities and differences across various television genres, particularly when dealing with programs with largely female audiences, such as daytime talk shows and soap operas. In the case of soap operas, it has been said that "they reinforce the status quo with respect to the nature of sex roles and interpersonal relationships in a patriarchal culture" (Rogers 1995, 325). Even the Home Shopping Network constructs and projects a purpose and position for its women viewers. Armed with televisions and telephones, these women are positioned as "the ideal consumer . . . and the domestic space as the ideal site of consumption" (White 1995, 153). Like Betty Rubble and Wilma Flintstone, such women pursue spending with vigor to the constant war cry . . . "Charge it!"

Women as Main Characters

(ELEM/MID) — Have students develop a list of television programs they watch in which women are the title or main characters (*Roseanne, Grace Under Fire, Caroline in the City, Ellen, Veronica's Closet, The X Files*). Do boys and girls watch these shows equally? Design a content analysis chart that would enable students to monitor and record important aspects of the characters and their lifestyles. These components could include: (1) Married/Single, (2) Wife/Mother, (3) Occupation (White-collar/Blue-collar), (4) City/Suburban/Rural, etc. Beyond these demographic factors, students might also assign other qualities to these female characters. These could include: (1) sense of humor, (2) intelligence, (3) independence, (4) attractiveness. Compare and contrast the characteristics that female and male students value in women on television.

That Was Then . . . This Is Now

(MID/HIGH) — *Where the Girls Are: Growing Up Female with the Mass Media* (Douglas 1994) provides a fascinating account of mass media representations of women and the relationship between media content and social developments. "American women," the author notes, "are a bundle of contradictions because much of the media imagery we grew up with was itself filled with mixed messages about what women should and should not do, what women could and could not do" (9). Re-runs of major television programs from the past (*I Love Lucy, Bewitched, I Dream of Jeannie, The Waltons, Happy Days, The Mary Tyler Moore Show*, etc.) offer students an opportunity to compare and contrast females in these shows with females in contemporary television programs. In fact, History and Social Studies classes exploring the 1950s, 1960s, and 1970s could use programs from this era as historical primary documents. Susan Douglas frequently makes connections between media representations and emerging social, political, and economic issues. The same year that Betty Friedan's *Feminine Mystique* was published, for example, television viewers were introduced to a very independent woman, albeit a witch, with a man's name (Sam[antha] in *Bewitched*).

Rock and Rule?

(MID/HIGH) — *Dream Worlds* is a creative, controversial, and somewhat contrived documentary about MTV's content and impact upon the adolescent male audience. Sexist and stereotypical music videos are seen as voyeuristic experiences and adolescent male fantasies that subjugate women by constructing images that are frequently violent and demeaning. Yet, there is another way of looking at women and music videos. Lisa Lewis, for example, argues that exposure through MTV "is contributing to an upsurge in female rock and roll musicianship . . . far from being absolute bastions of male desire, MTV is providing a unique space for the articulation of gender politics by female artists and audiences" (1995, 504). Survey your class to see how much music video your male and female students are exposed to. What are their favorite videos and what criteria do they assign for this status (e.g., the artist, the beat, the lyrics, the special effects, etc.)? Now ask the class to discuss the way males and females are represented in music videos. Start with their impressions and then select some examples to see if these impressions are representative. Older students can use key components of media literacy to discuss these images in terms of the audience and the creators.

Female Characters in Television Cartoons

(ELEM/MID) — Although there are many shows that feature women, the real concern is not whether they are represented but how they are represented. Boston media critic Vince Canzoneri (1984) looked at the images of females in cartoons. He noted the number of cartoon programs dominated by male characters and the relatively passive role of female characters featured.

Have students develop a list of all the television cartoon characters they are familiar with. They should create two lists, one for males and one for females. Then have them develop a list of adjectives to describe the characteristics of each character and a list of key verbs to describe the activities the characters normally engage in. Discuss the differences between the ways female and male cartoon characters are depicted.

View a television cartoon or assign students episodes of several different cartoons to watch at home. Have students present reports on how the program was similar to or different from the characteristics they described in class.

How Women Are Depicted on Television

(MID/HIGH) — In 1967, George Gerbner (1981) began a lengthy study of the depiction of women on television. The study looked at 5,000 major and 14,000 minor characters featured in 1,600 programs. He found that in television, men outnumbered women three to one, and most women did not work outside the home. A 1987 study reported that 75 percent of television's female characters work outside the home, which was actually 20 percent higher than in real life. A 1988 study still found men outnumbering women three to one on television, which also misrepresents the actual composition of society.

Introduce students to these statistics. Ask them why they think more women on television work than they do in real life. One possible response could be the dramatic need to locate the story away from the home. Ask students why they think images of working women increased on television between 1967 and 1987. Do they see any link between this and actual social changes? Are these patterns still true on television today? Ask students to explain why males are so overrepresented on television. Areas for discussion could include the influence of male writers, producers, and directors in a patriarchal entertainment industry and the belief that male characters offer more dramatic range than females.

Have the class conduct a statistical analysis of prime-time programs, dividing key characters into males and females. Then assign each student one or two different programs and have him or her report on the different ways the two genders are depicted. Areas to be considered could include occupation, interests, social position, income level, authority, appearance, and emotional stability. From the individual reports, compile a composite analysis of the images of men and women on television. Which program do students consider to be the most accurate, fair, and representative? Have them use specific incidents from episodes and story lines to justify their choice.

Creative Women in Television

(MID/HIGH) — In 1996, Jamie Tarses was appointed president of entertainment for NBC. This was the first time a woman had ever headed this division of a major television network. Within a year, Tarses became the subject of television talk shows when a man was appointed to oversee her work before the programs she had developed could find an audience. The glass ceiling that impedes the progress of women in corporate America is still evident in the giant conglomerates, of which the television industry is part. But some changes are taking place, however slowly.

In recent years, women have begun to make inroads into the creative side of television, and as a result, the way women are represented in some programs has changed. Linda Bloodworth Thomason is the creator and producer of *Designing Women*, Diane English created and produces *Murphy Brown*, Ester Shapiro developed *Dynasty*, and Carol Black co-created *The Wonder Years*. *China Beach*, on the other hand, although it dealt with women, was actually created by men and regarded by some as a male fantasy. Assign students several different television programs and have them develop a list of names of each program's writers and creators. Tabulate the figures to see how influential women are in the creative side of television. A 1989 report on this subject indicated that only 8 percent of directors were women and that female writers received only one-third the pay of their male counterparts. Select a female producer or writer and have the class write a letter commenting on what they like about her work. Also have students ask questions about career opportunities for women in television and the responsibility of the television industry to provide positive images of women.

FOCUS ON THE FAMILY: Is Prime Time a Fine Time?

In June 1996, *TV Guide* featured June and Beaver Cleaver along with an American flag in a cover story that asked, "What happened to Family TV?" How, they wondered, "did family time turn into cursing, conniving and carousing time?" (Rudolph and Hammer, 18). Lamenting the disappearance of quality images of family life typified by programs such as *The Waltons*, *Apple's Way*, *Family Ties*, *The Wonder Years*, and *My So Called Life*, a mother asked, "Would it do any harm to try a little tenderness earlier in the evening when some of the memories we make with our children are linked with the most powerful medium in our environment?" (Mitchard 1995, 17). Many adults are no doubt horrified by the demise of Ozzie and Harriet or Cliff and Claire Huxtable, especially since they seem to be replaced by increasingly unacceptable role models like Peg and Al Bundy, with their dismal representation of life in *Married with Children*. The Bundys, like the Connors (*Roseanne*), however, do not represent the whole picture. In many ways their existence, including their popularity, signifies the presence of an audience tired of fantasy families, hungry for images of working-class, or lower-middle-class life to which they can relate. Roseanne, for example, was four things women, especially television women, were not supposed to be: "working class, loud-mouthed, overweight, and a feminist" (Douglas 1994, 284). Keenly aware of television's saccharine representations of the family, suburbia, and motherhood, Roseanne drew upon our familiarity with these programs from the past. This included bringing some of television's most famous moms to her own home in Lanford, or parodying the past with her own all black-and-white episode in which she took on the appearance, if not the substance and sentiment, of perfect mothers like Margaret Anderson (*Father Knows Best*) and Donna Stone (*The Donna Reed Show*). Roseanne succeeded because "her mission was simple and welcome: to take the schmaltz and hypocrisy out of media images of motherhood" (284).

While many viewers may lament the passing of television's portrait of a kinder, gentler American family, researchers who have looked beneath the surface of these representations have come up with some interesting conclusions. While they agree that working-class families are generally depicted as more dysfunctional than middle-class families, the authors of a 1995 report in *The Journal of Broadcasting and Electronic Media* concluded that their study "yielded no support for the claim that family life and family relations have deteriorated across time in the television family" (Douglas and Olson 1995, 236). The study analyzed episodes of *The Honeymooners*, *I Love Lucy*, *Family Ties*, *Cosby*, *Roseanne*, *The Wonder Years*, and others. Episodes and interactions of major characters were coded for distribution of family power, satisfaction, and other factors.

❖**Reprinted with permission from News America Publications Inc., publisher of *TV Guide* magazine, copyright, July 13-19, 1996, News America Publications, Inc.**

The report documented "changed levels of relational openness and a general trend toward increased expression of affect in spousal relations" (236). One observation that would no doubt surprise many critics was that "most families were seen to provide more or less appropriate social models" (257).

Whether we approve or disapprove of how television depicts the family, over the years, including the 1990s, many of these programs have won critical acclaim. Located in Rome, Wisconsin, and centering on the family of Jill and Jimmy Brock, *Picket Fences* garnered 12 Emmy Awards. Describing the program, Matt Roush said, "In an hour we digest controversy, explore a complex and loving marriage, weigh the benefits

❖ Conservative groups like Focus on the Family lament the loss of television families like the Cleavers while researchers reject the claim that family life on television has deteriorated. Taken from the *Focus on the Family* magazine, August 1995, published by Focus on the Family. Copyright © 1995 by Focus on the Family. All rights reserved. International copyright secured. Used by permission. Photograph from FPG International.

of family and career, and are grandly entertained" (1993, 3d). The trials and tribulations of the Salinger family presented in Fox's *Party of Five* received a Golden Globe Award for best drama. The recurring presence and popularity of family representations on television offer teachers an opportunity to focus on the family as a major case study or unit to explore many of the major principles of media literacy described earlier in this book.

Media are commercial constructions. Any discussion of when and how television depicts the family cannot be separated from the fact that to succeed, these programs must gain and maintain an audience. In recent years, that audience has been fragmented and segmented, in part due to alternative programming evident in cable and by loss of viewers to the Internet and other entertainment sources. The fragmentation of the audience cannot be separated from the changing representation of the family. Explaining the demise of family time, *TV Guide* pointed out that 73 percent of American homes now have two or more television sets. Since parents and children no longer have to view together, producers are less inclined to create a program for an audience that may no longer actually exist. Television shows are produced and aired in the first place because network programmers and their sponsors believe they will deliver an audience, which will in turn purchase products promoted on the show. As such, the content can challenge, entertain, and engage but never bore or offend the audience. Safe programs like *Home Improvement* and *Cosby* typically have a longer life than cutting-edge programs. *Roseanne* and *The Simpsons* succeeded by breaking the rules. Marketing is a major aspect to explore in trying to understand not just how the family is depicted but also who the intended audience is. The animated series *King of the Hill* surprised many in the industry when it not only sustained but actually increased the ratings of *The Simpsons*, which it followed. Its demographics showed it won its time slot with men and women in the 18- to 34-year-old range and with men in the 18- to 49-age group. *Home Improvement*, unlike *The Wonder Years*, *The Brady Bunch*, *Roseanne*, and *Cosby*, featured only male children. Typically, the presence of both boy and girl characters gives both sexes in the audience an opportunity to relate and therefore strengthens the audience appeal. *Home Improvement* seems to appeal to boys in the audience who can relate to Mark and the other characters, while females in the audience are attracted by the good looks and teen idol appeal of the show's young stars. Animated series like *King of the Hill* tend to cost about 33 percent more to get off the ground than typical live action comedy, which costs about $750,000 per episode. But lucrative merchandising opportunities tend to offset this for cartoon characters. Fox is expected to receive some $1 billion from the sales of Simpsons-related merchandising and syndication by the end of the decade.

Media have unique forms. We noted earlier in this book that each medium has its own unique characteristics and attributes (movement, point of view, color, etc.). In the case of television genres, this includes the variation on the format and formula that have consistently characterized the codes and conventions of specific genres. Many representations of the American family have occurred in the context of the sitcom (*Cosby, Family Ties, The Wonder Years, Home Improvement, Roseanne*), while others have taken place in the context of dramas and, in the 1990s, dramedies (*7th Heaven, Eight Is Enough, The Waltons, Little House on the Prairie, Picket Fences, Party of Five*). By discussing their own perceptions of production patterns in these programs, students can begin to recognize recurring formulas in the writing, creation, and marketing of television genres. Gerard Jones, author of *Honey, I'm Home: Sitcoms Selling the American Dream*, says that sitcoms function with "different characters and different pretexts, but always the same basic structure: domestic harmony is threatened when a character develops a desire that runs counter to the group's welfare, or misunderstands a situation because of poor communication, or contacts a disruptive element outside" (1992, 4). Ultimately, he notes, "the wisdom of the group and its executive is proved."

Media messages contain values and ideologies. Jones recognizes that what the television-viewing public perceives to be mere entertainment actually represents the clear articulation of a value system within a commercial context. Describing the sitcom as "a corporate product" and "the Miracle Play of consumer society" (1992, 4), he articulates the values it has typically embodied. "It is an extension of the underlying assumptions of the corporate culture that has come to dominate American society. The ideals upheld by the sitcom are the ideals on which modern bureaucratic business and government are founded" (4). These include an emphasis upon consensus, a belief in the boss, especially a benevolent and responsive boss, and the value of compromise over confrontation.

Media messages have social and political consequences. Exposure to television's value system cannot be expected to be without impact. Whether television mirrors or makes the society that both produces and consumes it is a discussion of chicken-and-egg dimensions. Regardless of what side of that argument we come down on, television's content and value system cannot be called neutral. Heated discussions in Congress about television violence and the need for a V-chip or a more effective rating system are all predicated upon the assumption that exposure to television content somehow results in social consequences. While many people express concern about what they perceive as negative representations of family life on television today, others are concerned about the fantasy families they were raised on and the way these representations failed to prepare them for the world in which they grew up. Describing this disjuncture, Susan Douglas says, "After we'd watched the perfect, secure, harmonious families on *The Donna Reed Show* or *My Three Sons*, we watched our parents fight with each other, yell at us and hit us, and plot their divorces" (1994, 143). The towns of television's sitcoms were harmonious, happy places like Mayfield and Springfield, but on nightly news, young viewers growing up in the 1960s found American towns like Selma and

Birmingham that were hard to reconcile with televisionland. In the southern towns that filled the news reports, impressionable viewers saw places "where real parents lost their children to bombs planted in churches and where real teenagers were clubbed mercilessly by police" (143). For many, as Douglas notes, "spectatorship . . . even in the confines of your own home, was a politicizing event" (153).

While today's politics may be less turbulent than that of the 1960s, politics and social issues have now found their way into representations of the family, whether in sitcoms or dramas. Debates about ethics and morality infused almost every episode of *Picket Fences*, which was not afraid to criticize the Supreme Court, debate busing, challenge sex role stereotypes, or weigh the pros and cons of euthanasia. Nor was this simply the domain of informed and mature adults. Teenager Kimberly Brock was perfectly capable of articulating a position she knew was opposed to the views of her mother, her father, or both. The fact that parents and kids in today's television families are heard and seen talking with each other about complex issues is an enormous step forward. Regular viewers of *Home Improvement* (Tim), *Roseanne* (Dan), *The Simpsons* (Homer), and *King of the Hill* (Hank) might well conclude that television no longer believes that father knows best. For some, this might signify a rejection of the patriarchy and a decline in traditional family values. It might also, however, represent a more equitable and realistic representation of job sharing within the modern family. In their longitudinal study of television families, Lichter et al. found that television continued to promote the belief that wisdom resided with the older generation. While television viewers may more routinely see kids mouth off at their parents today than they did in the past, there is a level of openness and honesty associated with this. "The real change over time does not concern whether children or their parents know right. Rather, it comes in the circumstances and contexts surrounding presentations of parental wisdom. It is the issues under discussion that change over time, not the dynamics of the parent-child relationship" (1994, 167).

By modeling family life in which parents and children honestly and openly explore different points of view, television may create an environment that is true to American democratic ideals. Among the unanticipated outcomes of this type of programming, television might well develop healthier and happier children. Research has documented "wishful identification and parasocial interaction with favorite television characters" among children ages 7 to 12 (Hoffner 1996). Other studies have shown that family television series are particularly popular with children ages 2 to 11. These series frequently "center on ordinary everyday emotional situations that most children can expect to experience in their real lives" (Weiss and Wilson 1996, 19). As such, viewing these programs "may contribute to children's beliefs about the nature of emotions, how to express different emotions, what emotions are appropriate to express in particular situations . . . and how to control or regulate their emotional responses to various events in real life" (1).

Canadian researchers were able to use television programs about the family to facilitate parent-child interaction in homes where emotional conflict caused communication problems. The study, *Parents, Adolescents and Television* (Tierney 1978) used shows like *Eight Is Enough* to promote discussion between teens and their parents. "Watching the programs together generated discussion of important topics like sexual permissiveness, the pill, drinking, and personal relationships." Counselors might find that troubled teens could use characters and circumstances in today's television programs (*My So Called Life, 7th Heaven, Party of Five*) as catalysts to articulate their own worries.

For the most part, children and their parents tend to view programs about the family for relaxation, entertainment, and escape. But because these programs are located within the familiar context of the American family, they can potentially reflect, reinforce, and even undermine traditional images of family life. Because television operates on a ratings system, these programs are subject to public approval and the barometer of public opinion the ratings system offers. What became evident in the 1980s was that the

American family has more than one face. In fact, sociologists believe that television and other media representations can be read as a reflection of the nation's value system. The Huxtable family in *The Cosby Show* are an idealized image of the family. Jack Solomon (1988) says this represents the dream, not the reality. *U.S.A. Today* reported, "While Cosby offers positive models to learn from, the *Simpsons* act as negatives. The *Simpsons* use cynical caustic humor. They teach us vicariously through bad decisions. Cosby raises our expectations, while the *Simpsons* make us feel better about ourselves—our family will never be as bad as that" (1990, 3D).

(ELEM/MID) — Have students make lists of TV families and all the members of the family. Get the class to vote for their favorite television family. The class could break into small groups, with each group representing one television family and developing a presentation to the class on what they like about that family. Which family does the class think is the most realistic and which one is the least realistic? What reasons do they give?

❖ **The Camden family in *7th Heaven* functions as a representation of a Christian family. Entertaining as well as educational, the program models effective communication within a family context and has explored issues as diverse as the holocaust, substance abuse, and teen pregnancy. Used with permission of The WB Television Network. Photograph by James Sorenson for The WB, 1997.**

(MID/HIGH) — This assignment can be used in English and Social Studies classes but also has benefits in counseling. Assign one television family to groups of 3 or 4 students until the class is studying 6 to 10 TV families. Have them analyze the family according to the following elements:

- Members (age, sex, race)

- Occupation and income

- Neighborhood (city, suburban, or rural)

- Common conflicts or problems

- How problems are resolved

- Authority and control in the household

- Lifestyle (clothing, cars, recreation, vacations, luxury goods, etc.)

- Functional or dysfunctional

After students have provided profiles of the families, use census and other statistical information to compare and contrast these fictional families and their lifestyles to real life.

TV Teens and Tots

(MID) — In one episode of *Doogie Howser, M.D.*, the adolescent recorded the following memo in his diary: "When we're little, we want to be just like our dads. When we're teenagers we want nothing to do with them. When we're adult, we end up just like them." Like Kevin Arnold in *The Wonder Years*, Doogie takes viewers on a tour of adolescence from an unusually mature perspective. Doogie's genius enables him to be wiser than his years, although the program often points out that emotionally he is just like other teenagers with the same pleasures and fears. Kevin Arnold has the benefit of hindsight as voice-over narration takes us through his early adolescence in the late 1960s and early 1970s. Depictions of children and teenagers on television can be both beneficial and detrimental. They offer role models to young people, and they potentially offer students the chance to recognize that other kids, even fictional kids, feel the same way they feel. When Doogie Howser is reprimanded and grounded for underage drinking, young viewers have the opportunity to think about actions and consequences. When Alex Keaton confronts the death of a friend, adolescent viewers have the chance to reflect on their own mortality. When Janice has to accept that she's not the best cello player in the school, *Head of the Class* provides a forum for exploring self-image and self-esteem.

Statistically, Gerbner (1995) says, young people are underrepresented on TV, accounting for only one-third of their true numbers in the population. As an audience, however, teenagers can be quite influential. The Fox Network found success in 1991 with *Beverly Hills 90210*. Beefcake, good looks, and California cool captured 50 to 60 percent of teenagers watching television, making the show number two in the time slot, second only to *Cheers*. The show's creator said he devised the series because of the absence of intelligent programs for teenagers.

Provide the class with a list of the names of teenage characters on television, or have them generate their own list. Discuss which characters they think are most like and least like real teenagers.

While students will be familiar with current television programs, many of them will also be familiar with shows they grew up watching or with old television programs now widely seen on cable re-runs. The following list includes major characters that children and adolescents would be familiar with and might relate to. Remember to encourage them to update the list by contributing the names of characters in new programs.

The Cosby Show: Theo, Denise, and Vanessa Huxtable

Family Ties: Alex, Mallory, and Jennifer Keaton

Growing Pains: Mike, Carol, and Ben Seaver

Home Improvement: Brad, Randy, and Mark Taylor

Life Goes On: Becca, Paige, and Corky Thatcher

Married with Children: Kelly and Bud Bundy

Party of Five: Claudia, Julia, and Bailey Salinger

Roseanne: Becky, BJ, and Darlene Conner

The Simpsons: Bart, Maggie, and Lisa

(ELEM) — Ask students to develop a list of children who appear in television families. Which characters do your students most like and why? Have the students write a brief description of their favorite television child and then have them compare that child to themselves. Ask the children to start by listing all the ways the TV child is the same as and different from them. Develop a list of given names and surnames from television families. Mix the names up and have the class rearrange them so the right children are assigned to the right family.

Déjà View

(MID/HIGH) — This is an excellent activity to incorporate into History and Social Studies classes as an exciting and stimulating way of studying post-World War II America, with an emphasis on the 1950s and 1960s. Rather than having students simply read about these periods in textbooks, television programs from the era can be explored as primary documents of the way people lived and the values they held. In *Prime Time*, for example, the authors argue that television has in fact become "our common denominator . . . America's changing image of itself refracted through the lens of the American dream machine" (Lichter et al. 1994, 25). Students can explore the accuracy of television's image in any given era, comparing it with other primary documents such as magazines, newspapers, and family photograph albums from the time. Textbooks can then be used to flesh out the histories. While sitcoms like *I Love Lucy*, *The Brady Bunch*, *The Donna Reed Show*, and *My Three Sons* may give them a sense of what America found funny, even how people dressed and what our homes looked like, they totally ignored the reality of American society at the time, including polio, segregation, Vietnam, and student unrest. It would take Norman Lear (*All in the Family*) and a new generation of television writers and producers to bridge the gap between the world we lived in and television's window on the world. These and other shows from the 1970s address contemporary issues head on. Have students analyze television programs as a reflection of the time in which they were made. They should pay attention to the plot and what is said, but also concentrate on the set, which will give them clues about the lifestyle of the characters through such things as their appliances, furniture, clothing, cars, and modes of transportation.

1. How many members are there in the family? What does the family consist of? How does this compare to the composition of your parents' or grandparents' family at that time?

2. Do the parents work? What types of jobs do they do? Compare this to your parents or grandparents at that time.

3. Describe the income level and lifestyle of the family. Are they, for example, working-class, lower-middle-class, upper-middle class? What evidence are you using for this judgment?

4. Describe the environment in which the family lives. Is it rural, urban, or suburban? Do they own their own house, live in an apartment that they own or rent? What did your parents or grandparents live in at that time?

5. Pay careful visual attention to the family home. Make a note of the furniture and appliances. In what way are they different today? Try to find photos in your family albums that show appliances, fashions, and furniture from this period. Compare

them to the ones shown in the television program.

6. Listen carefully to the interaction between adults and children in the program. Make a list of words or phrases they use that you are not familiar with. Ask your parents if they used expressions like this or if they know what the expressions mean.

7. If there are any problems or conflicts in the program, make a list of them. Are similar problems present in today's television families? Were these problems common concerns for families when the program was made?

8. Does the program contain any references (visual or verbal) to real people such as politicians or to real social and political events or issues? If it does, develop a list of them for further research.

9. Does the program refer to school in any way? If so, how is it depicted?

10. Prices will be considerably different in these old programs. Make a list of all goods and prices referred to either visually or verbally.

11. In what way is the society in this program different from that of the world you live in?

Our Town

(MID/HIGH) — Thorton Wilder's *Our Town* remains one of the classic works of 20th-century American theater. Its representation of small-town life is in the tradition of Booth Tarkington's *Penrod* series and connected to literary classics like Thomas Wolfe's *You Can't Go Home Again*, Sinclair Lewis's *Mainstreet*, and other sensational fare, including *King's Row* and *Peyton Place*. Television, too, has found small-town America to be an entertaining and profitable setting for its storytelling, perhaps most successfully in Andy Griffith's Mayberry and, most offensively, in *The Dukes of Hazzard*. In recent years, two successful series, *Picket Fences* and *Northern Exposure*, have used Rome, Wisconsin, and Cicely, Alaska, respectively, as a microcosm to explore American society. Michael Pressman, who was involved in the development of *Picket Fences*, acknowledged that locating the series in the heartland of America's Midwest was a deliberate choice. "By choosing a small town, we could use this as a metaphor-society in microcosm. Major ethical issues are almost magnified by the setting instead of lost in the rush of city life" (Mitchard 1995, 28). Describing the world of Cicely, Alaska, and its audience appeal, critic Ron Powers called it a place "set off in glorious isolation from the rest of the world but urgently alive with its own rules, its own community of characters who collide and

scheme and get their feelings hurt. But who ultimately work things out. Who grow from experiences. Who survive. Who prevail as a community" (1991, 8). Ask students to make a list of television programs they regularly watch that deal with families and communities. Then ask them to describe the type of environment (city, suburban, rural, small town) in which the program is set. When you have a list of programs set in small towns, describe the character of the people and the characteristics of the town. Compare and contrast this to real small towns the students or their parents grew up in, are familiar with, have visited, etc. Compare and contrast television's small towns to those in some of the plays and novels mentioned earlier. Use census figures to determine how many Americans live in small towns. How does this compare to the representation of small-town life in television programs like *Murder She Wrote*? Discuss the dramatic reasons Michael Pressman advanced for explaining the choice of Rome, Wisconsin, as the setting for *Picket Fences*. It might be useful to introduce students to the theatrical and literary convention "willing suspension of disbelief" when discussing programs like *Picket Fences*. Because the town is small, most of the major issues and conflicts happen to a relatively small number of characters. It seems implausible that the Brock family would suffer the number of tragedies and conflicts that beset them. This, however, is to miss the point—that their family and their town is being used as a microcosm of the wider world beyond the town limits.

Marvelous Moms and Dumb Dads

(ELEM/MID) — Teachers wishing to explore sex role stereotypes and sex role socialization can encourage students to look at the way television programs depict parents. This can range from the rather bizarre fantasy families with parents like Herman and Lilly (*The Munsters*) and Morticia and Gomez (*The Addams Family*). In fact, the humorous excesses of these wacky families from television's past are not too far removed from television's current portrait of Pop as bumbling, benign, but basically inept. *Home Improvement* is one case in point. Tim "the toolman" Taylor may be the star of the series and his own *Tool Time*, but most of the wisdom comes from neighbor Wilson and wife Jill. In fact, Patricia Richardson's portrayal of Jill Taylor won *TV Guide*'s reader poll for most popular television mother. She also made an important distinction between television and real life when she said, "Being a Mom is much harder in real life. I mean, we solve the most complicated problems in 23 minutes on the show every week" (*TV Guide* 1996, 20). Assign students the task of monitoring television parents. Who is portrayed most accurately? Who is portrayed most fairly? What problems do parents typically face with their children? How do the children relate to each of their parents? If patterns of representation emerge, such as those suggested in the title of this exercise, try to explore why one parent is depicted more fairly than another. This is also a good time to explore television's representation of single-parent families.

Families on Television: Families and Television

(HIGH) — Bruno Bettelheim's *Uses of Enchantment* suggests that fairy tales help children process the way of the world, preparing them to understand their place in it. This notion has been applied to television sitcoms, which "show us our place in life . . . the families we'll grow into" (Friend 1993, 115). Assign this as the theme for a high school essay, asking students to discuss the premise and to provide examples of lessons viewers might learn about family life from watching television.

Big World, Small Screen says, "A healthy family life is critical to children and to many adults; we should place a high priority on gaining more knowledge about how television does and can contribute to it" (Huston et al. 1992, 40). Use this quote as the theme for a major essay or term paper, asking students to discuss ways in which television can hurt and help families.

RACIAL MINORITIES ON TELEVISION

"The media are not only a powerful source of ideas about race. They are also one place where these ideas are articulated, worked on, transformed, and elaborated" (Hall 1995, 18). How television depicts diversity, what it both reveals and conceals regarding the cultural contributions of ethnic minorities, cannot be ignored in any school curriculum that attempts to foster tolerance, challenge racism, and promote respect for all peoples. Monitoring television representations of ethnic minorities can include a head count, or statistical analysis of the number of depictions. However, emphasis should also be placed on the cultural context in which the depictions occur, which involves some degree of qualitative analysis. Tracing these patterns of representation over a period of time enables us to have a longitudinal perspective on the issue of how television represents race, how this relates to the reality of race relations in the United States, and what changes if any we would recommend. Beyond the demographic data and statistical analysis of how TV portrays minorities, researchers have also observed a broadly recurring theme. "The basic message is that everyone, regardless of race, creed, or color, deserves an equal chance at the good things in America. Bigotry and intolerance still exist but can be overcome when people learn about each other" (Lichter et al. 1994, 356).

In the mid-1980s, researchers found that black Americans were frequently depicted in a comedic context within a family relationship, which limited their roles and undermined depictions of power and assertiveness. A decade later, Hispanics were portrayed "within a narrow spectrum from villains to second bananas" (Greenberg and Brand 1994, 353). Television's depiction of black women has also been studied, especially within the context of cop, crime, and law drama. Describing minority women on *Hill Street Blues*, one study called them "the back drop of poverty, crime, and hopelessness on which the plots were based. They were hookers and drug addicts, abused wives and rape victims but rarely cops or public defendants or upstanding members of the community" (Rhodes 1995, 427). Similarly in the world of *L.A. Law*, these women "form the background of society . . . silent, nearly invisible characters found in back rows of the courtroom, on the street or in the jury box" (427). These depictions, as noted in the section on stereotyping, have the potential to affect not only the groups being represented but the majority culture as well, who can buy into the belief system that the media models regarding minorities. In the case of black children, research suggests they "tend to believe in the reality of television, to learn behaviors from televised models" (Greenberg and

Brand 1994, 274). Educators working with young children from minority groups need to be particularly aware of the impact the media can have on their self-concept and self-actualization. *Television and the Socialization of the Minority Child* (Berry and Mitchell-Kernan eds., 1982) is an important contribution to this realization. Discussing self-concept, Gloria Johnson Powell wrote, "A growing person's conception of his or her selfness comes into being through the reflected appraisal of others. What are the reflections of our race-conscious society that television mirrors or projects to the minority child viewer?" (1982, 124.)

One place where we might expect to see children encountering messages about diversity is in cartoons and other Saturday morning fare. Researchers in the 1990s reported that all racial minority characters featured in such programs were male. All regularly appearing minority characters were also black. Researchers found no depictions of Native Americans or Asian Americans, and only one Hispanic character. They concluded that these programs were "fairly empty as a carrier of multicultural information" (Greenberg and Brand 1994, 295). Unfortunately, researchers have also concluded that social studies textbooks are often containers and conveyors of inaccurate messages about race, gender, class, and disability (Sleeter and Grant 1992). As a result, both the curriculum of the classroom and the curriculum of the living room may do little to help the majority culture understand minority populations and little to help minority populations perceive themselves as individuals and groups valued by the mainstream media and its audience.

The Cosby Controversy

The Cosby Show dominated ratings throughout the 1980s. It was one of the most successful programs in television history, and many people were pleased to see its positive depiction of black family life. But not everyone was pleased. Some critics argued that the show was unrealistic and that the family life and social life presented were unattainable for most blacks. Some believed that blacks might aspire to the lifestyle of

the Huxtables but could never attain it. Some believed the program toned down color and race issues and succeeded with white television audiences by neutralizing the essence of black life and culture. Mark Miller wrote, "As a willing advertisement for the system that pays him well, Cliff Huxtable also represents a threat contained. Although dark skinned and physically imposing, he ingratiates himself with some childlike mien and enviable lifestyle, a surrender that must offer some deep solace to a white public" (1988, 74).

Oddly enough, one of the major criticisms of the program appears in a study actually funded by Bill and Camille Cosby. *Enlightened Racism: The Cosby Show, Audiences and the Myth of the American Dream* not only explored the content of the popular series, but also discussed the potential consequences of its race messages with a series of white and black audiences in specially selected focus groups. The study argued that television "affects how viewers make sense of the world" (Jhally and Lewis 1992, 35). One of the central charges made about the idealized world of the Huxtable family is that "these positive images can actually be counterproductive because they reinforce the myth of the American dream, a just world where everyone can make it and racial barriers no longer exist" (3). The researchers also supported one of the basic principles of media literacy, declaring that "the meaning of the show is different for different audiences" (50). Black audiences were offered a representation of black families that transcended white stereotypes and showed "black people as they would like to recognize themselves—strong, independent, intelligent—a mirror that shows the dignity of Black American life" (36). White viewers, however, processed Cosby on another level, one that led the researchers to actually conclude that "the show has a profoundly negative influence on racial equality in American society" (56). Many white respondents saw the success of the Huxtable family as evidence that all blacks could succeed if they wanted to work. The affirmation of the American Dream denied the existence of racism. "This attitude enables white viewers to combine an impeccably liberal attitude toward race, with a deep-rooted suspicion of black people" (110).

Noting that the condition of black Americans actually deteriorated during the time *The Cosby Show* dominated the ratings, the authors view the show's denial of class

not simply as escapist fare but as an ideological apparatus. Sustained by the massive presence of popular culture, the American Dream, they declare, is "insidious not innocent" (139). Moving from content to consequences, they argue that the dream, and *The Cosby Show* that reinforced it, "is part of a belief system that allows people in the United States to disregard the inequities that generate the nation's appalling record on poverty, crime, health, homelessness, and education" (139).

(HIGH) — Such concerns suggest that intentionally or not, television can have a social and political impact. Look at *The Cosby Show* and other shows depicting racial minorities. Have students consider the following questions: Do these shows present accurate insights into minority cultures?

- Do they address current controversial and social issues as they would affect these cultures?

- Do they foster white America's understanding of minorities, or do they present minorities in such a way that the central concerns of their lives in the real world are never manifested?

- Is this treatment unique to the way the media represent minority families, or do the media ignore social, political, and economic issues in the way they represent all families?

(ELEM/MID/HIGH) — Select a genre such as cartoons, sitcoms, or cop/crime and assign students the task of monitoring representation of minorities in these programs with reference to the research cited in the previous section. Students working with the cop shows, for example, might see if Rhodes's conclusions about minority women remain true today. Students working with cartoons and Saturday morning programs might attempt to validate or refute Greenberg and Brand's conclusion (1994) that they lack multicultural messages.

Middle-Class Minorities

(MID/HIGH) — It has been claimed that television's representation of middle-class minorities, including blacks, is romanticized and unrealistic. "The characters are never presented in situations where their racial identity matters" (Gray 1995, 435). Carefully read the section on *The Cosby Show* controversy and discuss differences between low-income and middle-class minorities as they are represented in the media.

What's Wrong with This Picture?

(MID) — Many of the most popular shows on television in the late 1990s were set in big cities with significant minority populations. This is true of *Seinfeld, Suddenly Susan, Friends, Caroline in the City,* and others. Despite the presence of major minority populations in these cities, minorities are almost entirely invisible from these popular programs. Have students come up with a list of programs set in big cities. Monitor these programs for the presence of minority characters. What factors might explain the presence or absence of minorities in certain programs? Is it true, for example, that they appear in cop/crime and medical programs but are almost invisible in sitcoms? What might explain this trend?

(ELEM/MID/HIGH) — Ask students to develop a list of all minority characters on television. Separate the list by groups, such as Hispanic, black, Asian, and Native American. Identify the characters as minor (supporting) or major (lead) characters. Identify the types of programs the characters appear in (comedy, drama, etc.). Classify the depiction of the characters as positive or negative. Examine the incomes, occupations, and lifestyles of the characters. Now compare these media representations of minorities to real life. How fair and accurate are the images?

TELEVISION AND HUMAN HEALTH

When the U.S. government banned cigarette advertising from television decades ago, it acknowledged that what we see and hear on television has the potential to affect our attitudes and actions. In the case of advertising, that is obvious in the various persuasion tools and techniques discussed earlier in this book. However, television's ability to influence is not restricted to the promotion of products during commercials. Sitcoms, dramas, cartoons, and other programming all model aspects of human life and can influence the way we think, talk, act, dress, and behave. Social learning theory tells us that this type of media modeling may result in direct imitation of behavior we see on television, or the more subtle process of identification in which we relate to and empathize with television characters. In the case of impressionable children and teens, this type of media modeling might affect a range of human health issues, including self-esteem, eating disorders, sex role socialization, violence, and the predisposition to consume alcohol and other drugs. In fact, some people look upon television as a drug and the viewing process as a habit. Marie Winn parlayed the concept into her successful book, *The Plug-In Drug* (1977). In a 1990 article for *Esquire*, Peter Hamill wrote, "Television works on the same imaginative and intellectual level as psychoactive drugs" (64). Interestingly, Hamill saw education as a tool for combating television and the culture of consumption. "Elementary and high schools must begin teaching television/media literacy as a subject . . . showing children how shows are made, how to distinguish between the true and the false, how to recognize cheap emotional manipulation" (64).

Clearly such a process could occur in a required or elective course on media literacy. It is vital, however, that existing courses integrate those aspects of media literacy that are compatible with their own content and goals. Since health education is part of the curriculum in most school systems throughout the country, teachers, administrators, and counselors need to recognize the influence television and other mass media might play in supporting or subverting the goals and objectives of that curriculum. In *Fateful*

Choices (1992) and *Great Transitions* (1995), the Carnegie Council on Adolescent Development articulated the way media messages might hurt or help the developing adolescent and supported media literacy as a viable educational strategy in the struggle to create healthy, happy young people.

TELEVISION AND SEX EDUCATION

In the case of sexuality, there is no doubt that television content both directly and indirectly makes reference to sexual circumstances and situations, and in the case of cable, increasingly depicts explicit physical interaction between characters. Studies report that the networks broadcast 65,000 instances of sexual material each year during the afternoon and prime time alone, without taking into account the explicit world of cable and late-night viewing. Further, a typical American child or teenager is said to view nearly 14,000 sexual references, acts, or innuendoes each year, while receiving fewer than 150 messages related to birth control, sexually transmitted diseases, or abstinence (Strasburger 1995). Putting that content in context, however, is more complex. When the new television ratings system was being developed in 1997, there was, for example, disagreement about what type of activity would or would not require that a program carry the label "S "for sexual content. While some people believe that a touch, a kiss, and a hug constitute sexual content, others believe that such a designation should be confined to more intimate interaction and acts of intercourse. Beyond the issue of definition, there is also the dramatic (or comedic) context in which sex is represented and, just as importantly, the social and psychological context in which viewers experience the message. Most adults, for example, are not looking for sexual information from television. Their real-life experiences have provided their primary understanding of sex. In the case of pubescent and adolescent viewers, however, curiosity and lack of experience magnify the importance of television's portrayals of sex. The significant point to emphasize here, as we have throughout this book, is the realization that "the effects of media (sex) are not entirely due to the nature of the material itself. They also depend on the context of the material and the content in which the person sees it" (Harris 1994, 256).

This can be further understood by returning to one of the primary principles of media literacy, which says that audiences negotiate their own meaning. In other words, we filter media messages based on our own nature, needs, values, attitudes, and experiences. How might these filters affect our response to television and sex? In a 1997 episode of *Party of Five*, Julia Salinger, a high school senior, becomes sexually active with her boyfriend. The couple are shown in bed on more than one occasion. The young woman purchases and provides condoms for the couple's protection. Is this a positive or negative depiction of sex? Is this responsible or irresponsible television? There is no single answer to either question. In fact, the real answer is, it depends. For the most part, it depends as much on who we are and what we think as it does on any intrinsic firm or fixed meaning with the program. Catholic educators opposed to both premarital sex and contraception would find the program objectionable. Health educators required to teach an abstinence-only curriculum might believe that the program contradicts and undermines their teaching. Some parents and health educators with a broader approach to sex education might regard a program that recognizes that some teens are sexually active and that models safe sex for them as an effective and responsible model.

Any meaningful attempt to address media messages about human sexuality needs to locate today's messages in some historical context. From the beginning, the depiction of sex in the mass media has been a controversial issue. In the days of silent movies, *The Kiss* created a scandal. Mae West was arrested for writing a play called *Sex* and became famous for her suggestive one-liners ("Is that a gun in your pocket or are you just glad to see me?"). The impact of movie messages on adolescent sexual attitudes and behavior was part of the Payne Fund studies of the early 1930s. In 1990, the rap group 2 Live Crew attracted national attention when they were arrested for obscenity in the lyrics. Years earlier, Ed Sullivan attempted to curtail the movements and lyrics of both Elvis Presley and the Rolling Stones because they were considered too suggestive. The reason why so much attention has been focused on television and other media messages related to sex in recent years has had less to do with media content (which has definitely become more explicit) and more to do with the changing social context. In particular, concerns about teen pregnancy and the ever-present threat of AIDS constitute a health crisis that has focused greater attention on what television tells young people about sex and, just as importantly, how these messages might influence them. But not everyone perceives a problem. In a *U.S. News and World Report* poll, "just 38 percent of the Hollywood elite were concerned about how TV depicted premarital sex, compared with 83 percent of the public" (Whitman 1997, 59).

What the Research Says

Concerns about television content are clearly predicated upon the belief that media messages influence the way young viewers think and behave. What do we know about the relationship between television's portrayal of sex and human sexual behavior? One of the most basic problems is the accuracy and reliability of the data on who's "doing it." A 1995 report for the Kaiser Family Foundation addressed this problem. "Research on sexual behavior, particularly with young people, is difficult. Parents, school boards, and health departments are reluctant to let researchers even talk with their children about sexual issues for fear of political fallout" (Brown and Steele, 19). Nonetheless, communication theory and the research that is available do point to some potential areas of influence. In *Television and Awareness Training,* Susan Franzblau said, "Television prescribes and manipulates how we interpret subtle sexual remarks. In fact, it probably helps us think about the remarks as sexual in the first place" (1977, 111). Sometimes the audience is cued and clued by program content, and at other times through canned laughter and other program conventions. One episode of *Roseanne* centered on her sister Jackie's concerns about her husband's inability to satisfy her sexually. When Roseanne says to her, "You mean he gets in the elevator but he won't go down?" the canned laughter placed in the context of the show's theme makes it fairly apparent that she's referring to oral sex. Stanley Baran's work on adolescent sexual self-image and television draws attention not just to program content but also to the viewing environment and context. Although movies are more explicit, television is afforded social sanction or approval because it is actually in the home. "Its impact may indeed be greater because it is constantly in the home (without apparent social restrictions), rather easily available, and it is indeed presented as enjoyable and attractive (1976a, 63).

In *Social Learning and Personality Development*, A. Bandura and R. H. Walters (1963) suggest that film and television characters serve as sexual informational models in our society because of the absence of real-life observational opportunities. In essence, because sexual behavior in our culture is private, occurring behind closed doors, children and adolescents must learn about it from other sources. In the absence of real and direct experience, *the media mediate*. It is not simply that young people do not have the opportunity to observe sexual interaction in our society that magnifies the potential influence of the media. "It is the fact that primary sex educators such as parents may supply only restricted or biased information . . . rarely discuss sexual activity or birth control, making a majority of teenagers dissatisfied with their parents' educational efforts" (Strasburger 1995, 41). By contrast, having learned that sex sells, television and other media discuss, describe, and demonstrate in detail many facets of human sexuality. The *Washington Post* commented, "Nowadays the cast of *The Nanny* crack wise about oral sex while the single women on *Cybil* trade quips about yeast infections" (Farhi 1996, 34). The media define what it is to be male or female, how couples communicate and interact, and how, when, where, and how often sex occurs. The authors of *Prime Time* concluded that "for adults on television, the question is no longer whether to have sex, but which kind of sex to try next . . . television leaves no stone unturned in its quest to educate the viewing public on the varieties of human sexual experience" (Lichter et al. 1994, 94). Beyond positions and matters anatomical, television also addresses values related to various aspects of human sexuality. "Television rarely says that adultery or prostitution or abortion are wise options that should be applauded. Instead, it criticizes censorship, homophobia, and puritanism while treating the victims of these evils in a generally sympathetic light" (94).

Although the content contained in these programs is not automatically synonymous with the content perceived or retained, there is a growing body of evidence that suggests that the values television carries and conveys about sexuality, like violence, do in fact affect the way we as a society perceive sex and violence. *Sex and the Mass Media* reported that television and other mass media "do play an important part in shaping America's sexual beliefs, attitudes, and behavior" (Brown and Steele 1995, 1). A report in *The Journal of Adolescent Health Care* concluded that "adolescents who rely heavily on television for information about sexuality will have high standards of female beauty and will believe that premarital and extramarital intercourse with multiple partners is acceptable" (Brown et al. 1990, 62). But it is not all clear-cut and consistent. In fact, Elizabeth Roberts argues that the mass media and television send many "inconsistent and contradictory messages about sexuality and sexual pleasure" (1983, 11) to young women.

In terms of sexual safety and preventing unplanned pregnancy, Roberts finds that the constant presence of sex in the media provides a measure by which many young people judge themselves, and that it may even push some of them toward sexual experimentation. Looking at the impact of media on adolescents' sexual satisfaction, Baran says: "The media may indeed serve as a contributing factor to an individual's piture of his or her sexual self. The virgin is not only forced to deal with peer pressure regarding his or her virginity, but apparently must also face and react to mass media pressure as well" (1976ba, 473). In one of the strongest statements about television's potential impact on young viewers, Richard Harris argues that sometimes the media can actually "change one's value or attitude. It may be that teenage girls watching Roseanne's daughter as she considers having sex with her boyfriend may also come to adopt those values. This is especially likely to happen if the TV characters holding those values are respected characters with whom viewers identify" (1994, 252).

Adolescent Sexuality

Like the subject of media violence, discussions of teen sex and media representations should try to avoid the blame game. Television may contribute to adolescent sexual development, but it neither creates nor causes it. That is a function of both biology and society. The sexual revolution of the 1960s hardly came about as a result of television. Mike and Robbie Douglas (*My Three Sons*) were never sexually active until they were married. Greg and Peter Brady (*The Brady Bunch*) didn't do it, nor did their sisters, Jan and Marcia. Richard may have chased after Patty and, once in a while, Cathy Lane (*The Patty Duke Show*), but their exploits were pretty much restricted to the malt shop and the hop, not so very different from the innocent, good clean fun of the earlier Andy Hardy films. Most television parents slept in single beds. Yet beyond this rather sexually sterile world of the television screen in the 1960s and 1970s, a sexual revolution was taking place. For the most part, the birth control pill contributed largely to those changing attitudes and behaviors. If media messages addressed sexuality head on in this period, it was most likely to have been in the form of rock music with song titles like "Give It to Me," "Let's Spend the Night Together," and "I Think We're Alone Now." Television, for its part, was slow to change, which reflects its conservative nature. "Television tends to follow change cautiously rather than leading it" (Huston et al. 1992, 38).

Once magazines, music, and the movies had pioneered a more daring approach to sex, television followed with programs like *Love American Style*. By the late 1970s, television was radically reassessing its depiction of children and teen sexuality. In one episode of *Mork and Mindy,* a boy referred to a girl as "a cute chick, a fox, real hot stuff." In *Eight Is Enough*, Nicholas, a boy not yet in his teens, found himself chased by a girl his own age. "She's warm for my form," he announced. In an episode of *Family*, 11-year-old Annie defended herself against the football hero who made his "first incomplete pass" and was "penalized 15 yards for illegal use of hands." *The White Shadow, The Waltons, Little House on the Prairie*, and TV movies such as "Thin Ice," "Coach," and "Anatomy of a Seduction" all pioneered more open, if sometimes sensational, images of adolescent sexuality. One of the most controversial shows was the series *James at 15*, which dealt with an adolescent losing his virginity and provoked criticism that it promoted adolescent sexuality. Richard Hawley wrote, "James's television plunge planted the anxiety producing notion in the mind of the adolescent viewer that he was sexually lagging behind not only the precocious kid down the block, but the Average American Boy character of James" (1978, 55).

But, whereas James lost his virginity, several programs, particularly those dealing with female adolescents, have cautioned against early sexual activity. In *Family*, Buddy faced her 16th birthday and increasing pressure from her boyfriend to have sex. Ultimately, she decided she was not ready for it. In *Eight Is Enough*, Tommy tried to persuade his girlfriend to go to bed with him, only to find himself denied. In a 1984 episode of *Family Ties*, 16-year-old Mallory was pressured by her boyfriend, Rick, to have sex. She, too, decided she was not ready. In the 1990s, Cybill's teenage daughter Zoe chose to be abstinent. No, she tells her mother, as she aggressively slices a phallic-looking vegetable, "Sean and I aren't having anything. Are you satisfied?" While the scene is played for laughs, Zoe's decision has been reached thoughtfully and is the subject of several different episodes of the program.

Not all TV teens, however, are abstinent, and not all TV parents ignore the sexuality of their children. Television has provided many realistic and responsible images of sexuality. In one episode of *Cagney and Lacey*, a mother told her son, "If you care enough about a girl to make love with her, you should care enough to keep safe." This episode was a recipient of the Nancy Susan Reynolds Award, given by the Center for Population Options to programs that demonstrate exemplary sexual responsibility. Other award-winners included an episode of *The Bronx Zoo* that showed schools distributing contraceptives, an episode of *Valerie*, the TV movie "Daddy," and an after-school special called "Teen Father." Early in the 1990 television season, viewers could watch Becky and Darlene (*Roseanne*) discussing being "felt up," hear Paul tell Kevin (*The Wonder Years*) that he was a virgin, or see Doogie Howser advocate the use of condoms. *Evening Shade* presented one interesting program in which a 15-year-old boy discussed the prospect of losing his virginity with both his father and his grandfather, who shared their own early sexual experiences. *Northern Exposure* depicted an adolescent male's loss of his virginity and his reaction to it.

While *My So Called Life* used Jordan Catalano as a stereotypical Lothario ready to hop into bed with anyone in a skirt, other programs during the 1980s and 1990s took a much more sensitive look at male sexuality, particularly the loss of virginity. When Paul loses his virginity in *The Wonder Years*, it not only surprises his friend Kevin Arnold, it also surprises and confuses Paul. What both boys expected to be an earth-shattering moment, auguring adulthood, turned out to be much more about anxiety and uncertainty. The event is never shown. What viewers witness instead is the two boys trying to make sense of the gap between expectations and experiences. Similarly, Vinnie Dalpino (*Doogie Howser*) loses his virginity in a manner that surprises both him and Doogie. Most of the program centers on the aftermath rather than the act. Interestingly, both these episodes of *The Wonder Years* and *Doogie Howser* feature female characters who initiate the sexual activity.

(MID/HIGH) — Ask the class to develop a list of teenage characters on television. Make sure the list includes males and females. Have them discuss each character in terms of how realistically they think the character's sexuality is depicted. Becky and Darlene in *Roseanne*, for example, have discussed menstruation and French kissing. But many adolescent characters are presented less openly. In *Head of the Class*, Eric is the school heartthrob, but there is little if any indication that he has actually had sex. A better program dealing with early adolescence is *The Wonder Years*. Kevin and his girlfriend, Winnie, struggled with peer pressure in one episode when they were forced to "make out" at a party. The prospect of kissing in a dark room sent them scurrying

home to the safety of family and the childhood they were not quite so anxious to leave. In *Doogie Howser, M.D.*, Vinnie is anxious to lose his virginity but throws up every time he gets too close. In other episodes, Doogie and his girlfriend, Wanda, almost have sex but decide they aren't ready—until a fall 1991 episode when they do.

Doogie Howser, M.D. has actually provided a strong source of sexual information for young viewers. Doogie and his girlfriend have talked about their parents' sexual activities ("geriatric sex perverts from Mars"), including the fact that they even had sex "in the afternoon!" Doogie has also regularly promoted contraception. In one episode he told kids, "You wouldn't jump out of a plane without a parachute, so don't have sex without a condom." In a parody of an American Express ad, he endorsed contraception with the slogan "The Condom: Don't Leave Your Pants Without It," and the ad began with the simple acknowledgment "You don't have to do it."

Initially, soap opera producers believed their audience was mainly adults. As the AIDS crisis grew, however, they became more aware that many young people were also watching. Creators of *Santa Barbara* acknowledged that young people did get sexual information from watching soaps. As a result of cooperation between program producers and educators, many soaps, such as *Days of Our Lives* and *The Young and the Restless*, began to integrate more responsible themes and scenes dealing with sexuality. Use a *TV Guide* or newspaper synopsis to discuss the way sex is presented in soaps. Ask your students which soaps they watch and why. Have students compare soap opera characters to real people. When sex is presented, is it shown as a normal part of a character's life, or are the characters sex-obsessed? Are there characters who could be classified as womanizers or nymphomaniacs?

An early study of pregnancy and motherhood in soap operas was called "Television's Romance with Reproduction" (Peck 1979). The study noted the pronatal tendencies in soap operas and commercials. There was, said Ellen Peck, a glorification of motherhood and the reproductive function and a parallel fear of the loss of ability to produce life. She found that commercials, by a cumulative process, idealized home and family life and conveyed the persistent and pervasive message that reproduction and large families were desirable. Look at the depiction of pregnancy and birth in today's soaps or prime-time programs such as *Roseanne*, *Growing Pains*, and *Married with Children*. Are Peck's conclusions still justified? Has more honest treatment of contraception or abortion changed the way soaps depict pregnancy? If abortion is presented, is there discussion of both sides of the debate?

Issues that frequently concern teens still often remain taboo. Anxiety about penis and breast size are seldom addressed except as a subject of humor. Female body odor seldom finds its way into programs, though many of them are sponsored by the manufacturers of female hygiene products that frequently sell insecurity, if not self-loathing, as part of their message. Other formerly taboo areas have been shattered, in more than one case by *Roseanne*. One program addressed premenstrual syndrome (PMS). Speaking about Roseanne, one female character said, "She's a wonderful woman when her estrogen isn't whipping her into a psychotic frenzy." Masturbation is the topic for a family discussion in another episode. Roseanne, Jackie, Dan, and other family members gather in the kitchen to discuss why DJ keeps locking himself in the bathroom. To Dan's embarrassment, the boy's

sister announces that her brother has finally found a friend that isn't imaginary, adding that "he's either very good at it, or he's very bad at it." The idea that masturbation is a suitable subject for television was reinforced when it left the world of the adolescent to enter the adult world of the hit series *Seinfeld*. While *Ellen*'s coming-out episode posted the highest ratings ever for the show, defeating the popular *E.R.*, teenagers looking for models of gay or lesbian adolescents on television still have a very difficult search. Surely it is now time that TV developed a healthy and happy adolescent comfortable with his or her sexual difference. Health educators and counselors can use programs like these to break the ice and help young people talk honestly and openly about their emerging sexuality. When the programs are positive, they have much to offer. When they are negative, they must be critiqued. Left unchallenged, these media messages can perpetuate myths and reinforce sexual stereotypes. Media educators exploring the subject of television representation can use adolescent sexuality as a case study, comparing and contrasting national surveys of adolescent sexuality with television teens. In fact, this subject offers an excellent opportunity for media educators to work in an interdisciplinary and cooperative way with counselors and health educators.

Fame and Shame

(MID/HIGH) — Ask students to nominate television episodes, special programs, or made-for-TV movies (*The Gloaming*) they believe have provided fair and useful information about sexual issues. Make sure they develop criteria for making their decision, such as treating a topic that is seldom covered. *L.A. Law*, for example, presented a program dealing with the rights and responsibilities of the mentally handicapped if they were sexually active. Gena Rowlands starred in "A Sudden Frost," a made-for-TV movie that looked at parents who discovered their son was gay and dying of AIDS. *Designing Women* has featured episodes that addressed sex education and sexual stereotyping in beauty pageants. When the class has discussed the nominees and

voted for the winner, have them prepare a letter of commendation to the network and the program producers. This process can also be done in reverse: By teaching students to be aware of stereotyping and bias, you can help them recognize media misrepresentations and distortion. They can select a single episode or an entire series they find sexually biased, offensive, or demeaning. Make sure their criteria are valid and that they do not select a program or episode because of an isolated line or incident. You might also want to draw their attention to comedy and its victims. In 1990 the comedian Andrew Dice Clay appeared on *Saturday Night Live* and provoked controversy with his sexist jokes.

Is Sex Funny?

(MID/HIGH) — In 1977 a study by Susan Franzblau, N. Sprafkin, and Eli Rubinstein found that sexually aggressive acts appeared in crime programs and less intimate acts such as kissing, embracing, and touching appeared in situation comedies. The dominance of sexual material in comedy programs, they reported, "supports the conventional notion that sex is a disturbing topic and is best handled humorously" (1977, 170). Situation comedies such as *Perfect Strangers*, *Spin City*, *Seinfeld*, *Anything but Love*, and *Growing Pains* often deal with bachelor or adolescent males constantly pursuing a female, only to fail. Sex in these programs is reduced to a chase, a game with an elusive prey. The humor of the situation (which is often not very humorous) has its traditions in bedroom farce and is reinforced by canned laughter, innuendo, and double entendre. Give students copies of *TV Guide* and have them study plots of situation comedies to see how many use sex as a plot. Look at program advertising in *TV Guide*. Do words and images also stress sex as a selling point of a program? Study one or two episodes of a situation comedy, noting examples of sexual contact and humor. How are the female characters presented? Is the dumb blonde or bubble-headed bimbo stereotype present? Compare the way these characters act to the way real people behave.

In addition to sitcoms, talk shows and variety shows often feature comedians who use sex to get a laugh. In 1990, Andrew Dice Clay and Sam Kinison provoked controversy by the sexist and prejudiced nature of their comedy, which often seemed to target women and gays. If humor has a victim, can it be funny? Ask students to put themselves in the place of those who are victimized by such jokes. If we laugh at a situation, do we unwittingly accept its existence?

Sexual Dysfunction

(HIGH) — In a review of *Equal Justice*, a 1990 crime series, *U.S.A. Today* described one of the young attorneys as "a handsome stud puppy." Despite his macho good looks and sex appeal, Chris was actually shown to be less secure when the action moved from the courtroom to the bedroom. In one episode he experiences temporary impotence and struggles to reconcile this with his own sense of masculinity. In an episode of *Spin City*, Michael J. Fox's character experiences performance anxiety and temporary impotence after he is named the sexiest man in New York City by a magazine. By dealing more openly and frankly with human sexuality, television offers the opportunity for an honest discussion of sexual dysfunctions including impotence, premature ejaculation, and frigidity. By using these examples, health educators can break the ice on a sensitive subject and help young people think about the causes of these problems and the available solutions. Use the questions in Fig. 5.1 to create a dialogue about sexuality.

Tuning into TV Sex

There's more to sex than sexuality. Indeed, there's more to a healthy sexuality than sexual behavior. It is all the ways we express what it means to be masculine or feminine in our culture, how we feel about our bodies, what it means to get married, divorced or remain single, to live alone or with friends. Throughout our lives we are sexual beings. Understanding sexuality is essential to our self-image, self-understanding and personal identity, and to the formation of human relationships. The following questions provide springboards of discussion and dialogue around issues of sexuality and sexual behavior.

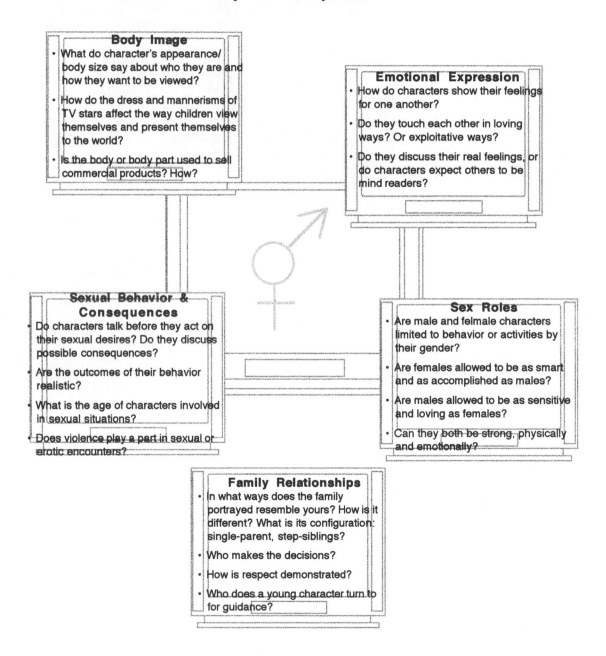

Body Image
- What do character's appearance/body size say about who they are and how they want to be viewed?
- How do the dress and mannerisms of TV stars affect the way children view themselves and present themselves to the world?
- Is the body or body part used to sell commercial products? How?

Emotional Expression
- How do characters show their feelings for one another?
- Do they touch each other in loving ways? Or exploitative ways?
- Do they discuss their real feelings, or do characters expect others to be mind readers?

Sexual Behavior & Consequences
- Do characters talk before they act on their sexual desires? Do they discuss possible consequences?
- Are the outcomes of their behavior realistic?
- What is the age of characters involved in sexual situations?
- Does violence play a part in sexual or erotic encounters?

Sex Roles
- Are male and female characters limited to behavior or activities by their gender?
- Are females allowed to be as smart and as accomplished as males?
- Are males allowed to be as sensitive and loving as females?
- Can they both be strong, physically and emotionally?

Family Relationships
- In what ways does the family portrayed resemble yours? How is it different? What is its configuration: single-parent, step-siblings?
- Who makes the decisions?
- How is respect demonstrated?
- Who does a young character turn to for guidance?

Fig. 5.1. **"Tuning in to TV sex: Using television for dialogue with your children" by Joan Garrity. Reprinted with permission from the Spring, 1989 issue of *Media&Values* published by the Center for Media Literacy, Los Angeles, CA 90010, USA.**

THE MEAN SCREEN: Television and Violence

Like the issue of television and sex, violence and television has been a consistently controversial subject. In the same way that sex and the screen was first studied in the early days of the talkies, the subject of visual violence also had its roots in the Payne studies of the 1930s, most noticeably in *Movies, Delinquency and Crime* (Blumer, 1933). By the 1950s, similar studies were under way when Congress investigated television's impact on juvenile deliquency. Any meaningful attempt to understand television's impact on either sex or violence must go beyond content to the broader context in which these media messages are both produced and consumed. In some ways, the subjects should be examined together, since violence and sex are often companions on the screen and off-screen as well, as is evident by crime statistics for both domestic violence and date rape. Exploring the relationship between television violence and social violence offers media educators an excellent case study to explore key principles of media literacy, including (1) media representations, (2) media influences and consequences, and (3) the commercial context and production process that maintains violence as a staple element in so many programs. Counselors and health educators dealing with issues of violence would also benefit from integrating the study of television violence into their programs. While the phrase "television violence" frequently conjures up images of cops, crime, shoot-outs, and bloody mayhem, such images are merely the

patina of a much deeper and pervasive presence throughout all programming. News, driven as it is by the "if it bleeds, it leads" credo, is perhaps the most violent program on television. Sporting events also frequently center on aggression as much as skill, and on some occasions viewing these programs seems to spill over into off-screen violence. "For too many households, the violence of football's most watched game is not confined to the TV screen. The Superbowl brings together many activities that may trigger a man predisposed to battering; intense viewing of sanctioned violence, heavy drinking, betting" (*Extra* 1993, 7). Children's play and fantasy programs are also pervaded with heavy recurring images of violence and an ideology that suggests violence is a socially acceptable way to solve problems. "The myth of redemptive violence is the simplest, laziest, most exciting, uncomplicated, irrational and primitive depiction of evil the world has ever known. Its orientation toward evil is one in which virtually all modern children (especially boys) are socialized in the process of maturation" (Wink 1993, 5). Exposure to television violence, it is argued, does more than merely entertain. Dr. George Gerbner, for decades now one of the most respected scholars of television content and effects, believes that what television shows, it also teaches. Symbolic violence, he says, "demonstrates power, who can get away with what against whom" (1981, 4).

Throughout the 1990s, concerns about television violence captured the attention of our Congress and our classrooms. Meeting in Los Angeles in 1995, the National Education Association highlighted "Respect, Responsibility, and Reason" as tools to foster safe communities and safe schools. In fact, the nation's schools were witnessing an increase in violent incidents including a growing number of cases of students and teachers bringing weapons to school. In the 1940s the biggest problems teachers faced were students talking out of turn, chewing gum, and running in the halls. By the 1980s, teachers listed assault, robbery, rape, drug abuse, pregnancy, and suicide as their major concerns (Zuckerman 1993). The Telecommunications Reform Act of 1996 included a provision for the V-chip, a device that would allow parents to block out programs with violent content. For President Clinton, the subject was clear, the solution simple: "What I'm trying to do is to challenge the industry to be aware, to just be self-conscious of what they're doing and the aggregate impact" (Murphy and Redicliffe 1996). "I see no alternative to solving this problem than to reduce the aggregate amount of violence . . . to which children are subject" (7/10/95). But violence is as American as apple pie, and its presence can be found well beyond our television sets and living rooms. The American Medical Association (AMA) prepares a National Report Card on Violence. In 1995 and again in 1996, they gave the nation a "D" rating for levels of violence including domestic violence, sexual assault, school violence, media violence, and workplace violence; a staggering 60,000 cases a year were reported. By the late 1990s, the AMA published its own *Physician's Guide to Media Violence*, urging doctors to consider the role the media played as part of a broader psychosocial evaluation of young patients with physical or psychological complaints. With violence seemingly endemic to American society, the chicken-and-egg problem once again emerges, allowing television's defenders

to argue that the medium merely reflects the level of violence in the nation. Others believe that children are less susceptible to television's influence than we believe. In an article called "Taming the Hysteria About Media Violence" that appeared in *Education Week*, Morris Freedman said, "Children are more resilient, armored, judicious, even more aesthetically discriminating than we allow ourselves to believe" (1996, 44).

Proponents of the V-chip, the new ratings system, and other attempts to regulate television's violent content argue that children need protection from toxic levels of television violence. They do not believe television merely mirrors violence in society. They believe television magnifies and distorts violence. In the process, they argue, it reinforces aggressive impulses among some members of the viewing audience and as such contributes to levels of violence in our homes, schools, and places of work. There is a growing body of evidence that suggests they are right. More than a quarter of a century has now passed since the Surgeon General's Committee reported in *Television and Growing Up* that there is a "preliminary and tentative indication of a causal relation between viewing violence on television and aggressive behavior" (1972). In the mid-1980s, the American Psychological Association "adopted the position that television violence has a causal effect on aggressive behavior" (1985). Evidence continues to find correlations between viewing violence and aggressive behavior or attitudes. "The accumulated research clearly demonstrates a correlation between viewing violence and aggressive behavior—that is, heavy viewers behave more aggressively than light viewers. Children and adults who watch a large number of aggressive programs . . . tend to hold attitudes and values that favor the use of aggression to resolve conflicts" (Huston et al. 1992). Dr. George Gerbner describes television as "the distinctive and dominant cultural force of our age" (1994, 37). He believes that "the repetitive lessons we learn from television . . . are likely to become the basis for a broader world view" (30). When these lessons concern violence, Gerbner believes television's mean screen and "mean world syndrome" cultivate potentially harmful attitudes. "Long term exposure to television, in which frequent violence is virtually inescapable, tends to cultivate the image of a relatively mean and dangerous world" (30). As such, television may predispose heavy viewers to think that the world is more threatening than it is, encouraging them to support a range of policies and strategies, both personal and public, including support for politicians and judges claiming to be tough on crime. These heavy viewers, he says, "are more likely to be dependent upon authority and susceptible to deceptively simple, strong, hardline approaches" (1995, 553). These reactions not only pervade their response to domestic issues but may also be evident in their attitude toward foreign policy, as studies of public opinion and the Gulf War indicated.

A Look at the Numbers: Violent Content and Context

In the mid-1970s, estimates suggested that American children and teenagers viewed approximately 1,000 rapes, murders, and assaults each year on television. During the 1980s, researchers documented an average of five violent acts per hour during adult programming. By the early 1990s, *Big World, Small Screen* concluded that by the time they complete elementary school, young students "will have witnessed at least 8,000 murders and more than 100,000 other assorted acts of violence. Depending upon the amount of television viewed, our youngsters could see more than 200,000 violent acts before they hit the schools and streets of our nation as teenagers" (Huston et al. 1992, 54). Writing in *The Journal of the American Medical Association*, Dr. Brandon Centerwall suggested that viewing violence exposed young children to what they perceive as "a source of entirely factual information regarding how the world works." As such, he suggested, it provides a repertoire of behaviors they may revert to in later life when faced with stress and conflict. "It is precisely at such moments that adolescents and adults are most likely to revert to their earliest, most visceral sense of what violence is and what its role is in society. Much of this sense will have come from television" (1992, 3060).

One of the most thorough reports on television and violence was actually funded by the television industry itself and provided not only a statistical analysis of the quantity of violence on television, but also examined the context in which violence occurred and the potential consequences both for characters in the programs and for the viewing audience. *The National Television Violence Study* (1995) looked at 2,693 programs on 23 different channels. In preparing the report, they defined violence as "any overt depiction of the use of physical force—or the credible threat of such force—intended to physically harm an animate being or group of beings" (3). This conservative definition did not take into account verbal or psychological aggression. Some of the key findings of the report included the following:

- Violence predominates on television and was present in 57 percent of programs studied.

- Researchers documented 18,000 violent interactions.

- Some 76 to 78 percent of violence perpetrators were white adult males.

- Violence is typically associated with three motives: personal gain (power, money, etc.), protection of self or others, and anger.

- Victims of violence are typically white adult males.

- In a majority (58 percent) of scenes, violence is neither rewarded nor punished.

- More than one-third of all violence is presented within a humorous context.

One of the most disturbing conclusions from the report was the observation that "in about three quarters of all violent scenes perpetrators go unpunished" (25). In the case of the type of violence children would most likely be exposed to, the researchers found that "children's series are less likely to show the pain of victims of violence, as well as any of its long-term consequences" (21). Showing violence without consequences deprives young viewers of any understanding of realistic consequences for such behavior. "Showing the negative consequences of television violence can serve to reduce the risk that viewers will imitate such portrayals" (16).

Looking and Learning: Consequences of Viewing Violence

Three decades ago, during one of the most turbulent years in American history, Fredric Wertham described television as a school for violence: "Whether crime and violence programs arouse a lust of violence, reinforce it when it is present, show a way to carry it out, teach the best method to get away with it, or merely blunt the child's (or adult's) awareness of its wrongness, television has become a school for violence" (1968). More recently the American Psychological Association has described lessons viewers may learn from watching television violence. In *Violence and Youth: Psychology's Response* (1993), they summarized these outcomes:

- Increases in aggression, anti-social behavior, and attitudes

- Increasing fear of becoming a victim, including mistrust

- Increasing appetite for more violence

- Increasing desensitization and callousness to violence and its victims

These outcomes are the result of what some researchers call Cognitive Social Information Processing. The theory suggests that television programs and movies provide young viewers with a series of stories and scenarios. By the process of observing the real world and the mediated world, "children encode or represent in memory scripts for behavior" (Dubow and Miller 1996, 125). These scripts function "like a stereotype, reflecting a set of expectations about the sequence of an event . . . they guide our information processing and facilitate our social behavior . . . and we behave according to the script" (125). Children who observe violence on television have no shortage of categories or contexts. One study divided violent behavior into classifications such as Serious Assault, Minor Assault, Harm to Property, Intimidation, Deception, Vandalism, Hostile Remarks, and Societal Harm. Noting that less than one violent act out of six was punished, the researchers reflected upon the way impressionable viewers might process such information and arrived at a disturbing conclusion. "We can see that the context would increase the probability that viewers would learn that committing these acts is a good thing (or at least a useful thing) (Potter et al. 1995, 515). If television frequently teaches young viewers that violence is a viable and socially sanctioned way to solve a problem, instructional intervention is necessary to prevent young people from responding impulsively to their emotions, while also providing them with the resistance skills necessary to seek peer mediation or alternatives to violence.

Understanding violent television content and the possible consequences of viewing that content is just the start of the process. Changing that content also requires understanding the social, economic, and industrial context in which these programs are produced and consumed. Marcia Kelly from Los Angeles-based Mediascope fully understands the complexity of the problem. No one accepts responsibility; instead they pass the buck in an endless blame game. "The writer will say that's what the producer wants me to write. The producer will say that's what the networks want. The networks will say that's what the advertisers want. The advertisers will say that's what the public wants. The question is how can we break the circle" (Rosenfield 1993, 23). George Gerbner looks at economics, marketing, and global packaging to explain the peril and power of television violence. Violence, he says, is "the product of a complex manufacturing and marketing machine" (1995, 554). As the networks and cable outlets fall into the ownership and control of fewer and fewer companies, creative independence and freedom from formula diminish. More and more emphasis is placed upon "dramatic ingredients most suitable for international promotion" (554). According to Gerbner, most producers find it difficult to break even on the license fees they are paid for domestic broadcasts. "They are forced into syndication and foreign sales to make a profit. They need a dramatic ingredient that requires no translation, speaks action in any language, and fits any culture. That ingredient is violence" (554). In short, in the name of profit at the international level, the creation and consumption of television violence at the domestic level are escalated. The price we may all pay for that remains to be calculated.

TV and Violence:
Challenging the Mythconceptions

There are several erroneous perceptions that are frequently expressed in any discussion about television or media violence. Exploring and exploding these mythconceptions can be a constructive exercise in critical thinking skills, whether working with students in a classroom or talking to parents at a PTO event. Anticipating these attitudes and preparing answers can help us rationally and logically consider the subject of television and violence.

1. *It didn't do me any harm.* It is not uncommon to hear adults say that they watched a lot of television or movie violence when they were young, and it didn't do them any harm. The most basic answer to this is quite simply that that was then, this is now. No matter how much an adult watched in the 1950s, 1960s, or 1970s, the visual and verbal violence to which children are exposed today

is greater quantitatively and qualitatively. Research makes it clear that today's TV is more graphic, explicit, and gratuitous than in the past. In addition, with many parents working, children often view these programs without adult supervision or guidance.

2. ***Shakespeare and the classics were violent.*** This argument suggests that violence is a traditional ingredient of classic literature, whether it be *Oedipus Rex, Macbeth,* or *Hamlet.* Two key differences must be stressed, however. The first and most significant is that when these dramas were performed on the stage or read, the violence was imagined, implied, or simulated. The movies first and then television have used special effects to portray all the pain, torture, and mayhem of these acts very, very graphically. Reading about a violent action has considerably less impact than actually witnessing the event. The second point is that in classic literature, the violence is integral to the plot and often historically accurate. Gerbner suggests that the reason for much of television violence is based on sales and marketing, not the integrity of the story.

3. ***Violence gives the people what they want.*** The "he who pays the piper" argument can be dismissed fairly easily almost any week of the television season by simply consulting the ratings published each week in *U.S.A. Today.* Sitcoms with low levels of violence and current affairs programs are often the most popular top 10 shows.

4. ***Controlling violence is censorship.*** Attempts to control television violence are often condemned as assaults on the First Amendment and free speech. In reality, this type of speech is far from free. We all potentially pay for a society that exposes impressionable children and teens to toxic levels of violence. In fact, how we pay might be the subject for a lengthy discussion when these misconceptions are raised. In addition, just as broadcasters have the right to produce whatever they wish, they must also be responsible in the way they use the public airwaves.

5. ***No one listens to me.*** While many people are concerned about violence on television, they also believe they can't make a difference. Remember that television works on ratings. It is responsive to numbers and viewer input. Calling, writing, or faxing a network or local affiliate can have an impact. So can letter writing from concerned citizens, especially if the views expressed are clear, concise, and polite. Don't attack, ask. And remember, television producers and broadcasters have children themselves. They don't want their products to hurt their families, and they take pride in what they create. They'd like to hear praise for positive programs (which helps keep them running) as well as concerns about other shows. Media advocacy and action from informed, articulate consumers is an exercise in grassroots democracy.

Getting Started: Defining Violence

(ELEM/MID/HIGH) — Ask the class to describe and define what they think "television violence" refers to. Do they include just acts of physical violence, or do they also include intimidation, verbal violence, and psychological violence? Look at the dictionary definition of "violence" and the way *The National Television Violence Study* defined the term.

Content, Consequences, and Causes

Under the three terms in the heading above, provide the class with a summary of some key findings from the research described in this section. Divide the class into three groups, with each group assigned to create a report or paper on one of these three areas. Remember, the section on consequences can describe what happened to the victims and the perpetrators, but it may also explore consequences for viewers. Where appropriate, students can use the Internet, taped samples from television, as well as newspaper and magazine articles as part of their reports.

Violence and Television Genres

(MID/HIGH) — It is very common to assume that most violence occurs in crime and police dramas. Violence, however, is also an inherent part of medical programs like *E.R.* and *Chicago Hope*. In fact, if we begin to divide television into genre categories, we might see that violence pervades many programs, such as news, sports, soap operas, and even a lot of talk shows if we include verbal violence in our definition. Break the class into small groups, with each group assigned the task of monitoring one genre. Have them record acts of violence and the context in which the violence occurs. This can include the motivation (e.g., protection, power, anger, etc.) as well as the socioeconomic classification, race, age, and gender of both the perpetrators and the victims.

Cartoon Violence: Fantasy and Reality

(ELEM/MID) — Young children cannot always distinguish between reality and fantasy. How do your students perceive violence in cartoons? Develop a list of all the cartoon programs your students watch and a list of the key characters in these programs. Ask students to describe the action and violence in each program. Which characters are the most violent? What types of acts do they commit? Why do they act this way? Do your students see the violence as justified and acceptable? If the students have play-action figures based on any of the cartoon characters, have them bring the figures to class. Look at the body language, clothes, and accessories of each character. Do they represent a violent nature? How do the advertisements during these cartoons reflect or reinforce violence?

What If You Acted Like That?

(ELEM) — Look at incidents of violence in cartoons or have students describe incidents they have seen. Try to get students to describe what would happen if they acted like a cartoon character. Would their parents be pleased if they hit someone, for example? Would they feel any physical pain if they hit a person? Does cartoon violence provide an accurate picture of what it feels like to be hit, hurt, blown up, run over, etc.?

Is Violence Funny?

(ELEM/MID) — Invariably, when we talk about cartoon violence, discussion centers on adventure cartoons such as *G.I. Joe* or *Masters of the Universe*. But violence has traditionally had a comedic element since the time of silent movies. What funny cartoons feature acts of violence? What type of violence typically occurs? Who commits the violence? Who is the victim? Is the violence depicted realistically? If not, what is missing from it? Have any of the students ever copied something they saw in one of these cartoons? What happened? Why do we laugh at these images of violence? Is violence funny?

Sticks and Stones

(ELEM) — Remind the children of the saying "Sticks and stones may break my bones, but words will never hurt me." Describe verbal violence. What TV programs do they watch in which characters are verbally violent to each other? Why do people act this way? In TV programs, this verbal violence is often meant to be funny. Is it funny in real life to say such things to other people?

Women as Victims: Voyeurism and Rape

(HIGH) — Domestic violence and rape have been persistent problems in our society. Sexual attacks against women have been on the increase, and date rape has become a major problem for young women, even on our college campuses. Research suggests that many rape victims never go to the police, and those who do often have to face the charge that "she asked for it" or "she really wanted it." Although rape is often depicted on television, the climate that promotes rape is usually more subtle in its presence. The voyeuristic nature of television persistently packages and parades women as sex objects to fulfill male fantasies. Women are more likely than men to be shown in swimwear, underwear, or provocative and revealing clothing. Women are also more likely than men to be the objects of innuendo, double entendre, or an unwelcome touch or gaze. Every one of these images creates the cumulative climate that dehumanizes women by representing them as objects. Discuss the way television depicts men and women in terms of this argument. Ask the class to provide examples of programs and advertisements that show women in such ways. You may choose to do a separate activity focusing solely on advertising.

The Functions of Visual Violence

(MID/HIGH) — It is pointless to claim that watching violence makes people violent. If that were true, our entire society would be violent. What research does suggest, however, is that under some circumstances, watching violence will encourage some viewers to actually commit violence or to be more tolerant of violence. Other people argue that watching violence actually channels their aggression and relieves their tension. Football, boxing, and ice hockey might be good examples of the latter. Introduce students to the following concepts. Then break students into groups and have each group develop arguments and evidence to support the claim they select.

- *Anesthetic:* By constantly showing acts of violence, television numbs viewers to the reality of violence, making us insensitive to it. Because we are insensitive to it, we are more likely to use it ourselves or accept other people using it.

- *Catharsis:* Violence on television is a form of social safety valve for letting off steam. Viewing violence enables the audience to vicariously experience violence and, therefore, reduces the likelihood that they will be violent.

- *Social sanction:* By constantly depicting violence, television models it and endorses it as an appropriate and valid behavior.

- *Social mirror:* Television neither creates nor condones violence; it merely mirrors and reflects the violent nature of society.

Rights Versus Responsibilities

(HIGH) — Addressing the Senate Commerce Committee on Television Violence, Attorney General Janet Reno said, "I want to challenge television to substantially reduce its violent programming now or else the government will have to intervene." In response, former NBC executive Michael Gartner wrote, "You're messing around with something more serious than violence. You're messing with freedom. As Attorney General you're not supposed to be attacking free speech, you're supposed to be defending it" (1993, 13a). Use these two points of view about television violence and freedom of speech for the subject of an essay or a debate.

ALCOHOL AND SUBSTANCE ABUSE

When we think about television and alcohol, most attention focuses on advertising. But the programs themselves frequently contain representations of people consuming alcohol and as such model attitudes and behaviors associated with alcohol and other substances. Two events from the 1997 television season demonstrate the mixed messages viewers may receive about alcohol. In an episode of *Spin City*, Michael J. Fox and two of his colleagues go to a bar after work. They order a "Stewart Surprise," named after one of their characters, with the express purpose of getting wasted. These are responsible, educated, middle-class young men, black and white, heterosexual and gay, who work in the office of the mayor of New York City, yet see no problem with getting drunk in public. Alcohol consumption is used in this script as a source of humor. In Fox's award-winning *Family of Five*, the subject of Bailey's alcoholism was an ongoing and central theme of the program for several weeks leading up to the season's dramatic conclusion. This representation of alcohol abuse and all its consequences was exemplary television. During commercial breaks and at the end of the show, characters from the program provided viewers with information about help for alcoholism. While some story lines deal with alcohol and substance abuse superficially, including miraculous cures, this series, like *Cagney and Lacey* before it, showed the long descent into addiction. Bailey denied that he had a problem. When friends and family asked, he became hostile and defensive. To recognize his problem, he had to bottom out, go as low as he could go. He crashed his car, injuring his former girlfriend. He failed to show up for a major sporting event, letting down his coach and his entire team. He got drunk and humiliated himself and his whole family at his little brother's birthday party. Finally, in an episode devoted almost entirely to the process of intervention, the family brought the problem to a head. Even in this segment, the show's writers moved from the abuser to the whole family, showing the pain, disagreement, and sense of betrayal family members often feel during an intervention. Bailey starts going to A.A., but he struggles with the 12 steps. He knows he has a problem, and he knows his recovery will be one day at a time. He tries to make amends to those he has hurt, but resists the idea of a higher power. He cannot "let go and let God." No simplistic solutions here, no miraculous recovery, just a long hard struggle on the road back to sobriety.

This story line helped increase the ratings for *Party of Five* and resulted in the ordering of a new series of episodes. Kathryn Montgomery says that this type of dramatic message is consistent with the industry's need to both entertain and make money. "Alcohol abuse has proved to be compatible with the needs of entertainment programming. It lends itself easily to dramatization, thus providing story materials for writers and producers. And the alcohol issue is relatively safe as opposed to such politically divisive topics as abortion or gun control" (1991, 19). During the 1980s and 1990s, health educators have attempted to work with the television industry to improve media representations of alcoholism and its consequences. Harvard University's School of Public Health set up the Harvard Alcohol Project with the express purpose of changing the television industry's attitude toward these depictions. Dr. Jay Winsten, the head of the project, stressed cooperation rather than confrontation, asking rather than demanding changes from the industry. The result was an increase in the number of story lines about alcohol, particularly in programs attracting impressionable audiences.

This was most dramatically and effectively demonstrated in the popular series *Growing Pains*. In an episode called "The Second Chance," Carol, the teenage daughter in the series, learns that her new boyfriend has died as a result of an auto accident and "just a few drinks." The background for this type of responsible storytelling can be found in several major developments during the 1980s. In 1982, for example, the Caucus for Producers, Writers and Directors created a White Paper urging a more responsible depiction of alcohol consumption and consequences. The following year, an Entertainment Industries Council was established to deglamorize depictions of alcohol and other substance abuse. In 1986 the Academy of Television Arts and Sciences established a Substance Abuse Committee. More than a decade later, this topic was still being presented responsibly in family series such as *7th Heaven*, which addressed alcohol abuse in fraternity hazings.

But if television can increase public awareness, helping parents and teens recognize the warning signs of alcohol or chemical dependency, it may also hurt by glamorizing or trivializing substance abuse. As popular and amusing as *Cheers* was, the series sent some very mixed messages. Sam Malone, a recovering alcoholic, worked in a bar. Looking at its 11-season run, one researcher concluded that *"Cheers* may have cultivated some of its millions of viewers to accept the perception that excessive beer drinking is an unproblematic activity" (Hundley 1995, 350).

In the 1980s, alcohol was present in more than 70 percent of dramatic programs during network prime time. Thirty-seven percent of major characters were depicted as drinkers, but only 1 to 2 percent were characterized as alcoholics. The consequences of consumption were minimized, with only 13 percent of the programs depicting harmful effects (Signorielli 1987). Drinking was also associated with positive characters. "The drinkers are not the villains or bit players, they are the good steady likable characters" (Jacobson et al. 1983). Researchers have also indicated that while underage drinking is not frequently shown on television, when it is, "adolescent drinking is often treated in a humorous fashion" (Strasburger 1995, 72). Since adolescence is by nature a time of transition, experimentation, even risk-taking, young people are potentially susceptible to media messages that glamorize drinking and other substance abuse. While the models established by parents in the home environment are a crucial element in decisions young people make regarding alcohol consumption, those decisions are also influenced by "their interpretations of television messages . . . and their desire to be like television characters who drink" (Austin and Meli 1994, 431).

(ELEM/MID/HIGH) — Health educators whose curriculum addresses alcohol and substance abuse can monitor television programs to find positive and negative examples of media representation. When series like *Party of Five* are popular with students, these characters can often communicate more successfully and effectively than a cold, cognitive list of the harmful consequences of substance abuse.

Students can be asked to create a list of programs they view regularly and to monitor both the frequency and content of alcohol consumption by characters in these programs. When programs are regarded as responsible, students can write to the networks and producers to commend the series. When programs depict this issue in a frivolous or irresponsible manner, students can write to condemn the episode and to suggest constructive changes they think would have been more responsible and accurate.

Kathryn Montgomery (1991) suggests the following criteria might be useful in monitoring these programs.

- Do they depict consumption as adult and glamorous?

- Is alcohol consumption gratuitous and unnecessary to the story or plot development?

- Does the program ignore the consequences of consumption (headache, aggression, hangover, missed work, etc.)?

- Does the program normalize drinking by suggesting that everybody's doing it?

- Is drinking depicted as funny and humorous?

- Is drinking presented as macho and the manly thing to do?

- Are characters with drinking problems realistically shown trying to recover, or is their recovery trivialized (e.g., Murphy Brown and Sam Malone [*Cheers*])? While Murphy Brown has been shown struggling with the temptation to drink, she, like Sam Malone, also spends a lot of time in a bar, which should be inconsistent with recovery. In fact, most of the cast of *Cheers* spent most of their time in a bar consuming alcohol with little, if any, shown consequences.

Television and Tobacco: Emmys and Phlemmys

Despite the fact that tobacco advertising has been absent from the nation's television screens for decades, TV representations are still capable of modeling messages about the consumption of tobacco by the way characters in series respond to pipes, cigarettes, cigars, and chewing tobacco. The American Lung Association (ALA) Thumbs Up, Thumbs Down Project monitored 238 individual television episodes in the mid-1990s and reported that only 15 percent featured tobacco use, compared to 86 percent of movies. Seeking to draw attention to the potential of television and movies to glamorize tobacco use while ignoring the consequences of consumption, they developed the Hackadamy awards and the Phlemmy awards, both timed to coincide with the major entertainment industry ceremonies. In the case of television and tobacco, they presented Phlemmies to programs that highlighted tobacco use, including a *Seinfeld* episode in which Kramer turned his home into a haven for smokers. They also acknowledged television's potential to send positive and balanced messages, presenting Pink Lung awards to *Spin City* and *Chicago Hope*. The American Lung Association's prestigious President's Award was presented to the producers of *Touched by an Angel* for one outstanding anti-tobacco program. The ALA has also developed guidelines for industry representations of tobacco products. These include avoiding glamorous messages that suggest smoking is cool, exciting, or fun; creatively substituting props for cigarettes and cigars to portray rebellion, nervousness, or other character traits; realistically depicting tobacco consumption, including personal and environmental consequences; and reducing the overall representation of tobacco use in television. Health educators can use these guidelines as a means to help students monitor and evaluate tobacco consumption by television characters. Students may also wish to choose their own recipients of Phlemmies, Coughscars, or Hackadamy awards, sending them to local network affiliates, national networks, or program producers. Guidelines for this work are available from the Thumbs Up, Thumbs Down Project of the American Lung Association, 909 12th Street, Sacramento, CA 95814.

EATING DISORDERS: Weighing the Consequences

Through relentless repetition, television messages may normalize, demonize, and socialize. What messages might television advertising and the programs they sponsor send to young boys and girls about body image and nutrition? Dr. Victor Strasburger, a pediatrician and adolescent medicine specialist, says that "along with aggression, obesity represents one of the two areas of television research in which the medium's influence achieves the level of cause-and-effect rather than simply being contributory (1995, 76). Researchers have also found that by the age of seven, children have processed norms of cultural attractiveness and prefer a playmate with a physical disability to a child who is obese (Feldman, Feldman, and Goodman 1988). How television contributes to obesity is a complex process that goes beyond a simple matter of television content. Researchers, for example, have demonstrated that in the 12- to 17-year-old population, the prevalence of obesity increases 2 percent for every additional hour of television the subjects view (Dietz and Gortmaker 1985).

The act of viewing television involves little physical activity. It is a principal source of physical inactivity for children. By engaging in non-physical pursuits, television prevents them from burning off calories and energy. One study suggests that viewing actually lowers their metabolic rate (Klesges, Shelton, and Klesges 1993). But television content also plays a role in contributing to obesity. "Programs portray eating and drinking practices that are probably not conducive to good health. Prime time programs contain frequent references to food—more frequent than those in commercials. Characters often eat snacks rather than organized meals, a practice known as grazing" (Huston et al. 1992, 68). Paradoxically, despite almost continuous consumption of food and drink by TV characters, only 12 percent of them are overweight, compared to 25 percent of the adult population (Kauffman 1980). It is hardly surprising that children who are the heaviest viewers of television are more prone to poor eating habits and unhealthy conceptions about food (Signorelli and Lears 1992). Heavy television viewers report consuming more sugar, cereal, candy, hot dogs, soda, and general snack foods than lighter viewers (Huston et al. 1992).

While television consistently models consumption, it also stresses body images that are unrealistic and often unattainable, particularly for women. "Television seems to have an obsession with thinness: 88 percent of all characters are thin or average in body build" (Strasburger 1995, 77). Adolescent girls are frequently preoccupied with body image. While anorexia nervosa and other eating disorders may result from a variety of circumstances and conditions, there is little doubt that cultural factors contribute to them. Television may well contribute to these disorders by telling young women that thin is in, that males will find them more attractive if they look like the women of *Baywatch* or *Beverly Hills 90210*, and that gaining weight is socially unacceptable. Young men may also receive these messages, as a result developing unrealistic expectations of young women and complicating the process further by communicating these expectations to them. It is a vicious cycle that needs to be broken.

(ELEM/MID) — Compare and contrast the body images of young men and women on television, in magazines, and in dolls such as Barbie. What patterns emerge? How are the people in the media similar to and different from the diversity of body images represented in the class?

Divide the class into groups and have them monitor the consumption of food and drink in television programs they routinely watch. Compare the findings and make a list of the type of food people consume and the circumstances under which they eat. Do the characters sit down for regular meals, or is there a lot of snacking and grazing as the research indicates? See if students can locate any examples of programs in which characters are on diets, are concerned about being overweight, or exhibit signs of eating disorders. Compare and contrast these representations to factual information about diet, nutrition, calories, and the food pyramid.

When studying nutrition and the food pyramid, start with a survey of the eating habits of your own students as well as their television viewing behaviors. Compare their daily intake of basic food groups with the recommended levels. Survey them for snacking between meals and during television viewing. What type of programs do they view? What type of food do they snack on? Make a list of the heaviest and lightest television viewers in your class and test their knowledge of food and nutrition. Is the research true for your class? Do the children who view the most television also have poor eating patterns and low levels of understanding about nutrition?

(ELEM/MID) — If the children spend several hours a day watching television, can we assume that this encourages them to be passive rather than active? Earlier in this chapter, we suggested that you survey students to discover what and how much your students watch. Using this instrument enables you to ascertain the times when students watch television. If a significant portion of the viewing occurs in daylight hours, it is fair to assume that this time could be spent more actively. You could modify the earlier survey to enable students who are involved in sports to identify themselves. Do they watch television more or less than students who are not in sports? It is possible that students who are involved in sports are actually more passive because they watch a lot of sports on television.

(ELEM/MID) — Ask students to select a favorite television program they watch regularly. Assign them the task of watching one episode and recording what each character eats and drinks. Many students can use a VCR to facilitate the accuracy of the record. Compile and tabulate the entire class record of food and drink consumption by popular television characters. Discuss the nutritional value of the food and how and when food is consumed. Do the characters snack frequently? Do they eat on the run? Is mealtime a family occasion? Do characters frequently eat in restaurants or at the office? Is the food consistent with their lifestyle, their size, and their weight? For example, do physically active and energetic characters have a diet that would help or hinder their activities?

(ELEM/MID) — Several television characters appear to be overweight (e.g., Drew Carey). Ask students to develop a list of programs featuring overweight people and a list of overweight characters. Which ones are men and which ones are women? Are the characters presented as healthy and happy? Does their weight seem consistent with what they eat and how frequently they eat in the programs? Are the characters dramatic or comedic? Comedy has often drawn on fat people as a source of humor. In what way (verbally or visually) is the characters' size used as a source of humor? Do the characters acknowledge that they are overweight, and do they try to do something about it? In *Roseanne*, episodes have dealt with dieting and exercise, but usually the character(s) return to their old habits.

In the mid-1980s the Caucus for Producers, Writers, and Directors developed a white paper on alcohol and television. In part the report asked, "Have any of us in Hollywood unwittingly glorified the casual use of alcohol in our projects? Have we written it as macho? Directed it as cute? Produced it as an accepted way of life? In short, are we subliminally putting a label of 'perfectly okay' on alcohol-related behavior?" (Caucus for TV Writers 1985, 22). If the industry has acknowledged the impact of their own image-making, health educators need to work with students, parents, and teachers so that they recognize these images and the inducements they may offer about alcohol, tobacco, substance abuse, and other potentially harmful products or behaviors.

REFERENCES

Adams, Anne, and Cathy Harrison, (1975). Using Television to Teach Specific Reading Skills. *Reading Teacher*, 29:1, 45-51.

American Psychological Association, (1985). *Violence on Television*. Washington, DC: APA Board of Social and Ethical Responsibility for Psychology.

———, (1993). *Violence and Youth: Psychology's Response*. Washington DC: APA.

Austin, Erica Weintraub, (1993). Exploring the Effects of Active Parental Mediation of Television Content. *Journal of Broadcasting and Electronic Media*, 37:2, 147-58.

Austin, Erica Weintraub, and Heidi Kay Meli, (1994). Effects of Interpretation of Televised Alcohol Portrayals on Children's Alcohol Beliefs. *Journal of Broadcasting and Electronic Media*, Fall, 417-35.

Bandura, A., and R. H. Walters, (1963). *Social Learning and Personality Development*. New York: Holt, Rinehart, & Winston.

Baran, Stanley, (1976a). Sex on TV and Adolescent Sexual Self Image. *Journal of Broadcasting*, 20:1, 61-88.

Baran, Stanley J., (1976b). How TV and Film Portrayals Affect Sexual Satisfaction in College Students. *Journalism Quarterly*, 468-78.

Barrie, Guner, (1994). The Question of Media Violence. In Jennings Bryant and Dolf Zillmann (eds.), *Media Effects: Advances in Theory and Research* (163-211). Hillsdale, NJ: Lawrence Erlbaum.

Barton, Richard, and Robert Miller, (1977). Television Literacy: Integrating the Symbolic Worlds of Educators and Students. *International Journal of Instructional Media*, 5:3, 229-34.

Bearinger, Linda. Study Group Report on the Impact of Television on Adolescent Views of Sexuality. *Journal of Adolescent Health Care*, 11:1, 171-74.

Bianculli, David, (1992). *Taking Television Seriously: Teleliteracy*. New York: Touchstone.

Blumer, Herbert, (1933). *Movies, Delinquency and Crime*. Chicago: University of Chicago Press.

Brown, Jane et al., (1990). Television and Adolescent Sexuality. *Journal of Adolescent Health Care*, 11:1, 62-70.

Brown, Jane, and Jeanne Steele, (1995). *Sex and the Mass Media*. Menlo Park, CA: Kaiser Foundation.

Brown, Jane, and Kim Walsh-Childers, (1994). Effects of Media on Personal and Public Health. In Jennings Bryant and Dolf Zillmann (eds.), *Media Effects: Advances in Theory and Research* (389-416). Hillsdale, NJ: Lawrence Erlbaum.

Bryant, Jennings, and Dolf Zillmann, (1994). *Media Effects: Advances in Theory and Research*. Hillsdale, NJ: Lawrence Erlbaum.

Buckingham, David, (1993). *Children Talking Television: The Making of Television Literacy*. London: Falmer Press.

Buckingham, David, and Julian Sefton-Green, (1994). *Cultural Studies Goes to School: Reading and Teaching Popular Media*. London: Taylor & Francis.

Burkhart, Alice et al., (1992). *Touch the World: Observations on the Use of CNN in the Classroom*. Chico: California State University.

Burr, Ty, (1997). The Kingdom Comes. *Entertainment Weekly*, May 16, 119.

Butsch, Richard, (1995). Ralph, Fred, Archie and Homer: Why Television Keeps Recreating the White Male Working Class Buffoon. In Gail Dines and Jean Humez (eds.), *Gender, Race and Class in Media* (403-12). Thousand Oaks, CA: Sage.

Cantor, Joanne, (1996). Television and Children's Fear. In Tannis Macbeth (ed.), *Tuning in to Young Viewers: Social Science Perspectives on Television* (87-116). Thousand Oaks, CA: Sage.

Canzoneri, Vince, (1984). What Parents Should Do About TV's Feminine Mistake. *TV Guide*, January 28.

Carnegie Council on Adolescent Development, (1992). *Fateful Choices*. New York: Carnegie Corporation.

———, (1995). *Great Transitions: Preparing Adolescents for a New Century*. New York: Carnegie Corporation.

Caucus for TV Writers, Producers, and Directors, (1985). Alcohol Guidelines for the Television Industry and Results. *Television and Families*, 8:3, 22.

Centerwall, Brandon, (1992). Television and Violence: The Scale of the Problem and Where to Go from Here. *Journal of the American Medical Association*, 267:22, 3059-63.

Collins, W. et al., (1978). Age-Related Aspects of Comprehension and Inference from a Televised Dramatic Narrative. *Child Development*, 49:2, 389-99.

———, (1995). How Kids Perceive TV. *Connect*, No. 9, Spring.

David, R., and R. Kubey, (1982). Growing Old on Television and with Television. In D. Pearl et al. (eds.), *Television and Behavior: Ten Years of Scientific Progress and Implications for the Eighties*, Vol. 2, *Technical Reports* (201-8). Washington, DC: U.S. Department of Health and Human Services.

Dietz, W. H. Jr., and S. Gortmaker, (1985). Television, Obesity and Eating Disorders. *Adolescent Medicine: State of the Art Reviews*, 4, 543-49.

Dines, Gail, and Jean Humez, (1995). Home, Home on the Remote: Does Fascination with TV Technology Create Male-Dominated Family Entertainment? In Gail Dines and Jean Humez (eds.), *Gender, Race and Class in Media* (362-66). Thousand Oaks, CA: Sage.

Doerken, Maurine, (1983). *Classroom Combat: Teaching and Television*. Englewood Cliffs, NJ: Educational Technology Publications.

Dominick, J., S. Richman, and A. Wurtzel, (1979). Problem-Solving in TV Shows Popular with Children. *Journalism Quarterly*, 56:3, 455-63.

Douglas, Susan, (1994). *Where the Girls Are: Growing Up Female with the Mass Media*. New York: Random House.

Douglas, William, and Beth Olson, (1995). Beyond Family Structure: The Family in Domestic Comedy. *Journal of Broadcasting and Electronic Media*, 39:2, 236-61.

Dubow, Eric, and Laurie Miller, (1996). Television Violence, Viewing and Aggressive Behavior. In Tannis Macbeth (ed.), *Tuning in to Young Viewers: Social Science Perspectives on Television* (117-48). Thousand Oaks, CA: Sage.

Durkin, Kevin, (1985). *Television, Sex Roles and Children*. Philadelphia: Open University Press.

Entertainment Weekly, (1997). Rating Nielsen Questions. April.

Ettema, James, and D. Charles Whitney, (1994). *Audiencemaking: How the Media Create the Audience*. Thousand Oaks, CA: Sage.

Ewen, Stuart, and Elizabeth Ewen, (1982). *Channels of Desire*. New York: McGraw Hill.

Extra, (1993). Superbowl Sunday: A Wake Up Call on Domestic Violence. March, 7.

Farhi, Paul, (1996). The Race for Ratings. *Washington Post*, weekly edition, June 17-23, 34.

Feldman, W., E. Feldman, and J. Goodman, (1988). Culture Versus Biology: Children's Attitudes Towards Thinness and Fitness. *Pediatrics*, 81, 190-94.

Fiske, John, and John Hartley, (1978). *Reading Television*. London: Methuen.

Fox, Mem, (1993). *Radical Reflections: Passionate Opinions on Teaching, Learning and Living*. San Diego: Harcourt Brace.

Franzblau, Susan, (1977). Television and Human Sexuality. In Ben Logan (ed.), *Television Awareness Training*. New York: Media Research Center Publications.

Franzblau, Susan, N. Sprafkin, and Eli Rubinstein, (1977). Sex on TV: A Content Analysis. *Journal of Communication*, 27:2, 164-70.

Freedman, Morris, (1996). Taming the Hysteria About Media Violence. *Education Week*, June 5, 44 and 47.

Friend, Tad, (1993). Sitcoms, Seriously. *Esquire*, March, 113-24.

Gabe, Donna, (1993). TV's Limited Version of Hispanics. *U.S.A. Today*, August 30, D1.

Gartner, Michael, (1993). Open Letter to Attorney General Janet Reno. *U.S.A. Today*, October 26, 13A.

Gerbner, George, (1981). Television: The American School Child's National Curriculum, Day In and Day Out. *PTA Today*, 6:7, 3-5.

———, (1995). Television Violence: The Power and the Peril. In Gail Dines and Jean Humez (eds.), *Gender, Race and Class in Media* (547-57). Thousand Oaks, CA: Sage.

Gerbner, George et al., (1994). Growing Up with Television: The Cultivation Perspective. In Jennings Bryant and Dolf Zillmann (eds.), *Media Effects: Advances in Theory and Research* (17-42). Hillsdale, NJ: Lawrence Erlbaum.

Giroux, Henry, (1997). *Channel Surfing: Race, Talk and the Destruction of Today's Youth*. New York: St. Martin's.

Goldstone, Bette, P., (1989). Visual Interpretation of Children's Books. *The Reading Teacher*, 42, April, 592-95.

Graves, Sherryl Brown, (1996). Diversity on Television. In Tannis Macbeth (ed.), *Tuning in to Young Viewers: Social Science Perspectives on Television* (61-86). Thousand Oaks, CA: Sage.

Gray, Herman, (1995). Television, Black Americans and the American Dream. In Gail Dines and Jean Humez (eds.), *Gender, Race and Class in Media* (430-37). Thousand Oaks, CA: Sage.

Greenberg, B. S., and J. E. Brand, (1994). Cultural Diversity on Saturday Morning Television. In G. Berry and J. K. Asamen (eds.), *Children and Television in a Changing Socio-Cultural World* (132-42). Newbury Park, CA: Sage.

Greenfield, Patricia, (1990). Video Screens: Are They Changing the Way Children Learn? *Harvard Education Letter*, March/April.

Gross, Larry, (1995). Out of the Mainstream: Sexual Minorities and the Mass Media. In Gail Dines and Jean Humez (eds.), *Gender, Race and Class in Media* (61-70). Thousand Oaks, CA: Sage.

Hall, Stuart, (1995). The Whites of Their Eyes: Racist Ideologies and the Media. In Gail Dines and Jean Humez (eds.), *Gender, Race and Class in Media* (18-22). Thousand Oaks, CA: Sage.

Hammil, Pete, (1990). Crack and the Box. *Esquire*, May 63-66.

Harris, Richard Jackson, (1994). The Impact of Sexually Explicit Media. In Jennings Bryant and Dolf Zillmann (eds.), *Media Effects: Advances in Theory and Research* (247-72). Hillsdale, NJ: Lawrence Erlbaum.

Hawley, Richard, (1978). Television and the Adolescent: A Teacher's View. *American Film*, 4:1, 52-56.

Healy, Jane, (1994). *Endangered Minds: Why Our Children Don't Think and What We Can Do About It*. New York: Doubleday.

Hoffner, Cynthia, (1996). Children's Wishful Identification with Favorite Television Characters. *Journal of Broadcasting and Electronic Media*, 40:3, 389-402.

Hundley, Heather, (1995). The Naturalization of Beer in *Cheers*. *Journal of Broadcasting and Electronic Media*. 39:3, 350-59.

Huston, Aletha, and John Wright, (1996). Television and Socialization of Young Children. In Tannis Macbeth (ed.), *Tuning in to Young Viewers: Social Science Perspectives on Television* (37-60). Thousand Oaks, CA: Sage.

Huston, Aletha et al., (1992). *Big World, Small Screen*. Lincoln: University of Nebraska Press.

Jacobson, M. et al., (1983). *The Booze Merchants: The Inebriating of America*. Washington, DC: Center for Science in the Public Interest.

Jhally, Sut, and Justin Lewis, (1992). *Enlightened Racism: The Cosby Show, Audiences, and the Myth of the American Dream*. Boulder, CO: Westview Press.

Jones, Gerard, (1992). *Honey, I'm Home: Sitcoms Selling the American Dream*. New York: St. Martin's.

Kauffman, L., (1980). Prime Time Nutrition. *Journal of Commuication*. Boulder, CO: Westview Press.

Kelley, Michael, (1983). *A Parent's Guide to Television*. New York: John Wiley.

Kelly, Hope, and Howard Gardner, (1981). *Viewing Children Through Television*. San Francisco: Jossey Bass.

Klesges, R., M. Shelton, and L. Klesges, (1993). Effects of Television on Metabolic Rate: Potential Implications for Childhood Obesity. *Pediatrics* 91, 281-86.

Krendl, Kathy, and Bruce Watkins, (1983). Understanding Television: An Exploratory Inquiry into the Construction of Narrative Content. *Educational Communication and Technology Journal*, 31:4, 201-12.

Kubey, Robert et al., (1995). Demographic Diversity on Cable: Have the New Cable Channels Made a Difference in the Representation of Gender, Race and Age? *Journal of Broadcasting and Electronic Media*, 39:4, 459-71.

The Learning Channel, (1994). *KNOW-TV: Changing, What, Why and How You Watch*. Bethesda, MD.

Leifer, Aimee, (1974). Children's Television: More Than Mere Entertainment. *Harvard Educational Review*, 44:2, 213-45.

Levy, Doug, (1996). CPR Success Rate Doesn't Match Hollywood's Version, Doctors Say. *U.S.A. Today*, June 13, D1.

Lewis, Lisa, (1995). Form and Female Authorship in Music Video. In Gail Dines and Jean Humez (eds.), *Gender, Race and Class in Media* (499-507). Thousand Oaks, CA: Sage.

Lichter, S. Robert et al., (1994). *Prime Time: How TV Portrays American Culture*. Washington, DC: Regnery Publishing.

Lieberman, David, (1996). Cable Threatens to Snatch Viewers. *U.S.A. Today*, September 16, B1.

Macbeth, Tannis, (1996). Indirect Effects of Television: Creativity, Persistence, School Achievement and Participation in Other Activities. In Tannis Macbeth (ed.), *Tuning in to Young Viewers: Social Science Perspectives on Television* (149-220). Thousand Oaks, CA: Sage.

Macbeth, Tannis, (1996). *Tuning in to Young Viewers: Social Science Perspectives on Television*. Thousand Oaks, CA: Sage.

Mayerle, Judine, and David Rarick, (1989). The Image of Education in Primetime Network Television Series, 1948-1988. *Journal of Broadcasting and Electronic Media*, 33:2, 139-57.

McKibben, Bill, (1993). Sometimes You Just Have to Turn It Off. *Esquire*, October, 67.

Mediascope, (1995). National Television Violence Study. *Executive Summary*. Los Angeles.

Meyer, Timothy, (1973). Children's Perceptions of Favorite Television Characters as Behavioral Models. *Educational Broadcasting Review*, 7:1.

Mielke, Keith, (1994). On the Relationship Between Television Viewing and Academic Achievement. *Journal of Broadcasting and Electronic Media*, 38:3, 3261-3366.

Miles, Betty, (1975). *Channeling Children: Sex Stereotyping on Prime-Time TV*. Princeton, NJ: Women on Words and Images.

Miles, Jack, (1997). Primetime's Search for God. *TV Guide*, March 29-April 24.

Miller, Mark Crispin, (1988). *Boxed In: The Culture of TV*. Evanston, IL: Northwestern University Press.

Mitchard, Jacquelyn, (1995). TV Heads for the Heartland. *TV Guide*, April 8, 28-29.

Montgomery, Kathryn, (1991). Alcohol and Television: And Now for Some Mixed Messages. *Media and Values*, Nos. 54-55, 18-19.

Murphy, Mary, (1995). Invasion of the Prime Time Boss Ladies. *TV Guide*, April 29, 11-12.

Murphy, Mary, and Steven Redicliffe, (1996). Clinton on Television. *TV Guide*, October 19, 46-50.

Nodelman, Perry, (1988). *Words About Pictures: The Narrative Art of the Children's Picture Books*. Athens: University of Georgia Press.

Nuland, Sherwin, (1996). Death, Dying and TV. *TV Guide*, June 27, 69-70.

Oliver, Mary Beth, (1994). Portrayals of Crime, Race and Aggression in Reality Based Police Shows: A Content Analysis. *Journal of Broadcasting and Electronic Media*, 38:2, 179-92.

Olson, Barry, and Peter Ross, (1992). Clinton on TV. *TV Guide*, November 21, 15.

Palmer, Edward, (1988). *Television and America's Children: A Crisis of Neglect*. New York: Oxford University Press.

Patureau, Alan, (1994). Southerners Love to Watch Themselves on TV. *Atlanta Journal and Constitution*, April 24, A3.

Peck, Ellen, (1979). Television's Romance with Reproduction. In E. Peck and J. Senderowitz (eds.), *Pronatalism: The Myth of Mom and Apple Pie*. New York: Thomas Y. Crowell.

Peggler, Tim, (1997). Church Blast for X Files. *The Age*, January 2, 5a.

Pezdek, Kathy, (1985). Is Watching TV Passive, Uncreative or Addictive: Debunking Some Myths. *Television and Families*, 8:2, 41-46.

Pezdek, Kathy, Arille Lehrer, and Sara Simon, (1984). The Relationship Between Reading and Cognitive Processing of Television and Radio. *Child Development*, 55:6, 2072-82.

Pfau, Michael et al., (1995). The Influence of Television Viewing on Public Perceptions of Physicians. *Journal of Broadcasting and Electronic Media*, 39:4, 441-58.

Postman, Neil, (1981). Childhood's End: The Tragedy of the Television Age. *American Educator*, 2:38, 20-26.

———, (1985). *Amusing Ourselves to Death*. New York: Viking.

Potter, James et al., (1995). How Real Is the Portrayal of Aggression in Television Entertainment Programming? *Journal of Broadcasting and Electronic Media*, 39:4, 496-516.

Powell, Gloria Johnson, (1982). The Impact of Television on the Self-Concept Development of Minority Children. In Gordon Berry and Claudia Mitchell-Kernan (eds.), *Television and the Socialization of the Minority Child*. New York: Academic Press.

Powers, Ron, (1991). Our Town. *TV Guide*, December 21, 8.

Quayle, Dan, (1993). *Washington Post*, weekly edition, December 20-26, 29.

Rapaczynski, Wanda, and Dorothy and Jerome Singer, (1982). Teaching Television: A Curriculum for Young Children. *Journal of Communication*, 32:2, 46-55.

Ravitch, Diane, and Chester E. Finn, Jr., (1987). *What Do Our 17 Year Olds Know?* New York: Harper & Row.

Rhodes, Jane, (1995). Television's Realist Portrayal of African-American Women and the Case of LA Law. In Gail Dines and Jean Humez (eds.), *Gender, Race and Class in Media* (325-31). Thousand Oaks, CA: Sage.

Roberts, Elizabeth, (1983). Teens, Sexuality and Sex: Our Mixed Messages. *Television and Children*, 6:4, 9-12.

Rogers, Deborah, (1995). Daze of Our Lives: The Soap Opera as Feminine Text. In Gail Dines and Jean Humez (eds.), *Gender, Race and Class in Media* (325-31). Thousand Oaks, CA: Sage.

Rosenfield, Megan, (1993). Tearing Away TV's First Amendment Figleaf. *Washington Post*, weekly edition, July 26-August 1, 63.

Roush, Matt, (1993). *U.S.A. Today*, 3D.

Rudolph, Ileane, and Mike Hammer, (1996). Imagine June Cleaver in a Bustier. *TV Guide*, July 13, 18-19.

Rushkoff, Douglas, (1994). *Media Virus! Hidden Agendas in Popular Culture*. New York: Ballantine Books.

Russo, Tom, (1997). King of Comedy. *Entertainment Weekly*, May 9, 53.

Salomon, Gavriel, and Tamar Leigh, (1984). Predispositions About Learning from Print and Television. *Journal of Communication*, 34:2, 119-35.

Shattuc, Jane, (1997). *The Talking Cure: TV Talk Shows and Women*. New York: Routledge.

Signorielli, N., (1987). Drinking, Sex and Violence on Television: The Cultural Indicators Perspective. *Journal of Drug Education*, 17:3, 245-60.

Signorielli, Nancy, and M. Lears, (1992). Television and Children's Conception of Nutrition: Unhealthy Messages. *Health Communication* 4, 245-57.

Singer, Dorothy, and Jerome Singer, (1994). *Creating Critical Viewers*. Denver: Pacific Mountain Network.

Singer, Dorothy, Jerome Singer, and Diana Zuckerman, (1981). *Teaching Television: How to Use It to Your Child's Advantage*. New York: Dial.

Sleeter, Christine, and Carl Grant, (1992). Race, Class, Gender, and Disability in Current Textbooks. In Michael Apple and Linda Christian-Smith (eds.), *The Politics of the Textbook*. New York: Routledge.

Smith, Lois, (1994). A Content Analysis of Gender Differences in Children's Television. *Journal of Broadcasting and Electronic Media*, 38:3, 323-27.

Solomon, Jack, (1988). *The Signs of Our Times*. Los Angeles: Jeremy Tarcher.

Stewart, David W., and Scott Ward, (1994). Media Effects on Advertising. In Jennings Bryant and Dolf Zillmann, (eds.), *Media Effects: Advances in Theory and Research* (315-64). Hillsdale, NJ: Lawrence Erlbaum.

Strasburger, Victor, (1995). *Adolescents and the Media: Medical and Psychological Impact*. Thousand Oaks, CA: Sage.

Surgeon General's Scientific Advisory Committee on Television and Social Behavior, (1972). *Television and Growing Up: The Impact of Televised Violence*. Washington, DC: U.S. Government Printing Office.

Tierney, Joan, (1978). *Parents, Adolescents and Television: Culture, Learning Influence*. Canada: Canadian Radio, TV and Telecommunications.

Time, (1996). Who Watches What?, June 3, 68.

Turow, Joseph, (1997). *Breaking Up America: Advertisers and the New Media World*. Chicago: University of Chicago Press.

TV Guide, (1990). March.

———, (1996). Reader Poll Results, August 17, 20.

U.S.A. Today (1990). June 12, 3D.

———, (1991). May 9, 10a.

———, (1996). Will This Nation Ever Grow Comfortable in Its Modern Skin? November 8, 14a.

Vandergrift, Kay, and Jane Anne Hannigan, (1993). Reading the Image. *School Library Journal*, January 20-25.

Weiss, Audrey, and Barbara Wilson, (1996). Emotional Portrayals in Family Television Series That Are Popular with Children. *Journal of Broadcasting and Electronic Media*, 40:1, 1-29.

Wertham, Fredric, (1968). In O. N. Larsen (ed.), *Violence and Media*. New York: Harper & Row.

White, Mimi, (1995). Watching the Girls Go Buy—Shop-at-Home Television. In Gail Dines and Jean Humez (eds.), *Gender, Race and Class in Media*. Thousand Oaks, CA: Sage.

Whitman, David, (1997). Was It Good for Us? *U.S. News and World Report*, May 19, 57-64.

Wink, Walter, (1993). Television and Media Violence. *Media and Values*, No. 62, 5.

Winn, Marie, (1977). *The Plug-In Drug*. New York: Bantam.

Xiaoming, Hao, (1994). Television Viewing Among American Adults in the 1990s. *Journal of Broadcasting and Electronic Media*, 38:3, 353-60.

Zuckerman, Mortimer, (1993). The Victims of TV Violence. *U.S. News and World Report*, August 2, 64.

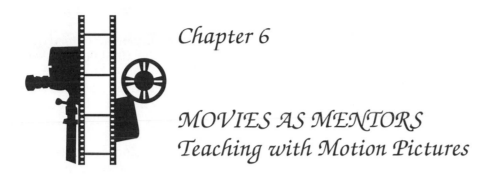

Chapter 6

MOVIES AS MENTORS
Teaching with Motion Pictures

More than 80 years ago, Thomas Edison's enthusiasm for the motion picture knew no bounds. "It is possible to teach every branch of human knowledge with the motion picture," he declared; "our school systems will be completely changed in ten years." (Saettler 1968, 8). As we now know, Edison was wrong. While movies continue to be potentially powerful technologies of instruction, they have historically been scorned and rejected by all but a few progressive teachers. Too often regarded as examples of low-brow taste and the excesses of pop culture, movies have historically been the subject of political attack, blamed for everything from social violence to teen pregnancy and the decline of the family. The 1996 presidential election provided Senator Dole with a forum to attack Hollywood and its creations. Dole, according to *Time* magazine, "accused the powers behind American movies of . . . flooding the country with nightmares of depravity" (Lacayo 1995, 26). Such assaults, however well meaning, serve to demonize film and to discourage a meaningful role for motion pictures in our classrooms and curricula.

Nor are the complaints restricted to political motivations. In 1997, Steven Spielberg developed a film study guide to accompany his release of the movie *Amistad*. Film critic Michael Medved complained that Hollywood was "pushing its own recklessly dishonest educational agenda," which "distorts a crucial episode in our history, using schools to shamelessly promote a commercial product" (Medved 1997).

In Australia, by contrast, educators and motion picture distributors work together cooperatively. For several years now, ATOM (Australian Teachers of Media) have published an outstanding series of interdisciplinary motion picture study guides. Now available in the United States, these beautifully designed, carefully researched, and well-written guides serve as outstanding teaching tools for the integration of motion pictures into the curriculum. At Appalachian State University, these study guides serve as models in undergraduate teacher preparation. Students are required to select a film of their own choice and work in cooperative groups creating an interdisciplinary curriculum unit based upon the movie. *The Wizard of Oz*, for example, includes a geography section on Kansas as well as a science section on tornadoes and rainbows. *Babe* includes a geography section on New South Wales as well as a comparative analysis of the movie's relationship to both *Animal Farm* and *Charlotte's Web*. Using computer scanning technology and color printers, these young teachers research, design, and create attractive study guides that use movies as teaching tools to explore the traditional curriculum. As such they move beyond a mere consideration of movies as product, emphasizing instead the instructional process by which teachers use these materials. Anyone who believes movies have little to say or a limited role in the curriculum should simply consider *Mr. Holland's Opus*. The film can be used as an exploration of teaching as a profession and school as an institution. Further, music teachers can explore Glenn Holland's methods and the way he turns the students on by connecting classical music to rock and roll. *Mr. Holland's Opus* also has something to say about special education, including education for the deaf, and it makes a positive statement about people with disabilities.

There is little doubt that movies, and American movies in particular, affect the way we think about individuals (*Gandhi*, *Malcolm X*), institutions, and issues. In the case of Oliver Stone's *Nixon*, *Newsweek* said, "Hopkins is Nixon. It's not imitation, it's alchemy. Hopkins grants us access to Nixon's wounded soul in a way that probably the real man never could have" (*Newsweek* 1995, 68). *Dead Man Walking*, *In Cold Blood*, *Let Him Have It*, and *I Want to Live* all represent powerful statements about the death penalty. *Mr. Holland's Opus* and *Dangerous Minds*, like *To Sir with Love* and *Up the Down Staircase*, provide the public with an insight into schools as institutions, teachers as individuals, and education as a process. While none of these films in and of themselves represents our total perception of our world, they do operate cumulatively to construct the way we think and feel about people and places. As such, they are capable of both helping and hurting the way young people perceive themselves and their world.

Movies are capable of bringing distant lands and different cultures to the classroom to enliven and enrich the study of these people and places. If a culture is stereotyped and misrepresented in a film, it is necessary for teachers to challenge these inaccuracies. When a portrayal is accurate and honest, movies bring the place to life in a way that textbooks and print cannot.

Motion pictures can also play an important role in promoting literacy and the enjoyment of literature. Film versions of books and plays can bring the characters to life and help students recognize universal themes and the human condition. Comparisons among various versions of a film can help students understand the role interpretation plays in literature. Mel Gibson's version of Hamlet can, for example, be compared to Kenneth Branagh's treatment or the classic Olivier version. All three can be explored through *Rosencrantz and Guildenstern Are Dead*. In the same way, Olivier's *Richard the III* can be compared to the 1996 version set in fascist 1930s England, and both can be explored through Al Pacino's *Looking for Richard*. *West Side Story* has long been used by teachers in an attempt to update Romeo and Juliet for today's teens. Nineteen ninety-six saw a new version of the story with a contemporary urban setting, a modern soundtrack, and the youthful appeal of Leonardo DiCaprio and Clare Danes.

The 1990 U.S. version of *Lord of the Flies* is an interesting contrast to the less stylish but more accurate 1963 British version. When students are excited by a movie, they often express interest in reading the book. Movies such as *The Neverending Story*, *Pagemaster*, *James and the Giant Peach*, and *Jumanji* can be explored as examples of fantasy genre with younger students, and brief clips from movies can be used as story starters to stimulate creative writing.

Although we think of film primarily as a visual medium, sound also plays a significant role. Imagine *Jaws* or *Psycho*, for example, without the tension and drama created by the music and sound effects. Music teachers can explore motion picture scores to see how they evoke particular moods and emotions. Biographies of classical and contemporary composers can also be useful in bringing individuals and the creative process to life. Some examples are *Amadeus* (Wolfgang Amadeus Mozart), *Immortal Beloved* (Beethoven), *Lisztomania* (Franz Liszt), *A Song to Remember* (Frederic Chopin), *The Music Lovers* (Peter Tchaikovsky), *Words and Music* (Richard Rogers and Lorenz Hart), *Deep in My Heart* (Sigmund Romberg), and *Night and Day* (Cole Porter).

Movies are also a very youth-oriented medium. Adolph Zukor once said, "The average movie-goer's intelligence is that of a 14-year-old child" (Considine 1985). If movies target young audiences, then parents, teachers, counselors, librarians, and media specialists need to monitor films and help students understand the views and values expressed in them. Social learning theory suggests that movies can model behavior and attitudes and that children and teens, impressionable as they are, may imitate such behavior or identify with such values. The repetitive nature of film, enhanced by multiple viewing made possible by cable programming and VCR technology, further increases the cumulative impact of movie messages and therefore their ability to influence. In 1990, for example, a 14-year-old Washington girl allegedly copied the behavior of a character in the movie *Heathers* by poisoning two 11-year-old playmates. Copycat tragedies also resulted when several teenagers were hit by cars after lying down in the road as characters did in the movie *The Program*. Although such instances are rare, the exception rather than the rule, they do demonstrate the social significance of movies when powerful film content comes into contact with impressionable young audiences. Adults charged with the responsibility of helping teens deal with the pressures and problems associated with substance abuse, sexual experimentation, dysfunctional families, abusive relationships, and self-esteem cannot afford to ignore the allure and social sanction often afforded by the silver screen. *Porky's*, *Animal House*, *The Basketball Diaries*, *Little Darlings*, and *The Last American Virgin*, among other titles, are potentially suspect in this area. On the other hand, *Zelly and Me*, *Rudy*, *Doll House*, *The Breakfast Club*, *Now and Then*, *Stand by Me*, *What's Eating Gilbert Grape?*, *Bless the Beasts and Children*, *This Boy's Life*, and many other films can be used to help young people understand their own lives and the process of growing up. A group of films from Ireland, including *War of the Buttons*, *Run of the Country*, and *Circle of Friends*, combine an exploration of adolescence with the observation of another country; it is possible for movies to be both inspirational and motivational.

Of course, like all instructional materials used in education, movies must be examined before use. Only by previewing a film for content, form, and language can teachers determine the suitability of the film for both advancing instructional objectives and addressing the nature and needs of the students. Pre-screening and post-screening strategies can only be meaningfully developed after a teacher has previewed a film and had time to prepare a lesson that takes advantage of the previewing process. Using films as filler or reward for work completed, or using movies as a means of electronic baby-sitting does a disservice to both the students and the movies. Properly selected and applied, however, movies can make a valuable contribution to students' comprehension, participation, and attention. As such, they offer educators a potentially powerful teaching tool.

FILM, ENGLISH, AND LANGUAGE ARTS

The curriculum area in which movies have most traditionally been accepted is clearly English, Literature, and Language Arts, where film versions of plays and novels have always been a valid and acceptable approach. But even here, the primacy of print continues to dominate the suspect cinema, which is frequently tolerated simply as a sugar-coated means of focusing student attention on books. "The cinema stands suspect, regarded as a flashy but floundering and intuitive child, clinging hard to literature's coattails and hoping to achieve through association with an established art form, a modicum of respect" (Peary and Shatzkin 1977, 2). As recently as 1995, the South Carolina Department of Education issued a new Language Arts Framework that referred to "thinking, speaking, listening, reading, and writing," without a single reference to visual media save for the ironic observation that "our children are more media-savvy and media dependent than earlier generations." (1995, 2)

Throughout the 1990s, English teachers wishing to bring film into their classrooms were offered a veritable treasure from which to choose. Buoyed in part by the success of the Merchant/Ivory productions (*Passage to India*, *Shadowlands*, *Howard's End*, *Room with a View*) that proved adaptations of literary classics could have life beyond the art houses, the film industry began to churn out a seemingly endless number of movies based on great plays and novels. These included Hawthorne's *Scarlet Letter*, Charlotte Brönte's *Jane Eyre*, Jane Austen's *Sense and Sensibility*, Arthur Miller's *The Crucible*, and

Thomas Hardy's *Jude the Obscure*. Describing Hollywood's sudden infatuation with Shakespeare as a "plethora of iambic pentameter," *Time* allowed *Romeo and Juliet* director Baz Luhrmann to explain the attraction. "His stories are full of sex, violence, tragedy, comedy, because he was first of all a great entertainer. IIis audience was 3000 drunken fighting people, bear baiters, and prostitutes" (Corliss, 1996, 90). The newsmagazine wryly observed that it sounded like Friday night at any big-city cinemaplex. *Othello, Hamlet, Richard the Third, Much Ado About Nothing,* and *Twelfth Night* were among some of the bard's plays to find their way to new audiences through the agency of cinema during this period.

So long as Hollywood continues to make movie versions of books like *Cry the Beloved Country, Little Women, Jude, Moll Flanders,* and other classics, English teachers will inevitably use them to advance the study of literature and bring drama to students in a way the printed word often cannot. While exploring the novel, however, it is also possible to look at the process of storytelling in both print and picture. In *American Cinema*, the outstanding Annenberg video series, one program seeks to explore decisions directors make "to most efficiently and effectively drive the story forward for the audience." This includes elements such as camera movement, composition of the frames, point of view, and the entire visual vocabulary at the director's disposal. Though some people may believe that the language of film is obvious, that what you see is what you get, in reality we need to be taught to both recognize and read its codes and conventions. "Anyone can see a film . . . but some people have learned to comprehend visual images, physiologically, ethnographically and psychologically with far more sophistication than others" (Monaco 1977, 125).

Like novels and plays, movies have plot, characters, themes, conflicts, resolutions, setting, and other elements in common. While the form and content are similar, there are ways in which they also differ. John Sayles directs, writes, and edits his films, including *Matewan, The Secret of Roan Inish, Passion Fish,* and *Brother from Another Planet*. In his book, *Thinking in Pictures*, Sayles distinguishes between the process of both creating and comprehending stories told in pictures and print. "Fiction relies more on the imagination of the reader," he says. "Trying to bring those pictures, those feelings to other people is a lot of what movie making is about" (1987, 8). By selecting key moments in a story, teachers can explore the ways words and pictures are used to advance the narrative and our understanding of characters and events. By providing students with the opportunity to discuss the similarities and differences, we widen their understanding of these storytelling forms and our understanding of young people as audiences. In *The Great Gatsby*, for example, how do students respond to Daisy's fascination for Gatsby's shirts as Fitzgerald describes it in words, compared to the way Mia Farrow's Daisy shows it? How does Fitzgerald's use of symbolism, such as Dr. Eckleburg's eyes and the green light across the bay, transfer to the screen in the hands of director Jack Clayton and writer Francis Ford Coppola?

DIRECTOR AS AUTHOR: *The Auteur Theory*

Dickens, Austen, Melville, Hemingway, Steinbeck—we all recognize the names of these authors. As novelists they labor alone, creating as individuals. But who writes a movie? These products are created collectively and cooperatively as part of an industry once called "the dream factory." Rather than being the vision of a single individual (presumably the director), they frequently represent the constraints of time; assumptions about the concentration span of the audience; various drafts, versions, and contributors; and a range of other factors. Despite the collective contribution made to a movie by the producer, editor, cinematographer, and others, film theorists have singled out some directors as auteurs or authors of their films. These filmmakers, it is said, have such vision and power in the industry that they are able to put their personal stamp on a story through the consistent use of film language, theme, and motif. In essence the auteur theory believes that the director is "the true creator of the film" (Tudor 1974, 122). While the concept had its origins in European film criticism, it came to be applied to American cinema, particularly to the work of directors such as John Ford, Howard Hawks, Alfred Hitchcock, and of course, Orson Wells. "These directors," it has been said, have been able to maintain a recognizable personal signature from film to film" (Monaco 1977, 245).

One example of this might be motifs. In general, motifs refer to a dominant and recurring image, idea, or theme in a single work or body of works. In some cases these can be relatively minor details, such as Hitchcock's penchant for women whose names start with *M:* Marion (*Psycho*), Miriam (*Strangers on a Train*), Melanie (*The Birds*), Margot (*Dial M for Murder*), Midge and Madeleine (*Vertigo*), and Marnie (*Marnie*). At the same time, motifs/themes can be much more psychologically significant. This is apparent with Hitchcock's predilection for stories featuring cold, jealous mothers and parent/child conflict (*Notorious*, *Psycho*, *North by Northwest*, etc.). Since these character traits are crucial to motivation, they are thematically central to the advancement of the story and our understanding of both people and plot. In the case of John Ford, particularly in westerns like *My Darling Clementine*, *The Searchers*, and *The Man Who Shot Liberty Valance*, a consistent worldview is evident. Ford's films are concerned with the process of bringing "civilization to a savage land, the garden to the wilderness" (Wollen 1968, 81). Ford locates characters such as Wyatt Earp, Ethan Edwards, and Tom Doniphon within a world "governed by a set of oppositions . . . garden versus wilderness, ploughshare versus sabre, settler versus nomad, European versus Indian . . . book versus gun . . . East versus West" (94).

Another director whose body of work clearly demonstrates continuity of theme and style is Stanley Kubrick. "If evidence of personal involvement and consistency of theme and style over an apparently heterogeneous range of projects distinguishes the true auteur, then Kubrick certainly qualifies" (Kagan 1991, xiii). Man versus machine, man versus nature, military madness—these are some of the themes evident in such different yet similar stories as *Spartacus*, *Dr. Strangelove*, *Barry Lyndon*, *Full Metal Jacket*, *2001*, *A Space Odyssey*, and *A Clockwork Orange*.

But not everyone believes in the auteur theory. Director Stanley Kramer unequivocally rejects it. "I don't believe in the auteur theory. Film is a concerted effort. It involves the work of a lot of people. The director just doesn't have that sort of overriding control and he has to depend upon the creative collaboration of writers, technicians, cameramen . . . everybody" (Spoto 1978, 13). While Kramer may not believe in the auteur theory, one wonders whether the theory might believe in him. Consciously or not, Kramer's films have consistently and courageously explored liberal and controversial themes and social issues, frequently during conservative times. This body of works includes racism and prejudice (*Home of the Brave*, *The Defiant Ones*, *Judgement at Nuremberg*, *Guess Who's Coming to Dinner*); nuclear proliferation (*On the Beach*); and environmentalism (*Bless the Beasts and Children*). Subject matter alone, however, is not sufficient evidence of an auteur. Storytelling style, the use of light and camera—these too must be taken into consideration and, as such, enable students and teachers to develop criteria to be critically applied when viewing a body of works from a single director. Which of today's current crop of directors would students nominate as auteurs? Surely Steven Spielberg's body of work, including *E.T.*, *Jurassic Park*, *Jaws*, *Close Encounters*, *Saving Private Ryan*, and *Schindler's List,* would be one obvious choice. Controversial director Oliver Stone certainly has a consistent way of re-examining the past in movies like *Platoon*, *The Doors*, *Nixon*, and *JFK*. But is he an auteur? Would Barbra Streisand make the cut for her efforts with *Prince of Tides*, *Yentl*, *The Mirror Has Two Faces*, and others? Many students will have seen *Awakenings*, *Big*, and *A League of Their Own*, but do they know that Penny Marshall directed all of them and that she used to be part of TV's *Laverne and Shirley*? Is it possible for a woman to be an auteur? Beyond the issue of gender, are there minority directors that could be auteurs? Would Spike Lee's *Get on the Bus*, *Crooklyn*, *Do the Right Thing*, and others show a consistency of theme and style?

(MID/HIGH) — Divide the class into groups and have each group select one auteur director to research. They should develop a list of films he made, the types of films he made, themes that appeared in the films, and awards and honors received by the director and the films. Each group should plan to make a brief class presentation on their findings, including showing one or two clips they think best demonstrate the director's work. After each group has presented their report, conduct a poll to see which current director(s) students think might qualify as auteur directors. Have a discussion to justify their opinions.

Some Important Academy Award-Winning Directors

Below is a partial list of directors who have won Academy Awards. You will note that Howard Hawks, Alfred Hitchcock, Fritz Lang, and Sam Peckinpah are missing from this list. Students should be made aware of this and reminded that, although George Lucas has directed some of the most successful movies in history, as of yet he has not received an Oscar for an individual picture. Many students will be familiar with the films of Lucas and Spielberg. Have them compile a list of films by each director and explore recurring themes, plots, and motifs. Can they find any similarities, for example, between *Close Encounters of the Third Kind* and *Poltergeist*? Where do *Jaws* and *The Color Purple* fit into Spielberg's body of work? Advanced students might enjoy exploring thematic links in two seemingly different Lucas movies, *American Graffiti* and *Star Wars*. One other current director, Oliver Stone, has also produced a body of work that might be studied in its entirety from an auteur perspective. His films include *Salvador*, *Platoon*, *Born on the 4th of July*, *Wall Street*, *The Doors*, and *JFK*. Can the students detect continuity in theme and style in these movies? *Caution:* Before showing one of these films, check your school district's policy on films.

Several actors have become directors and won an Academy Award for directing. Six of them are Warren Beatty, Robert Redford, Woody Allen, Clint Eastwood, Kevin Costner, and Mel Gibson.

Woody Allen (*Annie Hall*)
Warren Beatty (*Reds*)
Robert Benton (*Kramer vs. Kramer*)
Bernardo Bertolucci (*The Last Emperor*)
James L. Brooks (*Terms of Endearment*)
James Cameron (*Titanic*)
Frank Capra (*You Can't Take It with You*; *Mr. Deeds Goes to Town*; *It Happened One Night*)
Michael Cimino (*The Deer Hunter*)
Francis Ford Coppola (*The Godfather II*)
Kevin Costner (*Dances with Wolves*)
Clint Eastwood (*The Unforgiven*)
John Ford (*The Quiet Man*; *How Green Was My Valley*; *Grapes of Wrath*; *The Informer*)
Milos Forman (*Amadeus*; *One Flew over the Cuckoo's Nest*)
Mel Gibson (*Braveheart*)
George Roy Hill (*The Sting*)
Elia Kazan (*On the Waterfront*; *Gentleman's Agreement*)
David Lean (*Lawrence of Arabia*; *Bridge on the River Kwai*)
Joseph L. Mankiewicz (*Letter to 3 Wives*; *All About Eve*)
Mike Nichols (*The Graduate*)
Sydney Pollack (*Out of Africa*)

Robert Redford (*Ordinary People*)
Steven Spielberg (*Schindler's List*)
George Stevens (*Place in the Sun*; *Giant*)
Oliver Stone (*Platoon*; *Born on the 4th of July*)
Billy Wilder (*The Apartment*; *The Lost Weekend*)
William Wyler (*The Best Years of Our Lives*; *Ben Hur*;
    Mrs. Miniver)
Robert Zemeckis (*Forrest Gump*)
Fred Zinnemann (*From Here to Eternity*; *Man for All Seasons*)

The Common Elements of a Novel and Film

(ELEM/MID/HIGH) — Novels and films have several common elements, including characters, conflict/dilemma, setting, resolution, plot, and theme. Introduce each of these terms to the students. With younger students, a "three P" approach can be successful: people, place, and plot.

Characters. Have students pick their favorite film and, using the elements of a novel or film, analyze the film by its component parts. Younger students can deal with characters in broad terms as heroes and villains, whereas older students could consider aspects such as antagonist, protagonist, or anti-hero. Literary tradition and the theater have provided other staple roles that can still be found in films. These include the "everyman" character who often has the privileged position of being able to directly address the audience. Robert Bolt's *Man for All Seasons* has an interesting example of this. Many of Shakespeare's plays feature a fool or clown who, although appearing foolish, often sees more than the other characters. Spike Lee's controversial production *Do the Right Thing* (1989) provides a fascinating group of characters to consider from this perspective. (The film features strong language and some sexual situations and would be suitable only for high school seniors or for selected clips.) In addition to the central characters, students should consider the functions of Mother Sister, Mr. Mayor, Smiley, and Radio Rahine. *Caution:* Before showing a film, check your school district's policy on films.

Dilemma. The characters usually find themselves faced with a dilemma that is worked through in the unfolding of the plot or the events and action of the film. Sometimes characters are faced with dilemmas not unlike those that face average people. At other times ordinary people find themselves faced with extraordinary dilemmas. Consider the dilemmas in the films below. As an alternative, give students a list of dilemmas faced by characters in books and movies with which they should be familiar, and see if they can correctly identify each book or movie.

- A young boy finds an alien in his backyard. (*E.T.*)

- A lawyer believes he has been unjustly fired because he has AIDS and fights for his career. (*Philadelphia*)

- A small boy is forgotten by his parents when they go on vacation, and he has to singlehandedly stop burglars from breaking in. (*Home Alone*)

- A young girl suddenly finds herself and her dog transported to another world. (*The Wizard of Oz*)

- A teenage girl finds herself attracted to a strange autistic boy who thinks he can fly. (*The Boy Who Could Fly*)

- A president fights to save the United States from an alien invasion. (*Independence Day*)

- A young man buys a robot only to discover that it contains a mysterious message from a young woman asking for help. (*Star Wars*)

- A wounded soldier, crippled for life, returns home and tries to cope. (*Born on the 4th of July*)

- A farmer hears mysterious voices in his cornfield telling him, "If you build it, he will come." (*Field of Dreams*)

- An Italian pizzeria owner in a black neighborhood faces violence and hostility because he is not like them. (*Do the Right Thing*)

- A team of scientists attempt to chase and measure tornadoes. (*Twister*)

- A loner from the Australian outback finds himself in New York City, where he struggles to fit in. (*Crocodile Dundee II*)

- A boy meets two cyborgs from the future who return to Earth in the 1990s and battle for its future. (*Terminator II*)

- An inventor accidentally shrinks his children. (*Honey, I Shrunk the Kids!*)

- A young man falls in love with a beautiful girl, only to discover she's a mermaid. (*Splash*)

- A young man must choose between the honor of running for his country in the Olympic Games or observing his religious beliefs by refusing to run on a holy day. (*Chariots of Fire*)

You might also develop your own list of dilemmas based on films with which you think your students will be familiar.

Narrators and Voice-Overs

While it has been observed that "the most effective way of telling a story on the screen is to use the camera as the storyteller" (Bordwell, Staiger and Thompson 1985, 24), the voice-over narrator has been used to great advantage in the past as well as in more recent films like *The War*, *The Education of Little Tree*, *How to Make an American Quilt*, and *Last of the Dog Men*. As such, the film narrator can be connected to classic literary techniques. *Moby Dick*, for example, opens with the words "Call me Ishmael." Nick Carraway introduces himself at the beginning of *The Great Gatsby*: "In my younger and more vulnerable years, my father gave me some advice that I've been turning over in my mind ever since." *Legends of the Fall* commences with the Native American storyteller saying, "Some people hear their own inner voices with great clearness." Harrison Ford introduces himself at the start of *Presumed Innocent*: "I am a prosecutor. I am part of the business of accusing and punishing. I explore the evidence of a crime and determine who is charged." This technique can be explored to help students recognize literary devices and styles. It can also be employed to foster their own journals. Young adult novels and films can model this. One good example can be found at the beginning of S. E. Hinton's *The Outsiders*. Ponyboy's voice-over opens the film as we see his hand writing, "When I stepped out into the bright sunlight from the darkness of the movie house." Following are some other examples of voice-over narration in motion pictures.

Risky Business: "The dream is always the same. Instead of going home, I go to the neighbors. I ring, but nobody answers."

The Outsiders: "When I stepped out into the bright sunlight from the darkness of the movie house."

Member of the Wedding: "It happened that green crazy summer when Frankie was 12 years old. This was the summer when for a long time, she had not been a member."

The Piano: "The voice you hear is not my speaking voice but my missing voice. I have not spoken since I was six years old."

What's Eating Gilbert Grape?: "My brother Arnie's about to turn 18. My family's planning a big party for him."

Goodfellas: "To me, being a gangster was better than being president of the United States."

A River Runs Through It: "My father was a Presbyterian minister and a fly fisherman."

How to Make an American Quilt: "For as long as I can remember, my grandmother and her friends have been part of a quilting bee. I remember sitting under the quilting frame pretending that I was surrounded by a forest of friendly trees."

Sunset Boulevard: "Yes, this is Sunset Boulevard in Los Angeles, California. It's about 5 o'clock in the morning. That's the homicide squad."

Gilda: "To me a dollar was a dollar in any language. It was my first night in the Argentine and I didn't know much about the local citizens."

Manhattan: "Chapter 1. He adored New York City. He idolized it out of all proportion. No, make that he romanticized it out of all proportion."

Equus: "Afterwards, he says, they always embrace. The animal digs his sweaty brow into his cheek and they stand in the dark for an hour, like a necking couple."

The Valley of the Dolls: "You've got to climb Mt. Everest to reach the valley of the dolls. It's a brutal climb to reach that peak."

All About Eve: "The Sara Siddons Award for distinguished achievement in theater is perhaps unknown to you."

The Barefoot Contessa: "I suppose when you spend most of your life in our profession, you develop what could be called an occupational point of view."

Other suggested titles: *Love Story, Summer of '42, Matewan.*

And Then What Happened?:
Movies as Motivators and Story Starters

(ELEM/MID) — When writer's block sets in and students stare blankly at an empty page, motion pictures can inspire and jump-start those sluggish minds. A simple strategy for this is to take a dramatic moment from a film, show it to the class, and turn off the set just at the climactic moment. After the class has finished groaning and complaining, ask them, "And then what happened?" Their job is to complete the scene. An alternative approach is to have them write a story that ends where the clip began. The clip you show should be 5 to 10 minutes long, no more. It is better if the students are not familiar with the film; remember, you are using the images to inspire them and to stimulate their imaginations. They should not write an end they already know.

Rebel Without a Cause has a very good scene that has been successfully used this way. The clip, generally known as "the chickie run" scene, centers on two teenage males caught up in a game of chicken. The boys take their cars to a cliff over the ocean. The object of the dare is for the boys to drive rapidly to the edge of the cliff; the first one to jump out of his car is a chicken. The scene appeals to students because it has action, fast cars, young people, a peer group theme, and a sense of danger. Make sure you are thoroughly familiar with the scene before using it, so you can stop it before one of the boys goes over the cliff. Before showing the clip, you might tell the class they are going to see a story about four young people—Judy, Jim, Buzz, and Plato. Depending on the level of your class, you might also introduce them to concepts such as conflict and resolution. This same scene has very good applications in Social Studies and in any discussion about peer pressure. *Caution:* Before showing the clip, check your school district's policy on films.

Chain of Events, Sequencing, and Narrative Structure

(MID/HIGH) — Meaning in motion pictures is derived from the way we interpret the chain of events. We are conditioned from our early experiences with movies to intuitively understand that not all things are shown. If we see the hero leave his office and head for the subway, we do not, for example, have to watch his subway journey. When we next see him opening his front door, we mentally fill in the blanks and know how he got there. Sometimes, however, when a film cuts from one scene to another, there is a disruption to the continuity that leaves us wondering what has occurred between the scenes. Two highly acclaimed 1989 movies, *Driving Miss Daisy* and *Born on the 4th of July*, have moments like this. In the first film, Miss Daisy attends a banquet for Martin Luther King, Jr. The next time we see her, she is ill and has regressed into her youth, thinking she is still a teacher. It is difficult to know how much time has elapsed between the King dinner and this scene. Often this is clearly the intention; on other occasions, the disruption seems less intentional. *Born on the 4th of July* has a similar problem when Ron Kovic (Tom Cruise) arrives at the railway station and is met by his high school sweetheart. The jump from one moment in the film to this is abrupt, and consequently it is difficult to read this scene.

Because film is merely an illusion of reality, its time frame is not accurate. Dramatic conventions as well as technology enable the filmmaker to "telescope" time. In the movies, time can be compressed or expanded. Flashbacks and flash-forwards are two methods by which this occurs. Explain these two terms to students and have them come up with examples of films that employ these techniques. Some important examples are *Casualties of War, Citizen Kane, D.O.A., Double Indemnity, Home of the Brave, Lost Weekend, Mildred Pierce, Once upon a Time in America, The Joy Luck Club*, and *Sunset Boulevard*.

In the space of about two hours, a film can deal with a day in the life of one character, a character's entire life, or the lives of several generations. *The Breakfast Club* takes place on one day when a group of high school students find themselves in detention on a Saturday. *Ferris Bueller's Day Off* takes place in one 24-hour period, chronicling the adventures of a high school student who cuts class. *Same Time Next Year, The Color Purple, Gandhi, Forrest Gump*, and *When Harry Met Sally* are films that occur over several decades. Divide the class into three groups and have each group create a list of films that occur (1) in a single day, (2) over a brief period of time, and (3) over several years.

What sort of problems have to be considered when dealing with films that take place in one day or over several years? Stories that operate on the "day in the life of" format tend to require either a very special individual, a special set of circumstances, or a willing suspension of disbelief. *Ferris Bueller's Day Off*, for example, is fun but hardly believable. However, an epic such as *The Color Purple* requires more time to tell the story and needs makeup, sets, and costumes that convey the different times in which the film is set. *Same Time Next Year* achieved this transition from one period to the next through music and a series of still images highlighting key events in each era.

Chain of Events and *Jurassic Park*

(MID/HIGH) — The sequencing of events in the first 20 minutes of *Jurassic Park* is particularly skillful; in fact, most of the key characters have been introduced, the death of Muldoon has been foreshadowed, and the key conflicts and dilemmas have been established. Since most students will be familiar with the film, this 20 minutes could be used to see how each major scene sets up the rest of the drama.

Scene 1. Islar Nublar, Costa Rica. The worker is killed by the unseen animal in the cage. We already know there's a problem with safety and security.

Scene 2. The insurance agent arrives to investigate the safety of the park following the death of the worker. Now we know the future of the park is at risk.

Scene 3. The excavation at the Badlands. It introduces the paleontologists, Alan Grant and Ellie Satler, but just as significantly, it includes Grant's speech on the pack nature of the animals and their resemblance to birds. Hammond, the owner of Jurassic Park, also arrives during this scene to ask for their support.

Scene 4. Dennis Nedry appears in this scene. His size, appetite, and greed set him up as the villain as he plots to deliver "viable embryos" and notes, "I've got an 18-minute window." Now, of course, if anything goes wrong with the schedule, we have been alerted to the time constraints.

Scene 5. The journey to the island and the first spotting of the dinosaurs. The scene introduces Ian Malcolm, whose belief in chaos theory will raise serious questions about the safety of the project. It also shows a shift in perspective from the person of the insurance agent, who initially says, "This is not a weekend excursion, this is a serious investigation of the stability of the island." Once he has seen the dinosaurs, however, he exclaims, "We're gonna make a fortune with this place." The scientists are awestruck, noting simply, "They're moving in herds."

Excellence in Editing

(ELEM/MID/HIGH) — As we have seen, editing represents decisions about what to leave out, what to put in, and the transitions in between. Sometimes the cuts are from one location to another, from one group of characters to another, or from one moment in time to another. At other times the editing represents rapid cutting to build pace, tension, and excitement centering on one moment. The threat of the attacking shark in *Jaws*, for example, is enhanced by the editing. In fact, *Jaws* and *Jurassic Park*, both created by Steven Spielberg, use editing in similar ways. As *Jurassic Park* opens, there is a problem with an unseen animal being handled at the loading cage. The death of the worker is never seen, his destruction simply implied by clever editing and excellent sound effects as his body, then his arm, and finally his hand disappear inside the cage. While this may sound gruesome, in fact no blood appears in the scene, and it demonstrates how sound and editing shape a film. Running the scene without the sound is another way to help students recognize the role these elements play. Examine the following list of films that have won Academy Awards for editing and have students discuss the types of films that tend to win this award. Show students one or two scenes from these films and have them discuss the editing and what impact it had on the scene. Interesting examples include the shark attack in *Jaws*, the chariot race in *Ben Hur*, the dock fight at the end of *On the Waterfront*, the showdown sequence in *High Noon*, the final attack sequence in *Star Wars*, and the opening sequence of *West Side Story*. *Caution:* Before showing one of these films, check your school district's policy on films.

(MID/HIGH) — After the class has examined a scene closely and discussed it, have them write the scene as though it were in a novel. In follow-up discussion, talk about problems involved in the process. What can the camera and editing do that words cannot?

National Velvet (1945)
The Best Years of Our Lives
    (1946)
High Noon (1952)
On the Waterfront (1954)
Around the World in 80 Days
    (1956)
Bridge on the River Kwai (1957)
Ben Hur (1959)
West Side Story (1962)
How the West Was Won (1963)
Mary Poppins (1964)
Sound of Music (1965)
In the Heat of the Night (1967)
Patton (1970)
The French Connection (1971)
Cabaret (1972)
The Sting (1973)

The Towering Inferno (1974)
Jaws (1975)
Rocky (1976)
Star Wars (1977)
The Deer Hunter (1978)
All That Jazz (1979)
Raging Bull (1980)
Raiders of the Lost Ark (1981)
Gandhi (1982)
The Right Stuff (1983)
The Killing Fields (1984)
Witness (1985)
Platoon (1986)
The Last Emperor (1987)
Born on the 4th of July (1989)
Dances with Wolves (1990)
Schindler's List (1993)
Forrest Gump (1994)

Screenwriters

Most film discussion centers on the look of the film. Attention can also be focused on the language, writing, dialogue, and speeches by selecting scenes from films that have been honored for their writing. Show clips and discuss the quality of the writing with students. The following is a partial list of writers who have won an Academy Award for Best Screenplay.

Matt Damon and Ben Affleck (*Good Will Hunting,* 1997)
Billy Bob Thornton (*Slingblade,* 1996)
Quentin Tarantino and Roger Avary (*Pulp Fiction,* 1994)
Jane Campion (*The Piano,* 1993)
Tom Schulman (*Dead Poets Society,* 1989)
John Patrick Shanley (*Moonstruck,* 1987)
Woody Allen (*Hannah and Her Sisters,* 1986)
William Kelley (*Witness,* 1985)
Robert Benton (*Places in the Heart,* 1984)
Horton Foote (*Tender Mercies,* 1983)
John Briley (*Gandhi,* 1982)
Colin Welland (*Chariots of Fire,* 1981)
Bo Goldman (*Melvin and Howard,* 1980)
Steve Tesich (*Breaking Away,* 1979)
Nancy Dowd and Waldo Salt (*Coming Home,* 1978)
Marshall Brickman (*Annie Hall,* 1977)
Paddy Chayefsky (*Network,* 1976)
Robert Evans (*Chinatown,* 1974)
Jeremy Larner (*The Candidate,* 1972)
Francis Ford Coppola and Edmond North (*Patton,* 1970)
William Rose (*Guess Who's Coming to Dinner,* 1967)
James Webb (*How the West Was Won,* 1963)
William Inge (*Splendor in the Grass,* 1961)
Nathan Douglas and Harold Jacob Smith (*The Defiant Ones,*
    1958)
Paddy Chayefsky (*Marty,* 1955)
Budd Schulberg (*On the Waterfront,* 1954)

Billy Wilder (*Sunset Boulevard*, 1950)
Robert Sherwood (*The Best Years of Our Lives*, 1946)
Billy Wilder and Charles Brackett (*The Lost Weekend*, 1945)
Julius G. Epstein, Philip Epstein, and Howard Koch
  (*Casablanca*, 1943)
Herman Mankiewicz and Orson Wells (*Citizen Kane*, 1941)

Genre Studies

Classic American cinema, it has been said, was driven by "the dialectic between genre and auteur . . . the clash between an artist's sensibility and the classic mythic structures of the story types" (Monaco 1977, 246). Traditional film genres include the gangster film, the screwball comedy, horror films, and of course, the most American of all genres, the western. The concept of genre suggests that motion picture story types can be analyzed in identifiable groups with their own codes, characteristics, and conventions. Traditional gangster films like *The Public Enemy* and *Little Caesar*, for example, deal with what is generally referred to as "the rise and fall" of the criminal. The western, as we have noted in discussing John Ford's films, frequently addresses itself to the frontier, rugged individualism, the law, and of course, the landscape, which provides the physical and psychological terrain of the tale. But while the stories are familiar, the variations and reworking of the themes can tell us much about the times in which they were both produced and consumed. Clint Eastwood's *The Unforgiven* and Sam Peckinpah's *The Wild Bunch* are considerably different in mood and tone from *Shane* or *The Magnificent Seven*. Genre studies are certainly relevant in English and literature as they help students recognize and appreciate archetypical elements. But genre studies also go well beyond the English curriculum. Stuart Kaminsky has noted in *American Film Genres* that "the roots of genre are not solely in the literary tradition, but in the fabric of existence itself. Genre films deal just as surely and deeply with social issues, considerations of life and death, and the unknown as do art films" (1974, 5). The relationship between cinema and society that can be discovered in genre analysis is explored later in this chapter in the sections addressing history and social studies.

(ELEM/MID/HIGH) — Essentially, "genre" refers to a story type or category of story types. Introduce students to the term and give them one example, perhaps the western. The western is an easy place to begin genre studies. It is the most American of genre forms, and all students have some sense of what happens in a western.

Break the class into groups and assign each group one of the following topics: (1) typical names/people/characters, (2) typical names/places/location/setting, and (3) plot/events/incidents. Each group has to develop a descriptive list of the characters, environment, and incidents we can expect to encounter in a western. They will have some background in this area simply from having watched television. The research can, however, be supplemented with various readings listed in this chapter and a TV movies viewing guide. The groups can divide work among members so that one member might develop a list of western film titles and another might compile a list of stars or directors who are best known for westerns. Each group should make a presentation to the class, and there should be discussion and classification of the information.

The simple process of defining a western can be a thought-provoking exercise. Is it, for example, set in the American West? Is it set in the West during a particular period of time? In *Go West*, the Marx Brothers were clearly in the American West at a particular point in time; nonetheless, this comedy is not a western in the true sense of the genre. Similar problems arise with *Blazing Saddles*, which is clearly a comedy set in the West. *Black Robe* and *The Last of the Mohicans* are westerns set in the East. In terms of the iconography of the western, horses are a dominant feature. Westerns have sometimes been called "horse operas." But will your students accept technology in their westerns? *The Wild Bunch*, a classic western of the late 1960s, features automobiles, and *Butch Cassidy and the Sundance Kid* features a bicycle. Another interesting aberration is *Westworld*, which looks like a western but is actually science fiction. *Zachariah* had classic elements of the western, including black hats and white hats, but this "electronic western," with Country Joe and the Fish, is certainly not what we mean by a typical western. Finally, Sergio Leone developed an important series of westerns. Because they were Italian, they became known as "spaghetti westerns." Select a series of clips from important westerns to demonstrate the form and format of the genre. Compare the clips to the students' reports. These short categories might help in formulating research on the western and serve as a model for approaching other genres.

ELEMENTS OF WESTERNS

Characters

Doctor (sometimes alcoholic)
Newspaper editor
Sheriff/deputy
Saloonkeeper/barman
Dancehall girl (sometimes prostitute)
Female schoolteacher
Banker
Gambler
Indians
Cavalry
Scout
Preacher/missionary
Gunslinger
Hero/loner

Locations

Town
Fort
Plains
Indian village
Jail
Ranch

Plots

Showdown/shoot-out
Cattle rustling
Jail break
Cleaning up corrupt town
Gold rush
Indian attack
Journey of wagon train
Struggle between farmers and ranchers

In the Beginning

(MID/HIGH) — A useful way to approach genre studies is to select a group of films from one genre and watch the first 5 to 10 minutes of each. In the case of westerns, films such as *Johnny Guitar*, *The Wild Bunch*, and *Dances with Wolves* provide strong, contrasting openings. Students can be assigned various tasks as they watch. One group might study the landscape, environment, and setting. Another group might make notes on the music and the mood it creates. Other areas for analysis are the key characters and the way the plot begins. Using four or five clips, each about six minutes long, would occupy only one lesson. The students could write up their reports overnight and class discussions and presentations could occur the next day. Listed below are a group of westerns that provide interesting material for contrast and comparison using the opening sequences. Remember, this exercise can be used with any genre. *Caution:* Before showing one of these films, check your school district's policy on films.

1. *The Plainsman:* An interesting beginning. The titles will look familiar to anyone who has seen *Star Wars*. The prologue is important and demonstrates the use of dramatic license, compressing characters and events to suit the dramatic format. Clip can be stopped after the Lincoln assassination.

2. *Stagecoach:* Often regarded as the quintessential western. It has John Ford's familiar milieu of Monument Valley and a cast of characters that defined the human elements of a western. Clip can be stopped when Doc and Dallas board the coach.

3. *She Wore a Yellow Ribbon:* One of the classic cavalry films. The opening establishes the characters, conflict, and tone. Clip can be stopped when John Wayne says, "Six more days and I retire."

4. *The Searchers:* The arrival of the hero and the landscape are classic elements of this western. Stop clip after the supper sequence.

5. *Soldier Blue:* A very interesting contrast, particularly in terms of the music, prologue, and treatment of women. Stop clip when the payroll is attacked.

For another activity, ask the class to come up with a list of other genres, such as gangster/crime, horror, science fiction, fantasy, musical, war, and love story. The approach used with the western can be applied to any of these genres, with students working individually or in groups.

And They All Lived Happily Ever After

The successful resolution of the conflict usually brings closure to the story. Sometimes order is restored when the lone gunfighter or hero defeats the villain and cleans up the town or village. At other times the man gets the woman and they find true love. Sometimes, however, the conclusion is much grimmer. At the end of *Magic*, the dummy has finally destroyed its ventriloquist master and the camera provides closure as it pulls back from inside the cabin, distancing us from the victim and the frame. *Psycho* concludes with a similar cinematic technique, with Norman's crimes explained, the loose ends tied up, and two personalities merged in the image of Mother's skull superimposed over Norman's face. The camera pulls back as the car emerges from the lake and the curtain closes on our voyeurism.

Sometimes students may find that the end of a movie seems unsatisfactory. Discuss this with them. What end would they have preferred? Why do they think the director closed the film the way he or she did? More advanced students may think that the conclusion is inconsistent with the character. These issues can also be connected to classic conflict and characters in literature. The closure of *Hamlet*, for example, leaves much room for discussion, which could even be conducted in the form of a post-mortem or coroner's inquest. Whereas Shakespeare's plays often end tragically, Hollywood, particularly in the 1950s, seemed intent on providing a happy ending no matter how unrealistic or inconsistent it might be. Often that closure involved restoring the patriarchy or asserting the dominance of a male figure. *Rebel Without a Cause* closes by banishing the mother to the periphery of the frame and action as Jim reconciles with his father. Nicholas Ray did the same thing at the end of *Johnny Guitar*, which finds Vienna washed clean of her sins and literally crawling on her hands and knees to Johnny. *Mildred Pierce* closes with the male detective shedding light on the murder, and a new day as the once dominant Mildred symbolically steps into the light and returns to her former husband.

Even recent films such as *Kramer vs. Kramer* and *Ordinary People* establish closure through male bonding and banishing the female. But current films are much less likely to have a happy ending. Sure, the guy still gets the girl (*Top Gun*), but in cleaning up the world, the hero may be killed (*Terminator II*). Mature motion pictures such as *Presumed Innocent* also close with a much stronger sense of moral ambiguity and uncertainty. For the story to succeed, the end must do more than make us feel good. It must be plausible and consistent with the characters and context. Teachers can explore this element of movies to help students think about literature and their own writing.

The Fantasy Genre: A Case Study. Some of the most enduring classics of children's literature are fantasies. *Peter Pan*, *The Wizard of Oz*, *Alice in Wonderland*, and *Charlotte's Web* are just a few examples. Picture books by Chris Van Allsburgh and novels by Susan Cooper, Russell Hoban, Natalie Babbitt, and Lloyd Alexander, to name just a few, provide current examples of the fantasy genre in children's literature. These books stimulate children's imagination and can be used to develop analytical skills as students consider the elements of the genre or compare and contrast film and book versions of the same story. The most basic rule of thumb in a fantasy is to expect the unexpected. The everyday laws of nature do not apply. Everyday worlds are replaced by encounters with strange environments. Dorothy visits Oz, Peter Pan and the Darlings go to Never-Never Land, and Alice falls down a rabbit hole and winds up in Wonderland. Many recent movies give children the opportunity to follow heroes and heroines on quests to strange lands, where they encounter exotic creatures, magical spells, and the trials and tests that confront such travelers. *Labyrinth* and *Legend* are two good examples. One of the most enjoyable modern film fantasies is *The Neverending Story* (1984).

The film opens in the modern world where the central character, 10-year-old Bastian, feels alone and frightened. His mother has died. He is afraid of the school bullies who beat him up, and his father does not understand him. The boy is troubled at school and bothered by dreams about his mother. When he tries to confide in his father, he is told, "We each have responsibilities and we can't let Mom's death become an excuse for not getting the old job done . . . you're old enough to get your head out of the

clouds and start keeping both feet on the ground." When Bastian leaves for school, both feet are rather quickly off the ground as the bullies pursue him and throw him in a dumpster.

These two incidents at the start of the film clearly create a sense of Bastian's alienation at school and at home. Before moving into the fantasy, both episodes should be explored with students so they understand the boy's circumstances. His only real joy in life comes from reading. In a mysterious bookstore, he excitedly tells the equally mysterious owner all the titles he has read. This scene also provides an opportunity to talk to children about the value of reading. The bookstore owner initially doesn't even want to talk to Bastian. Because he's a modern child, the bookstore owner is sure Bastian is not interested in books: "The video arcade is down the street. Here we just sell small rectangular objects called books and they require a little effort on your part." The book with which Bastian leaves the store is the beginning of his journey as he enters the land of Fantasia and shares the quest of Atreyu. *Caution:* Before showing the film, check your school district's policy on films.

The following questions and activities are designed to help teachers explore part or all of the film with students.

1. The initial fantasy sequences introduce us to a common element of the genre in the form of the fantastic creatures: the Rock Eater, the Racing Snail, and the Night Hob riding the giant bat. Have students make a list of the characters. Others are seen shortly as the adventurers arrive at the Ivory Tower. Compare these exotic characters to those found in the cantina sequence of *Star Wars*. Ask students to compare and contrast the Emerald City with the Ivory Tower.

2. At the Ivory Tower we learn the dilemma facing the kingdom of Fantasia. What is it? How can Atreyu help Fantasia and how do the people at court initially react to him? What is the primary quest he is given and what conditions are established?

3. Another key element of the fantasy genre is fantastic lands, places, and environments. In this movie some are just referred to, and others, such as the Swamp of Sadness, are featured. Make sure students keep a list of places, such as the Silver Mountains, the Desert of Shattered Hopes, and the Sea of Possibilities.

4. Atreyu's quest actually takes him on a series of secondary missions and trials. In one adventure, he has to find the Morla. Why? In what way is the Morla like Yoda in *Star Wars*? How is he different? Another mission sends Atreyu to the southern oracle. Why does he go there and what tests does he have to endure? Ultimately, Atreyu must find a new name for the empress. How does this involve Bastian?

5. *The Neverending Story* features a rich cast of heroes and villains. Students should make a list of each group and describe the characteristics of each individual. Villains would include the Nothing and Smork, and some students may even put the bullies in this group. The heroic characters would include Atrax the pony, Falkor the flying luckdragon, the empress, Urgle the gnome, and her husband, the scientist Engywook. Some of these characters are more helpful than heroic. Use this distinction to have students explore each character's role in the story.

6. In *Star Wars* the great evil is the Empire and the dark forces of Lord Darth Vader. In this story the evil is the Nothing. Is the Nothing a character or a presence and force? *Star Wars* referred constantly to the power of the Force. In this film such a force is also implied. Just as Luke Skywalker must blind himself with the helmet and go inside himself to master the Force, Bastian must conquer his own fears. Those fears actually feed the force. We are told that Fantasia is dying "because people have begun to lose their hopes and forget their dreams." The film takes on an almost political tone with the statement "People who have no hopes are easy to control, and whoever has the control has the power." This concept could be explored with more advanced students.

7. Throughout the film, action constantly shifts from the world of Fantasia to Bastian's hideout at school where he reads books. A series of incidents begins to suggest that he is part of the world of the story and that its characters are aware of his presence. What incidents begin to suggest this? In what way can we say that Bastian goes on a quest, as well as Atreyu?

8. If Luke Skywalker learns the power of the Force and Dorothy learns there's no place like home, what does Bastian learn about life? In what way is his growth from his journey similar to the knowledge gained by the Scarecrow, the Cowardly Lion, and the Tin Man?

A Selection of Key Films of Various Genres

Westerns

The Plainsman (1936)
Stagecoach (1939)
My Darling Clementine (1946)
She Wore a Yellow Ribbon (1949)
The Gunfighter (1950)
Broken Arrow (1950)
High Noon (1952)
Shane (1953)
Johnny Guitar (1954)
The Searchers (1956)
Rio Bravo (1959)
The Magnificent Seven (1960)
How the West Was Won (1962)
Cheyenne Autumn (1964)
Hombre (1967)
The Good, the Bad and the Ugly (1967)
Butch Cassidy and the Sundance Kid (1969)
The Wild Bunch (1969)
Once upon a Time in the West (1969)
True Grit (1969)
Little Big Man (1970)
The Missouri Breaks (1970)
Soldier Blue (1970)
A Man Called Horse (1971)
McCabe and Mrs. Miller (1971)
The Cowboys (1971)
Pat Garrett and Billy the Kid (1973)
The Outlaw Josey Wales (1976)
The Shootist (1976)
Windwalker (1980)
Heaven's Gate (1980)
Silverado (1985)
Young Guns (1988)
Dances with Wolves (1990)
The Unforgiven (1992)
Geronimo: An American Legend, (1993)
Legends of the Fall (1994)

Science Fiction

The Day the Earth Stood Still (1951)
The Thing (1951, 1982)
War of the Worlds (1953)
Them (1954)
Tarantula (1955)
1984 (1956, 1984)
Forbidden Planet (1956)
The Fly (1958, 1986)
The Time Machine (1960)

Fantastic Voyage (1966)
2001: A Space Odyssey (1968)
Silent Running (1971)
A Clockwork Orange (1971)
Soylent Green (1973)
Zardoz (1974)
Rollerball (1975)
Man Who Fell to Earth (1976)
Logan's Run (1976)
Star Wars (1977)
Close Encounters of the Third Kind (1977)
Alien (1979)
Black Hole (1979)
E.T. (1982)
Tron (1982)
Dune (1984)
Starman (1984)
Running Man (1987)
Total Recall (1990)
Terminator II (1991)
Jurassic Park (1993)
Stargate (1994)
Demolition Man (1994)
Independence Day (1996)
Contact (1997)
Men in Black (1997)
Armageddon (1998)

Fantasy

The Wizard of Oz (1939)
Thief of Baghdad (1940)
Cabin in the Sky (1943)
The Secret Life of Walter Mitty (1947)
5000 Fingers of Dr. T. (1953)
20,000 Leagues Under the Sea (1954)
Seven Faces of Dr. Lao (1964)
Willy Wonka and the Chocolate Factory (1971)
Bedknobs and Broomsticks (1971)
The Little Prince (1974)
Lord of the Rings (1978)
Watership Down (1978)
Heaven Can Wait (1978)
Dragonslayer (1981)
Excalibur (1981)
The Neverending Story (1984)
Legend (1985)
Cocoon (1985)
Labyrinth (1986)
Willow (1988)
Big (1988)
Field of Dreams (1989)
The Santa Clause (1994)

The Mask (1994)
Hocus Pocus (1994)
The Secret of Roan Inish (1995)

Horror
Dracula (1931)
Frankenstein (1931)
Dr. Jekyll and Mr. Hyde (1932, 1941)
King Kong (1933)
The Wolfman (1941)
Cat People (1942, 1982)
Invasion of the Body Snatchers (1956, 1978)
Psycho (1960)
Whatever Happened to Baby Jane? (1962)
Rosemary's Baby (1968)
Night of the Living Dead (1968)
Play Misty for Me (1971)
The Exorcist (1973)
Carrie (1976)
Halloween (1978)
The Shining (1981)
The Howling (1981)
An American Werewolf in London (1981)
Nightmare on Elm St. (1984)
Silence of the Lambs (1991)
Wolf (1994)
Interview with the Vampire (1994)

Mary Shelley's Frankenstein (1995)

Gangster/Crime
The Public Enemy (1930)
Little Caesar (1930)
Scarface (1932, 1983)
Dead End (1937)
Angels with Dirty Faces (1938)
The Roaring Twenties (1939)
Dillinger (1945)
They Live by Night (1947)
White Heat (1949)
Joe Macbeth (1955)
Al Capone (1959)
The Rise and Fall of Legs Diamond (1960)
Pretty Boy Floyd (1960)
Bonnie and Clyde (1967)
The St. Valentine's Day Massacre (1967)
The Godfather (1972)
Once upon a Time in America (1984)
The Untouchables (1987)
Miller's Crossing (1990)
Goodfellas (1990)
Mobsters (1991)
Bugsy (1991)
Billy Bathgate (1991)
Casino (1995)
L.A. Confidential (1997)

FILM AND ART EDUCATION

In *Lust for Life*, the Academy Award-winning movie about Vincent Van Gogh, the Dutch painter engages in an angry confrontation with Gauguin. All he sees when he looks at his art, Gauguin tells him, is someone who paints too fast. "You look too fast," Vincent yells back. Understanding and appreciating the art of motion pictures require that we learn how to look. Michael Chapman, cinematographer of *Taxi Driver* and *Raging Bull*, believes that "the cinematographer's job is to tell people where to look" (*Visions of Light* 1992). But while the camera and the director may tell us *where* to look, we do not necessarily know *how* to look.

The idea that we need to be taught to "read" film or television seems strange and even absurd to many in a society that frequently asserts "Seeing is believing" or "What you see is what you get." Others find the whole idea elitist, believing that meaning in movies is manifestly obvious. Still others draw distinctions between fine arts and the excesses of mass media and pop culture. Such a distinction has been challenged by Angella Dalle Vacche in *Cinema and Painting: How Art Is Used in Film.* "While some may feel that film does not belong to the history of art, the fact is that filmmakers often use painting to shape or enrich the meaning of their work" (1996, 1). She compares sets from Vincent Minnelli's *An American in Paris* to paintings by Renoir and Rousseau and describes Gene Kelly dancing through Lautrec drawings. Murnau's *Nosferatu*, an example of German expressionist cinema, is said to "thrive on . . . the legacy of German Romantic landscape painting" (6). Anyone who has seen *Spellbound* by Alfred Hitchcock is well aware of the contributions of Salvador Dali in the

❖Film as art: *Lust for Life* brought Van Gogh to life and won an Oscar for Anthony Quinn's portrayal of Paul Gauguin. *Lust for Life* copyright © 1956 Turner Entertainment Co. Used with permission.

surrealistic dream sequence sets that he designed. *The Wizard of Oz*, one of the best known and most loved American films, also has connections to the world of fine art. The twister sequence and the set design for the yellow brick road are both reminiscent of American regionalist art, including the paintings of Grant Wood. Of today's contemporary directors, perhaps no one is more keenly aware of the relationship between cinema and visual arts than Peter Greenaway. While some may find his movies excessive, indulgent, and even offensive, many of them contain outstanding composition and design, not to mention period re-creations. Of particular interest here is the 17th-century world of *The Draughtsman's Contract* and *Prospero's Books,* the latter based on Shakespeare's *The Tempest.*

But appreciating the art of film involves more than simply recognizing art in film. Seeing a relationship between fine art and the movies is part of the process, but this must be expanded to include an understanding of the language of film and the way elements such as design, lighting, composition, and point of view create meaning. While English teachers may use movies to explore narrative, archetypes, and literary codes and conventions, art educators can use movies to explore the relationship between story and style, form and content.

MISE-EN-SCENE: Reading Design and Composition in Movies

Taken from French film theory, the concept of mise-en-scene (placement within a frame) offers us a way to conceptualize the visual composition of a movie and the contribution the image makes to the story and our understanding of elements such as character, motivation, plot, and setting. Louis Giannetti says, "Mise-en-scene in the movies resembles the art of painting in that an image of formal patterns and shapes is presented on a flat surface and enclosed within a frame" (1976, 149).

Types of Shots

Types of shots include the following:

1. *Establishing or long shot:* Usually used to establish the primary location at the beginning of a film or to designate a change to a major new location. *Psycho, The Lost Weekend,* and *West Side Story* open with excellent examples of establishing shots.

2. *Close-up shot:* The character or object fills most of the frame. When used with props, symbolism is almost always implied. *Ordinary People*, for example, uses close-ups of the napkins and napkin rings to symbolize Beth's need for order, control, and neatness.

3. *Medium shot:* Sometimes designated as medium close-up (MCU). If a close-up shows a character's head and shoulders, the MCU would show a waist-up view.

4. *Extreme close-up:* Camera comes in very tight, concentrating on a hand, eye, etc. The end of the shower sequence in *Psycho*, for example, fills the screen with just one eye of the murdered woman.

5. *Dolly shot:* Camera is mounted on a dolly and moving.

6. *Tracking shot:* The movements of the character are tracked, or followed, by a moving camera.

7. *Pan shot:* Abbreviated term for "panoramic." The camera swivels in a horizontal plane to scan the scene.

(ELEM/MID/HIGH) — Introduce students to the above key terms and ask them for a definition and a purpose or context in which each would be used. Look at brief clips from motion pictures to get some examples of these shots. Lavish musicals are often good sources for dolly, pan, and tracking shots.

Following are two brief plot descriptions. Give these outlines to students and have them indicate what type of shot they would use for each action. Discuss the reasons for the decisions they make.

Scene 1

A platoon of soldiers marches across
   the desert.
Some of the soldiers worry about the
   mission they are on.
The enemy opens fire.
One of the platoon is hit.
His friend is shocked.

Scene 2

The story opens in San Francisco.
Three young women walk along a
   crowded street.
They stop for a traffic light.
The light turns green.
As they cross the street, a car lunges at
   them.
One woman is hit.
The car speeds away.
The two friends offer assistance.

The Four P's

1. *Point of View (POV)*. "A frame
   is not a neutral border; it produces
   a certain vantage point onto the
   material within the image . . . the
   frame is important because it actively defines the image for us"
   (Bordwell and Thompson 1979,
   109). POV generally refers to camera position/perspective approxi-
   mating the position of a character,
   so the audience frequently sees the
   action from the POV of one character or another. POV can also be
   understood as the perspective the
   camera and director give us on a
   character, location, or object. Two
   common camera angles are the low
   angle (tilt-up) and the high angle
   (tilt-down). Neither perspective is
   neutral, and both carry and activate
   cultural codes and conventions that
   shape how an audience constructs
   meaning. The high-angle tilt-down
   usually implies weakness, vulnerability, and loss of power. The expression "looking down on
   someone" actually reinforces this.
   The first sequence in the bar in
   Nicholas Ray's *Johnny Guitar* provides an outstanding example of
   POV in both the camera angle and
   the dialogue. ("Look at her up there
   staring down on us.") The low angle
   or tilt-up, on the other hand, usually conveys power and authority.
   Those who are shot from a low angle
   are typically those who are in control. Once again the cultural convention "looking up to someone"
   connects to this visual technique,

❖**Low-angle perspective empowers the
threatening figure of the devil in the
fantasy *Legend*. Copyright © 1998 Gail E.
Haley.**

which has its origins in the Renais-
sance and in the stained glass windows of cathedrals, which forced
our eyes upward to a higher
authority. Typically the tilt-up has
been assigned to men, but there
are examples of female characters,
especially femme fatales, who are
seen this way. Billy Wilder's *Double Indemnity* clearly introduces
Barbara Stanwyck this way. "Neff
is in the foyer looking up at the
white goddess; when Phyllis looks
down at him, his diminished size
suits the position of a thrall in the
goddess' presence" (Dick 1980,
480). *Superman II* features a good
example of both high and low angle in the sequence when Clark
drops his glasses in the fire and
Lois discovers he is Superman.

Teachers should be aware that students will go through various stages as they learn this visual vocabulary. Initially they will "spot the shot." They will then gradually develop the skills to interpret the shot and understand why the director selected that POV. This means they must put the shot within the wider context of the story. *Mr. Holland's Opus*, for example, opens with a high-angle shot looking down on Holland. Under normal circumstances this might suggest weakness and vulnerability. However, it is used in this case to allow us to see the piano keys. Holland's body language as he conducts and the energy and spirit of the music make it quite clear that he is anything but weak and vulnerable. The tilt-down on a piano player is actually a cinematic convention, a composition of the frame necessary to show the action, as is evident by looking at sequences from *The Competition, Shine,* and *The Piano.* The victim/villain or power/vulnerability convention associated most of the time with high- and low-angle shots is readily demonstrated in hugely popular films such as *Mission Impossible.* When the Tom Cruise character is interrogated by Max (Vanessa Redgrave), she is given the tilt-up or low angle. When he realizes he has been set up by his own bosses, he runs to a building and the camera pulls back, looking down on him at the bottom of a spiral staircase.

Elia Kazan's *On the Waterfront* carefully used POV during pivotal scenes. The recipient of an Oscar for Best Picture, the film offers many opportunities to explore mise-en-scene. In a scene rife with religious symbolism (shadows of crosses, stoning), the priest visits the waterfront to offer last rites to a murdered worker. "Boys, this is my church," he declares. As he stands over the body

❖ The low angle typically empowers men, but in *Mission Impossible*, Vanessa Redgrave is privileged by this perspective as she interrogates Tom Cruise. The fact that she is called Max reinforces the gender bias of this POV. Copyright © 1998 Gail E. Haley.

❖ High-angle shots typically belittle those seen this way, making them weak and vulnerable. *Mission Impossible* locates Tom Cruise in the vortex of the spiral staircase as the mystery threatens to engulf him. Copyright © 1998 Gail E. Haley.

deep in the loading hole (hell), the POV looks down on him and up at the union bosses who dominate the waterfront. Undeterred by the insults and objects thrown at him, the priest denounces the bosses, rallies the workers, and, in the final shot, is actually elevated head and shoulders above the bosses as he and the slain worker are lifted up in an image of resurrection.

Point of view, however, involves much more than a simple choice of high or low angles. In *Jaws*, especially during the beach sequences, Spielberg frequently positions his camera at water level, making the impending or implied attack even more threatening. Fight sequences in *Raging Bull* employ subjective camera work to establish the boxer's perspective. "The camera movement and the editing during the fight scenes are like Jake's style of fighting—all punches and stops . . . the cinematography captures Jake's fighting style with quick editing, camera movement, and close-ups" (Connelly 1993, 76).

If camera work and mise-en-scene can make us identify with the character of the boxer, it is evident that the look and composition of a film are about much more than aesthetics. It is equally important that we come to recognize the social significance and ideology implicit in the way film constructs our perspective and positions our point of view. In terms of the western, Hilger suggests that "the distance and angle from which audiences see characters and settings are basic techniques filmmakers use to shape responses" (1995, 10). In a fascinating and detailed study of the relationship between the form and content of the western genre, Hilger argues that the typical white characters are privileged with more close-ups while we are distanced from the savage and brutal Indians. An equally brilliant essay on the relationship between film form and content can be found in Robert Burgoyne's discussion of *JFK*. While much debate centered on the relationship between fact and fiction in Stone's controversial movie, Burgoyne sees an aesthetic at work. Exploring what he calls "broken narratives," "the profusion of stylistic forms," and "cubistically competing perspectives," Burgoyne describes Stone as using "anti-narrative techniques in order to express both the loss and the refiguration of a unified national identity" (1996, 115-19).

2. *Posture.* Posture or body language are key clues in reading a character's mood and reaction. No one can watch James Dean in *East of Eden* or *Rebel Without a Cause* without becoming aware of how the actor used his body to convey his inner conflict. Also watch Conrad's rapidly changing body language in the family photograph sequence of *Ordinary People*.

3. *Props.* Analyzing the function of props in a frame or scene promotes awareness of metaphor and symbolism. On the most basic level, this can be handled through the western convention of white hats for good guys and black hats for bad guys. On a more sophisticated level, it can be used to consider the function of the baseball bat in *The Natural*, the stuffed birds in *Psycho*, the dinner plate in *Ordinary People*, and the milk bottle in *Rebel Without a Cause*. One major thing to notice about the use of props is that the importance of the object is usually signified by the shot the director uses, typically a close-up. When Robert Redford closes in on the napkin rings in the drawer (*Ordinary People*), we know he is trying to tell us something about Beth, in the same way he does with the broken plate. Immediately before Nicholas Ray begins the classic confrontation between James Dean and his parents (*Rebel Without a Cause*), his close-up occupies the entire screen with a shot of Judy's compact. When everyday objects are shown from such a privileged perspective, it serves as a visual exclamation mark, and the director is saying,

"This is important; I am telling you something with this object." By presenting the object to us in this way, the director indicates that it will play some pivotal role in the story or that it has symbolic significance. Composing the frame in this way represents the use of "an isolating device, a technique that permits the director to confer special attention on what might otherwise be overlooked in wider context" (Giannetti, 1976, 53).

4. ***Position.*** Position refers to placement within the frame and is usually considered in conjunction with other elements. Placing a character at the top of the stairs, for example, usually involves a tilt-up and promotes a different response than placing the character at the bottom of the stairs. Excellent symbolic use of staircases can be seen in *Johnny Guitar* and *Rebel Without a Cause*.

Sample Scenes for Teaching Mise-en-Scene

Using the two scenes described from *Rebel Without a Cause* and *Ordinary People*, teachers can help students first recognize and then read POV, props, posture, and position. Once students are familiar with these elements, they will begin to recognize them naturally in their own recreational viewing.

Ordinary People (1980)

(MID/HIGH) —This film belongs in every high school media center. It won multiple Academy Awards, including Best Picture and Best Director. The novel is popular in English classes, and the subject matter of adolescent suicide and dysfunctional families has applications in the areas of health and counseling. Many sequences lend themselves to analysis of the mise-en-scene. The one selected here centers on taking a family photograph. Fast-forward the videotape until you find this sequence. Posture, position, and props are highly active in this scene. Mention this to the students before you show the clip. After they have seen it, ask them questions based on the guidelines set out below. Some visual variations might be useful here because many students may be inhibited about answering verbally. Some students might be more comfortable doing stick figure drawings in their books or on the board to show the positions of key characters at different points in the scene. You might also select several students to play key characters and ask them to re-enact the postures and positions of the characters. Role play is very useful in understanding body language

and how movies use it. *Caution:* Before showing this clip, check your school district's policy on films.

- The scene opens with Beth, the grandfather, Conrad the teenage son, and the husband/father (Calvin) arranged left to right across the frame while the grandmother takes a photograph.

- The next picture to be taken is of "the young people," so the grandfather joins his wife. The characters are now arranged left to right: Beth, Calvin, and Conrad.

- Conrad's grandfather tells him to change places, "over in the middle between your mother and your father." There is a progressive change in the boy's body language. Watch his hands and arms.

- In the photo when Calvin kisses his wife, watch his posture. "Come on, you can do better than that."

- Calvin wants to take a photograph of Conrad and Beth. Look at the expression and posture of mother and son as Calvin tries to get the picture he wants.

- A very angry Conrad screams, "Give her the goddamn camera!" and walks away. What does he do and how do his posture, his position, and the point of view convey his feelings?

- What is Beth's reaction to the incident? What two props does she use as a form of displacement activity?

- Watch the camera angle and the position of the camera in the kitchen sequence with Beth and her mother.

- The motif of the broken home is repeated several times in the film. What is ironic about Beth's comment, "You know, I think this can be saved. It's a nice clean break"? Stop film here.

❖ "It's a nice, clean break; I think it can be saved." Robert Redford employs props symbolically throughout *Ordinary People*. Copyright © 1998 Gail E. Haley.

Rebel Without a Cause (1955)

(MID/HIGH) —Sociologically this is one of the most important films of its decade because it reveals the fragmentation of the family in the post-World War II United States and shifts juvenile delinquency to white middle-class families. The entire film lends itself to mise-en-scene analysis, from the very beginning, when Jim (James Dean) is seen in a fetal position playing with a toy monkey, until the conclusion, when his father finally stands up for him and his mother is banished to the edge of the frame.

This is a complex but exciting scene to analyze and should be attempted only after students have had practice exercises with some of the shorter scenes recommended in this chapter. Fast-forward the video after the car crash. The scene begins just as an extreme close-up of Judy's compact fades out. The scene commences with Jim arriving home and getting a drink. *Caution:* Before showing this clip, check your school district's policy on films.

- The milk bottle is a major prop. Note how the director centers attention on it and how Jim uses it to soothe and cool himself. The bottle and its color invoke both purity and a maternal bond.

❖James Dean soothes himself with the milk bottle, one of many props Nicholas Ray employs to advance our understanding of his characters in *Rebel Without a Cause*. Copyright © 1998 Gail E. Haley.

- Jim enters the living room and curls up on the couch in a fetal position. The posture recalls the opening of the film and further invokes the mother/milk metaphor.

- In a startling POV shot, Jim's mother comes down the stairs and enters the living room. The shot, of course, is subjective, reflecting the boy's perspective, but it also symbolizes the sexual imbalance in the family because Mother wears the pants in the Stark household. In Jim's world, everything is upside down because his father offers no real male role model. He is henpecked and even wears an apron.

- Jim confesses that he was in an accident in which a boy was killed. Two pivotal elements are active in this sequence. The stairway clearly functions as a power base, and the shifting positions and postures of the mother, father, and son on the stairway reinforce this function. Sketching the movement of the characters at key points helps us understand the symbolic role of these elements. When the son confesses his behavior to his parents, he sits at the bottom of the stairs and his parents stand. When he begins to assume moral responsibility, he rises and is now head and shoulders above his parents, who want him to cover up the crime. At times in this sequence, the staircase railing seems to suggest a prison, and the father even seems to resemble a prisoner in the dock of a court. At times Jim turns his back on his parents, and a window further fragments the frame. When the mother moves above Jim on the stairs, the power structure of the family is evoked, with the son clearly trapped between his mother and his weak father. Unable to assert himself, the father sits at the bottom of the stairs. The scene now features a series of tilt-ups and tilt-downs that empower the mother and disempower the father.

- There is constant interaction between the visual devices and the verbal content. The son finally pleads, "Dad, stand up for me," and drags his father from the chair.

- When the boy finally runs from the house in frustration, he kicks in a portrait of his grandmother, symbolically turning his anger on the matriarchal structure of the family.

❖ **Jim's changing posture, and his position on the stairs, display a dynamic and complex interaction of mise-en-scene and narrative in** *Rebel Without a Cause.* **Copyright ©** **1998 Gail E. Haley.**

- Finally, Jim's clothes in this sequence symbolize his all-American nature. He wears a white T-shirt, blue jeans, and a red jacket. The red jacket ties in with his name (Stark) and symbolizes that he wears his heart on his sleeve. This is in marked contrast to the tough, unfeeling gang members in their black leather jackets. In an earlier scene, it is a black leather jacket that traps one teenager in a car and leads to his death. After James Dean's death, shortly before the release of this film, the red nylon jacket became an icon to thousands of American kids who identified with Dean's "rebel without a cause."

(ELEM) — Teachers wishing to use some of these concepts with younger children might select films with less serious themes. *Honey, I Shrunk the Kids!* has a very good use of perspective or point of view, as does *Superman II*.

MOTIFS

Motifs can generally be conceptualized as a series of recurring visual and verbal references repeated throughout a film as a means of stressing a particular theme or message. In *Psycho*, for example, Hitchcock plays with references to voyeurism. He uses mirrors, mirrored sunglasses, Norman's spying eyes, peepholes, and the dead cold eyes of the stuffed birds as part of this. The birds also represent a motif. Norman has stuffed them, as he did his mother. Janet Leigh's character is named Crane, and in the milk and sandwich sequence we are told that she "eats like a bird." *Nick of Time*, a thriller that deals with a political assassination, opens with a series of images of guns, watches, and clocks and repeats these throughout the film, much of which is shot in real time.

David Lean's *Dr. Zhivago* uses vision as a central theme. "A complex of shots featuring windows and other transparent, translucent and semi-opaque surfaces structure the film. This recurrent motif implies most obviously an inside/outside dichotomy" (Anderegg 1984, 126). The warmth, comfort, and security of inside life are contrasted with the cold, threatening, and conflict-ridden world outside. In *The Graduate*, Mike Nichols uses a transportation motif, bookending the opening and the end of the film. Benjamin arrives in Los Angeles by plane and is carried coldly and mechanically through the airport's moving pathway. The film closes with Benjamin and Elaine boarding a bus with no idea where they are going or what lies ahead. A similar device is evident in *Midnight Cowboy,* with Joe Buck's bus trip from Bible Belt to Broadway at the start and the final trip to Florida with Ratso at the end.

Forrest Gump uses a complex series of visual, verbal, and musical motifs related to birds and flying, particularly for the character of Jenny. The film starts and ends with an image of a bird feather blowing in the wind, a song she will later sing. At one point Jenny talks about trying to turn into a bird to fly away from her troubles. Later, in a suicidal state, she asks Forrest, "Do you think I could fly off this bridge?" Jenny moves to California and becomes trapped in a self-destructive world of drugs and abusive relationships. We see her step to the edge of her window about to jump as the soundtrack plays Lynyrd Skynrd's "Freebird." When Jenny dies and Forrest stands by her grave, he wonders if everyone has a destiny or if people are "just floating around accidentally, like on a breeze." On a more complex level, Jenny can be read as the incarnation of the 1960s, not simply as a flower child but as a deflowered child spoiled by her times and susceptible to every self-indulgent whim and hedonistic fad of the era. A victim of the SDS (Students for a Democratic Society) and LSD, her death signals a rejection of the 1960s as surely as Lieutenant Dan's marriage to an Asian represents a reconciliation with Vietnam.

❖**The motif of flight, signaled by the feather, is used as a bookend at both the opening and the end of *Forrest Gump*. Copyright © 1998 Gail E. Haley.**

(MID/HIGH) — Select two or three scenes from a movie to demonstrate motif—the start and end of *The Graduate*, for example. Ask the students to discuss what they have in common. Introduce them to the concept of motif. Continue to link form and style to story content by exploring graphics devices used during movie titles and credits. Two good examples are the watches and gun already described in *Nick of Time* and the windswept title letters used in *Twister*. *Caution:* Before showing any of the films, check your school district's policy on the films.

❖*The Graduate* also bookends with a motif of transportation, opening the film as the plane arrives in Los Angeles and closing as Benjamin and Elaine board the bus. Copyright © 1998 Gail E. Haley.

The Question of Color

The role color plays in the meaning of a movie is one of the most obvious ways of beginning to introduce students to the language of visuals. Cultural codes and conventions have traditionally drawn on color to represent moods and character. Most students, for example, are capable of explaining the symbolic significance of saying someone is "yellow" or rather "green." They intuitively know what it means when someone tells them, "I feel blue today," and they all recognize and respond to the role color plays in controlling traffic, whether they are drivers or pedestrians. Moving this awareness from their own day-to-day life into the realm of moviemaking can be a relatively easy step. Most students will be familiar with the *Wizard of Oz*, and it does not require too much discussion to get them to explain that the black and white sequences of the film represent the reality of Kansas while the color sequences are used for Dorothy's journey over the rainbow to Oz. Older students can be challenged by asking them why Steven Spielberg made the decision to shoot *Schindler's List* in black and white instead of color.

For Spielberg, the consummate entertainer and special-effects wizard, color would not do. Black and white would validate and authenticate the subject matter while, at the same time, recalling the black-and-white photographs and newsreel images through which most of us first became acquainted with the Holocaust. For the director it meant a radical departure from his successful mode of moviemaking. "My problem is, I have too much command of visual language. I don't want a style similar to anything I'd done before. I tried to pull the events closer to the audience by reducing the artifice. For the first time, I felt free to abandon form, to tell the story of a life" (Sanello 1996, 224).

Another life that came to the screen in glorious black and white was that of boxer Jake La Motta in Martin Scorcese's *Raging Bull*. A far cry from the bicentennial sentimentality of *Rocky*, the film presents a portrait of a protagonist who is less than heroic. Shot by Michael Chapman, the look of the film is intimately related to both its meaning and feeling. The use of black and white recalls film noir and the 1940s era when the story was set and film noir was in style. Scorcese used a high-contrast film stock to make this movie, and he used the blacks, whites, and grays for specific purposes. "It also helps create a documentary feel and complements the objective narrative style" (Connelly 1993, 74).

Chapman's photography recalls the black-and-white boxing photographs of *Life* magazine in the same way that Gregg Toland's work in *The Grapes of Wrath* resembles the WPA (Works Progress Administration) depression photographs of Walker Evans, Dorothea Lange, and others. In so doing, these cinematographers establish the relationship between moviemaking and other visual arts.

The choice to use color or black and white can become a major focus for studying the work of individual directors. Roman Polanski, for example, used black and white for *Repulsion* but color for *Chinatown*, which clearly had a film noir feeling and setting. Mike Nichols used color for *The Graduate* but black and white for the gritty drama *Who's Afraid of Virginia Woolf?* Stanley Kubrick used color for *A Clockwork Orange* but black and white for *Dr. Strangelove*. Elia Kazan chose color for *East of Eden* but black and white for *On the Waterfront*. Woody Allen shot *Manhattan* in black and white, but used color for *Annie Hall*. Finally, Peter Bogdanovich used color for his depression-era period piece, *Paper Moon*, while choosing black and white for *The Last Picture Show*. Clearly, these directors made design decisions about the relationship between form and style as they selected color or black and white. Sometimes the subject matter of a film is quite simply better conveyed in one form or another. The grim, real-life death-penalty dramas *I Want to Live* and *In Cold Blood*, for example, were shot in black and white, while more recently Tim Robbins addressed the same subject matter (*Dead Man Walking*) in color.

The contribution color makes to a movie and its meaning is, however, more complex than a simple decision to use either color or black and white. In the case of Spike Lee's *Malcolm X*, for example, the use of color throughout the film is associated with the evolution of the character and signifies his journey from street punk to political leader. Production designer Wynn Thomas developed the look of the film in three phases, with color signifying Malcolm's status at the time. The film opens at the time of Malcolm's youth. He is a wild, restless hustler, and the zoot suits and infusion of color contribute to this feel. The second stage of the movie is the prison period. It is a time of rebirth for the hero, and the early color is drained from the film, replaced by combinations of gray, white, and blue. The final phase represents a period of maturity and manhood. For this part of the film Lee and Wynn used earth colors to convey Malcolm's strength and commitment. Interestingly enough, with the exception of the Islamic flag, red is absent from this section of the film until the assassination scene. *The Last Emperor* also uses color to address a character's progression. In *Visions of Light*, cinematographer Vittoria Storraro describes the use of orange to represent the royal family and forbidden city, yellow for the emperor's personal identity and affinity with the sun, and green, which is associated with the tutor and knowledge. In *Lawrence of Arabia*, costume and color are also used to indicate the hero's growing identification with the Arab cause and the gradual transformation from idealism to moral ambiguity.

(ELEM/MID/HIGH) — Select scenes from some of the movies described and present them to students to consider in terms of the director's decision to use color or black and white. The obvious one to start with is the twister sequence in *The Wizard of Oz*, followed by the shift to the color fantasy sequences.

Film Noir

(HIGH) — In the 1940s a whole style of film emerged based upon black-and-white cinematography and bleak, brooding human themes. The psychological mood of these films reflected a peculiar mixture of neurosis, psychosis, and paranoia that could not have been evoked if the films had been shot in color. Shadows dominate the films, and much of the action occurs at night. Teachers wishing to work with this sub-genre can update the style with Kenneth Branagh's 1991 hommage, *Dead Again* or appropriate scenes from *L.A. Confidential*. One episode in the Annenberg videotape series *American Cinema* is also dedicated to film noir and widely available for purchase and/or rental. Art teachers familiar with the city paintings of Reginald Marsh (*Death Avenue, Lunch*) can compare the "isolation and the brooding tension" (Hirsch 1981, 81) in these images to the unstable cities of film noir.

Key films from this style include:

The Maltese Falcon (1941)
Double Indemnity (1944)
Mildred Pierce (1945)
Scarlet Street (1945)
The Blue Dahlia (1946)
The Big Sleep (1946)
Gilda (1946)
The Postman Always Rings Twice (1946)
The Killers (1946)

Kiss of Death (1947)
Lady in the Lake (1947)
The Big Clock (1948)
Key Largo (1948)
Sorry, Wrong Number (1948)
Lady from Shanghai (1948)
The Naked City (1948)
Sunset Boulevard (1950)

Art teachers may want older students to look at some of these films to study the ways the visual elements convey the mood and tone of the film. English teachers might want to trace the literary origins of the films by looking at novels and short stories by Dashiell Hammett, Raymond Chandler, and James M. Cain.

German Expressionism

(HIGH) — Study of film noir can be connected to a study of German expressionist cinema and expressionist painting in Germany. This is a fascinating movement to study because it can be integrated into art, social studies, and history. The films emerge most strongly in the period after World War I, when Germany's defeat leaves the country in psychological and social turmoil. This period is depicted in literature by the Berlin stories of Christopher Isherwood and in motion pictures such as *Cabaret, The Damned*, and *The Serpent's Egg*.

Expressionist art represented a radical departure from the past. Lotte Eisner calls it "the apocalyptic doctrine of Expressionism" (1969, 9). She notes that as early as 1920, "the movement had tended to sweep aside all the principles which had formed the basis of art until then" (10). Expressionist art manifested itself in the look of German cinema. The sets, architecture, props, and lighting conspire to create the brooding, mystical, satanic landscapes that convey the national nightmare represented in this disturbing body of films. Art teachers can provide students with examples of these films to view or clips from several of them. In addition to drawing students' attention to chiaroscuro and other visual effects, teachers may wish to integrate history into these lessons by looking at the role of the artist in times of social, political, and economic turmoil.

Key films of the era that are now widely available include:

The Golem (1920)
The Threepenny Opera (1920)
Dr. Mabuse the Gambler (1922)
Nosferatu (1922)
The Cabinet of Caligari (1924)
Metropolis (1926)
M (1931)

Among the German directors of these films are Fritz Lang, who left Germany and settled in the United States. His German expressionist background merged into U.S. film noir in movies such as *The Big Heat*, *Ministry of Fear*, and *Scarlet Street*.

Art Deco

(HIGH) — If German expressionism says something about the nature of German society after World War I, art deco can certainly be read as a reflection of the United States at the same time. Howard Mandelbaum and Eric Myers write that "art deco was closely allied to the fantasies of wealth and elegance prevalent in America between the wars" (1985, 1). The term "encompasses everything from the ornate zigzags of the movement's infancy in the 20s through the stripped down, streamlined geometric form of 30s Moderne" (1). Hollywood's use of art deco can be seen in various ways in films of the period, and students can look at the overall effect or the specific designs of art directors such as Cedric Gibbons and Van Nest Polglase. Areas to look for include everything from the studio logo at the start of the film to furnishings, sets, and lighting. The worlds created in these films are opulent and lush. Their fantasies reverse the nightmare of expressionism. The action occurs in grand hotels, enormous ballrooms, expensive nightclubs, lavish penthouses, and oceanliners. They fuse technology and the good life. By creating such images Hollywood reinforced and promoted their presence in U.S. architecture and styles of the times. Perhaps the most obvious example is the movie palaces where the products of the "dream factory" were shown. Major buildings in New York City also emerged as part of the deco movement. Advertising, graphic art, and design also showed the strong influence of art deco.

Teachers looking for brief film clips to present the period might want to look at the extravagant sets and geometric choreography of Busby Berkeley (*Footlight Parade*, *Gold Diggers of '33*) or the elaborate sets and dance numbers in Fred Astaire and Ginger Rogers movies (*Gay Divorcee*, *Top Hat*). *Caution:* Before showing any of these films, check your school district's policy on films.

Key films of the period include:

Trouble in Paradise (1932)
Footlight Parade (1933)
Gold Diggers of '33 (1933)
The Gay Divorcee (1934)
Top Hat (1935)
Swing Time (1936)
Shall We Dance (1937)

Cinematography, Art Direction, and Costumes

Visions of Light: The Art of the Cinematographer is an invaluable teaching tool for any teacher attempting to help students appreciate the contribution the cinematographer makes to a movie. With detailed scenes from movies such as *The Godfather*, *Citizen Kane*, and *The Last Emperor* and featuring interviews with leaders in the craft, the videotape is an important addition to any library media center. While acting and directing are obviously central to the advancement of any story, the style, set, location, look, and feel of a film all create the atmosphere that make a good movie successful. Art director Leon Barasacqu has said that a "set must take into account the psychology and behavior of those intended to inhabit it" (Mandelbaum and Myers 1985, 1). How can one attempt to distinguish between the characters of a film and the environment in which they function?

Fred Astaire and Ginger Rogers are inseparable from the BWS (big white sets) and lush deco environments they dance their way through. How can one understand Charles Foster Kane (*Citizen Kane*) without exploring the physical world he constructs for himself from the excesses of the operahouse to his prison/mansion?

(ELEM/MID/HIGH) — Costumes, sets, photography, lighting, and visual effects all contribute to the look of a film. Sometimes the effects bring to life something beyond our imagination. Sometimes the sets and costumes lavishly and perhaps accurately create a bygone era. Gotham City comes to life as a brooding presence in *Batman* (1989) largely due to the art direction. Comic-book style and color were skillfully re-created in the 1990s *Dick Tracy*. The battle sequence set on the beach in *Glory* (1989) shows the power of cinematography to evoke emotion and paint a portrait of epic grandeur.

Turn-of-the-century New York is lovingly re-created in *The Age of Innocence*. Stuart England is exquisitely presented in the costumes and sets of *Restoration,* while the England of the Edwardian era is showcased in *Howard's End*.

Costumes and sets that re-create an era also bring the past to life and can be explored in film and history classes, thereby integrating the arts into these disciplines. (See "Fashions and Film" section later in this chapter.) By selecting examples from films that have won awards in these areas, teachers can draw students' attention to the role of these elements in creating the overall look of the film. This process can be facilitated if the sound is turned off when students look at the clips. Older students can analyze these compositions in depth, and younger students can be asked to describe the mood and feeling the images create. In the case of *Batman*, they should have strong reactions to Gotham City. *Caution:* Before showing any of these films, check your school district's policy on films.

Partial List of Academy Award-Winners
Cinematography

Titanic (1997)
Braveheart (1996)
Legends of the Fall (1994)
Schindler's List (1993)
Dances with Wolves (1990)
Glory (1989)
The Last Emperor (1987)
The Mission (1986)
Out of Africa (1985)
The Killing Fields (1984)
Fanny and Alexander (1983)
Gandhi (1982)
Reds (1981)
Tess (1980)
Apocalypse Now (1979)
Days of Heaven (1978)
Close Encounters of the Third Kind (1977)
Bound for Glory (1976)
Barry Lyndon (1975)
The Towering Inferno (1974)
Cries and Whispers (1973)
Cabaret (1972)
Fiddler on the Roof (1971)
Ryan's Daughter (1970)
Butch Cassidy and the Sundance Kid (1969)
Romeo and Juliet (1968)
Bonnie and Clyde (1967)

Who's Afraid of Virginia Woolf? (1966, black and white)
Man for All Seasons (1966, color)
Ship of Fools (1965, black and white)
Dr. Zhivago (1965, color)

Art Direction/Set Decoration
Restoration (1995)
The Madness of King George (1994)
Schindler's List (1993)
Dick Tracy (1990
Batman (1989)
The Last Emperor (1987)
Room with a View (1986)
Out of Africa (1985)
Amadeus (1984)
Fanny and Alexander (1983)
Gandhi (1982)
Raiders of the Lost Ark (1981)
Tess (1980)
All That Jazz (1979)
Heaven Can Wait (1978)
Star Wars (1977)
All the President's Men (1976)
Barry Lyndon (1975)
The Godfather II (1974)
The Sting (1973)
Cabaret (1972)
Nicholas and Alexandra (1971)
Patton (1970)
Hello, Dolly! (1969)
Oliver (1968)
Camelot (1967)
Who's Afraid of Virginia Woolf? (1966, black and white)
Fantastic Voyage (1966, color)
Ship of Fools (1965, black and white)
Dr. Zhivago (1965, color)

REELING IN THE YEARS: Film in History and Social Studies

More than a hundred years have now passed since the invention of the motion picture. From its inception it seems it has been a controversial creation, widely accused of having negative social consequences. Calls for motion picture censorship quickly followed in the wake of *The Kiss*, produced in 1896. "Their unbridled kissing," wrote one critic, "magnified to gargantuan proportions, and repeated thrice, is absolutely loathsome" (Karney 1995, 20). In 1915, when movies were still silent, passions ran high about *The Birth of a Nation*. The editor of the *New York Post* accused the film

of being "a deliberate attempt to humiliate millions of American citizens by portraying them as complete animals" (113). In Boston, thousands marched to complain about the film, and more than 6,000 signatures were collected against the film by members of the NAACP. Almost 80 years later, Ed Guerrero complained that "the representation of black people on the commercial screen has been one grand, multifaceted illusion. Blacks have been subordinated, marginalized, positioned, and devalued" (1993, 2). On the eve of the Academy Award ceremony in 1996, a cover story in *People Magazine* proclaimed, "the film industry says all the right things, but its continued exclusion of African-Americans is a national disgrace" (1996).

Nor has concern about the influence of film content centered only on movie representations of sexuality or minorities. The Pulitzer Prize-winning author of *Vietnam: A History* has said, "Friends who teach high school and college courses on Vietnam tell me that for most of their students, *JFK* is the truth" (Karnow 1995, 273). Widely condemned by scholars and politicians "as a preposterous, even alarming deformation of reality" (270), Oliver Stone's *JFK*, like many movies dealing with historical issues, figures, and events, came to be perceived as reality by impressionable young audiences with no other source of information. Stung by criticism of *JFK*, Oliver Stone presented *Nixon* with a series of disclaimers in the opening titles, suggesting that the movie is "an incomplete historical record" with certain events "condensed" or "conjectured." Of course, those who sit through the powerful epic are likely to find the picture worth considerably more than a thousand words, while the disclaimers fade from memory.

There is nothing new about Hollywood's interest in history. Since its inception, the motion picture industry has drawn upon historical figures (*Young Mr. Lincoln, St. Joan, Patton*); events (*The Alamo, The Charge of the Light Brigade, Titanic, Saving Private Ryan*); and periods (*The Red Badge of Courage, Elizabeth and Essex, Spartacus, The Three Musketeers*) as the subject matter for its storytelling. Many such movies, both from the past and from more contemporary times, have won critical and commercial acclaim, including *Braveheart, Schindler's List, Gandhi,* and *A Man for All Seasons.* Successfully bringing the past to life, however, means creating substance beneath the surface. For movies to have validity in our classrooms, particularly for period pieces, they must be able to re-create the past carefully while also bringing to our attention and comprehension an understanding of the characters and the historical conditions and circumstances in which they functioned. *Jefferson in Paris* and *The Madness of King George* are useful examples of movies set in the same time period. However, while one succeeds, the other fails. In the case of *Jefferson in Paris,* one

critic wrote, "the film certainly delivers spectacle, lingering on lots of 1780s decor . . . and eye-poppingly teased, bouffanted and curlicued hairpieces. Yet only King George moves beyond that to find the humanity of an ailing monarch. The pretentious Jefferson never penetrates beneath the surface of its waxworks ensemble" (Daly 1995, 116). Many films set in the past have daringly explored new perspectives and challenged the dominance of traditional white Eurocentric perspectives (*Soldier Blue, Dances with Wolves, Platoon*). The emergence of an increasingly successful and visible community of black filmmakers has added a more mature voice and vision to representations of the African-American experience (*Do the Right Thing, Malcolm X, Boyz 'n' the Hood, Waiting to Exhale, Menace II Society*). Even mainstream, white Hollywood directors have become increasingly capable of realistically representing aspects of African-American life. Evidence of this can be found in Clint Eastwood's direction of *Bird,* documenting the life of jazz legend Charlie Parker, as well as in Edward Zwick's *Glory* and Richard Pearce's *The Long Walk Home. Glory* has been praised as "the first feature film to treat the role of the black soldier in the American Civil War" and "one of the most powerful and historically accurate movies ever made about that war" (McPherson 1995, 128). *The Long Walk Home* takes for its subject matter the 1955 Montgomery bus boycott, initiated when Rosa Parks refused to give up her seat on a bus. Historian Jacqueline Jones says it is "a Hollywood film that gets pretty nearly right a small but compelling piece of Southern history" (Jones 1995, 262). Films such as these can clearly make a major contribution to our understanding of the past, facilitating classroom discussion and debate while bringing people and events from the distant past to life for today's students.

However, not all movies, past or present, are as honest or accurate in their representations. An indispensable aid to History and Social Studies teachers working with film is *Past Imperfect: History According to the Movies* (Carnes 1995). Two films singled out for criticism in this volume are *Abe Lincoln in Illinois,* which is dismissed as "confused chronology and sanitized historical narrative"

(Neely 1995, 126), and the more recent *Mississippi Burning*. Another example of cinema and civil rights, the story is set in Mississippi in 1964 when the movement attempted to register black voters, thereby challenging the state's white political machinery. The film has been condemned as "an atrocious distortion of history." Historian William Chafe said, "According to the way Hollywood presents the story, events of that summer are reduced to a fight between the local white racists on one hand and, on the other, heroic FBI agents sent to the rescue of submissive, illiterate, quaking black people unable and unwilling to stand up for themselves" (1995, 276).

The ability of movies to powerfully shape our perception of the past has, in recent years, been considerably enhanced by increasingly sophisticated computer technologies and special effects that manage to almost seamlessly fuse the past with the present and the living with the dead. Anyone who has seen Forrest Gump's encounter with President Kennedy is sure to have marveled at such techniques, which won Oscars for editing and visual effects, among others. Similarly, *JFK*, which garnered Oscars for cinematography and editing, merges archival footage with re-creations, truth with speculation, in an engaging way that blurs the boundaries between documentary and fiction film. For serious students of history, the film raises significant "issues concerning the limits of fact and fiction and the erosion of the presumed boundaries between documentary and imaginative reconstruction" (Burgoyne 1996, 113). Add to these techniques the presence of cable and VCRs in our homes, both of which provide the repetition necessary to make a message more powerful, and we begin to conceptualize how "reel" history could well become a substitute for real history. The implications of this, for any teacher concerned with creating responsible citizens for a democratic society, should be quite daunting.

Historical Evidence:
Forrest Gump, Independence Day, and Others

Despite Hollywood's ability to both hurt and help the way our students perceive themselves and their world, we have yet to raise a generation of public school educators who comprehend the ways that entertainment films can be integrated into history and social studies. Writing in *American History/American Film*, Arthur Schlesinger recognizes this problem: "Social and intellectual historians draw freely on fiction, drama, paintings, hardly ever movies. Yet the very nature of film as a supremely popular art form guarantees that it is the carrier of deep enigmatic truth" (1979, 1x).

Schlesinger argues that when properly studied, motion pictures provide significant clues about the inner and outer nature of the society that both produced and consumed the movies. A proper reading of movies as more than mere entertainment "offers the social and intellectual historian significant clues to the tastes, apprehensions, myths, inner vibrations of the age" (x).

This symbiotic relationship between cinema and society, the way in which movies both show and shape, mirror and make, reflect and reinforce their culture is also acknowledged by Robert Sklar. In *Movie-Made America*, he writes that films "by their content and control . . . help shape the character and direction of American culture as a whole" (1975, v). In his study of depression America and the movies, Andrew Bergman argued that "every movie is a cultural artifact . . . and as such reflects the values, fears, myths, and assumptions of the culture that produces it" (1971, xiii). The origins of such theories can be traced to Siegfried Kracauer's classic 1947 study, *From Caligari to Hitler*. Kracauer believed that "the films of a nation reflect its mentality in a more direct way than any other artistic media" (5). Because movies were made collectively and consumed by the masses, he argued, they represented a form of social barometer that could reveal "the patterns of a people at a particular time" (5). Perhaps no film in recent time has so invited this form of speculation than *Forrest Gump*. It has been described as "a reassuring fantasy of a man who in an almost mythic way, can transcend our divisions and heal the scars of the past" (Chumo 1995, 11). Well-known critic Gene Siskel believes that the film was a national therapy session for a deeply troubled country. "The viewing of *Forrest Gump* has become almost a religious experience for a grieving nation, for an America that still hasn't come to grips with the last 30 years of political assassinations, White House corruption, a war that wasn't won, sexual abuse, scandals, and drive-by shootings" (3).

Not everyone agreed that the message and meaning of the movie were so therapeutic. In *The Persistence of History*, Vivian Sobchack calls the film "a fantastic dream in which ignorance and niceness win out over historical consciousness and meaning" (1996, 1). While the film has a feel-good quality, it actually presents for its central character a man-child, blown in the buffeting winds of time, like the feather at the start and end of the film, with little understanding of his place in those times. The film tells us "not to worry; one can be in history and make history without paying attention and without understanding" (2).

In summer 1996, journalists, critics, and social historians used exactly such concepts as they attempted to explain the social significance of *Twister* and the so-called new cycle of disaster films scheduled for release throughout the year. Grossing more than $100 million in its first 12 days of release, *Twister* not only pulled in a national audience, but seemed to be doing very well in the small towns accustomed to the threats of tornadoes. In the process it landed a cover story not only on *Entertainment Weekly* but also in *Time* magazine. In its wake were *Independence Day*, *Deep Impact*, *The Arrival*, *Phenomenon*, *Volcano*, and *Titanic*. These production patterns and the astounding audience response to some of the films offer the social historian rich material for analysis and speculation. Dean Devlin, producer of *Independence Day*, observed that "trends are always a reflection of what's happening in the world. Having gone through fires and riots and floods in the last

few years, Hollywood has been inspired" (Wells 1996, 17). *New York* magazine believed that the alien apocalypse, the destruction of the White House, and the death of the First Lady in *Independence Day* tapped into social fears and anxieties. "The trailer feeds into suspicion of the government, the mass revolt against authority, the millennium, and the future—it's not surprising that people are cheering at these images" (Callahan 1996, 15). Not to be outdone, *Time* ran a cover story declaring "Aliens Have Landed." They, too, saw social significance in the new wave of science fiction films. "Most of us can't program our VCRs. We have the tools of science in our hands and we're afraid of them . . . the American theology of the 50s— the middle class' belief in the government's bland benevolence is dying. Rising expectations have given way to escalating suspicions about those in power" (Corliss 1996, 59).

The distance of time does, however, allow us to draw some conclusions about production patterns evident during the first cycle of disaster films (*Airport*, *The Towering Inferno*, *Earthquake*, *The Poseidon Adventure*, etc.). Coming as they did in the early 1970s, such films reflect a country mired in Vietnam, the aftermath of political assassinations, and big-city riots. The society they depict is one in crisis, trying to solve "its social and cultural problems through the ritualized legitimization of strong male leadership, the renewal of traditional moral values, and the regeneration of institutions like the patriarchal family" (Ryan and Kellner 1988, 52). They also "warn about the dangers of unrestrained corporate capitalism and show how the unchecked pursuit of profits leads to catastrophe" (52).

This relationship between cinematic messages and the social conditions at the time of production offers older history students an opportunity to engage in a form of cinematic archaeology, attempting to discern meaning in patterns of production and consumption. In working with Kracauer's notion of the mirror metaphor, we must, however, employ discipline, not just speculation, as we look at pieces of the puzzle. In his study of small-town America in film, Emanuel Levy raises these concerns: "The reflection theory is not adequate. One needs to be more specific asking what particular aspects of the film (narrative structure, thematic conventions, style) reflect what aspects of the social structure" (1991, 81).

On the lighter side, films like *Bill and Ted's Excellent Adventure, Back to the Future, Peggy Sue Got Married,* and *The Philadelphia Experiment* can all be used to motivate young people to think about their own place in time and what they would do or change if they could move backward or forward in time. The 1960 version of *The Time Machine,* with its Oscar for special effects, is another useful movie, especially when linked to 1979's *Time After*

Time, which has H. G. Wells pursuing Jack the Ripper through history. On a more serious note, films like *December* and *Swing Kids* can locate today's teenagers in World War II America and Europe, giving them some sense of what it may have been like to be young and at war. Movies like *Driving Miss Daisy, Nixon, Malcolm X,* and *Forrest Gump,* which span several decades of the 20th century can also be used to give students a sense of pivotal moments in the nation's recent past. *Caution:* Before showing any of these films, check your school district's policy on films.

Historical Authenticity

(MID/HIGH) — The real process here is to develop students' ability to analyze and read films for historical accuracy. By comparing a movie version with historical accounts, students develop analytical skills. Areas they can concentrate on include the chronology of events; the depiction of historical figures; the visual validity of the sets, environment, and costumes; and the accuracy of the language. The language provides an interesting and often amusing approach because so often it reflects the vocabulary and slang of the audience rather than those of the period in which it was set. When the soothsayer warns Julius Caesar to "beware the Ides of March," is it unlikely, for example, that Caesar's response was "One day's as good as another?" In *Becket,* which is set in the 12th century, the bishop of London refers to King Henry II as an "adolescent," despite the fact that the term was not coined until the 20th century. In Titanic, acclaimed for its attention to period detail, Jack

Dawson (Leonardo DiCaprio) refers to a lake in Wisconsin, which was man-made and in fact, was not in existence at the time the film is set.

Bonnie and Clyde (1967) is a useful film to consider from the perspective of historical evidence. Certainly the real Clyde Barrow and Bonnie Parker looked nothing like the glamorous screen versions played by Warren Beatty and Faye Dunaway. Although the physical resemblance may not be accurate, the circumstances under which the characters died and the impact of the depression on average Americans are much more authentic. Several scenes in the film can be usefully compared to photographs from the Dust Bowl era. The Farm Security Administration (FSA) photographs in *In This Proud Land* (Stryker and Wood, 1973) are particularly suitable. Given the role the still camera plays in *Bonnie and Clyde,* the thematic link is also important. *Caution:* Before showing this film, check your school district's policy on films.

Cultural Values

(HIGH) — Some of the distortion and glamorization in *Bonnie and Clyde* can be understood if we realize that films must appeal to an audience. The function of film is not to provide a historically accurate record, but to create an entertaining vehicle that will attract audiences and make money. The nature of this attraction, however, actually provides historians with a second approach to movies as historical evidence. This approach argues, as did Kracauer, that films reflect the views

and values of those who pay to see them. In the case of *Bonnie and Clyde,* director Arthur Penn made this perfectly clear when he said, "We wanted to make a modern film whose action takes place in the past" (Hillier 1973, 11). Penn was also interested in the role of myth in U.S. history. He said that when Bonnie and Clyde were killed, they were regarded as folk heroes by many people. Interestingly enough, the youthful audience of the 1960s found something appealing about the 1930s gangsters—the film was a commercial success. A fashion line based on the period developed, and Faye Dunaway appeared on the January 12, 1968, cover of *Life* in an article on film and fashion. English singer Georgie Fame had a hit record with "The Ballad of Bonnie and Clyde," which featured the sound of machine guns echoing the bloody conclusion of the film.

Bonnie and Clyde can, therefore, be seen as an interesting case study of film as historical evidence. Its violence and hipness mirror something of the generation gap of the 1960s and Americans' reaction to the Vietnam War and President Kennedy's assassination. A year after the film was released, the Tet offensive and the assassinations of Robert Kennedy and Martin Luther King, Jr. provided further evidence of the violent nature of U.S. society.

Two other films by Arthur Penn are worth noting. *The Left-Handed Gun* (1958) is an interesting story of Billy the Kid that examines another U.S. myth, but can also be read as an extension of 1950s juvenile delinquency. In this version, Billy is a kind of crazy, mixed-up kid in the mold of James Dean's *Rebel Without a Cause*. Another film, *Little Big Man* (1970), was a Native American/cavalry story, but Penn saw it as much more than that. The movie, he said, addressed "what was really the fate of the Red Indians at the time of Custer. Obviously the analogy with the Negroes is great" (Hillier 1973, 11).

Primary and Secondary Evidence

(MID/HIGH) — The 20th century is the only period in history during which the motion picture has been present. The motion picture camera recorded the past as it actually happened, and Hollywood has reinvented the past by continuing to set stories in it. For historians this means we have an opportunity to compare and contrast a period as it saw itself to the way we have seen it with hindsight. Changes in historical characters, for example, reflect the changing nature of society. Billy the Kid and General George Custer have undergone major transformations over the years. Teachers wishing to use this approach could select a topic or period from the following list and study the difference between films made at the time (primary documents) and those made after the event (secondary documents). Magazines, photographs, books, and newspapers can all be used to supplement this approach. Decade-by-decade suggestions are provided in upcoming sections.

In working with films from the list on page 306, teachers should keep in mind that these represent only a handful of films made in any given period. Although many of the films are worth viewing in their entirety, teachers are again encouraged to select brief, 5- to 10-minute clips for analysis and comparison. This guideline to the decades is, by nature, a generalization. The links made between film and society should be taken as suggestions rather than conclusions. Teachers and students should have the opportunity to investigate and test these associations. Remember, these connections are based on the concept that films can be read as a reflection of society. How we read them and what we read into them need to be balanced against other historical evidence, such as textbooks, journals, and magazines. In addition, the video revolution continues to make new materials available for teachers. Two useful sources are *The Video Encyclopedia of the Twentieth Century* and *The March of Time* newsreels.

The 1930s: Overview. The single most dominant factor of the 1930s was the Great Depression. Its presence is visible in many of the films of the era, either overtly or blatantly. The gangster films clearly reflect the little man's struggle to succeed. A populist series of films by Frank Capra reflect rural, middle-American values versus big-city corruption. *Mr. Smith Goes to Washington* is an excellent example. The Andy Hardy series that started in 1937 is another good example of small-town American values in the tradition of Booth Tarkington's Penrod stories. The musicals, however, remain one of the most important and least understood reflections of the era. *Top Hat* and other musicals with Fred Astaire and Ginger Rogers are pure escapism. They provided a cathartic release and extravagance for movie audiences of the depression. The Warner Brothers musicals are almost social commentaries. The Shanghai Lil sequence at the very end of *Footlight Parade* features images of FDR and is consistent with the studio's support for Roosevelt and the New Deal. *Gold Diggers of '33* offers two outstanding depression-era songs, "We're in the Money" and "Forgotten Man." This era is captured particularly well in a compilation documentary called *Brother, Can You Spare a Dime?* (1975). Propaganda films such as Germany's *Triumph of the Will* and the U.S. films *The River* and *The Plough That Broke the Plains* can be used by teachers to show society in the 1930s as well as the growing power of the motion picture.

Period
1930s
  [primary]
The Public Enemy (1931)
Little Caesar (1931)
Wild Boys of the Road (1933)
Footlight Parade (1933)
Gold Diggers of '33 (1933)
Top Hat (1935)
Swing Time (1936)
Mr. Smith Goes to Washington (1939)

  [secondary]
Grapes of Wrath (1940)
Bonnie and Clyde (1967)
They Shoot Horses, Don't They? (1969)
Lady Sings the Blues (1972)
Sounder (1972)
The Way We Were (1973)
Paper Moon (1973)
Bound for Glory (1976)
Honky Tonk Man (1982)
The Journey of Natty Gann (1985)
Mobsters (1991)
Billy Bathgate (1991)
Fried Green Tomatoes (1991)

Period
1940s
  [primary]
Meet John Doe (1941)
Mrs. Miniver (1942)
Casablanca (1942)
Double Indemnity (1944)
The Lost Weekend (1945)
Spellbound (1945)
Mildred Pierce (1945)
The Best Years of Our Lives (1946)
Gentleman's Agreement (1947)

The Boy with Green Hair (1948)
Home of the Brave (1948)
Mr. Blandings Builds His Dream Home (1948)
The Snakepit (1948)
Pinky (1949)
Knock on Any Door (1949)

  [secondary]
Saving Private Ryan (1998)
Red Sky at Morning (1970)
Summer of '42 (1971)
The Way We Were (1973)
New York, New York (1977)
Yanks (1979)
Raging Bull (1980)
Swing Shift (1982)
Guilty by Suspicion (1991)
Swing Kids (1991)
December (1991)

Period
1950s
  [primary]
I Married a Communist (1950)
The Day the Earth Stood Still (1951)
On the Waterfront (1954)
Executive Suite (1954)
The Caine Mutiny (1954)
The Blackboard Jungle (1955)
Rebel Without a Cause (1955)
Marty (1955)
Invasion of the Body Snatchers (1956)
The Man in the GreyFlannel Suit (1956)
I Want to Live (1958)
The Defiant Ones (1958)
Blue Denim (1959)
On the Beach (1959)

  [secondary]
The Last Picture Show (1971)
Grease (1978)
September 30, 1955 (1978)
The Atomic Cafe (1982)
Daniel (1983)
Desert Bloom (1986)
Quiz Show (1994)
The Long Walk Home (1990)

Period
1960s
  [primary]
The Apartment (1960)
The Ugly American (1963)
A Hard Day's Night (1964)
Failsafe (1964)
Dr. Strangelove (1964)
The Pawnbroker (1965)
Who's Afraid of Virginia Woolf? (1966)
Bonnie and Clyde (1967)
The Graduate (1967)
In the Heat of the Night (1967)
Wild in the Streets (1968)
Bob and Carol and Ted and Alice (1969)
Easy Rider (1969)
The Green Berets (1969)
The Wild Bunch (1969)

  [secondary]
American Graffiti (1973)
Coming Home (1978)
Purple Haze (1982)
The Right Stuff (1983)
1968 (1986)
1969 (1988)
Mississippi Burning (1988)
JFK (1991)
The Doors (1992)
Heaven and Earth (1993)
Nixon (1995)

The 1940s: Overview. World War II is the dominant aspect of films of the early 1940s. The classic example would be *Casablanca.* The war also saw the first sophisticated use of motion pictures as propaganda and training vehicles. Frank Capra's *Why We Fight* series, available on video, gives students interesting insights into Hollywood's role in the war. As a lighter approach, teachers might want to use cartoons from the era. *The Private Snafu* series is available, as are several of the Daffy Duck cartoons that pushed the war effort for civilians and soldiers. For understanding U.S. society after the war, there is no better film than *The Best Years of Our Lives,* which deals with social adjustment. Maladjustment is reflected in many of the so-called social problem or issue-oriented films. Film noir, covered earlier in this chapter, also reflects the darker side of the United States after the war. Of interest for war's impact on society are the number of movies dealing with trauma, psychosis, and alienation. *Spellbound* and *The Snakepit* both examined mental illness. *The Lost Weekend* took on alcoholism. *Pinky* and *The Gentleman's Agreement* addressed racism, prejudice, and anti-Semitism. On a much lighter note, *Mr. Blandings Builds His Dream Home* is a comedy about the growth of both the suburbs and advertising in U.S. life.

The 1950s: Overview. The period between 1946 and 1964 in U.S. society was dominated by the baby boom. It is not surprising when we look at films from the era that we see evidence of the presence and power of teens. It was the age that gave us James Dean, Gidget, and rock and roll. It also reflected a growing tension between young people and their parents. Juvenile delinquency moved to white, middle-class suburbs (*Rebel Without a Cause*). Teens clashed with their teachers in movies such as *The Blackboard Jungle.* Sex was often a cause of conflict, evident in *Blue Denim, A Summer Place* (1959), and *Peyton Place* (1957). For adults, the era seems to suggest the continual struggle to get ahead and achieve power, money, and prestige (*The Man in the Grey Flannel Suit, Executive Suite*). The atomic jitters of the cold-war era, so well documented in 1982's *The Atomic Cafe,* show up in science fiction fare

from the period. *On the Beach,* set in Australia, dealt with the end of the world after an atomic war. It would be an interesting companion piece for 1983's *The Day After. The Day the Earth Stood Still* preaches the need for cooperation in a nuclear era. Cooperation is also stressed on a racial level in *The Defiant Ones,* which clearly reflects the United States after the court order to desegregate public schools. The various mutants and monsters of movies such as *Them* and *Tarantula* (1955) are also allegories. They represent either fear of science that has endangered humanity or fear of communism. One other major trend throughout the era was the epic or biblical film. These include *The Robe* (1953), *The Ten Commandments* (1956), and *Ben Hur* (1959). In part they reflect an escape from the present to the safety of the past. Technologically, they also reflect Hollywood's struggle to attract adult audiences away from television through the development of cinemascope and film spectacle.

The 1960s: Overview. The 1960s remain one of the most talked-about and least understood eras, often due to the media's emphasis on certain highly visible but not necessarily representative elements of the period. The 1960s were actually more like two decades, with the election of Lyndon Johnson in 1964 marking the beginning of the second stage. Undoubtedly the period between 1960 and 1969 was turbulent and traumatic. The Vietnam War and the civil rights movement were the most visible evidence of this disturbance. *The Ugly American,* made in the year of President Kennedy's assassination, is a useful glimpse at U.S. involvement in Southeast Asia and its consequences. The nuclear nightmare fed by the Cuban missile crisis of 1962 was highly visible in films such as *Failsafe* and *Dr. Strangelove, Or How I Stopped Worrying and Learned to Love the Bomb.*

The youth revolution and the generation gap show up in *Easy Rider, The Graduate,* and *Wild in the Streets.* Changing sexual attitudes in the wake of the birth-control pill are evident in many films of the era, including *Bob and Carol and Ted and Alice, Midnight Cowboy, The Sterile Cuckoo,* and *Who's Afraid of Virginia Woolf?* These films represented major changes in motion picture censorship and ratings and reflect the liberalization of U.S. society in the 1960s. In part, this liberation was manifested in new themes and in part through stronger language. It was also evident in the more graphic depiction of violence, whether in westerns such as *The Wild Bunch* or gangster films such as *Bonnie and Clyde*. The civil rights films are dealt with in more detail later in this chapter. Finally, we have to remember that alongside all of this turmoil, there were many extremely successful family films during this decade. These include *Mary Poppins* (1964), *My Fair Lady* (1964), *The Sound of Music* (1965), *Camelot* (1967), and *Oliver!* (1968).

Exploring the 1970s and 1980s

The 1970s are perhaps still a little too close for us to see clearly. Nonetheless, some patterns seem evident in films of the era, and these patterns might prove useful for examination. The Vietnam War is indirectly addressed in both *Patton* and *M*A*S*H*, which provide strikingly different images of war. George Patton's speech early in the film, as he is dwarfed by the U.S. flag, is well worth looking at. *Catch-22*, made the same year, clearly indicates the visibility of war in the national consciousness. Westerns such as *Little Big Man* (1970) and *Soldier Blue* can also be read as allegories of the Vietnam War. *Boys in the Band* (1970) and *Carnal Knowledge* (1971) are two of many films of the era to provide evidence of changing sexual attitudes. The women's movement changed attitudes about women and, as a result, notions of masculinity. Films such as *Alice Doesn't Live Here Anymore* (1975), *An Unmarried Woman* (1978), *Norma Rae* (1979), and *Kramer vs. Kramer* (1979) all showed women rethinking their roles. *The Great Santini* (1979) and *Kramer vs. Kramer* also reflected the need for men to be nurturing and giving rather than simply providers and punishers. The generation gap that had begun in the 1950s and exploded in the 1960s took on a new element in the 1970s. *The Exorcist* (1973) stunned audiences around the world with its images of a demonically possessed child. The child or teen as a monster out of control seemed a popular motif in the 1970s, as evidenced by *Carrie* (1976), *The Omen* (1976), and *Halloween* (1978). President Gerald Ford called Watergate the "national nightmare," and films of the 1970s might suggest that a nightmare had replaced the American dream. At times this appears allegorically in the so-called disaster films. *The Poseidon Adventure* (1972), the *Airport* series, and *The Towering Inferno* (1974) all imply that we cannot trust leaders or technology. Something is wrong in the system, and it threatens us all. One need only look at Jack Lemmon's Oscar-winning performance in *Save the Tiger* (1973) to understand images of corporate corruption and despair. If the White House is tainted (*All the President's Men*, 1976), so, too, are television stations (*Network*, 1976) and nuclear power plants (*The China Syndrome*, 1979). It is not surprising that the era that experienced the energy crisis, oil embargoes, acid rain, pollution, and Love Canal also warned us about our water. "Just when you though it was safe to go back in the water," *Jaws* (1975) observed, there is something else lurking just below the surface waiting to get you. Is it any wonder so many Americans joined George Lucas in outer space (*Star Wars*, 1977) and wished "may the Force be with you"? Escapism from Watergate and the Vietnam War fed a nostalgia wave evident in *The Way We Were* (1973), *Summer of '42* (1971), *American Graffiti* (1972), *Grease* (1978), and others. Those who stayed earthbound contemplated the fall of Saigon and the cost of the war (*Coming Home*, 1978; *The Deer Hunter*, 1978) or disappeared into the disco phenomenon of *Saturday Night Fever* (1977).

Looking back to an era that is still very close, several trends do seem evident in films of the 1980s. The family was still being redefined. *Ordinary People* (1980), *On Golden Pond* (1981), and others explored family relationships. As more and more Americans got older, so-called gray power began to exert an influence on the box office. *The Trip to Bountiful* (1985), *The Whales of August* (1987), *Cocoon* (1985), and *Driving Miss Daisy* (1989) were some of the numerous films that provided rich images of the elderly. The impaired and disabled also attracted new attention in films such as *Children of a Lesser God* (1986), *Rain Man* (1988), and *Born on the 4th of July* (1989). U.S. foreign policy in the Reagan era, with its stridently anti-Soviet tone, is evident in films such as *Missing in Action* (1984), *Rambo: First Blood, Part II* (1984), *Red Dawn* (1984), and *Rocky IV* (1985). The Vietnam War's continued impact on the U.S. consciousness is seen in several important films, including *Platoon* (1986) and *Born on the 4th of July*. Materialism, corporate takeovers, and the cost of a booming economy show up in *Wall Street* (1987) and *Working Girl* (1988).

Throughout the 1980s, reflecting the drug crisis in U.S. society, the film industry also changed its depiction of alcohol and drug use. The casual consumption evident in *Annie Hall* (1977) and *The Big Chill* (1983) gave way to much more serious depictions of alcoholism and addiction in movies such as *Less Than Zero* (1987) and *Bright Lights, Big City* (1988). In *10* (1979) and *Arthur* (1981), Dudley Moore played a lovable drunk, but as the truth emerged about Betty Ford, Liza Minnelli, Elizabeth Taylor, John Belushi, and others, Hollywood decided it was time to get *Clean and Sober* (1988). Finally, several interesting films dealt with the black experience in the United States. These include *The Color Purple* (1985), *Native Son* (1986), *A Soldier's Story* (1984), and *Glory* (1989). Perhaps the most controversial of these films was one made by independent black producer Spike Lee. *Do the Right Thing* (1989) created enormous debate, and Lee was nominated for an Academy Award for his screenplay. Interestingly enough, the main story of the 1980s, AIDS, was almost totally ignored by the film industry.

Pictures of the Past

There is a popular belief that wherever history is concerned, Hollywood always gets it wrong. What is overlooked, however, is the astonishing amount of history Hollywood has got right and the immense unacknowledged debt which we owe to the commercial cinema as an illuminator of the story of mankind (Fraser 1988, xi-xii).

(ELEM/MID) — When beginning a new topic about some historical period, character, or event, start by asking the children what they know about the subject. Use the board to compile a list of their entry-level knowledge. Alongside it, build up a source list indicating where the students may have gotten their ideas and impressions. This list might include other classes, books, word of mouth, and, of course, the media, including film and television. If they have misconceptions about the topic you are covering, and if these came from the media, take time to discuss these misconceptions. You might want to make a distinction between deliberate lying and dramatic license. The important thing is to use the opportunity to get students to realize that history did not always happen the way Hollywood shows it.

When studying a particular historical period, character, or event, use the resources listed in this chapter to locate a film on that subject. Select a brief, 5- to 10-minute clip from the film to bring to life some aspect the class is studying. This might include the lifestyle of people at a given time, making note of their clothes, housing, furniture, occupations, modes of transportation, and speech. If you select a historical figure, have the students talk or write about the way they imagined the person and compare it to the film depiction.

(ELEM/MID) — This exercise can concentrate on one character from a single film, or you may want to select several characters from several different films. The objective is to develop students' visual literacy and critical thinking skills by having them note differences and similarities between primary documents of historical figures and the secondary documents represented by Hollywood's depiction of these figures.

The primary documents can include statues, paintings, and photographs of famous people. They must all have been made at the time the individual lived. Advanced classes or groups might investigate the authenticity of these documents. Would a painter or photographer, for example, flatter a patron or client and leave out some physical defect or imperfection? The following list gives examples for this exercise.

- Bonnie and Clyde (photographs compared to film *Bonnie and Clyde*, 1967)
- Cleopatra (statue or coin compared to movie *Cleopatra*, 1963)
- Julius Caesar (statue or coin compared to movie *Julius Caesar*, 1953)
- Michelangelo (statues, self-portraits compared to movie *The Agony and the Ecstasy*, 1965)
- Henry VIII (portraits by Hans Holbein compared to films such as *Man for All Seasons*, 1966, and *Anne of a Thousand Days*, 1969)
- Saint Thomas More (portrait by Hans Holbein compared to *Man for All Seasons*)
- Charles I (portraits by Anthony Van Dyck compared to movie *Cromwell,* 1970)
- Napoleon (portraits by Jacques Louis David compared to films such as *Desiree*, 1954, and *Waterloo*, 1971)

- Franklin Roosevelt (photographs compared to the film *Sunrise at Campobello*, 1960)
- Richard Nixon (photographs, portraits and documentary video compared to *Nixon*, 1995)

The exercise can concentrate simply on physical features, with students discussing similarities and differences between the actors and the people they portray. Teachers might also focus attention on clothes, jewelry, furnishings, and other elements present in primary documents. These can be located in most encyclopedias and in various art histories. Students can be given the task of tracking the pictures down as research. Postcards found at various major museums traditionally feature important historical portraits, and these can be laminated and labeled to build up a pictorial file of important historical characters. Secondary sources include the films themselves and photographs from the films that are published in various film guides and journals. Motion picture stills are also available from several major dealers, and these can be collected and filed in the media center. *Entertainment Weekly* classifieds is a good starting point.

Fashions and Film

Costumes are particularly important in creating a sense of the period. Sometimes meticulous research is done to re-create the time. Other films are full of historical inaccuracies in terms of the look they assign to a period. Look at the following list of films that have won Academy Awards for costuming and you will get some sense of how often the award has gone to a historical or period film. Working with some of these examples, help students understand the concept of historical accuracy in the way a film looks. Teachers can also point out the fact that films have often influenced fashion and set trends.

Writing in *Hollywood and History: Costume Design and Film*, Edward Maeder noted: "When we try to recreate historical costumes, a problem arises. Our vision is so influenced by contemporary style that we cannot be objective, and the result is always interpretation" (1987, 9). Maeder's comments are made in what served as the catalog for a major exhibit mounted by the Los Angeles County Museum of Art. Below is a list of several historical films, some with the catalog's comments on the costumes featured in that film.

- *Cleopatra* (1963). Elizabeth Taylor has 65 costume changes. "It evoked the past while incorporating the stylistic influences of the day."
- *The Egyptian* (1954). Two years of research on the costumes.

- *Gone with the Wind* (1939). Vivien Leigh's hats were not in style during the Civil War and actually reflect 1930s fashion. During the 1860s, women's dresses would have been cut to conform to the corset. In this film they are cut to the bosom, also reflecting 1930s fashion.

- *The Great Gatsby* (1974). "The costumes on both the men and women appear to be historically correct."

- *Romeo and Juliet* (1968). "The costumes are probably the most accurate ever produced for a film of this period."

- *Spartacus* (1960). Kirk Douglas appears as a Roman slave sporting a very contemporary 1960 hairstyle.

- *The Three Musketeers* (1974). "A triumph of historical accuracy."

- *The Virgin Queen* (1955). This story of Elizabeth I is described as "a stand-out for its historical accuracy." It "broke new ground in Hollywood make-up and hairstyle."

The following films all influenced contemporary fashion at the time they were shown.

Cleopatra (1963)
Tom Jones (1963)
Dr. Zhivago (1965)
Bonnie and Clyde (1967)
The Great Gatsby (1974)
Saturday Night Fever (1977)

(MID/HIGH) — Advanced students could be assigned the task of researching fashion and film. Select one of the films just listed or another film that had an impact on fashion, and have students examine old copies of *Life, Look, Ebony, Saturday Evening Post, Esquire*, etc., to find evidence of these trends in advertising or articles. The cover of *Life* (January 12, 1968), for example, featured a story on *Bonnie and Clyde* fashions.

Partial List of Academy Award Winners for Best Costumes

Restoration (1995)
Age of Innocence (1993)
Cyrano de Bergerac (1990)
Henry V (1989)
The Last Emperor (1987)
Room with a View (1986)
Ran (1985)
Amadeus (1984)
Fanny and Alexander (1983)
Gandhi (1982)
Chariots of Fire (1981)
Tess (1980)
All That Jazz (1979)
Death on the Nile (1978)
Star Wars (1977)
Fellini's Casanova (1976)
Barry Lyndon (1975)
The Great Gatsby (1974)
The Sting (1973)
Travels with My Aunt (1972)
Nicholas and Alexandra (1971)
Cromwell (1970)
Anne of a Thousand Days (1969)
Romeo and Juliet (1968)
Camelot (1967)

What's Wrong with This Picture?

(ELEM/MID/HIGH) — Have you ever seen a film in which something struck you as being completely out of place? Sometimes this can be a problem with continuity. In *Camelot*, for example, a montage sequence shows King Pelinore, even though he has not yet arrived in Camelot at this point of the story. In *Jagged Edge*, Glenn Close appears in one courtroom sequence in which she inexplicably goes through several changes of clothes. In *Presumed Innocent*, Harrison Ford is interviewed on the courthouse steps by a reporter with no tape in the recorder. In *Die Hard 2*, Bruce Willis makes a call from a Pacific Bell phone, despite the fact that he's in Washington, D.C. In *Born on the 4th of July*, Tom Cruise is shown in a hospital in 1968 while the soundtrack features Don McLean's "American Pie," which was not released until 1971. These are all minor problems with continuity, editing, or props, but they can be useful and intriguing examples that encourage students to be more alert and become more visually literate. Sometimes the problems deal with historical accuracy. When a television miniseries about Napoleon showed a character with a cigarette lighter, viewers called to ask how that was possible. Apparently a rudimentary form of lighter was developed around this time. The incident demonstrated that audiences will note small things that seem obviously out of place. It also demonstrated that if historical accuracy is used, our knowledge of even small things can be improved. One scene in *Gone with the Wind* shows light-bulbs in street lamps, despite the fact they were not in use at the time. Ask students if something they have seen in movies about the past has ever seemed to be impossible, untrue, or inaccurate. If they have few ideas, you might want to offer one or two examples.

- Jousting sequences in medieval films: Do we ever see the knights lifted onto their horses? Isn't the armor too heavy for them to climb back up when they fall off? Why is this ignored?

- Cleopatra's entry into Rome in the 1963 film *Cleopatra* is incredible for its sheer excess. Who are all these people? Where did they come from? How far is Rome from Egypt? Consider the logistics of moving all these people, animals, and equipment this distance.

In *God Bless You, Buffalo Bill* (1983), Wayne William Sarf provides intricate details of historical inaccuracies and anachronisms in westerns. These include the use of cavalry costumes and flags that were either never used or used in a different era from the one depicted. Sarf draws particular attention to the number of westerns featuring the Colt .45 Peacemaker, even though the gun had not been available during the period in which the films are set. Mistakes involving weapons are common in westerns because the producers either had not done their research or because the drama would have been undermined if characters had to reload their guns constantly.

(MID/HIGH) — Collect a series of images of the American West, using photographs from the period and paintings by Charles Russell and Frederic Remington, and have students compare these to the images in movies. The movie images can come from brief film clips or movie books or stills. Develop a list for students to work on, including such things as clothes, hairstyles, towns, homes, furnishings, tools, and so on. Are there any groups of people who seem to be overrepresented or underrepresented? Remember that in all media analysis, it is important to draw the attention of students to what is left out of the frame as well as to what is put into it. (*Premiere* magazine regularly features a section called "The Eyes Have It" that notes mistakes in continuity and accuracy.)

Mirrors, Windows, and Frames

(HIGH) — *From Caligari to Hitler* popularized the notion that movies were somehow mirrors that reflected society. Although the mirror metaphor raises interesting possibilities for historians, it is often forgotten that mirrors can conceal as well as reveal, can reverse reality, and can even distort the image they reflect. If movies supposedly reflect the society that creates them, we have to be very careful in determining just how that reflection occurs. Two useful examples serve to demonstrate the latent nature of this reflection.

The first is juvenile delinquency. When it comes to the movies and juvenile delinquency, most people think immediately of the 1950s and films such as *The Wild One* and *Rebel Without a Cause*. Actually, juvenile crime was very evident in movies in the 1930s. *Dead End* and *Crime School* are two examples. In 1938, Warner Brothers made *Angels with Dirty Faces*. The following year, at the outbreak of war in Europe, the studio made *Angels Wash Their Faces*. This was an attempt to create a patriotic, positive image of U.S. life. This mood created an artificial image that actually concealed the growing problem of juvenile delinquency. From 1939 to 1945, while juvenile delinquency increased in the United States, images of it in movies declined. As historical evidence, then, the movies do not accurately reflect this problem in U.S. society. What they do reflect is the desire to create a very positive view of U.S. life. Movies such as *Yankee Doodle Dandy* (1942), although set in another age, are clearly part of the U.S. war effort.

The second example is the Vietnam War. With the rare exception of *The Green Berets* (1968), the Vietnam War was largely invisible in U.S. movies of the time despite the fact that it dominated society and filled the nation's newspapers and television screens. To find reflections and references to Vietnam, we need to look beyond the manifest meaning and investigate the latent presence of the war in movies of the period. Westerns made during this time can often be read as allegories of Vietnam. *The Wild Bunch* (1969) certainly reflects the increasingly violent nature of a country bogged down in Vietnam and the Kennedy and King assassinations. *Little Big Man* (1970) depicted the Washita River massacre of 1868, and *Soldier Blue* (1970) dealt with the Sand Creek massacre of 1864. In both cases, the Native Americans can be interpreted as Vietnamese and the cavalry as less than virtuous U.S. soldiers. The controversial court martial of Lt. William Calley, Jr., for the My-lai massacre in South Vietnam provides a backdrop against which these films can be analyzed. In *The Western*, Phil Hardy makes the link very specific, calling *Soldier Blue* "a displaced reaction to the revelations of American atrocities in Vietnam" (1983, 372).

Civil Rights in Cinema and Society: A Case Study

(HIGH) — The civil rights movement and racial attitudes in general provide a rich and rewarding area for students to investigate through motion pictures. For the purposes of this timeline, emphasis is placed on the 1950s and 1960s, when most of the landmark legislation of the civil rights era was passed. However, *Get on the Bus*, Spike Lee's response to the 1995 Million Man March on Washington, along with a number of relatively contemporary films, such as *Ghosts of Mississippi*, can be used to update the subject. Teachers can also use the primary and secondary evidence methods already demonstrated by comparing movies like *The Defiant Ones* (made in the 1950s) with *The Long Walk Home* (set in the 1950s).

Using motion pictures as historical evidence, students can be exposed to films from *Birth of a Nation* (1915) to *Do the Right Thing* (1989) and *Jungle Fever* (1991), and asked to analyze the content of the films in terms of developments in U.S. society at the time. Although the examples given in this case study deal mainly with images of blacks in U.S. film, it must be noted that changes in the depiction of one minority often bring changes in the depiction of another. There are certainly parallels between the improved image of blacks in U.S. films and improved images of Native Americans. The following timeline provides significant dates for developments in civil rights and cinema and should be used as a reference when dealing with this topic.

Civil Rights, Cinema, and Society: Timeline

1863 13th Amendment abolishes slavery.

1868 14th Amendment makes former slaves citizens.

1896 *Plessy vs. Ferguson* decision by Supreme Court upholds the concept of "separate but equal." Precedent is used to justify segregation.

1909 National Association for the Advancement of Colored People (NAACP) formed.

1915 *Birth of a Nation* produced. Remains highly controversial because of its depictions of blacks and the Ku Klux Klan.

1927 Al Jolson appears in blackface in *The Jazz Singer*.

1930s Major images of blacks include the song-and-dance man Bill Robinson (*The Little Colonel, The Littlest Rebel*) and the comic Stepin Fetchit.

1934 *Imitation of Life* produced. Mulatto stereotype that depicts a black girl's desire to "pass" as white.

1939 *Gone with the Wind*. Hattie McDaniel wins Academy Award for Best Supporting Actress for her stereotypical role of Mammy.

Daughters of the American Revolution (DAR) bans black singer Marian Anderson from singing at Washington, D.C.'s Constitution Hall. Eleanor Roosevelt invites Anderson to sing at the Lincoln Memorial and resigns from the DAR.

1940s Two-and-a-half million southern blacks move north. Blacks serve in World War II, usually in segregated units.

1947 The film *The Gentleman's Agreement* deals with anti-Semitism.

1948 Paramount case ends with a legal ruling forcing separation of film distribution from film production, allowing independent film producers to find theaters to show their films.

Stanley Kramer makes *Home of the Brave*, which openly addresses blacks' service in the war and the prejudice they faced.

By executive order, President Harry Truman desegregates the military.

1949 *Pinky* and *Intruder in the Dust*, two of the new "black problem" films that give new visibility to the issue of racial prejudice, are released.

1950 *No Way Out*, starring Sidney Poitier, is a breakthrough film because Poitier plays a doctor and middle-class black life is represented.

Delmar Daves makes the western *Broken Arrow*. The broken arrow of the title is a Native American symbol of peace. Despite the fact that Cochise is played by a white (Jeff Chandler), the film represented a major improvement on the traditional image of Native Americans as blood-thirsty savages.

Ralph Bunche becomes the first black to win the Nobel Prize for Peace.

1951 Sidney Poitier stars in *Cry, the Beloved Country*, which deals with conditions for blacks in South Africa.

1954 *Brown vs. Topeka Board of Education* Supreme Court decision makes segregated schools illegal.

1955 Rosa Parks refuses to sit at the back of the bus in Montgomery, Alabama.

Bad Day at Black Rock examines small-town prejudice.

1956 *The Searchers*, a John Ford western, continues to look more sympathetically at Native Americans.

The King and I is released, a lavish and successful musical with an interesting anti-slavery subplot (note *Uncle Tom's Cabin* sequences).

1957 Civil Rights Act passed, the first such legislation since Reconstruction.

Miscegenation theme appears in *Island in the Sun*.

1958 Stanley Kramer makes *The Defiant Ones*, with Sidney Poitier and Tony Curtis. The message is that blacks and whites must work together. Nominated for Best Picture, it wins Oscars for Best Cinematography and Best Screenplay.

1960 John F. Kennedy elected president.

Formation of Student Nonviolent Coordinating Committee.

Civil Rights Act aimed at helping blacks register to vote.

1961 Freedom Riders active in attempts to improve conditions for blacks in southern states.

Raisin in the Sun examines black life and housing conditions in the North.

James Meredith registers at University of Mississippi, supported by troops sent by President Kennedy.

1962 *To Kill a Mockingbird* made into motion picture. Nominated for Best Picture, it wins Oscars for Best Actor and Best Screenplay.

1963 Martin Luther King, Jr., leads march on Washington, D.C., and delivers "I have a dream" speech.

Sidney Poitier becomes first black to win Best Actor Oscar, for his role in the film *Lilies of the Field*.

President Kennedy assassinated; Lyndon Johnson becomes president.

1964 Civil Rights Act passed, outlawing discrimination in public facilities and hiring.

Martin Luther King, Jr., wins Nobel Prize for Peace.

John Ford makes *Cheyenne Autumn*, dealing with white treatment of Native Americans.

1965 Black Muslim leader Malcolm X is assassinated.

Voting Rights Act ends literacy tests for voting in some southern states.

Major riots and destruction in Watts (Los Angeles, California). Kerner commission later blames white racism for many conditions in the Watts area.

1966 Black Panther movement formed. A more militant group than the civil disobedience devotees of Dr. King, they assert "Black power" and "Black is beautiful."

1967 Thurgood Marshall becomes first black appointed as a justice of the Supreme Court.

In the Heat of the Night wins Best Picture Oscar for its story of a black detective's struggle with racism in the South.

Guess Who's Coming to Dinner nominated for Best Picture. It wins two Oscars. Directed by Stanley Kramer, it deals with a romance between a white woman and a black man.

Blacks represent 30 percent of box-office receipts in major cities.

1968 Martin Luther King, Jr., assassinated.

Race riots.

Robert F. Kennedy assassinated.

Riots at Democratic National Convention in Chicago.

Richard Nixon elected president.

Passage of the Civil Rights Act for fair housing.

1969 Gordon Parks becomes first black to direct a major motion picture for a major studio when he makes *The Learning Tree*.

1970 *Little Big Man* and *Soldier Blue*, both westerns, depict white atrocities against Native Americans.

1971 The movie *Shaft* develops the image of "superspade."

Melvin Van Peebles makes *Sweet Sweetback's Baadasssss Song*.

1972 Sympathetic treatment of blacks in *Sounder* and *Lady Sings the Blues*.

1973 Tom Bradley becomes first black mayor of Los Angeles.

This timeline deals with the major period of civil rights changes and legislation in the United States. It provides some evidence of a relationship between the issues and images in movies and the events taking place in society at the time. Although some of these relationships can no doubt be dismissed as coincidence, it seems likely that broader patterns do suggest a correlation between social attitudes and the views and values expressed in movies. This concept suggests that history teachers and students could find films to be an interesting area for exploration and analysis as historical evidence, whether dealing with civil rights or any other topic. The 1980s provided useful examples to update this approach in films including *A Soldier's Story* (1984), *The Color Purple* (1985), *Do the Right Thing* (1989), *Glory* (1989), and *Driving Miss Daisy* (1989). Also during this period, the Oscar for Best Supporting Actor was awarded to Louis Gossett, Jr. (*An Officer and a Gentleman*) and to Denzel Washington (*Glory*), and the Oscar for Best Supporting Actress was awarded to Whoopi Goldberg (*Ghost*).

The scenes in the following exercises have been selected to help teachers develop strategies for integrating the film-as-history approach into the curriculum. The film clips can be shown individually or in a group. If only one clip is used, teachers should introduce it as an exercise in reading historical documents. Based on their reading and classwork, students would be asked to draw on prior knowledge and analytical skills to name the period in which the film was made and to provide evidence to support their answer. Students could recognize that the themes and ideas expressed in the film belong to a particular period. If two or more clips are used, they should be sufficiently different so that students can be asked to compare and contrast them and place them in chronological order. *Caution:* Before showing any of these films, check your school district's policy on films.

Comprehension questions help students analyze characters and understand their motivations. When students watch the clips, this method provides a context in which they can understand the material. Teachers might focus attention on what happened, to whom it happened, how it happened, and why it happened. This context can be applied to the study of almost any period to help students respond both affectively and cognitively to history.

Cinema and Civil Rights:
Additional Case Studies

(MID/HIGH) —

Raisin in the Sun (1961). This particularly strong and important film makes an interesting companion to *To Kill a Mockingbird*, which was made the following year. The latter film looks at blacks through the eyes of children and liberal white society. *Raisin in the Sun*, on the other hand, is essentially a black film in which whites are only incidental to the plot.

The film is set in Chicago and provides an interesting insight into the extended family. The central characters of the Younger family are Lena, the matriarch; her adult son, Walter Lee; his wife, Ruth; his sister; and Travis, his young son.

Lena's husband has recently died and she is expecting a $10,000 insurance check. For the first time in their lives, the family will have money and be able to realize some of their dreams. It becomes evident, however, that they do not see eye to eye on how to spend the money. Although the family appears in danger of breaking apart, they find unity in their response to the white prejudice they are forced to endure.

The first 10 minutes of the film provide a strong sense of the difficult conditions the family lives in. Have students make a list of these conditions. They include sharing a bathroom with other tenants, no bedroom for Travis, and lack of money.

Walter Lee is a complex and interesting character. He is also prejudiced himself, particularly toward women. He is very unhappy that his sister wants to be a doctor. Walter Lee considers this man's work and tells her to be a nurse. Several times early in the film, Walter Lee argues with his wife, his mother,

and his sister. He feels misunderstood and says he lives in the "world's most backward nation of women." Teachers can use this to discuss different levels of prejudice or the status of black and white women in the United States in the early 1960s.

At one point in the film, Walter Lee, feeling depressed and misunderstood, goes to a bar to drown his sorrows. Fast-forward to this scene and show the sequence when he arrives home drunk. He finds his sister about to go out on a date. She is wearing Nigerian clothes and playing tribal music. Her date is a successful, conservative black man who does not share her view of her rich ancestry: "Let's face it, baby, your heritage ain't nothin' but some bunch of raggedy spirituals in some grass huts." How does she respond to this claim? Teachers can link this episode to the growth of the concept of Afro-American culture in the 1960s. Phrases such as "Black is beautiful" can be discussed. The musical *Hair* has some interesting songs about black self-image during this period that could be used to provide further examples of the image of blacks during the 1960s.

The same sequence provides further evidence of Walter Lee's prejudice. Have students watch for his conversation with his sister's date. What prejudices do they detect? "How come all you college boys wear all them faggoty-looking white shoes?" Walter Lee says. He does not hold education in high esteem, saying all it teaches is "how to read books and talk proper and wear faggoty white shoes." Why would Walter Lee be so negative about education and the way George dresses?

Later in the film, the family decides to use the insurance money to buy a new home. Scan to the scene when a white man knocks at their door. He is balding and seems rather meek and timid. He is a representative of the improvement association for the housing subdivision they are moving to. At first, Walter Lee thinks the man is a form of welcoming committee. His sister is more suspicious and cynical. The white man tells them: "We feel that most of the trouble in this world exists because people don't sit down and talk to each other. We don't try hard enough in this world to understand the other guy's point of view. . . . You've got to admit that a man, right or wrong, has the right to have the sort of neighborhood he lives in a certain kind of way." Although he assures them that "race prejudice simply doesn't enter into it," he points out that the white community of the subdivision does not want them to move in, saying, "Negro families are happier when they live in their own communities." Use this scene to discuss notions of prejudice and bigotry. Have the students discuss what they think the Younger family should do in the face of this opposition. Remind students of the passage of the Fair Housing Act in the late 1960s. On November 9, 1953, *Life* magazine ran an article on the riots in Chicago at the Trumbull Park housing project that resulted when blacks moved into a white neighborhood. Refer to this story as a background to this incident in the film.

Do the Right Thing (1989) also features characters who think people of different races and nationalities would be better off if they stuck to their own kind. One or two scenes from that film could be used for comparison. Students might also be directed to recent events that illustrate this problem. In the late 1980s, for example, the city of Yonkers, New York, clashed with the courts over an issue related to racial themes.

In the Heat of the Night (1967). This scene begins shortly after the start of the film. The police officer, Warren Oates, arrives at the railway station at night and finds Sidney Poitier waiting for the train. Start the clip as the policeman says, "On your feet, boy." The main scene centers on the interrogation of Virgil Tibbs (Sidney Poitier) at the police station by the senior officer, Gillespie, played by Rod Steiger. The clothes, cars, salary, and racial attitudes will help students identify the period in which the film is set. Those who are familiar with *Mississippi Burning* (1988) will recognize the depiction of southern law officers. It is important, however, that they note the subtle indications that Gillespie is not completely negative. There are several developments in his response to Tibbs both before and after he discovers that Tibbs is also a police officer. Stop the scene when Gillespie says, "Because I'm not an expert, officer!"

- How does Gillespie react to Virgil's name?

- Virgil corrects his interrogator's speech, replacing "who" with "whom." What insights does this give us into the two lead characters?

- Why is it important for the audience to hear the train whistle during this sequence, and how does Gillespie respond to it?

- Why does Gillespie think the money that Tibbs has is stolen?

- Why is the phrase "162 dollars and 39 cents a week" repeated several times during the scene?

- What evidence is there that the arresting officer did not follow proper procedure during the arrest?

- Tibbs turns out to be "the number one homicide expert" in his division, and Tibbs's boss wants him to work on Gillespie's case. How does he respond and why?

- Gillespie reluctantly turns to Tibbs for help. Why? How do this mutual need and cooperation reflect the time in which the film was made?

- Compare Tibbs to Poitier's character in *Raisin in the Sun*, made at the start of the decade.

MOVIES, STEREOTYPING, AND SOCIAL STUDIES

How we are seen determines in part how we are treated; how we treat others is based on how we see them. Such seeing comes from representation.—Richard Dyer

Despite the well-documented reciprocal relationship between cinema and society and the abundance of texts (Hilger 1995; Guerrero 1993; Norden 1994) and journals devoted to this subject, Social Studies Methods classes in our teacher preparation programs continue to pay scant attention to America's most popular art form. In the process they fail to help young teachers conceptualize the way in which movie representations of minorities, people with disabilities, gays, and other groups might affect both public perceptions and public policy.

Ironically, America's standard of living will increasingly depend upon growing trade ties with other countries and cultures, which will in turn depend upon our understanding of, and respect for, these groups. Within our own borders, the composition and character of the American population is experiencing ethnogenesis. "We are approaching an age," said *Time* magazine, "when the average U.S. resident as defined by census statistics will trace his or her descent to Africa, Asia, the Hispanic world, the Pacific Islands, Arabia—almost anywhere but Europe" (1990). By the end of this century, the Hispanic population is expected to increase by 21 percent, the Asian population by 22 percent, and the black population by 12 percent. By the year 2010, it is expected that 38 percent of Americans under the age of 18 will be minorities. These changes represent a challenge both to the traditional content of the curriculum and to those who deliver it. Flexibility, sensitivity, and tolerance to difference and diversity will be needed in this era of transition.

In such times, movies can either hurt or help our understanding of ourselves and others. Evidence of this approach was found during 1996 and 1997 at the University of Wisconsin, River Falls. The National Endowment for the Humanities sponsored a program called Cinematic Representations of America's Ethnic Minorities. Targeted at History, English, and Social Studies teachers in Minnesota and Wisconsin, the program explored stereotyping, Manifest Destiny, pluralism, and immigration. Participants were required to develop their own multicultural curriculum units employing film and literature. Given latent hostility to Native Americans in some communities in these states and the growth of the Asian-American population in previously German and Scandinavian areas, such a program might well foster understanding not only of movies but also of other ethnic groups.

Throughout this book we have argued that media and other representations are much more than mere entertainment. While we may turn on our televisions or go to a cineplex to relax and be entertained, we are also always being taught and socialized. Social learning theory, with its emphasis on imitation, identification, informal learning, and modeling, suggests that consciously or otherwise, we are susceptible to the influence of movie messages and representations. This is particularly true when we have little other source of knowledge and no direct or immediate experience of the people, place, circumstance, or situation that is the subject of the cinematic story. In recent times, movies like *The Joy Luck Club*, *Mi Familia*, and *Mississippi Masala* have presented both an informative and engaging look at the changing face of the American family and nation. *Heaven and Earth*, part of Oliver Stone's Vietnam trilogy, details "a Vietnamese woman's painful odyssey from a peaceful childhood in a peasant village to a lifetime of upheaval in both Vietnam and the U.S." (Maltin 1996, 572). When Lilly returns to America with her soldier husband, he tells his family, "She knows exactly what she's got and she knows exactly what she's leaving behind." But as the movie progresses, Lilly finds herself caught between two worlds and accepted in neither. Her boys will not talk Vietnamese and pretend to be Mexican. Years later, when she returns to her village, she finds her mother and brother cannot accept the person she has become. This film has a great deal to say about courage, culture, identity, and survival.

Movie representations of minorities have historically not all been so sensitive, however. In fact, the relationship between screen image and social influence has resulted in some major studies that document the film industry's depiction of various groups. The mirror model established by Kracauer's *From Caligari to Hitler* in 1947 was the basis for a number of books that began to emerge at the time of the women's movement. As the largest minority of all, women and their representation in film were the subject for Molly Haskell's *From Reverence to Rape*. Haskell documented what she called "the big lie, women's inferiority," arguing that the film industry was "dedicated for the most part to reinforcing the lie . . . through the myths of subjection and sacrifice" (1973, 3). *From Sambo to Superspade: The Black Experience in Motion Pictures* (Leab 1975) claimed that ever since the film industry began, "the human dimension has been lacking in the movie treatment of the black" (5). Donald Bogel's 1974 study of the same subject described the various movie representations in its title, *Toms, Coons, Mulattoes, Mammies and Bucks*. Native American stereotypes were the subject of *From Savage to Nobelman* (Hilger 1995). While the author saw an improvement in movie representations, he concluded "that they are ultimately too bad or too good to be believable . . . westerns have used images of the Savage or the Noble Red Man to show the superiority of their heroes . . . and the values of white culture" (1). The expectations of the white audience are also seen as shaping the film industry's response to Chicanos. Describing the narrative genre conventions of the Hollywood formula, Keller writes that its dominant elements were to "provide wish fulfillment" and "communicate Americanism."

As such, "it was the influence of the formula on the development of the movie's theme or message that really did damage to minority and other out groups" (1985, 25). Perhaps the most out group in American society has always been homosexuals. Movie stereotypes have included "sissies," "faggots," "dykes," "hustlers," and a host of other readily identifiable, frequently despisable, dehumanizing categories. Despite the presence of such characters in films like *Staircase, The Fox, The Killing of Sister George, Cruising*, and *Boys in the Band*, it is not the representation so much as the lack of it that has been criticized. Writing in *The Celluloid Closet*, Vito Russo claims, "invisibility is the great enemy, it has prevented the truth from being heard. There never have been lesbians or gay men in Hollywood films. Only homosexuals" (1981, 246). While *Torch Song Trilogy, The Bird Cage*, and *In and Out* seem to represent more sympathetic treatment of this group, as well as the public's willingness to pay to see such stories, there is still a major area of invisibility. With rare exceptions, like the character of David in *Torch Song Trilogy*, the gay or lesbian adolescent is almost entirely missing from mainstream American film. By contrast, French movies like *Wild Reeds* are capable of depicting both homosexual and heterosexual awakening with sensitivity, not sensationalism. On the rare occasions that American films have featured teenage homosexual experiences, as in *Ode to Billie Joe*, they have killed the characters off. Counselors faced with confused teenagers questioning their sexuality, on the one hand, and a homophobic student body and community, on the other hand, need to address these stereotypes. Movies and other media can both hurt and help in this process.

Stereotypes, Conventions, Clichés, and Social Attitudes

A stereotype is a hackneyed or unoriginal representation of a group. The stereotype attributes characteristics and qualities belonging to some members of a group to *all* members of that group. These can include physical characteristics and appearances as well as the views, values, beliefs, and behavior of the group. Stereotypes are exaggerations and generalizations. Although no harm may be intended by those who repeat the stereotype, the impact can still be detrimental.

The film industry does not invent stereotypes. It repeats existing stereotypes, but in the process, reinforces and perpetuates them. This is potentially harmful because it prevents us from understanding other members of our society and robs them of dignity and self-respect. Perhaps the worst stereotyping was the way the Nazi Ministry of Propaganda depicted Jews in films such as *The Eternal Jew*.

Although it is clear that stereotypes can be damaging, the media still uses them because they are immediately recognizable. In a short television program or a motion picture, there is not always enough time to flesh out a character. Using a stereotype permits the creators to present the audience with a familiar character type. Stereotypes are therefore part of the codes and conventions of filmmaking. Attempting to break those codes can be very controversial.

One such controversy exploded in 1991 following the release of *Thelma and Louise*. The depiction of women in the movies has been the subject of several outstanding books, including Molly Haskell's *From Reverence to Rape* (1973) and M. Rosen's *Popcorn Venus* (1974). More recently, feminists such as Ann Kaplan have focused attention on Hollywood's depiction of women as sex partners, mothers, and workers. Kaplan notes, for example, that although films such as *Sex, Lies and Videotape* and *9½ Weeks* give new honesty to expressions of female sexuality, they continue to do so "within a patriarchal imagery" (1991, 5). Into this arena came *Thelma and Louise*, a buddy movie in which the buddies were women. Screenwriter Callie Khouri said she wanted to see what would happen when women were placed in positions traditionally occupied by men, with control of the car, the gun, and the action. Haskell called the film "a breakthrough . . . very radical in the way it threatens men" (1973). Not all critics, however, were as enthusiastic. John Leo wrote an essay in "The Society" section of *U.S. News and World Report* describing the film as "very disturbing . . . toxic feminism" that espoused "nihilistic and self destructive values" (1991, 20). He concluded by saying, "This is a quite small hearted, extremely toxic film, about as morally and intellectually screwed up as a Hollywood movie can get" (20). Throughout the summer, the debate about women in the movies continued. *Time* said women's roles "fall into three

stereotypes: butch, babe and babysitter" (1991, 66) and concluded that "actresses may have better body tone, but most of their roles are dispiriting to anyone who harbors the hope that American movies will some day grow up" (67). The depiction of women on screen should always be considered in terms of their roles in the film industry. As of January 1992, *Premiere* magazine indicated that only 18 percent of top billed actors were females; only 15.5 percent of screenwriters at movie studios were women; on average, female directors received an annual salary of $40,000 while men were paid $85,000; and women writers received 63 cents for every dollar earned by male writers (17). If the depiction of a group that constitutes more than half of U.S. society can be so constricted and controversial, stereotyping of other groups in the culture provides an important avenue for promoting both critical thinking and critical viewing skills. Several films in recent years have generated controversy because of stereotypes and negative depictions. These include *The Color Purple*, *Sixteen Candles*, *Big Trouble in Little China*, *A Fish Named Wanda*, and *Crazy People*. Make a list of others.

(ELEM/MID/HIGH) — Have students create a list of particular groups that are often seen in the movies and describe each group's characteristics. This can include both their physical appearance and the way they act and behave. Give students the following list and have them describe the way each group is depicted in films and provide some specific movie titles to support their assertions.

Australians
Dumb blondes
Feminists
Hispanics
Homosexuals
Italian Americans
Jocks
Native Americans
Nerds
Southerners
Teamsters
Teenagers

Some films actively attempt to examine and expose these stereotypes. *The Breakfast Club* centers on a group of high school students who are locked into various cliques. They are prisoners of their perceptions, and in the course of the film they come to understand each other better. Unfortunately, the same movie that asks teenagers to judge each other fairly tends to stereotype their parents. *Pretty in Pink* is another teen film that deals with peer pressures and perceptions. The story concentrates on a working-class girl and a wealthy boy and the misconceptions they have about each other. Brief scenes from each film could be used to help middle school and high school students deal with stereotyping on a level that would be very relevant to them. *Caution:* Before showing any of these clips, check your school district's policy on films.

Sometimes clichés and conventions also subvert our understanding of individuals, issues, or institutions. Adult movie-goers would recognize the unhappy homosexual who will die by the end of the film, the racist southern politician or policeman, and the alcoholic or drug addict miraculously saved by the "love of a good woman." Neat endings, happy or otherwise, may be good box office, but they can prevent us from seriously examining our society and the issues that confront it.

Image and Influence: Beyond the Blame Game

A 1996 review of *Trainspotting*, a movie about heroin-addicted teens in Edinburgh, observed, "the movie will doubtlessly be accused of glorifying heroin, and, in a sense, it will stand guilty as charged. . . . It is a brutally honest depiction of the fun of drugs" (Gleiberman 1996, 57). Almost from its inception, the film industry has attracted controversy and concern about the impact of its images on impressionable children and teens. In the early 1930s, the Payne Fund studies investigated the influence movies had on this audience. Researchers at the time were particularly interested in the values and content of movies and how they might influence attitudes and behaviors related to sex, violence, and crime. Film and other mass media were particularly successful in Hitler's Germany in promoting and perpetuating negative attitudes about Jews that helped make the Holocaust possible. In the United States, the House Committee on Un-American Activities (HUAC) investigated the film industry looking for communist influences both behind the scenes and on the screen. Dramatic re-creations of this era can be found in *The Front*, *The Way We Were*, and *Guilty by Suspicion*.

In the 1950s, movies such as *The Wild One* and *The Blackboard Jungle* were accused of inciting juvenile deliquency. Similar charges were made about *The Warriors* in the late 1970s. In 1991, *Boyz 'n' the Hood* and *New Jack City* were both blamed for violence following screenings. After the attempted assassination of President Reagan, claims were made that the assailant had been influenced by the motion picture *Taxi Driver*. When Clark Gable wore no undershirt in *It Happened One Night* (1934), undershirt sales in the United States declined. *American Gigolo* (1980) was said to have contributed to the sale of gravity boots. The film *10* (1979) apparently contributed to a renewed interest in Maurice Ravel's *Bolero*.

Often, however, we have no idea what impact movies have on impressionable young audiences. We do not know whether or how film affects their views, values, and perceptions of others. The impact can be very subtle. In *Reel Politics*, Terry Christensen argues that movies have created negative impressions of the political process and actually serve as a form of narcotic by distracting us from issues of the day: "They have disparaged politics in general, presenting it as evil and corrupting. . . . This image reflects and reinforces popular prejudices but it also helps to entrench alienation and apathy. Movies that reinforce, reassure, or warn us to stay away from politics keep us passive" (1987, 222). Like most media, movies are capable of creating our ideas and impressions of individuals, institutions, and issues. It is also evident that they do not affect everyone in the same way. How do movies exert an influence on audiences? Communication theory indicates that film and other media messages are likely to have their greatest impact when:

1. The idea is simplified.

2. The idea/image is repeated.

3. The audience has little or no context in which to place the information and no way of judging it.

4. The image is given social sanction by being screened in the family home.

As we introduce students to the issue of film content and social attitudes, we need to be aware of several points. The messages of the movies need to be considered both individually and cumulatively. A negative image of a Native American in one film may have little or no influence. When that image is repeated in hundreds of films and reinforced in other media, however, it is likely that the stereotype will become accepted by many people, including our students. Our attempt to analyze movie messages is not intended as an exercise in finger-pointing. We are trying to describe the content of movies and to understand the forces and factors that shape that content as well as the possible social consequences of the content. We are not attempting to assign blame or to create a victim/villain model. It is also important to understand that some areas of this work may result in discomfort or denial. Identifying media messages and studying their impact on society inevitably means coming to terms with the way the media may have shaped some of our own attitudes and perceptions. In addition to realizing that movies and other media may influence us, there is also an opportunity for the liberating experience that comes when we recognize that we can reject media messages when we find them to be sexist, racist, stereotypical, or in other ways offensive. Thus, our students, who are part of a youth market, can begin more consciously to select films to see. Finally, as students become more sophisticated viewers, they can begin to detect changes in movie representations of various groups and connect these to changing social conditions. The positive public reception for films like *Rain Man*, *My Left Foot*, and *Scent of a Woman*, for example, cannot be separated from the passage of the Americans with Disabilities Act, which President Bush signed in 1990. Whether these movies shaped public attitudes and then legislation followed, or whether the movie content merely reflected changing attitudes in the audience, is a chicken-and-egg discussion of some interest. The "Cinema and Civil Rights" section of this chapter provides a more detailed analysis of this symbiotic relationship. The remainder of this chapter explores movie representations of various groups, as well as regions of the country including Appalachia and the South. History and Social Studies teachers as well as media specialists and counselors should find these sections and the films they list useful in several areas of the curriculum.

Alcoholism and Addiction

Speaking at American University in Washington, D.C., the week after California and Arizona voters approved initiatives to legalize marijuana for medicinal purposes, National Drug Policy Director Barry McCaffrey asserted that such votes did not affect federal law and that drugs like these "destroy you physically, mentally and morally." But McCaffrey did much more than condemn cocaine and other illicit substance. "Hands down," he told his audience, "the most dangerous drug in America is alcohol. We've got 10 to 18 million Americans addicted to this mildly addictive substance."

According to the drug czar, 47 percent of Americans have family members, loved ones, or employees who are trapped in the process of alcoholism or drug addiction of one form or another (CSPAN 11/13/96). The same year this speech was made, Nicholas Cage won an Academy Award for his work in *Leaving Las Vegas*. The film centers on the final days of a man on a suicidal drinking binge. Also showing that year was *Trainspotting*, "an exuberant black comedy of youthful nihilism" and heroin addiction that one writer reviewed as "Syringe Benefits" (Gleiberman 1996, 56). The arrest of Robert

Downey Jr. highlighted the continued problem and presence of drug addiction in the film industry, leading to a cover story on *Entertainment Weekly* that addressed "Heroin's Hold on Hollywood" (8/9/96).

With statistics showing increased consumption of alcohol and illegal drugs among teenagers, media representations of both alcohol and drug consumption must be featured in classroom discussions and explorations intended to reduce at-risk behavior in our young people. The tragic drug-related deaths of River Phoenix and Kurt Cobain underline the fact that youthful success often comes with a price—one that some of our young people are apparently willing to pay. While textbooks and formal instruction can categorize the chemical content and social consequences of substance abuse for students, too much of such presentations remains coldly cognitive. Movie representations, on the other hand, whether shown in their entirety or in selected scenes, tend to function in the affective domain, engaging the feelings and emotions of our students. The balance between the cognitive skills of analysis and the personal involvement of the affective domain can provide a suitable context in which to explore this very real social problem while also analyzing stereotypes and media representations. When these stories center on youthful characters, such as in *The Basketball Diaries* and *Trainspotting*, the likelihood of engaging students is even greater.

The old stereotype of the skid-row bum and wino is no longer the typical image. The context for alcoholism and addiction is frequently varied from the work-related pressures that encourage Denzel Washington's drinking in *Courage Under Fire*, to family pressures confronted by Meg Ryan in *When a Man Loves a Woman*, and the traumas of war and personal injury that Ron Kovic battles in *Born on the 4th of July*. The recovery process is also frequently shown in detail, especially when a character is engaged with a sponsor and a 12-step program like Alcoholics Anonymous (*Clean and Sober, Days of Wine and Roses*). Unfortunately, even good films can trivialize the recovery process, as is evident in Goldie Hawn's spectacular and largely painless recovery from alcoholism in the hit comedy *The First Wives Club*.

The treatment of alcoholism and drug addiction in movies and the mass media extends back at least as far as the cult classic *Reefer Madness*, made in the 1930s. Throughout the 1980s, as these social problems attracted more and more attention, Hollywood found itself under pressure to change the way it depicted drug use. Casual and recreational use of drugs can be seen in popular films such as *Annie Hall* (1977) and *The Big Chill* (1983). When it was claimed that such images glamorized and endorsed drug use, films began to change their depiction of drugs. *Less Than Zero* (1987) and *Bright Lights, Big City* (1988), both aimed at the teen market, presented very bleak images of the impact of drugs on young people. The adult market has also been targeted by Michael Keaton's *Clean and Sober* (1988). Teachers wishing to work with the issue of society and drugs, whether in social studies, counseling, or health education, can now locate many of the important films that have dealt with these topics in the last 50 years. These include Academy Award-winning films such as *The Lost Weekend* (1945) and *Days of Wine and Roses* (1962). Teachers are reminded that such themes can be integrated into English and Literature classes. Of particular interest, for example, are Eugene O'Neill's *Long Day's Journey into Night* (1962) and Edward Albee's *Who's Afraid of Virginia Woolf?* (1966). In what way do the films confirm or challenge social stereotypes about alcoholism and addiction? Are women and men both shown to be vulnerable? Do income level and class tend to play any role in addiction? How realistic are representations of the recovery process? When a character succumbs to the disease, is it clear why recovery was not possible? An example of this approach can be used with *When a Man Loves a Woman*. The film was generally well received, and it does have some strong moments, particularly late in the story when Meg Ryan's character addresses an AA meeting after six months of sobriety. However, there are aspects of alcoholism that are never addressed, often because of the high income level of the family. Unlike thousands of American families affected by alcoholism, the Greens never discuss loss of income, insurance coverage, or the cost of detox and the prolonged stay in a treatment center. The husband never once speaks to a counselor, therapist, doctor, or friend during the period before his wife is admitted or during her hospital stay. His wife works in a school but never once makes reference to how she got time off for treatment, whether the job will be there when she gets back, or whether anyone at school knew she was drinking. Since she works with students and says she started drinking at 4 a.m., there seem to be some gaps in terms of her job performance. Finally, Alice's decline into binge drinking is more talked about than shown. We see her tipsy at a restaurant and later that night; we see her fall out of a rowboat; we see her sneaking drinks and hiding bottles. The low point comes when her daughter catches her drinking: "My bottom was 184 days ago when my little girl watched me wash down aspirin with vodka and I hit her." While alcoholism is a mysterious disease, those afflicted by it do search,

often desperately, for the reason. Alice is never shown doing this. Rather, in brief, passing moments the cause is casually referred to as an alcoholic father, genetics, a mother who made her feel worthless, and that she is lonely when her husband is away on business. Thus, while we learn something of the relationship between the husband and wife, there's a good deal we do not learn about alcoholism in terms of both cause and cure. A conceptual framework using key categories can be employed to analyze movies addressing both alcoholism and addiction. *Caution:* Before showing any of these films, check your school district's policy on films.

Using categories such as (1) The Chemical, (2) The Cause, (3) The Consequences, and (4) The Cure, have students compare and contrast media representations with textbook materials and literature from groups such as AlAnon, Narcotics Anonymous, and AA.

Barfly (1987)
Basketball Diaries (1995)
Bird (1995)
The Boost (1988)
The Boy Who Drank Too Much (CBS, 1980)
Bright Lights, Big City (1988)
Clean and Sober (1988)
The Country Girl (1954)
Days of Wine and Roses (1962)
The Death of Richie (1977)
Desert Bloom (1986)
Easy Rider (1969)
A Hatful of Rain (1957)
A Hero Ain't Nothin' but a Sandwich (1978)
Ironweed (1987)
Lady Sings the Blues (1972)
Leaving Las Vegas (1995)

Less Than Zero (1987)
Long Day's Journey into Night (1962)
The Lost Weekend (1945)
The Man with the Golden Arm (1955)
My Own Private Idaho (1991)
Panic in Needle Park (1971)
Sarah T.: Portrait of a Teenage Alcoholic (NBC, 1971)
A Star Is Born (1937, 1954, 1976)
Syd and Nancy (1986)
Trainspotting (1996)
When a Man Loves a Woman (1994)
Wired (1989)

Disabilities

He didn't want to be called crippled just like I didn't want to be called stupid. —Forrest Gump

In *The Cinema of Isolation: A History of Physical Disability in the Movies*, Martin Norden asserts that the film industry has depicted "stereotypes so durable and pervasive that they have become mainstream society's perception of disabled people and have obscured if not outright supplanted disabled people's perception of themselves" (1994, 3). In the process, people with disabilities have been reduced to objects of pity and scorn as the movies pander "to the needs of the able-bodied majority" (1).

Oddly enough, such criticism came in the midst of a seemingly significant number of films that achieved both critical and popular success while addressing stories about physical disability as well as mental and emotional disorders. Al Pacino was honored with an Academy Award for his performance as a blind military officer in 1992's *Scent of a Woman*. In 1990, Robert DeNiro was nominated for an Oscar for his work in the movie *Awakenings*, which was nominated as Best Picture of the year and told the story of an individual struggling against a disease that kept him asleep for years. The year before, *My Left Foot* received Oscar nominations, and Daniel Day Lewis won a Best Actor Oscar for his performance as Christy Brown, an Irish artist with cerebral palsy. Lewis beat out Tom Cruise, who was nominated for his portrayal of Ron Kovic, a paralyzed Vietnam War veteran in *Born on the 4th of July*. Dustin Hoffman won the Academy Award for Best Actor in 1988 for his role in *Rain Man*, which dealt with the subject of an idiot savant's growing relationship with his estranged brother. *Rain Man* was also awarded Best Picture of the year. Marlee Matlin received the 1986 award for Best Actress for her role as a young deaf woman in *Children of a Lesser God*, which was also nominated for Best Picture. *Mask* (1985), *Frances* (1982), and *The Elephant Man* (1980) all received Oscar nominations for their stories about the disabled and impaired. John Voight's portrayal of a paraplegic Vietnam veteran in 1978's *Coming Home* earned him the Best Actor award, and the movie also won for Writing.

In fact, the Academy of Motion Picture Arts and Sciences has routinely singled out pictures and performances that deal with this subject matter. John Mills was honored for playing a misshapen mute in *Ryan's Daughter* (1970). Louise Fletcher received her 1975 Best Actress award for *One Flew over the Cuckoo's Nest*, drawing attention to the hearing-impaired by signing her speech. In 1968, *Charly* received the Oscar for Best Actor, which went to Cliff Robertson for his portrayal of a retarded man who becomes the subject of a scientific experiment. Perhaps the most famous performance was Patty Duke's Oscar-winning depiction of Helen Keller in 1962's *The Miracle Worker*. But even before relatively modern times, images of the disabled and the Oscar went hand in hand, evidenced by Jane Wyman's win as a deaf mute in 1948's *Johnny Belinda* and Harold Russell's win playing an amputee like himself in *The Best Years of Our Lives* (1946). His special award was presented "for bringing hope and courage to other veterans" (Maltin 1996, 104).

The period since the publication of *The Cinema of Isolation* has witnessed Disney's successful and sympathetic marketing of Quasimodo in *The Hunchback of Notre Dame*; an Oscar-nominated performance by Jodie Foster as *Nell*, an isolated and fearful woman with communication disorders; and Holly Hunter's win for *The Piano*, in which she plays a woman who has renounced speech. Best Picture and Best Actor for 1994 went to *Forrest Gump*. Hugely popular, the film might be regarded as problematic; in fact, on one level the movie represents a denial of disability since Forrest miraculously overcomes polio and seems unencumbered by his low I. Q. Whether the fantasy nature of the film invalidates such claims is a matter of personal opinion.

As a debilitating and deadly disease that frequently brings with it social scorn and ostracism, AIDS might also be included in the category of films depicting disability. *Long Time Companion*, *And the Band Played On*, and Academy Award-winning,

Philadelphia are all important contributions.

But merely listing a number of films on a given topic, or even indicating what awards and high honors they have received, is not an indication of the nature of the representation. The awards may indicate that a role was well played or a story well written. They do not necessarily indicate that these portraits of people with disabilities were honest, accurate, sensitive, or representative. In fact, the industry could be chastized for patting itself on the back for performances in which the cast simply pretended to be disabled. For those who hold such a belief, perhaps the tragic accident of Christopher Reeve may serve as a better model. His disability and long rehabilitation continue to attract national attention, and he has served as a high-profile speaker on behalf of people with disabilities at events such as the Academy Awards ceremony in 1996 and the Democratic convention in Chicago the same year.

But that is the real world, and Reeve is not playing a role. When it comes to on-screen performances, Norden's *Cinema of Isolation* refers to the "divisive behavior" indicative in the movie industry's "penchant for constructing warped social imagery" (1994, 1). He does, however, also acknowledge occasions when a story is well presented. One such story is 1993's *Passion*

Fish, which deals with an actress who is paralyzed as a result of an accident. Initially full of self-pity and resentful of others, she forms a relationship with Chantelle, an African American, and they grow together. "The women help each other, learn from each other, and grow to appreciate the world around them in a refreshingly understated way" (310).

Exploring movie representations of disabilities and mental illness can be a valuable part of any attempt to understand the relationship between film and society. "By looking at the depiction of madness in the cinema, one can gain a better understanding of how the popular conception of madness changes over time" (Fleming and Manvell 1985, 19). Whether the movies merely reflect changing social attitudes or actually serve to reinforce or alter those attitudes is open for discussion.

In special education, and in mainstreaming situations where students need to recognize that being different is not being disabled, and that having a disability does not mean that someone is a disabled person, these movie representations can play an important role. Selected, previewed, and shown in their entirety or as excerpts, they can promote sensitivity, understanding, and challenge stereotypes. *Caution:* Before showing any of these films, check your school district's policy on films.

Agnes of God (1985)
And the Band Played On (1993)
Angie (1994)
The Best Years of Our Lives (1946)
Birdy (1984)
Born on the 4th of July (1989)
The Boy Who Could Fly (1986)
Charley (1968)
Children of a Lesser God (1986)
Coming Home (1978)
Dangerous Woman (1993)
The Deer Hunter (1978)
The Elephant Man (1980)
Equus (1977)
The Fisher King (1991)
Forrest Gump (1994)
Frances (1982)
Harvey (1950)
Ice Castles (1979)
Scent of a Woman (1992)

I Never Promised You a Rose Garden (1977)
Johnny Belinda (1948)
Long Time Companion (1990)
Man Without a Face (1993)
Mask (1985)
The Miracle Worker (1962)
My Left Foot (1989)
Nell (1994)
Nuts (1987)
One Flew over the Cuckoo's Nest (1975)
Orphans (1987)
Passion Fish (1992)
Philadelphia (1993)
Prince of Tides (1991)
Rain Man (1988)
Regarding Henry (1991)
Ryan's Daughter (1970)

Snakepit (1948)
Splendor in the Grass (1961)
Stoneboy (1984)

*Tell Me That You Love Me,
    Junie Moon* (1970)
Voyage Around My Father
    (1983)
The Waterdance (1992)
The Whales of August (1987)

The South and Appalachia

If movie representations can affect our perception of addiction and disabilities, they can also influence the way we think about other countries and cultures. Even in the United States, movies and the mass media may influence our understanding about ethnic groups and whole regions of the country, particularly when we have had limited direct contact and experience with these people and places. One such example is the way Hollywood has depicted the American South. In *The Celluloid South*, Edward Campbell acknowledges the powerful role the film industry has played in shaping the public's perception. "Whatever the image, benign or evil, the cinema insured that the South was a distinctive section which drew unrelenting curiosity . . . despite the growth of urban centers and heavy industry in the region. The survival of the South in the popular imagination owes more to the cinema than any other force" (1981, 191). Much of the perception of the South, it is true, has its roots in the literary contributions of William Faulkner, F. Scott Fitzgerald, and of course, Tennessee Williams. The world of plantations, political corruption, family skeletons, belles, slaves, and long hot summers, however, represents only part of the picture.

Two of our last four presidents have come from the South. The election of Jimmy Carter in 1976 represented the emergence of the New South. Yet, despite the reality and visibility of commercial and technological centers like Atlanta or Raleigh-Durham's Research Park Triangle, old stereotypes persist both on the screen and in real life. South Carolina's senior senator, Strom Thurmond, and North Carolina's Jesse Helms exist for much of the nation as caricatures of southern politicians exemplified by Charles Laughton's role in *Advise and Consent*.

While the South actually encompasses a range of subcultures, including the Cuban presence in Florida, the Cajun and Creole contribution to Louisiana, the bluegrass traditions of the southern mountains, and affluent coastal communities like Hilton Head, the cinematic stereotypes are much narrower and less diverse. The cinematic South is a place where *Smokey and the Bandit* meets Tennessee Williams. It is a world of eccentrics, racists, lynchings, cross burnings, inbreeding, rednecks, good old boys, plantations, belles, and mint julips. Families, in fact whole communities, are depicted for the most part as dysfunctional (*Prince of Tides, The Great Santini*) or just a little crazy (*Steel Magnolias, Fried Green Tomatoes*). While these representations are evident in older films like 1941's *The Little Foxes* and 1958's *Cat on a Hot Tin Roof*, it is true that more recent contemporary and successful films like *Driving Miss Daisy* continue to dwell on a narrow range of character and story types. In reality, of course, the South is both privately and publicly more successful than its screen heritage might suggest. Atlanta secured the 1996 Olympic Games. The leadership of the Republican Party is controlled by men from Georgia, Texas, and Mississippi. The president and vice president of the United States are both from southern states.

If the South has been rather narrowly defined in film, perhaps no part or subculture of the region has been more stereotyped than Appalachia, which, for the most part, seems to be a world of coalminers and moonshiners (*Coalminer's Daughter, Matewan*). J. W. Williamson is the author of *Hillbillyland: What the Movies Did to the Mountains and What the Mountains Did to the Movies*. He believes that the hillbilly "mirrors us and like most mirrors he can both flatter, frighten and humiliate . . . he now mirrors an undeniable possibility in American manhood. In other words, we want to be him and we want to flee him" (1995, 2). While these images can be found in pictures from the past like 1941's *Tobacco Road*, they are also evident in more recent movies such as 1989's *Winter People*, 1991's *Cape Fear,* and 1994's *Nell*. There is something profoundly different and disturbing about these mountain people. While they are rural, they are not the decent, friendly farmers we recognize in *The River, Country,* or *Places in the Heart*. In our hearts and heads, whether played as cartoonishly dumb or devilishly dangerous, the hillbilly is a disturbing encounter. "He reminds us symbolically of filth, of disgusting bodily functions. Why else is he so frequently pictured with outhouses? That particular prop links the hillbilly . . . to an uncomfortable and unwelcome opening in history we have tried to forget . . . the pain and heartache of living in the dirt of the frontier" (3).

No film better conveys the encounter between the Old and the New South, and the cultural clash that occurs when city slickers encounter hillbillies, than 1972's *Deliverance*. The story actually symbolically acknowledges the destruction of the past and the rebirth of the New South. While audiences all over the world recall the brutal rape of Bobby (Ned Beatty) by the mountain men, these men, their families, their traditions, and their whole lifestyle are being raped and penetrated by progress. The film opens with the building of a new dam that will displace many of the mountain people and bury their homes beneath a wall of water. This dam will bring electricity and the comforts of suburban living to the people of nearby Atlanta. Bobby, Drew, Ed, and Lewis leave these complacent comforts to run the river while it is still possible to do so. Their encounters with the place and the people, both physical and psychological, offer students interesting insights into stereotyping and social misconceptions. While the contemptuous and judgmental Bobby derisively dismisses these people as the worthless result of inbreeding, the more sensitive Drew is able to recognize and respect their skills, evident in the now famous dueling banjo sequence. In this sense, while the film employs stereotypes, it also explores and challenges them.

Another film rich in respect for the community it depicts is John Sayles's *Matewan*. Based on a 1920 strike at a coal mine in southern West Virginia, the film "succeeds admirably in creating a sense of time and place . . . its evocation of the texture of the miner's world. Through music, regional accents, and numerous local characters, Sayles successfully creates a sense of the Matewan community" (Foner 1995, 206). Though the mayor of the town had worried that the film would result in another story about a bunch of hillbillies, the final version dispelled such concerns. It must also be acknowledged that much of the reason for this was that John Sayles is an independent director, running his own production company without studio financing and therefore free from much of the formulaic storytelling that frequently dominates the industry. As such, movie representations of the South can be compared and contrasted to the diversity of the real South. At the same time we should ask students to explore not only media content but also media control and ownership of the production process. A final word should be said about movie representations of southern women, since they frequently occur in stories that have received critical and commercial acclaim, thereby attracting national and international audiences to stories about the South. These include Academy Award-winning performances by Sally Field in *Norma Rae* and *Places in the Heart*, Sissy Spacek as Loretta Lynn (*The Coalminer's Daughter*), Jessica Tandy in *Driving Miss Daisy*, and Jodie Foster as detective Clarice Starling in *Silence of the Lambs*.

All the King's Men (1949)
Angel Baby (1961)
Ballad of the Sad Cafe (1991)
The Big Easy (1987)
Blaze (1989)
Cat on a Hot Tin Roof (1958)
Coal Miner's Daughter (1980)
Cool Hand Luke (1967)
Crimes of the Heart (1986)
The Defiant Ones (1958)
Deliverance (1972)
Dollmaker (1984)
Driving Miss Daisy (1989)
Everybody's All-American (1988)
Fried Green Tomatoes (1991)
Glory (1989)
Gone with the Wind (1939)
I Am a Fugitive from a Chain Gang (1932)
In the Heat of the Night (1967)

Inherit the Wind (1960)
Intruder in the Dust (1949)
The Little Foxes (1941)
The Long Hot Summer (1958)
Macon County Line (1974)
Matewan (1987)
Mississippi Burning (1988)
Norma Rae (1979)
Places in the Heart (1984)
Ramblin' Rose (1991)
Shy People (1987)
Smokey and the Bandit (1978)
Song of the South (1946)
The Sound and the Fury (1959)
Sounder (1972)
Southern Comfort (1981)
Steel Magnolias (1989)
Sweet Bird of Youth (1962)
Tobacco Road (1941)
Winter People (1989)

THE WORLD OF WORK: School on the Screen

> *Sometimes you need Mr. Chips, sometimes you need Dirty Harry.*—William Bennett, U.S., Secretary of Education, 1988

So far, we have explored the way in which movies and other mass media can shape our perception of minorities and ethnic groups, regions of the country, and entire countries and cultures. If we accept the fact that these media messages constitute part of the way we look at and think about such groups, it is also possible that movies and other media can affect our perception of various occupations and professions, both by whose stories they choose to tell (doctors, lawyers, police officers) and by those who are largely ignored (vets, architects, accountants, engineers). One group frequently depicted in movies is soldiers. While we may come to understand something of the calling and the individual conflict in which these cinematic soldiers are engaged, we are also presented with a portrait of the military as an institution (*An Officer and a Gentleman*, *A Few Good Men*, *Barry Lyndon*, *Full Metal Jacket*, *Platoon*, *Courage Under Fire*). The Pentagon certainly cares enough about the image of the military as an institution that it traditionally lends its considerable support to films it regards as pro-military (*Top Gun*), while denying support to those it regards as negative (*Platoon*). This support was institutionalized during World War II when Hollywood and the Pentagon came to understand that "politics, profits, and propaganda could reinforce each other to create symbols of a unified harmonious society" (Koppes and Black 1987, 328). These films, whether criticizing the military or supporting it, represent the filter and frame through which we conceptualize military life. Frequently this includes our perception of other countries, and our relationships with them as our allies. Their causes are defined while our enemies are demonized. This process is described in *Celluloid Wars*, which examines the relationship between cinematic representations of the military and the nation's experience of war. "Movies have been an intregal part of the American experience. They combine myth, folklore and political and social messages in a way that *both reflect and direct* America's world view" (Wetta and Curley 1992, xv).

One profession whose members have become increasingly concerned about the way the media depicts them are the clergy. *Hollywood Versus Religion,* a videotape produced by Focus on the Family, intended to address this form of representation. Hosted by well-known film critic Michael Medved, the program accuses the film industry of "one-sided, vicious and unfair stereotyping." In the past, the program suggests, priests, ministers, men of the cloth, personal faith and the church as an institution were respected by society and cinema. Pointing to Hollywood hits like *Boy's Town*, *Angels with Dirty Faces*, *Going My Way*, and *The Bells of St. Mary's*, the show explores these positive images. Interestingly enough, these were all made in the late 1930s and 1940s when pro-American messages were being created as part of the war effort. According to Medved, this positive image began to change in the late 1960s. Today, he says, whether presenting individual religious figures, everyday believers, or the church as an institution, the message is relentlessly negative irrespective of denomination. *Misery* and *A Few Good Men* are typical examples of films in which the openly Christian characters are presented as crazed killers. While the program makes no attempt to link Hollywood's message to changing public perceptions of the church or various scandals that have emerged in real life, it nonetheless makes an interesting case about media representations. As a Hollywood insider, Medved knows how the industry works. When he says, "Nothing in movies happens by accident," he points to a deliberate attempt on the part of filmmakers to damage the church. This view was reinforced by the publication of *Seeing and Believing: Religion and Values in the Movies*. The author describes what she calls "the frequency of slurs about religion" in the movies, and she regards this as "evidence of North America's anxiety about religion" (Miles 1996, ix). While Medved seems content to blame the industry, Miles sees a more symbiotic relationship, suggesting that "we as a society seek evidence that will substantiate and reinforce our belief that religious practices are ineffective, and that religious beliefs are wrong, misguided and dangerous" (ix). There is no difficulty finding contemporary films that, at the very least, question religion. *At Play in the Fields of the Lord*, *The Mission*, *Priest*, *Mass Appeal*, *Agnes of God*, and others are all good examples. It is also possible to find films that support faith and spirituality, whether on an individual or an institutionalized level (*Shadowlands*, *Little Buddha*, *Chariots of Fire*, *The Chosen*, *Seven Years in Tibet*).

One of the most interesting ways to show the relationship between social reality and media representations is to explore school on the screen, or the way movies depict education as a process, school as an institution, and both teachers and students as individuals. Since your students will have had many years of experience with teachers, principals, and the day-to-day routine of school, they will all have a body of personal experience to draw upon as they consider Hollywood's depiction of school. It is also highly likely that they will have seen a number of movies about school (*Dangerous Minds*, *Mr. Holland's Opus*, *The Breakfast Club*, *Dead Poet's Society*) and will have some strong feelings about some of them. Thus, studying representations of school in the media provides them with a very concrete opportunity to compare their personal experiences to those the film industry depicts and then make a record of these movies. Undergraduates in teacher preparation at Appalachian State University employ such an approach as part of their own program. This popular assignment asks them to compare and contrast movie representations of teachers, communities, students, and administrators with those in the real world. In the process, they also explore curriculum content and teaching methods.

While *Mr. Holland's Opus* and *Dangerous Minds* are two recent examples of rather positive portraits of teachers, this has not always been the most common image provided by Hollywood. In 1980, *The Secondary Teacher* observed that "today, with alarming and relentless repetition, the image of the teacher is that of a victim, a voyeur or worse." Further it is suggested, "any analysis of school on the screen will show the teacher at the mercy of students, parents and administration, or as a morally suspect individual" (Considine, 13). Five years later, *The Cinema of Adolescence* asserted that "the changing image of school and particularly the school teacher can be read as a reflection of changes not only within the American school system but within the nation itself. Most astounding of all these changes is the increasingly negative portrayal of the school teacher" (Considine 1985, 114).

Tracing movie representations of education back to the 1930s, this work noted that even the most beloved teachers often started as failures. *Goodbye Mr. Chips*, which garnered an Oscar for Robert Donat's performance, is one such example. The boys get the better of Arthur Chipping, who is shown as weak and ineffectual at the start of the film. Finally, the headmaster intervenes, telling him, "Our business is to mold men. Above all it demands the ability to exercise authority." Trapped between the dictates of the administration and a desire to employ his own methods, "Chips" becomes something of a Caligula of the classroom. "Perhaps you don't mind being hated," one of his students suggests. What transforms Chips into the beloved teacher audiences remember is not his teacher training, nothing he finds in textbooks, nor the support of colleagues or administrators. He is transformed as both a person and a pedagogue by that old cliché—the love of a good woman. Hence he becomes a better teacher through the support of a total outsider to the profession.

This outsider knowledge became much valued in both film and television portrayals of teachers. The 1980s hit series *Head of the Class* featured a stimulating and effective teacher who was, in fact, an actor basically substituting as a teacher. Sidney Poitier's Mark Thackeray in *To Sir with Love* is one of the screen's most loved teachers, but he is really an engineer. In the working-class environment where he teaches, education is regarded as a disadvantage. The principal, conforming to stereotype, is well meaning but inept. The other teachers range from naively optimistic to scathingly cynical. To succeed, Thackeray must throw out the curriculum and teach what he thinks is important.

Another teacher who throws out the formal curriculum for one of her own is Jean Brodie (*The Prime of Miss Jean Brodie*). Much more morally ambiguous than *To Sir with Love*, which clearly presented the hero-teacher, *Jean Brodie* is symptomatic of much of the generation gap of the late 1960s. Although the film is set in Scotland during the 1930s, the clash between Brodie and the administration, and the assertion of artistic freedom and open sexuality are particularly indicative of attitudes of the 1960s. Brodie says, "I am a teacher, first, last, and always . . . I influence them to be aware of the possibilities of life, beauty, honor, courage. I have dedicated and sacrificed my life to this profession." Brodie's energy and conviction are in stark contrast to the timid, colorless teachers that surround her. It is easy for movie audiences, like her students, to be drawn into her charm. But her lessons about life go well beyond any concept of curriculum or locus parentus. Fascinated by the fascist states of Franco and Mussolini, her political teachings contribute to the death of one student. Another is designated by Brodie as a suitable mistress for the art teacher. For all her appeal and energy, Brodie stands condemned. At the end of the film a student tells her, "You're dangerous and unwholesome and children should not be exposed to you."

The private world of Brodie's Marcia Blane School for Girls is not far removed from the world John Keating finds himself in (*Dead Poet's Society*). In fact, both films present the formulaic story and set with one engaging, dedicated teacher surrounded by bored but eager students, unsupportive hard-line administrators, and ineffectual colleagues. Despite the fact that the screenplay won an Oscar, much about the story follows such stereotypes of school. Set at a New England prep school in 1959, it places the school and the students on the cusp of Kennedy's New Frontier. In his inaugural address, Kennedy will say that the torch has been passed to a new generation of Americans. As if to signify this theme, the film's title appears as a candle is lit. The world of Wellton Academy, its routine, and its rituals are the focus of this opening ceremony. The headmaster calls upon the boys to declare the four pillars: Tradition, Honor, Discipline, Excellence. Later in their rooms, the boys will rephrase this: Travesty, Horror, Decadence, Excrement. John Keating arrives at this school as a breath of fresh air, even though he himself is a graduate of the school. Before we ever see him teach, the film makes a point of showing us the dull drill-and-practice routine and tedium of the Latin, trigonometry, and science classes. Keating's methods are in stark contrast. The revolutionary nature of his approach is signified as he enters the classroom for the first time whistling "The 1812 Overture." Immediately he removes the boys from the classroom and has them contemplate photographs of now dead former students. "We are the food for worms, lads . . . *carpe diem*. Seize the day. Make your lives extraordinary." Unsure what to make of the lesson or the new teacher, the boys call the experience "weird," "spooky," "but different." In a world of routine and numbing conformity, Keating's difference is alluring to these future doctors, lawyers, and bankers. It is especially attractive to Neale Perry, whose father pushes him to succeed, requiring him to attend summer school and insisting that he give up his role as assistant editor of the school annual. It is Perry who is called upon by Keating to read the introduction of the textbook on understanding and appreciating poetry. Once again the classroom seems to be a ritualized world of rules, regulations, and guidelines. Keating startles the boys when he tells them to rip out that section of the textbook. He dismisses the chapter as "excrement," immediately aligning himself with language the boys had used earlier. In place of the textbook technique, Keating wants the boys to "learn to savor words and language. This is a battle, a war, and the casualties could be your hearts and souls." By the end of the film, Neale Perry is the casualty, taking his own life when his father withdraws him from school because he disobeyed him and performed in a play. The father and the school administration blame Keating for leading the boy astray. The film ends with order restored and Keating's replacement returning to textbook traditions. The camera looks down on Keating, but at the same time, it looks up at the boys—not all of them, to be sure, but many who now stand on top of their desks, as Keating had once done. These are the Keating converts, who now will look at the world in a very different way, the way he advocated.

In *Dangerous Minds*, it is the teacher, Luanne Johnson, who must learn to look at the world in a different way. "Who are these kids, rejects from hell?" she asks after her first encounter with her class. The kids have an attitude and an answer: "You don't understand nothin'. You don't come from where we live. You're not bussed here . . . you're just here for the money." Luanne

Johnson is a former marine. She has completed her education classes but has not had the required term of supervised teaching. Nonetheless she finds herself hired to work with a group of kids who seem to take pride in causing teachers to have breakdowns. Her students, she is told, are "bright kids with little or no educational skills and what we politely call a lot of social problems."

While the language the kids use and their hostile in-your-face attitude are profoundly different from the politeness of Wellton Academy, they are merely an extension of 1955's *Blackboard Jungle* and 1967's *To Sir with Love*. The teachers in all three films encounter a curriculum that fails to engage the students. They also encounter a hard-line administration more intent on enforcing policy than on engaging pupils. Ms. Johnson is called to the office of the black principal, Mr. Grandey. She is told that she must "follow the curriculum dictated by the Board of Education." "You're going to have to go along with our policies even if you don't agree with them." Like Dadier (*The Blackboard Jungle*) and Thackeray (*To Sir with Love*) before her, Ms. Johnson quickly discovers that the answers cannot be found in textbooks. She laughs at the guidelines in *Assertive Discipline* and struggles to find her own teaching strategies. Ostensibly an English teacher, her first lesson is karate skills. Her colleague has told her that to be able to teach them, "all you've got to do is get their attention." The karate lesson works. She teaches parts of speech by using sentences the students can relate to. "Never shoot a homeboy," she writes on the board, and distributes candy bars as a reward to students who correctly identify nouns and other parts of speech. She challenges them with the poetry of Bob Dylan and Dylan Thomas, once again offering inducements like a night at a fancy restaurant or a trip to an amusement park for successfully completing the assigned work.

But she makes mistakes along the way and has to learn from them. "I made it worse, I made you look bad in front of the others," she admits to Raoul after she has tried to prevent a fight. From the boy's perspective, he had no choice except to fight. "In our neighborhood, if you don't stand up, you can't walk down the street because everyone will attack you." Johnson begins to realize that to understand who these kids are, she has to understand where they come from. She wins the respect of Emilio, the class leader and the most difficult student to reach, when she visits some of the families. "That's cool," he tells her. Winning him over is the key to succeeding with the class in the same way Thackeray must win over Denim.

Johnson can reach out and motivate many of these young people. She can encourage Raoul and Kelly. She can help them deal with pregnancy and poverty and poor self-esteem. But she cannot save them all. While she tells them, "There are no victims in this classroom," some of them are clearly victims of an indifferent society and school system. This point is hammered home when Emilio is shot and killed because of the rigid, inflexible rules and attitudes of the principal. *Dangerous Minds*, like *Dead Poet's Society, Teachers,* and *Up the Down Staircase*, uses the death of a student to demonstrate the cold indifference of the education system. If most teachers come off badly in these films, the administrators consistently fare worse. Parents, for their part, are either totally absent from the plot or are presented as simply one more obstacle and problem for the hero-teacher and student-victims to deal with.

Against this background, the Oscar-nominated *Mr. Holland's Opus* presents an optimistic, if idealized, vision of American education. Not since *Good Morning Miss Dove* (1955) has a movie devoted itself to tracing the lifelong career and contribution of a teacher in a single community. Glenn Holland is a musician who looks upon his introduction to teaching as a stopgap, something to fall back on. The movie traces his experiences in an Illinois school as he teaches generations of young people to appreciate music, whether the classics, rock, or the marching band. While the film skirts some of the central problems of the 1960s and 1970s, including drugs, the sexual revolution, and the generation gap, it does depict what a dedicated and inspired teacher can

achieve. It also shows some of the costs of that commitment. Both Holland's wife and son complain at various points in the movie that he cares more about his students than about them. As Mrs. Jacobs, the school principal, Olympia Dukakis presents a refreshingly human and warm face to what is usually a sterotype. By late in the film, her retirement signals the arrival of the numbers-crunchers. Acrimonious meetings result in budget cuts to both the drama and music programs. An angry Holland tells the administrators, "How little you people care, how lazy you've become. You people are willing to create a generation of children who will not have the ability to think, or create, or listen."

It is not possible in this short section to address all movie representations of school as an institution or education as a process. Moving from the fictional world of some of these movies to real-life stories can help students compare and contrast reality with dramatizations of reality. Two very useful films to achieve this are *Stand and Deliver* (1987), the true story of teacher Heime Escalante, set in the East Los Angeles barrio and chronicling the story of how one teacher's methods contributed to success on the Advanced Placement Calculus Test at a time when the school had given up on these kids; and *Lean on Me* (1989), the story of controversial New Jersey high school principal Joe Clark. Clark's methods, which included expelling hundreds of students and firing teachers, were so controversial that he landed a cover story in *Time* magazine (2/1/88). Made by John Alvidsen, director of both *Rocky* and *The Karate Kid*, the film suffers from some of the emotional excesses of both movies. It does, however, raise many important questions about real problems facing real students, teachers, and administrators. Not everyone will agree with Clark's solutions, but he does have a positive, upbeat message: "If you can conceive it, you can believe it, and you can achieve it."

REFERENCES

American Film Institute, (1992). *Visions of Light: The Art of Cinematography.* Videotape.Washington, DC.

Anderegg, Michael, (1984). *David Lean.* Boston: Twayne Publishing.

Annenberg Collection, (1995). *American Cinema.* Videotape series including "The Hollywood Style," "Film Noir," "The Combat Film," and "The Western." 1-800-LEARNER.

Ascher-Walsh, Rebecca, (1995). Does Hollywood Have a Jewish Problem? *Entertainment Weekly*, 28-31.

Beaver, Frank, (1994). *Oliver Stone: Wakeup Cinema.* New York: Twayne Publishers.

Bergman, Andrew, (1971). *We're in the Money: Depression America and Its Films.* New York: Harper Colophon.

Bogel, D., (1974). *Toms, Coons, Mulattoes, Mammies and Bucks.* New York: Bantam.

Bordwell, David, and Janet Thompson, (1979). *Film Art.* Reading, MA: Addison-Wesley.

Bordwell, David, Janet Staiger, and Kristin Thompson, (1985). *The Classical Hollywood Cinema.* New York: Columbia University Press.

Burgoyne, Robert, (1996). Modernism and the Narrative of Nation in JFK. In Vivian Sobchack (ed.), *The Persistence of History: Cinema, Television and the Modern Event.* New York: Routledge.

Callahan, Maureen, (1996). Trends/Alienation. *New York*, May 20, 151.

Campbell, Edward, (1981). *The Celluloid South: Hollywood and the Southern Myth.* Knoxville: University of Tennessee Press.

Carnes, Mark C. (ed.), (1995). *Past Imperfect: History According to the Movies.* New York: Henry Holt.

Cawelti, John G. (ed.), (1973). *Focus on Bonnie and Clyde.* Englewood Cliffs, NJ: Prentice Hall.

Chafe, William, (1995). Mississippi Burning. In Mark Carnes (ed.), *Past Imperfect: History According to the Movies.* New York: Henry Holt.

Chatham Hill Foundation, (1994). *Hollywood vs. Religion.* Dallas, Texas. Videotape.

Christensen, Terry, (1987). *Reel Politics: American Political Movies from the* Birth of a Nation *to* Platoon. New York: Blackwell.

Chumo, Peter, (1995). You've Got to Put the Past Behind You Before You Can Move On: Forrest Gump and National Reconciliation. *Journal of Popular Film and Television,* Spring, 2-7.

Connelly, Marie Kathleen, (1993). *Martin Scorcese.* Jefferson, NC: McFarland.

Considine, David, (1980). School on the Screen: From Mentors to Murders. *The Secondary Teacher*, No. 6, 13-17.

———, (1985). *The Cinema of Adolescence.* Jefferson, NC: McFarland.

Corliss, Richard, (1996). The Invasion Has Begun. *Time,* July 8, 58-64.

———, (1996). Suddenly Shakespeare. *Time,* November 4, 88-90.

Costanzo, William, (1992). *Reading the Movies.* Urbana, IL: National Council of Teachers of English.

Daly, Steve, (1995). For King or Country. *Entertainment Weekly*, September 15, 116-17.

Dick, Bernard, (1980). *Billy Wilder.* Boston: Twaybe Publishing.

Dyer, Richard, (1993). *The Matter of Images: Essays on Representation.* London: Routledge.

Eisner, Lotte, (1969). *The Haunted Screen.* London: Secker & Warburg.

Entertainment Weekly, (1996). Heroin's Hold on Hollywood. August 9, cover.

Ferro, Marc, (1988). *Cinema and History.* Detroit: Wayne State University Press.

Fleming, Michael, and Roger Manvell, (1985). *Images of Madness: The Portrayal of Insanity in the Feature Film.* Cranbury, NJ: Associated University Presses.

Foner, Eric, (1995). Matewan. In Mark Carnes (ed.), *Past Imperfect: History According to the Movies.* New York: Henry Holt.

Fraser, G., (1988). *The Hollywood History of the World.* New York: Beach Tree.

French, Philip, (1973). *Westerns.* London: Secker & Warburg.

Giannetti, Louis, (1976). *Understanding Movies.* Englewood Cliffs, NJ: Prentice Hall.

Gleiberman, Owen. (1996). Syringe Benefits. *Entertainment Weekly,* July 19, 56-57.

Guerrero, Ed, (1933). *Framing Blackness: The African American Image in Film.* Philadelphia: Temple University Press.

Hardy, Phil, (1983). *The Western.* New York: William Morrow.

Haskell, Molly, (1973). *From Reverence to Rape: The Treatment of Women in the Movies.* New York: Holt, Rinehart & Winston.

Henry III, William, (1990). Beyond the Melting Pot. *Time,* April 9, 28-31.

Hilger, Michael, (1995). *From Savage to Nobleman: Images of Native Americans in Films.* Lanham, MD: Scarecrow Press.

Hillier, Jim, (1973). Arthur Penn. In John Cawelti (ed.), *Focus on Bonnie and Clyde* (7-14). Englewood Cliffs, NJ: Prentice Hall.

Hirsch, Foster, (1981). *Film Noir: The Dark Side of the Screen.* New York: Plenum.

Horowitz, Joy, (1989). Hollywood's Dirty Little Secret. *Premiere*, March, 56-64.

Jones, Jacqueline, (1995). The Long Walk Home. In Mark Carnes (ed.), *Past Imperfect: History According to the Movies*. New York: Henry Holt.

Kagan, Norman, (1991). *The Cinema of Stanley Kubrick*. New York: Continuum.

Kaminsky, Stuart, (1974). *American Film Genres*. Dayton, OH: Pflaum.

Kaplan, E. Ann, (1991). Sex, Work and Motherhood. *Metro*, 85, 3-11.

Karney, Robyn, (1995). *Chronicle of the American Cinema*. New York: Dorling Kindersley.

Karnow, Stanley, (1995). JFK. In Mark Carnes (ed.), *Past Imperfect: History According to the Movies*. New York: Henry Holt.

Keller, Gary D., (1985). *Chicano Cinema: Research, Reviews and Resources*. Tempe, AZ: Bilingual Review Press.

Koppes, Clayton, and Gregory Black, (1987). *Hollywood Goes to War: How Politics, Profits and Propaganda Shaped World War 2 Movies*. New York: Free Press.

Kracauer, Siegfried, (1947). *From Caligari to Hitler*. Princeton, NJ: Princeton University Press.

Lacayo, Richard, (1995). Violent Reaction. *Time*, June 12, 24-30.

Leab, Daniel, (1975). *From Sambo to Superspade: The Black Experience in Motion Pictures*. Boston: Houghton Mifflin.

Leo, John, (1991). Toxic Feminism on the Big Screen. *U.S. News and World Report*, June 10, 20.

Levy, Emanuel, (1991). *Small Town America in Film: The Decline and Fall of Community*. New York: Continuum.

Life, (1953). Night Watch, November 9, 57-60.

Maeder, Edward, (1987). *Hollywood and History: Costume Design in Film*. New York: Thames & Hudson.

Maltin, Leonard, (1996). *1997 Movie and Video Guide*. New York: Signet.

Mandelbaum, Howard, and Eric Myers, (1985). *Screen Deco*. New York: St. Martin's.

Mapp, E., (1974). *Blacks in American Film: Today and Yesterday*. Metuchen, NJ: Scarecrow.

Maynard, R., (1972). *Africa on Film: Myth and Reality*. Rochelle Park, NJ: Hayden.

McBride, Joseph, and Michael Wilmington, (1974). *John Ford*. London: Secker & Warburg.

McPherson, James, (1995). Glory. In Mark Carnes (ed.), *Past Imperfect: History According to the Movies*. New York: Henry Holt.

Medved, Michael, (1997). Spielberg Film Warps History, Deceives Students. *U.S.A. Today*, December 9, 15A.

Miles, Margaret, (1996). *Seeing and Believing: Religion and Values in the Movies*. Boston: Beacon Press.

Monaco, James, (1977). *How to Read a Film*. New York: Oxford University Press.

Neely, Mark, (1995). The Young Lincoln: Two Films. In Mark Carnes (ed.), *Past Imperfect: History According to the Movies*. New York: Henry Holt.

Newsweek, (1995). *Nixon: The Movie, the History, the Controversy*, December 11, 68.

Norden, Martin F., (1994). *The Cinema of Isolation: A History of Physical Disability in the Movies*. New Brunswick, NJ: Rutgers University Press.

Peary, Gerald, and Roger Shatzkin, (1977). *The Classic American Novel and the Movies*. New York: Ungar Publishing.

Rosen, M., (1974). *Popcorn Venus: Women, Movies and the American Dream*. New York: Avon.

Russo, Vito, (1981). *The Celluloid Closet: Homesexuality in the Movies*. New York: Harper & Row.

Ryan, Michael, and Douglas Kellner, (1988). *Camera Politica: The Politics and Ideology of Contemporary Hollywood Film*. Bloomington: Indiana University Press.

Saettler, Paul, (1968). *History of Instructional Technology*. New York: McGraw Hill.

Sanello, Fran, (1996). *Speilberg: The Man, the Movies, the Mythology*. Dallas: Taylor Publishing.

Sarf, W., (1983). *God Bless You Buffalo Bill: A Layman's Guide to History and the Western Film*. Rutherford, NJ: Fairlegh Dickenson University Press.

Sayles, John, (1987). *Thinking in Pictures: The Making of Matewan*. Boston: Houghton Mifflin.

Schlesinger, Arthur, (1979). Introduction. In J. O'Connor and M. Jackson (eds.), *American History/American Film*. New York: Ungar Publishing.

Sklar, Robert, (1975). *Movie-Made America: A Cultural History of American Movies*. New York: Vintage.

Sobchack, Vivian, (1996). *The Persistence of History: Cinema, Television and the Modern Event*. New York: Routledge.

South Carolina Department of Education, (1995). *English Language Arts Framework*. Columbia, SC.

Speech Communication Association, (1996). *Speaking, Listening and Media Literacy Standards for K Through 12 Education*. Annandale, VA: SCA.

Spoto, Donald, (1978). *Stanley Kramer: Film Maker*. Hollywood: Samuel French.

Stryker, Roy, and Nancy Wood, (1973). *In This Proud Land*. New York: Rapaport Printing.

Time, (1983). *The Outsiders*, review. April 4, 78.

——, (1991). Why Can't a Woman Be a Man? August 5, 66-67.

Tudor, Andrew, (1974). *Theories of Film*. London: Secker & Warburg.

Vacche, Angela Dalle, (1996). *Cinema and Painting: How Art Is Used in Film*. Austin: University of Texas Press.

Wells, Jeffrey, (1996). Flirting with Disaster. *Entertainment Weekly*, May 17.

Wetta, Frank, and Stephen Curley, (1992). *Celluloid Wars: A Guide to Film and the American Experience of War*. New York: Greenwood Press.

Williamson, J. W., (1995). *Hillbillyland: What the Movies Did to the Mountains and What the Mountains Did to the Movies*. Chapel Hill: University of North Carolina Press.

Woll, Allen, (1980). *The Latin Image in American Film*. Berkeley and Los Angeles: University of California Press.

Wollen, Peter, (1968). *Signs and Meaning in the Cinema*. London: Secker & Warburg.

In the last five years a growing number of videotapes, books, journals, and other materials have been published and produced that support the development of media education. It is not possible to list systematically all of these materials in this section. Most of the books referred to throughout this book are available through two major centers as well as through virtual bookstores such as *Amazon.com*. In the United States, the closest thing to a one-stop shopping experience for both American and "foreign" items is *The Center for Media Literacy in Los Angeles.* They can be contacted at 1-800-226-9494 or faxed at 213-931-4474. The abbreviation CML next to an item in the list below indicates that it can be accessed through this organization. In Canada, Toronto's *Theatre Books* provides access to an enormous number of materials, including U.S., British, and Australian media literacy resources. The phone is 202-949-0511, or they can be faxed at 204-949-0013. Catalogs are available from both companies.

MEDIA LITERACY ORGANIZATIONS, PERIODICALS, AND WEBSITES

Association for Media Literacy. The flagship media literacy organization in Canada and the source of much impetus and inspiration for the U.S. media literacy movement. Publishes newsletter called *Mediacy*. 41 Pinewood Ave., Toronto, Ontario M6C 2 V2.

ATOM (Australian Teachers of Media). Perhaps the most respected media education organization in the world. Publishes *METRO*, and an outstanding series of movie study guides designed by and for teachers. 3rd Floor, 17 St. Andrews Pl., East Melbourne, Victoria 3002. c/o Locked Bag 9 Collins St., East Melbourne, Victoria 3003. Fax: 61-3-9651-1311. E-mail: atomvic@netspace.net.au. Website: http://www.cinemedia.nct/ATOM.

British Film Institute. The center for media education and teacher training in the UK. Excellent source for curriculum documents, frameworks, evaluation instruments, and guidelines. 21 Stephen St., London W1P 2LN. Fax: 0171-580-8434.

Center for Literacy. Publishes *Literacy Across the Curriculum*. Represents a holistic approach to literacy in all its manifestations. 3040 Sherbrooke St. West, Montreal, Quebec, Canada H3Z 1A4.

Center for Media Education. Kathryn Montgomery. Particularly concerned with government policy, regulation, and issues of citizenship. 1511 K St. NW, Suite 518, Washington, DC 20005. Phone: 202-628-2620. Website: www.cme.org/cme.

Center for Media Literacy. Elizabeth Thoman, Executive Director. Formerly the Center for Media and Values with an emphasis on Catholic media education. Now more broad-based, it serves as a major distribution center for media literacy materials and publishes a short newsletter called *Connect*. 4727 Wilshire Blvd., Suite 403, Los Angeles, CA 90010. Website: http://www.medialit.org.

Clipboard is a media education newsletter from Canada published by Father John Pungente, whose major contribution to media literacy other than this publication has been his work as head of the Jesuit Communication Project and his creation of the series *Scanning Television* and *Scanning the Movies*. 60 St. Clair Ave. East, Suite 1002, Toronto, Ontario M4T 1N5. Fax: 416-515-0467. E-mail: pungente@epas.utoronto.ca.

Media Education Foundation. Founded by Sut Jhally and including an impressive board (Naoim Wolf, Jean Kilbourne, Noam Chomsky), the group focuses on the production and distribution of media education materials. 26 Center St., Northhampton, MA 01060. Fax: 413-586-8938.

Media Literacy On-line Project. The principal media literacy website with links to numerous other media literacy sites and sources. Established by the University of Oregon. Website: http://interact.uoregon.edu/MediaLit/HomePage.

National Telemedia Council. Hosted the 1995 National Media Literacy conference. They win the longevity award with media literacy roots in the 1950s. Publishes *Telemedium: The Journal of Media Literacy*, the most professional and nationally focused U.S. publication in the field. Glossy, visual, and contemporary, it typically includes activities for classroom teachers as well as articles from major figures in the field including Barry Duncan, Renee Hobbs, and David Considine. 120 East Wilson St., Madison, WI 53703. Phone: 608-257-7712. Fax: 608-257-7714. E-mail: NTelemedia@aol.com.

New Mexico Media Literacy Project. Publishes a newsletter, *The State of Media Education*, that addresses media literacy events and developments within New Mexico. Albuquerque Academy, 6400 Wyoming NE, Albuquerque, NM 87109. Contact Bob McCannon: 505-828-3264. Website: http://www.aa.edu.

Recommended Periodicals

In addition to newsletters and journals published by various media literacy organizations, there are a number of useful publications that make a valuable addition to any collection. They are available either through subscription or in some cases from bookstores.

General Media Content

Entertainment Weekly. An invaluable source of information about television, advertising, movies, and multimedia, including ratings and revenues. c/o Time Inc., 1675 Broadway, New York, NY 10019.

Journal of Broadcasting and Electronic Media. Scholarly articles addressing a wide range of media formats and issues, including television, advertising, and news. Published quarterly by the Broadcast Education Association, 1771 N. St. NW, Washington, DC 20036-2891.

News on Children and Violence on the Screen. UNESCO International Clearinghouse on Children and Violence on the Screen. Nordicom, Goteborg University, Sweden. Fax: +46-31-773-4655.

News

Columbia Journalism Review. Published monthly, it provides an industry insider look at what journalists themselves have to say about their own profession and coverage. Columbia University, 101 Journalism Building, 2950 Broadway, New York, NY 10027.

Extra. Published by FAIR (Fairness and Accuracy in Media). Bimonthly publication from media watchdog group. Includes in-depth analysis and criticism of how news media covered particular stories. PO Box Congers, New York, NY 10920-9930. Phone: 1-800-847-3993.

Advertising

ADbusters: Journal of the Mental Environment. Critical, frequently humorous, and satirical spin on advertising with highly popular spoofs of major advertising images. Fights fire with fire through concept known as culture jamming. Teenagers tend to love it. The Media Foundation, 1243 West 7th Ave., Vancouver, BC V6H 1B7 Canada. Phone: 604-736-9401. E-mail: adbusters@adbusters.org.

Advertising Age. Published weekly, it provides an industry insider look at advertising, including revenues and various campaign tactics and strategies. Published weekly. 965 East Jefferson, Detroit, MI 48207-3185,

VIDEOTAPES

Overviews and Introductions

Creating Critical Viewers. Videotape and workbook developed by Dorothy and Jerome Singer from Yale University. Includes lessons on advertising, stereotyping, and news. Distributed through NATAS (National Academy of Television Arts and Sciences). Renee O'Leary, c/o NATAS, 111 West 57th St., Suite 1020, New York, NY 10019.

The Crisis of the Cultural Environment: Media and Democracy in the 21st Century. Dr. Gerbner discusses media policy including issues of control and the information superhighway. Media Education Foundation. Phone: 1-800-897-0089.

The Electronic Storyteller: Television and the Cultivation of Values. Perhaps the most respected voice in television effects research, Dr. George Gerbner explores television's representation of gender, class, and race. Media Education Foundation. Phone: 1-800-897-0089.

Kids Talk TV: Inside/Out. Includes segments on television news, stereotyping and production techniques. Aimed at children 9 to 11 as a tool to promote critical viewing and thinking skills. CML. Phone: 1-800-226-9494.

Media Literacy: The New Basic? Produced at Rutgers University in 1996. Hosted by John Merrow, it aired on PBS in late 1996. Journalists Walter Cronkite and Hugh Downs discuss the need for media literacy. They are supported by academics from the field, including David Considine and Renee Hobbs. Program also features classroom teachers and their students in several locations describing activities and strategies they have engaged in to promote media literacy. California Newsreel, 149 9th St., San Francisco, CA. Phone: 415-621-6196. Fax: 415-621-6522.

Scanning Television: Videos for Media Literacy in Class. Developed by John Pungente, Gary Marcuse, and Neil Andersen, the program provides extensive clips and a teacher's guide. Forty clips are presented with written material that supports the context for viewing, including components for before viewing and after viewing. c/o Gary Marcuse, 1818 Grant St., Vancouver, BC Canada. Fax: 604-251-9149.

Teach the Children. 1992. Another creation from Rutgers University, it provides an entertaining and informative overview of television's impact on children and the need to respond to that influence. Media Education Laboratory, Rutgers University, Newark, NJ. Phone: 415-621-6196.

Tuning in to Media: Literacy for the Information Age. The program grew out of Harvard University's Media Education Institute. Hosted by Renee Hobbs, it features academics, teachers, and clips from television programs to advance its argument. CML. Phone: 1-800-226-9494.

Advertising and the Consumer Culture

The Ad and the Ego. Powerful and controversial, the program explores the impact of advertising on everything from the economy to the environment and our values as human beings. Fast-paced and dynamic, it comes with a curriculum guide to facilitate use of particular segments in bite-sized portions. California Newsreel, 149 9th St., San Francisco, CA. Phone: 415-621-6196. Fax: 415-621-6522.

Advertising and the End of the World. Sut Jhally and the Media Education Foundation address these basic questions in this program: How do we become happy? What is Society? How far into the future can we think? In an era of conspicuous consumption, how do we learn to locate our authentic selves when we are surrounded by mass-produced dreams? Phone: 1-800-897-0089. Fax: 1-800-659-6882.

Buy Me That. Actually three programs (Buy Me That Too and Buy Me That 3), the series is excellent in elementary and middle school, providing the opportunity to examine everything from the marketing of toys to fast food. Enjoyable and eye-opening, it can be purchased as single programs or a series. CML. Phone: 1-800-226-9494.

Consuming Images. Excellent for high school and beyond, this was part of the Public Mind series Bill Moyers created for PBS in the late 1980s. Phone: 1-800-344-3337.

Listening to America: Countdown to Election 92. Bill Moyers and Kathleen Hall Jamieson track candidates' messages in the 1992 election and voter response. Includes presentation and discussion of various spots used in the controversial campaign that pitted incumbent George Bush against Bill Clinton and independent Ross Perot. Films for the Humanities and Sciences. Phone: 1-800-257-5126.

Selling Weapons. Part of the series *America's Defense Monitor.* An unusual look at the role of advertising and marketing in promoting various weapons systems in Congress. Raises significant issues about democracy and special-interest groups. Tape #547. Center for Defense Information. Phone: 202-862-0700. Fax: 202-862-0708.

The Thirty Second President. Bill Moyers and PBS provide a fascinating look at the history of advertising and presidential politics. Phone: 1-800-344-3337.

Health and Protection

The Discovery of Dawn. An important program for early adolescent and adolescent females as well as males. It documents the causes, symptoms, and effects of eating disorders through the struggles of an 18-year-old victim of anorexia nervosa. Added bonus is the presence of actress Andie MacDowell (*Four Weddings and a Funeral, Green Card*). Ask for other programs from this company. Newist/CESA 7, University of Wisconsin Green Bay. Phone: 1-800-633-7445. Fax: 414-465-2576.

The Glitter: Sex, Drugs and the Media. Human Relations Media, New York. Comes with

extensive teacher kit, handout materials, and guidelines. Good starting point for this topic for middle school and high school students. Features teens and teachers discussing media influences, along with media literacy leaders, including David Considine and Elizabeth Thoman. Phone: 1-800-431-2050.

Pack of Lies: The Advertising of Tobacco. Jean Kilbourne and Rick Pollay provide opportunities to analyze techniques and persuasions used in cigarette marketing. Media Education Foundation. Phone: 1-800-659-6882.

Selling Addiction. Videotape and printed materials from Center for Media Literacy and Scott Newman Center. Hosted by Ms. Michael Learned (The Waltons), it examines the way alcohol and tobacco are targeted at various groups, including youth, women, and minorities. CML. Phone: 1-800-226-9494.

Slim Hopes: Advertising and The Obsession with Thinness. An important program, it features Jean Kilbourne and explores the fashion industry, idealized images of beauty, and the consequences of these media myths. Media Education Foundation. Phone: 1-800-659-6882.

Still Killing Us Softly. Jean Kilbourne provides an eye-opening look at advertising images of women and the impact these images might have on female self-esteem and the way men perceive women. Available from Cambridge Documentary Films, Inc. (617) 484-3993; http://www.shore.net/~cdf

Motion Pictures

American Cinema series. Can be bought as single tape or series. Includes The Studio System, Film Noir, The Western, The Combat Film, and others. Textbook also available. American Cinema/American Culture. From the Annenberg Collection. Phone: 1-800-LEARNER.

Hollywood Versus Religion. Interesting program about the issue of media representation. Film critic Michael Medved explores examples of Hollywood distortion and stereotyping of the clergy and faith. Chatham Hill Foundation, PO Box 7723, Dallas, TX 75209. Also available from Focus on the Family, Colorado Springs, CO.

Making Grimm Movies. Filmmaker Tom Davenport takes viewers behind the scenes to explore techniques, style, and composition employed in the creation of Appalachian folktales. Comes with study guide. Suitable for middle school and older. CML. Phone: 1-800-226-9494.

Visions of Light: The Art of Cinematography. Greg Toland, William Fraker, Vittorio Storaro, and other award-winning cinematographers explore the light, point of view, and composition of dozens of major movies. The American Film Institute. Washington, DC. Phone: 202-828-4090.

News

The Language of War. Excellent for high school and beyond, particularly in Social Studies and English classes. Examines the misuse of language, persuasion, and propaganda techniques. Tape #440. Center for Defense Information. Phone: 202-862-0700. Fax: 202-862-0708.

Lines in the Sand. Short but important videotape addressing the press coverage of the Gulf War and the way the government and Pentagon controlled public perception of the conflict and issues. CML. Phone: 1-800-226-9494.

The Myth of the Liberal Media. Series from Center for Media Education. Includes programs on The Filters of News, Domestic Issues, and International Issues. Features Edward Herman and Noam Chomsky. Phone: 1-800-897-0089.

What Makes News. Videotape from Center for Media Literacy that looks at how the U.S. media cover and construct stories from the Third World and the reasons for this. Phone: 1-800-226-9494.

Why America Hates the Press. Focuses on the blurring of the lines between news, entertainment, and politicking. Profiles Jack Germond, Cokie Roberts, and Bob Woodward. PBS. Phone: 1-800-344-3377.

Violence and the Media

Beyond Blame. An extensive boxed set with handouts, guidelines, and support materials. Can be purchased as single parts (*Elementary, Middle, Town Hall Meeting*, etc.) or as a whole. CML. Phone: 1-800-226-9494.

Does TV Kill? A documentary from PBS Frontline featuring Bill Moyers and a panel as they explore the historical background and contemporary relevance of this controversy. CML. Phone: 1-800-226-9494.

Dreamworlds: Desire, Sex and Power in Music Video. Two parts. Controversial and compelling, it explores the content and consequences of the representation of men and women in music videos. Of particular importance is the focus on potentially impressionable adolescent/early adult audience still formulating their sense of self. Manipulative editing techniques that mirror those used in music videos are problematic and rape scenes make this potentially too strong for some viewers. Center for Media Education. Phone: 1-800-659-6882.

The Killing Screens. Jean Kilbourne introduces Dr. George Gerbner, who examines in graphic detail the cumulative body count reference and potential consequences of film and television violence. Center for Media Education. Phone: 1-800-659-6882.

INDEX

Dr. David Considine is Media Studies Co-ordinator in the College of Education at Appalachian State University, North Carolina. In 1994 the National Telemedia Council presented him with the Jessie McCanse Award for individual contributions to media literacy. The following year he chaired the first National Media Literacy Conference. A frequent presenter of keynote addresses and workshops at both the national and international level, his writings have appeared in *Educational Technology*, *School Library Journal*, *The Journal of Media Literacy*, and numerous other publications.

He is featured in the PBS program *Media Literacy: The New Basic*, as well as in AMC's *Homeward Bound: The American Family in Film*, and the HRM program *The Glitter: Sex, Drugs and the Media*. In 1998 he served as the national expert for the development of Minnesota's year 10 critical viewing skills assessment. He has worked as a consultant for the Office of National Drug Control Policy at the White House, as well as for national anti-tobacco groups (ASSIST) and for AODA (Alcohol and Other Drug Abuse) programs. For the last several years he has been a featured speaker for the Discovery Network's KNOW-TV programs, presented throughout the country.

More than 25 years ago, **Gail E. Haley**'s Caldecott Medal acceptance speech for the children's book *A Story, A Story* commented on television's impact on children's development. Today as an author, illustrator, and media literacy advocate, she continues to link the literacies, exploring the relationship between print and picture, page and screen.

Together with her husband, Dr. Considine, she presents V.I.E.W. (Visual Information Education Workshops) throughout the United States, working with teachers, librarians, parents, and children. She has been a regular featured speaker and workshop leader for Wisconsin's Center for Excellence in Critical Thinking. She has conducted workshops and made keynote addresses for children's literature and library/media programs in Canada, Australia, and the United Kingdom. In 1997 she worked for the American International Schools in Africa, and in 1998 Discovery Communications Network invited her to present storytelling and puppetry programs for the opening of its flagship store in Washington, DC.